Victoria Crosses on the Western Front
Battles of the Scarpe 1918 and Drocourt–Quéant Line

Victoria Crosses on the Western Front Battles of the Scarpe 1918 and Drocourt–Quéant Line

26 August–2 September 1918

Paul Oldfield

Pen & Sword
MILITARY

First published in Great Britain in 2021 by
Pen & Sword Military
an imprint of
Pen & Sword Books Ltd
47 Church Street
Barnsley
South Yorkshire
S70 2AS

Copyright © Paul Oldfield 2021

ISBN 978 1 52678 803 0

The right of Paul Oldfield to be identified as the Author of this Work has been asserted by him in accordance with the Copyright, Designs and Patents Act 1988.

A CIP catalogue record for this book is available from the British Library

All rights reserved. No part of this book may be reproduced or transmitted in any form or by any means, electronic or mechanical including photocopying, recording or by any information storage and retrieval system, without permission from the Publisher in writing.

Typeset in Ehrhardt by
Mac Style
Printed and bound in the UK by TJ Books Ltd, Padstow, Cornwall

Pen & Sword Books Ltd incorporates the imprints of Pen & Sword Archaeology, Atlas, Aviation, Battleground, Discovery, Family History, History, Maritime, Military, Naval, Politics, Railways, Select, Social History, Transport, True Crime, and Claymore Press, Frontline Books, Leo Cooper, Praetorian Press, Remember When, Seaforth Publishing and Wharncliffe.

For a complete list of Pen & Sword titles please contact

PEN & SWORD BOOKS LIMITED
47 Church Street, Barnsley, South Yorkshire, S70 2AS, England
E-mail: enquiries@pen-and-sword.co.uk
Website: www.pen-and-sword.co.uk

Or

PEN AND SWORD BOOKS
1950 Lawrence Rd, Havertown, PA 19083, USA
E-mail: Uspen-and-sword@casematepublishers.com
Website: www.penandswordbooks.com

Contents

Master Maps vii
Abbreviations ix
Introduction xii

Battle of the Scarpe 1918 (Master Maps 1 & 2) 1

397. LCpl Henry Weale, 14 Royal Welsh Fusiliers, 26 August 1918, Bazentin-le-Grand, France
398. Sgt Reginald Judson, 1 Auckland, NZEF, 26 August 1918, Bapaume, France
399. Lt Charles Rutherford, 5 Canadian Mounted Rifles, CEF, 26 August 1918, Monchy-le-Preux, France
400. Lt David Macintyre, Argyll & Sutherland Highlanders att'd 1/6 Highland Light Infantry, 27 August 1918, Near Hénin & Fontaine-lès-Croisilles, France
401. Lt Col William Clark-Kennedy, 24 Battalion (Victoria Rifles), CEF, 27 August 1918, Chérisy, France
404. 2Lt James Huffam, 2 Duke of Wellington's (West Riding), 31 August 1918, St Servin's Farm, Haucourt, France

Battle of the Drocourt–Quéant Line (Master Map 2) 31

414. CSM Martin Doyle, 1 Royal Munster Fusiliers, 2 September 1918, Riencourt-lès-Cagnicourt, France
415. CPO George Prowse, Drake Battalion, RND, 2 September 1918, Pronville, France
416. LCpl William Metcalf, 16 Battalion (Canadian Scottish), CEF, 2 September 1918, Cagnicourt, France
417. Lt Col Cyrus Peck, 16 Battalion (Canadian Scottish), CEF, 2 September 1918, Cagnicourt, France
418. Pte Walter Rayfield, 7 Battalion (1st British Columbia), CEF, 2–4 September 1918, Villers-lès-Cagnicourt, France
419. Sgt Arthur Knight, 10 Battalion (Canadians), CEF, 2 September 1918, Villers-lès-Cagnicourt, France
420. Pte Claude Nunney, 38 Battalion (Ottawa), CEF, 1-2 September 1918, Dury, France

421. Capt Bellenden Hutcheson, RCAMC att'd 75 Battalion (Mississauga) CEF, 2 September 1918, Dury, France
422. Pte John Young, 87 Battalion (Grenadier Guards), CEF, 2 September 1918, Dury, France
423. LSgt Arthur Evans, 6 Lincolnshire, 2 September 1918, Southwest of Étaing, France

Biographies 70
Sources 313
Useful Information 318

Index 322

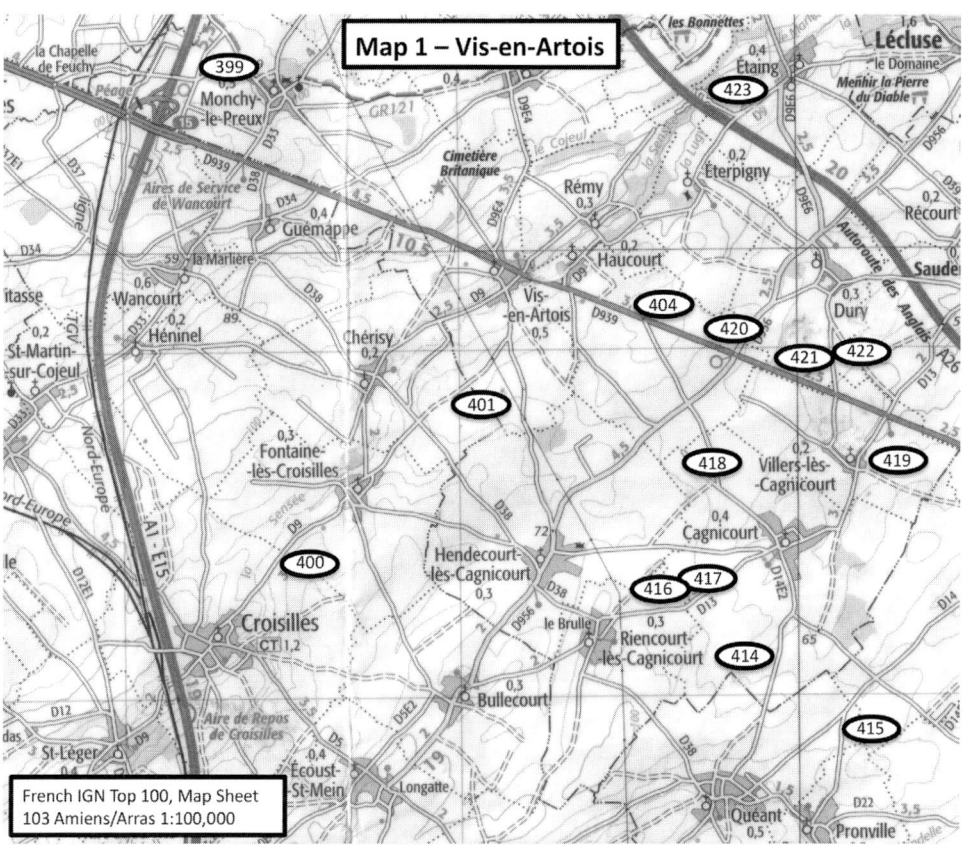

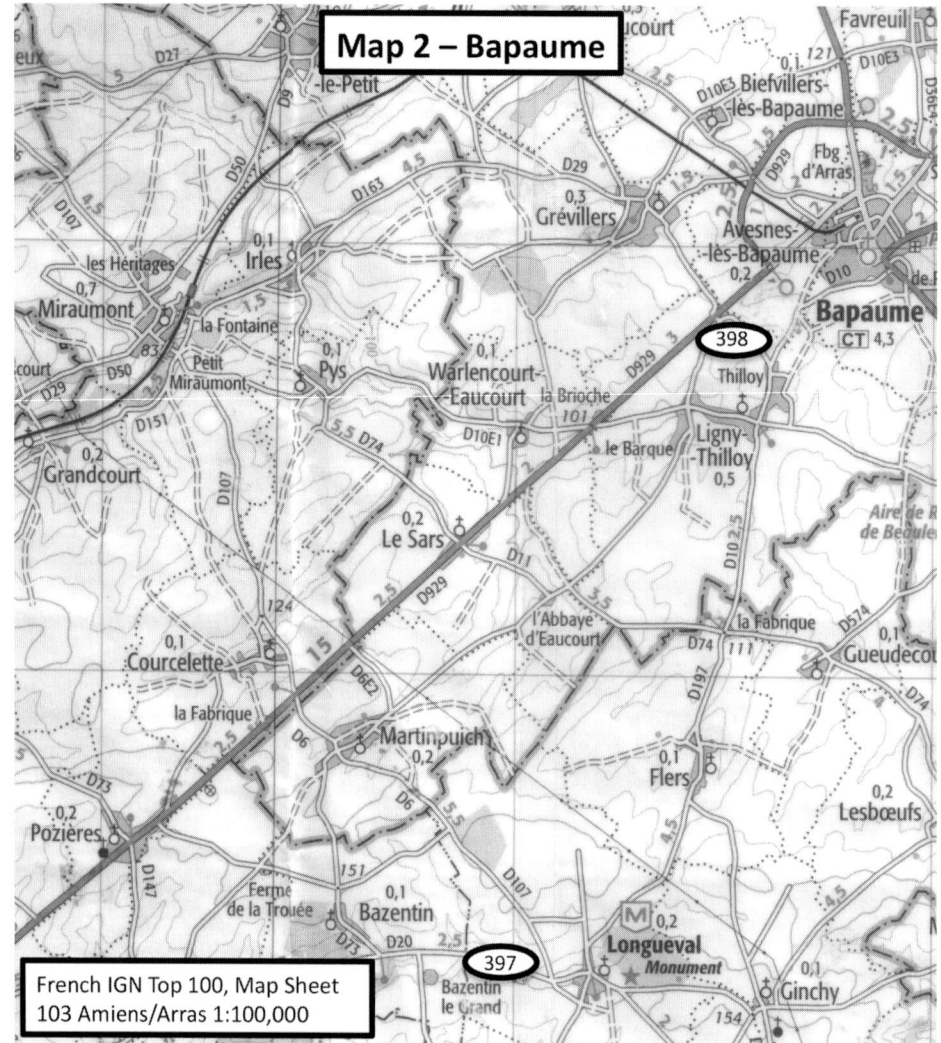

Abbreviations

AB	Bachelor of Arts
ADC	Aide-de-Camp
ADMS	Assistant Director Medical Services
AFS	Advanced Flying School
AIF	Australian Imperial Force
AMF(L)	Allied Command Europe (ACE) Mobile Force (Land)
ARICS	Associate Royal Institute of Chartered Surveyors
ASC	Army Service Corps
Att'd	Attached
BC	British Columbia
BD	Bachelor of Divinity
BEF	British Expeditionary Force
BM	Brigade Major
Brig Gen	Brigadier General
BSc	Bachelor of Science
Bty	Battery (artillery unit of 4–8 guns)
CAMC	Canadian Army Medical Corps
Capt	Captain
CASC	Canadian Army Service Corps
CB	Companion of the Order of the Bath
CBE	Commander of the Order of the British Empire
CCS	Casualty Clearing Station
CEF	Canadian Expeditionary Force
ChB	Bachelor of Surgery
C-in-C	Commander-in-Chief
CMG	Companion of the Order of St Michael & St George
CO	Commanding Officer
Co	County
Col	Colonel
Cpl	Corporal
CQMS	Company Quartermaster Sergeant
CRA	Commander Royal Artillery
CSgt	Colour Sergeant
CSM	Company Sergeant Major

Cty	Cemetery
CWGC	Commonwealth War Graves Commission
CWM	Chartered Wealth Manager
DADMS	Deputy Assistant Director Medical Services
DCM	Distinguished Conduct Medal
DD	Doctor of Divinity
DL	Deputy Lieutenant
DSO	Distinguished Service Order
Dvr	Driver
FCSI	Fellow of the Chartered Institute of Securities and Investments
FTS	Flying Training School
FRICS	Fellow Royal Institution of Chartered Surveyors
GCB	Knight Grand Cross of the Order of the Bath
GCMG	Knight Grand Cross of the Order of St Michael & St George
Gen	General
GHQ	General Headquarters
GOC	General Officer Commanding
GSO1, 2 or 3	General Staff Officer Grade 1 (Lt Col), 2 (Maj) or 3 (Capt)
HE	High Explosive
HMHS	Her/His Majesty's Hospital Ship
HMNZHS	Her/His Majesty's New Zealand Hospital Ship
HMS	Her/His Majesty's Ship
HMT	Her/His Majesty's Transport/Troopship/Hired Military Transport
JP	Justice of the Peace
KCB	Knight Commander of the Order of the Bath
KCMG	Knight Commander of St Michael and St George
Kia	Killed in action
Kms	Kilometres
LCpl	Lance Corporal
LG	London Gazette
LLB	Bachelor of Laws (Legum Baccalaureus)
Lt	Lieutenant
Lt Col	Lieutenant Colonel
Lt Gen	Lieutenant General
Maj	Major
Maj Gen	Major General
MA	Master of Arts
MB	Bachelor of Medicine
MBA	Master of Business Administration
MBE	Member of the Order of the British Empire
MC	Military Cross
MID	Mentioned in Despatches

MM	Military Medal
MO	Medical Officer
MSM	Meritorious Service Medal
NB	New Brunswick
NSRD	Nova Scotia Regiment Depot
NSW	New South Wales
NWF	North West Frontier
OBE	Officer of the Order of the British Empire
OC	Officer Commanding
OCB	Officer Cadet Battalion
OTC	Officers' Training Corps
PPCLI	Princess Patricia's Canadian Light Infantry
Pte	Private
RAF	Royal Air Force
RAP	Regimental Aid Post
RCR	Royal Canadian Regiment
RE	Royal Engineers
RFA	Royal Field Artillery
RGA	Royal Garrison Artillery
RNVR	Royal Naval Volunteer Reserve
RSM	Regimental Sergeant Major
Sgt	Sergeant
SMLE	Short Magazine Lee Enfield
SNCO	Senior non-commissioned officers
Spr	Sapper
SS	Steam Ship
TA	Territorial Army
TF	Territorial Force
Tr	Trench
VAD	Voluntary Aid Detachment
VC	Victoria Cross
WO1 or 2	Warrant Officer Class 1 or 2

Introduction

The tenth book in this series continues the story of the Hundred Days, the final and relentless advance by the Allies leading to the Armistice. The Hundred Days resulted in the award of 119 VCs; almost a quarter of the 492 land forces VCs awarded for the Western Front between 1914 and 1918. This book covers sixteen of them, ten of which were awarded to Dominion troops, mainly Canadians.

As with previous books in the series, it is written for the battlefield visitor as well as the armchair reader. Each account provides background information to explain the broad strategic and tactical situation, before focusing on the VC action in detail. Each is supported by a map to allow a visitor to stand on, or close to, the spot and at least one photograph of the site. Detailed biographies help to understand the man behind the Cross.

As far as possible chapters and sections within them follow the titles of battles, actions and affairs as decided by the post-war Battle Nomenclature Committee. VCs are numbered chronologically 397, 398, 399 etc from 26th August 1918. As far as possible they are described in the same order but, when a number of actions were fought simultaneously, the VCs are covered out of sequence on a geographical basis in accordance with the official battle nomenclature. As a result it may appear that 402, 403 and 405–413 are missing. However, they appear in the next volume in the series under the Second Battle of Bapaume, allowing the whole of the Battles of the Scarpe 1918 and the Drocurt-Quéant Line to appear in this volume.

Refer to the master maps to find the general area for each VC. If visiting the battlefields it is advisable to purchase maps from the respective French and Belgian 'Institut Géographique National'. The French IGN Top 100 and Belgian IGN Provinciekaart at 1:100,000 scale are ideal for motoring, but 1:50,000, 1:25,000 or 1:20,000 scale maps are necessary for more detailed work, e.g. French IGN Serie Bleue and Belgian IGN Topografische Kaart. They are obtainable from the respective IGN or through reputable map suppliers on-line.

Ranks are as used on the day. Grave references have been shortened, e.g. 'Plot II, Row A, Grave 10' will appear as 'II A 10'. There are some abbreviations, many in common usage, but if unsure refer to the list provided.

I endeavour to include memorials to each VC in their biographies. However, every VC is commemorated in the VC Diary and on memorial panels at the Union

Jack Club, Sandell Street, Waterloo, London. To include this in every biography would be unnecessarily repetitive.

Every reasonable effort has been made to reduce errors to the minimum and facts have been cross-checked as far as possible. Any remaining mistakes are mine alone.

Thanks are due to too many people and organisations to mention here. They are acknowledged in 'Sources' and any omissions are my fault and not intentional. The continuing contribution of fellow members of the 'Victoria Cross Database Users Group', Doug and Richard Arman, is very much appreciated, as is the cooperation of Steve Lee and the Memorials to Valour website team.

Paul Oldfield
Wiltshire
January 2021

Battle of the Scarpe 1918

26th August 1918

> 397 LCpl Henry Weale, 14th Battalion, The Royal Welsh Fusiliers (113th Brigade, 38th Division), Bazentin-le-Grand, France
>
> 398 Sgt Reginald Judson, 1st Auckland (1st New Zealand Brigade, New Zealand Division), Bapaume, France
>
> 399 Lt Charles Rutherford, 5th Canadian Mounted Rifles (8th Canadian Brigade, 3rd Canadian Division), Monchy-le-Preux, France

On 26th August 1918 a new phase in the Allied offensive (Hundred Days) opened, when First Army joined in to the north of Fourth and Third Armies, in what became known as the Battle of the Scarpe 1918. Previously First Army had only engaged in small-scale operations to pin down enemy reserves and to take advantage of any opportunities presented by the offensives to the south. GHQ's new orders were for Third Army to continue to advance eastwards, protected on the right by Fourth Army, with First Army cooperating on the left.

Fourth Army's orders for the 26th were to give the demoralised enemy no rest and to take every opportunity to press on, including at night. Considerable advances were made across the Army's frontage. Third Army's right and centre (V, IV and VI Corps) continued to drive eastwards, while XVII Corps on the left was to incline to the southeast to capture Croisilles, in conjunction with First Army. It was to maintain contact with VI Corps on the right and cooperate with the Canadian Corps (First Army) on the left. There was no set zero hour, but corps were ordered to start as early as possible. However, in some cases orders did not filter down until early in the morning and a violent thunderstorm also caused delays.

V Corps met stiff resistance, particularly from machine gun posts and their fire grew in severity as the light improved. 38th Division was on the extreme right of V Corps and Third Army, in contact with Fourth Army. It was to clear Bazentin Woods, capture High Wood and advance towards Longueval. 113th Brigade on the right attacked at 4 a.m., but 115th Brigade on the left did not commence its advance until over two hours later.

On the previous day 113th Brigade had captured Mametz Wood. It had also taken part in its capture on 10th July 1916. The advance on 26th August 1918 was well supported by a creeping barrage and machine guns. However, the leading battalion,

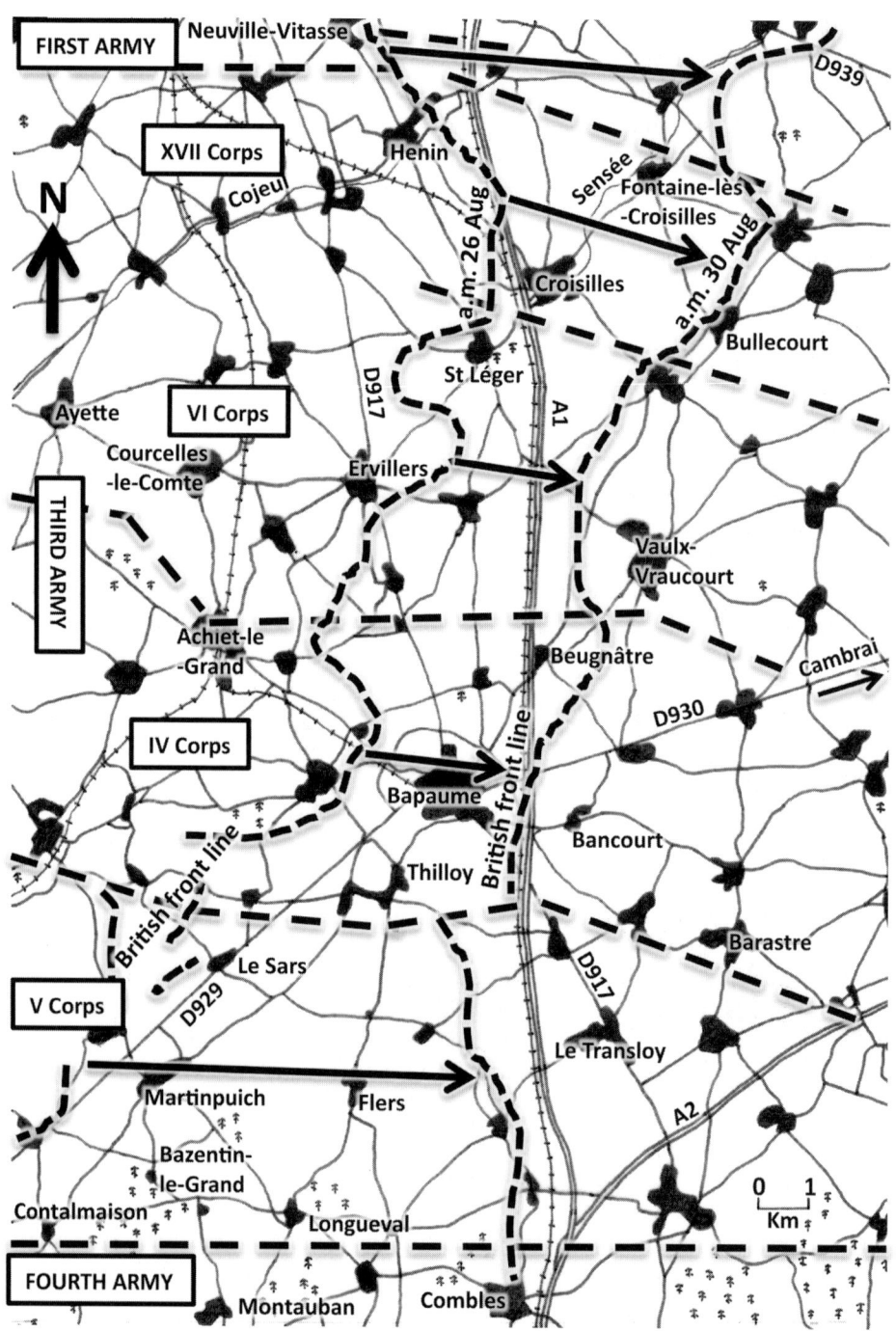

Third Army 26th–30th August 1918.

13th Royal Welsh Fusiliers, immediately came under heavy fire and, within a few minutes, the supporting units (14th and 16th Royal Welsh Fusiliers on the left and right) were heavily involved. The advance was exposed to flanking fire from High Wood on the left and Montauban on the right. 13th Royal Welsh Fusiliers was checked and slipped to the right. To fill the gap B Company, 14th Royal Welsh Fusiliers came up on the left and took Bazentin-le-Grand just after 7 a.m. By 9 a.m., 16th Royal Welsh Fusiliers on the right was held up and 2nd Royal Welsh Fusiliers (attached to establish a series of posts along the right boundary) sent two companies to guard the right flank.

Soon after 10 a.m., 115th Brigade began the attack on High Wood. 17th Royal Welsh Fusiliers moved to the north and 10th South Wales Borderers to the south of the lightly held Wood, which was secured by 12.30 p.m. The Brigade then came up against a strong enemy force to the east and established a line on the high ground.

Meanwhile in 113th Brigade, having secured Bazentin-le-Grand, B Company, 14th Royal Welsh Fusiliers pushed on to a crossroads on the Longueval–Contalmaison road, but was forced back to the crossroads at Bazentin-le-Grand. Two platoons of C Company surrounded a strongpoint on the left flank and, when 10th South Wales Borderers (115th Brigade) came up on the left, C Company captured the strongpoint, taking thirty prisoners and two machine guns, before going on to the Windmill.

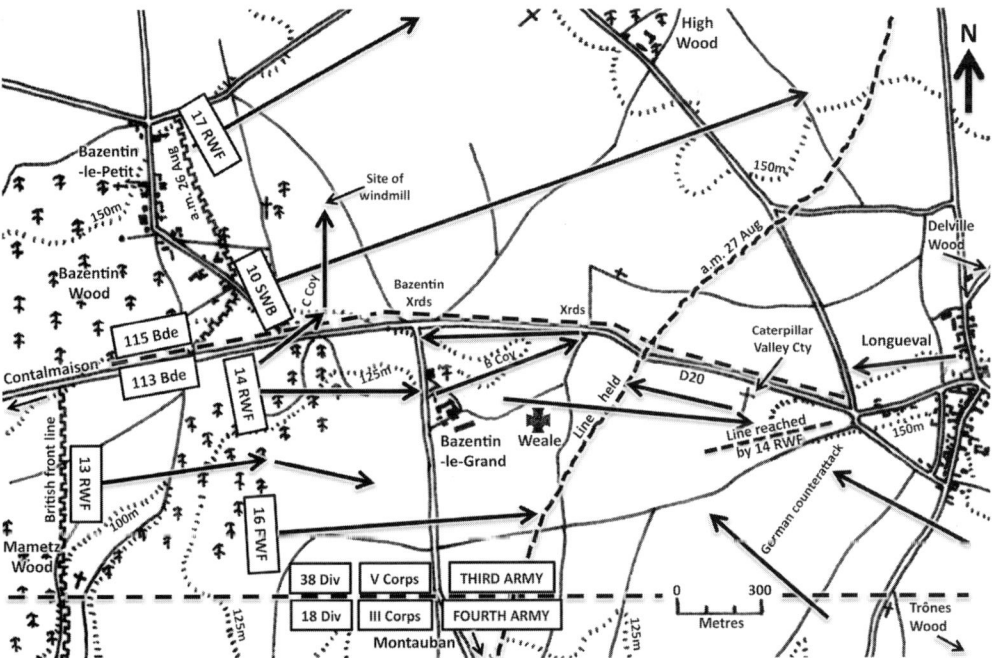

Leave Longueval on the D20 westwards. Pass Caterpillar Valley Cemetery on the left and continue for 300m to where the road bends first to the right and then left. Park safely here and cross the road to the south side for a view towards Bazentin-le-Grand and the ground over which Weale won his VC.

Elsewhere in 113th Brigade, 13th and 16th Royal Welsh Fusiliers remained bogged down. However, 14th Royal Welsh Fusiliers (less the C Company platoons at the Windmill) on the left continued the advance, with A Company on the right, D Company in the centre and the other two platoons of C Company on the left. This daring move turned the flank of the Germans holding up 13th Royal Welsh Fusiliers and one hundred prisoners and eight machine guns were taken. 14th Royal Welsh Fusiliers took up position on the ridge 900m west of Longueval with A and D Companies holding the front, C Company in support and B Company in reserve.

14th Royal Welsh Fusiliers was by then 900m ahead of its flanking units and very exposed. At 5 p.m. a determined counterattack from Delville and Trônes Woods fell upon it. The attack failed to force the Battalion off the ridge, but the CO decided that he could not remain there and withdrew to about 500m east of Bazentin-le-Grand, where his flanks were more secure. The Brigade's right flank was reinforced by 6th Dragoon Guards and touch was made with 18th Division (III Corps, Fourth Army), which had taken Montauban.

It is not entirely clear when in this action **Lance Corporal Henry Weale** performed the deeds for which he was awarded the VC. The citation states that when the adjacent battalion was held up he was ordered to deal with the enemy machine gun posts. His Lewis gun failed but, undaunted and on his own initiative, he rushed the nearest post and killed the crew. He then went for the other posts. The crews fled as he approached, hotly pursued by Weale. His action cleared the way for the advance and inspired his comrades. It is possible that this action took place when two platoons of C Company captured the strongpoint on the left flank and went on to the Windmill. However, it seems more likely to have been later, when 14th Royal Welsh Fusiliers turned the flank of the Germans holding up 13th Royal Welsh Fusiliers.

From just south of the D20 road, which is on the right. Bazentin-le-Grand is amongst the trees on the left and Bazentin-le-Petit is just left of centre, also mainly surrounded by trees. 14th Royal Welsh Fusiliers attacked from Bazentin-le-Grand towards the camera position.

The rest of V Corps also had mixed results. 17th Division made some progress, attacking at 5 a.m., but the advance was held up 650m west of Flers. By evening 21st Division's outpost line had been advanced just 275m.

IV Corps' main objective was Bapaume and zero hour was set for 6.30 a.m. On the right, 63rd Division was opposed by two German divisions in its advance towards Thilloy, in support of the New Zealand Division. Its right was unable to move and the left, although it managed to reach the northwest outskirts of Thilloy, was heavily enfiladed from the left and had to fall back.

The New Zealand Division in the centre of IV Corps, already ahead of its flanking divisions, was to seize Bapaume and the high ground to the east. There was to be no frontal assault. Instead 1st New Zealand Brigade, south of the town, was to conform to the movements of 63rd Division on its right. 3rd New Zealand (Rifle) Brigade was to pass through 2nd New Zealand Brigade to the north of the town towards Bancourt, in cooperation with 5th Division. There was no creeping barrage but a battery of field artillery was attached to each battalion.

During the night, 1st New Zealand Brigade side slipped to the north and, as a result, faced an unknown front. In addition wires connecting Brigade HQ had been cut by shellfire and there was uncertainty about 63rd Division's zero hour to the south. The intention was to send forward strong patrols to maintain contact with the enemy and conform to the movements of friendly troops to the south and north. If Bapaume was encircled, the Brigade was also to assist in clearing it.

2nd Wellington on the right advanced in daylight in support of 63rd Division. Only a short advance was possible. Another attempt in the evening was stopped by enemy machine gun posts. 15th Company, 1st Auckland, which had been attached to 2nd Wellington from 12.30 a.m., was sent to assist. A bombing section, consisting of **Sergeant Reginald Judson** and four men, pushed through 2nd Wellington's line. They rushed forward under intense fire and captured a machine gun post in a sap. While his men were consolidating, Judson continued along the sap alone for another 200m. He bombed two more machine gun posts and then climbed out of

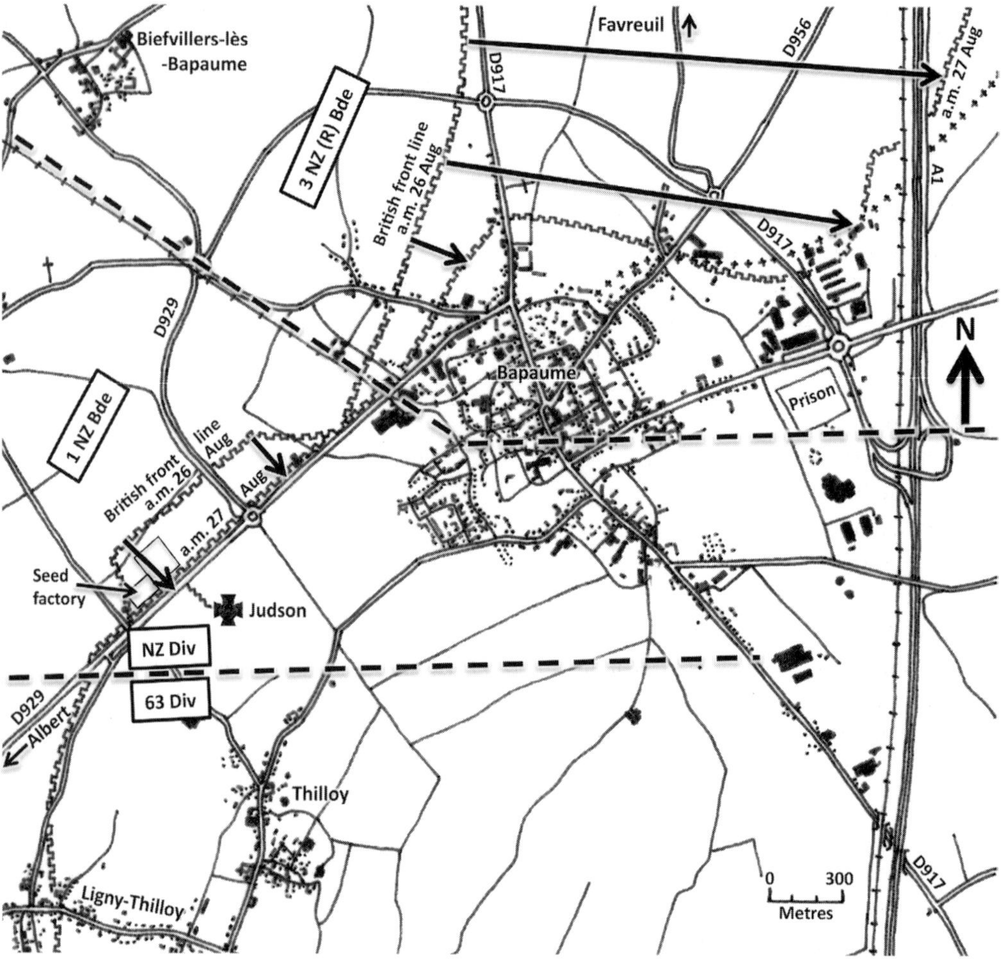

6　Victoria Crosses on the Western Front – Battles of the Scarpe 1918

The site of Judson's VC action is adjacent to the very busy D929. There is space to park on the grass verge on the southeast side of the road, opposite the huge Exélience seed production factory, but it is not advisable to do so. A slow drive past is suggested.

The sap cleared by Judson crossed the road (D929) on the left and headed across the field on the right towards the end of the line of bushes and beyond. Bapaume is in the centre distance.

the trench and ran ahead of the enemy. Standing on the parapet he ordered a party of two officers and ten men to surrender. They fired at him but undaunted he threw a bomb and jumped down among them. He killed two and the rest fled, allowing Judson to capture the two machine guns. This gallant action saved many lives and enabled the advance to continue a little further. However, patrols continued to be severely harassed by machine gun fire from Bapaume and only advanced as far as the Albert–Bapaume road. A renewal of the attack in the late evening was abandoned. 1st New Zealand Brigade's position could not improve until progress was made on its right. During the night, 1st Auckland took over 2nd Wellington's line and became responsible for the whole Brigade front.

3rd New Zealand (Rifle) Brigade advanced with three battalions. Despite the fire from the outskirts of Bapaume on the right and Beugnâtre on the left, the Bapaume–Beugnâtre road was reached. However, the Brigade could progress no further. Another attempt was made at 6 p.m., in conjunction with 5th Division to the north, but Bapaume still held out. Elsewhere the Brigade advanced 450m but once again was brought to a halt by heavy machine gun fire. The line fell back a little to the Bapaume–Cambrai railway.

On the left of IV Corps, 5th Division attacked towards Beugnâtre to cover the New Zealand Division to the south. Great difficulties were encountered in finding the start positions in heavy rain and pitch darkness. However, all was ready by zero hour. Beugnâtre was taken and a line was established 200m beyond it, in contact with the divisions on both flanks.

VI Corps attacked with 62nd and Guards Divisions. The former made some progress but did not achieve all its objectives. The latter was exhausted and its part was cancelled as it was expected that the advances to the north would clear the enemy in that area. In the event it was found that St Léger Wood had been abandoned and 1st Guards Brigade was able to occupy posts along its eastern edge, which had been the original objective.

On the left flank of Third Army, XVII Corps had two tasks. On the right, 56th Division was to cooperate with VI Corps to the south in the capture of Croisilles, an outwork of the formidable Hindenburg Position. On the left, 52nd Division was to cooperate with the Canadian Corps on the right flank of First Army as it progressed

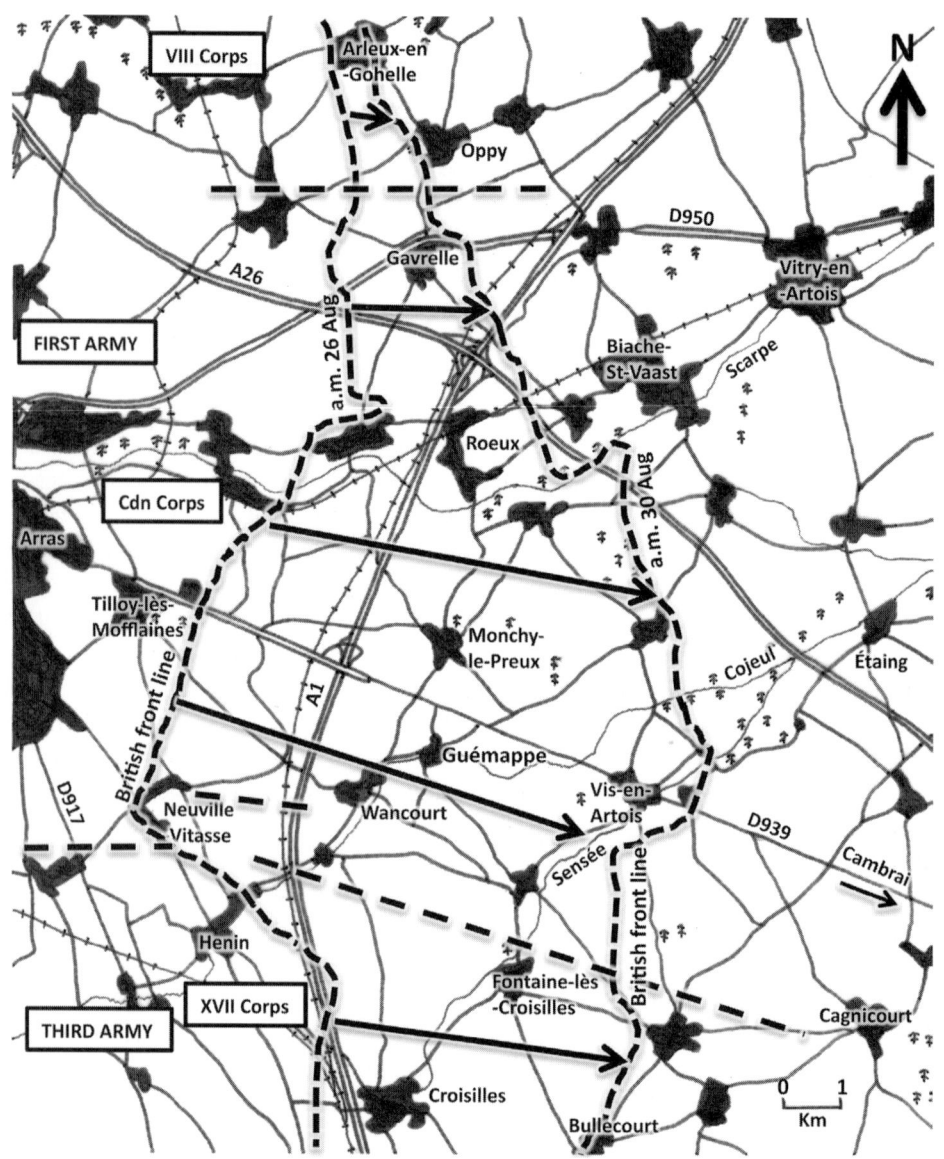

First Army gains 26th–30th August 1918.

southeast along the Hindenburg Position. Each division had two brigades of heavy artillery attached. 56th Division ran into uncut wire in front of Croisilles and, because the Guards Division attack to the south had been cancelled, it stood fast. 52nd Division was to advance into the Cojeul valley and gain the ridge beyond. 155th Brigade in reserve, commanded by Brigadier General James Forbes-Robertson VC, was then to cooperate with the Canadians in clearing a triangular pocket between

Wancourt and Neuville Vitasse. The first phase was completed in darkness with few casualties. The second phase commenced at 3 p.m. in cooperation with 2nd Canadian Division. The dry Cojeul was crossed and the northern end of Hénin Hill was occupied without difficulty. The line was extended to the left to maintain contact with the Canadians. All of XVII Corps' objectives were gained.

Only the right wing of First Army was engaged on 26th August. This included the Canadian Corps and part of VIII Corps to the north. First Army's objective was to breach the Drocourt–Quéant Line and then to swing southeast and drive into the flank of the enemy resisting Third Army. This required the Canadian Corps to exploit to the east and southeast towards the line Wancourt–Guémappe–Monchy-le-Preux.

The Canadian Corps had 2nd and 3rd Canadian Divisions and 51st Division in the line, with 15th Division in reserve. 1st and 4th Canadian Divisions were still moving north from the Fourth Army area to rejoin the Corps. The ground in front was dominated by three hill features. About five kilometres in front was Monchy-le-Preux on its own hill, north of the Arras–Cambrai road. This village had been fiercely fought over the previous year. In front of Monchy and protecting it were Orange and Chapel Hills, the latter astride the Arras–Cambrai road.

The Canadian Corps was to attack between Neuville Vitasse and the Scarpe on a frontage of 6,500m. When 2nd and 3rd Canadian Divisions' first objective was secured, and a defensive flank had been formed facing south, 2nd Canadian Division was to work along a trench to join up with 52nd Division (Third Army), in order to cut off any Germans remaining in the area between Wancourt and Neuville Vitasse. This second objective, east of the Cojeul, was 2,500m beyond the first, 800m east of Wancourt and just west of Guémappe and Monchy-le-Preux. 51st Division, north of the Scarpe, was given no clearly defined objectives and was to be ready to exploit any success south of the river.

On 23rd August a preliminary operation at the junction of Third and First Armies, by the right of 2nd Canadian Division and 52nd Division on the left of Third Army, made a small advance against Neuville Vitasse. Most of the village was taken on the 24th.

The Canadian Corps had fourteen brigades of field artillery allocated, including those within 2nd and 3rd Canadian Divisions. Also deployed were those from 15th, 16th and 39th Divisions, plus three Army brigades. In addition there were nine brigades of heavy artillery. Although a company of nine tanks of 3rd Tank Brigade was allotted to each Canadian division, they did not arrive until about 5.30 a.m. and zero hour was at 3 a.m. Above, two squadrons of RAF fighters flew low to maintain touch with the advance, while four more attacked ahead of it. The ground was complicated, being intersected by a number of valleys and dominated by the ridge running from Tilloy-lès-Mofflaines through Chapel and Orange Hills to Monchy-le-Preux. Three German divisions faced the Canadian Corps. However, the advance to the first objective (Green Line) was completed successfully in the dark, the defenders having been surprised by the early hour of the assault. Resistance stiffened as the advance progressed and there was some sharp fighting before the objective trench was taken at about 6.30 a.m.

In 2nd Canadian Division, 6th Canadian Brigade was on the right to secure the flank and 4th Canadian Brigade was on the left to make the main attack. 5th Canadian Brigade, with No.1 Company, 2nd Canadian Machine Gun Battalion attached, was in support. It was to be prepared to pass through 4th Canadian Brigade to exploit success or operate south of the Cojeul. The first objective was Minorca Trench, including Neuville Vitasse and Chapel Hill, and involved an advance of about 2,700m. The final objective was the enemy main line of resistance west of Guémappe.

6th Canadian Brigade moved forward to establish the defensive right flank. 27th and 28th Battalions moved southwards to mop up the area as far as the boundary with 52nd Division. The Brigade ran into some machine gun posts and rifle grenades had to be used to clear them. In one instance a tank had to overcome the resistance. At the same time, 4th Canadian Brigade moved off to make the main attack on the left, supported by a machine gun barrage. The outpost line was overrun quickly and Chapel Hill was captured shortly after 6 a.m. By then it was daylight, making it easier for tanks to cooperate. However, it also gave the Germans better observation to use their field artillery to knock out a number of tanks. The second objective was captured by 7.30 a.m. but by then the right of the Brigade was approaching Guémappe and came under heavy fire from Monchy to the north.

In 3rd Canadian Division, 8th Canadian Brigade was to make the attack, initially planned for 4.30 a.m. but later changed to 3 a.m. This required special messengers to be sent forward to warn battalions, companies and platoons. Some of the assault troops only just made it into their assault positions before zero hour. The three assault battalions (from south to north 5th, 2nd and 4th Canadian Mounted Rifles) formed up south of the Scarpe in no man's land and set off on time. 5th Canadian Mounted Rifles reported that the supporting barrage was somewhat ragged and a number of shells fell short, inflicting some casualties, including killing OC A Company. However, they avoided the enemy artillery as it fell on the front line positions. Careful attention was paid to maintaining direction in the dark and this was successful. Less resistance was encountered than expected. 4th Canadian Mounted Rifles on the left advanced along the riverbank and outflanked Orange Hill. This allowed 2nd Canadian Mounted Rifles in the centre to turn sharp right and seize the Hill from the north just after 4 a.m.

In the first 900m of the advance, 5th Canadian Mounted Rifles encountered fire from a few trench mortars, 5.9" guns and machine guns. However, as Halifax Trench was neared the machine gun fire intensified and there was strong opposition. This was overcome by the Lewis gunners and rifle grenadiers. Sixty prisoners, six machine guns, two light trench mortars and three anti-tank rifles were seized. However, contact was lost with 2nd Canadian Mounted Rifles on the left, although

Battle of the Scarpe 1918   11

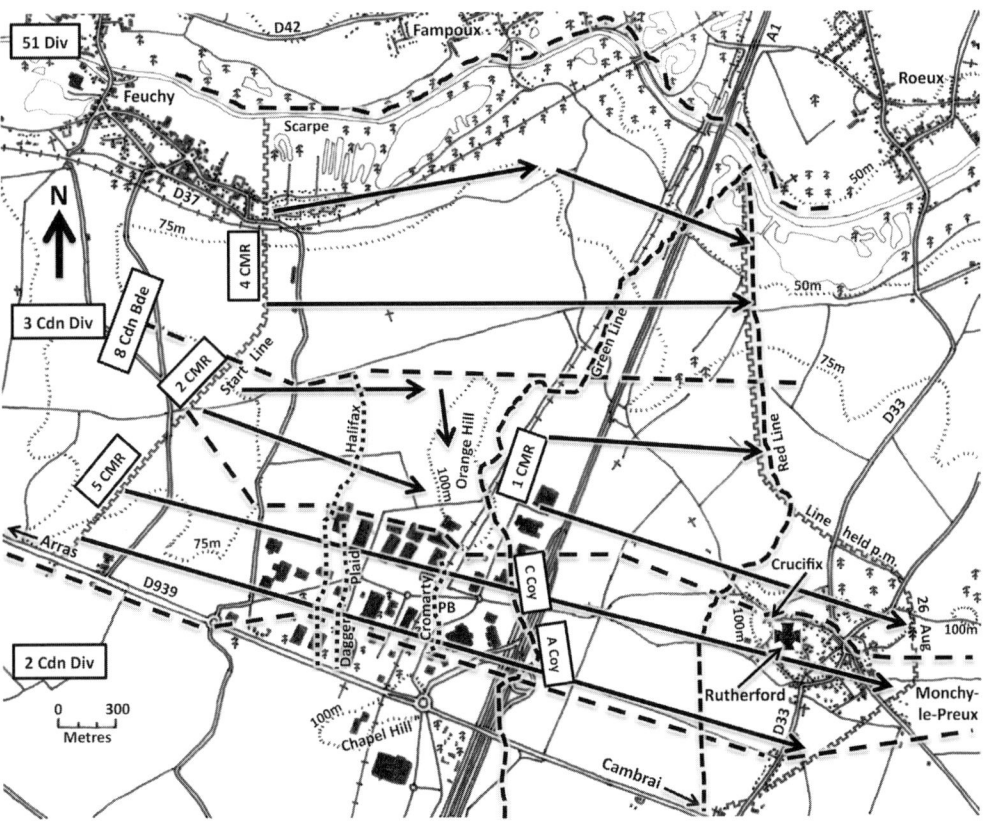

The abbreviation PB = pillbox.
Approach Monchy-le-Preux from the south on the D33 off the main D939 Arras–Cambrai road. After 450m turn left onto a farm track (boundary between 2nd and 3rd Canadian Divisions) and continue for 150m. It is quite firm going. Stop here and look right towards the village. The two pillboxes captured by Rutherford were amongst the houses at the left hand end of the village. The crucifix is amongst the buildings and is not visible from here. Rejoin the D33 and turn left towards the village. Pass the cemetery on the right and 100m beyond turn left. Follow this road as it bends to the right for 450m. At the crossroads look left to see the crucifix at the end of a small open area. This was the location of the first pillbox captured by Rutherford. Turn left and continue to the fork in the road. Stop here to look back into Monchy along the direction of advance.

this was restored at dawn. The advance continued without a pause, leaving mopping up to a previously detailed party. Dagger and Plaid Trenches were crossed but, as the advance approached Cromarty Trench, resistance stiffened, particularly from a pillbox and a machine gun on the left front. Using smoke, rifle grenades and the Lewis guns, the advance pushed on steadily and Cromarty Trench was rushed. The advance then continued without a pause to the first objective (Green Line), which was reached simultaneously by the two leading companies at 5.30 a.m.

5th Canadian Mounted Rifles on the right and 1st Canadian Mounted Rifles on the left, behind 2nd and 4th Canadian Mounted Rifles, continued the attack towards Monchy. 5th Canadian Mounted Rifles had A Company on the right,

C Company on the left, D Company in support and B Company in reserve. 5th Canadian Mounted Rifles swept on without encountering any opposition until the second objective (Red Line) was approached. The assault troops were subjected to the fire of two artillery pieces at point blank range, together with heavy machine gun fire. The objective was taken at 6.40 a.m., together with the two guns, five machine guns and over one hundred prisoners.

Two strong parties were organised to continue the attack on Monchy. One, provided by A Company under Lieutenant Warren Peter Loggie, was to work around the southern outskirts. The other, provided by C Company under **Lieutenant Charles Rutherford,** was to work through the centre of the village. The remainder of both companies were to follow their respective party.

Loggie's party advanced until it was held up by a pillbox. Meanwhile Rutherford had moved some distance ahead of his party to reconnoitre. He observed a party of about forty Germans standing outside a pillbox near the Crucifix. Rutherford waved his revolver at them and motioned them to come forward. They stayed put and motioned for him to come to them. Rutherford acted boldly and knew that if he showed any hesitation the Germans would undoubtedly have resisted. He told the German party that they were his prisoners. However, an English speaking officer disputed this and wanted Rutherford to go into a dugout, which he refused to do. He informed the German that his own men had the party surrounded and that they must surrender immediately. After some discussion one German soldier threw

From the fork in the road looking towards Monchy-le-Preux. C Company attacked from right to left to the right of the road. The Crucifix is hidden amongst the trees around the buildings.

down his rifle and took off his equipment. The others followed him and forty-five surrendered, including two officers, with three machine guns.

In the smoke and dust Rutherford could not see his party and he could hear a German machine gun firing about fifty metres away. Rutherford told the German officer to have this firing stopped and he would ensure that his own men also ceased firing. The German officer agreed and Rutherford rushed back fifty metres to where he could see his men. In his absence, shelling had become so heavy that the sergeant had ordered the assault party back to safer ground. Rutherford signalled them to hurry up. By his quick thinking and bold action Rutherford had recovered what could have been a critical situation.

From the high ground Rutherford could see that the right party was held up by heavy machine gun fire from another pillbox. He directed the remainder of his party to press on eastwards to the outskirts of the village. Keeping a Lewis gun section with him, he attacked and captured the pillbox, together with thirty-five prisoners and three machine guns. This unlocked the deadlock and the right party was then able to advance again.

Meanwhile the main body of Rutherford's party advanced along the main street, captured another pillbox with two machine guns and took thirteen prisoners, including an officer. They seized the high ground on the eastern outskirts of Monchy at 7.35 a.m. The remainder of the two leading companies arrived and a line was established in East Trench at 8 a.m. Close touch had been maintained with 1st Canadian Mounted Rifles on the left throughout this action. This Battalion had secured the north and northeast of the village. A defensive right flank was established by 5th Canadian Mounted Rifles along Circle Trench, as 20th Battalion had not advanced beyond the Red Line. Artillery fire from Saddle Lane was silenced by subjecting the area to Lewis gun fire. Horse teams coming forward to recover various guns were forced to withdraw by the Lewis gunners. The Germans shelled Monchy heavily for the next twenty-four hours. 5th Canadian Mounted Rifles suffered relatively light casualties in this attack – seventeen killed or died of wounds, 158 wounded and six missing. About 300 prisoners were taken in total.

The opposite view from the previous picture. The road on the right leads to the fork. The Crucifix is beyond the open area and is where the first pillbox captured by Rutherford was located in 1918. The lane to the left leads to the D33.

From the track off the D33 looking northeast. Monchy-le-Preux church is on the right and the fork in the road is beyond the bushes on the far left. The second pillbox captured by Rutherford was on the edge of the buildings in the centre. The Crucifix is hidden by the trees just left of centre.

About 7.20 a.m. the brigade commander ordered 4th Canadian Mounted Rifles to push on and assist 1st Canadian Mounted Rifles. The same order was passed to 2nd Canadian Mounted Rifles to support the 5th.

At 11 a.m. orders were issued by HQ 2nd Canadian Division to 6th and 4th Canadian Brigades to continue the advance southeast, with new boundaries being designated. 6th Canadian Brigade was to capture the high ground south of Wancourt beyond the Cojeul. 4th Canadian Brigade was to advance between Wancourt and the Arras–Cambrai road. At the same time, 7th Canadian Brigade in 3rd Canadian Division was to pass through 8th Canadian Brigade and, with the belatedly arrived tanks, exploit forwards.

Two battalions of 6th Canadian Brigade attacked at 4.30 p.m. Hostile machine gun fire was ineffective until they reached the top of the slope above the Cojeul, where there was uncut wire. They were held up there for the rest of the day and suffered heavy losses. However, contact was maintained with 52nd Division on the right. A night attack, carried out at 4.30 a.m. next morning, was entirely successful.

4th Canadian Brigade's task to capture Guémappe involved advancing down the ridge and crossing a significant depression. 18th Battalion in support passed through 21st Battalion, one of the two assault battalions in the morning. Machine gun posts were gradually overcome with the assistance of the artillery and the village fell about 5 p.m. A line was consolidated 275m beyond. At 7.45 p.m., 20th Battalion, protected by an artillery barrage, met little opposition and came up in line with 18th Battalion.

7th Canadian Brigade passed through 8th Canadian Brigade shortly after Monchy had been captured. It advanced almost 900m until being stopped by fire from the front and both flanks. All four supporting tanks were knocked out. German counterattacks against Monchy failed but did prevent the Canadians from making further progress.

51st Division had three objectives, each about 800m beyond the previous one. If all went well for the Canadians to the south, the third objective was Greenland Hill, with its commanding observation to the east. At 8.30 a.m. news arrived that the Canadians had seized Monchy-le-Preux and 51st Division was ordered forward.

152nd and 153rd Brigades advanced against little resistance and the first objective was secured about midday. The advance continued at 7 p.m. and the second objective was taken. To keep abreast of 3rd Canadian Division, the advance continued to Roeux, on the Scarpe, and the western slope of Greenland Hill, where the left flank was formed by 154th Brigade.

On the night of 26th/27th August in VIII Corps, 8th Division patrols occupied the enemy front line and part of the support line. The advance averaged 900m on a frontage of 3,650m.

The extension of the BEF offensive northwards by First Army had made a most successful start. That night the Germans facing the French Third and First Armies and the British Fourth and Third Armies began preparations for a withdrawal to commence on the night of 27th/28th August. The new line was up to thirty kilometres in front of the Hindenburg Line, except near Arras, where it joined the front positions, and was chosen for its suitability for resisting tank movement.

27th August 1918

> 400 Lt David Macintyre Argyll & Sutherland Highlanders attached 1/6th Battalion The Highland Light Infantry (157th Brigade, 52nd Division) Near Hénin & Fontaine-lès-Croisilles, France
> 401 Lt Col William Clark-Kennedy 24th Battalion (Victoria Rifles) CEF (5th Canadian Brigade, 2nd Canadian Division) Chérisy, France

On 27th August the German Eighteenth, Second and Seventeenth Armies began a retirement from south of the Somme northwards almost to Arras, where it pivoted at the end of the Drocourt–Quéant Line. The move was covered by increased German air activity. There were also intense barrages, partly to use up stocks of ammunition that would otherwise have been abandoned. Single guns were used to delay the follow up. British progress was more marked in the south than in the north, where First Army faced the Drocourt–Quéant Switch. The French First Army also began to move forward on the 27th. Haig urged Foch for other forces to join the offensive.

Fourth Army made steady progress but came up against stiff resistance in places. Third Army ordered all four corps to continue the advance that had commenced the previous day. V, IV and VI Corps were to continue eastwards, while XVII Corps on the left was to advance southeast astride the Hindenburg Line in cooperation with the Canadian Corps (First Army) to the north. Tanks were to be used sparsely to allow time for reorganisation and refitting. The British troops and staff were tiring and needed fresh formations to reinvigorate the offensive. Coordination of efforts was noticeably lacking on the 27th. At the same time German reinforcements were arriving and resistance stiffened. They held on to ground for as long as possible in order to recover stores and ammunition.

V Corps' divisions attacked at various times from as early as 1 a.m. to as late as 9 a.m. A short advance was made; but newly arrived German divisions stopped all further movement, mainly by intense machine gun fire. IV Corps made almost no progress, including against Bapaume. VI Corps ordered its divisions to take advantage of any enemy weakness resulting from the flanking movement of XVII and Canadians Corps to the north. Some progress was made but in places gains had to be abandoned.

XVII Corps ordered 56th Division to maintain pressure against Croisilles, while 52nd Division advanced southeast along the Hindenburg front line. In 56th Division, 167th Brigade was to remain facing Croisilles, while 169th Brigade advanced to the north of the village, including crossing the Sensée valley, with the objective being the Hindenburg front line. The advance did not commence until 9.20 a.m. and this late start affected the right of First Army to the north. Three companies led the advance. The one on the right was halted by enfilade machine gun fire from Croisilles after 400m. However, the other two companies advanced about 1,500m to a trench north of the village, where they were stopped by uncut wire and heavy frontal fire. Later, after 52nd Division had taken Fontaine-lès-Croisilles on the left, the leading companies were reinforced and managed to reach the objective.

During the attack at 7 a.m. on 24th August, 56th Division had made the main effort towards Croisilles, while 52nd Division conformed to its movements on its left. In 52nd Division, 157th Brigade led with 1/6th and 1/5th Highland Light Infantry, right and left respectively, and 156th Brigade followed on the left in echelon. 1/6th Highland Light Infantry crossed Boiry Reserve Trench and came under heavy machine gun fire soon afterwards. By 7.45 a.m. it was held up by the British barrage. However, despite these setbacks, 157th Brigade took Hénin with little difficulty and the first objective on the Hamelincourt–Héninel ridge was reached at 9 a.m. Pressing on towards the objective in the Hindenburg Line, the leading battalions were ahead of the troops on the right and were enfiladed from that flank. They also ran into the British heavy artillery barrage, which should have lifted off the Hindenburg Line. The artillery eventually moved back 450m, where it was of no assistance to the assaulting troops. Had it lifted immediately the Hindenburg Line here would have been taken swiftly. The battalions reorganised but another attack

Battle of the Scarpe 1918 17

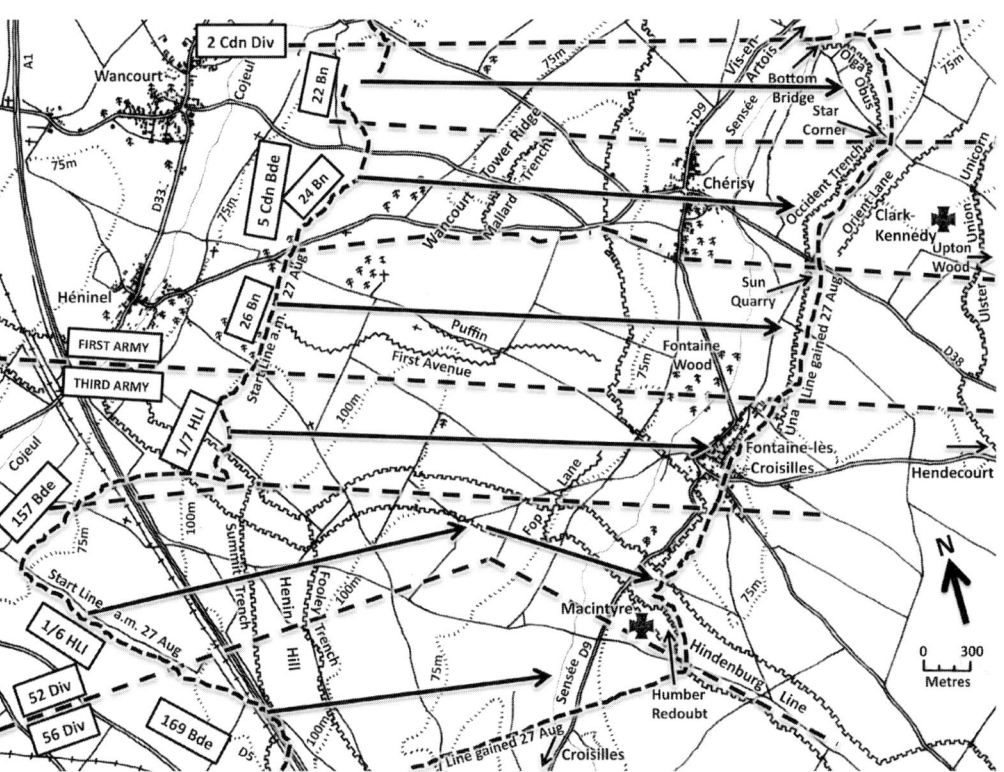

Leave Fontaine-lès-Croisilles on the D9 southwestwards towards Croisilles. On leaving the village the road bends left and then right. After the second corner, drive for 1,000m and park in the track entrance on the left. There is another track 500m before this one, but ignore it. Walk up the hill to the southeast for 400m to the crest and look left towards Fontaine-lès-Croisilles. Humber Redoubt was about 200m into the field on a direct line between where you are standing and the church in the village. For an overview of the area around Humber Redoubt and the Hindenburg Line, return to the village. Go around the left and right bends to the t-junction and continue round to the left. After seventy-five metres the priority route swings right. Turn left here, essentially straight on, and follow this track to the west for 1,000m to where there is a right fork. Just south of this point is where Fop Lane crossed the Hindenburg Line support trench. Park here and look southeast with the village to the left. Humber Redoubt was on the spur beyond the Sensée.

To visit the site of Clark-Kennedy's VC action, turn off the main Arras - Cambrai road (D939) in Vis-en-Artois onto the D9 southwest towards Chérisy. After 300m turn left signed for Québec Cemetery and after another 200m turn right at the fork with the football stadium on the right. Go on another 100m and take the left fork. Follow it for almost 400m and turn right at the next fork. Follow this track for 900m to the track junction at Québec Cemetery. This is Star Corner. Park here and walk along the track to the southeast for 175m to where Orient Lane crossed at right angles. Walk on another 200m to the crest to look towards Ulster and Union Trenches.

failed to penetrate thick wire entanglements covered by artillery, trench mortars and machine guns. In addition the Germans brought more machine guns to bear on the exposed right flank. At 6.30 p.m. Brigade HQ ordered the advanced posts to be withdrawn and the first objective to be held. **Lieutenant David Macintyre**, Adjutant 1/6th Highland Light Infantry, was in the firing line throughout the day and exhibited extreme coolness under heavy fire. He was an inspiration to all. The day's operations cost the Battalion 177 casualties, including twenty-one killed and died of wounds. However, the main event for which Macintyre was awarded the VC took place on 27th August. On that day he was the acting second in command, as there were only six officers left in the Battalion.

Orders were late in arriving on the night of 26th/27th August and it was not until 3.05 a.m. that 52nd Division, in common with 56th Division, issued its instructions. The intention was for 155th Brigade to carry out a preliminary operation to clear the Hindenburg Position for 800m and then the main attack, by 157th and 156th Brigades, was to follow at 10 a.m. to seize Fontaine-lès-Croisilles and then Riencourt. The orders to 155th Brigade did not reach their destination and, as a result, there was no preliminary operation. A gap opened between 56th and 52nd Divisions.

In the rearranged plan 157th Brigade advanced at 9.36 a.m., sixteen minutes after the barrage commenced, to clear the northern end of Hénin Hill. It was then to advance eastwards along the trenches of the Hindenburg Line to take Fontaine-lès-Croisilles, while 155th Brigade mopped up on Hénin Hill as far as Fop Lane. At 10.03 a.m., 156th Brigade was to come up on the left of 157th Brigade and advance to Hendecourt, while on the right 56th Division advanced from the southern end of Hénin Hill to take Croisilles.

157th Brigade set off on time with 1/6th Highland Light Infantry on the right and 1/7th Highland Light Infantry on the left. 1/5th Highland Light Infantry in support had two companies detailed to mop up in Fontaine-lès-Croisilles. The supporting guns were late taking up their positions and the barrage was not particularly effective at first, although it improved as the attack progressed. Thick bands of barbed wire, well covered by machine guns and trench mortars, were

From the track running southeast off the D9 road looking over the site of Macintyre's VC action around Humber Redoubt.

encountered from the outset. Casualties were heavy but, with great determination, ways were found through the wire and the opposing strongpoints were overcome in Summit and Fooley Trenches. The Germans were forced off Hénin Hill to lines of resistance further back, where more barbed wire was encountered. However, by 12 p.m. the Sensée had been passed and the troops pressed on towards Fontaine-lès-Croisilles, which was taken by 12.15 p.m.

Captain Macintyre distinguished himself in the initial attack by reconnoitring and leading his men forward to create gaps in the barbed wire. On another occasion he organised a party to cut gaps under very heavy machine gun fire. When the advance progressed beyond the Sensée, it became clear that 56th Division had been unable to take Croisilles and was still held up on the eastern slopes of Hénin Hill. This resulted in 157th Brigade being fired upon by machine guns and trench mortars from the right flank and also from the rear. It was not possible to continue the advance.

Before the attack the main resistance had been expected on the left flank and this is where the 157th Brigade reserve was situated. The heavy fire from the right flank prevented the reserve from being switched to where it might have been able to influence the outcome. An attempt to coordinate a combined attack by 155th and 169th Brigades, the former commanded by Brigadier General James Forbes-Robertson VC, to clear the trenches holding up 56th Division and 157th Brigade came to nothing.

While all this was going on, 156th Brigade attacked on the left and took Fontaine-lès-Croisilles, together with 500 prisoners and more than eighty machine guns. However, further advance was not possible due to the Canadians being held up further north. 157th Brigade became engaged in a ferocious battle as the Germans tried to infiltrate behind the right flank of 1/6th Highland Light Infantry. This area was critical as it held the key to Croisilles for both sides. About 2 p.m., when the line was held up, Macintyre led a party that included Sergeant James Smith and Macintyre's batman, Private Andrew Taylor, through the German barrage. They destroyed a machine gun post in a pillbox at Humber Redoubt. Three Germans were killed and eleven were captured, together with five machine guns. Macintyre's party then went on to dispose of three more pillboxes.

52nd Division wanted to renew the attack but, with every brigade engaged and facing southwest as well as east, it was decided to consolidate the positions held. There was also a shortage of ammunition and a few hours later aircraft dropped supplies. 1/6th Highland Light Infantry clung to its gains despite being under fire from front, right and rear. When 1/6th Highland Light Infantry was ordered to form a defensive line, Macintyre was relieved in the firing line and went to reconnoitre the exposed right flank. While doing so a machine gun opened fire on him from close range. Without hesitating, he rushed it alone and put the team to flight. He returned to the Redoubt with the gun, where he continued to supervise consolidation. The Battalion suffered 158 casualties in this action, including sixteen killed and nine designated 'not yet diagnosed nervous' (shellshock). That night 52nd Division was relieved by 57th Division. 157th Brigade was relieved by 172nd Brigade and withdrew to a bivouac area by 11 a.m. on the 28th.

In First Army, the Canadian Corps was to continue the advance, while a defensive flank was formed north of the Scarpe. The Canadian Corps issued its orders at 7.10 p.m. on the 26th. If the Drocourt–Quéant Line was found to be held strongly, it was to be left for an attack on subsequent days. The objective for 2nd and 3rd Canadian Divisions was the Fresnes–Rouvroy Line, along the high ground beyond the Sensée, on the line Fontaine-lès-Croisilles – Vis-en-Artois – Boiry-Notre-Dame. This involved an advance of about 3,200m. Although eight tanks were allocated to each division, only four could be produced by 14th Tank Battalion and two of these were knocked out early on. Zero hour, set for 4.55 a.m., was changed to 10 a.m. for 2nd Canadian Division on the right in order to coordinate movements with 52nd Division (Third Army). It also allowed time for 5th Canadian Brigade and the tanks to come forward and for reconnaissance to take place.

2nd Canadian Division was to secure Chérisy and Vis-en-Artois and then advance another 1,800m eastwards. A further objective was Cagnicourt; but this would entail a total advance of eight kilometres, through heavily defended positions, and seemed unlikely to be achieved. 5th and 4th Canadian Brigades, on the right and left respectively, were to lead.

The opposite view to the first picture.

5th Canadian Brigade, with 29th Battalion (6th Canadian Brigade), attached as a reserve, was to advance through Wancourt Tower Ridge, supported by eight tanks of 14th Tank Battalion and No.1 Company, 2nd Canadian Machine Gun Battalion. Three battalions led: from right to left these were 26th, 24th and 22nd, with 25th Battalion in support. All were in position by 8.20 a.m., having suffered few casualties in the move forward. The barrage opened on time and soon after zero an aircraft patrol reported that the enemy were retiring along Puffin, Parnell and First Avenue Trenches. Soon after zero the German barrage fell on the old front line and began to creep backwards close behind the advancing infantry, who pressed on.

Mallard Trench was captured, where a large number of prisoners, machine guns and trench mortars were taken. Thereafter enemy small arms fire slackened but artillery fire increased, including a large proportion of gas shells. On the right, 26th Battalion had crossed the almost dry Sensée by midday and large numbers of prisoners were streaming back. Shortly afterwards 24th and 22nd Battalions, in the centre and on the left, crossed either side of Chérisy, having captured the village. In the advance to this point 24th Battalion had been under heavy machine gun fire and some gas shelling.

There was a pause here for thirty minutes for reorganization before the barrage moved on again. When the advance resumed the supporting artillery barrage lifted off Occident Trench, which was seized by 24th Battalion. The artillery was only able to cover the infantry for a short time before the batteries were out of range and had to move forward. As soon as the barrage ceased, fierce resistance was met from machine guns and field gun batteries brought into action in the open south of Upton Wood. 24th Battalion advanced to about 135m from Ulster and Union Trenches. The Battalion was under fire from the front and both flanks, as it was ahead of both flanking units. An outpost line was established in Orient Lane with the main line in Occident Trench.

Lieutenant Colonel William Clark-Kennedy, CO 24th Battalion, went to Brigade HQ and reported that the infantry were held up 450m east of the Sensée. The line held by the three assault battalions was within 150m of Ulster Trench but there was no contact with units on the flanks. The CO of 22nd Battalion, Major

Arthur Edouard Dubuc DSO, had been wounded and Clark-Kennedy had taken command of both battalions. Artillery was brought forward to engage the German guns near Upton Wood and troops moving on the Hendecourt road. This prompt action stopped any possible German counterattack.

26th Battalion on the right was in contact with 7th Royal Scots in Una Lane. The latter was within the Canadian area and arrangements were made for 26th Battalion to take over the line as far as the Corps boundary in Fontaine Wood with one company. The Germans shelled the valley east of Chérisy heavily but elsewhere shelling was scattered and largely ineffective. There was a great deal of machine gun fire from the high ground east of Fontaine-lès-Croisilles. At this time the RAF appeared to be unaware of the line of forward troops, as a flight of Sopwith Camels was reported firing on friendly troops around Sun Quarry for fifteen minutes about 5.30 p.m. There was also a gap on the left flank between 22nd Battalion and 19th Battalion (4th Canadian Brigade). The latter sent a platoon to fill this gap and, later in the evening, 22nd Battalion took over this area.

Corps instructions were not to attempt too much if resistance was strong. Attempts to get forward were met with heavy machine gun fire. Without an effective barrage it was not possible to make progress and a halt was called until the next day. Machine guns were brought up to protect the flanks. The line consolidated was Fontaine Wood–Una Lane–Sun Quarry–Occident Trench–Orient Trench, Star Corner, Obus–Olga–Bottom Bridge. 24th Battalion suffered 252 casualties that day, including ten officers and the RSM.

In 4th Canadian Brigade, 18th Battalion, assisted by 43rd Battalion (3rd Canadian Division) on the left advanced parallel with the Arras–Cambrai road. Vis-en-Artois was occupied with little difficulty. However, beyond the Sensée the barrage was soon out of range and the enemy fire intensified. The infantry managed to press on for 450–550m beyond the stream and established a small bridgehead.

3rd Canadian Division's advance was led by 9th Canadian Brigade. Overnight rain added to the difficulties of assembling and it was still raining at zero hour. 52nd and 58th Battalions attacked at 4.55 a.m. with 116th Battalion in support. However, on the right 43rd Battalion had to wait until 10 a.m. to advance in conjunction with 2nd Canadian Division. Eight tanks appeared but were either knocked out or otherwise incapacitated.

52nd Battalion cleared Bois du Vert and 58th Battalion took, lost and retook Bois du Sart. 116th Battalion passed through 52nd Battalion but was met with such heavy fire from Boiry-Notre-Dame and in enfilade from Artillery Hill and Jigsaw Wood to the north that it was unable to progress. About midday 43rd Battalion came up on the right. A heavy artillery barrage came down at 1 p.m. and 116th Battalion tried again but, after making considerable progress, was forced to fall back. On the left Pelves was still held by the Germans and fire from it prevented movement on that flank. Meanwhile 43rd Battalion had gained touch with 2nd Canadian Division in Vis-en-Artois. That night 8th Canadian Brigade took over the line on the right.

North of the Scarpe 51st Division's objective was Greenland Hill. The attack started well but was forced back by a counterattack and the Hill was lost, although some progress was made on the flanks. Overall 27th August was a disappointing day, except for the Canadian Corps. The relief of 2nd and 3rd Canadian Divisions was postponed and both were ordered to continue the advance on the 28th, with the intention of breaking through the Fresnes–Rouvroy Line and seizing Cagnicourt, Dury and Étaing.

28th August 1918

The advance continued on 28th August, a warm day following a night of rain. Fourth Army's progress was more marked than the other Armies because the enemy withdrawal behind the Somme moved back further than in the north. The Australian Corps' divisions started at various times and probed ahead. They had an exhausting day advancing through a maze of old trenches and barbed wire. However, considerable advances were achieved in following up the retreating enemy, with many prisoners and machine guns being taken. III Corps also achieved its objectives with some heavy fighting at times.

Third Army's corps were to continue their advance in the same directions as on the 27th. However, if the enemy held on to their positions in strength, the day was to be spent resting and bombarding points of resistance and lines of approach for the future. As a result only a few small advances were made, mainly where the Germans pulled back and abandoned positions. XVII Corps took Croisilles and advanced 1,800m. 56th Division was then ordered to move southeast towards Bullecourt, while 57th Division advanced on Riencourt and Hendecourt. Preparations were also made for the bombardment and capture of the Drocourt–Quéant Line on 30th August. Zero hour was set for 12.30 p.m. In 56th Division, 167th Brigade advanced to occupy what was thought to be the abandoned village of Croisilles. Stiff resistance was met but was overcome and the objective was gained. The advance to Bullecourt by 169th Brigade came under heavy machine gun fire and encountered deep uncut wire. Direction was lost and the advance arrived in front of Hendecourt in 57th Division's area. There were heavy casualties but the village was captured and a few parties of 57th Division arrived there. However, under fire from three sides, they eventually had to fall back 450m to a trench northwest of Hendecourt. The advance towards Bullecourt fell short by 1,100m. 57th Division's objective, a trench about 550m short of the Bullecourt–Hendecourt road, was taken after overcoming considerable opposition.

First Army's orders to the Canadian Corps were confusing. It was to advance to the line Cagnicourt–Dury–Étaing and be prepared to attack the Drocourt–Quéant Line on 30th August. However, the line of villages was beyond the Drocourt–Quéant Line. The first objective for 2nd and 3rd Canadian Divisions was a trench line about 1,100m beyond the start positions. The Army objective was the Drocourt–Quéant

Line about 3,200m beyond. 51st Division on the left was to conform. Plouvain and Greenland Hill were its objectives but these were not attacked until the 29th. There were no tanks and zero hour for 2nd Canadian Division was 12.30 p.m., the same as for XVII Corps.

In 2nd Canadian Division, 5th and 4th Canadian Brigades were to continue the advance, with 6th Canadian Brigade in close support. The first objective was the Fresnes–Rouvroy Line and the second the Drocourt–Quéant Line. The night was quiet, with just a few scattered shelling incidents and intermittent bursts of machine gun fire. The artillery was able to provide a supporting barrage but there were no tanks available. Although 22nd and 24th Battalions were weak and exhausted, it was considered better for them to continue the advance and to retain 25th Battalion for use in emergency. In any case, moving 25th Battalion into an assault position would alert the Germans.

5th Canadian Brigade was hit by heavier fire than that experienced the previous day. 24th Battalion was led by C Company on the right and D Company on the left, supported by A and B Companies respectively. The Battalion pushed forward but was halted by the uncut wire in front of Ulster and Union Trenches. Repeated attempts to get through were driven back by the intense machine gun fire from the strongly held objective trenches. The Battalion was also under heavy shell fire throughout, which added to the casualties. Lieutenant Colonel Clark-Kennedy was wounded early on in the leg and was unable to move. Major Georges Philas Vanier MC (a future Canadian Governor General), commanding 22nd Battalion, lost his right leg in this action. Clark-Kennedy amalgamated the remnants of 22nd and 24th Battalions and, in spite of his wound, continued to direct the force against the German positions from a shell hole. By his leadership and example he was able to maintain the precarious position. At 3 p.m. 24th Battalion was holding Union Trench and 26th Battalion was believed to be in Ulster Trench. The artillery was requested to bring back the barrage. Having reported the situation to Divisional

Looking from the track southeast of Québec Cemetery in the direction of 24th Battalion's attack.

HQ, 5th Canadian Brigade was ordered to make good Ulster and Unicorn Trenches. 25th Battalion sent forward a company to each forward battalion. The company on the right reached the wire in front of Ulster Trench and the one on the left reached the wire in front of Unicorn Trench. Due to the heavy machine gun fire they were unable to progress further and joined the remnants of the assault battalions. By 5.30 p.m. the situation was more clear and settled. Only then did Clark-Kennedy agree to be carried back, leaving the Battalion under the command of Lieutenant Frederick Henry Morgan MC, assisted by Lieutenants Harold Richard Tanner MC and William McMurray MC, until Major Patterson Lindsay Hall MC arrived to assume command of the composite 22nd/24th Battalion.

4th Canadian Brigade was exhausted from two days of heavy fighting and could muster the strength of one battalion. The obstacle of uncut wire in front of the Fresnes–Rouvroy Line was too much. The Brigade was held up by Ocean and Opera Trenches and the attack stalled.

That night 2nd Canadian Division was relieved by 1st Canadian Division. The relief was conducted in difficult conditions and for 5th Canadian Brigade was not completed until 8.30 a.m. next morning. 24th Battalion was relieved by 13th Battalion by 2.30 a.m., having suffered another 162 casualties. 5th Canadian Brigade suffered 1,296 casualties before being relieved, including 117 killed. 24th Battalion's share was 414 casualties, including Clark-Kennedy and nineteen other officers.

3rd Canadian Division enjoyed more success. The night before the attack the Division's front had been reorganised and divided between the three brigades, from the south 8th, 9th and 7th. This was done in order to attack the Fresnes–Rouvroy Line in strength. The brigades were allotted different start times so that all five brigades of field artillery could support each infantry brigade in turn. 7th Canadian Brigade set off at 5 a.m. and took Pelves. 9th Canadian Brigade had a battalion of 8th Canadian Brigade (4th Canadian Mounted Rifles) attached in exchange for 43rd Battalion, which could not be disengaged. It started its advance at 11 a.m.

4th Canadian Mounted Rifles and 52nd Battalion took the first objective and advanced to the western edge of Boiry-Notre-Dame and the road running south from it. 52nd and 58th Battalions then swung north, with the latter clearing the village, and captured Artillery Hill. 42nd Battalion and Princess Patricia's Canadian Light Infantry (7th Canadian Brigade) captured the high ground and Jigsaw Wood, north of the village, by 3 p.m. They joined up with 49th Battalion in Pelves.

On the right 8th Canadian Brigade advanced at 12.30 p.m. 43rd Battalion and 5th Canadian Mounted Rifles had been shelled heavily earlier due to the movement of 9th Canadian Brigade. Considerable opposition was met but the enemy front line on Seventy Ridge was rushed. The western part of Rémy and Rémy Wood to the north of it were reached but not Haucourt. That night 3rd Canadian Division was relieved by the British 4th Division, which was reinforced with Brutinel's Brigade to guard against counterattacks on the vulnerable left flank near Pelves.

The three days of hard fighting by 2nd and 3rd Canadian Divisions resulted in 5,801 casualties. However, they had advanced eight kilometres on a widening front, through a maze of strongly defended trenches and had captured part of the Fresnes–Rouvroy Line. More than 3,300 prisoners were taken as well as fifty-three guns and 519 machine guns.

31st August 1918

> 404 2Lt James Huffam 5th attached 2nd Duke of Wellington's (West Riding) (10th Brigade, 4th Division) St Servin's Farm, Haucourt, France

The Allied Commanders-in-Chief met on 29th August and decided to continue the offensive. Haig issued his orders later in the day. First Army was to attack the Drocourt–Quéant Line south of the Scarpe, with the aim of reaching the line Bourlon Wood–Arleux–Sensée River. The cavalry was then to strike southeast into the rear of the enemy opposing Third and Fourth Armies, while they held the enemy's attention.

4th Division had been relieved in the Pacaut area on 23rd August and moved to join the Canadian Corps. On the night of 28th/29th August it relieved 3rd Canadian Division north of the Arras–Cambrai road, with 10th Brigade on the right and 11th Brigade on the left. Brutinel's Detachment was attached to guard against counterattacks from the direction of Hamblain. To the south of 4th Division was 1st Canadian Division and to the north was 51st Division. 1st Canadian and 4th Divisions were instructed to carry out small operations in order to secure good start positions (Yellow Line) for the attack on the Drocourt–Quéant Line by midnight on 30th August. This meant launching a number of minor operations to complete the capture of the Fresnes–Rouvroy Line and the Vis-en-Artois Switch, which joined the Drocourt–Quéant Line about 1,600m west of Cagnicourt.

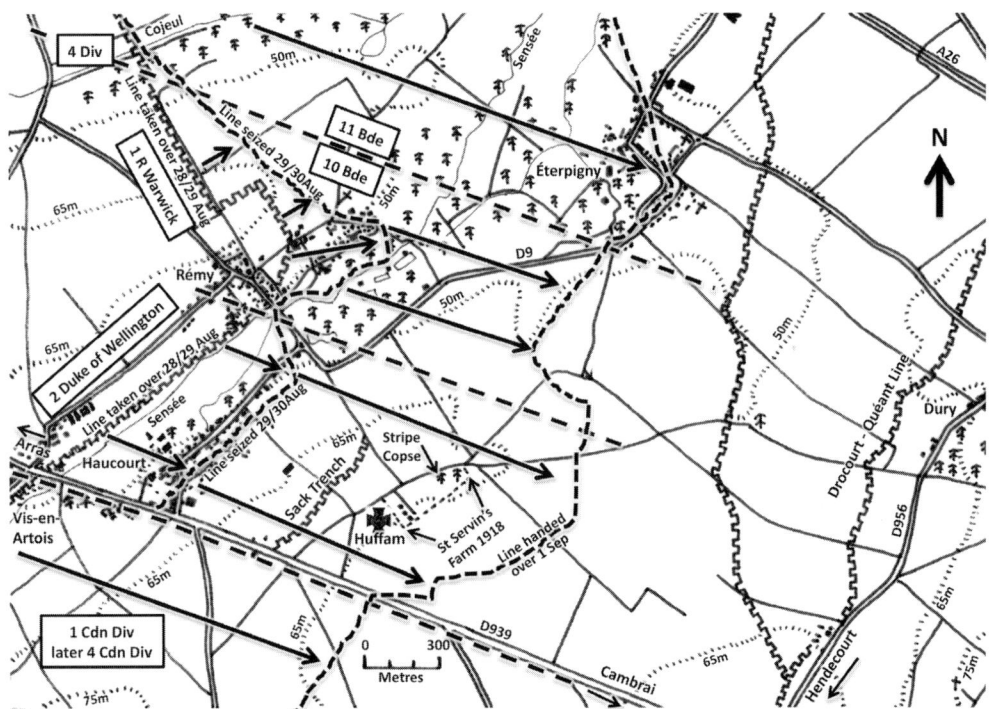

Drive southeast through Vis-en-Artois on the D939 Arras–Cambrai road. Pass the Vis-en-Artois Memorial on the left and continue to the top of the hill. Pass the water tower on the right and 150m beyond turn left into a gravel lane. Continue for 250m to a junction. Huffam's VC action was just beyond it, in the field on the right. New buildings on the site of St Servin Farm can be seen beyond. Return to the D939 and turn right. After 525m turn right onto the D9 through Haucourt. Follow for 450m to the church on the left, where there is a memorial to Huffam next to the village war memorial and a memorial to a Blenheim crew shot down on 22nd May 1940.

On 29th August, Brutinel's Detachment advanced almost 900m to seize Bench Farm and Victoria Copse north of Boiry-Notre-Dame, with some posts being established right up to the Scarpe. 10th Brigade advanced to secure the line east of Haucourt and Rémy. On the left, 1st Royal Warwickshire was ordered to gain the eastern edge of Rémy with zero hour set for 4 p.m. However, the Battalion achieved the objective by peaceful penetration by 7.45 p.m. instead. On the right, 2nd Duke of Wellington's had SOS artillery support on call and zero hour was set for 10 p.m. It established posts to the east of Haucourt by 2.30 a.m. on 30th August.

Throughout 30th August, Third and Fourth Armies pressed on with varying degrees of success. First Army made preparations for the forthcoming attack on the Drocourt–Quéant Line, with the 6″ Howitzers continuing to cut lanes in the wire in front of it. South of the Arras–Cambrai road, 1st Canadian Division surprised the enemy by attacking northwards and seized the Vis-en-Artois Switch, an advance of over three kilometres. North of the road, 4th Division attacked at 4 p.m. The

From the track junction looking northeast. Buildings on the site of St Servin's Farm are in the trees to the right of the track in the centre. The attacks by 2nd Duke of Wellington's came from the left. Huffam's VC action was in the ploughed field on the right.

Germans observed some troops moving into position and casualties were suffered due to heavy and persistent machine gun and artillery fire, including some gas shells. This attack was across swampy ground, in places waist deep in water, but fortunately the enemy did not resist strongly.

In 10th Brigade on the right, 2nd Duke of Wellington's took St Servin's Farm and 1st Royal Warwickshire seized the high ground further north, albeit with heavy

The area around St Servin's Farm from the southeast on the Cagnicourt road.

casualties to its two left companies. However, with both flanks exposed to fire, the company in the Farm had to abandoned its gains and the troops fell back to the first objective in Sack Trench. 2nd Duke of Wellington's lost thirty-eight killed and 170 wounded or missing in this action.

On the left, 11th Brigade seized Éterpigny. That evening Brutinel's Detachment on the far left also advanced and was then relieved by 33rd Brigade (11th Division). To the north, 51st Division made an advance of 450m and then it and 11th Division transferred to XXII Corps, thus shortening considerably the Canadian Corps front.

Next day, 31st August, the Australian Corps in Fourth Army gained a foothold on Mont St Quentin. This action was part of the Second Battle of Bapaume and will

be covered in the next volume of this series. In Third Army, Écoust-Saint-Mein and Longatte were retaken by VI Corps and XVII Corps took Bullecourt. IV Corps was pushed back 450m in places but the lost ground was recovered later.

First Army continued preparations for the attack on the Drocourt–Quéant Line, which was later rescheduled for 2nd September. 1st Canadian Division captured Hendecourt Château and the Crow's Nest, in cooperation with 57th Division (XVII Corps) to the south. 4th Canadian Division moved its 12th Canadian Brigade into the line between 1st Canadian and 4th Divisions. Both 4th Divisions were ordered to push ahead in line with 1st Canadian Division. By the evening, 4th Canadian Division had advanced its outposts 900m. The left made another attack at 8.40 p.m. in cooperation with the right of 10th Brigade. However, the enemy was too strong and this attack failed.

Earlier, at 2.30 p.m., 10th Brigade sent 2nd Duke of Wellington's to retake St Servin's Farm, which had to be abandoned the previous day, in order to join up with the left of the new Canadian line. B Company led on the left and A Company on the right, with C and D Companies in support. D Company, 2nd Seaforth Highlanders was in reserve. The Farm and surrounding wood (Stripe Copse) were taken but the position was again subjected to heavy fire from three sides. The Germans counterattacked with heavy artillery support at 6 p.m. and recovered the lost ground. During this fighting **Second Lieutenant James Huffam** took three men and rushed a machine gun post that was being set up on the western face of the wood. Having secured it, a heavy counterattack forced him to pull back, fighting all the way. The SOS barrage was called for and fell on the Farm, which forced the Germans to pull back from the western face.

10th Brigade ordered another attempt be made, with zero hour set for 8.45 p.m. 2nd Duke of Wellington's retook the Farm and wood and established a line 450m beyond. However, the right had to draw back a little and throw back a defensive flank. Undaunted by the odds against him in this attack Huffam, accompanied by only two men, rushed a machine gun post that was holding up the whole advance. It was captured with eight prisoners. In addition to these two incidents, Huffam performed with the utmost gallantry throughout the operations from 29th August to 2nd September. In total the Battalion took sixty-one prisoners, nine machine guns and a field gun. It suffered seventy-two casualties. Another twenty-two men were admitted to hospital; this might have been due to influenza but the war diary is not specific.

2nd Seaforth Highlanders advanced on the left and relieved 1st Royal Warwickshire, which was by then down to just four officers and about 150 men, by 5.15 a.m. Another advance was made on 1st September. This line was handed over to 12th Canadian Brigade as its start line for the forthcoming attack on the Drocourt–Quéant Line. The Canadians continued to make small improvements to their positions prior to the attack and the final preparations are covered in the next section.

Battle of the Drocourt-Quéant Line
2nd September 1918

414 CSM Martin Doyle 1st Royal Munster Fusiliers (172nd Brigade, 57th Division) Riencourt-lès-Cagnicourt, France

415 CPO George Prowse Drake Battalion (189th Brigade, 63rd (Royal Naval) Division) Pronville, France

416 LCpl William Metcalf 16th Battalion (Canadian Scottish) (3rd Canadian Brigade, 1st Canadian Division) Cagnicourt, France

417 Lt Col Cyrus Peck 16th Battalion (Canadian Scottish) (3rd Canadian Brigade, 1st Canadian Division) Cagnicourt, France

418 Pte Walter Rayfield 7th Battalion (1st British Columbia) (2nd Canadian Brigade, 1st Canadian Division) Villers-lès-Cagnicourt, France

419 Sgt Arthur Knight 10th Battalion (Canadians) (2nd Canadian Brigade, 1st Canadian Division) Villers-lès-Cagnicourt, France

420 Pte Claude Nunney 38th Battalion (Ottawa) (12th Canadian Brigade, 4th Canadian Division) Dury, France

421 Capt Bellenden Hutcheson Royal Canadian Army Medical Corps att'd 75th Battalion (Mississauga) (11th Canadian Brigade, 4th Canadian Division) Dury, France

422 Pte John Young 87th Battalion (Grenadier Guards) (11th Canadian Brigade, 4th Canadian Division) Dury, France

423 LSgt Arthur Evans 6th Lincolnshire (33rd Brigade, 11th Division) Southwest of Étaing, France

On 1st September 1918 the Australian Corps in Fourth Army completed the capture of Mont St-Quentin and Péronne, turning the entire enemy position on the Somme. This famous action is covered in the next volume in this series. Most corps in Third Army made ground and First Army made the final moves up to the Drocourt–Quéant Line (hereafter D-Q Line). Despite a number of setbacks, by nightfall the flanks of Third and First Armies were in position at their junction and ready for the assault next day.

The main event on 2nd September was the assault on the D-Q Line by First Army but the advance also continued elsewhere. Although Fourth Army was showing signs of exhaustion, it pressed on and reinforced earlier successes rather than give the enemy any respite. The Australian Corps finished clearing up on Mont St-Quentin and in Péronne. III Corps on the left of Fourth Army attacked with three divisions, including the 74th in its first action since arriving from Palestine. Some progress was made but there were considerable difficulties. In general the advance fell short of expectations.

Third Army ordered the advance to continue in order to assist First Army on the left flank. On the right, V Corps was to complete the capture of Saillisel and le

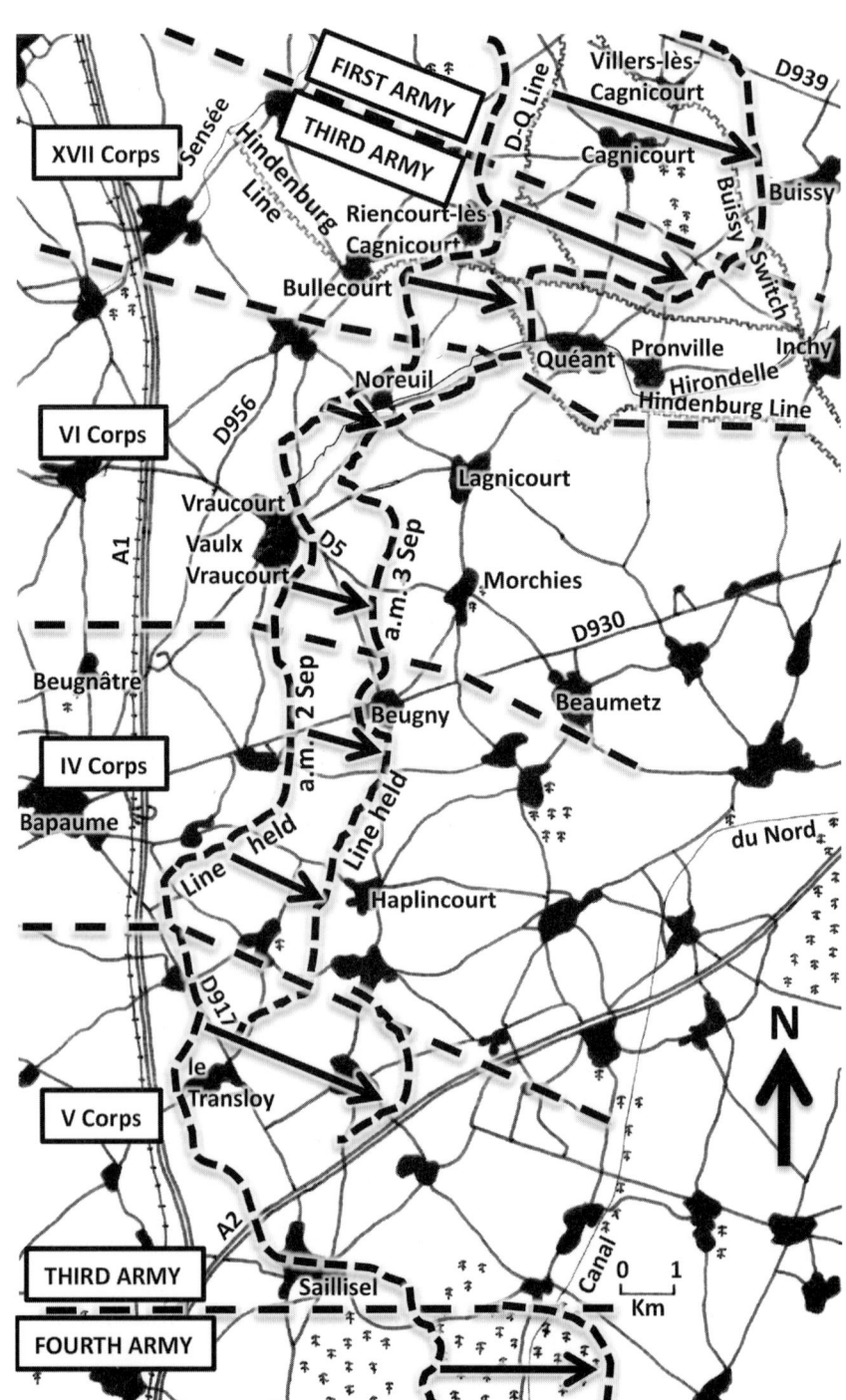

Third Army on 2nd September.

Transloy and push on towards the Canal du Nord. IV Corps was to take Haplincourt and Beugny, then also push on towards the Canal du Nord. Having taken Morchies and Lagnicourt, VI Corps was to head towards Beaumetz. On the left, XVII Corps was to cooperate with the Canadian Corps in First Army. All Mark V tanks were held in Army reserve.

V Corps advanced with 38th Division on the right, 17th Division in the centre and 21st Division on the left, with the main objective being le Transloy. Results were disappointing but some progress was made. IV Corps attacked with 5th Division on the left, the New Zealand Division in the centre and 42nd Division on the right. All objectives were reached except Beugny; although it had been entered it was lost in a counterattack.

VI Corps attacked at 5.30 a.m. with 3rd and 62nd Divisions, each supported by a company of 12th Tank Battalion (Mark IVs). A company of 6th Tank Battalion (Whippets) remained under Corps control. Little warning was given to the tanks and there was no time to rehearse with the infantry. The ground over which they were to operate, reportedly firm and good going, turned out to be clayey with steep sided sunken roads to impede progress.

On the right, 62nd Division, led by 187th Brigade, was well supported by field and heavy artillery, machine guns and eight tanks. The attack was launched fifteen minutes after IV Corps on the right and this alerted the Germans, who put down a barrage on the front line before the three battalions set off. At first casualties were light and by 6.50 a.m. the right had reached the Beugny–Vaulx Vraucourt road and the left had taken Vaulx Wood. However, six of the tanks had been lost and a counterattack recaptured the Wood. It was retaken by the divisional pioneer battalion at 2.30 p.m. and this position was then held.

On the left, 3rd Division was led by 8th Brigade, supported by a battalion from each of the other brigades on the flanks. On the right was 7th King's Shropshire Light Infantry, in the centre was 2nd Royal Scots and on the left was 1st Royal Scots Fusiliers, each with a section of A Company, 3rd Machine Gun Battalion attached. Ten Mark IV Tanks and eight Whippets were allocated. The Mark IVs were to operate against all trenches between the start line and objective, while the Whippets operated in the Noreuil valley and south and east of Lagnicourt.

Advancing behind an effective barrage, fired by seven field and two heavy brigades, and supported by nine Mark IV tanks and two machine gun companies, progress was initially good, except that seven tanks came to grief. Noreuil was taken and the outskirts of Lagnicourt were reached but, on the right, 7th King's Shropshire Light Infantry was forced back to Vraucourt Switch southwest of Noreuil. 1st Royal Scots Fusiliers on the left and 2nd Royal Scots in the centre only managed to reach an extension of the same trench (MacAulay Avenue) east of Noreuil by about 10 a.m.

Around 1 p.m. it was reported that 62nd Division on the right had been forced back almost to Vaulx-Vraucourt. A defensive flank was thrown back until 62nd Division regained its former positions. The attack was resumed in the late afternoon, with

2nd Suffolk assisting 7th King's Shropshire Light Infantry on the left. By 8 p.m. the road between Vaulx-Vraucourt and Lagnicourt had been reached. However, in order to avoid confusion when the Guards Division passed through, it was decided to withdraw all forward troops to Vraucourt Switch by 4.15 a.m. on 3rd September.

During the initial advance **Lieutenant Colonel Richard West**, CO 6th Tank Battalion, rode ahead to reconnoitre. When he reached the forward infantry he found that most officers were already casualties. He took charge, riding up and down the line with his orderly, encouraging the infantry and ensuring that the line held. He was eventually killed, but his intervention ensured there was no withdrawal. It is unclear precisely where West's action took place, but the evidence points to 7th King's Shropshire Light Infantry's area. Eight Whippet tanks were to operate on the Battalion's right flank with 62nd Division, but 7th King's Shropshire Light Infantry reported that none were seen during the morning. Notwithstanding this it is known that West was killed on the ridge southeast of Vraucourt Switch, close to the boundary with 62nd Division. This is the area across which 7th King's Shropshire Light Infantry advanced and later fell back to Vraucourt Switch. It seems a reasonable assumption that this is where West rallied the retiring troops and ensured that the line of this trench was held. West's VC was awarded for his actions on this day and also on 21st August at Courcelles (see the previous volume in this series for the account of this action and his biography).

XVII Corps' orders were issued on the evening of 31st August. Preliminary operations to take Riencourt-lès-Cagnicourt and the area to the south of it were completed on 1st September. The Corps' objective was the southern part of the D-Q Line but, with few tanks available, no frontal assault was to be made. Instead, if the Canadian Corps was successful on the left, 172nd Brigade (57th Division) was to pass through on the right of the Canadians, then turn south and roll up the D-Q Line facing the rest of XVII Corps. 52nd Division on the right would conform. It was hoped that the final objective, a section of the Hindenburg Position west of Quéant, would be reached in contact with the Canadians. At this point 63rd Division, recently transferred from IV Corps, was to pass through 57th Division to exploit towards Inchy on the Canal du Nord. This whole area had been fought over heavily in April 1917. The night before the attack, No.102 Squadron RAF bombed villages behind the German front. Low flying aircraft would also follow the advance and No.12 Squadron RAF was to provide the contact patrols.

At 5 a.m. a barrage was fired on the left of XVII Corps by five brigades of field artillery. It consisted of fifteen percent smoke, forty-five percent shrapnel and forty percent HE. After eighty-four minutes this barrage was to cease and four of the field brigades were to switch their fire to an east-west line through the D-Q Line, about 175m south of the boundary with the Canadian Corps. Six minutes later it was to creep southwards to cover the advance of 172nd Brigade (57th Division) down the D-Q Line. Meanwhile at 6 a.m. the seven brigades of heavy artillery were to switch from counter battery fire. Until 7.15 a.m. they were to concentrate on the triangle

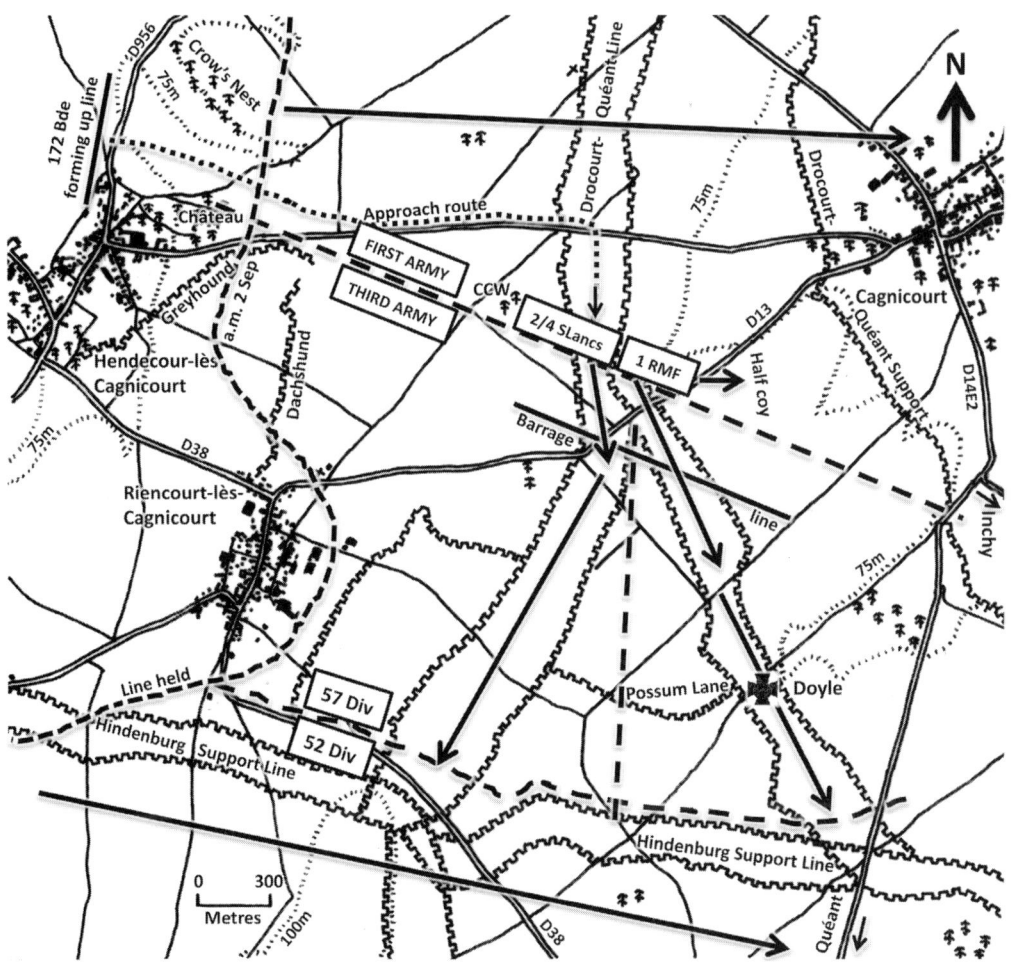

This abbreviation is used – CCW = Calling Card Wood.
In the centre of Cagnicourt drive southeast on the D14E2 towards Inchy-en-Artois. After 350m take the right fork and follow the track for 1,550m to a junction on the right. This track is shown as being private on some old and barely readable signs. However, when I used it, all I got was a wave from two friendly farmers. It is up to you if you use it or not. At the track junction you are just about on the westernmost trench cleared by 1st Royal Munster Fusiliers. Look back the way you came. The easternmost trench cleared by 1st Royal Munster Fusiliers crossed the track about 200m closer to Cagnicourt. Both trenches headed off downhill from this point and joined Possum Lane just before the line of bushes in the low ground. The precise location of Doyle's VC actions within D-Q Line is not known.

between the southern end of the D-Q Line and the Hindenburg Position and also on Quéant and a few other places.

Thirty minutes after zero two battalions of 172nd Brigade were to follow behind the Canadian right flank along the Cagnicourt road and halt where it crossed the D-Q Line. They were to meet two tanks commanded by Lieutenant Knight near

Calling Card Wood. 1st Royal Munster Fusiliers was to lead, followed by 2/4th South Lancashire. Once in position the two battalions were to face right and wait for the barrage at zero plus ninety minutes. At that time the two battalions were each to follow one of the tanks. 2/4th South Lancashire was to clear the western fork of the D-Q Line, while 1st Royal Munster Fusiliers rolled up the eastern fork as far as the Green Line. 9th King's was in support in Greyhound and Dachshund Avenues. A Company, 57th Machine Gun Battalion attached one section to each assault battalion for consolidation and two sections remained with the support battalion.

1st Royal Munster Fusiliers had moved forward at 2 a.m. and occupied trenches west of Hendecourt, prior to moving forward again at 3 a.m. At 4.48 a.m. it formed up on a taped start line 450m west of the line Crow's Nest–Hendecourt Château. Despite the tanks not arriving, and a heavy German barrage that included gas shells, the troops moved through the gap created by the Canadians twelve minutes after zero hour, formed right and took up their assault positions. At zero plus ninety minutes the barrage fell and, supported by flanking fire from 57th Machine Gun Battalion in the front line on the right, the two battalions swept down the D-Q Line trenches, clearing them with bomb and bayonet. At the same time the Canadians encountered problems on their right and 1st Royal Munster Fusiliers sent half a company to assist.

On the right, 2/4th South Lancashire had a similar experience to 1st Royal Munster Fusiliers. When 52nd Division was held up on the right, a company was sent to form a defensive flank. 9th King's also sent a company to support 2/4th South Lancashire.

Both forks of the D-Q system were cleared, but considerable opposition was met, particularly after the barrage ended at 7.15 a.m. 1st Royal Munster Fusiliers overcame a number of machine gun and trench mortar positions and took many prisoners. The Battalion pushed on 900m and established itself in Possum Lane. A counterattack was dealt with and by 8.40 a.m. all objectives had been taken.

Looking southeast along the two trench lines of the Drocourt–Quéant Line to Possum Lane.

172nd Brigade was relieved the following afternoon. It had captured almost 1,000 prisoners, 110 machine guns, thirty minenwerfer and two anti-tank rifles. Two 77mm field guns captured by 1st Royal Munster Fusiliers were later appropriated by the Canadians. The Brigade suffered 203 casualties, including 134 in 1st Royal Munster Fusiliers.

During the attack, **CSM Martin Doyle** in 1st Royal Munster Fusiliers took command of his company due to casualties amongst the officers. Some men were cut off by the enemy and he led a party to their rescue. By great skill and leadership he worked his way close to them and, having killed several of the enemy, extricated the party. He carried back a wounded officer under heavy fire and some time later observed a tank in difficulty. Despite the intense fire, he rushed forward and routed the enemy who were in the process of trying to get into the tank and prevented another party from launching an attack. However, machine gun fire on the tank made it impossible to move the wounded. Single-handed, Doyle rushed the machine gun. About twenty metres along a trench he encountered a German officer with a machine gun under his arm. The German ordered Doyle to put up his hands, but Doyle shot him in the chest with a revolver that he had taken from the tank. Doyle pressed on, picked up a rifle and bayonet and came upon the machine gun crew. He bayoneted three of the four Germans (the citation says that he took three prisoners) and then returned to the tank, which was on fire and the enemy were again swarming around it. The party was in danger of being taken prisoner. Doyle carried a badly wounded sergeant in the tank to a place of safety, while under heavy fire. Not content with this outstanding performance, he then carried another wounded man to safety under heavy fire. Later, when the enemy counterattacked his company's position, he demonstrated great power of command and drove back the attack, taking many prisoners in the process.

At 8.45 a.m. 156th Brigade (52nd Division) advanced to follow on the success of 57th Division. The Brigade pushed almost 1,200m along the Hindenburg front line as far as the D-Q front line. Uncut wire was then encountered and the right

and centre were held up. Enemy resistance stiffened but it was outflanked and by 3 p.m. the line as far as the outskirts of Quéant had been taken. In the evening the Hindenburg support line was occupied as far as the Quéant–Cagnicourt road. 155th Brigade followed on the right of 156th Brigade, entered the Hindenburg front position at 5 p.m. and continued beyond the Hirondelle stream, where it was out of contact with 3rd Division to the south. That night patrols found Quéant had been abandoned.

63rd Division's advance at 8.10 a.m. was predicated on the success of 57th Division. 188th Brigade was to lead, with the battalions of 189th Brigade on call and 190th Brigade in reserve. The objective was the Quéant–Marquion railway (Red Line), between the Hindenburg support line and the right of the Canadians on the high ground east of Quéant. If possible the advance was to continue to Inchy.

The assault troops moved up through Calling Card Wood and set off over the Cagnicourt–Quéant road at 8.10 a.m. 188th Brigade was led by 2nd Royal Irish Regiment and 1st Royal Marines. Despite a few setbacks and lack of artillery support at the start (all guns were supporting 57th and 52nd Divisions until 9.30 a.m.), the advance swept on at great speed until being held up by machine guns in the Hindenburg and D-Q support lines. The Anson Battalion reinforced the centre and artillery and machine guns were brought to bear. At 1 p.m. the attack was renewed and Queer Street and the Quéant–Buissy road were reached just short of the Red Line objective.

189th Brigade assembled around Calling Card Wood at 10.40 a.m., where it suffered some casualties to artillery fire. At 1 p.m. it was ordered to send one battalion to extend the left of 188th Brigade and then swing southwards in order to turn the enemy position from the northern flank. The objective was the railway (Red Line). The Drake Battalion, commanded by **Commander Daniel Beak**, set off at 1.30 p.m. It passed through Cagnicourt and made a wide sweep to the left through Bois de Bouche to reach 188th Brigade's line in Queer Street.

Heavy machine gun fire was received from the Hindenburg support line. Beak detailed a platoon to clear that section and then to work forward to the railway to protect his right flank, while the rest of the Battalion attacked over the open towards Pronville at 6.30 p.m. A number of enemy posts were outflanked before reaching the Red Line on the railway and contact was made with the Canadians on the left near Inchy Station. The advance continued over the ridge in front of 188th Brigade, broke through the Hindenburg support line and entered Pronville. The Pronville–Inchy road was also reached by two companies, cutting off the enemy's retreat and netting a large bag of prisoners, machine guns, mortars and field guns. However, despite its success, at the end of the day the Drake Battalion was isolated east of Pronville. This was the second action for which Beak was awarded the VC, the previous being at Logeast Wood on 21st -25th August (see the previous volume in this series).

During the advance of the Drake Battalion, part of **Chief Petty Officer George Prowse**'s company was cut up by machine gun fire from a strongpoint and was

Battle of the Scarpe 1918   39

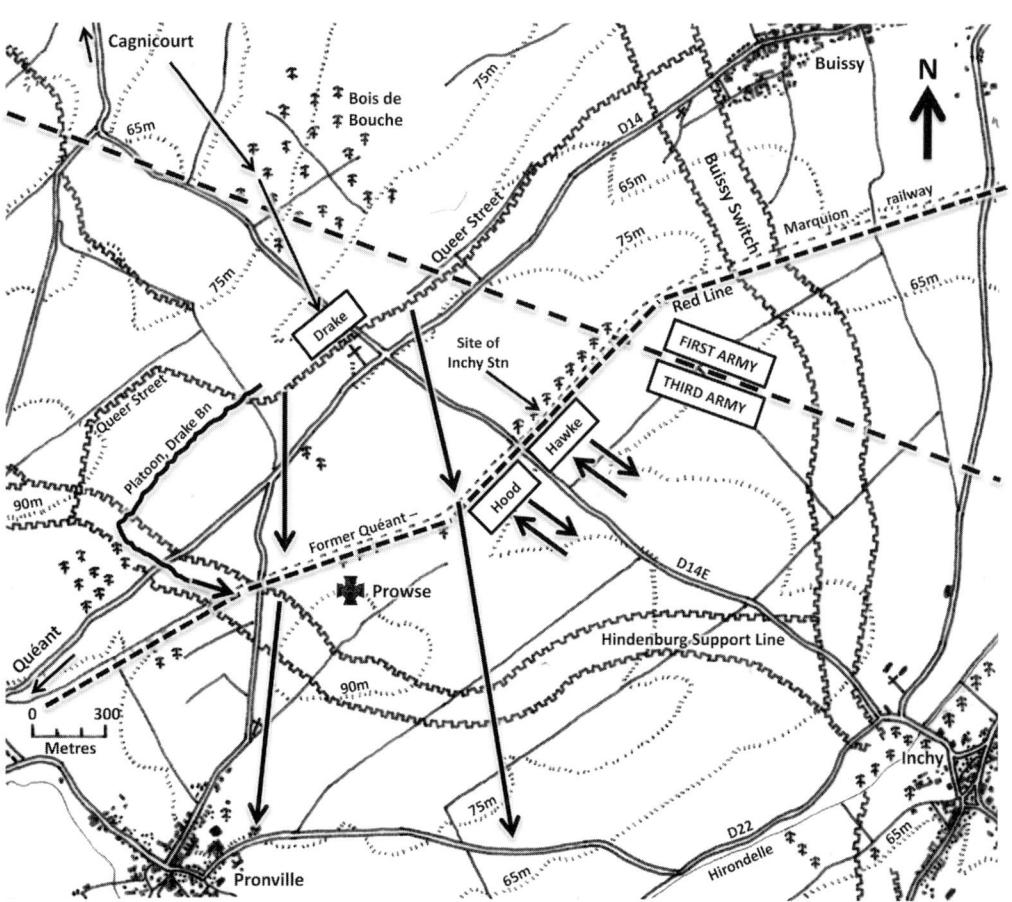

In Pronville drive northwards along a minor road past the village cemetery on the right towards the D14. 250m beyond the cemetery stop on the crest and look to the north. The Drake Battalion attacked towards this position. The former Quéant–Marquion railway runs left to right 300m in front, marked by a line of bushes. Drive on to the junction with the D14 and park safely in one of the track entrances to see the reverse view.

badly disorganised. Remaining cool he collected the men that were available and led them forward to capture the strongpoint, taking twenty-three prisoners and five machine guns. He then took a patrol onto the vital high ground in the face of heavy opposition. A German limber crew, who were trying to recover ammunition, was observed and Prowse attacked it singlehanded, killing three men and capturing the limber.

At 6.30 p.m. 189th Brigade was ordered to attack with two battalions to capture Inchy. The Hood and Hawke Battalions set off with artillery support at 7.30 p.m. The Hood Battalion was to work eastwards along the Hindenburg support line, while the Hawke Battalion advanced north of the Cagnicourt–Inchy road to capture a section of Buissy Switch. They met fierce resistance and were held up by heavy

From the D14 looking south towards Pronville and the high ground where George Prowse led a patrol and captured the limber.

machine gun fire. Little progress could be made in daylight. Fighting continued at night but nothing more was gained and they fell back to the Red Line. The attack was renewed next day.

Two days later, while covering the advance of his company with a Lewis gun section, Prowse observed two machine guns in a concrete emplacement holding up the battalion on the right. Rushing forward with a small party, he captured the post and killed six of the enemy. He was the only survivor of the party but the action allowed the battalion to continue. Prowse bagged thirteen prisoners and the two machine guns.

The success of the whole day hinged upon the Canadian Corps in First Army breaching the D-Q Line. This formidable position consisted of a front and support system, each with numerous concrete pillboxes and covered by thick wire

The reverse view with the high ground on the right. The D14 is marked by the line of bushy topped trees.

entanglements. The front line was mainly along a crest or forward of it, whereas the support line was on the reverse slope throughout. Behind the southern half was the Buissy Switch, which connected with the Hindenburg support line.

In the days preceding the attack the Canadian Corps improved its positions to gain the most advantageous start line. This included an ingenious operation by 1st Canadian Brigade on 30th August. XVII Corps to the south had captured Hendecourt behind the Fresnoy–Rouvroy Line. Using this breach as a starting point, the Brigade attacked northwards from Third Army's area. The attack by 1st and 2nd Battalions set off at 4.40 a.m. behind a complicated barrage that instead of advancing away from the front had to move from right to left. The move caught the defenders by surprise and the line was rolled up quickly, destroying two enemy battalions in the process. The 3rd Battalion attacked frontally on the left and cleared the trenches southwards.

First Army's orders were issued at 7.45 p.m. on 31st August. The operation had been scheduled for 1st September but the senior commanders decided not to launch

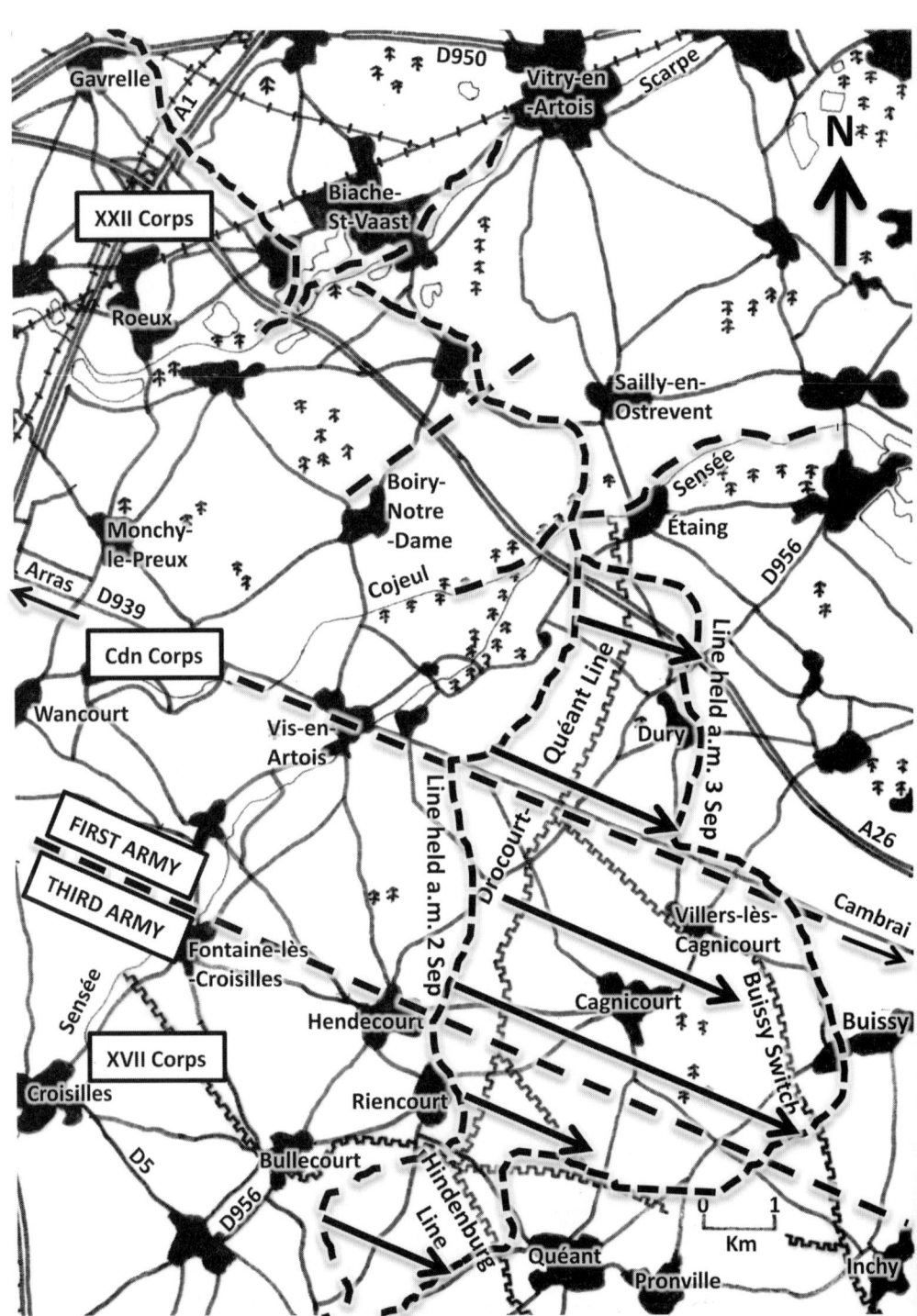

First Army on 2nd September.

the attack until the conditions were right. On the right, the Canadian Corps was to breach the D-Q Line, exploit rapidly to seize crossings over the Canal du Nord and gain the high ground beyond. 3rd Tank Brigade, a regiment of cavalry and 17th Armoured Car Battalion were attached. XVII Corps (Third Army) to the south was to cooperate fully and exploit the breach to the southeast. The left flank of the Canadian Corps was to be secured by XXII Corps exerting continuous pressure on the enemy. On the left of First Army, VIII Corps was also to maintain pressure and use its artillery to engage hostile batteries able to fire into the left flank of the Canadians.

First Army also had 1st Brigade RAF in support and the Cavalry Corps was at four hours notice to move. Such was the strength of the D-Q Position, that General Sir Henry Wilson, Chief of the Imperial General Staff in London, sent Haig a message on 29th August. He associated the D-Q Line with the Hindenburg Line and pointed out that the War Cabinet would become anxious if there were heavy casualties without success. Haig kept this to himself and his plans and orders remained unchanged.

The advance continued on 31st August by 1st Canadian and 4th Divisions. That night 4th Canadian Division moved 12th Canadian Brigade into the line between the two divisions. On the morning of 1st September, 2nd and 3rd Canadian Brigades captured the Crow's Nest, a strongpoint overlooking the D-Q Line. Despite three counterattacks the position was held. Fighting for advantageous start positions continued almost until zero hour. The Germans knew an attack was coming and launched a number of counterattacks late on 1st September, in particular at the junction of the two Canadian divisions. The Germans also pushed forward their outpost zone, which was already 1,600m deep in places.

The Canadian Corps attack was led by three divisions, from the south 1st Canadian, 4th Canadian and 4th Divisions. 1st Division and the Canadian Independent Force (previously known as Brutinel's Force/Brigade/Detachment) was in reserve. Lieutenant General Sir Arthur Currie's plan was to break through the D-Q Line astride the main Arras–Cambrai road, then swing left and right to roll up the rest of the Line from north and south, rather than take it by frontal assault. The reserves of the two flanking divisions were concentrated on their inner flanks. As soon as the Red Line had been secured, the Canadian Independent Force was to push along the Arras–Cambrai road to seize crossings over the Canal du Nord ahead of the main advance.

There were four objectives but only the first two are relevant to the action as the third (Blue Line) and fourth (Brown Line), beyond the Canal du Nord, were not reached. The first (Red Line) was the high ground from Cagnicourt to Dury, south of Étaing beyond the D-Q support line. The advance to the second objective (Green Line) was to commence three hours after zero, which was set for 5 a.m. This objective overlooked the Canal du Nord and the Sensée. Two companies of Mark V tanks were allocated to each attacking division. The noise of them assembling was covered by low flying aircraft. The tanks were to set off in time to be at the first German trench just ahead of the infantry. After the first objective tanks were only to be used to mop up on the flanks. The Canadian Corps had twenty field and eleven heavy brigades of artillery in support.

Aerial activity was considerable. Night bombers struck three defended villages (Saudemont, Écourt-St-Quentin and Palluel) and also billeting areas and airfields. No.8 Squadron was detailed to cooperate with the tanks, while No.73 Squadron picked off anti-tank guns and Nos.5 and 52 Squadrons worked with the attacking divisions. No.6 Squadron cooperated with the cavalry and day bombers attacked railway stations in Douai, Marquion and Valenciennes and some of the Sensée bridges. Four squadrons in 1st Brigade RAF (Nos.54, 64, 208 and 209) singled out various villages to complement the heavy artillery programme. A few aircraft were specially detailed to attack trains. Nos.22 and 40 Squadrons protected the low flying aircraft and the armoured cars, while also attacking German kite balloons.

1st Canadian Division was led by 3rd and 2nd Canadian Brigades. Each had three batteries of machine guns and a company of 14th Tank Battalion attached.

A number of abbreviations are used – CN = Crow's Nest, CCW = Calling Card Wood, BW = Butt Wood (site of), TC = Trigger Copse.

The map shows the start and final positions for battalions but not all positions occupied during the day or where leapfrogging took place. Drive north through Hendecourt-lès-Cagnicourt on the D956. Pass the church on the left and, after 200m, turn right and immediately take the left fork. Follow this lane past the football pitch on the right for 1,800m to the first wind turbine on the right. Just after it, turn right and continue for 450m with Calling Card Wood on the left. Park at wind turbine PA1-14 on the right. Walk southeast along the track south of Calling Card Wood for 525m. This is where D-Q Line front line crossed the track. Look left into the field where Metcalf's VC action took place to the east of Calling Card Wood. Continue along the track to the southeast for another 150m. Look half left towards Cagnicourt. Peck ran up the slope out of the shallow re-entrant to the D-Q Line support trench in the field in front of you. He led his Battalion in taking D-Q Support, which ran about 200m in front of the water tower at Cagnicourt.

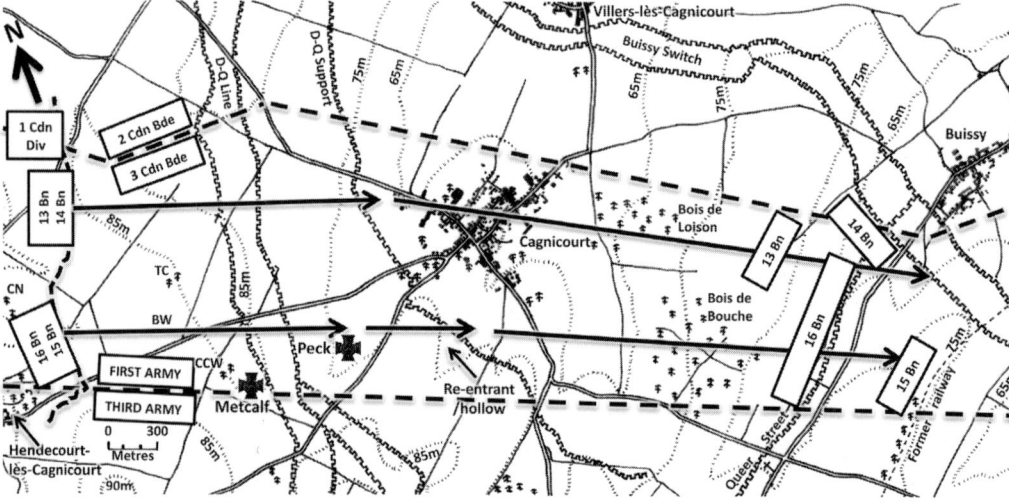

1st Canadian Brigade was to pass through after the capture of the Buissy Switch, between the first and second objectives, to capture Buissy and Baralle. As the thick belts of wire in front of the D-Q Line had only recently come into range of the heavy and medium artillery, it was not possible to destroy them before the assault commenced. It was therefore decided to cut it in certain places and to rely on the tanks to create more lanes.

3rd Canadian Brigade was to attack on a frontage of 1,450m towards Cagnicourt with 16th Battalion on the right and 13th Battalion on the left. Three tanks were to move ahead of 16th Battalion into the D-Q Line. Unless called upon they would then rendezvous at Calling Card Wood. Similarly, three tanks would precede 13th Battalion and rendezvous at Butt Wood. Two other tanks were to support 172nd Brigade on the right flank. At the first objective (Red Line) 15th and 14th Battalions were to pass through to capture Cagnicourt, Bois de Bouche and Bois de Loison. Four tanks were to encircle Cagnicourt and Bois de Loison, while another two encircled Bois de Bouche. 13th Battalion was then to pass through 14th Battalion to mop up the Buissy Switch (Green Line). 15th Battalion would be in support and 16th Battalion in reserve. The creeping barrage would end at the Red Line. Thereafter heavy artillery would engage sections of ground for specific times and a mobile field artillery brigade was attached to the Brigade.

16th and 13th Battalions assembled behind 15th and 14th Battalions with some difficulty in the darkness and almost featureless terrain. While the CO and company commanders of 16th Battalion were meeting in a dugout to finalise the orders for the attack, a shell seriously wounded the MO, Capt Cathcart, in the trench outside, a huge loss just before the men went into battle. The attack started on time at 5 a.m. Enemy artillery fire opened almost immediately but was light at first and the advance proceeded quickly. The wire had to be cut by hand in places and, where necessary, tanks fired smoke to cover the wire cutters. Resistance was overcome quickly and the two trenches of the D-Q Line front system were taken along with many prisoners. The advance continued without the tanks and 13th Battalion captured the support line by 7.30 a.m., having suffered light casualties.

16th Battalion attacked with No.1 Company on the right and No.2 Company on the left, supported by Nos.4 and 3 Companies respectively. The right boundary was on the Hendecourt–Cagnicourt road. Assembly was slow in the dark, the move forward taking many hours, although over no great distance. No.2 Company was only partly in position by zero hour and No.1 Company found it difficult making contact with 57th Division on the right. To complicate matters, as the troops moved into their start positions, Germans sprang up in front of them to surrender. Prisoners reported that the Germans were due to attack at 6 a.m.

When the advance began the enemy barrage was light and at first crowds of Germans came through the smoke to surrender. One supporting battery was firing short and caused some casualties. The ground began to rise towards the D-Q Line and a German convoy was seen racing back along the Hendecourt–Cagnicourt road. An area of shell holes and concrete emplacements was passed through without opposition and more Germans surrendered. After 550m machine gun fire was received from Trigger Copse, which was engaged by the Lewis guns, while a platoon each from Nos.1 and 4 Companies swung round to the south. They outflanked the German position, which surrendered readily. The advance resumed until thick bands of wire, much of it intact, were reached and they came under heavy machine gun fire from the right, where 57th Division was not making a frontal attack. All eight officers in Nos.1 and 4 Companies became casualties and the men were mixed up. Losses were so heavy that these companies were effectively out of action as formed units for the rest of the day. However, small groups of men pressed on. The hold up was observed by the Brigade commander, who ordered two tanks forward to assist.

The right of 16th Battalion was within thirty metres of the second belt of wire when the artillery barrage lifted off the D-Q front line. The defenders were quick to set up numerous machine guns and open fire. The advance slowed again and progress was only made by short rushes. However, by the time that they had reached the wire, the enemy had brought up more machine guns and forced the attackers into cover.

In No.1 Company, 4 Platoon on the extreme right was sheltering in shell holes. Eighteen years old Lieutenant Alex Campbell-Johnston led another rush but it faltered after five metres in the face of heavy fire. Campbell-Johnston was killed in the wire (Dominion Cemetery, Hendecourt-lès-Cagnicourt–I C 25). Any exposure brought renewed fire from the front and right. After a short while a tank was heard approaching from the left about one hundred metres behind. They tried to signal the tank but were not seen, so settled down to fire rifle grenades at the enemy trench,

From the D-Q front line looking northwest. The Canadian attack came from left to right. The D-Q front line ran from this position over the high ground to the left of the group of wind turbines on the right. The copse on the left is Calling Card Wood and to the right of it, in the distance, is Trigger Copse. Metcalf guided the tank in the open ground in the centre.

while the German machine guns poured heavy fire at the approaching machine. As it got closer the Germans threw bundles of grenades at it.

Lance Corporal William Metcalf MM calmly walked over the bullet swept ground and guided the tank towards the trench that was holding up the advance, using signal flags to point out targets. He walked ahead on the right of the tank as it approached the line held by 4 Platoon from the left rear. As Metcalf guided the tank along the trench, the Platoon took advantage of the reduction in enemy fire and rushed forward again. The trench was seized and the tank went on about 450m but was knocked out fifteen minutes later. Seventeen machine guns were found in this section of trench and all had been in use. It seems inconceivable that Metcalf could have carried out these actions without being hit. Later, although wounded, he continued to advance until ordered to get into a shell hole and have his wound dressed.

172nd Brigade came up on the right flank and initially occupied the trench held by Nos.1 and 4 Companies before turning south. Meanwhile on the left flank, No.2 and 3 Companies had met little resistance and, having overtaken the barrage beyond Trigger Copse, rushed through a gap in the first two belts of wire. When the barrage lifted off the D-Q front line, 16th Battalion rushed it. On arrival most of the enemy were found standing on the fire step with their hands up. One man levelled his rifle at the CO, **Lieutenant Colonel Cyrus Peck**, who was in the centre of the first wave, but a comrade knocked the weapon out of his hands and the entire group of about thirty Germans surrendered. The trench was found to be well constructed and strongly manned, with up to three times as many defenders as attackers, but they were demoralised and had no fight in them.

Having sorted out the prisoners and reformed the Battalion, Peck led it forward again towards the D-Q intermediate support line, about 225m away. Gaps in the wire were sufficient to allow the attackers to pass through. On reaching the trench the garrison surrendered without a fight. The Battalion had by then crossed the crest and was still heading southeast towards the D-Q Support line down a bare

Looking northeast from roughly the area of the D-Q intermediate support line towards Cagnicourt in the distance. Running across the middle of the picture is the re-entrant/hollow sloping down to the left. Beyond it, just in front of the village, was the D-Q Support line.

slope and across a shallow re-entrant. As soon as the advance recommenced it came under heavy fire from high ground on the right flank. Although the fire caused some casualties, it did not halt the advance initially. However, when about 200m from the D-Q Support, the Battalion came under even heavier fire from it and a trench running along the southeast side of the Riencourt–Cagnicourt road.

The attack stalled again. Peck realised that the first priority was to gain concealment from the enemy fire, so he ordered smoke grenades be thrown to form a screen. Peck was in a shell hole with Lieutenant Dunlop, the Battalion Intelligence Officer, discussing their next moves, when they came under machine gun fire from the right. This was being directed against a tank that was in difficulty in the hollow on the right of the Battalion. The tank was engaging the Germans' full attention. Taking advantage of this, Peck ordered Dunlop to return to the intermediate support line under cover of the smoke screen to find out the situation there. He returned

The reverse view to the previous picture, from just behind the D-Q Support line, looking southwest. 16th Battalion attacked towards this position across the re-entrant/hollow in the centre. On the right is Calling Card Wood with Trigger Copse beyond it in the right distance. In the left distance is the church in Riencourt-lès-Cagnicourt.

unhurt and reported that the trench was held in strength with British troops on the right. Peck was about to return to the intermediate support line himself when another tank came down the slope and attracted a hail of machine gun fire. The tank continued until it was only a short distance from the shell holes occupied by the forward elements of 16th Battalion.

The tank halted and then turned to return the way it had come. Peck disregarded the heavy fire and ran after the tank, standing directly in front of it to gain its attention. He ordered it forward again, which it did, but when he returned to the shell holes, the tank once again retired towards the intermediate support line without explanation. This left the forward elements of 16th Battalion in a very dangerous situation. Peck and Dunlop ran back to the intermediate support line under heavy fire. Peck admitted that the speed was 'out of keeping with my avoirdupois'. There he found some Royal Munster Fusiliers crossing to the 16th Battalion's left, away from their direction of advance. Despite his remonstrations they continued. Perhaps this was the half company sent by 1st Royal Munster Fusiliers to assist 16th Battalion and Peck had no knowledge of it. The reinforcement is not mentioned in his after action report.

Peck turned his attention to the situation in front of his own Battalion. He ordered the machine gun officer to direct all his fire against the ridge to the south and the

right flank of the D-Q Support line. He then arranged for the artillery forward observation officer to bring down fire on the same locations. Having subdued the enemy fire to a degree, Peck organised the troops in the D-Q intermediate support into an attacking formation and led them down the slope to join the leading waves in their shell holes. Peck then led this more substantial force forward and seized the Battalion's objective in the D-Q Support line.

Large numbers of troops could be seen advancing on the left flank towards Cagnicourt but the right flank was still of concern. It was not clear where the British troops on that flank were. Lieutenant Green was sent to find out and found a party of 1st Royal Munster Fusiliers whose orders were to act as a link with the Canadians. However, due to the stream of machine gun and field gun fire from the high ground it was clear that the enemy still held Cagnicourt. German aircraft had been very busy and frequently swooped down to machine gun and bomb.

Between 8 a.m. and 9 a.m., 15th and 14th Battalions passed through the leading battalions. By then they were beyond the range of the supporting artillery and progress was made by platoon and section rushes. 15th Battalion's right was protected by 16th Battalion and later by 3rd Battalion (1st Canadian Brigade). It suffered casualties but fought forward slowly and took Bois de Bouche. By 1.30 p.m. the Battalion had reached the Quéant–Marquion railway. The open right flank was closed by British troops at 6 p.m. 14th Battalion took Cagnicourt, where it surprised the Germans in the cellars, and consequently had few casualties. Bois de Loison was seized and, after a rapid dash over 1,800m of open ground, the Battalion was in part of the Buissy Switch by 11.15 a.m. There the Germans resisted strongly and fighting continued until nightfall. 13th Battalion held the left flank facing north. During the afternoon the artillery was called upon to break up German reinforcements threatening from Buissy Switch.

3rd Canadian Brigade took 2,800 prisoners that day, in addition to 200 machine guns, twenty-nine guns and twenty trench mortars. The Brigade suffered 926 casualties, with 16th Battalion losing 203 officers and men, of whom thirty-eight were killed. In his post-action report, Peck noted that the Battalion had lost twenty-seven officers in as many days.

On the left of 1st Canadian Division, 2nd Canadian Brigade was to capture the Vis-en-Artois Switch and D-Q Line within its boundaries and Villers-lès-Cagnicourt. Attached to it was No.2 Company, 14th Tank Battalion, with nine tanks, and No.2 Company, 1st Canadian Machine Gun Battalion (less one battery). 2nd Brigade CFA was in direct support. 7th Battalion was to lead the attack with five tanks on a frontage of 900m. 10th Battalion, with the tanks previously attached to 7th Battalion, was to pass through after the D-Q Line fell (Red Line), with 8th Battalion in support and 5th Battalion in reserve. The remaining four tanks were kept in reserve to replace casualties. One battery of 2nd Brigade CFA was detached to 7th Battalion and then to 10th Battalion after the Red Line. A battery of machine guns was detached to 7th, 8th and 10th Battalions and two trench mortars to every

Battle of the Scarpe 1918   51

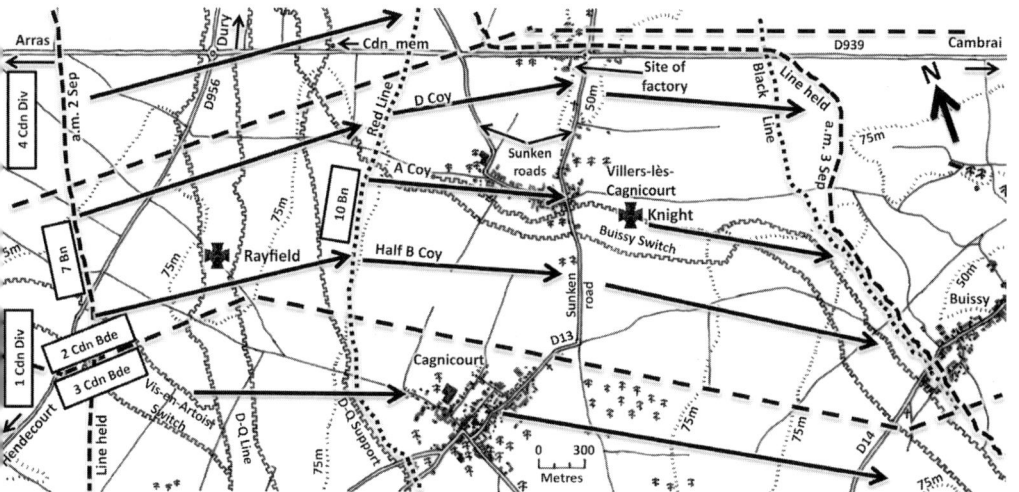

The area in which Rayfield's VC action took place is all but featureless. Leave the centre of Cagnicourt on the minor road to the northwest. After 1,400m turn left onto a pavé track leading to Dominion Cemetery after 550m. The Cemetery sits on the junction of the Vis-en-Artois Switch and the D-Q Line. There are sweeping views from here to the north over the ground fought over by 10th Battalion. Return to the road and turn sharp left. Follow it for 900m to the north, which is probably where Rayfield's VC action took place. If you wish to stop, choose your spot wisely as the road is narrow and the verges can be very soft in wet weather.

To visit the site of Knight's VC action, turn off the main D939 Arras–Cambrai road onto the D13 and drive into Villers-lès-Cagnicourt. At the crossroads turn left and follow the single lane track for 650m to the top of the rise. Park carefully on the verge to ensure that other vehicles can pass and to avoid getting bogged in. Turn back to face the village. The two trenches of Buissy Swtch ran through the field to the left parallel with the track. Return to the village and go straight over at the crossroads to the church where there are memorials to Metcalf, Peck, Rayfield and Knight on the outside of the south side of the tower.

battalion in the Brigade. The attack was preceded by a rolling barrage, including ten percent smoke, moving forward ninety metres every five minutes. At the Black Line, 1st Canadian Brigade was to continue the advance.

Nos.3 and 1 Companies, 7th Battalion, right and left respectively, set off at zero hour and passed through 5th Battalion, which was fighting for an ill-defined front line east of the Hendecourt–Dury road (D956). It had been engaged in hand to hand fighting all night for the start line. In support on the right was No.4 Company and on the left No.2 Company. The ground here was vital for both sides, as it provided visibility over the other side's rear areas. Inevitably, 7th Battalion immediately came under the fire of advanced machine gun posts about 135m east of the Hendecourt–Dury road.

No.3 Company suffered a number of casualties but the enemy posts were gradually overcome. The advance then continued more rapidly to the main D-Q Line by when the tanks were in the lead. Keeping up with the barrage, the Company had little difficulty in taking the forward system of the D-Q position. It continued into the D-Q Support system, which was defended by only a few machine gun posts and they were overrun quickly.

No.1 Company had a similar experience. The tanks helped to clear machine gun posts and the infantry was able to reorganise, covered by the barrage, before moving on. Heavy casualties were inflicted on the retiring enemy. Hostile fire from the D-Q Support system was silenced by concentrated small arms fire. Thereafter the opposition came from isolated machine gun posts along a slight rise in the ground. The objective was reached in the northern end of Buissy Switch. German field guns opened fire from just in front of a wood but concentrated small arms fire silenced them and forty gunners surrendered.

Large numbers of prisoners (estimated at up to 700) were taken and casualties were comparatively light. The Germans used large quantities of gas before and during the attack but there were few casualties as a result. The Red Line was reached at 7.30 a.m. Casualties amounted to twenty-five killed, ninety-two wounded and ten missing.

During this attack **Private Walter Rayfield** pushed ahead of his company and assaulted a trench occupied by a large number of the enemy. He bayoneted two of them and took ten prisoners. Later, while under constant rifle fire, he engaged in a dual with a German sniper, who had caused three casualties. He worked around to a flank, shot the sniper dead and rushed that section of trench. The enemy there was demoralised and another thirty surrendered to him. Then, regardless of heavy machine gun fire from the front and flank, he left cover and carried in a wounded comrade. It is not clear from the sources in which company Rayfield was serving. However, the descriptions favour No.3 Company, although that is by no means certain.

From the minor road northwest of Cagnicourt. Rayfield's VC action was probably somewhere in the near to middle distance.

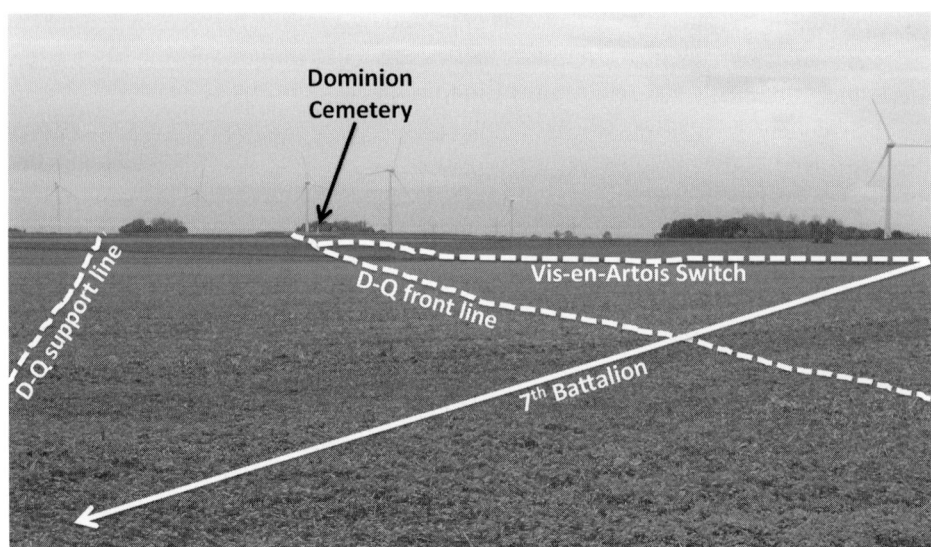

Just after 8 a.m., 10th Battalion passed through 7th Battalion at the Red Line and was then beyond the range of the supporting barrage, which to that point had been excellent. Half of B Company on the right was to maintain contact with 3rd Canadian Brigade. A Company in the centre was to attack along Buissy Switch and mop up Villers-lès-Cagnicourt, before going on to the final objective. D Company on the left was to advance astride the Arras–Cambrai road to mop up the factory north of Villers-lès-Cagnicourt and other obstacles. It had two tanks attached. The other half of B Company was in support behind A Company, while C Company remained in reserve with one tank. 6th Battery CFA and F Battery, 1st Canadian Machine Gun Battalion were attached. Scouts led the way, followed by three battle patrols (one per leading company) and then the main force of the leading companies.

Within forty-five minutes five tanks had been knocked out as they crossed a skyline. The advance came to a halt in the face of heavy machine gun fire. There was also field gun and minenwerfer fire from the front, left flank and left rear, particularly from the high ground south of Villers-lès-Cagnicourt. The unit on the left was well behind and the enemy in Buissy Switch and trenches northwest of Villers-lès-Cagnicourt resisted strongly with bombing parties. A frontal assault was not possible in the face of this fire and companies were ordered to work their way forward slowly, taking advantage of cover and any opportunity to outflank enemy positions.

6th Battery CFA came forward to deal with the enemy resistance points. The Battalion also brought captured enemy guns into action. The attached machine guns subjected enemy resistance points to direct fire. Under cover of this the infantry managed to get around the flanks and made steady but slow progress.

B Company on the right kept up with the other companies and maintained contact with 3rd Canadian Brigade on the right flank. In the centre A Company encountered more resistance in Villers-lès-Cagnicourt and the attack became more methodical as the village and Buissy Switch were gradually taken.

The wood at the northwest end of Villers-lès-Cagnicourt was taken with thirty-five prisoners. The advance continued to establish a line in the sunken road at the eastern end of the village and a party bombed along the southern trench of Buissy Switch. It met with considerable resistance but succeeded in taking forty-two unwounded prisoners and eight machine guns, as well as killing another twenty-five enemy.

D Company encountered stiff resistance from the sunken road running north from Villers-lès-Cagnicourt. It was eventually overcome with sixty-one unwounded prisoners and thirteen machine guns being taken. A number of British tank crewmen, who had been taken prisoner by the Germans earlier in the day, were released. About 4 p.m. the Factory fell and D Company established a line in front of it and along the sunken road to the south. Here the enemy suffered heavy casualties and another twelve prisoners were taken with eight machine guns. The Company

The northern trench of Buissy Switch ran parallel with and about 100m to the left of the track on the right. The attack came out of the village of Villers-lès-Cagnicourt towards the camera position and on past the left side of this view. The church in the right middle ground is where the memorials to Metcalf, Peck, Rayfield and Knight are located.

came under heavy fire as it passed through a hedge and most of those who attempted it were killed or wounded.

The centre and left of the Battalion just about surrounded Villers-lès-Cagnicourt and mopping up started from the rear. The two support platoons of B Company went to assist A Company and captured a battery of field guns that the Germans were trying to withdraw.

A line was established along the sunken road south of Villers-lès-Cagnicourt and a short pause followed to allow more artillery to be brought up. The Germans made a number of small counterattacks all along the line. The opportunity was taken to finish clearing Villers-lès-Cagnicourt. Two more tanks of 14th Tank Battalion were sent forward to assist at 3 p.m. By 5 p.m. the village had been taken but the Germans pushed the Battalion back a little. A halt was made there until the supporting artillery (2nd Brigade CFA and some heavy guns) could be arranged for a renewed attack. In the meantime two tanks that had progressed along Buissy Switch were knocked out by a field gun firing over open sights, before they reached Villers-lès-Cagnicourt. 7th Battalion arranged for ammunition and other supplies to be passed forward.

The advance by 10th Battalion resumed at 6 p.m. behind a renewed but less intense barrage than was normally expected. However, it proved to be adequate and the advance was more rapid than earlier in the day. Two platoons attacked along the sunken road east of Villers-lès-Cagnicourt, while another two drove the enemy out of the northern trench of Buissy Switch. At the same time A and B Companies dealt with the area on the right. The attack along the sunken road stalled in the face of machine gun fire. However, the troops rallied, reorganised and continued until the sunken road became shallow and the remnants of the garrison fled. On the right there was also heavy fighting. German aircraft managed to gain superiority in this area and some casualties were caused by their machine guns. The German planes were also quick to call in artillery support.

Initially the attack along the northern trench failed to make progress against a strong enemy force with a plentiful supply of bombs. Lieutenant G Watt reorganised

the two platoons into one due to the casualties and sent a section under **Sergeant Arthur Knight** ahead. Under heavy machine gun and trench mortar fire, Knight led his men forward and was soon in the thick of hand-to-hand fighting, which lasted for at least ten minutes. He continued alone, bayoneting a number of machine gun and trench mortar crewmen. The survivors fell back in some confusion and were followed closely, resulting in seventy-five prisoners being taken. Another one hundred Germans were killed or wounded. About thirty tried to get into a tunnel leading to the rear but Knight dashed towards it, killed an officer and two NCOs and forced the remainder to surrender. The advance continued and, when the enemy again held it up, Knight rushed forward and routed them before they had had time to reorganise. He died of wounds the following day.

B Company mopped up the trench and provided enfilade fire to support C Company in the northern trench. Both companies then manned the captured trench. The forward line was held from the right by B, A and C Companies.

It was not until 11 p.m. that resistance in Buissy Switch was overcome and the objective (Black Line) was reached. Contact with 3rd Canadian Brigade was established in Queer Street on the right. The northern flank was exposed as the troops on the left had been held at the Red Line. 8th Battalion provided two platoons to establish eight outposts along the Arras–Cambrai road to cover the threatened flank, in contact with 4th Canadian Division. Casualties had been so severe that Battalion HQ was thinned out to provide men for the companies. Overnight the positions were adjusted so that, by dawn on 3rd September, the line was held by two companies of 10th Battalion on the right and a company of 8th

Villers-lès-Cagnicourt church. The memorials to Rayfield, Peck, Metcalf and Knight are in a square on the outer wall on the right.

Battalion on the left. 1st Canadian Division thus ended the day having breached both systems of the D-Q Position and had made inroads into Buissy Switch.

2nd Canadian Brigade took 450 prisoners, of whom one hundred were wounded. By the time that the Brigade was relieved late on 3rd September, it had captured twenty-three mortars, thirty-six guns and 242 light and heavy machine guns. Casualties from 30th August until 3rd September were 135 killed, 663 wounded

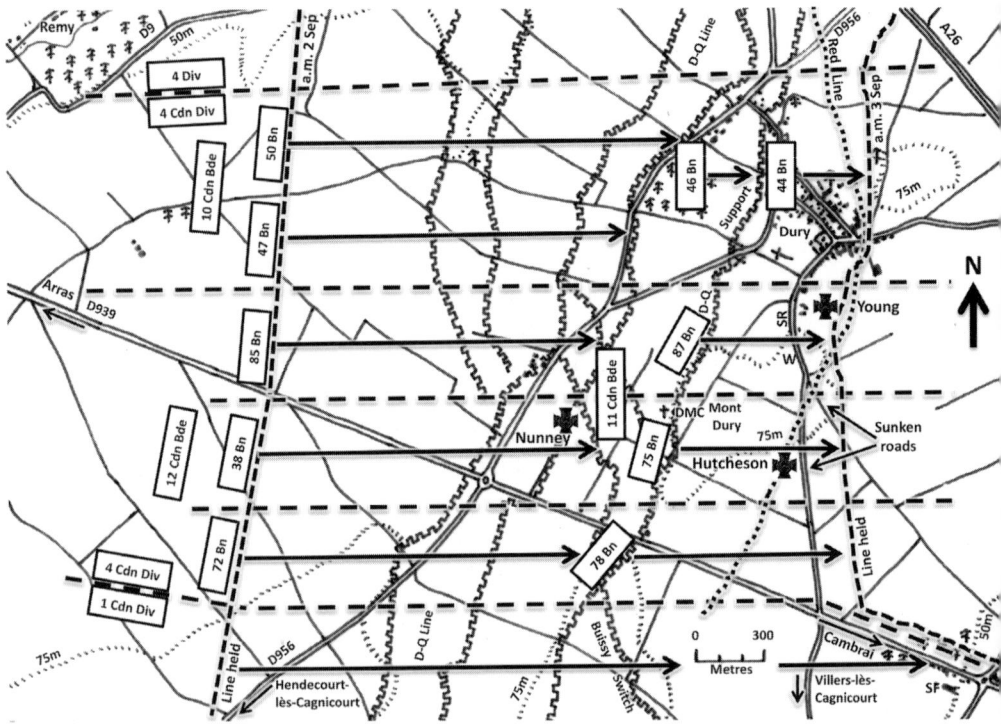

A number of abbreviations are used – W = windmill, SF = sugar beet factory, DMC = Dury Mill Cemetery. There is a café in Dury.

The best view over the scene of Nunney's VC action is from Dury Mill Cemetery, which is close to the junction of the D-Q Line and D-Q Support line. Approach Dury off the main D939 Arras - Cambrai road on the D956. After 900m take the minor road half right up the hill. Pass the communal cemetery on the right and take the next right. There is a small chapel on the corner with memorials to Nunney and Hutcheson. Continue past Dury Crucifix Cemetery on the left to the junction with the water tower and turn right. After 100m turn right again onto a rough track and follow it for 750m to Dury Mill Cemetery. Look westwards. 38th Battalion advanced towards this position between the roundabout on the D939 and the farm surrounded by trees in the low ground. The precise location of Nunney's VC action is not known but was probably between Dury Mill Cemetery and the D956.

Return 750m to the last junction. Young was active in the area to the south of this point, mainly between the road (sunken in places) and the line held that evening, which was parallel with the road and about 250m east (left) of it. Continue southwards for 350m to a fork. Just south of here was 75th Battalion's northern boundary. Hutcheson was active all over the area to the south from the crest of the ridge on the right, where the trees of Dury Mill Cemetery can be seen 150m east (left) of the road. Continue almost to the junction with the D939 and look back to see the sunken part of this road.

and forty-one missing. Of interest in the Brigade HQ war diary, in addition to a long list of enemy equipment captured, is a list of British equipment salvaged. This included 718 rifles, 172 sets of webbing, 161 water bottles, 158 steel helmets, 3,059 Mills grenades and 129,200 rounds of small arms ammunition. By contrast a wheelbarrow, a broom and two signal flags were also recovered. When 10th Battalion was relieved early on 4th September, its casualties amounted to twenty-nine killed, 193 wounded and eleven missing.

4th Canadian Division was led by 12th and 10th Canadian Brigades on the right and left, with twenty-five tanks of 9th Tank Battalion and nine of 11th Tank Battalion in support. It was late in the planning when, due to casualties, it had been decided to shorten 4th Division's front to the north and insert 10th Canadian Brigade into the line alongside 12th Canadian Brigade. For the former this entailed a sixteen kilometres approach march, followed by relief in place and assembly, all in darkness, immediately before the attack.

12th Canadian Brigade was supported by twenty-four tanks of 9th Tank Battalion, a battery of 3rd Brigade CFA, some 6″ Newton Stokes mortars, No.3 Company, 4th Battalion Canadian MGC, half a company of 12th Battalion Canadian Engineers, an NCO and four men of the Canadian Corps Cavalry and stretcher-bearers from 12th Canadian Field Ambulance. The frontage of the Brigade was 1,350m wide up to the Red Line. Thereafter it narrowed to just 450m before extending to 2,250m as it approached the Canal du Nord. Four lines of trenches, strongly constructed and heavily wired, had to be captured. In front was an outpost zone up to 1,600m deep. The Arras–Cambrai road and Mont Dury had to be taken on time to allow 11th Canadian Brigade and the Independent Force to pass through at 8 a.m. It was also vital in order to allow the artillery to move forward.

The Brigade advanced at 5 a.m. with 72nd Battalion on the right, 38th Battalion in the centre and 85th Battalion on the left. 78th Battalion, initially in reserve, was to form an advanced guard after the Brigade crossed the Red Line, with 11th Canadian Brigade on the left. At the Black Line, 72nd and 38th Battalions were to resume the lead to the Green Line and then press on to secure crossings over the Canal du Nord. Finally 85th Battalion was to pass through to the Blue Line.

72nd and 85th Battalions had been under pressure from enemy counterattacks the previous day. They had fought hard to retain their positions even before the operation against the D-Q Line commenced. About 6.30 p.m. on 1st September, an attack developed against 38th Battalion. The advanced posts of B Company were in danger of being overrun and were reinforced by the other two platoons of the Company. The SOS flare was fired to bring down an effective artillery barrage. During this attack **Private Claude Nunney**, who was at Company headquarters, proceeded through the barrage to the outposts, going from post to post to give confidence and encouragement to the men there by his own example. The enemy was repulsed after a short fight.

Assembling the assault battalions was achieved in difficult circumstances and there was no opportunity for proper reconnaissance. Some of the forward enemy posts were so close to the start line that they were unaffected by the barrage. Twenty-two tanks of 9th Tank Battalion had not arrived by zero hour and did not appear until after the enemy wire had been crossed. The front and support systems of the D-Q Line were taken with little difficulty, except on the left of 85th Battalion in the sunken road. Three tanks were lost. The guns of 3rd Brigade CFA engaged strongpoints and the machine guns suppressed much of the enemy fire to allow the infantry to progress. The advance continued across a shallow valley but, on reaching the crest of Mont Dury, 72nd and 38th Battalions were hit by machine gun fire. This was sited in depth and in enfilade from the direction of Villers-lès-Cagnicourt, beyond the range of the supporting artillery. There were heavy casualties but they pressed on and, aided by the tanks, reached a sunken road from Dury to the Arras–Cambrai road, close to the Red Line.

38th Battalion was led by A Company on the right and B Company on the left supported by C and D Companies respectively. Except for one machine gun post, little opposition was encountered and the first objective in the D-Q Line was taken on time. Rifle grenades were used freely to engage strongpoints. On the left, the right of 10th Canadian Brigade lost direction and crossed 38th Battalion's front. There was some confusion before the officers managed to change direction and bring their men back to their proper positions. During this phase of the attack Nunney again displayed great dash and was continually in advance of his comrades. His fearless example helped to carry the company forward to its objective.

C and D Companies took up the lead. They came under heavy machine gun fire and scattered shelling but seized the last D-Q Line. Advancing again they crossed a

From Dury Mill Cemetery, the wall of which can be seen on the right, looking west. The roundabout at the junction of the D939 and D956 is on the left amongst the trees. 38th Battalion attacked towards the middle of the picture. Nunney's VC action was probably in the fields in the centre, this side of the D956, which runs from the roundabout in front of the farm buildings on the right.

valley and came under heavy fire as they reached the crest of the hill. The fire came from Dury and a windmill on the left, posts to the front, and the wood of Villers Château and the factory on the right. The two companies were in advance of both flanking units and suffered heavy casualties. C Company extended its front to the right, almost to the Arras–Cambrai road and reached its objective on a frontage of 725m.

Enemy machine guns poured fire over the entire ridge and, except for one straight trench, there was no cover. The sunken road was reached after the garrison of machine gun and trench mortar teams had been destroyed. However, heavy mortar fire forced the attackers to fall back behind the road into shell holes. 78th Battalion and 11th Canadian Brigade arrived but were unable to continue the advance due to the heavy fire. A and B Companies, 38th Battalion had reorganised by then and reinforced C and D Companies, adding to the growing congestion in the area. It proved impossible to reach the right of C Company but the unit on the right sent a party of an officer and twelve men to help. Trench mortars and two field guns continued to fire on the line held. German infantry occupying a building in front were driven out by the 6″ Newton mortars. Unable to move forward, 11th Canadian Brigade took over the line and 38th Battalion was withdrawn. The Battalion claimed to have taken 325 prisoners, four trench mortars and forty machine guns.

In following the leading battalions, 78th Battalion suffered considerable casualties just crossing the ground already seized. It continued the advance at 8 a.m. but there appeared to be no support on the right, where the troops were making use of the trenches to progress at a more steady rate. In contrast, 78th Battalion faced open ground and was forced to advance as rapidly as possible. With little artillery available, only a small amount of territory was gained beyond the sunken roads. The armoured cars were late in arriving and did not go forward until 9 a.m. A more vigorous attempt was made between 10.30 a.m. and 11.30 a.m.

Little more was achieved by 12th Canadian Brigade that day. A field gun, some anti-tank guns and masses of machine guns were taken, in addition to 1,259

prisoners. The Brigade suffered 967 casualties: 38th Battalion – 232 (269 according to the Battalion war diary), 72nd Battalion – 225, 78th Battalion – 250 and 85th Battalion – 260.

10th Canadian Brigade, led by 47th and 50th Battalions had much the same experience as 12th Canadian Brigade. Having negotiated intact wire obstacles, it overran both trenches in the front line system of the D-Q Position and many prisoners were taken. 46th Battalion then passed through and seized the support line, which passed through Dury, after overcoming some flanking machine gun fire from the right. Nine machine guns and 120 prisoners were taken. The Brigade's objective was secured by 7.30 a.m.

At 8 a.m. the second phase commenced. 11th Canadian Brigade passed through with 78th Battalion (12th Canadian Brigade) and 44th Battalion (10th Canadian Brigade) on the right and left flanks respectively. 75th and 87th Battalions led with 54th and 102nd Battalions in support respectively. Attached to the Brigade were a battery of field guns, two mobile 6" Newton mortars (one to each leading battalion) and twenty-four Vickers machine guns (eight to each leading battalion and eight in reserve) from No.2 Company, 4th Canadian Machine Gun Battalion. However, after the Red Line the artillery was out of range. Later the support battalions were to pass through to capture bridgeheads over the Canal du Nord and the high ground to the east (Blue Line).

Many casualties were suffered in the approach march and the advance had to go ahead without the benefits of the artillery barrage or tank support. However, the field battery and the Brigade Trench Mortar Battery were on call. Two 3" Stokes mortars were attached to each assault battalion. It appears that 11th Canadian Brigade actually passed through 12th Canadian Brigade on the D-Q Support line instead of the Red Line. The high ground of Dury Hill was gained but, in the approach to it, 85th and 38th (12th Canadian Brigade) Battalions had veered outwards leaving the

Looking south from the junction of 75th Battalion's northern boundary with the Red Line on the road running south from Dury to the D939, which is out of sight in dead ground in the middle distance. Hutcheson was active all over this area.

area around the windmill open. As a result patrols of 75th and 87th Battalions had gone forward assuming that 12th Canadian Brigade had already gone on. As soon as this was realised the battalion commanders decided to seize the Red Line. There were many casualties and heavy fire from machine guns and field guns was met on the far side. There was also congestion as units ran into each other as the advance slowed. 54th Battalion was ordered to disperse itself in greater depth to avoid this.

At 10 a.m. 75th and 87th Battalions made another attempt to progress and managed to establish a line 175m in front of the sunken roads after hard fighting. At 11 a.m. the Brigade commander made a personal reconnaissance and found 87th Battalion in the sunken road as far south as the windmill, with outposts 175m ahead. The leading company of 102nd Battalion was also there having pressed forward too quickly. 75th Battalion continued the line to the south, with a company of 54th Battalion on the right flank. The enemy machine guns holding up the advance were too far away to be engaged by the mortars or outmanoeuvred by the infantry. Communication forward from battalion HQs was difficult and the Brigade HQ radio was knocked out five minutes after being set up. Maintaining wires was also difficult. The Brigade commander realised that further progress was not going to be made without artillery support. In addition, unnecessary casualties were being suffered due to congestion and crowding in the forward areas. As a result he pulled back 75th Battalion in the centre into reserve and closed up 54th and 87th Battalions to fill the gap. 102nd Battalion remained in support. At the same time stragglers from 12th Canadian Brigade were sent back. 11th Canadian Brigade suffered 952 casualties in this action.

The machine guns attached to 75th Battalion were bombed on their way to the assembly area. Only two gun teams were still effective afterwards and they went into Brigade reserve to be replaced by the eight guns in reserve. The Battalion was led by C and D Companies on the left and right respectively, with B Company in support and A Company in reserve. In front a patrol was to maintain contact with 12th Canadian Brigade and keep the CO appraised of the situation. At 7.15 a.m. the patrol reported that 12th Canadian Brigade was occupying the D-Q Support line but there

was no sign of any troops further ahead. At 8 a.m. the leading companies pressed on from the D-Q Support line and immediately came under fire from the sunken road, the windmill and the right flank. C Company's left flank was open but reached the sunken road. D Company came up on the right. A platoon of A Company was sent to replace casualties in C Company and allow the advance to continue. Both leading companies pushed on 175m beyond the sunken road but could advance no further due to the machine gun fire. A Company moved up to the sunken road in support and B Company was in reserve. A 6" Newton mortar and the attached machine guns kept the enemy under fire and low flying British aircraft also rendered valuable assistance. About 12.20 p.m. the Brigade commander ordered the Battalion to press on while he tried to obtain tank and artillery support. Immediately after this the CO was wounded while on reconnaissance. All afternoon enemy aircraft machine-gunned and bombed the line. No further forward movement was made and by 8.30 p.m. the Battalion had been relieved by 54th Battalion. It suffered 305 casualties, including the CO and twenty-one other officers. In addition to taking 132 prisoners, the Battalion captured eighteen machine guns.

Captain Bellenden Hutcheson RCAMC was attached to 75th Battalion and accompanied it through the D-Q Support line. With utter disregard for his personal safety, he remained in the open until every wounded man had been attended to. With his medical team, he worked along the crest attending to the wounded when the Battalion was held up short of its objective. The fire was intense and they reached the wounded by crawling or running stooped. When the fire became too hot, they had to flatten out on the ground.

Hutcheson dressed the wounds of Captain Robert Dunlop MC who had been hit in the abdomen by a bullet as he led his company over the crest. About twenty to thirty minutes later Hutcheson was near Dunlop again, when he told him that he had also been hit in the thigh as he lay there. Hutcheson put him in a shell hole and, as Dunlop had an abdominal wound, it was necessary to get him back to the casualty clearing station as quickly as possible for an operation. So Hutcheson and 139240 Corporal Hedley Harry Mennell stopped three or four German prisoners and pressed them into service as stretcher-bearers. An enemy field gun then fired on them and Hutcheson was knocked into the shell hole with one of the Germans on top of him. Mennell was also knocked to the ground. The other two Germans, wounded and shrieking, ran off toward the Canadian lines. Hutcheson struggled to get out from under the German, who was groaning and crying, and spoke to him sharply to get him to remove his weight. Dunlop told Hutcheson that the German was badly hit. Hutcheson then saw that his face was grey and a wound in his thigh was spurting blood from the severed femoral artery. Hutcheson applied a tourniquet and then noticed that the whole side of his chest was torn out. He died in less than a minute. Meanwhile the field gun continued to fire every ten to fifteen seconds. Hutcheson, Mennell, Dunlop and another wounded man lay in the shell hole sheltering from the shelling, the machine gun and rifle fire and low

The reverse of the previous view, looking at the sunken section of the road from Dury to the D939, which is behind the camera.

flying planes swooping down. Shortly afterwards the enemy fell back and the fire slackened, enabling them to get Dunlop and the other casualties back a few hundred metres to a trench in which the wounded were being collected. Dunlop died of his wounds on 7th September (Terlincthun British Cemetery, Wimille, France).

Later Hutcheson was lying near the CO, the adjutant, Sergeant Geoffrey McCullogh (Battalion scout) and several others, when the firing ahead subsided somewhat. The CO ordered McCullogh to go forward to find out what progress was being made on the right flank. After covering about sixty metres there was a single shot followed by a burst of machine gun fire, and McCullogh fell, shot through the pelvis. The Germans were 90–270m ahead in the sunken road. Without hesitating, Hutcheson rushed forward in full view of the enemy and still under heavy fire to tend the wounded McCullogh. Hutcheson managed to get him into a shell hole and dressed his wounds. After a few minutes Hutcheson crawled away to deal with other casualties. McCullogh was recovered a short time later. Hutcheson remained until every casualty had been removed from the battlefield. About fifty prisoners were retained to assist in clearing the wounded. Hutcheson's coolness and devotion to duty resulted in many lives being saved. During the day he was knocked to his knees when a bullet deeply scored his steel helmet but did not penetrate. Amongst Hutcheson's medics, Corporal Harry Mennell received the DCM and 139003 Lance Corporal George Adnitt the MM for their work that day.

87th Battalion also set off at 8 a.m. It was clear that the sunken road was still held by the enemy and heavy fire was being received, particularly from the windmill. B Company was on the right and D Company on the left, with A Company in support and C Company in reserve. Cresting the ridge, the leading companies came under very heavy machine gun and shell fire from both flanks. The left flank was also open but they pressed on. However, they were unable to advance further than a line

Looking south along the sunken road from Dury to the D939, which is out of sight in the distance in dead ground, as is the sugar factory crossroads. In the foreground and leading off to the right is the track leading to Dury Mill Cemetery, which is marked by a dense clump of trees just left of the telegraph pole. The windmill was to the right of the road in the centre about where it starts to disappear into lower ground.

135–175m east of the sunken road south of Dury due to heavy fire from Villers-lès-Cagnicourt, a sugar beet factory at the crossroads northeast of the village and also artillery firing from a ridge about 1,600m east of the sunken road. The supporting 3″ Stokes mortars had run out of ammunition and the 6″ Newton mortar was out of action. The companies were reorganised and rearranged to hold the gains and the advance ended for the day. The Battalion was relieved late on 3rd September, having suffered 331 casualties. Fifty prisoners were taken, in addition to two bomb throwers, two light machine guns, an anti-tank rifle and an anti-tank gun.

During the action on 2nd September, **Private John Young** was a stretcher-bearer with D Company. The Company suffered heavy casualties as it advanced over the ridge. In spite of the complete absence of cover, and without the slightest hesitation, he went into the open fire-swept ground to dress the wounded. He exhausted his stock of dressings on more than one occasion and returned, still under intense fire, to Company HQ for further supplies. He continued this work for over an hour and thereby saved many lives. Later, when the fire slackened, he organised and led stretcher parties to bring in the wounded. He continued to show the greatest valour and devotion to duty over the following two days.

At the end of the day, 4th Canadian Division was on its first objective but, until the artillery was brought forward, it was unable to progress. The Independent Force armoured cars made a few unsuccessful attempts to rush ahead but had to be satisfied with engaging enemy positions either side of the Arras–Cambrai road.

On the left of the Canadian Corps only 12th Brigade advanced in 4th Division. It had a frontage of 1,375m and a considerable amount of artillery in support (five field artillery brigades, a battery of 8″ Howitzers, three batteries of 6″ Guns), in addition to nine tanks of 11th Tank Battalion and forty-eight machine guns of 4th and 11th Machine Gun Battalions. The tanks found marshy ground and were forced to move

around to the north to catch up with the infantry in the front D-Q system. Frontal fire was negligible but heavy flanking fire was received from Étaing and Prospect Farm. Due to an error the tanks attacked Étaing Wood 800m south of the village and therefore did not stop the enfilade fire. However, both D-Q systems were taken with few casualties and the first objective was reached. At 8 a.m., 11th Brigade passed through but came under fire from Prospect Farm, which by then was in the rear. Despite making some progress, the line was pulled back to the second trench of the D-Q Support system. Later in the day, 12th Brigade seized Prospect Farm but machine guns in Étaing Wood continued to block progress towards Étaing. The day ended with 11th and 12th Brigades, somewhat intermingled, holding the D-Q Support system but with the left bent back through Prospect Farm, south of Étaing, which was not captured until the following morning.

Although the defences were strong, German resistance in the D-Q Position was not as fierce as expected and both front and support systems fell, albeit in places after heavy fighting. Although more distant objectives were not taken (they were optimistic), the Canadian Corps had still achieved a spectacular success. The D-Q Line had been overrun on a frontage of 6,400m and the Buissy Switch was captured, as were the villages of Villers-lès-Cagnicourt and Cagnicourt.

Orders were issued for all three divisions of the Canadian Corps to continue the advance next day, with the intention of at least gaining observation over the Sensée and Canal du Nord. However, during the night the defenders slipped away and by the end of 3rd September the Corps had closed up to the Canal du Nord, while on the left 4th Division had cleared along the Sensée. In this action (1st–3rd September) 6,000 prisoners were taken by the Canadian Corps, which suffered 5,622 casualties.

XXII Corps, on the left of the Canadians, did not attack but exerted pressure on the enemy and used its artillery to cover the flank. 33rd Brigade (11th Division) had taken over the line east of Boiry-Notre-Dame from the Canadians on the night of 30th–31st August. In the line 6th Lincolnshire on the right and 7th South Staffordshire on the left were some way ahead of 4th Division (Canadian Corps).

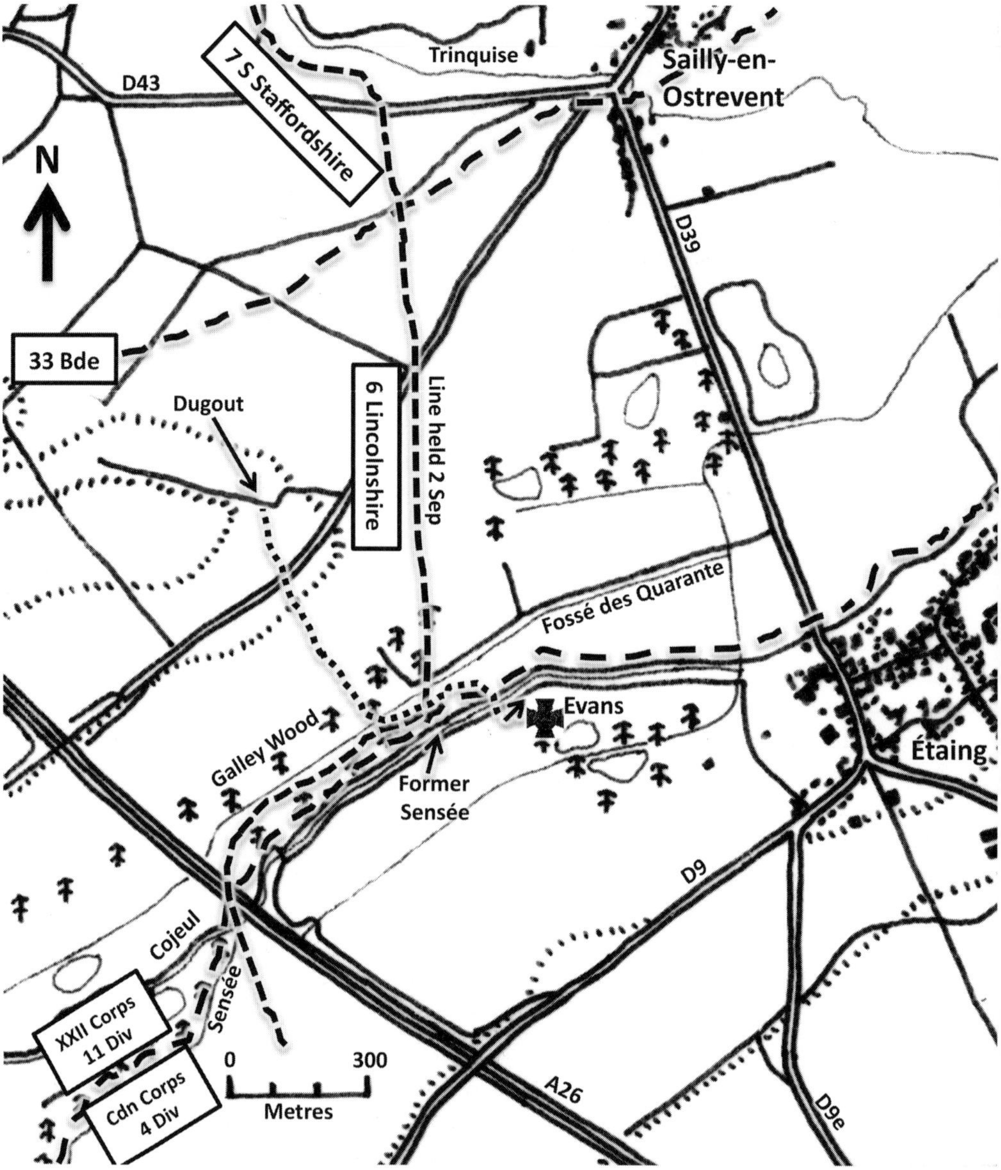

Drive through Étaing northwards on the D39 towards Sailly-en-Ostrevent. Take the last turning on the left as you leave the village and park on the grass verge. Walk along this track to the west. After 200m there is a causeway across the diverted Sensée, marked by the deep ditches either side. Continue straight ahead. Running parallel with the track on the right is a line of scrub. This was the line of the Sensée until it was diverted and filled in. Keep going for 775m around a left hand bend until a track crosses the former Sensée on the right. There was a bridge crossing here in 1918 and it is probably where the patrol regained the north bank after the VC action. Turn back to face Étaing. There is a small copse to the right of the track, which you passed while walking to this point. Just in front of it is where the German post was located.

Patrols on the night of 31st August brought back valuable information about enemy dispositions at Sailly-en-Ostrevent and Étaing.

During the attack on 2nd September, 33rd Brigade covered the left flank of 4th Division on the opposite bank of the Cojeul and Sensée rivers. 6th Lincolnshire was tasked to protect the flank by breaking up enemy counterattacks and seizing any opportunities to move the line forward should the enemy retire. Patrols were to push forward to maintain contact with the enemy and keep up the pressure.

A small patrol, consisting of an officer and five men, set out from a dugout at 11.45 a.m., passed through Galley Wood and reached the north bank of the Sensée. It turned northeast and headed towards Étaing. Its orders were to maintain contact with 4th Division. It moved for some distance before spotting a German sentry on the far bank about 350m in front of the British lines. Suspecting that there was a post nearby, **Sergeant Arthur Evans** volunteered to cross the river (about six metres wide and unfordable) to reconnoitre, while the remainder covered him.

Using cover along the bank he passed the sentry without being seen and swam the river, emerging on the far bank behind the enemy post, which was concealed amongst trees. He crawled up behind the sentry, who was not alert, and shot him with a revolver. The No.2 on the machine gun in the post turned round and Evans shot him as well. Two other men ran back and were shot down by the rest of the patrol on the north bank. The machine gun was mounted on a pile of logs and there were also three bivouacs. Evans discovered four other men. They threw up their hands and he sent them across the river over a small bridge consisting of a number of tree trunks. While two men guarded the prisoners on the north bank, the rest of the patrol crossed to join Evans.

They moved along the south bank towards Étaing and, after sixty-five metres, discovered an unoccupied trench. Evans went on alone until coming under heavy fire from the direction of Étaing. Two men were in the trench but Second Lieutenant A Barrett, the patrol leader, was standing on top and was shot through the thigh and fell into the trench. Evans returned and ordered one man to go back and fetch the prisoners to help. With the other man he moved Barrett into the water amongst the sedges, where there was cover from the intense fire. They moved through the water to the bridge from where the four prisoners carried Barrett back to safety. Evans' actions not only destroyed a machine gun post and brought in a number of prisoners but led to the identification of key enemy units. One of the two men left at the bridge with the prisoners, 53053 Private John William Broughton, was killed in the fire-fight (Vis-en-Artois Memorial). The rest of the patrol returned at 2 p.m.

Overall the day's fighting had been a considerable success, particularly the storming of the D-Q Line by the Canadian Corps. It was becoming clear that in open warfare the BEF was superior to the enemy. Its artillery was much better and was well supplied with ammunition. Machine gun posts that had previously held up advances were being dealt with more effectively with improved tactics. Older

The track in the centre running away from the camera leads back to Étaing. The line of scrub to the left of it is the former Sensée. In the foreground the track heading off to the left is where there was a bridge in 1918. To the right of the central track is a small copse, just in front of which was the German machine gun post. The patrol approached from Galley Wood on the far left and moved along the left (north) bank of the Sensée to engage the machine gun post.

On the same track closer to Étaing. The church is in the far left distance. The former Sensée is just left of the track. The small copse seen in the previous picture is in the centre and the machine gun post was in the field just to the right of it. The camera position is where Evans crossed the Sensée to emerge behind the enemy post.

soldiers were surprised that in a few days they had advanced across areas that in 1916 and 1917 had taken months and with enormous casualties.

The results of the day's fighting had an immediate effect on the German high command. They recognised that their positions were no longer tenable and ordered an immediate retirement behind the Sensée, Canal du Nord and Hindenburg positions, pivoting on Étaing. Rearward movement began that night, with the whole retirement to be completed on 9th September. This entailed pulling back up to twenty-nine kilometres. All the gains from the March offensives and in the Lys salient won in April would be abandoned.

Biographies

LIEUTENANT COLONEL WILLIAM HEW CLARK-KENNEDY
24th Battalion (Victoria Rifles) CEF

William Clark-Kennedy was born on 3rd March 1879 at Dunskey House, Portpatrick, Wigtownshire, Scotland. His father, Captain Alexander William Maxwell Clark-Kennedy JP DL (26th September 1851–21st December 1894), born at Rochester, Kent, served in the Coldstream Guards and was promoted captain in 1874. The family home was at Knockgray, Carsphairn. He married Lettice 'Lottie' Lucy née Hewitt (1st January 1853–13th August 1939), born in Dublin, Ireland, on 4th February 1875 at Meenglas, Co Donegal, Ireland. They were living  at Henbury House, Sturminster Marshall, Dorset in 1881. In 1891 they were living at 72 Eaton Place, London. He was Secretary of the Colonial Mutual Life Assurance Society, 29 Cockspur Street, London. Alexander was appointed JP and DL Kircudbrightshire and JP Dumfriesshire and Dorsetshire. He was a fellow of the Linnaean Society, Royal Geographical Society, Zoological Society, Society of Actuaries and Society of Actuaries (Scotland). He was the author of several works on science, travel and poems. Alexander died at his home at 19 Eccleston Square, London and Lottie at Knockgray, Carsphairn. William had seven siblings:

The current Dunskey House seen here was built in 1901-04 for the Orr-Ewing family, replacing the earlier house of 1706, where William was born in March 1879. Some fragments of the old house were incorporated into the new structure. The old house was owned by the Hunter-Blair family and was extended c.1830.

- John William James Clark-Kennedy (7th November 1875–19th June 1939), born in Scotland, emigrated to South Africa where he married Phyllis Elizabeth Ashburnham (1895–24th December 1976) on 6th April 1918. He served as a lieutenant colonel in the South African Police. They had a daughter:

Eccleston Square, London, where William's father died in December 1894.

Knockgray, Carsphairn.

- Margaret Lettice Frances Ashburnham Clark-Kennedy (c.1921–2010), born in South Africa, married John Ellis Spencer BA psc (1914–2002) in 1947 at Weston super Mare, Somerset. John was commissioned in the Royal Artillery on 29th August 1935 and was promoted lieutenant 29th August 1938, acting captain 17th July 1940, temporary captain 17th October 1940–10th January 1942 and 13th June–27th October 1942, war substantive captain 28th October 1942, captain 28th August 1943, acting major 28th July 1942, temporary major 28th October 1942–14th May 1947 and 28th July 1947–28th August 1948, major 29th August 1948, acting lieutenant colonel 5th August–6th September 1945 and 24th September–8th November 1945, temporary lieutenant colonel 11th October–30th December 1956 and lieutenant colonel 31st December 1956. He was supernumerary from 31st December 1959 and retired on 31st March 1961. In 1939 he was serving in 11th Field Regiment RA, living with his mother at Yeomans, Axbridge, Somerset. Margaret and John lived at Hill Farm, Swalcliffe, Oxfordshire. He died at Penrith, Cumbria and she at Southampton, Hampshire. They had six children – Henrietta Frances Spencer, John Spencer, Lavinia Spencer, Teresa Spencer, Olivia Spencer and Victoria Veronica Spencer.
- Alexander Clark-Kennedy, born and died 1877 at Dumfries.
- Lettice Eleanor Clark-Kennedy (9th January 1878–17th April 1926), born in South Kensington, London, died unmarried at St Colme House, Aberdour, Kircudbright, Dumfriesshire.
- Leopold James Clark-Kennedy (27th March 1881–1st July 1932), born at Sturminster, Dorset, was educated at Westminster School, London. He died at Dumfries.
- Alice Arthur Clark-Kennedy (13th July 1882–24th October 1961) died unmarried at The Liggate, Carsphairn, Castle Douglas, Galloway.

- Alexander Kenelm Clark-Kennedy (18th December 1883–19th April 1917) was educated at Ashburnham School, London, Westminster School, London September 1898–July 1902 and Trinity College, Cambridge (BA 1905). Alexander became a HM Inspector of Factories at the Home Office on 31st July 1906. He was commissioned in the Galloway Rifles in October 1906 and promoted lieutenant in August 1907. He was appointed Secretary to the Employment of Children Act 1909 and by January 1912 was a first division clerk in the Home Office. He was reappointed an Inspector of Factories on 13th August 1912. He was also Honorary Secretary of the Elizabethan Club for twelve months. His address was 6 West Eaton Place, Middlesex. Alexander was embodied in 1/5th King's Own Scottish Borderers at the outbreak of the Great War and sailed for Gallipoli in May 1915. Appointed temporary captain on 11th May and landed on 6th June. He suffered from diarrhoea, dysentery followed in early September and rheumatic fever on 15th September. He left the unit on 28th September, embarked at Lancashire Landing on 30th September and was evacuated to Mudros. Tranferred to Malta aboard HMHS *Grantully Castle*, arriving on 6th October. A medical board there at the Blue Sisters Hospital next day found he was unfit for General Service for one month. The hospital was ordered to be evacuated and he was transferred to Britain aboard HMHS *Panama*, arriving at Southampton on 16th October. A medical board at Caxton Hall, London on 22nd October found him unfit for General Service for three months and Home Service for two months. He was granted leave to 22nd December. Another medical board at Caxton Hall on 3rd January 1916 found him unfit for General Service for three months and Home Service for one month but fit for light duties. A medical board at the Military Hospital, Ripon on 9th February found him fit for General Service. He embarked on HMT *Aragon* at Devonport on 4th April, disembarked at Alexandria, Egypt on 15th April and joined the Base Depot, Mustapha. He was admitted to 19th General Hospital, Alexandria with pyrexia on 19th April, returning to the Base Depot on 29th April and rejoined the Battalion at Kantara,

Three battles were fought by the Egyptian Expeditionary Force around Gaza, which was captured during the Third Battle on 7th November 1917. Medical facilities were set up there, including casualty clearing stations and later general and stationary hospitals. The first burials in the cemetery were troops killed during the capture of the city. These were added to by medical units but two-thirds of the total were concentrated after the war. During the Second World War, Gaza was the AIF HQ and Australian hospitals were there. The RAF had an airfield at Gaza. Gaza War Cemetery now contains 3,217 Commonwealth burials of the First World War (781 unidentified) and 210 Second World War burials. There are thirty post-war burials and 234 graves of other nationalities.

Egypt on 4th May. Alexander was killed during the Second Battle of Gaza (Gaza War Cemetery – XVIII A 3).

* Archibald Douglas Hewitt Clark-Kennedy (30th July 1888–18th September 1918), born in London, was educated at Westminster School from 1902. He applied for a commission on 23rd March 1910, described as 5′ 10″ tall and working in life insurance at 20 Grosvenor Street, Edinburgh. He was commissioned in 4th Royal Scots in 1910 and the Bombay Light Horse in 1912. He was commissioned in 5th Royal Scots Fusiliers as a lieutenant and temporary captain on 12th July 1915 and was MID. Archibald was killed near Moeuvres, France and was buried about two and a half kilometres east-southeast of Pronville. In 1920 his remains were exhumed and buried in (Quéant Road Cemetery, Buissy – VII D 20). On 21st November 1918 his brother, William, wrote to the War Office from the Ritz Hotel, Piccadilly, London requesting a death certificate so that a claim on a life insurance policy could be progressed. Archibald left effects valued at £290/9/11 to his mother. His address was given as 41 Albany Street, Edinburgh.

Archibald Douglas Hewitt Clark-Kennedy's grave, on the right, in Quéant Road Cemetery. Percy Cherry VC is also buried here. His story is told in the fourth book in this series, *Victoria Crosses on the Western Front: 1917 to the Eve of Third Ypres*. Another notable burial is Chaplain 4th Class Maurice Berkeley Peel MC & Bar, son of 1st Viscount Peel, a former Speaker of the House of Commons, and grandson of Prime Minister Sir Robert Peel.

William's paternal great-grandfather, Lieutenant General Sir Alexander Kennedy Clark-Kennedy KCB KH (1781–1863), served in the Peninsular War and at Waterloo with 1st Royal Dragoons. In a charge at Waterloo he was involved in the capture of the Eagle of the French 105th Regiment of the Line. He was Colonel of 6th Dragoon Guards 1860–62 and Colonel of the Scots Greys from 1862.

William's paternal grandfather, Lieutenant Colonel John Clark-Kennedy CB (21st September 1817–18th December 1867), obtained a cornetcy by purchase in 7th Dragoon Guards in October 1833, a lieutenancy in March 1837 and a captaincy in December 1841. He exchanged to 18th Royal Irish Foot and took part in the China Expedition 1842, during which he was present at the investment of Nankin. Appointed Assistant Quartermaster-General to the force under Major General Sir George Charles d'Aguilar (1784–1855) during the combined naval and military operations on the Canton River in 1847, when the forts of the Bocca

Lieutenant General Sir Alexander Kennedy Clark-Kennedy.

The Eagle of the French 105th Regiment of the Line. In December 1804, Napoléon I distributed *aigles* to the regiments based on the eagle standards of Roman legions. He insisted that the troops should defend the standards with their lives. The eagle had the same significance to French regiments as the colours did to British regiments. To lose one would bring shame to the regiment. Two eagles were captured during the Battle of Waterloo. 1st Dragoon Guards captured the eagle of the 105th and it can be seen in the National Army Museum in Chelsea. The Royal Scots Greys captured the eagle of the 45th and it is held in the Royal Scots Dragoon Guards Museum in Edinburgh Castle.

Tigris, the Staked Barrier, and the city of Canton were taken. He also served in the Second Sikh War 1848–49, during which he was present at the first siege of Mooltan as ADC to Lieutenant General Sir William Whish (1787–1853), at the action at Soorjkoond (attached to Brigadier Frederick Markham (1805–55), commanding 2nd Infantry Brigade), at the second siege and fall of the city and citadel, the capture of the port of Cheniote and the Battle of Goojerat. Appointed ADC to Brigadier Armine Simcoe Henry Mountain (1797–1854) and took part in the pursuit of the Sikhs and the passage of the Jhelum. Attached to the staff of Major General Sir Walter Gilbert (1785–1853), he was present at the surrender of the Sikh army and guns, and in the forced march on Attock, which drove the Afghans across the Indus. As ADC to Brigadier Colin Campbell (1792–1863) he was in the advance upon and occupation of Peshawar on 21st March 1849. He served in the Crimea from December 1854 and was present at the siege of Sebastopol, where he commanded the right wing of the 18th Royal Irish, leading Eyre's Brigade in the assault of 18th June 1855, and was wounded in the neck. He was appointed Assistant Adjutant-General at Headquarters on 10th August and was in the assault of 8th September 1855. He was

William's paternal grandmother was born at Witham, Essex. Occupation of the area dates back to Neolithic times and there was a Roman temple alongside the Roman road from Colchester to London. Witham appears in the Domesday Book of 1086. The manor was given to the Knights Templar in 1148 and north of the town is Cressing Temple, the earliest foundation of Templar lands in Britain. Witham was a centre for the wool trade until its decline in the late 17th century. In the 18th century Witham was briefly an affluent spa town. On 1st September 1905, a London to Cromer express train derailed whilst travelling through the station. Ten passengers and a porter were killed and seventy-one passengers were seriously injured. The town expanded in the late 1960s and 1970s as a result of overspill from London and again in the early 2000s. A famous resident was Dorothy L Sayers, author of detective fiction, who died there in 1957.

afterwards appointed Assistant Quartermaster-General at Aldershot, Hampshire and in February 1860 Commandant of the Military Train. John married Frances Eleanor née Walford (c.1824–2nd April 1857), born at Witham, Essex, on 2nd October 1850 at St George Hanover Square, London. Frances died at Downham, Norfolk. John married Charlotte Isabella Cust (16th May 1828–24th November 1914), born at Charles Street, Mayfair, London, on 8th September 1859 at Belton, Grantham, Lincolnshire. John was posted on special service to Cairo, Egypt in connection with the Abyssinian expedition and died of dysentery there. Charlotte was living at 6 West Eaton Place, London at the time of her death, leaving effects valued at £38,465/15/6 (£4.3M in 2019). In addition to Alexander, John had four other children from his two marriages:

- Arthur John Clark-Kennedy (26th February 1857–27th November 1926), born at the Grange, Farnham, Surrey, married Alice Maud Appleton (24th September 1859–23rd July 1893), born at Baltimore, Maryland, USA, on 29th September 1880 in Boston, Massachusetts, USA. They had three children – Arthur Robert Windsor Stuart Clark-Kennedy (1884–1945), Hew Desborough George Armistead Clark-Kennedy (1889) and John Nigel Douglas Clark-Kennedy (born and died 1890). They were living at St Hélène, Guernsey, Channel Islands in 1891. Alice died at Croydon, Surrey. Arthur married Ethel Clark Bell (née Dobrée) (1858–13th October 1939), born at Sculcoates, Yorkshire, on 13th September 1895. She had married John Charles Bell (1853–93) on 8th November 1884 at Westminster and was the eldest daughter of NF Dobrée of Guernsey, Channel Islands. John and Ethel lived at Langhargh Hall, Beverley, Yorkshire. He died at 43 Pall Mall, London leaving effects valued at £42,450/8/10 (£5.1M in 2018). John and Ethel

Bell had two children – Una Clara Margaret Bell (1885–1959) and John Dobrée Bell (27th September 1887–30th October 1918), who was commissioned in the Royal Field Artillery on 12th September 1914. He disembarked at Le Havre on 10th May 1917 and was posted to 38th (Army) Brigade RFA on 15th May. He was admitted to 7th Stationary Hospital, Boulogne (not yet diagnosed sick slight) 25th–28th June. He was in hospital sick again on 1st July and joined the Artillery Base Depot, Le Havre on 22nd July. John was granted leave to Britain 19th–29th August, extended to 9th September for medical reasons. Medical boards on 8th and 21st September found him unfit for General & Home Service for up to three months and light duties for up to six weeks. He eventually recovered and disembarked at Boulogne on 17th August 1918. He joined HQ XIX Corps Intelligence from Second Army on 10th September and was appointed 4th class agent, Intelligence Corps on probation on 18th September. He was serving as

Throughout the Great War, Boulogne and Wimereux housed numerous hospitals and medical establishments. The cemetery at Terlincthun was begun in June 1918 when space for burials in the civil cemeteries of Boulogne and Wimereux was exhausted. By July 1920 the cemetery contained more than 3,300 burials and it remained open as burials from isolated sites and other burials grounds throughout France, where maintenance could not be assured, were concentrated there. Wimille was devastated in the fighting there 22nd–25th May 1940 as the garrison of Boulogne fought a delaying action to cover the withdrawal to Dunkirk. There was also fighting there in 1944. The cemetery was damaged in 1940 and during the German occupation. The cemetery now contains 4,378 Commonwealth burials of the Great War, more than 200 war graves of other nationalities, plus another 149 burials from the Second World War. In the background is the Column of the Grande Armée, intended to commemorate a successful invasion of Britain that never occurred. It now commemorates the first distribution of the Imperial Légion d'Honneur by Napoleon. The first stone was laid by Marshal Soult on 9th October 1804 but the project lacked funds and work stopped in December 1811. Work restarted in 1819 but it was not completed until 1838. In 1840 Louis-Napoleon landed a small body of supporters at Boulogne and took refuge in the park around the column, where they raised the imperial flag before fleeing to the beach, where he was arrested. A statue of Napoleon I in coronation costume was completed in time for the return of his remains to Paris on 15th December 1840. The statue was raised to the top of the column on 15th August 1841. It was noted in Britain that the new statue had its back to England. The column and statue were damaged in 1944 and the park became a German naval cemetery. One of the burials was Klaus Dönitz, son of Admiral Karl Dönitz. The original statue was replaced and the restoration was inaugurated on 24th June 1962, in the presence of Charles de Gaulle.

The 13th century Beaulieu Palace House was originally the gatehouse of Beaulieu Abbey. Following the Dissolution of the Monasteries the estate was bought by Thomas Wriothesley, 1st Earl of Southampton in 1538. It is still owned by his descendants, the Barons Montagu of Beaulieu. The house was extended in the 16th and 19th centuries. During the Second World War, Palace House was a Special Operations Executive training facility. In the grounds is the National Motor Museum.

a Lieutenant when he was admitted to 8th Red Cross Hospital, Boulogne with influenza on 25th October and died there on 30th October 1918 (Terlincthun British Cemetery, Wimille – IX B 10). John had married Dorothy Aird Briscoe (born 1894), born at Wandsworth, in 1916 at Lewisham and they had a son, Peter March Dobrée Bell (1916–94). Dorothy married Henry Lionel Dymoke (1894–1965), in 1919 at Amersham, Buckinghamshire. He was an actor, known as Lionel Dymoke. Henry and Dorothy had two sons – Lionel Dorian Dymoke (1921–2004), who became a rear admiral, and Michael Rollo Dymoke (1925). The marriage ended in divorce and Henry married Barbara Blanche Rees (1905–82) in 1944 and they had a son, John Dymoke (1945). Arthur and Ethel's marriage was dissolved by divorce. Ethel did not remarry and died at Brook Cottage, Higher Hawsker, near Whitby, Yorkshire. Arthur Clark-Kennedy married Hon Helen Cecil Douglas–Scott–Montagu (7th March 1890–21st May 1969), born at Beaulieu, Hampshire, on 12th December 1916 at Bloomfield, New Jersey, USA. She was the eldest daughter of James Walter Edward Douglas-Scott, 2nd Baron Montagu of Beaulieu (1866–1929) and Cecil Victoria Constance Kerr (1866–1919). The marriage was dissolved by divorce in 1925. Arthur Clark-Kennedy married Dorothy Kate Robb (29th August 1895–6th January 1942), born at Westminster, London, on 27th July 1925 at Wandsworth, London. They were living at Farnham Grange, Surrey and at Avenue du Longchamp 255, Uccle, Belgium at the time of his death there. She died at Wandsworth.

- Minnie Frances Clark-Kennedy (January 1861–2nd January 1928), born at St George Hanover Square, London, married Sir George Francis Hampson 10th Bt (14th January 1860–15th October 1936), born at Marylebone, London, on 1st June 1893 at St George Hanover Square. He was educated at Charterhouse School and Exeter College, Oxford. He became a tea planter in the Nilgiri Hills, India and developed an interest in Lepidoptera. After returning to England he became a civil servant and volunteered at the Natural History Museum. He wrote, The Lepidoptera of the Nilgiri District 1891 and Lepidoptera Heterocera of Ceylon

1893 as Parts 8 & 9 of Illustrations of Typical Specimens of Lepidoptera Heterocera of the British Museum, followed by The Fauna of British India, Including Ceylon and Burma: Moths, in four volumes 1892–96. He became an assistant at the Museum in March 1895 and was promoted to acting assistant keeper in 1901. He then worked on a Catalogue of the Lepidoptera Phalaenae in the British Museum, in fifteen volumes 1898–1920. They were living at 36 Tedworth Square, London in 1897 and at 62 Stanhope Gardens, Kensington in 1911. They were living at Thurnham Court, Maidstone, Kent at the time of their deaths there. He left effects valued at £72,157/0/10 (£4.9M in 2018). They had three children:
  ° Marjorie Eleanor Hampson (1895–1963).
  ° Dennys (later Sir Dennys) Francis Hampson (1897–1939) was educated at Wellington House, Westgate and Eton College January 1911–July 1915, where he was in the OTC. When he applied for a commission on 25th August 1915 an assessment by the CO of Eton College OTC said of him, 'Very reliable….. Probably make a steady conscientious officer without much initiative or leadership'. He was commissioned in 4th Royal West Kent (TF) on 22nd September and was attached to 71st Provisional Battalion TF. He was serving with 65th Provisional Battalion at Great Yarmouth when he had a medical in London on 27th October 1916. His commission was relinquished when he entered the Royal Military College, Sandhurst on 3rd November 1916. He was dismissed from Sandhurst with two other office cadets for 'ragging' another cadet. Later the case was reviewed and it was decided that it was not as serious as first believed, although the Commandant's decision was not reversed. The three were allowed to apply for Special Reserve commissions. Dennys enlisted on 3rd February 1917, with service reckoning from 22nd February, when he had a medical at the Central London Recruiting Depot, Whitehall. He was posted to the Rifle Brigade Depot (S/31725), described as 6' 4" tall, weighing 130 lbs and his religious denomination was Church of England. He was posted to G Company, 5th Battalion at Minster, Isle of Sheppey on 27th February. He applied for a commission on 9th March and was posted to No.19 Officer Cadet Battalion, Pirbright on 5th May. He was commissioned in the Rifle Brigade on 29th August 1917 and served with 8th Rifle Brigade. He received a glancing wound, which fractured the left scapula, on the Somme on 28th March 1918. He embarked at Le Havre on 9th April and disembarked at Southampton next day for treatment at King Edward VII Hospital from 10th April. He applied for a wound gratuity from the Red Cross Hospital, 10 Percival Terrace, Brighton on 21 May 1918. A medical board on 16th April found him unfit for Category A Service for three months and for C1 for one month. A medical board on 18th June found him unfit for Category A & B Service for three months but fit for C1. He was granted leave to 9th July and reported to 5th Reserve Battalion, Isle of Sheppey next day. Medical boards followed on 26th September, 21st

March 1919, 24th July and 13th August, which found him unfit for Category A & B Service from three to twelve months. He was found fit for C1 Service on 26th September and reported to Southern Command Depot for duty. However, the next board found him unfit for Category C1 for two months and he was sent to an officers' hospital. The following boards found him fit for C1. He was demobilised on 29th August 1919 and relinquished his commission on 1st April 1920, retaining the rank of lieutenant. Sir Dennys was living at Thurnham Court, Maidstone, Kent at the time of his death at the Grand Pump Room Hotel, Bath, Somerset. He left effects valued at £61,821/9/4 (£3.9M in 2018).
  ° Honoria Mary Hampson (1900–33).
- Isabella Charlotte Clark-Kennedy (1864–16th August 1923) served in the French Red Cross in the Great War as a canteener from May 1916. She was a spinster living at Harestock Lodge, near Winchester, Hampshire at the time of her death, leaving effects valued at £26,850/9/10 (£1.45M in 2018).
- Harriet Sophia Clark-Kennedy (24th February 1867–22nd February 1948), born at Westminster, London, married Lieutenant Colonel Stewart Lygon Murray (5th July 1863–27th April 1930) on 26th November 1895 at St Gabriel's Church, Warwick Square, London. He was the eldest son of Sir Herbert Harley Murray KCB, Governor of Newfoundland. Stewart was living at Casa-di-Cura, Borgo, Trento, Verona, Italy at the time of his death. She was living at Red Cottage, Potten End, Berkhamsted, Hertfordshire at the time of her death there. They had three children – Elsie Dorothea Isabel Murray (1897–1989), Christian Charlotte Murray (1904–98) and Joan Margaret Vere Murray (1909–93).

His maternal grandfather, James Hewitt, 4th Viscount Lifford (31st March 1811–20th November 1887), born at Merrion Square, Dublin, Ireland, was baptised on 27th June 1811 at St Marylebone, London. The lineage began with James Hewitt, 1st Viscount Lifford, Lord Chancellor of Ireland, who was elevated to the peerage of Ireland in 1768 as Baron Lifford of Lifford, Co Donegal and was created a viscount thirteen years later. James' principal place of residence was Meenglas, Ballybofey, Co Donegal, Ireland. He owned over 11,000 acres of prime land. Together with fellow landlord, Sir Samuel Hayes, he helped to expand Ireland's railways in the 1850s. Their representations to Parliament helped to secure funding to begin the Finn Valley Railway Co in May 1860. The construction of the line between Strabane and Stranorlar began at the end of the summer of 1861 and, after a lot of hold-ups, infighting and huge expense, the line opened on 7th September 1863. James married Lady Mary Acheson (27th July 1809–13th March 1850) on 9th July 1835. She was the daughter of Archibald Acheson, 2nd Earl of Gosford (1776–1849), and Mary Sparrow (1777–1841). Mary died at Monellan House, Donaghmore, Co Donegal following complications with the birth of her daughter, Isabella. James married Lydia Lucy late Purdon-Coote née Wingfield-Digby (13th August 1828–28th April

1919) on 9th December 1851 at Coleshill, Warwickshire. She was the daughter of the Reverend John Digby Wingfield-Digby and Ann Eliza Wyldbore-Smith and the widow of Charles Purdon-Coote of Ballyclough Castle, Co Cork (1823–3rd September 1848), who she married in 1846. Charles served as a lieutenant in 3rd Dragoon Guards and was appointed DL and JP. They lived at Bearforest, Co Cork and had two children. Maria Coote (c.1834–82) married Henry M Smythe on 3rd December 1855 and lived at New Parl, Co Roscommon. She died as a result of a gunshot to the head at Barbaville, Co Westmeath. Charles Purdon Coote (1847–93) married Harriette Louisa Maxwell on 22nd June 1871. He was Gentleman Usher to the Lord-Lieutenant of Ireland and was appointed DL and JP Co Cork. Charles and Harriette had four children. James Hewitt died at Meenglas, Ballybofey and Lydia at Ardendee, Kirkcudbrightshire, Scotland. In addition to Lettice, James had thirteen children from his two marriages:

- James Wilfrid Hewitt (12th October 1837–20th March 1913), later 5th Viscount Lifford, born at Astley, Coventry, Warwickshire, was educated at Rugby School, Warwickshire. He was commissioned in 4th Regiment of Foot in 1856, transferred

William's maternal grandfather, James Hewitt, 4th Viscount Lifford, was born at Merrion Square, Dublin. The square was laid out after 1762 and was complete by the beginning of the 19th century. It was one of three residential squares built on the Southside as the demand for Georgian townhouse residences grew. Aristocrats and the wealthy sold their Northside residences and moved into the new developments. Three sides of Merrion Square are lined with Georgian redbrick townhouses and the west side abuts the grounds of Leinster House. The centre is a public park, which contains a statue of Oscar Wilde. Since the 1950s many of the houses have been used for office accommodation. The poet, novelist and satirist, Oscar Wilde, lived at No.1 from 1855 to 1876, the poet, WB Yeats, at No.82 and Daniel O'Connell at No.58. Until 1972 the British Embassy was at No.39 but it was burned down during a demonstration following the Bloody Sunday shootings in Londonderry, Northern Ireland. The headquarters of St John Ambulance was at No.40 during the Great War and later moved to No.14. Amongst its other notable residents was the writer, Sheridan Le Fanu.

to 3rd Regiment of Foot on 16th January 1857 and was promoted lieutenant that year. He was Honorary Colonel of the Donegal Royal Field Reserve Artillery. James married Annie Frances Hodgson (1847–23rd April 1927) on 4th July 1867 at Lillington, Warwickshire. She was the eldest daughter of Sir Arthur Hodgson KCMG. They were living at Austin House, Broadway, Worcestershire at the time of their deaths without issue.

- A stillborn son delivered on 2nd April 1839 at Loughhall, near Armagh, Ireland.
- Mary Anne Hewitt (1840–20th March 1913), born at Astley Castle, Warwickshire, married John Gathorne Wood JP (18th September 1839–3rd August 1929) on 4th September 1866. John was commissioned in 17th Foot and resigned on 5th September 1862. He was appointed DL Hampshire on 14th June 1899. They lived at Shalden Manor, Alton, Hampshire and both died there. He left effects valued at £61,105/1/9 (£3.6M in 2018). They had five children – Archibald Henry Wood (1868–1921), Ernest Gathorne Wood (1869–1948), Wilfrid Edward Wood (1871–1900), Gertrude Mary Wood 1875 and Mary Millicent Wood 1880. John had married Susan Mary Pennefather (20th January 1842–18th December 1864), born in Wicklow, Ireland, on 9th December 1862 at St Stephen's, Dublin. She died at Hastings, Sussex. They had two children – Evelyn Emily Wood (1863–1911) and Edith Susan Mary Wood (1864–1947).
- Evelyn John Hewitt (19th July 1842–4th July 1867) died in-service as a lieutenant in the Royal Artillery.
- Archibald Robert Hewitt, later 6th Viscount Lifford (14th January 1844–22nd May 1925), married Helen Blanche Geach (22nd October 1859–4th June 1942), born at Marylebone, London, on 5th December 1878 at St George Hanover Square, London. They were living at Hill House, Lyndhurst, Hampshire at the time of his death there. She was living at Weston House, Weston Corbett, near Basingstoke, Hampshire at the time of her death at Fenwick Cottage Hospital, Lyndhurst. They had four children:
    ◦ Hon Norah Hewitt (1879–1983) never married and died at Kendal.
    ◦ Rt Hon Evelyn James Hewitt, later 7th Viscount Lifford (18th December 1880–5th April 1954), was educated at Haileybury College. He served in the Militia 6th August 1901–9th October 1902 and was embodied for 306 days for service in the South African War on operations in Cape Colony January to 31st May 1902 (Queen's Medal with two clasps). He served in the East Indies 28th November 1902–8th December 1906 and was commissioned in the Dorsetshire Regiment from the Militia on 26th August 1903. Promoted lieutenant 9th April 1905 and captain 26th May 1910. During the Great War he was Staff Captain HQ 34th Brigade 2nd April 1915–15th August 1916. He was appointed acting major 16th–21st August 1916, acting lieutenant colonel 22nd August–22nd October and acting major 6th Dorset 22nd December 1916–8th April 1917. He was promoted temporary lieutenant colonel to command 6th Duke of Cornwall's Light Infantry 9th April 1917–2nd June 1918. Promoted

major 22nd October 1917 and commanded 4th East Lancashire 3rd June 1918–5th January 1920. Awarded the DSO (LG 3rd June 1916), DSO Bar (LG 3rd June 1918) and was Mentioned in Despatches three times (LG 13th July 1916, 18th December 1917 and 24th May 1918). Promoted lieutenant colonel on 24th November 1920 and had transferred to the Regular Army Reserve of Officers by December 1923. He married Charlotte Rankine Walker née Maule (27th September 1883–2nd April 1954), born at 8 Laverbank Terrace, Trinity, Leith North, Edinburgh, on 8th July 1919 at Beverley, Yorkshire. She was the daughter of Sir Robert Maule (1852–1931) of Edinburgh and the widow of Captain Edgar Wilmer Walker (1875–28th October 1914), 3rd attached 1st East Yorkshire, who died on active duty at Armentières, France (Ration Farm Military Cemetery, La Chapelle-d'Armentières). He was the son of Rear Admiral Charles Walker of The Hall, Beverley, Yorkshire. Charlotte and Edgar married on 17th April 1906 at St Andrew's Church, St George, Edinburgh. Edgar was a barrister at law and lived at Ramsdale Bank, Belmont Road, Scarborough. She was living at Prospect House, Sallins, Co Kildare, Ireland in the early 1920s. Edgar's date of death varies between 26th and 29th October 1914. It is recorded as 28th October in probate and other documents but the CWGC date is 29th October. As Edgar's next of kin, Charlotte received a gratuity of £250 and a pension of £100 per year. They had a son, Francis Robert Walker, born in February 1910, who received a gratuity of £83/6/8 and a compassionate allowance of £18 per year, increasing to £24 per year on 1st March 1915. Evelyn and Charlotte were living at Pinchbeck, Gullane, East Lothian at the time of their deaths there, just three days apart.

○ Hon Archibald Rodney Hewitt (1883–1915), born at Torquay, Devon, was educated at Dulwich College and spoke German and French. He trained at the Royal Military College, Sandhurst and was commissioned in the East Surrey Regiment on 22nd October 1902. He was promoted lieutenant 18th June 1904 and captain 18th May 1910. He served in India 15th October 1903–24th August 1910 and passed the Paymaster course in 1906 and the School of Musketry with distinction in August 1909. Archibald was appointed adjutant 1st June 1911–31st May 1914. He served in 2nd Battalion during the Great War, was awarded the DSO (LG 9th November 1914) and was killed in action (Ypres (Menin Gate) Memorial, Belgium).

○ Hon Anne Rachel Millicent Hewitt (1885–1967).

Archibald Rodney Hewitt's name on the Ypres (Menin Gate) Memorial.

- Cornwallis Charles Hewitt (3rd March 1847–4th September 1889) was Prebendary of Tuam, Co Galway, Ireland. He married Maria Hayes (c.1848–19th August 1882) on 7th December 1881 at Calcutta, India. She was the daughter of Sir Edmund Samuel Hayes (1806–60), 3rd Bt, and Emily Pakenham (1819–83). She died at Darjeeling, India without issue.
- Edward Hewitt (31st March 1848–4th September 1931) married Evelyn Frances Charlotte Stronge (c.1866–17th June 1956) on 10th December 1890. She was the daughter of Edmond Robert Stronge (1822–1900) JP BA and Charlotte Newman Henderson, of Lizard Manor, Co Londonderry, Ireland. Edward was appointed JP Wiltshire and Denbighshire. They were living at 17 Royal Crescent, Bath, Somerset at the time of his death there. She was living at 29 St James Square, Bath at the time of her death there, leaving effects valued at £158,736/12/1 (£3.9M in 2018). There were no children.
- Isabella Hewitt (9th March 1850–19th March 1924), born at Monellan House, Donaghmore, Co Donegal, Ireland, married Richard Southby (31st July 1838–11th December 1921), born at Chieveley, Berkshire, on 7th January 1879. They were living at Wendover, Christ Church Road, Cheltenham, Gloucestershire at the time of his death there. She died at Artillery Mansions Hotel, Victoria Street, Westminster. They had four children:
    ◦ Richard Edward James Southby (1879–80).
    ◦ Olivia Mary Anne Southby (1881–1925).
    ◦ Evelyn John James Southby (1882–1937) married Vera St John Kneller (1892–1970) in 1913 at Poole, Dorset. He died at Uckfield, Sussex. Vera married Oliver A G St John Kneller (1878–1959) in 1938 at Bournemouth, Hampshire. Oliver had married Edith Maud Knapp (1877–1934) in 1909 at St George Hanover Square, London.
    ◦ Archibald Richard James Southby (1886–1969) married Phyllis Mary Garton (1886–1974) in 1909 at Epsom, Surrey, where she was born. They had a son.
- Hon Alice Anne Hewitt (16th September 1854–11th February 1943), born in Dublin, Ireland, married Sir Samuel Hercules Hayes, 4th Bt (3rd February 1840–6th November 1901), of Drumboe Castle, Co Donegal, Ireland on 25th July 1878. He was the brother of Maria Hayes who married Alice's half brother, Cornwallis. Samuel was commissioned in 10th (North Lincoln) Regiment of Foot on 13th March 1858 and was promoted lieutenant on 30th August 1859. He transferred to 2nd Regiment of Life Guards as a lieutenant on 25th March 1862 and was promoted captain on 27th February 1867. He retired from the Army in 1872 (last in the Army List December 1871) and became a magistrate, DL for Co Donegal and High Sheriff of Donegal 1884–87. Samuel died at Funchal, Madeira. She was living at Sahn Creggan, Ballybofey, Co Donegal at the time of her death there.
- Hon William James Hewitt (6th April 1856–28th October 1948), born at Astley, Warwickshire, was a factor. He married Evelyn Frances Carey (6th April

James Francis Hewitt's name on the Ploegsteert Memorial.

1862–21st October 1946), born at Knightsbridge, London, on 26th April 1887 at Winchester, Hampshire. She was the youngest daughter of Lieutenant General Francis Carey. They were living at St Colme House, Aberdour, Fife in 1914, where both subsequently died. They had two sons:
- ○ James Francis Hewitt (1888–1914) served as a lieutenant in 1st Cameronians. He joined the Battalion on 22nd September 1914 and was killed in action on 26th October 1914 (Ploegsteert Memorial, Belgium).
- ○ William George Hewitt (1892–1914) was educated at Edinburgh Academy and Christ Church College, Oxford, where he was a corporal in the OTC. He served as a second lieutenant in 3rd attached 2nd Royal Scots from 8th August 1914 and was reported missing on 13th October, later wounded and finally killed in action on 14th October 1914. He was buried just north of Croix Barbée and was exhumed post-war for burial in Vieille-Chapelle New Military Cemetery, La Couture, France.

• Hon Georgina Rosamund Hewitt (31st August 1857–9th May 1887) married John Kenelm Digby Wingfield-Digby MP JP (2nd September 1859–25th December 1904), born at Blythe Hall, Coleshill, Warwickshire, on 13th December 1883 at Stranorlar, Co Donegal. He was the son of Captain John Digby Wingfield-Digby (1832–88) and Maria Madan (1833–1909). They lived at Coleshill Park, Warwickshire and Sherborne Castle, Dorset. He was elected MP for Mid Somerset in March 1885 and, when that seat was abolished, represented North Dorset 1892–1904. Georgina died at 21 Wilton Street, Grosvenor Place, London. John married Charlotte Kathleen Digby (14th July 1863–5th February 1935), born at Moylough, Co Galway, on 5th June 1890 at St James's Palace, Westminster, London. John died at Sherborne Castle, Dorset leaving effects valued at £73,769/16/10 (£8.6M in 2019). Charlotte was living at The Court, Chetnole, Dorset at the time of her death there. John had eight children from his two marriages:

William George Hewitt's grave in Vieille-Chapelle New Military Cemetery.

- Lydia Mary Wingfield-Digby (1884–87).
- Frederick James Bosworth Digby Wingfield-Digby (1885–1952) married Gwendolen Marjory Fletcher (1884–1975) at Sherborne in 1909. They had two daughters.
- Georgina Rosamund Lettice Wingfield-Digby (1887–88).
- Kenelm Essex Wingfield-Digby (1891–1972) was commissioned in the Royal Artillery from the Special Reserve on 22nd May 1912. He was promoted lieutenant 22nd May 1915, captain 8th August 1916 and war substantive major 31st December 1917. He last appears in the Army List in September 1920. Kenelm married Mary E Paget at St George Hanover Square, London in 1916 and they had a son in 1921. Kenelm married Agusta/Augusta Jonasdottir Magnuss (1915–72) at Sturminster, Dorset in 1950. They had a son in 1952. Kenelm was living at The Priory House, Greenhill, Sherborne, Dorset at the time of his death, leaving effects valued at £132,960 (£1.9M in 2018).
- Kathleen Venetia Wingfield-Digby (1892–1982) married Reginald Walker in 1914 at Sherborne.
- Dorothy Charlotte Edith Wingfield-Digby (1894–1918).
- John Reginald Wingfield-Digby (1896–1988) married Margaret B Holford (1906–80) in 1930 at Sherborne. They had three children. John married Stella M Furnival née Bradwell (born 1930), born in Chester, in 1970 at Hendon. She had married Herbert Neil Furnival (1919–75) in 1959 at Chapel-en-le-Frith, Derbyshire.
- Robert Almarus Wingfield Digby Wingfield-Digby (1901–74).

• Hon George Wyldbore Hewitt (16th November 1858–23rd April 1924), born in Ireland, married Elizabeth Mary Rampini on 24th January 1891 in Calcutta, Bengal, India. He died at his home at Field House, Hursley, near Winchester, Hampshire. She died at Gifford House Nursing Home, St Giles Hill, Winchester on 24th May 1959. They had two sons:
  - Denis George Wyldbore Hewitt (1897–1917) was awarded a posthumous VC for his actions on the opening day of the Third Battle of Ypres.
  - Alan William Wingfield Hewitt (1900–87).
• Hon Anne Elizabeth Hewitt (1860–5th September 1957) died unmarried at Beechmount Castle, Douglas, Kirkcudbrightshire.

William was educated at St Andrews School, Southborough, Tunbridge Wells, Kent until

Denis George Wyldbore Hewitt VC. His story is related in the fifth book in this series published in 2017, *Victoria Crosses on the Western Front: Third Ypres 1917*.

86 Victoria Crosses on the Western Front – Battles of the Scarpe 1918

Westminster School, within the precincts of Westminster Abbey, traces its origins to a charity school established by the Benedictine monks of the Abbey. It dates back to at least the 14th century and is one of the original nine public schools defined by the Clarendon Commission of 1861. Although Henry VIII dissolved the monasteries, he ensured that the School survived by royal charter. In 1967, the first female pupil was admitted. Westminster has an impressive list of famous alumni, including:

- Dido Armstrong (born 1971), musician.
- Tony Benn (1925–2014), Labour politician.
- Helena Bonham Carter (born 1966), actress.
- Sir Adrian Boult (1889–1983), conductor.
- Nick Clegg (born 1967), Liberal Democrat leader and Deputy Prime Minister.
- Augustus Henry Fitzroy, 3rd Duke of Grafton (1735–1811), British Prime Minister.
- Sir John Gielgud (1904–2000), actor and director.
- Ben Johnson (1573–1637), poet and dramatist.
- Nigel Lawson (born 1932), Conservative Chancellor of the Exchequer.
- Lord Andrew Lloyd Webber (born 1948) composer and producer.
- AA Milne (1882–1956), author and journalist.
- Kim Philby (1912–88), intelligence officer and double agent for the KGB.
- Charles Cotesworth Pinckney (1746–1825), ADC to George Washington in 1777, defeated by Thomas Jefferson in 1804 for the US Presidency.
- Henry Purcell (1659–95), composer.
- Lord John Russell (1792–1878), British Prime Minister.
- Field Marshal FitzRoy James Henry Somerset, 1st Baron Raglan (1788–1855), lost his right arm at Waterloo and was C-in-C in the Crimean War. There is a statue of him in Dean's Yard at the School.
- Sir Peter Ustinov (1921–2004), actor, writer and director.
- Charles Wesley (1707–88), Methodist preacher and hymn writer.
- Sir Christopher Wren (1632–1723), architect, scientist and co-founder of the Royal Society.

Five other former Westminster pupils have been awarded the VC - Edmund Henry Lenon (1830-93), William George Hawtry Bankes (1836–58), Nevill Maskelyne Smyth (1868–1941), Arthur Martin-Leake VC & Bar (1874–1953) and Richard Wakeford (1921–72).

1893 and Westminster School, London June 1893–1896. He was employed by the Standard Life Assurance Co 1896–99 and emigrated to Canada in 1902, where he worked for the company. He was transferred by Standard Life to Johannesburg, South Africa in 1910.

William married Katherine 'Kate' Florence Reford (3rd June 1877–11th August 1966) in Montréal, Québec on 5th September 1914. They lived there at 260 Drummond Street and 290 Peel Street. Her address in early 1919 was 157 St James Street, Montréal. There were no children.

Kate's father, Robert Wilson Reford (1st August 1831–15th March 1913), born at Moylena, Co Antrim, Ireland, emigrated to Canada with his family in 1845 and settled in Toronto, where he had a successful wholesale grocery business. By the early 1860s he and his partner, John Dillon, had purchased an import business from William Ross. He married Margaret McCord (c.1838–c.1863) on 6th November 1862 at Mount Pleasant, Brant Co, Ontario. There were no children. In 1866 Robert moved to Montréal to establish the Robert Reford Co, a general steamship agency representing a number of steamship lines operating out of London, Newcastle, Glasgow, Antwerp and some Mediterranean ports. Robert married Katharine 'Kate' Sherriff née Drummond (16th January 1844–28th February 1938) on 12th September 1866 at Stirling, Scotland, where she was born. They returned to Canada, where she was a member of St George's Anglican Church for many years and was one of Montréal's best-known residents. In 1871 Robert was described as an importer and they were living at 301 Peel Street. In 1881 he was described as a merchant and they were living in St Antoine, Montréal. In 1882 he created the Mount Royal Milling & Manufacturing Co (later Mount Royal Rice Mills Ltd) and in 1890 it purchased SV *Thermopylae* to transport rice from China to its mill in Victoria, British Columbia. He was a shipping agent in 1891, a merchant in 1901 and in 1911 was running a steamship company. That year he represented Cunard in Montréal as general

William's father-in-law, Robert Wilson Reford (1831–1913). During the Great War his company handled about ninety-five troopships at various Canadian ports, moving 139,000 soldiers. In the 1920s immigration to Canada increased and, as general agents for Cunard and other lines, much of the Company's business was focused on passenger traffic. During the Second World War the company helped organise convoys leaving Halifax for Europe. From 1945 the Company operated exclusively as general steamship agents, representing companies in Europe, South America, Asia and Australia. Since 2004 it has acted exclusively as vessel and port agents, serving ship owners and charterers. The Company was a founding member of the Shipping Federation of Canada in 1903 and played a leading role in the development of the marine transportation industry in Canada. It is the oldest Canadian steamship agency and five generations of the Reford family have been involved in its management.

agents for Canada, an association that lasted until 1945. The Company continues as the oldest Canadian steamship agency. Kate was living at 260 Drummond Street, Montréal in 1915 and died at her home, 3468 Drummond Street, Montréal. She is buried with her husband in Mount Royal Cemetery, Montréal. In addition to Kate they had five other children, all born in Montréal:

St George's Anglican Church on Stanley Street, opposite Place du Canada, was designated a National Historic Site in 1990. The original church opened on 30th June 1843 on Saint Joseph (now Notre-Dame) Street. It was the second Anglican congregation in Montréal and was built to accommodate the overflow of parishioners from Christ Church Cathedral. The congregation grew as the city expanded and land at the corner of Peel Street and De la Gauchetière Street was chosen as the site of the current church. The land had been a Jewish cemetery 1775–1854. The church opened on 9th October 1870. Only the pulpit was retained from the old church, which became a factory for organ-maker Samuel Russell Warren. When St Jude Church and Church of the Advent closed, their parishioners joined St George's. The bell tower was completed in 1894. The architecture of the church is classic English Gothic revival. The ceiling beams are among the largest in the world and the exposed double-beam hammer roof is second in the world only to Westminster Hall in span. The tapestry originates from Westminster Abbey, where it was used during the coronation of Queen Elizabeth II in 1953.

- Robert Wilson Reford (19th August 1867–15th November 1951) was educated at Upper Canada College, Toronto and Lincoln College, Sorel. In 1888 he worked as a purser aboard a Thomson Line vessel in the Mediterranean. The following year he went to Victoria, British Columbia as assistant manager of the Mount Royal Rice Mills, founded by his father in 1882. While there he was in charge of SV *Thermopylae*. From 1891 he worked in shipping offices in Antwerp and Paris before returning to Montréal, where he joined Robert Reford Co as Secretary-Treasurer. He was made a partner in 1906 and succeeded to the presidency of the Company on the death of his father in 1913 until 1945. Robert was President of the Montréal Board of Trade in 1912 and during the Great War he was vice-president of the Montréal Branch of the Canadian Patriotic Fund. In 1919 he was made a director of Cunard Steamship Co. He was also a director of the Lake of the Woods Milling Co Ltd, Keewatin Flour Mills, Inter City Baking Co and the New Brunswick Railway. He was President of the Shipping Federation of Canada 1920–30 and of the Québec Division of The Navy League of Canada 1920–22. He was the first vice-president of the Montréal Canadian Club, vice-president of the Association of Canadian Clubs and President of the Canadian Club 1915–16. He was also a councillor of the Montréal Sailor' Institute and Shipping Federation. Robert was an art collector. He

SV *Thermopylae* (991 tons), an extreme composite clipper, launched on 19th August 1868 by Walter Hood & Co, Aberdeen for the Aberdeen Line, was designed for the China tea trade. *Cutty Sark* was built to rival her. She sailed for Melbourne from Gravesend on 7th November, arriving in a record sixty-three days on her maiden voyage. She went to Newcastle, New South Wales and loaded for Shanghai, making that passage in a record twenty-eight days. *Thermopylae* cut two days off the record for the Foochow, China to London run. However, this was beaten by another two days by *Sir Lancelot* just two weeks later. In 1872 *Thermopylae* raced *Cutty Sark* from Shanghai to London, arriving seven days ahead after *Cutty Sark* lost her rudder. In a single day she covered 358 knots but *Cutty Sark* holds the record with 363 knots. *Thermopylae* made her last passage in the tea trade, leaving Foochow on 30th October 1881 and arriving 107 days later. From 1882 she was involved in the Australian wool trade. The Aberdeen Line sold her in 1890 to Robert Reford Co for the rice trade between Rangoon and Vancouver, British Columbia. She once completed the Shanghai to Victoria route in twenty-nine days. She was sold in 1895 to the Portuguese Government as a training ship named *Pedro Nunes*. On 13th October 1907, before Amelia de Orleans, Queen of Portugal, she was torpedoed with full naval honours off Cascais.

acquired one of the first Kodak cameras in 1888 and became one of Canada's most prolific amateur photographers. On 12th June 1894 at St Paul's Church, Montréal he married Mary Elsie Stephen Meighen (23rd January 1872–8th November 1967), born at Perth, Lanark County, Ontario, daughter of Robert and Elsie Meighen and niece of George Stephen, 1st Baron Mount Stephen. She became President of the Women's Canadian Club in Montréal, first director of the Montréal Maternity Hospital and convener of the Québec Battlefields Association 1908. In 1902, they built their home at 300 Drummond Street, Montréal. They had two sons – Robert Bruce Stephen Reford (1895–1972) and Lewis Eric Reford (1900–83).

- Andrew Drummond Reford (23rd June 1869–12th November 1948) was a clerk in a rice mill office in 1891, a merchant in 1901 and was employed by a steamship company in 1911 living with his parents. He was a lieutenant in 3rd Field Battery, Canadian Artillery and served as a lieutenant and assistant quartermaster with 2nd Canadian Mounted Rifles in the South African War (Queen's South Africa Medal with clasps – Cape Colony, Transvaal & South Africa 1902). He was a captain in 3rd Field Battery, Canadian Artillery and 5th Royal Highlanders of Canada before the Great War. He enlisted as a lieutenant for overseas duty with 13th Battalion CEF at Valcartier on 21st September 1914. He was described as 5′ 9½″ tall, weighing 148 lbs, with dark complexion, brown eyes, grey hair and his religious denomination was Church of England. He sailed with his unit on

3rd October aboard RMS *Alaunia* and served with 17th Battalion at Tidworth, Hampshire. On 19th March 1915 he transferred to the Royal Artillery. On 12th May 1917 he was tried by field general court martial for drunkenness on 26th April, while attached to 298th Army Field Artillery Brigade Ammunition Column. He was dismissed from the service on 2nd June 1917. Andrew lived at The Guard House, Knowlton, Québec. He married Anne Marie de Nonancourt (6th December 1880–21st October 1958), daughter of Commandant Marie Ernest de Nonancourt and Catherine Bidalot. They had two children:
  ◦ John Reford, who married Diana Rosemary Trafford, daughter of Major Sigismund William Joseph Trafford and Lady Elizabeth Constance Mary Bertie on 3rd March 1951.
  ◦ Sophia Reford, who married Jacques Sourdille of Paris, France.
- Grace Simonton Reford (26th July 1871–5th August 1875).
- Edith Eleanor Margaret Reford (16th August 1874–31st August 1970) married Hartland Brydges MacDougall (born 10th March 1876) on 25th April 1899 at St George's Anglican Church, Ste-Anne-de-Bellevue, Montréal. He was a stockbroker when he enlisted in the CEF on 10th May 1915 and was appointed captain the same day, described as 5′ 9¾″ tall, with dark complexion, brown eyes, black hair and his religious denomination was Church of England. His address was 381 Mountain Street, Montréal. He served in 42nd Battalion and sailed for Britain on 10th June 1915. He was admitted to 7th Stationary Hospital, Boulogne 18th–22nd October 1916 and was attached to the Canadian Section, GHQ 3rd Echelon for temporary duty 12th–16th December and 3rd Division HQ as acting field cashier on 22nd January 1917. He returned to his unit on 19th March. Hartland was promoted temporary major and was appointed Deputy Assistant Adjutant General at the War Office, London and was posted for instructional duty with the British Military Mission in Washington DC on 19th January 1918. He was posted to Casualty Company on 10th December 1918 and demobilised on 12th December. He was brought to the notice of the Secretary of State for War for valuable service on 24th March 1919. They had five children:
  ◦ Grace Edith MacDougall (1900–83).
  ◦ Katherine Lorna MacDougall (1901–90) married as Price.
  ◦ Hartland Campbell MacDougall (1905–97) married Dorothy Molson, eldest daughter of Lieutenant Colonel Herbert Molson (1875–1938) MC CMG, President of Molson Brewery.
  ◦ Robert Reford MacDougall (1908–80) married Margaret Meredith Cape, daughter of Lieutenant Colonel Edmund Graves Meredith Cape.
  ◦ Peter Lewis MacDougall (1913–73).
- Lewis Lawrence Reford (5th March 1879–31st May 1949) was educated privately and at McGill University, graduating in arts in 1900. He was a chief engineer in 1901 living with his parents. He graduated in medicine in 1904 and studied neurosurgery at John Hopkins. In 1911 he was appointed to the Royal Victoria

Hospital, Montréal and became a noted neurosurgery pioneer. Lewis joined the CEF as a captain in the Canadian Army Medical Corps on 5th March 1915. He was described as 5′ 9″ tall, weighing 151 lbs, with fair complexion, blue eyes, fair hair and his religious denomination was Church of England. His address was 307 Pine Avenue West, Montréal and later 287 Drummond Street. He allotted $40 per month from his Army pay to his wife. He joined 3rd Canadian General Hospital and sailed with the unit for Britain on 6th May aboard SS *Metagama*. Lewis joined the Military Hospital, Shorncliffe, Kent on 1st June. The unit proceeded to France on 18th June aboard SS *Huanchaco*, set up at Dannes-Camiers and was ready to receive casualties on 7th August. Amongst the staff were Major John McCrae, who wrote In Flanders Fields, and Captain Francis Scrimger VC. Lewis proceeded to the CAMC Training Centre in England on temporary duty on 14th December and was attached to the Canadian Casualty Discharge & Exercise Depot on 9th February 1916. He embarked for France on 8th April and rejoined 3rd Canadian General Hospital. He was granted leave 25th April–2nd May and was admitted to 14th Stationary Hospital, Boulogne on 31st July with suspected German measles. He was evacuated to Britain on HMHS *Cambria* on 17th August with typhoid and was admitted the same day to 1st London General Hospital, Camberwell until 31st August. A medical board at 86 Strand, London that day found him unfit for service for one month. A medical board there on 15th September found him unfit for service for two months and he was granted leave until 15th November. He returned to Canada, embarking on RMS *Olympic* on 18th September and arriving on 30th September. His leave was extended to 15th January 1917 and then to 15th February. He returned to France on 26th February to rejoin 3rd Canadian General Hospital. Lewis was granted fourteen days leave to Paris from 10th December, extended on 25th December until 4th January 1918 and then to 8th January. He was promoted temporary major on 10th January and was again granted leave to Paris 25th–27th April. On 26th May he was posted to the CAMC Depot, Shorncliffe, Kent and reported sick on 29th May. He was admitted to 1st Scottish General Hospital, Aberdeen on 19th June with pyrexia of unknown origin. On 27th June he was transferred to the Canadian Officers' Convalescent Hospital, Matlock Bath, Derbyshire. A medical board there on 11th July found him fit for General Service and he joined 14th Canadian General Hospital, Eastbourne on 28th July. Lewis was treated there for bronchitis 2nd–11th December 1918 and 6th–9th March 1919. He embarked for Canada on HMT *Regina* at Liverpool on 20th May and disembarked at Halifax, Nova Scotia on 28th May for demobilisation on 6th June 1919. Lewis married Jean Cassils McIntyre (18th September 1879–18th October 1970) on 4th May 1915, daughter of Duncan McIntyre, first vice president and later president of the Canadian Pacific Railway and a founder of the Bell Telephone Company of Canada. They lived initially at 317 Drummond Street, Montréal.

Prince Arthur William Patrick Albert, Duke of Connaught and Strathearn (1st May 1850–16th January 1942), was the seventh child of Queen Victoria. In 1866 he attended the Royal Military Academy Woolwich and was commissioned as a lieutenant in the Royal Engineers on 18th June 1868. He transferred to the Royal Artillery on 2nd November 1868 and on 2nd August 1869 to the Rifle Brigade. He served in South Africa, Canada 1869, Ireland, Egypt 1882 and India. In Canada he was involved in defending against the Fenian Raids. In January 1870 he visited Washington DC and met President Ulysees S Grant. Arthur was appointed C-in-C Bombay Army December 1886–March 1890. He was then GOC Southern District in Portsmouth until 1893. He commanded Aldershot District Command until 1898. On 26th June 1902 he was promoted to field marshal. He was C-in-C Ireland 1900–04, with the dual appointment of GOC III Corps from October 1901, and was Inspector-General of the Forces 1904–07. He was Governor General of Canada 3rd October 1911–11th November 1916, the only British prince to hold the appointment.

William served in the Imperial Yeomanry, Rhodesian Horse and later Paget's Horse as a trooper during the Second Boer War. He saw action in Cape Colony, Orange Free State and Transvaal (MID). He was discharged in 1902 and the following year joined the Canadian Militia (5th Royal Highlanders of Canada). William was one of the chief organisers of the St Andrew's Ball of 1913 at which the Duke and Duchess of Connaught were guests of honour.

William had a medical at Valcartier on 28th August 1914 and was attested on 23rd September. He was commissioned in 13th Canadian Infantry Battalion with the rank of captain backdated to 22nd September 1914. He was described as a company manager, 5′ 9½″ tall, weighing 141 lbs, with fair complexion, blue eyes, brown hair and his religious denomination was Church of England. William sailed for Britain with the First Canadian Contingent, embarking on RMS *Alaunia* at Québec on 25th September and arriving at Plymouth, Devon on 16th October.

Further training was carried out on Salisbury Plain, Wiltshire before moving to France on 9th February 1915 and rejoining 13th Battalion on 1st April. He was in action during the German gas attack at

RMS *Alaunia* (13,405 tons), a Cunard Line ship built in 1913. When war broke out she was requisitioned as a troopship and was widely employed bringing Canadian troops to Europe, supporting the Gallipoli campaign, carrying troops to Bombay and returning to the North Atlantic route in 1916. On 19th October 1916, outbound for New York from London, she struck a mine in the English Channel laid by *UC-16* and sank off Hastings, Sussex with the loss of two crewmen. Cunard named another vessel RMS *Alaunia*, which was in service 1925–57.

Ypres in April 1915 and was reported killed on 25th April. This was corrected two days later to 'alive and well'. He was knocked over three times by shells, the third time being completely buried and rendered unconscious. The men on either side of him were killed but he managed to dig himself out, although the enemy was close by, and managed to return to his own lines with valuable information. **Awarded the French Croix de Guerre with Bronze Palm, LG 30th March 1916**.

William was promoted temporary major on 24th April. **Awarded the DSO for his actions in the attack on Festubert in May 1915, LG 14th January 1916.** He was admitted to 3rd Canadian Field Ambulance on 29th May and No.4 Casualty Clearing Station with a back injury. He was discharged to duty on 31st May and was appointed Staff Captain, HQ 3rd Canadian Brigade on 27th November. William was granted leave 3rd–13th December 1915 and 1st–15th April 1916. On 18th June he was appointed GSO3, HQ 2nd Canadian Division and was attached to HQ 3rd Canadian Brigade on 17th September. He was promoted major and appointed Brigade Major, HQ 5th Canadian Brigade on 3rd October 1916. He was granted ten days' leave from 22nd January 1917. William was involved in the capture of Vimy Ridge in April. Leave was generous at this time as he was granted ten days on 6th June, ten days on 3rd September and thirty days on 27th November, all in Britain.

William was promoted temporary lieutenant colonel and assumed command of 24th Battalion on 30th December. **Awarded the CMG for services rendered in connection with military operations in France and Flanders, LG 3rd June 1918**. He was granted fourteen days leave in England on 24th June 1918. **Awarded**

The Most Distinguished Order of Saint Michael and Saint George was founded on 28th April 1818 by George, Prince Regent (later King George IV). The Order was originally awarded to those holding commands or high position in the Mediterranean territories acquired in the Napoleonic Wars but was extended to holders of similar offices or positions in other territories of the Empire. It is currently awarded to those who hold high office or who render extraordinary or important non-military service in a foreign country. There are three classes:

- Knight Grand Cross or Dame Grand Cross (GCMG).
- Knight Commander (KCMG) or Dame Commander (DCMG).
- Companion (CMG).

People are appointed to the Order rather than being awarded it. It is the sixth-most senior in the British honours system and was opened to women in 1965. The British Sovereign appoints all other members of the Order on the advice of the Government. The next-most senior member is the Grand Master, currently the Duke of Kent. The Order includes 125 GCMG, 375 D/KCMG and 1,750 CMG. Members of the Royal Family appointed to the Order do not count towards the limit, nor do foreign honorary members. The original home of the Order was the Palace of St Michael and St George in Corfu. Since 1906, the Order's chapel has been in St Paul's Cathedral, London.

a Bar to the DSO for his actions during the Battle of Amiens on 8th August 1918. The Battalion reached its objectives and on several occasions at great risk he personally directed the capture of strongpoints obstinately defended by the enemy. The success of his Battalion was due in no small degree to the example, courage and resourcefulness of its commander, LG 11th January 1919.

Awarded the VC for his actions at Chérisy, France on 27th–28th August 1918, LG 14th December 1918. He was admitted to 4th Canadian Field Ambulance and No.1 Casualty Clearing Station the same day and to 3rd General Hospital, Le Tréport, France on 29th August. He was evacuated to Prince of Wales Hospital, London on 3rd September, on the held strength of the Québec Regiment Depot, Bramshott from 2nd September. He transferred to the Imperial Order of the Daughters of the Empire Canadian Red Cross Hospital, 1 Hyde Park Place, London on 13th September. A Medical Board on 18th October at 13 Berners Street, London recommended one month sick leave and to attend outdoor treatment. He was living at Garland's Hotel, Suffolk Street, London at the time. A Medical Board on 19th November in London found him fit for General Service. He was discharged on 26th November and returned to France to join 2nd Canadian Division on 13th January 1919. William was attached to HQ 5th Canadian Brigade on 15th January and returned to Britain on 20th February for posting to 2 Repatriation Depot, South Ripon, Yorkshire. A medical at 13 Berners Street on 28th February found him fit for discharge. The VC, CMG and DSO & Bar were presented by the King in the ballroom at Buckingham Palace on 1st March. William sailed for Canada aboard SS *Melita* on 28th March and was struck off strength of

The Prince of Wales General Hospital, Tottenham Green East, Tottenham. Dr Laseron decided to found a hospital to train ladies to nurse the sick poor and the Evangelical Protestant Deaconesses' Institution and Training Hospital opened in a converted cottage in 1867. John Morley, a City merchant, donated Avenue House on the east side of Tottenham Green to the Institution and it moved there in 1868. Avenue House was replaced in 1881 and in 1887 further extensions were added. The Prince and Princess of Wales (later King Edward VII and Queen Alexandra) opened the new buildings. In 1899 the Institution was renamed Tottenham Hospital and it became a district general hospital. In 1907 another extension was opened by King Edward VII and Queen Alexandra and the name was changed to Prince of Wales General Hospital. Adjoining property was purchased in 1917 and in 1923 a further extension was opened. In 1932 the Prince of Wales (later King Edward VIII and Duke of Windsor) opened an Out-Patients wing and another Nurses' Home. By 1972 the Hospital had 200 beds but by 1983 it had largely closed. In 1993 the four-storey red brick building was converted into thirty-eight apartments named Deaconess Court. The two-storey hospital building to the north was also converted for residential use as 2a Elliot Court.

By 1915 there was a need for more hospital accommodation for officers. A townhouse on the Bayswater Road was obtained and Colonel and Mrs AE Gooderham of Toronto paid for its conversion into a hospital for Canadian officers. It was run by the Daughters of the Empire (Mrs Gooderham was President) and the Canadian Red Cross was responsible for maintenance. The Daughters of the Empire Canadian Red Cross Hospital for Officers was officially opened by Princess Louise, Duchess of Argyle, on 11th May 1916. Although intended for Canadian officers, other nationalities were received. The Hospital had twenty-five beds, most overlooking Hyde Park. It closed on 20th September 1919. The Imperial Order of the Daughters of the British Empire was inaugurated in 1900 in a surge of patriotism caused by Canadian soldiers departing for the Second Boer War. Membership increased greatly during the Great War. The money raised was used to purchase hospitals, hospital ships and ambulances as well as military aircraft, in addition to providing field comforts. The Order still exists as a charitable organisation in Canada, dedicated to improving the quality of life for children, young adults and those in need, through scholarships, bursaries, awards and education projects.

the CEF at Halifax, Nova Scotia on 7th April 1919. He gave his address as 157 St James Street, Montréal. William was **Mentioned four times – in Sir John French's Despatch of 15th October 1915 (LG 1st January 1916) and in Sir Douglas Haig's Despatches of 7th November 1917, 7th April 1918 and 8th November 1918 (LG 28th December 1917, 28th May 1918 and 31st December 1918 respectively).** William rejoined the Militia and was promoted brevet lieutenant colonel.

William returned to his job with Standard Life Assurance Co and became a manager. He was appointed a director of Guardian Insurance Co of Canada in 1927 and Chairman in 1943. He was also Chairman of the Advisory Board of the Guardian-Caledonian group of insurance companies. William retired from Standard Assurance Co in November 1945. He was a member of Saint Paul's Freemason Lodge (No.12) of the Canadian Constitution, (renumbered 374), meeting in Montréal, where he was the Secretary. William was a keen sportsman, particularly fond of fishing and shooting.

William attended two VC reunions – the VC Dinner at the Royal Gallery of the House of Lords, London on 9th November 1929 and the VC Centenary Celebrations at Hyde Park, London on 26th June 1956. With his wife, Kate, he sailed from New York to Southampton, Hampshire aboard RMS *Mauretania*, arriving on 17th December 1952. They sailed the same route aboard RMS *Queen Mary*, arriving on 18th April 1956. They also travelled from Montréal to Greenock, Scotland, arriving on 16th July 1960.

William died in Montréal on 25th October 1961 and is buried in the Reford family plot (Lot 258, Pine Hill Section) in Mount Royal Cemetery, 1297 Chemin de la Forêt, Outremont, Montréal. He is commemorated in a number of other places:

SS *Melita* was laid down at Barclay, Curle & Co, Glasgow in 1913 for the Hamburg America Line. However, the Great War broke out and she was purchased by Canadian Pacific when launched in 1917. She entered service on 25th January 1918 with a maiden voyage from Liverpool to St John, New Brunswick. She operated on the Canadian Pacific's Liverpool–New York route and made a Glasgow–Bombay voyage in 1919 for the British government. *Melita* was on the Antwerp–St John service 1922–27 and returned to the Britain–Canada service until March 1932. In October 1925, *Melita* made a routine call to Antwerp to collect passengers for Canada. On the night of 20th October, Captain Arthur Honeywell Clews was asleep in his cabin when First Officer Towers entered and shot him in the head with a revolver. He was disarmed by other officers and was locked in his cabin. Towers held a grudge because of lack of promotion within the company. Discussions were held between the company agent, local police and embassy staff. It was agreed that because it was a British ship and all involved were British, the Southampton police would investigate when the ship arrived in port. Thomas Augustus Towers was tried at Winchester Assizes for the murder of Captain Clews and the attempted murder of two other officers. He was committed to Broadmoor as criminally insane at the King's pleasure. After making 146 Atlantic crossings, Melita was used for cruising until sold for scrap in Genoa in 1935. However, she was bought from the breakers by Italy, renamed *Liguria* and was used as a troop transport. She was damaged in an air attack on Tobruk in 1940 and was scuttled there in January 1941. The hulk was raised and scrapped in 1950.

- Montréal, Québec
    - Memorial tablet in the Museum of Royal Highlanders of Canada, Bleury Street, which also commemorates the Regiment's other VCs – Dinesen, Good, Fisher, Gregg and Croak.
    - Path named after him in Field of Honour Cemetery, 703 Donegani, Pointe-Claire.
- Ontario
    - Victoria Cross obelisk to all Canadian VCs at Military Heritage Park, Barrie dedicated by Princess Royal on 22nd October 2013.
    - Named on one of eleven plaques honouring 175 men from overseas awarded the VC for the Great War. The plaques were unveiled by the Senior Minister of State at the Foreign & Commonwealth Office and Minister for Faith and Communities, Baroness Warsi, at a reception at Lancaster House, London

on 26th June 2014 attended by The Duke of Kent and relatives of the VC recipients. The Canadian plaque was unveiled outside the British High Commission in Elgin Street, Ottawa on 10th November 2014 by The Princess Royal in the presence of British High Commissioner Howard Drake, Canadian Minister of Veterans Affairs Julian Fantino and Canadian Chief of the Defence Staff General Thomas James Lawson.
  ◦ Plaque No.11 on the York Cemetery VC Memorial, West Don River Valley, Toronto dedicated on 25th June 2017.
* Two 49 cents postage stamps in honour of the ninety-four Canadian VC winners were issued by Canada Post on 21st October 2004 on the 150th Anniversary of the first Canadian VC's action, Alexander Roberts Dunn VC.
* United Kingdom
  ◦ A Department for Communities and Local Government commemorative paving stone was dedicated at Carsphairn Parish Church, Carsphairn, Castle Douglas, Kircudbrightshire, Scotland on 27th August 2018.
  ◦ Family headstone in the private cemetery, Knockgary Estate, Dumfries & Galloway, Scotland.
  ◦ Memorial paving stone unveiled outside Freemason's Hall, Covent Garden, London on 25th April 2017 by the Duke of Kent.

William Clark-Kennedy's gravestone in Mount Royal Cemetery.

Victoria Cross Grove, Dunorlan Park, Tunbridge Wells.

The memorial plaque just north of Chérisy alongside the D9 Vis-en-Artois road.

- ○ Victoria Cross Grove, Dunorlan Park, Tunbridge Wells dedicated on 8th May 1995 to honour the ten Borough of Tunbridge Wells VC holders – Charles Lucas, Matthew Dixon, William Temple, John Duncan Grant, Douglas Belcher, William Addison, Eric Dougall, William Clark-Kennedy, Lionel Queripel and John Brunt.
- ○ A VC memorial was dedicated by the Princess Royal at the Victoria Cross Grove on 13th October 2006, marking the 400th anniversary of Royal Tunbridge Wells and the 150th anniversary of the Victoria Cross.
• Plaque at the northern end of Chérisy, France on the D9.

In addition to the VC, CMG and DSO & Bar, he was awarded the Queen's South Africa Medal 1899–1902 (clasps Cape Colony, Orange Free State, Transvaal & South Africa 1901), 1914–15 Star, British War Medal 1914–20, Victory Medal 1914–19 with Mentioned-in-Despatches Oakleaf, Efficiency Decoration (Canada), George VI Coronation Medal 1937, Elizabeth II Coronation Medal 1953 and French Croix de Guerre 1914–18 with Bronze Palm. The location of his medals is not known.

10864 COMPANY SERGEANT MAJOR MARTIN DOYLE
1st Battalion, The Royal Munster Fusiliers

Martin Doyle was born on 25th October 1891 at Cloonagh, Gusserane, New Ross, Co Wexford, Ireland. His father, Laurence 'Larry' Doyle (15th June 1859–1949), a labourer born at Ballycullane, Tintern, Co Wexford, married Bridget née Fardy (c.1861–1931) on 28th November 1882 at Ballycullane, Tintern, Co Wexford. They were living at Dunmain, Co Wexford in 1901 and at Ballykelly, near New Ross in 1909. Martin had six sisters:

• Ann Doyle (born 20th December 1883) married as Maher.
• Ellen 'Nellie' Doyle (13th November 1885–25th February 1966) married Thomas Cooney (1872–16th December 1942) on 19th August 1912. They both died in Ballykelly, Co Wexford. They had seven children including:
   ○ Patrick Cooney (1913–19).
   ○ Johannah Ita Cooney (1915–87) married Patrick Joseph Maddock (1914–97) and they had three children.
   ○ Laurence Cooney (1917–45).
   ○ Patrick Enda Cooney (1922–2011) married Julia Courtney (1921–97), born at Kanturk, Co Cork, in 1957 at Ilford, Essex. She died in London and he at Chelmsford, Essex. They had a daughter.
   ○ Bridget Mary Cooney (died 2012).

Biographies 99

The port of New Ross dates back to at least the 6th century when St Abban of Magheranoidhe founded a monastery there. It is at an important crossing point on the River Barrow. The Anglo-Norman, William Marshall, conquered the region in early 13th century and a borough of English and Welsh settlers grew up around his motte. Marshall was made Earl of Pembroke by King John in 1199. The town of New Ross was granted a Royal Charter in 1207. It was fought over in the Irish Confederate Wars in the 1640s and resisted a siege in 1643 but fell to Oliver Cromwell in 1649. There was also a battle there in the 1789 rebellion.

The nationalist politician, John Edward Redmond (1856–1918), was the MP for New Ross 1881–85. He led the moderate Irish Parliamentary Party 1900–18 and the paramilitary Irish National Volunteers. He was instrumental in September 1914 in the passing of the Irish Home Rule Act, granting limited self-government to Ireland. However, Home Rule was suspended for the duration of the Great War. Redmond called on the National Volunteers to join the British Army and support the war effort, thereby ensuring the implementation of Home Rule after the war. However, after the 1916 Easter Rising, Irish opinion shifted in favour of full independence and Redmond's party lost its dominance in Irish politics.

The Kennedy family homestead, ancestral home of US President John F Kennedy (1917–63), is eight kilometres south of New Ross. JFK visited in 1963 and spoke at the spot where his great-grandfather, Patrick Kennedy, boarded the famine ship, *Dunbrody*, in 1848 to emigrate to America. A replica of the ship is moored at New Ross.

Liverpool FC's football ground is named Anfield, after the old town land of Annefield, just outside New Ross.

- Catherine 'Kate' Doyle (21st January 1888–14th December 1923) married John Spencer, a labourer, at the Roman Catholic Church, Ballykelly, New Ross on 9th February 1914. She died at the Auxiliary Hospital, New Ross. They had five children including William Alfred Spencer (1915) and Mary Frances Spencer (1917), both born at Abbey View, New Ross.
- Bridget 'Ciss' Doyle (25th March 1895–2nd April 1922), a domestic servant, married James Doyle (sic) (born c.1885), a labourer, at the Roman Catholic Church, Ballykelly, New Ross on 10th June 1915. They were living at Old Court, New Ross at the time.

- Elizabeth 'Lizzie' Doyle (25th October 1895–6th April 1985), a servant, married James Ryan (16th April 1900–30th January 1984), a carpenter, at the Roman Catholic Church at New Ross on 7th February 1923. They had eleven children including:
    ◦ Nancy Ryan (1924–95) married Jimmy Ryan (sic) (died 1985) and they had eight children.
    ◦ Cissie Ryan (1926–40).
    ◦ Elizabeth 'Bessie' Ryan (1927–93) married Brian Barnwell (died c.1998) and they had eight children.
    ◦ Kathleen Ryan (born 1928) married James 'Jimmy' Grangel in 1950 in Essex and they had at least a daughter.
    ◦ Moira Ryan (1932–56).
    ◦ Jim Ryan (1935–2014) married in April 1963 (spouse not known) and they had nine children.
    ◦ Eileen Ryan (born and died 1937).
- Mary 'Mollie' Agnes Doyle (19th November 1900–22nd September 1990) married James William 'Billy' Marston (23rd January 1899–1974), born at York, Yorkshire, in 1926 at Croydon, Surrey. He was a canteen manager in 1939, by when they were living at 2 Cross Street, Oakham, Rutland. He died at Southwark, London and she at Peterborough, Northamptonshire. They had two children:
    ◦ James Laurence Marston (1927–2014), born at Bath, Somerset, married Doris Ethel Grant (1930–70), born in London, in 1960 at Pancras, London. They had two children. James married Muriel Williams (1929–2005) in 1988 at Croydon, Surrey.
    ◦ Marie P Marston (born 1930), born at Romford, Essex, married Leonard Henry Groom (1927–91), born at Paddington, London, in 1951 at Ealing, London. They had two sons.

Very little is known about Martin's grandparents. His paternal grandfather, also Martin Doyle, married Anna née Ryan. His maternal grandfather is understood to be Patrick Fardy (c.1796–1868), who married Mary Fardy (c.1813–80). Martin was educated at Gusserane National School and Cushinstown School, both in New Ross, Co Wexford. He was employed as a farm worker.

On 12th March 1909 Martin enlisted in 4th Royal Irish Regiment, Special Reserve at Waterford and joined at Kilkenny (3889 & 9962). He added four months to his age and was described as 5′ 5″ tall, weighing 129 lbs, with grey eyes, brown hair and his religious denomination was Roman Catholic. He transferred to the Regular Army on 28th December 1909, served in India with the 1st Battalion and won the Battalion lightweight novice boxing competition in 1913. He returned to Ireland in 1914, transferred to the Royal Dublin Fusiliers (40342) and went to France on 19th December 1914. He was promoted sergeant in 1915 and transferred to 1st Royal Munster Fusiliers in March 1918 (10864).

Awarded the MM for his actions on 27th March 1918 when the Battalion was in reserve during an attack. The troops in front were driven back and the Battalion counterattacked. Harbonnières and Vauvillers were taken and 900m of open ground was crossed with heavy casualties. The enemy trench was reached but another trench forty metres on was still held. Between was a barn in which the enemy positioned a machine gun. Doyle called for volunteers and charged. He reached the barn alone, bayoneted two Germans and took the machine gun, LG 13th September 1918. He was captured by the Germans later in the March retreat and was treated badly but escaped after a counterattack. While out of the line, he won the 57th Division open mile race.

Mary Street in New Ross, where Martin and Charlotte lived.

Appointed acting company sergeant major in August 1918. **Awarded the VC for his actions near Riencourt, northwest of Quéant, France on 2nd–3rd September 1918, LG 31st January 1919.** The VC was presented by the King in the quadrangle at Buckingham Palace on 8th May. He was discharged from the Army in July 1919.

Martin married Charlotte Mary Kennedy (born 1st May 1891), of New Ross, on 25th November 1919 in Dublin. She was living with her aunt, Anastasia Kennedy (born c.1862), at Mary Street, New Ross in 1901. They lived at 18 Mary Street, New Ross. She reportedly died in 1978 at Kimmage, Dublin. They had four children:

- Bridget Doyle (born 4th October 1920) married as Wade and lived in London. They had a daughter, Gemma Wade.
- Laurence Anthony Doyle born at New Ross in 1922.
- Maria Doyle (born 16th June 1928) lived in Dublin.
- Charlotte Doyle (born 31st January 1935), known as Gemma, lived in Milwaukee, Wisconsin, USA.

Charlotte's father, Richard Kennedy (c.1865–31st December 1930), a sailor, married Mary née Culleton (born c.1864–6th February 1928) on 1st September 1889 at New Ross. In addition to Charlotte they had another daughter, Anastasia Kennedy, born at Mary Street, New Ross on 19th August 1903. By then Richard was a sea captain. Both Mary and Richard died at Mary Street, New Ross.

Martin Doyle meets Queen Mary at the VC Garden Party at Buckingham Palace on 26th June 1920, while serving in the IRA.

Martin became a member of the Royal Munster Fusiliers Old Comrades' Association shortly after his discharge. However, whilst working for the British Army at Ennis, Martin was recruited as an intelligence officer for the Irish Republican Army (IRA) with the Mid Clare Brigade, during the War of Independence 1920–21. It is assumed that he was feeding information to the IRA on British activities. He came under suspicion at one time and considered taking to the hills with his rifle. On another occasion he went to Kilrush on a mission and, due to faulty information, almost fell into a trap. Ironically he was a member of the IRA when he attended the VC Garden Party at Buckingham Palace on 26th June 1920. He was also in the VC Guard at the interment of the Unknown Warrior on 11th November 1920 and was a member of the Irish party at the unveiling of the Cenotaph on 13th November 1920. Martin attended the VC Dinner at the Royal Gallery of the House of Lords, London on 9th November 1929.

Martin enlisted in the Irish Free State Army in February 1922 and fought in the Civil War. He served in Waterford, Kilkenny and South Tipperary and was wounded in the left arm in early 1923. He continued to serve in 2nd and 20th Infantry Battalions and at the School of Instruction before retiring from the Army in 1938 as a sergeant major. He was on the strength

23 Larkfield Park, Kimmage, where Martin lived when he worked for Guinness.

When Sir Patrick Dun, a prominent physician, died in 1713, he left property in Co Waterford in trust to the Royal College of Physicians of Ireland. In 1788 the College set up a clinical hospital in a house on Clarendon Street, Dublin but high costs forced it to close in 1790 and its equipment was distributed to other hospitals. In 1792 a house on Wellington Quay was leased by the College and it opened as Sir Patrick Dun's Hospital. By February 1793 it had moved to Lower Exchange Street. The School of Physic Act 1800 entrusted eight commissioners to establish a hospital able to hold thirty patients. Land on Grand Canal Street was selected, with a 998-year lease from May 1802. It was completed with Parliamentary aid and opened for clinical instruction on 25th October 1808. Services transferred to St James' Hospital in 1986 and Sir Patrick Dun's Hospital closed. Since the mid-1990s the building has been used by the superintendent registrar of births, deaths and marriages to host civil ceremonies.

Martin Doyle's grave in Grangegorman Cemetery.

of 2nd Battalion Reserve Regiment until 25th January 1939. The Free State Army was reluctant to let him go as he was described as 'an excellent NCO, a very good Vickers machine gun and rifle instructor, and someone who could not be replaced without serious inconvenience to the service'. He worked for Guinness as a security officer and lived at 23 Larkfield Park, Kimmage, Dublin, owned by the Irish Soldiers and Sailors Trust.

In February 1924 Martin was impersonated by a man in Rugby, Warwickshire for financial gain. The impostor was exposed by someone who knew the real Martin Doyle during the war.

Martin developed pneumonia and was admitted to Sir Patrick Dun's Hospital, Dublin, where he died on 20th November 1940. He is buried in Grangegorman Cemetery, near McKee Barracks, Blackhorse Lane, Cabro, Dublin (also known as Blackhorse Cemetery). The grave was paid for by the Old Comrades' Association and his widow. His headstone bears the badge of the Royal Munster Fusiliers. He is commemorated in a number of other places:

- A Department for Communities and Local Government commemorative paving stone was dedicated at the Cross of Sacrifice in Glasnevin Cemetery, Dublin on 11th November 2018.
- Irish VC Memorial, National Memorial Arboretum, Alrewas, Staffordshire.
- Blue Plaque on his former home at New Ross, Co Wexford, Ireland.

Irish commemorative paving stones in Glasnevin Cemetery, Dublin.

In addition to the VC and MM he was awarded the 1914–15 Star, British War Medal 1914–20, Victory Medal 1914–19 and George VI Coronation Medal 1937. The VC was offered for sale by Sotheby's on 1st March 1984 but was withdrawn at the last minute. It was auctioned by Spink's on 7th November 1995 and was purchased for £19,000 by Lord Ashcroft. The VC is held by the Michael Ashcroft Trust, the holding institution for the Lord Ashcroft Victoria Cross Collection and is displayed in the Imperial War Museum's Lord Ashcroft Gallery.

On 26th May 1942 the Irish government approved the Service (1917–1921) Medal for persons who were members of Óglaigh na hÉireann (Irish Republican Army), Na Fianna Éireann (Irish nationalist youth organisation), Cumann na mBan (Irishwomen's Council) and the Irish Citizen Army for not less than three months prior to 11th July 1921. The medal was issued with a bar to those on active service 1st April 1920–11th July 1921. Without the bar it was issued to those whose service was not deemed to be active military service, but were members of these organisations. It is understood that the medal was awarded to Martin posthumously.

The Service (1917–1921) Medal without bar.

41788 LANCE SERGEANT ARTHUR EVANS (ALIAS WALTER SIMPSON)
6th Battalion, The Lincolnshire Regiment

Arthur Evans was born on 8th April 1891 at 33 Caradoc Road, Seaforth, Lancashire. It has been assumed that Arthur was a stepson of Robert and Eleanor Evans but this is not so. The anomaly is thought to arise from an interview given by his sister, Eleanor, to the *Bolton Journal and Guardian* on 1st November 1918, when Arthur was still serving as Walter Simpson. Eleanor was his next-of-kin and in order to cover her brother's change of name declared that he was her stepbrother. Arthur's father, Robert Evans (born c.1854), born at Wigan, Lancashire, married Eleanor Ann née McCann (1856–1916), born at West Derby, Lancashire, in 1879 in Liverpool, Lancashire. She was a general servant in 1871 living with her mother and siblings. Robert was a storekeeper in an engine works in 1881 and they were living with her father at 16 Myrtle Street, Birkenhead, Cheshire. In 1890 they moved to Seaforth, Lancashire. He was a timekeeper in an engineering works in 1901 and they were living at 33 Caradoc Road, Seaforth. He later gained employment as an accountant in a cotton mill. By 1911 they had moved to 2 Hawarden Grove, Seaforth. Arthur had five siblings:

- Sarah Evans (born 1879), born at Birkenhead, Cheshire, was a nursing sister in charge of the children of Captain Robert James Cecil Charles Edward Willis (1894–1979), of Esher, Surrey in July 1937. Captain Willis lost his first wife in 1936 and remarried in 1938. A Sarah Evans, born on 15th July 1879, single and a nurse (retired) was living on her own at 26 Somerton Avenue, Lowestoft, Suffolk in 1939. Another single Sarah Evans, born on 12th March 1879, was a patient at St Faith's London County Council Hospital, London Road, Brentwood in 1939. It has not been possible to ascertain if either of these ladies was the VC's sister. The death of a Sarah Evans born in 1879 was registered in October 1969 at Deben, Suffolk.
- Eleanor Evans (born 1880) was a domestic servant at 9 Queensgate, Halliwell, Bolton, Lancashire in 1911. She was living at 99 Davenport Street, Bolton in 1921.
- John 'Jack' Robert Evans (1884–25th February 1933), born at Seacombe, Cheshire, was an apprentice coppersmith in 1901. He served during the Great War as a corporal in the Royal Engineers, enlisting in September 1914. He was badly wounded on the Somme in 1916 and lay out in no man's land for three days before being rescued. Jack married Annie Gertrude Bolton (1886–11th February 1945) on 31st August 1918 at St George's Church, Bolton-le-Moors, Lancashire. She

was an assistant in a drapers' shop in 1911, living with her parents at 48 Church Street, Bolton. They lived at 9 Forshaw Avenue, St Anne's-on-Sea, Lancashire. Jack never fully recovered from his wounds and died there. Annie died at The Memorial Hospital, St Anne's-on-Sea. They had a son:
  ○ Noel Cherry Evans (born 1921), born at Fylde, Lancashire, served as a corporal in the RAF during the Second World War. He married Dorothy M Worrall (born 1922), born at Runcorn, Cheshire, in 1955 at Bucklow, Cheshire.
- James Arnold Evans (born 8th September 1885) was a baker's messenger in 1901 and a painter in 1911. He served during the Great War as a corporal in 11th King's (Liverpool). He was gassed in 1916 before serving in Ireland with 3rd (Home Service) Garrison Battalion, Northumberland Fusiliers. He was a ship's painter in 1939, living on his own at 47 Newman Street, Liverpool.
- Alice Gwendoline Evans (23rd February 1895–October 1992), born at Seaforth, Lancashire, was living at 48 Church Street, Bolton c.1918. She died unmarried at Loughborough, Leicestershire.

Arthur's paternal grandfather was John Robert Evans (c.1833–95), a labourer. His maternal grandfather, Samuel McCann (c.1811–1883), born in Co Antrim, Ireland, married Margaret Jones (1808–26th March 1851) on 3rd November 1840 at St John the Baptist Church, Walton-on-the-Hill, Lancashire. They were living at Stanhope Street, Toxteth Park, Lancashire at the time. Margaret had married Miles Jones (c.1804–c.1834), a painter born in Liverpool, on 14th September 1828 at St Mary's Church, Edge Hill, Walton-on-the-Hill. Miles and Margaret had two children, both born in Liverpool:

- Alexander Jones (1831–89) married Jane Rose (c.1830–1906) on 25th December 1855 at St Anne's (Richmond) Church, Liverpool. He was a paper ruler and she was a book sower. They were living at 6 Mansfield Street, Liverpool. He was a bookbinder in 1861 and they were living at 7 Hanover Street, Halifax, Yorkshire. By 1871 they were living at 6 Elvington Street, Hulme, Lancashire and at 33 Radnor Street, Hulme in 1881. Jane was living with her family at 36 Princess Street, Broughton, Salford in 1891. She subsequently died there. They had five children – Alice Jones 1852, Richard Miles Jones 1858, Alexander Jones 1860, William Jones 1862 and James H Jones 1870.
- Mary Jones (born c.1833).

Samuel was a seaman in 1841 and they were living at South Side, New Bird Street, Liverpool. Margaret died at 64 Lime Kiln Lane, Liverpool and is buried at St Michael's Church there. He married Ellen née Hughes (c.1821–73), born at Tranmere, Cheshire, on 4th July 1852 at St Nicholas Church, Liverpool. They were living at Fazakerley Street, Liverpool at the time. By 1861 he was a ship's rigger and they were living at 105 Hopwood Street. In 1871 she was living with her family at 32 Leadenhall Street, Everton but Samuel was not with her at the time of the Census. Ellen died at West Derby, Lancashire and is buried in Anfield Cemetery. By 1881 Samuel was a ship watchman (dock) and was living with his children at 16 Myrtle Street, Birkenhead. In addition to Eleanor, Samuel had six children from his two marriages:

- Samuel William McCann (born 28th December 1844).
- Ellen McCann (1847–51).
- William Arnold McCann (c.1854–1906) was a gasfitter in 1871, living with his mother and siblings. He married Mary Ellen Thomas (c.1855–1912), born at St Helens, Lancashire, on 12th July 1874 at Everton. Her name was Mary Helen Thomas on her marriage certificate but she signed it Mary Ellen Thomas. By 1891 William was a tinman and gasfitter and they were living at 6 Bentinck Lane, Birkenhead. By 1901 he was a canned meat examiner and they were living at 31 Hope Street. Ellen was living with her sons, Samuel, a driller in a shipyard, and Albert, a waiter in a restaurant, at 22 Hope Street in 1911. They had six children including – William Arnold McCann 1878, John Isaac McCann 1884, Samuel Arnold McCann 1888, Mary Emily McCann 1891 and Albert Bramhall McCann 1892.
- John Isaac McCann (22nd December 1858–1940) married Mary Jane Kilshaw (18th September 1860–1912) in 1883. He was a ship's rigger in 1911 and they were living at 49 Cleveland Street, Birkenhead. They had six children – Charlotte McCann (1891–1934), Mary Eleanor McCann (1893–1900), Samuel Arnold McCann (1894–1955), Ethel McCann (1896), Elsie McCann (born and died 1900) and John Isaac McCann (1904–81).
- Sarah Sowerby McCann (1861–1955) married Joseph William Gurnell (26th March 1860–1910), born at Birkenhead, on 6th October 1881 at St Nicholas, Liverpool. They were living at Dale Street, Liverpool at the time. Joseph was a seaman steward in 1881, living with his cousin, Charles Clarke, a plasterer, and his family at 9 Cleveland Street, Birkenhead. He was a general labourer in 1901 and they were living at 14 Peter Street, Wallasey, Cheshire. She was a charwoman in 1911 living with her children at 9 Platt Street, Seacombe, Lancashire. They had thirteen children – Elizabeth Gurnell 1881, Samuel Gurnell 1883, Elizabeth Gurnell 1884, Emily Gurnell 1887, Mary A Gurnell 1889, Joseph Gurnell 1890, Sarah Gurnell 1891, John Gurnell 1894, Emma Gurnell 1896, Thomas Gurnell 1898, Annie Gurnell 1900, Flora Gurnell 1903 and Ellen Gurnell 1908.
- James Arnold McCann (1867–1915), a mariner, married Letitia Emma Skelton (born 1863) on 6th July 1896 at St Thomas Church, Seaforth, Lancashire. Her birth was registered as Emma Skelton at West Derby. James was living at 33 Caradoc Road and she at 6 Tuscan Street, Seaforth at the time of their marriage. He was a docks gatekeeper in 1901 and they were living at 50 Caradoc Road. Living with

them were his mother-in-law, Mary Jane, and brother-in-law, Benjamin Skelton, a general labourer. They were living at 2 Tattersall Road, Litherland, Lancashire in 1911. They had five children including – John Arnold McCann (1897–1984), Isabella Grace McCann (1898), George Albert McCann (1900–76) and Reginald Gordon McCann (1903).

Arthur was educated at St Thomas's School, Seaforth until 1905. His father found him a job in a Liverpool office as a porter. However, this did not suit him and he joined the Royal Navy on 2nd July 1909 at Chatham, Kent for twelve years (K2552). He was described as 5′ 4½″ tall, with light brown hair, blue eyes and fair complexion. He was appointed the same day as a stoker aboard HMS *Acheron* and joined HMS *Pembroke II* on 19th November. He transferred to HMS *Indomitable* on 17th December. On 30th August 1910 he was charged with theft and sentenced to forty-two days' detention. He rejoined HMS *Indomitable* on 12th October and was sentenced to fourteen days' detention (offence not known) on 9th November. He rejoined HMS *Indomitable* on 24th November but on 1st December 1910 he was discharged as 'services no longer required'.

What follows is based mainly on the interview given by his sister, Eleanor Evans, to the *Bolton Journal and Guardian* in November 1918 and should be treated with some caution. After leaving the Royal Navy, he reportedly joined the Merchant Navy, jumped ship in New York and travelled across America. He was next heard of in charge of a gang of 1,000 labourers working on the Panama Canal. He then joined a company exploring the jungles of Central and South America with an Australian and a Scot. He contracted malaria and had to be carried out of the jungle to the coast to recover. He moved to Cuba and then the USA, living in Detroit, Michigan,

HMS *Northumberland* (10,584 tons), the last of the three Minotaur class armoured frigates built in the 1860s, was powered by a two-cylinder trunk steam engine and was also fitted with five masts until 1875-79, when two were removed in a refit. She was part of the Channel Squadron and occasionally served as flagship. In 1869 she helped tow a floating dry-dock to Madeira, where other ships continued with it to Bermuda. She was anchored at Funchal, Madeira, on Christmas Day 1872, when a storm parted her anchor chain and she drifted onto the ram bow of HMS *Hercules*. *Northumberland* was damaged below the waterline but was able to steam to Malta for repairs. She was assigned to 1st Reserve Squadron at Portland 1890-91 and Devonport 1891-98. She was hulked in 1898 as a stoker's training ship at the Nore and was renamed HMS *Acheron* on 1st January 1904. She served as a coal hulk at Invergordon 1909-27 and was renamed C8 in 1909 and C68 in 1926. Sold in 1927, she was renamed *Stedmound* for service at Dakar until being scrapped in 1935.

HMS *Indomitable* (20,420 tons), one of three Invincible class battlecruisers, was launched on 16th March 1907 and commissioned on 25th June 1908. Immediately afterwards she carried the Prince of Wales to Canada. *Indomitable* was armed with eight 12″ guns, mounted in four hydraulically powered turrets, sixteen 4″ guns (reduced to twelve in 1915), a 3″ anti-aircraft gun, supplemented later by a 3 Pounder and a 4″ gun, plus five 18″ submerged torpedo tubes. She was assigned to the Nore Division, Home Fleet and became flagship of Rear Admiral S Colville, commanding 1st Cruiser Squadron. She transferred to the Mediterranean in August 1913 to 2nd Battlecruiser Squadron and later 3rd Battlecruiser Squadron. She was involved in trying to hunt down the German ships *Goeben* and *Breslau* in the Mediterranean when war broke out and bombarded Turkish fortifications protecting the Dardanelles. At the Battle of the Dogger Bank in 1915 she helped to sink the German cruiser *Blücher* and towed the damaged battlecruiser HMS *Lion* to safety after the battle. She damaged the German battlecruisers *Seydlitz* and *Derfflinger* during the Battle of Jutland the following year. *Indomitable* was sold for scrap in 1921.

The Panama Canal under construction. It is eighty-two kilometres long and connects the Atlantic and Pacific Oceans across the Isthmus of Panama. France began work in 1881 but the project stalled due to engineering difficulties and a high mortality rate. The Americans took over in 1904 and opened the Canal on 15th August 1914. It was one of the most difficult engineering projects ever undertaken. The USA controlled the territory surrounding the Canal until 1977, when joint control commenced with Panama, which took over independently in 1999. The original locks are thirty-four metres wide and wider locks were constructed 2007–16. Annual throughput has increased from 1,000 ships in 1914 to 14,702 in 2008.

Talavera Barracks, Wellington Avenue, Aldershot, built 1854–59 as part of Wellington Lines, was named after one of Wellington's victories in the Peninsular War. It was demolished in the early 1960s to make way for new married quarters, Talavera Park Estate, which in turn were demolished in the 1990s for more modern housing.

Buffalo and Niagara Falls, taking any work he could find to finance his travels. In 1912 he sailed from New York on a four-master to Australia and then to Liverpool, arriving at the end of 1913. On his return he found that the family had moved to Bolton, Lancashire and he lived there with his sister, Eleanor, and brothers. However, he soon tired of the quiet life.

Arthur enlisted in 1st King's (Liverpool) Regiment at Talavera Barracks, Aldershot, Hampshire on 11th May 1914 (11930), described as 5′ 6″ tall, weighing 149 lbs, with brown hair and blue eyes. He embarked on SS *Irrawaddy* for France at Southampton on 12th August 1914 and was involved in the actions at Mons, retreat to the Marne, the Aisne and First Battle of Ypres. He was badly wounded at Festubert

SS *Irrawaddy* (5,066 tons), launched on 10th August 1903 by Denny & Co at Dumbarton for the Burmah Steamship Co, passed to the Trinidad Shipping & Trading Co Ltd in 1914 and was renamed *Maraval*. In 1921 she transferred to the Bermuda & West Indies Steamship Co Ltd and was scrapped in 1933 in Genoa, Italy.

in May 1915 and was evacuated to Manchester for treatment. **Mentioned in Sir John French's Despatch dated 31st May 1915, LG 22nd June 1915.** By then he was serving with 3rd King's (Liverpool) and was a sergeant.

What happened next is unclear. He may have returned to the front and served with the Devonshire and the North Staffordshire Regiments for a short period. However, he may have deserted and rejoined the Merchant Navy and this would account for the change of name to Walter Simpson. It is claimed that he was awarded the Mercantile Marine War Medal, but this has not been proved. It is known that he served in 43rd Training Reserve Battalion (20353), which formed from 10th (Reserve) Battalion, King's Own (Royal Lancaster Regiment) on 1st September 1916 at Wareham, Dorset. He transferred to 2/4th Lincolnshire and served in Ireland for a period between April 1916 and January 1917, when the Battalion moved to England. It crossed to France in early February 1917.

The Mercantile Marine War Medal was established in 1919. It was awarded by the Board of Trade to mariners of the British Mercantile Marine (later Merchant Navy) for service at sea during the Great War. Qualification was one or more voyages through a danger zone or service at sea for six months between 4th August 1914 and 11th November 1918. Coastal mariners (pilots, fishermen, lightship and post office cable ship crews) could also qualify. There was no minimum qualifying period for those killed or wounded by enemy action, or those taken prisoner. All recipients also received the British War Medal but the award of the Mercantile Marine War Medal did not count for the award of the Victory Medal or either of the two Stars. Members of the Royal Navy, seconded to man defensive weapons on merchant ships, could also qualify. A total of 133,135 Mercantile Marine War Medals were awarded.

Arthur is believed to have been gassed and wounded at Poelcapelle, Belgium on 9th October 1917, whilst manning a machine gun. During this action he was buried by a shell burst and was reported killed in action. He had actually regained consciousness to find himself buried with only his face exposed. Two comrades found him and dug him out. If this part of his military career is correct, he must have already transferred to 6th Lincolnshire, as it was involved in the Battle of Poelcapelle on 9th October in 33rd Brigade, 11th Division. Conversely 2/4th Lincolnshire in 177th Brigade, 59th Division was not there. He was evacuated to Bath, Somerset for hospital treatment. When discharged he was granted leave to Bolton before going to Ireland. It is assumed that he joined 3rd (Reserve) Lincolnshire in Cork, where he was based until the spring of 1918. He returned to France and rejoined 6th Lincolnshire.

The chateau of Aubencheul-au-Bac was used as a hospital during the war but was destroyed almost at the end of the conflict.

Awarded the VC for his actions southwest of Étaing, France on 2nd September 1918, LG 30th October 1918. In the London Gazette dated 31st March 1919 his name was changed from Walter Simpson back to his real name of Arthur Evans. **Awarded the DCM for his actions on 6th/7th October 1918 while in command of a platoon of C Company on a fighting patrol. He was ordered to clear the area from the north of Chateau Aubencheul-au-Bac to the Canal de la Sensée. He rushed a strong enemy post, killing ten of the occupants and wounding several others. A prisoner he brought back yielded valuable information. He showed excellent leadership and the utmost disregard of all danger, LG 12th March 1919.** The VC was presented by the King at Vincent Barracks, Valenciennes, France on 6th December 1918.

On a leave in Bolton, Arthur promised his sister, Eleanor, that he would *bring home the VC and peace, not in pieces*. After the VC action he sent her the revolver he used at Étaing with a note, *The carrier and 'it' swam the river. Its internals are getting a little rusty but perhaps Jack (his brother) will oil it. Don't be afraid of it – I've extracted all its teeth!*

Arthur served as a company accountant 6th March–5th April 1919 and was discharged to the Reserve on 19th November 1921 (4792840). After a few months living with his sister, Eleanor, in Bolton, he found employment as a bank messenger with Lloyd's Bank British Empire Exhibition Branch, Wimbledon in the summer of 1922. He was lodging there at 20 St George's Road.

Arthur married Ellen Maud Whitaker (8th October 1892–1977), born at Chiswick, at Kingston Register Office on 9th April 1924. She was a housemaid in 1911 at 63–65 Western Road, Brighton, Sussex. She also lived at Woodside, Wimbledon, London at one time. It

Vincent Barracks, Valenciennes, where the VC investiture took place.

is understood that they met when living in the same lodgings at 20 St George's Road. They had one son, Arthur George Evans, born c.1933 in Australia.

Ellen's father, (c.1863–1916), born at Thirsk, Yorkshire, married Lydia née Ledger (1869–1933), born at Streatley, Berkshire, in 1889 at Bradfield, Berkshire. He was a steam engine maker/turner in 1901 and they were living at 143 Havelock Road, Preston, Sussex. By 1911 they had moved to 50 Sandgate Road, Preston and he was a turner engineer. In addition to Ellen they had another four children including:

Arthur receives the VC from the King.

- Margaret Lydia Whitaker (3rd May 1890–1969), born in Kennington, London, married Benjamin Funnell (1882–1958), born at Brighton, at Steyning, Sussex in 1909. He was a fireman with the London, Brighton & South Coast Railway in 1911 and they were living at 48 Sandgate Road, Brighton. They had two sons – Alfred F Funnell 1915 and Archibold S Funnell 1917.
- Violet Kathleen 'Kate' Whitaker (1st December 1894–28th February 1975), born at Chiswick, London, was a servant at 176 Ditchling Road, Brighton, Sussex

Arthur and Ellen married at Kingston Register Office in April 1924.

63–65 Western Road, Brighton, where Ellen worked as a housemaid in 1911, is now a fast food outlet.

in 1911. She was a spinster, living at Everleigh, 106 Wargrave Road, Twyford, Berkshire, at the time of her death there.
* Lydia Florence Whitaker (born 1904), born at Steyning, Sussex, married Ernest Claud Carey (13th January 1889–1968), born at Tunbridge Wells, Kent, at Steyning in 1921. He served as a private in the Sussex Yeomanry (3310) and the Royal Sussex Regiment during the Great War (G/16600). He was a motor driver in 1939, living at 35 Ellen Street, Hove, Sussex. Lydia was not with him at the time of the Census. They had a daughter, Molly Carey, in 1926.

On 28th July 1924 Arthur appeared before Wealdstone Police Court for stealing £500 while a messenger with Lloyd's Bank. In his defence he claimed to have been led astray, was duped by a second party and had not gained financially from the theft. The prosecution claimed that he alone had taken the money, which had not been recovered. However, he had voluntarily alerted the authorities to the loss and admitted his guilt. Several testimonials to his previous good character and details of his exceptional war service were submitted. As a first offender he was bound over to be of good behaviour for twelve months in the sum of £10. However, because of his war record the case was widely reported. He lost his job and reputation. With unemployment high, he stood little chance of finding work and decided on a fresh start abroad.

They emigrated to New Zealand, arriving in January 1925, and settled at Tauranga, Bay of Plenty, North Island, where he was employed as a clerk for six months with Armstrong Whitworth, prior to enlisting in the New Zealand Permanent Defence Staff as a staff sergeant on 1st July 1925. He was posted to the Nelson, Marlborough & West Coast Regiment in Southern Command at Christchurch, where he was employed

Wealdstone Police Station and Magistrate's Court was later part library until it became entirely a police station. It was built 1908–9 on the High Street and was Grade II listed in 1998. The entrance on the right was the Police Station and on the left, the Magistrates Court.

Tauranga is the country's fifth-largest city and the most populous in the Bay of Plenty. It was settled by Māori in the late 13th century and by Europeans early in the 19th century. It became a city in 1963 and is one of New Zealand's main centres for business, trade, culture, fashion and horticultural science, The port is New Zealand's largest in terms of gross export tonnage (Albert Percy Godber).

as Sub Area Sergeant Major, Area 9B at Greymouth, South Island. He transferred to the same appointment in Area 9C at Blenheim on 26th September 1926. Arthur chose to be discharged on 25th November 1927 on health grounds, claiming that the New Zealand climate did not suit him. He had been suffering from stomach pains and chest problems.

They emigrated to Australia in 1928 and he was employed as a clerk in Sydney, New South Wales. He enlisted as a private in the Australian Tank Corps on 17th October 1932 (311052) and was promoted sergeant within a few weeks and staff sergeant after six months. His health began to suffer again and he was discharged on 13th March 1934.

While in Australia, Arthur attended the first AIF Reunion Dinner at Sydney Town Hall on 8th August 1928, the tenth anniversary of the commencement of 'The Big Push', with fellow VCs Bede Kenny, G Cartwright, G Howell, P Storkey, J Whittle, W Currey, WE Brown and BA Wark. He attended a luncheon at Government House in November 1929 given by the Governor of Australia, Sir Dudley de Chair, with thirteen other VCs – W Jackson, J Hamilton, B Kenny, A Sullivan, W Currey, G Cartwright, P Storkey, J Ryan, J Whittle, JE Newland, BA Wark, J Maxwell and G Howell. Arthur also attended the wedding of Walter Ernest Brown VC DCM at Christ Church, Bexley, New South Wales on 4th June 1932, with fellow VCs B Wark, J Hamilton, G Howell, W Currey, TJB Kenny, A Sullivan and G Cartwright.

Arthur was admitted to the Prince of Wales Military Hospital, Randwick, Sydney, New South Wales in January 1936 suffering from carcinoma of the bowel, possibly induced by the mustard gas attack at Poelcapelle in October 1917. He

Sydney Town Hall, where the first AIF Reunion Dinner was held on 8th August 1928, was built in the 1870–80s. Its Centennial Hall contains the world's largest pipe organ, built in 1886–89. Before the opening of Sydney Opera House, the Town Hall was Sydney's main concert hall.

Government House, overlooking Sydney Harbour, built in 1837–43, was temporarily the residence of the Governor-General of Australia 1901–14, when it reverted to the residence of the Governor of New South Wales, except for 1996–2011. The building, grounds and furnishings are listed on the New South Wales State Heritage Register.

The Society for Destitute Children, formed in 1852, established the Asylum for Destitute Children and opened the first building in March 1858 in Paddington, Sydney. It became 4th Military General Hospital during the Great War and afterwards was a rehabilitation hospital for returning servicemen. In 1920 the Prince of Wales (later King Edward VIII) visited the hospital and it was renamed Prince of Wales Hospital. In 1953 it became a state hospital and a teaching hospital in 1962. Since then it has amalgamated with Prince Henry Hospital, Royal South Sydney Hospital and Eastern Suburbs Hospital (Sardaka).

Arthur Percy Sullivan (1896–1937) was awarded the VC for his actions with the North Russia Relief Force on 11th August 1919. He was under training in the AIF in England when the Great War ended and transferred to the British Army to serve in 45th Royal Fusiliers. The VC was presented at Government House in Adelaide on 13th July 1920 by the Prince of Wales. In 1937 Sullivan was selected to join the Australian Coronation Contingent for the coronation of King George VI. The Contingent comprised one hundred soldiers, twenty-five sailors and twenty-five airmen. Sullivan was the only VC. He is seen here about to hand over Arthur Evans' ashes to Mr W Ratcliffe of the British Legion at Lytham St Annes. On 9th April 1937, Sullivan attended an afternoon tea in St James's with fifty members of the Contingent. He left early in order to get ready for a reunion dinner that evening at the Royal Fusiliers HQ in the Tower of London. It was getting dark as he returned to his accommodation at Wellington Barracks on Birdcage Walk, when he was mobbed by autograph hunters. He attempted to avoid them, slipped and struck his head against the kerb. A cyclist crashed into him at the same time. The barracks guard carried him to the orderly room and he was taken to hospital but died soon afterwards. The Contingent cancelled all scheduled activities for three days. The inquest was conducted over his coffin and the coroner found that his death was accidental, caused by a fracture to the base of the skull and lacerations to the brain. It was concluded that the fatal fall occurred before the cyclist hit him. Sullivan's funeral took place in the Guards Chapel, Wellington Barracks on 13th April and he was cremated at Golders Green. On 12th May, as the Australian Coronation Contingent marched in the coronation parade, a gap was left in the ranks. His ashes were returned to his family in Sydney (Trove).

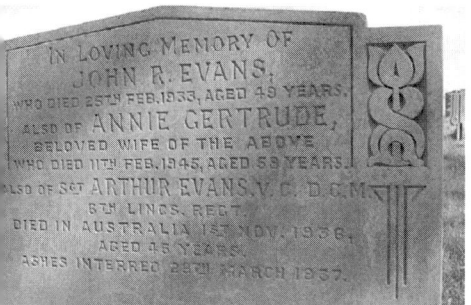

Arthur's ashes were interred in his brother John's grave in Lytham Park Cemetery on 29th March 1937. The comedian, Les Dawson, and his first wife, Meg, are also buried there.

died there on 1st November 1936. His funeral, at Rookwood Cemetery, Sydney, New South Wales, was the first military funeral in Australia at which the volleys over the grave were fired from revolvers. The firing party was formed by personnel from the Australian Tank Corps. The coffin was drawn through Sydney's streets on a gun carriage, preceded by the Royal Australian Artillery Band. Seven Australian VCs were present – P Storkey, TJB Kenny, JW Whittle, WM Currey, W Jackson, J Hamilton and G Cartwright. The wife of GJ Howell was also present. Following cremation at the North Suburbs Crematorium, Sydney, his ashes were placed in an oak casket and interred at Rookwood Cemetery, Sydney.

Arthur's great friend, Arthur Percy Sullivan VC, who was in the Australian contingent at the coronation of King George VI, carried Arthur Evans' ashes to Britain. They were re-interred in the grave of his brother, John, in Lytham Park Cemetery, Regent Avenue, Lytham St Annes, Lancashire (Church of England Section A, Grave 483) on 29th March 1937. A military funeral was held at the graveside. The grave was re-discovered in the early 1990s, restored by the Royal Anglian Regiment and re-dedicated in April/May 1992. On 9th April 1937, Arthur Sullivan was on Birdcage Walk, London when he slipped, fell backwards and suffered a major injury to his head. He died later in hospital, was cremated at Golders Green and, rather ironically, his ashes were transported back to Australia.

Arthur Evans is commemorated in a number of other places:

- Evans Crescent, Canberra, Australian Capital Territory.
- A Department for Communities and Local Government commemorative paving stone was dedicated at Bowersdale Park, Seaforth Road, Liverpool, Lancashire on 7th September 2018.
- Memorial at Rimrose Hope Church of England Primary School, Thomson Road, Seaforth, Liverpool.
- His VC action featured in Issues No. 677 and 1231 of the Victor Comic entitled *The Man who never Was!* on 9th February 1974 and *A True Story of Men at War* on 22nd September 1984.

Ellen returned to England following her husband's death but nothing is known of her later life or what became of her son. She died in Brighton, Sussex.

In addition to the VC and DCM he was awarded the 1914 Star with 'Mons' clasp '5th Aug.–22nd Nov. 1914', British War Medal 1914–20, possibly the Mercantile

There are memorial photographs to Arthur Evans VC and Eric Bell VC at Rimrose Hope Church of England Primary School, Seaforth, Liverpool. Both attended St Thomas Church of England School on Thompson Road, later renamed William Gladstone Church of England Primary School, after the Prime Minister who was educated at a preparatory school at Seaforth Vicarage before attending Eton College 1821–27. It closed in August 2008. William Gladstone and Beach Road Schools combined in the new Rimrose Hope Church of England Primary School.

Marine War Medal 1914–18 and Victory Medal 1914–19 with Mentioned-in-Despatches Oakleaf. The VC group was sold at a Spink auction on 27th–28th November 2019 for £235,000.

The award of the Mercantile Marine War Medal has not been proved. There is a gap in his Army service record that might be explained by service in the Merchant Navy. However, no conclusive evidence of the award has been found, although two Arthur Evans and a Walter Simpson received the Medal. However, none has the correct place and year of birth:

- Arthur Evans, born in Birkenhead 1893.
- Arthur Evans, born in Liverpool 1885.
- Walter Simpson, born in Birkenhead 1888.

SECOND LIEUTENANT JAMES PALMER HUFFAM
5th attached 2nd Battalion, The Duke of Wellington's (West Riding Regiment)

James Huffam was born on 31st March 1897 at the Armoury, Dunblane, Perthshire, Scotland. Huffam is an old Kentish family that can be traced back through the Normans in Avranches to the Vikings. Amongst its famous ancestors are Richard de Hougham, Prior of Dover and Robert de Hougham, who was with Richard I at the siege of Acre in Palestine in 1189–91 during the Crusades. James' father, Edward Valentine Huffam (14th February 1861–20th January 1936), born at Walworth,

Surrey, enlisted in 5th Regiment of Foot in London (2325) on 26th April 1879. His next of kin was his brother, William, until he married. He was described as 5′ 5″ tall, with fresh complexion, grey eyes and brown hair. He was serving in 1st Battalion, 5th (Northumberland Fusiliers) Regiment of Foot at Cambridge Barracks, Portsmouth, Hampshire in 1881. That year the Regiment became the Northumberland Fusiliers. He was promoted lance corporal on 10th March 1881 and was awarded Good Conduct Pay of 1d per day from 26th April. Promoted corporal on 8th August. He gained 2nd Class Education on 20th June 1883 and was promoted sergeant that August. He was reduced to corporal on 4th June 1884 and forfeited Good Conduct Pay with effect from 31st May. He was reduced to private on 17th August 1884 and passed to the Army Reserve on 6th September. Edward rejoined on 29th October and was promoted lance corporal on 4th October 1885. He was awarded Good Conduct Pay of 1d per day on 8th October 1885 and was promoted corporal on 10th March 1886. He was awarded Good Conduct Pay of 2d per day from 8th October 1887 and he was promoted lance sergeant on 7th May 1888. Edward married Dorothy McDonald née Roughead (22nd April 1864–26th May 1926) on 21st September 1884 at Spittal, Berwick-upon-Tweed, Northumberland, where she was born. Edward was a staff sergeant, serving with 3rd Black Watch (Royal Highlanders), by 5th April 1891, when he was based at Queen's Barracks, Barrack Street, Perth, Perthshire, Scotland. He was a colour sergeant with 4th Volunteer Battalion, Black Watch in 1901, by when they were living at 66 Princes Street, Perth. Edward was discharged on 30th November 1905 from Perth having given three months notice. His trade was given as cabinet carver and his intended place of residence was 4 Blenheim Place, Spittal. His conduct and character were assessed as Very Good and he would have been entitled to six Good Conduct Badges had he not been promoted. Edward and Dorothy were living at 2 West Street,

Cambridge Barracks was created by converting late 18th century warehouses into military accommodation. The first unit to occupy the barracks was the 9th Regiment. In 1856–58 the barracks were extended to provide accommodation for units in transit for overseas. About the same time the barracks were named after the Duke of Cambridge, who had recently died. After the Great War the barracks were disused and became derelict. In 1926 the officers' quarters were taken over by Portsmouth Grammar School. The soldiers' blocks were taken into the adjacent Clarence Barracks but were later acquired by the School, which now occupies the entire former barracks site (Gary Allman).

Spittal, in 1911 and later at 119 High Street, Berwick-upon-Tweed. Edward was a County Court High Bailiff in 1916. They were living at The Cottage, High Street, Berwick-upon-Tweed in 1918. Dorothy died at Tweedmouth, Berwick-upon-Tweed. Edward was living at Wavering, Mansefield Road, Tweedmouth at the time of his death there. James had six siblings:

James' mother was born at Spittal, on the opposite bank of the Tweed to Berwick-upon-Tweed. The name derives from a shortened form of hospital, as a hospital dedicated to St Bartholomew was built there in the Middle Ages to care for lepers (Berwick Record Office).

 * Alfred Meek Huffam (24th October 1887–1966), born at 2 Barrack Street, Perth, was a coachbuilder in 1911, living with his parents. He served for five years in 4th Volunteer Battalion, Royal Highlanders as a private and lance corporal. Alfred enlisted in 1/7th Northumberland Fusiliers (2110 & 290348) on 7th September 1914, described as 5′ 8″ tall, with fresh complexion, blue eyes and brown hair. He was promoted lance corporal on 28th November. He embarked at Folkestone and disembarked at Boulogne on 21st April 1915 and was promoted corporal on 27th April and sergeant on 26th June. He was

High Street, Berwick-upon-Tweed, where the Huffam family lived.

in hospital with influenza 15th–21st March 1916 and was promoted WO2 and appointed CSM on 6th October. Alfred was admitted to 2/2nd (Northumbrian) Field Ambulance with skin disease on 24th October and transferred to No.3 Casualty Clearing Station next day. He was transferred by 18 Ambulance Train to 1st Canadian General Hospital, Étaples on 31st October/1st November. He joined 30th Infantry Base Depot on 8th November and rejoined the Battalion on 18th November. Alfred was Mentioned in General Sir Douglas Haig's Despatch of 18th November 1916, LG 29th December 1916. He applied for a commission while CSM of D Company, 1/7th Northumberland Fusiliers on 4th January 1917 and returned to Britain on 15th February. He was taken on strength of 75th Territorial Force Depot on 17th February and was granted a month's leave. He joined No.10 Officer Cadet Battalion, Gailes on 7th April and was commissioned in 5th attached 1/6th Duke of Wellington's on 1st August 1917. Alfred suffered gunshot wounds to the chest and lower jaw on 10th October 1918. He embarked at Boulogne and disembarked at Folkestone on 21st December and was treated at 3rd London General Hospital, Wandsworth. A medical board on 23rd January 1919 found him unfit for Category A Service for six months and for C1 for two months. He remained in hospital and was awarded a wound gratuity of £104/3/4. He was promoted lieutenant on 1st February 1919 and was sent on leave for five months from 22nd March. A medical board on 28th August found him unfit for Category A for six months, for B & C1 for three months and he remained in hospital. Another wound gratuity of £145/16/8 was paid. He qualified for a wound pension of £50 from 12th October 1919 to 11th October 1920. Medical boards on 6th November, 4th February 1920 and 3rd March found him unfit for Category A & B permanently and for C1 for periods from one to four months. He remained in hospital pending transfer. Alfred relinquished his commission on account of ill health on 3rd April 1920, retaining the rank of lieutenant. He married Violet Adeline N Young (24th September 1891–1974) in 1922. He died at Lewes, Sussex and she at Hove, Sussex.

- John Henry Huffam (23rd August 1889–7th January 1937), born at Victoria Barracks, Perth, was educated at Southern District School, Perth. As a boy he tried to enlist in the Royal Navy but was rejected due to his teeth. He was a collector for an insurance company in 1911, living with his parents. John enlisted in York in 17th Northumberland Fusiliers (17/1381) and 85th Training Reserve Battalion (formerly 30th (Reserve) Battalion, Northumberland Fusiliers) (TR/5/40282) and joined at Hull on 19th April 1915. He was described as a railway guard, 5′ 5½″ tall, weighing 174¾ lbs, with fresh complexion, grey eyes, brown hair and his religious denomination was Baptist. He was living at 10 Park Parade, Harrogate, Yorkshire. He was promoted acting lance corporal on 2nd August. He was posted to 28th Reserve Battalion on 10th August and 32nd Reserve Battalion on 30th October. He was promoted corporal on 1st December and qualified in musketry at Fulford Barracks, York on 23rd December. He was promoted sergeant on 29th January 1916 and was admitted to 1st Northern General Hospital on 30th July with a fistula. He had an operation on 2nd August and was sent to a convalescent home on 10th September. He was on the strength of 80th Training Reserve Battalion from 1st September. Having recovered, he embarked at Folkestone on 10th May 1917 and disembarked at Boulogne next day. He joined 34th Infantry Base Depot, Étaples on 12th May and made a will on 18th May, leaving everything to his wife. John joined 17th Northumberland Fusiliers (Pioneers) on 6th June. He applied for a commission on 14th October, giving his permanent address as Cross View, Abbey Road, Scone, Perthshire. The application was supported up the chain of command, but the Commander of 32nd Division, Major General Sir Cameron Shute, wrote that he will require considerable training. John returned to Britain on 28th November on the strength of 85th Training Reserve Battalion and was granted leave until 12th November. He joined 5th (Reserve) Battalion, Highland Light Infantry, Lowland Reserve

Brigade, Bridge of Allan on 13th December. He was reprimanded for being absent from early morning parade on 16th January 1918 and again for showing lights after 10.15 p.m. on 10th March. John joined No.9 Officer Cadet Battalion, Gailes on 22nd March and was commissioned in the Machine Gun Corps on 29th October 1918. He embarked at Folkestone and disembarked at Boulogne on 21st May 1919 and joined 6th Battalion, Machine Gun Corps on 26th May. The Battalion moved to Ireland and he was admitted to hospital in Cork on 8th September. A medical board on 7th October found him unfit for Category A & B for one month but fit for C1 and he was granted leave 7th–28th October, then to report to Grantham. He was discharged on 1st November 1919 from No.1 Dispersal Unit, Ripon, Yorkshire, giving his address as 148 Main Street, Spittal, Berwick-upon-Tweed. He relinquished his commission and retained the rank of second lieutenant on 13th November 1920. John married Margaret Campsie Lindsay (6th January 1889–10th January 1989), a teacher, on 12th May 1916 at Crossview, Scone, Perthshire, where she was born. They were living at 104 Victoria Road, Darlington, Co Durham at the time of his death there. She died at Blakiston, South Australia and is buried in St James Anglican Cemetery there. They had three children, all born at Berwick-upon-Tweed:

Fulford Cemetery is near the barracks and military hospital at Fulford, which was in use during the Great War. The cemetery has a CWGC plot containing 104 Great War and 115 Second World War burials. There are also fifteen war graves of other nationalities within the war graves plot. The graves of more than fifty German servicemen were moved to the German cemetery on Cannock Chase. Buried in the cemetery is Barbara Jane Harrison (24th May 1945–8th April 1968), a stewardess on a British Overseas Airways Corporation Boeing 707 flight to Sydney, Australia when an engine fell off the aircraft on takeoff from Heathrow, London. An emergency landing was made as the fire on the port wing intensified. She opened the rear gallery door so that passengers could escape. She was alone helping the passengers out of the aircraft and directing others to another exit. With flames and explosions all around her, she was overcome while trying to save an elderly person. For her gallantry she was awarded a posthumous George Cross, the only one awarded to a woman in peacetime. Only four women have received the honour and she is the youngest female recipient.

- ° Edward Valentine Huffam (born 1917) married Suzanne Morgan in 1946 at Darlington, Co Durham. They had three children.
- ° Catherine Hutchinson Huffam (born 1919).
- ° Ian Lindsay Huffam (1921–93).
- Elizabeth Clara Marjorie Huffam (2nd July 1891–3rd March 1944) trained as a nurse at Leeds General Infirmary, Yorkshire 1914–17. She moved to New York, USA and lived at 143 East 53rd Street. She returned to Britain and served as a nursing sister in Queen Alexandra's Imperial Military Nursing Service (208368) during the Second World War. She served with No.4 Casualty Clearing Station in France before being evacuated to England in June 1940. She was serving at No.58 General Hospital, Ormskirk, Lancashire on 12th February 1941. Elizabeth died unmarried at the Auxiliary Military Hospital, Askham Richard, Yorkshire and is buried in Fulford Cemetery, York (Section 2, Row I, Grave 2).
- Dorothy Frances Lily Huffam (5th March–12th April 1893) was born at Kirkcaldy, Fife.
- Harry Harold Huffam (18th May 1895–21st August 1915), born at 125 Links Street, Kirkcaldy, was a joiner's apprentice in 1911, living with his parents. He served as a private in 1/7th Northumberland Fusiliers (2107) and was killed in action (Houplines Communal Cemetery Extension, near Armentieres, France – II E 32).
- Dorothy Gertrude Beatrice Huffam (12th April 1898–1937), born at the Armoury, Dunblane, Perthshire, married John Sidney Mole (8th March 1898–1976) on 24th November 1926 at Berwick-upon-Tweed. He was a pumping station attendant with the London North Eastern Railway in 1939, living with his brother Bertram, a confectioner and Air Raid Precautions Warden, at 20 Magdalene Drive, Berwick-upon-Tweed. He married Harriet Trowbridge (11th August 1917–1998) in 1941.

Harry Harold Huffam's grave in Houplines Communal Cemetery Extension.

James' paternal grandfather, Alfred Meek Huffam (21st July 1804 14th January 1895), born at Tooley Street, Southwark, London, was apprenticed to William Johnstone, a goldsmith, for seven years as an engraver. He became a Freeman of the Company of Goldsmiths on 2nd July 1828. He married Fanny née Cox (30th March 1821–26th November 1904), born at St Pancras, London, in 1843 at Lambeth, London. Alfred was also a landscape painter in 1851, when they were living at 16 Burdett Street, Newington, Surrey. By 1861 they were living at 5 Low Docton

The Worshipful Company of Goldsmiths, one of the Great Twelve Livery Companies of the City of London, has its headquarters at Goldsmiths' Hall. The Company originated in the 12th century and received a Royal Charter in 1327. It was first established as a guild for the goldsmith trade and the term *hallmark* derives from precious metals being inspected and marked at Goldsmith's Hall. In 1891 the Goldsmiths' Company founded Goldsmiths' Technical and Recreative Institute, later Goldsmiths' College of the University of London.

Goldsmiths' Hall, a Grade 1 listed building in the City of London, has been in the same location since 1339. The first hall was rebuilt in 1407. The second hall, built c.1634–36, was restored after the Great Fire of London in 1666 and was demolished in the late 1820s. The third and present hall was completed in 1835 and the inaugural dinner was attended by the Duke of Wellington and Sir Robert Peel. During the Blitz a bomb hit the southwest corner but the building largely survived and was restored after the Second World War.

Street, Newington, by 1881 at 4 Goldsmith Building, Shoreditch and by 1891 at 35 Chalcot Crescent, St Pancras. Alfred died at Islington, London and Fanny at West Ham, London. In addition to Ernest they had eleven other children:

* Clara Frances 'Fanny' Huffam (19th August 1839–10th February 1923), born at Islington, London, married William Read (3rd April 1839–11th October 1936), a parochial clerk, on 17th February 1869 at Pancras, London. They were living at 51 Warden Road, St Pancras in 1871, at 36 Chalcot Crescent, St Pancras in 1881, at 35 Chalcot Crescent in 1891, at 33 St George's Road, St Pancras in 1901 and at 153 Adelaide Road, South Hampstead in 1911. She was living at 37 Ainger

Road, Primrose Hill, London at the time of her death there. He died at Hendon, Middlesex. They had two sons:
  ◦ Alfred John Read (1877–1947).
  ◦ Herbert Edward Read (1880–1967) was a mill foreman and married Ann Sarah Warne (née Edwards) (1878–1943), born at Islington, in 1916 at Wandsworth, London. Ann had married George Henry Warne (1877–1913), a rag sorter, in 1901 at Shoreditch. They were living at 10 Martins Buildings, Wandsworth in 1911 with their two children. Herbert enlisted on 19th February 1917 at Wandsworth Town Hall in the Inland Water Transport Corps RE (WR315110), described as 5′ 6¾″ tall and weighing 148 lbs. His address was 21 College Street, Putney Bridge Road, London. He served with 57th Traffic Company RE, Richborough New Wharf, Sandwich, Kent. He was absent without leave from Richborough, Kent 16th–20th June and was confined to barracks for seven days. Again at Richborough he was absent without leave 11th–19th September and was confined to barracks for another seven days. Appointed unpaid acting lance corporal on 11th July 1918 and paid from 16th January 1919. Appointed paid acting corporal on 17th January. He was demobilised from No.2 Dispersal Unit, Shorncliffe on 28th January and transferred to the Class Z Reserve on 17th February 1919. Herbert was a municipal officer in 1939, recorded as single and living at 63 Eton Avenue, Hampstead, London. Ann's death was registered at Chelsea, London and Herbert's at Hampstead, Greater London.
- William Alfred Huffam (28th February 1841–28th March 1924), born at Hackney, Middlesex, was a shoemaker. He married Christina Mitchell Robertson (born 9th July 1853), born in Glasgow, Lanarkshire, in 1876 at Marylebone, London. They were living at 2 Buckingham Street, Marylebone in 1881, at 63–66 Christopher Buildings, North Street, St Marylebone in 1901 and at 82 High Street, Camden Town, London in 1911. He died at Hampstead. They had nine children:
  ◦ Fanny Mary Huffam (1878–1928) married William James Wise in 1899 at Marylebone, London.
  ◦ Jessie Annie Huffam (born 1880).
  ◦ Archibald Owen Huffam (1881–1902) served as a trooper in the Imperial Yeomanry (31559) during the Second Boer War. He died of disease at Elandsfontein, South Africa on 8th January 1902.
  ◦ Harold Hugh Huffam (born 1883).
  ◦ Edwin Robin Huffam (born 1885).
  ◦ Frederick Ralph Huffam (1886–1953).
  ◦ Christina May Huffam (born 1889).
  ◦ Margaret Alice Huffam (born 1892).
  ◦ Nellie Winifred Huffam (1894–1997).
- Henry Huffam (6th November 1842–13th October 1914), born at Shoreditch, London, was a clerk living at Albany Road, Southwark at the time of his marriage

to Elizabeth Windridge (1843–1932), born at Atherstone, Warwickshire, in 1865 at Camberwell, London. Henry was a tobacco and cigar warehouseman in 1871 and they were living at 75 Elsted Street, Walworth, London. By 1881 he was a tobacconist and they were living at 52a Old Kent Road, Southwark. They were still there in 1891. By 1901 they had moved to 98 Waleran Buildings, Old Kent Road, London and were still there in 1911. He died at Southwark, London and she at Battersea, London. There were no children.
- John Samuel Huffam (4th March 1845–3rd April 1921), born at Hoxton Old Town, Shoreditch was indentured as an apprentice in the Merchant Navy on 2nd September 1861. He emigrated to New Zealand and was shipwrecked on the journey but was rescued by a following New Zealand bound ship. He married Charlotte Ayland (31st October 1857–12th April 1942), born in Cardiff, Glamorgan, on 30th April 1879. She emigrated to Canterbury, New Zealand aboard SV *Marlborough* on 14th December 1878. They were living at 191 Westminster Street, St Albans, Christchurch in 1916. He died at Canterbury. She was living at Brown Street, Waitara, New Plymouth by February 1924 and at Fairton, Canterbury by July 1924. They had nine children:
    ◦ Clara Huffam (1880–1945).
    ◦ Cecelia Louise Huffam (1881–1960) married Benjamin Brown in 1912 and they had a son.
    ◦ Elizabeth Huffam (1883–1971) married George William Plowman (1876–1962) in 1910. They had at least four children.
    ◦ Ernest Edward Huffam (1884–1944) married Alice Valentine Walker (1889–1958) in 1908. They had at least seven chidren.
    ◦ Walter Charles Huffam (1886–1915) enlisted in the Canterbury Infantry Battalion at Addington on 26th August 1914 (6/1036). He was described as a labourer for Canterbury Frozen Meat Co at Fairfield, 5′ 8″ tall, weighing 146 lbs, with dark complexion, brown eyes, dark brown hair and his religious denomination was Church of England. He was living at Fairton Ashburton. Walter departed New Zealand on HMNZT *11 Athenic* on 15th October and disembarked in Egypt on 4th December. He died of wounds received at Gallipoli on 27th April 1915 and was buried at sea between Gallipoli and Alexandria (Lone Pine Memorial, Gallipoli).
    ◦ Harold Thomas Huffam (1888–93).
    ◦ Charlotte May Huffam (born 1896) married Harold Twentyman Wilson (born 1889) in 1920.
    ◦ Holly Gladys Huffam (1898–1901).
    ◦ Victor Claude Huffam (1901–89) married Isabella May McKenzie in 1932.
- Walter Huffam (born 17th January 1847), born at Shoreditch, emigrated to the USA.
- Cleopas Frank Huffam (25th February 1849–12th May 1908), a fancy leather goods worker born at Camberwell, London, married Sarah Sophia Stone

SS *Athenic* (12,234 tons), built by Harland & Wolff in Belfast for the White Star Line in 1901, carried 121 first, 117 second and 450 third class passengers. She was also equipped to transport frozen meat. *Athenic* was the first of three identical ships built for the London–Wellington, New Zealand route. The others were *Corinthic* 1902 and *Ionic* 1903. On 13th February 1902, *Athenic* sailed from London on her maiden voyage to Wellington via the Canary Islands, Cape Town and Hobart. When war was declared, *Athenic* was in Wellington and was requisitioned as a troopship. She was one of the transports carrying the Main Body as HMNZT 11 *Athenic*, including the Canterbury Infantry Battalion (less one company). She left Wellington and sailed via Hobart, Albany, Colombo and Aden before arriving in Alexandria, Egypt to disembark on 3rd December 1914. She was the largest troopship sent from New Zealand and acted several other times as a transport during the Great War. In 1928 she was taken over by a Norwegian company and renamed SS *Pelagos* but remained on the New Zealand route until the outbreak of the Second World War. She was torpedoed in 1944 but was refloated the following year and continued in service until being scrapped in 1962.

(c.1858–1919), born at Newington, Surrey, on 23rd May 1875 at Christ Church, Southwark, London. They were lodging at 31 Lorrimore Street, Newington, London in 1881. He died at Lambeth, London and she at Southwark, London. They had nine children:

° Alfred Frank Huffam (1876 1930) married Jane Elizabeth Bentley (1876–1968) in 1899 at St Saviour, London.

The Lone Pine Memorial, Gallipoli, Turkey where James's cousin, Walter Charles Huffam, is commemorated.

- Ernest Joseph Huffam (1878–82).
  - William Cleopas Huffam (1880–1930).
  - Edward Charles Valentine Huffam (1882–1957).
  - Lily Sophia Huffam (born 1885).
  - Alice Adelaide Huffam (1888–1909).
  - Walter Charles Huffam (born and died 1891).
  - Arthur Ernest Huffam (1892–1961).
  - Sidney John Huffam (1895–1970) married Dorothy Georgina W Platt (born 1898) in 1921 at Southwark. They had three children.
- Mary Hannah Huffam (15th February–15th May 1851).
- Alfred Josiah Huffam (born 28th February 1853). His birth was registered as Huffham at Newington, Surrey. He moved to Canada.
- Sarah Jessie Huffam (10th July 1856–12th January 1858).
- Ralph Ernest Arthur Huffam (15th July 1858–15th February 1861).
- Ernest Arthur Huffam (4th April 1867–1945), a cabinetmaker, married Susan Belle Havell (25th February 1872–1973), born at Wandsworth, London, in 1895 at Islington, London. They had a daughter prior to their marriage, Sylvia Annie Huffam (1894–1959), who never married. They were living at 201 Fulbourne Road, Walthamstow in 1911. They both died at Epping, Essex. They had four daughters, none of whom married – Ivy Marguerite Huffam (1896–1930), Irene Constance Huffam (1900–15), Jennie Lilian Huffam (1901–02) and Gladys Rosaline Huffam (1903–78).

His maternal grandfather, John Roughead (5th June 1824–1889), born at Spittal, Northumberland, married Elizabeth née Palmer (c.1837–83), also born at Spittal, in 1861 at Berwick-upon-Tweed. He was a fisherman and they were living at 13 Middle Street, Spittal in 1871 and at 14 West Street in 1881. In addition to Dorothy they had five other children, all born at Spittal:

- Margaret Roughead (1862–1918) was a servant to the Whittie family at 50 Main Street, Tweedmouth, Northumberland in 1881. She married Michael Patterson (born c.1853), a labourer in a manure works, born in Ireland, in 1882. They were living at 24 Middle Street, Tweedmouth in 1891. Michael died before 1911. Margaret was living with her children at 76½ Middle Street, Spittal in 1911. They had eight children:
  - Richard Patterson (1883–1954).
  - Elizabeth Palmer Patterson (1884–1971) married Robert Cox in 1910 and they had five children.
  - John Patterson (born 1887).
  - Catherine Patterson (born 1890).
  - William Patterson (born 1894).
  - Lily Jane Patterson (born 1895).

- ○ Margaret Ellison Patterson (born 1898).
- ○ Michael Patterson (born 1902).
- Benjamin Roughead (born and died 1863).
- William Roughead (born and died 1869).
- Thomas Roughead (1870–2nd January 1951) was living at 73 Sunnyside, Cramlington, Northumberland at the time of his death at the General Hospital, 418 Westgate Road, Newcastle-upon-Tyne, Northumberland.
- John Roughead (1874–10th September 1938) was a labourer at a manure works in 1891, boarding with his sister Margaret and family. He married Margaret Cromarty (23rd July 1878–3rd August 1950) in 1898 at Berwick-upon-Tweed. Margaret was living with her mother at 2 Sandstell Road, Berwick-upon-Tweed in 1881. John was a fireman in a chemical works in 1901 and they were living at 5 Middle Street, Tweedmouth. By 1911 he was a fisherman and they were living at 51 Middle Street, Spittal. They had thirteen children:
  - ○ John Roughead (born and died 1899).
  - ○ Mary Ann C Roughead (1899–1966) married Andrew Westwater Fife (1902–66) in 1922. They had three children.
  - ○ Elizabeth Palmer Roughead (1901–03).
  - ○ Margaret 'Maggie' Roughead (1902–15).
  - ○ Dorothy Roughead (1903–80) married Harry K Gilchrist in 1927.
  - ○ John Roughead (1905–74) married Mary H Sanderson in 1933 and they had a son.
  - ○ Evelyn Benjamin Roughead (born and died 1907).
  - ○ James Cromarty Roughead (born and died 1908).
  - ○ Christina Roughead (1910–84) married George Rowntree in 1935 and they had a son.
  - ○ Lily Roughead (1912–97) married Thomas McDonald in 1938 and they had a daughter.
  - ○ Thomasina Roughead (1914–74) married James G Smith in 1939.
  - ○ Harry Harold H Roughead (1916–85) married Stella Todd in 1951.
  - ○ Thomas H Roughead (1919–90) married Minnie Dinsdale in 1940.

James was educated in Berwick-upon-Tweed and at Perth Academy, Perthshire. He was a joiner's apprentice in 1911. He enlisted on 21st February 1915 in 2/7th Northumberland Fusiliers (7/3082) and transferred to 1/7th Battalion to be with two of his brothers on 6th June and went to France on 28th June. He was promoted corporal in September 1915 and sergeant in May 1916. James returned to England on 23rd August 1917 and joined one of the two Officer Cadet Battalions at Oxford on 26th August. He was commissioned into 5th Duke of Wellington's on 30th January 1918 and was posted to the same unit as his older brother, Alfred, 1/6th Battalion. James returned to France on 24th May and was attached to 2nd Battalion.

Perth Academy, founded in 1696, has a strong connection to Perth Grammar School, founded in the 12th century. The name Perth Academy first appears in 1542. By the 1800s it was cramped and a new building was needed. Work started in October 1803 and it was in use in 1807. In 1915 the Academy amalgamated with Sharp's Institution in Perth. The school moved to its present site in 1932. Until 1968 the school was selective and in 1971 became comprehensive. Large extensions were added in 1990.

Awarded the VC for his actions at St Servin's Farm, Haucourt, southeast of Vis-en-Artois, France, on 29th–31st August and 1st September 1918, LG 26th December 1918. The VC was presented by the King in the ballroom at Buckingham Palace on 12th April 1919. James received a gold watch and a cheque from the people of Berwick-upon-Tweed after the investiture. He was promoted lieutenant as a Regular officer on 30th July.

James was seconded for service with the Indian Army as a temporary lieutenant in the Indian Army Reserve of Officers with seniority from 30th January 1919 (corrected the following year to 30th January 1918) from 8th April 1920. He served in 1/9th Gurkha Rifles, commanded by Lieutenant Colonel George C Wheeler VC at Peshawar and Dehra Dun. James returned from India to serve with 2nd Duke of Wellington's in Palestine from 30th January 1921. On 16th October 1922 he was seconded to the Royal Air Force. He was posted as a flying officer under instruction at No.4 Flying Training School, Abu Sueir, Egypt from 22nd November. On 5th March 1924 he was posted to No.55 (Bombing) Squadron, Hinaidi, Iraq and was supernumerary from 9th June 1926, returning to Army service on 15th October. He then served with the 1st Battalion for a year before being seconded to the Royal West African Frontier Force (Sierra Leone Battalion) 30th November 1927–7th October 1933. He was appointed temporary captain 2nd June 1928–11th July 1929, was promoted captain on 29th July 1929 and rejoined the 1st Battalion in October 1933 for service in Aldershot and Malta. He attended the Royal West African Frontier Force Dinner at the Savoy Hotel, London in 1935.

George Campbell VC (1880–1938) was awarded the VC as a major in 2nd Battalion, 9th Gurkha Rifles for his actions on 23rd February 1917 at Shumran on the Tigris in Mesopotamia.

No.4 Flying Training School (FTS) is currently based at RAF Valley in Anglesey, Wales and manages Advanced Fast Jet Training. It formed on 1st April 1921 at Abu Sueir, Egypt to train pilots, primarily for squadrons in the Middle East. Here ground crew are being instructed. On 1st September 1939 it moved to RAF Habbaniya, Iraq. The Habbaniya Air Striking Force was created from the School. Rebels gathered south of Habbaniya airfield and the instructors and more experienced pupils manned the aircraft. On 2nd May 1941, the School attacked the enemy positions and the battle lasted for five days before the rebel forces retreated. The School flew 584 sorties, fired 100,000 rounds and dropped forty-five tons of bombs. On 1st July 1941 the School disbanded. On 3rd February 1947, it reformed at Heany, near Bulawayo, Southern Rhodesia. The School disbanded again on 26th January 1954. The RAF's Advanced Flying Schools (AFS) in the early 1950s provided a step between elementary flying training and the operational conversion units. On 1st June 1954, No.205 AFS at Middleton St George was renumbered No.4 FTS. It moved to Worksop in June 1956 and absorbed No.211 FTS. On 9th June 1958, No.4 FTS again disbanded. Its role was carried on by No.7 FTS at RAF Valley until 15th August 1960 when it renumbered as No.4 FTS again. Students from the Jet Provost came through onto the Gnat for advanced jet training. In 1965 the Red Arrows formed. The Gnat was replaced by the Hawk by late 1979.

James married Constance Marion Huffam (11th January 1911–12th February 1998), born at Malton, Yorkshire, on 23rd April 1935 in St Paul's Anglican Cathedral, Valletta, Malta. Two branches of the family, separated 350 years before, were brought together by the marriage. The ancestor who linked them was Thomas Huffam in 1659. One of Constance's predecessors was Christopher Huffam, rigger to the Navy, who was one of the godfathers to the author Charles John Huffam Dickens (1812–70). They were living at 13 New House, Park Street, St Albans, Hertfordshire in 1948 and at 58 Silverston Way, Stanmore, Middlesex in 1967.

St Paul's Pro-Cathedral, officially The Pro-Cathedral and Collegiate Church of St Paul, in Independence Square, Valletta. A pro-cathedral is a church with cathedral status. The Cathedral was commissioned by the Dowager Queen Adelaide during a visit to Malta and was built between 1839 and 1844. Queen Adelaide laid the foundation stone on 20th March 1839. In 1938 the under-croft was transformed into a gas proof air raid shelter and was used by scores of citizens during air raids in the Second World War. The Cathedral was damaged and the roof collapsed but it avoided other serious damage (Martin Furtschegger).

Constance died at Newtownabbey, Co Antrim, Northern Ireland. They had two children:

- Robert Huffam (born 6th March 1936), born in Malta, trained at the Royal Military Academy Sandhurst, Surrey and was commissioned into the Duke of Wellington's Regiment on 27th July 1956. He was promoted lieutenant on 27th July 1957, temporary captain 1st–26th July 1962 and captain on 27th July 1962. Robert last appears in the Army List in March/Spring 1966. He was living in Carrickfergus, Co Antrim, Northern Ireland in 2006.
- Marian 'Ann' Huffam (born 13th December 1939) was born at Ripon, Yorkshire.

Charles John Huffam Dickens (1812–70), the writer and social critic, who created some of the best-known fictional characters, is regarded as the greatest novelist of the Victorian era.

Constance's father, Leonard William Huffam (20th May 1869–7th April 1945), a bank manager born at Hull, Yorkshire, married Annis Burland née Todd (1870–18th November 1921), born at Pontefract, Yorkshire, on 8th January 1904 at Malton Priory, Yorkshire. He was commissioned in 1st Volunteer Battalion, The Prince of Wales's Own (West Yorkshire Regiment) on 4th April 1900 and was appointed temporary lieutenant while serving in South Africa on 17th April 1901. Promoted lieutenant 16th November 1901 and captain 28th March 1906. Embodied on 3rd October 1914. Appointed temporary captain on 21st July 1916. He was a temporary captain in the Labour Corps from 9th March 1917 with seniority backdated to 21st July 1916. Annis died at Scarborough, Yorkshire. He was living at Ackworth Cottage, Cloughton, near Scarborough, Yorkshire at the time of his death at 8 Stepney Road, Scarborough. In addition to Constance they had two sons:

Malton Priory was founded as a Gilbertine monastery about 1150. It was the only order initiated in England. After the Dissolution it was bought in 1540 by Robert Holgate, former master of the Gilbertine Order and Bishop of Llandaff. In 1545 he became Archbishop of York and founded three grammar schools in Yorkshire, including Malton School on part of the monastic site. The Priory church is now a parish church, the only church of the Gilbertine Order still in regular use. However, its reduction in size was carried out somewhat clumsily and there was a major restoration in the 19th century.

- William Henry Huffam (3rd April 1905–26th February 1962), born at Selby, Yorkshire, married Jean Heather Campbell (10th November 1905–8th November 2000), born at Horsham, Victoria, Australia, on 28th April 1930 at Geelong, Victoria. He enlisted in the Royal Australian Air Force on 26th February 1940 at Laverton, Victoria and was commissioned as a flying officer. He was serving at 76 Operational Base Unit, Learmonth, Western Australia at the time of his discharge on 27th November 1945. He was a sheep farm overseer and they were living at 51 Retreat Road, Corio, Victoria in 1954. They had two children including William Henry Huffam, who married Anne Bowman in 1957.
- John Leonard Huffam (10th April 1906–15th July 1988), born at Malton, married Alice Rae Kemp (17th December 1911–1999) on 31st August 1937 at Aberdeen, Scotland. He was a timber merchant and Air Raid Precautions Warden in 1939 and they were living at 41 Overland Road, Cottingham, Yorkshire. He was living at 27 Hull Road, Cottingham, North Humberside at the time of his death at Beverley, Yorkshire. Alice died at Ulverston, Lancashire. They had a daughter, Vivian A Huffam (born 1939).

In October 1936, James went to India with the 2nd Battalion and served at Nowshera. He returned to England, retired on 30th August 1938 and was appointed the civilian Adjutant RAF Dishforth, Yorkshire. James was recalled from the Regular Army Reserve of Officers to the Duke of Wellington's Regiment on 24th August 1939 and was promoted major the same day, with seniority from 1st August 1938. He was appointed Deputy Assistant Provost Marshal with the BEF at Dieppe, France in April 1940 and was subsequently evacuated (Mentioned in a War Office Despatch dated 20th December 1940, LG 20th December 1940). He was appointed OC L Traffic Control Group, Southern Command, Winchester in November 1940 and Deputy Assistant Provost Marshal, Eastern Command in 1941. He was posted to 153 HQ Provost Company, Dunstable, Bedfordshire in April 1942 and was appointed Assistant Provost Marshal at HQ Division, Tenby, Pembrokeshire in January 1945. James became the Army Recruiting Officer at St Alban's on retiring in August 1945.

James was a Freemason, being Initiated into Saint David's Lodge (No.393), Berwick-on-Tweed on 17th February 1920. He was Passed on 16th March and Raised on 20th July. He resigned on 31st March 1966. On 16th August 1928, whilst serving with the Royal West African Frontier Force in Sierra Leone, he joined the Rokell Lodge (No.2798) of the English Constitution, meeting in Freetown. He resigned in December 1933. He then joined the Maguncor Lodge (No.3806) on 29th March 1956. He was installed as Worshipful Master on 3rd October 1960 and was still a member at the time of his death. In the Knights Templar Degree he was Installed as a Knight in the Crystal Palace Preceptory (No.257), which meets in Mark Masons' Hall. In the Rose Croix of Heredom, he was Perfected as a Prince Rose Croix between 1957 and 1964. In the Mark Degree he was a member of the Maguncor Lodge of Mark Master Masons (No.833) and was Invested as a Grand

Golders Green Crematorium was the first crematorium in London. It is secular, accepting all faiths and non-believers. The crematorium gardens are Grade I listed in the National Register of Historic Parks and Gardens. Amongst the numerous famous people cremated there, in addition to fourteen VCs, are:

- Actors – Cicely Courtneidge, Joyce Grenfell, Jack Hawkins, Gordon Jackson, Sid James, Ivor Novello, Peter Sellars, Henry Irving, Vivien Leigh, Peter O'Toole, Wendy Richards and Arnold Ridley.
- Architects – Edwin Lutyens and Charles Rennie Mackintosh.
- Comedians – Tommy Handley, Bernie Winters, Peter Cook and Kenneth Horne.
- Composers – Lionel Bart, Eric Coates and Ralph Vaughan Williams.
- Military - Admiral of the Fleet 1st Baron John Fisher, Field Marshal 1st Earl of Ypres John French and Admiral of the Fleet Sir Dudley Pound.
- Musicians/singers – Larry Adler, Marc Bolan, Jack Bruce, Ray Ellington, Bud Flanagan, Matt Munro, Keith Moon, Ronnie Scott and Amy Winehouse.
- Politicians – Stanley Baldwin, Ernest Bevin and Neville Chamberlain.
- Sportsmen – Don Revie.
- Royalty – Princess Louise Duchess of Argyll and Princess Louise Margaret Duchess of Connaught & Strathearn.
- Writers – Kingsley Amis, Enid Blyton, Bram Stoker, AJP Taylor, TS Eliot, WS Gilbert, Henry James, Rudyard Kipling and HG Wells.
- Others – Sigmund Freud, Hughie Green, Alexander Korda and Anna Pavlova.

Steward on 13th June 1967. After 1961 he was a member of the Secretariat of Mark Grand Lodge until his death.

James attended a number of VC Reunions–the VC Centenary Celebrations at Hyde Park, London on 26th June 1956 and the first five VC & GC Association Reunions at the Café Royal, London on 24th July 1958, 7th July 1960, 18th July 1962, 16th July 1964 and 14th July 1966.

James collapsed on Stanmore Park Golf Course, Middlesex on 16th February 1968 and died later at Edgware General Hospital, Burnt Oak, Stanmore. He was cremated at Golders Green Crematorium, Hoop Lane, London on 21st February 1968 and his ashes were scattered in the Garden of Remembrance (Crocus lawn, Section 30). He is commemorated in a number of other places:

The VC memorial at Golders Green Crematorium (Sarah Kellam).

James Huffam's memorial paving stone outside Freemason's Hall, London.

- One of fourteen VCs named on a plaque dedicated at Golders Green Crematorium on 7th April 2013. The others are – Lieutenant General Sir Fenton John Aylmer, Major The Viscount Alexander Edward Murray Fincastle, Lieutenant Colonel Thomas Colclough Watson, Colonel Edward Douglas Brown-Synge-Hutchinson, Corporal James Upton, Brigadier The Rt Hon Sir John George Smyth, Lieutenant Leonard Maurice Keysor, Lieutenant Colonel William John Symons, Rear Admiral The Hon Edward Barry Stewart Bingham, Lieutenant Commander Percy Thompson Dean, Lieutenant Colonel Sir Brett Cloutman, Corporal Arthur Percy Sullivan and Major Parkash Singh.

James Huffam's memorial plaque, on the far left, outside Haucourt Church on the right.

- Memorial paving stone unveiled outside Freemason's Hall, Covent Garden, London on 25th April 2017 by the Duke of Kent KG.
- A Department for Communities and Local Government commemorative paving stone was dedicated at Dunblane Railway Station, Station Road, Dunblane, Stirlingshire on 31st August 2018.
- Plaque outside Haucourt Church, Rue du Général de Gaulle, about 750m northwest of St Servin's Farm.

In addition to the VC he was awarded the 1914–15 Star, British War Medal 1914–20, Victory Medal 1914–19, 1939–45 Star, Defence Medal, War Medal 1939–45 with Mentioned-in-Despatches Oakleaf, George VI Coronation Medal 1937 and Elizabeth II Coronation Medal 1953. The location of his medals is not known.

CAPTAIN BELLENDEN SEYMOUR HUTCHESON
Canadian Army Medical Corps, attached 75th Battalion (Mississauga) CEF

Bellenden Hutcheson was born on 16th December 1883 at Mount Carmel, Wabash Co, Illinois, United States of America. His father, also Bellenden Hutcheson (28th August 1856–23rd January 1931), born at Syracuse, Onondaga Co, Illinois, married Luella/Louella née Wiley (December 1864–1911), born in Cincinnati, Ohio, on 27th March 1883 in Wabash Co. Bellenden senior was an engineer and machinist and they were living at Township 16, Range 1 West, Mound City, Pulaski Co, Illinois in 1900. They were living at Mounds Ward 2, Pulaski Co in 1910. Luella died at Mount Carmel, Wabash Co and Bellenden at Cairo, Alexander Co, Illinois. Bellenden junior had four siblings:

- Frederick Buteel Hutcheson (born 14th November 1885) with his brother, Roderick, owned and managed the Hutcheson Lumber Co at Jackson, Madison Co, Tennessee. He married Mary and they were residing at New Southern Hotel, Jackson in 1937. He had died by 1942 when his widow was still living at New Southern Hotel.
- Roderick John Hutcheson (26th December 1887–23rd October 1946) owned a lumber wholesale business and served as a second lieutenant with the International Red Cross during the Great War. He married Mae (1900–52) and they were living at 17 Northwood, Jackson, Madison Co, Tennessee in 1937. He subsequently died there from acute alcoholism. They had a daughter, Susan W Hutcheson, c.1932.

Mount Carmel, the largest of the eight precincts of Wabash Co and is the county seat, known as 'Little Egypt'. The County was formed in 1824 to avert an armed confrontation between the militias of Albion and Mount Carmel after the county seat was moved.

Biographies 137

Cincinnati, the government seat of Hamilton Co, Ohio, was first settled in 1788. It was the first city founded after the Revolution and is therefore the first purely 'American city'. The introduction of steamboats on the Ohio River in 1811 opened up the city's trade and in the 19th century it was a boom town. The Miami and Erie Canal in 1827 further stimulated business. By the end of the 19th century there had been a shift from steamboats to railroads and Cincinnati's growth slowed. The city was referred to as the 'Paris of America' due to its many ambitious architectural projects. Cincinnati was a 'border town' 1810–63 between the free state of Ohio and the slave state of Kentucky. It became a focal point for escaping slaves. In 1884 outrage over a manslaughter verdict, widely believed to be a clear case of murder, triggered the Courthouse Riots in which fifty-six people were killed and over 300 were injured. A number of famous people came from the city or settled there:

- Rutherford Birchard Hayes (1822–93), 19th US President, moved to Cincinnati in 1850 and was the city solicitor 1858–61.
- William Howard Taft (1857–1930), 27th US President.
- Neil Alden Armstrong (1930–2012), the first man to walk on the Moon, taught at the University and later died in the city.
- Doris Day (1922–2019), actress, singer and animal welfare activist.
- Tyrone Edmund Power III (1914–58), film, stage and radio actor.
- Medal of Honor recipients – Christian Albert, Edward William Boers, John Cook, Manning Force, John R Fox, Webb Hayes and Heinrich Hoffman.
- Steven Allan Spielberg (born 1946), Oscar-winning film director known for *Jaws* (1975), *ET* (1982), *Jurassic Park* (1993), *Schindler's List* (1993), *Amistad* (1997), *Saving Private Ryan* (1998) and many other films.
- Howard Andrew 'Andy' Williams (1927-2012), singer best known for 'Moon River', who sold more than 100 million records worldwide.
- The Isley Brothers musical group.
- Cordelia Elizabeth 'Betty' Cook (1919–96), US Army Nurse Corps during the Second World War and was the first woman to receive the Bronze Star and Purple Heart.

- George Courtenay Hutcheson (3rd September 1896–18th February 1955) was working for Artman Nicholls & Co at Metropolis, Illinois in June 1918. He enlisted as a private in Company A, 74th Engineers on 31st August 1918. He married Mary Louise Sweeney (c.1906) in 1929 in Illinois. He was a buyer for a timber company in 1930 when they were living at 164a Arlington Avenue, Jackson, Madison Co. By 1937 they had moved to 333 Westwood, Jackson. By 1940 he was a co-owner in the family lumber company, still living at 33 Westwood. He was a lumber inspector at the time of his death at the Veterans Affairs Hospital, Murfreesboro, Rutherford Co, Tennessee. Mary was secretary of Jackson-Madison Girl Scouts in 1958, living at 125 Walnut, Jackson. They had two daughters – Mary Courtenay Hutcheson c.1929 and Katherine B Hutcheson c.1935.
- Florimel Hutcheson (3rd April 1890–20th May 1967) was a doctor's receptionist in 1940, lodging at 603 Walnut, Cairo, Alexander Co, Illinois. She never married.

Bellenden's paternal grandfather, also Bellenden Hutcheson (1st March 1831–30th August 1901) was born at Bath, Somerset, England. He emigrated to the USA and lived at Oswego, New York State. He married Mary née Jones (born c.1829), born at Bradford, Yorkshire, England, in 1852. Bellenden enlisted in the Union Army and was paid for by the state of New York 1st–16th May 1861. On 17th May he transferred to B Company, 24th (New York Volunteers) Regiment at Elmira and was commissioned as a first lieutenant on 4th July with rank from 1st May. He was promoted captain on 25th September with rank from 7th August and was detached to Chief of First Army Corps Ambulances on 26th September 1862. He was accused of being absent without leave 3rd February–23rd March 1863 and was placed in close arrest. On 21st March 1863 he was dismissed for being in the City of Washington without proper authority, in violation of General Orders, and desertion of his command whilst it was under orders to move. However, testimonials from his superior officers caused the decision to be revoked on 28th October 1868 and he was deemed to have been honourably discharged upon tender of resignation with effect from 14th January 1863. Meanwhile in 1865 he was appointed adjutant and first lieutenant in 48th Regiment of Infantry, National Guard in New York. Bellenden was a prominent churchman and a licensed lay reader in central New York. For several decades he was Inspector of Lighthouses and Harbor Improvements on the Great Lakes. He was the editor of *The Sample Case* in 1894, living with his children, Edith and Robert, at 140 North Garfield Avenue, Columbus, Franklin Co, Ohio. He died at Columbus, Ohio and is buried in Riverside Cemetery, Oswego, Oswego Co, New York. Mary was living at 24 Wilson Avenue, Columbus Ward 3, Franklin Co, Ohio in 1910. In addition to Bellenden they had six other children:

- Mary E Hutcheson (1855–11th November 1940), born at Syracuse, Onondaga Co, New York. She was an authoress in 1910 living with her mother. By 1940 she was an art teacher living with her sister, Kate, at 2422 Indianola Avenue, Columbus, Franklin Co, Ohio. She never married and died at Blendon, Franklin Co.

Biographies 139

Bellenden's paternal grandfather was born at Bath, Somerset. The city is best known for its Roman baths in the valley of the Avon but settlement goes back to the Mesolithic period. Bath Abbey was founded in the 7th century and was rebuilt in the 12th and 16th centuries. In the 17th century the curative properties of the spring water made Bath a popular spa town. Beau Nash was prominent in the city's social life 1705–61. Bath suffered three air raids during the Second World War as part of the Baedeker Blitz. More than 400 people were killed and 19,000 buildings were damaged or destroyed. In 1987 Bath became a UNESCO World Heritage Site. Amongst the many famous people who were either born or lived in Bath are:

- Emperor Haile Selassie of Ethiopia spent four years there in exile 1936–40.
- William Arnold Ridley OBE (1896-1984) playwright and actor best known for playing Private Godfrey in *Dad's Army* 1968–77.
- Thomas Gainsborough (1727–88), portrait and landscape painter.
- Kenneth Charles Loach (born 1936), television and film director particularly known for covering social issues in television plays such as *Up the Junction* (1965) and *Cathy Come Home* (1966) and films *Poor Cow* (1967) and *Kes* (1969).
- William Pitt, 1st Earl of Chatham (1708–78), British Prime Minister 1766-68, was MP for Bath 1757–66.
- Christopher Francis Patten, Baron Patten of Barnes (born 1944), was Conservative MP for Bath 1979–92 and the 28th and final Governor of Hong Kong 1992–97.
- Jane Austen (1775-1817), the author, lived there in the early 19th century.
- Charles John Huffam Dickens (1812-70), the author and social critic, was a frequent visitor and set much of the *Pickwick Papers* in the city.
- Mary Wollstonecraft Shelley (1797–1851) author of *Frankenstein*.
- Sir Roger Gilbert Bannister (1929–2018) ran the first sub four minute mile.
- Sir Clive Ronald Woodward OBE (born 1956) rugby union player and Bath coach, who coached England 1997–2004, including victory in the 2003 Rugby World Cup.
- Rear-Admiral Sir William Edward Parry (1790–1855), Arctic explorer whose 1819 expedition through the Parry Channel was the most successful in the quest for the Northwest Passage.
- Henry 'Harry' John Patch (1898–2009), briefly the oldest man in Europe, was the last surviving combat soldier of the Great War of any nation.

Oswego, on Lake Ontario in north-central New York, is the county seat of Oswego Co and became a major port and railway hub. A trading post was established in 1722 and was fortified as Fort Oswego, named after the Iroquois place name. The Oswego Canal, a branch of the Erie Canal, reached the area in 1829. The city was incorporated in 1848 and was the home of the *Oswego Water Cure* establishment in the 1850s. The first fort, on the site of the current Fort Ontario, was built by the British in 1755. It was destroyed by the French during the French and Indian War and the British began another on the site in 1759. During the American Revolution, the British abandoned the Fort and it was destroyed by American troops in 1778. In 1782 the British reoccupied it and did not concede it to the United States until 1796, thirteen years after the end of the Revolutionary War. During the War of 1812 the garrison was overwhelmed by the British but they were defeated near Oswego later that month. The US military maintained Fort Ontario until it was abandoned in 1901. During the Second World War the Fort was used to house 982 Jewish refugees from Europe, the only such effort by the USA during the War. In 1946 the Fort was transferred to the state of New York and was used to house veterans and their families. Development as a historic site began in 1949 and it has been restored to its 1867-72 appearance. Amongst the notable people to have lived at Oswego is Mary Edwards Walker MD (1832-1919), Civil War surgeon and the only woman to receive the Medal of Honor.

- Frederick Lester Hutcheson (born 1861) in Oswego Co, New York.
- John Kyrie Hutcheson (1866–1947) married Edith J Maitland (born February 1865), born in Canada, in 1887. He was a conductor on the railroad in 1900 and they were living on Pearl Street, Madison, Norfolk Co, Nebraska. She was later living with her children on Pierce Street, Council Bluffs, Ward 3, Pottawattamie Co, Iowa, recorded as a widow. They had five children – Emily Hutcheson 1887, Bessie Hutcheson 1889, Guy Hutcheson 1891, Jack Hutcheson 1895 and Robert Hutcheson 1903. John married Hattie Bell Patterson (née Baker) (18th November 1875–25th September 1943), born at Plymouth, Indiana, on 30th June 1925 at Coon Rapids, Iowa. He was an electrician and she was a member of Faith Chapter Order of the Eastern Star of Coon Rapids. Hattie had married Joseph Patterson

Bellenden's paternal grandmother was born in Bradford in the West Riding of Yorkshire, which became a municipal borough in 1847 and a city in 1897. It rose to prominence in the 19th century as an international centre for textile manufacture and became the 'wool capital of the world'. The population grew from 6,393 in 1801 to 182,000 by 1850. The textile industry in Bradford fell into decline in the mid-20th century but the city has since become a tourist destination. In June 2009 Bradford became the world's first UNESCO City of Film. Amongst the famous people who were born or lived there are:

- David Hockney (born 1937), painter, draftsman, printmaker, stage designer and photographer.
- Frederick Theodore Albert Delius (1862–1934) composer.
- John Boynton Priestley (1894–1984) novelist, playwright, screenwriter, broadcaster and social commentator.
- Sir Edward Victor Appleton GBE KCB (1892–1965), who discovered the ionosphere, 1947 Nobel Prize winner and pioneer in radiophysics.

(c.1866–15th October 1921), a photographer born in Wisconsin, on 23rd May 1894 at Albion, Boone Co, Nebraska. They moved to Essex Co, Iowa in 1901 and to Coon Rapids in 1909. Joseph and Hattie had three children – Roy E Patterson c.1899, Gertrude Patterson c.1901 and Raymond J Patterson c.1912, who was serving in the US Army in Florida in 1943.
- Edith Diana Hutcheson (4th September 1869–3rd November 1930) was a church organist and never married. She died at Columbus, Franklin Co.
- Kate B Hutcheson (2nd August 1871–15th November 1950), born in New York, was a teacher at a kindergarten in 1910, living with her mother. By 1940 she was a music teacher living with her sister, Mary. She died at Hardin, Franklin Co, Ohio.

- Robert Bulteel Hutcheson (30th April 1873–24th September 1952), born in Oswego Co, married Mary Agnes Bennett (September 1879–1956), born in Ohio. He was a general bookkeeper in 1919 and they were living at Westerville, Franklin Co. Mary was the auditor of the Scioto Country Club, Upper Arlington, Ohio in 1934. He died at Columbus, Franklin Co, Ohio.

Nothing is known of his maternal grandparents. Bellenden was educated at Illinois High School, Mound City, Illinois until 1901 and then at Northwestern University Medical School, Chicago, Illinois, from 1902. He practised medicine and surgery in Iowa before moving to Illinois, where he served as house surgeon at Alexian Brothers Hospital, Chicago.

Bellenden is believed to have renounced his US citizenship in 1915 in order to join the Canadian Army but reclaimed it after the war. His motives for joining the Canadian Army were mixed. He was in sympathy with the Allied cause and was English by descent. His great grandfather served under Lord Nelson and lost an eye at Trafalgar. The third factor was to gain surgical experience and adventure. He joined the Canadian Army on 6th November 1915 and was appointed lieutenant and MO of 97th Overseas Battalion CEF at

Mound City (population 692), on the Ohio River close to where it joins the Mississippi, is in southern Illinois about eight kilometres north of Cairo and is the seat of Pulaski Co. The first class to graduate from Mound City High School was in 1888. The original Mound City High School has since been demolished.

The Alexian Brothers (Cellites or Beghards), a Roman Catholic male nursing order, originated during the bubonic plague in the 13th century. The Brothers were associated with the chapel dedicated to Alexius of Rome, who had served for many years in a hospital at Edessa in Syria, and became known as the Brothers at St Alexius Chapel and later more simply as the Alexian Brothers. In the early 20th century the Brothers had four hospitals in the USA, the first built in Chicago in 1866. It was destroyed in the Great Fire in October 1871 and was rebuilt the following year. The Chicago hospital has become the Alexian Brothers Medical Center and Rehabilitation Hospital in Elk Grove Village and the St Alexius Medical Center and Behavioral Hospital, in Hoffman Estates. In January 2012 the Alexian Brothers Health System became part of St Louis-based Ascension Health, the largest Catholic and non-profit health system in the USA.

Halifax was founded in 1749. HMS *Shannon* captured the frigate USS *Chesapeake* in a naval engagement off Halifax during the War of 1812. The invasion force that landed at Washington in 1813 and burned the Capitol and White House set out from Halifax. Although Nova Scotia joined the Canadian confederation, Halifax retained a British garrison until 1906 and the Royal Navy remained until 1910, when the newly created Royal Canadian Navy took over the dockyard. In 1912 Halifax was the hub for recovery operations following the sinking of RMS *Titanic*. One hundred and fifty victims of the disaster are buried there. During the Great War the port became a major departure point for Canadian forces to Europe. In both world wars it was a key assembly point for trans-Atlantic convoys. On 6th December 1917 the town suffered a devastating explosion when the French SS *Mont-Blanc*, carrying high explosives, collided with the Norwegian SS *Imo* in the Narrows. About 2,000 people were killed and 9,000 were injured.

Exhibition Camp, Toronto on 14th December. He was described as 5′ 8½″ tall, weighing 143 lbs, with blue eyes and his religious denomination was Episcopalian. He sailed from Halifax, Nova Scotia aboard RMS *Olympic* on 18th September 1916, arriving at Liverpool, Lancashire on 25th September. He was promoted captain the same day.

Bellenden was attached to the Royal Canadian Regiment & Princess Patricia's Canadian Light Infantry Depot at Seaford, Sussex on 3rd November. He was appointed acting Senior Medical Officer with 13th Provisional Brigade at Seaford, Sussex on 18th November but returned to the RCR & PPCLI Depot on 21st November. Two days later he was attached as acting Deputy Assistant Director Medical Services Canadians, Shoreham, Sussex and as acting DADMS Staff, Seaford on 2nd December. He transferred to 7th Reserve Battalion there on 1st January 1917. The Battalion was formed by absorbing the RCR & PPCLI Depot. He was attached to DADMS Seaford from ADMS Brighton for medical base duties on 8th January.

On 11th January, Bellenden was admitted to Raven's Croft Military Hospital, Seaford. He was diagnosed with pleurisy and transferred to Perkins Bull Hospital for Convalescent Canadian Officers, Putney Heath, London on 25th January. A medical board at 76 Strand, London on 6th March found him fit for General Service and he resumed the duties of Senior MO, 3rd Reserve Brigade on 8th March. He

A school was established in 1895, by sisters Isabel and Margaret Mullins, at Bournside, Kenley, Surrey. Shortly afterwards it moved to a larger house nearby, Raven's Croft, which was adopted as the name of the school. In 1904 it moved to a house at Warlingham, Surrey and in 1909 to new premises built in Sutton Avenue, Seaford, Sussex. When the large military camp was built nearby in 1915, the school moved to South Cliff, Eastbourne. The School was then used as Raven's Croft Military Hospital. In November 1916 it had a capacity of one hundred beds. The School returned after the Great War but when the Second World War broke out it was evacuated to Devon. In 1951 economic pressure led to an amalgamation with Blatchington Court School. When the

School ran into financial difficulties again in 1959, the parents came to the rescue, enabling a company to be formed. However, the financial situation did not improve and Raven's Croft School closed in 1965. The land has since been developed into a residential site.

was posted to the CAMC Depot, Shorncliffe, Kent on 16th March and sailed for France on 22nd March. Next day he was a supernumerary at 7th Canadian General Hospital, Boulogne on the strength of CAMC General. He was attached to 2nd Canadian Stationary Hospital on 8th April, to 11th Canadian Field Ambulance on 11th April and to 76th (Army) Brigade RFA on 14th April. He joined the latter

When war broke out, William Perkins Bull KC (1870–1928), a Canadian lawyer and businessman living in London, tried to enlist but was refused. The Perkins Bulls began to invite Canadian officers on leave to their home at 7 Heathview Gardens for dinners and other events. These gatherings developed into a wartime institution and their home became a hostel for the Canadians. Up to twenty-four could be accommodated. Many guests were convalescing and in 1916 Mrs Perkins Bull suggested that the vacant house across the road, 9 Heathview Gardens, be used as a convalescent hospital. The Perkins Bull Hospital for Convalescent Canadian Officers opened in July. The Hospital was affiliated to Queen Alexandra's Military Hospital, Millbank and had twenty-five beds, later thirty-two. The Hospital was visited by King George V and Queen Mary and the Prime Ministers of Canada and other allied countries. As so many wartime romances started there, the Hospital became known as the 'Perkins Bull Matrimonial Bureau'. The Hospital closed in the summer of 1919, having seen about 1,000 Canadians pass through the two houses as guests or patients. Notable patients were the flying ace, William Avery 'Billy' Bishop VC CB DSO MC DFC ED (1894–1956), and future Governor General of Canada, Georges Vanier (1888–1967), who lost a leg during the war. No.9 has since been divided into apartments. No.7, seen here, was the home of Sir Ernest Shackleton (1874–1922) 1911–13, who led three expeditions to Antarctica.

to assist with casualties during the Battle of Vimy Ridge. 76th Brigade RFA was supporting the Canadian Corps and the gun crews were quartered in cellars. After several had been blown in, Bellenden and some of the uninjured set to work digging out the injured while the bombardment continued. Gas shells and high explosive were intermingled. Bellenden dressed the wounded, gave morphine when necessary and ensured that the injured were evacuated.

Bellenden was attached to 11th Canadian Field Ambulance on 29th April and to 75th Battalion on 2nd May. He was granted ten days' leave on 21st September. In November 1917, on the way up to Passchendaele, he was hit by a fragment of shell while passing the Cloth Hall in Ypres. The back of his raincoat and tunic were torn out but he sustained no injury other than a severe contusion. On 21st December he was admitted to 13th Canadian Field Ambulance with trench fever (pyrexia of unknown origin), transferred to 12th Canadian Field Ambulance next day and to No.22 Casualty Clearing Station on 30th December. On 1st January 1918 he was transferred by 19 Ambulance Train to No.1 British Red Cross, Duchess of Westminster Hospital, Le Touquet and to No.8 Convalescent Home for British Officers (Michelham Convalescent Home), Dieppe on 21st January. On 19th February he was discharged and rejoined 75th Battalion on 23rd February.

Awarded the MC for his actions on 8th August 1918. When the Battalion reached its jumping off point, the enemy artillery was very heavy and many casualties were sustained. He worked unceasingly in attending to and dressing the wounded whilst under heavy fire in the open ground between Beaucourt and Le Quesnel, immediately north of the Amiens – Roye road. He continued his treatment of the wounded while passing through Le Quesnel several times during the mopping up operations. He supervised the collection of the wounded into a cellar during lulls in the shelling. As he, 139003 Lance Corporal John George Adnitt and 629281 Private Walter James Marigold, were attending to some wounded near a street corner, a company of 4th Canadian Mounted Rifles and some tanks pushed through the village. A shell landed in their midst and six men went down. The three medics ran to help. The company commander and three other men were killed and the CSM had his leg blown off above the knee. The wounded were dressed and they got them into shelter. One of the dead was carrying phosphorous bombs, which set his clothing alight and could not be extinguished. Later in the day, when the enemy had been pushed back and it was quieter, Bellenden observed that the body had been almost incinerated. A day or so later he came across a temporary German tent hospital and he and his men dressed nearly one hundred enemy wounded so that they could be evacuated, LG 2nd December 1918.

Awarded the VC for his actions at Dury, east of Arras, France on 2nd September 1918. LG 14th December 1918. He was granted fourteen days' leave from 15th September to 3rd October. He did not want to go at that time as he was trying to arrange leave at the same time as his brother, who was serving as a lieutenant in the American 42nd Infantry Division (Rainbow Division). He was granted another fourteen days' leave from 16th January to 8th February 1919. He returned to Britain on 2nd May and joined CAMC Casualty Company, Witley, Surrey. The VC and MC were presented by the King in the quadrangle of Buckingham Palace on 22nd May.

Bellenden returned to Canada aboard RMS *Mauretania*, embarking on 31st May, disembarking on 6th June, and was taken on strength of No.2 District Depot, Toronto. He transferred to the Army Medical Corps Training Depot, Toronto on 11th June. He was posted for duty under ADMS HQ Ottawa on 17th June and was attached to Clearing Services Command, Quebec on 30th June. He returned to the strength of No.2 District Depot on 3rd October. Next day he reported sick at St Andrew's, Toronto for an irritating ischio-rectal scar that resulted from an operation fourteen years previously. He also had an operation for haemorrhoids and a hernia eight years previously. No operation was required on this occasion and he was

RMS *Mauretania*, seen here while being fitted out, was built by Wigham Richardson and Swan Hunter for Cunard Line and was launched on 20th September 1906. She was the world's largest ship until RMS *Olympic* was completed in 1911. *Mauretania* gained the eastbound Blue Riband on her maiden return voyage in December 1907 and the westbound for the fastest transatlantic crossing in 1909. She held both records for twenty years. When the Great War broke out *Mauretania* made a dash for safety in Halifax, Nova Scotia, arriving on 6th August. Shortly afterwards she was requisitioned as an armed merchant cruiser but was unsuitable and resumed civilian service on 11th August. Lack of passengers crossing the Atlantic caused *Mauretania* to be laid up in Liverpool until May 1915, when she filled the void left by the sinking of *Lusitania*. She became a troopship and carried troops to Gallipoli. Because of her high speed, she was able to avoid U-boats and *Mauretania* became a hospital ship until 25th January 1916. In late 1916 she became a troopship again and was requisitioned by the Canadian government to carry troops from Halifax to Liverpool, including thousands of American troops the following year. *Mauretania* returned to civilian service in September 1919 and had an extensive overhaul in 1920. In 1921 she was removed from service after a fire and returned in March 1922 after her boilers had been converted to oil, which reduced her top speed. In 1923 a major refit was commenced on the turbines and she returned to Atlantic service in 1928. In 1930 she became a cruise ship. When Cunard Line merged with White Star Line in 1934, *Mauretania*, *Olympic* and *Majestic* were not required and were withdrawn from service. *Mauretania* completed her final Atlantic crossing from New York to Southampton in September 1934. In May 1935 her furnishings and fittings were auctioned and on 1st July she departed Southampton for Rosyth. On the way she stopped at her birthplace on the Tyne, drawing large crowds. The ship's bell is in the reception of Lloyds Registry in London.

sent on leave until 10th December. Bellenden was demobilised on 12th December 1919 in Toronto. He gave his address as 800 Commercial Avenue, Cairo, Illinois, USA.

Bellenden married Frances Rand Young (30th December 1889–September 1975) on 1st December 1919 at Kentville, Kings Co, Nova Scotia. She was probably born in Nova Scotia and was a nurse when they met before the war. He refused to marry her then for fear of making her a widow. Bellenden and Frances travelled from Canada to Port Huron, Michigan, USA on 24th December 1919 and later lived at 3003 Park Place West, Cairo, Illinois. They had a son:

Commercial Avenue, Cairo, Illinois, where the Hutchesons lived.

- Bellenden Rand Hutcheson (born 30th July 1922), born in Illinois, USA, was educated in Canada (BSc MB MD), qualified as a doctor and is believed to have been on the teaching staff at The Harvard School of Public Health, teaching Public Health Practice. He married Rosemary Dodge and they were living at Apartment 104, 1150 Coast Village Road, Santa Barbara, California in 1980. They had at least a son:
  ◦ Bellenden Rand Hutcheson Jr (1962–2012), born at Boston, Massachusetts and known as Rand, was educated at Dexter School, Phillips Exeter Academy, New York University, Columbia University and the University of Michigan. He taught Old English at Marshall University before becoming a Trusts and Estates attorney in the Estate Planning groups of the Boston law firms of Bingham Dana (later Bingham McCutchen) and Rackemann, Sawyer & Brewster. He was a partner at the Worcester law firm of Erskine & Erskine and at the Amherst law firm of Brown, Hart & Kaplan. He went into solo practice at 6 Market Street, Northampton, Massachusetts. Rand was author of *Old English Poetic Metre* and numerous articles on both medieval English and linguistics as well as on estate planning. He married Eva Rosenn and the marriage ended in divorce. They had two children – Sarah Hutcheson and Bellenden Ian Hutcheson. He died at Northampton, Massachusetts.

Bellenden and Frances.

Frances' father, William Young (1866–29th December 1900), born in Nova Scotia, married Margaret Rebecca née Rand (born 10th October 1865), born at Cornwallis, Kings Co, Nova Scotia, on 9th February 1888 at Canning, Kings Co. They lived at Kentville, Kings Co and he died there. She was living with her children at Upper Dyke Village, Kings Co in 1901. By 1921 she was a farmer, living with her children, George and Constance, at Shipman Corner, Upper Dyke Village, Kings Co. In addition to Frances they had nine other children, all born in Kings Co:

 * John Young (born 25th November 1888) was living with his mother in 1911.
 * Thomas Kenneth Young (15th December 1890–24th May 1977) joined HMS *Excellent* on 11th August 1915 and was commissioned as a temporary sub lieutenant RNVR on 13th August, with seniority from 10th August. In his service record his year of birth is recorded as 1892. He was posted to HMS *Teutonic* on 29th September and HMS *Moldavia* on 14th January 1916. Appointed temporary acting lieutenant on 11th August and was posted to HMS *Endymion*. Posted to HMS *Excellent* on 4th November. Promoted temporary lieutenant 1st September with seniority from 10th August 1917. Thomas was granted leave in Canada 1st–30th September, sailed for Britain aboard HMS *Columbella* and was discharged from HMS *Moldavia* to the Depot on 4th January 1918. To Devonport on 8th January and HMS *Endymion* on 19th January. He was admitted to Haslar Royal Naval Hospital on 21st November with influenza and to a convalescent hospital with pneumonia on 13th December. He was discharged to duty on 14th February 1919 and was found fit on 10th March. Thomas was demobilised in Canada on 9th April 1919, giving his address as Fairview, Kentville. He married Frances Clark (18th January 1907–20th April 1978), born at Bloomville, New York, on 18th September 1944 in New York, USA. Thomas was appointed lieutenant in the Royal Canadian Naval Reserve on 22nd August 1941 (823 72 31). He was promoted lieutenant commander on 1st January 1943 and is understood to have transferred to the US Naval Reserve. He was serving aboard USS LCS (L) (3) 126 sailing from Okinawa, Japan to Jinsen, Korea on 18th November 1945 and from Tsingtao, China to Guam on 11th December 1945. He was a salesman living with his family at Elmore Drive, Homestead, Dade Co, Florida in 1952. He applied for US citizenship on 5th November 1952 and was described as 5' 7½" tall, weighing 135 lbs, with fair complexion, blue eyes and gray-brown hair. They both died in Dade Co. They had a daughter, Margaret Young (born 1947).
 * George Renny Young (born 8th April 1892) served for six months in 14th King's Canadian Hussars and 6th Canadian Mounted Rifles before enlisting in 25th Battalion CEF on 19th May 1915 at Halifax, Nova Scotia. He was attested next day, described as a farmer, 5' 11" tall, weighing 150 lbs, with fair complexion, grey eyes, dark brown hair and his religious denomination was Presbyterian. He was commissioned as a lieutenant with seniority from 19th May. The unit sailed from Canada aboard SS *Saxonia* on 20th May and arrived in England on 29th May. He

was struck off strength of 25th Battalion on 14th September and transferred to 17th Reserve Battalion on 24th September. He was drafted to 25th Battalion in France on 3rd November and joined the unit there on 11th November. He was admitted to 6th Canadian Field Ambulance with bronchitis 15th–19th February 1916 and to Nos.12 and 10 Casualty Clearing Stations with a contused right foot 5th–16th April. George was granted eight days leave from 26th April and transferred to HQ Canadian Training Division, Shorncliffe on 15th June. He sailed to Canada aboard SS *Grampian* on 23rd June for instructional purposes/transport duties. He was suffering from nausea, vomiting, diarrhoea and headaches. On 3rd July he was taken on strength of the Nova Scotia Highland Brigade and on 12th July of 185th Battalion at Aldershot, Nova Scotia. He was found fit for overseas service on 28th August, transferred to 185th Battalion on 1st September and sailed with the Battalion from Halifax, Nova Scotia aboard RMS *Olympic* on 12th October, arriving in Liverpool on 18th October. George was attached to 85th Battalion at Witley on 3rd January 1917 and transferred to it on 24th January. He returned to France with the Battalion on 10th February. He was admitted to 11th and 12th Canadian Field Ambulances on 4th May and transferred to 7th General Hospital, St Omer with mumps 5th–26th May. On 29th June he was wounded in the ear and left shoulder when a shell fragment struck his helmet. He was unconscious for fifteen minutes but the wounds were not serious and no bones were broken. He was admitted to 11th Canadian Field Ambulance and No.21 Casualty Clearing Station the same day and transferred to 20th General Hospital, Camiers the following day. He transferred by hospital ship to 3rd London General Hospital, Wandsworth Common on 6th July also suffering from trench fever. While there he was on the held strength of the Nova Scotia Regiment Depot, Bramshott. A Medical Board in London on 14th September found him unfit for service for one month. He was discharged and granted leave until 14th October. While on leave he suffered from Dhobie's Itch and was treated at 2nd Scottish General Hospital, Craigleith, Edinburgh 11th October–15th November. As a result he was struck off strength of 85th Battalion on 29th October. A medical board at 13 Berners Street, London on 16th November found him unfit for General Service for two months and Home Service for one month. A subsequent board there on 17th December found him unfit for General Service for one month but fit for Home Service. He was convalescent until 20th December and rejoined 17th Reserve Battalion. He was admitted to 12th Canadian General Hospital, Bramshott with bronchitis/myalgia on 4th January 1918. A medical board there on 23rd January found him unfit for General Service for one month but fit for Home Service and he returned to 17th Reserve Battalion. However, a medical board at Bramshott on 22nd February found him unfit for General Service for three months but fit for Home Service. He was admitted to 12th Canadian General Hospital with indigestion 15th March–27th April and was on the held strength of the NSRD until returning to 17th Reserve Battalion on 28th April. A medical board at Bramshott on 1st

May recommended no service for six months due to chronic appendicitis. He was readmitted to 12th Canadian General Hospital on 6th May on the strength of the NSRD. He transferred to the Canadian Convalescent Officers Hospital, Matlock, Derbyshire 7th May. A medical board there on 10th May found him unfit for General Service for two months but fit for Home Service and he was attached to 17th Reserve Battalion on 19th May. A medical board at Bramshott on 10th July found him unfit for service for one month but fit for a command depot. He joined the Officers Casualty Company, Bexhill on 15th July and ceased to be attached to 17th Reserve Battalion. A medical board at Bexhill on 14th August found him fit for General Service and he transferred to 17th Reserve Battalion on 24th August. George was admitted to 12th Canadian General Hospital with bronchitis 7th–18th November and was taken on strength of NSRD, Ripon on 3rd December. He was admitted to 3rd London General Hospital, Wandsworth with appendicitis on 4th December and they were removed on 6th December. He transferred to the Canadian Red Cross Officers' Hospital, 17 North Audley Street, London on 18th December, to Perkins Bull Convalescent Hospital on 8th January 1919 and to the Canadian Convalescent Officers Hospital, Matlock on 23rd January. A medical board at Bramshott that day found him unfit for General Service for one month but fit for Home Service. A medical board at Matlock on 5th February found him fit for General Service and he rejoined 17th Reserve Battalion on 10th February. George was admitted to the Military Hospital, Ripon, Yorkshire with bronchitis 3rd–12th March. He transferred to the Canadian Concentration Camp, Kinmel Park, Rhyl on 29th March and sailed for Canada from Liverpool on 7th May aboard SS *Celtic*. George was demobilised on 21st May 1919. By then he weighed just 139 lbs. He was living with his mother in 1921.

- William Mather Young (born 25th October 1893) was a sailor (quartermaster) when he emigrated to the USA, arriving at Boston, Massachusetts on 23rd October 1914. He applied for US citizenship on 15th January 1915. He enlisted in the Cyclists Battalion (405) at Halifax, Nova Scotia on 20th April, described as 5′ 10″ tall, weighing 155 lbs, with light complexion, brown eyes, light brown hair and his religious denomination was Church of England. He sailed for England aboard RMS *Caledonia*, arriving on 24th June and was posted to Shorncliffe, Kent. He was admitted to Bevan Military Hospital, Sandgate 2nd–20th August with general vaccinia. He went to France on 15th September and joined 2nd Canadian Division Cyclists Company. William was attached to 5th Brigade Reserve Battalion 7th January–15th February 1916 and to the Assistant Provost Marshal 20th April–29th May. He was granted leave 30th May–9th June. From 31st May his unit formed part of the Canadian Corps Cyclists Battalion. He was admitted to No.2 Divisional Rest Station with pyrexia of unknown origin on 23rd June and transferred to the North Midlands Casualty Clearing Station, Mont des Cats on 27th June. He rejoined the unit on 1st July and was on duty in Paris 11th–18th July. He was attached to the Canadian Corps Salvage Company

12th–27th September and was wounded on the Somme on 8th October. He was admitted to St John's Ambulance Brigade Hospital, Étaples with severe gunshot wounds to the right hand, arm and eye on 10th October. He was evacuated on HMHS *Brighton* and transferred to 1st Southern General Hospital, Edgbaston, Birmingham, Warwickshire on 12th October. He was on the held strength of the Canadian Casualty Assembly Centre, Folkestone from 13th October. He transferred to Highbury Auxiliary Hospital, Moseley, Birmingham on 4th November, the former home of Joseph Chamberlain, and to the Canadian Convalescent Hospital, Bearwood, Wokingham, Berkshire on 26th January 1917. He reported to the Canadian Convalescent Depot, Hastings for physical training on 30th January and to the General Depot, Hastings on 10th March. William was taken on strength at Chiseldon, Wiltshire on 12th April and was appointed unpaid acting lance corporal on 9th June while on a musketry course. He was struck off strength to the General Depot, Chiseldon on 3rd July and then to 2nd Canadian Command Depot, Shorncliffe on 18th July. William was discharged from No.2 Canadian Discharge Depot, London on appointment to a commission in the RNVR. His address was c/o Mrs E Percy Champion, 11 Rollscourt Avenue, Herne Hill, London.

- Ella Young (born 7th November 1894) travelled to Boston, Massachusetts in 1914 bound for the Deaconess Hospital there.
- Dorothy Marion Young (born 17th February 1896) was single in 1950 when she travelled to New York from Québec aboard SS *Manchester Port*.
- Emma Young (born 16th December 1897).
- Catherine Jane Young (born 14th January 1899).
- Constance 'Willie' Irene Young (born 18th February 1900) was a teacher at Naparima Girls High School, San Fernando, Trinidad and Tobago in 1924. She was appointed principal in 1927 and returning to Canada aboard SS *Canadian Skirmisher* on 5th July 1928. She was still employed as a teacher in 1950, living at 521 West 121st Street, New York.

Bellenden was a member of staff of St Mary's Hospital, Cairo, Illinois and was the City Health Officer at the same time. He was appointed acting assistant surgeon of the US Public Health Service. He was also a member of the American Medical Association and Illinois State Medical Society. He attended the VC Dinner at the Royal Gallery of the House of Lords, London on 9th November 1929. He travelled to the British Embassy, Washington DC on 9th June 1939 to be presented to King George VI and Queen Elizabeth during their tour of North America. During that visit he accompanied the Royal party to Arlington Cemetery to lay a wreath at the Tomb of the Unknown Soldier.

Bellenden died of cancer at Cairo, Illinois on 9th April 1954. He is buried in Rose Hill Cemetery, Mount Carmel, Alexander Co, Illinois (Sect B, Lot 145, Grave C). He is commemorated in a number of other places:

St Mary's Hospital, Cairo, Illinois. Cairo, at the confluence of the Ohio and Mississippi rivers, is the southernmost city in Illinois and the seat of Alexander Co. Fort Defiance was built there during the Civil War by Union General Ulysees S Grant to control access to the rivers. The naval station for the Mississippi River Squadron was established there in September 1861. As a result Cairo was an important Union supply base and training centre. The city's population peaked at 15,203 in 1920. Charles Dickens visited in 1842 and it became his prototype for the nightmare City of Eden in *Martin Chuzzlewit*. The Illinois Central Railroad arrived in 1855. The city is very low lying and is completely enclosed by levees and floodwalls. Cairo has had a turbulent history of race relations, including the November 1909 lynching of black resident William James, who was accused of murdering Anna Pelly, a white woman, although there was no evidence. Approximately 10,000 people gathered for the lynching but the rope broke and James survived, but the mob then shot him more than 500 times. The body was dragged to the scene of the murder, his head was cut off, mounted on a pole and his body was burned. The mob lynched another man at the jail who was also unconnected with the murder. The Governor of Illinois deployed eleven companies of militia to prevent further violence. A slow economic decline began in the early 20th century, partly due to the construction of bridges over the rivers and traffic bypassing the city. Racial tension increased again in the 1960s with the Civil Rights Movement and violence reached a peak during 1969. African-Americans boycotted white businesses throughout 1970. As the economy suffered so the population declined from a peak of 15,203 in 1920 to just 2,831 in 2010. Cairo was the original destination for Huck and Jim in Mark Twain's *The Adventures of Huckleberry Finn*.

- Illinois
    - Captain Bellenden S Hutcheson VC MC MD Day, celebrated annually in Mount Carmel since December 2016.
    - Memorial in Mount Carmel Court House.
- Ontario
    - Captain Bellenden Seymore Hutcheson VC Armoury, 70 Birmingham Street, Etobicoke, Toronto was opened by Lieutenant Colonel Justin Neil CD, CO Toronto Scottish Regiment (Queen Elizabeth the Queen Mother's Own) on 12th September 2009. There is a painting of the VC action in the Armoury.
    - Victoria Cross obelisk to all Canadian VCs at Military Heritage Park, Barrie dedicated by Princess Royal on 22nd October 2013.
    - Plaque No.80 on the York Cemetery VC Memorial, West Don River Valley, Toronto dedicated on 25th June 2017.

- Named on two of eleven plaques honouring 175 men from overseas awarded the VC for the Great War. The plaques were unveiled by the Senior Minister of State at the Foreign & Commonwealth Office and Minister for Faith and Communities, Baroness Warsi, at a reception at Lancaster House, London on 26th June 2014 attended by The Duke of Kent and relatives of the VC recipients. The Canadian plaque was unveiled outside the British High Commission in Elgin Street, Ottawa, Ontario on 10th November 2014 by The Princess Royal in the presence of British High Commissioner Howard Drake, Canadian Minister of Veterans Affairs Julian Fantino and Canadian Chief of the Defence Staff General Thomas James Lawson. The United States plaque is at Arlington National Cemetery, Arlington Co, Virginia, USA.
- Two 49 cents postage stamps in honour of the ninety-four Canadian VC winners were issued by Canada Post on 21st October 2004 on the 150th Anniversary of the first Canadian VC's action, Alexander Roberts Dunn VC.
- Communities and Local Government commemorative paving stones for the 145 VCs born in Australia, Belgium, Canada, China, Denmark, Egypt, France, Germany, India, Iraq, Japan, Nepal, Netherlands, Newfoundland, New Zealand, Pakistan, South Africa, Sri Lanka, Ukraine and United States of America were unveiled at the National Memorial Arboretum, Alrewas, Staffordshire by Prime Minister David Cameron MP and Sergeant Johnson Beharry VC on 5th March 2015.
- Plaque on the outside wall of a small chapel near Dury Crucifix Cemetery, France.

The grave of Bellenden and Frances Hutcheson in Rose Hill Cemetery.

Memorial plaques for Hutcheson and Young on the wall of the chapel opposite Dury communal cemetery. The lane on the right leads to Dury Crucifix Cemetery.

Captain Bellenden Hutcheson VC Armoury, Toronto.

In addition to the VC and MC he was awarded the British War Medal 1914–20, Victory Medal 1914–19, George VI Coronation Medal 1937 and Elizabeth II Coronation Medal 1953. The VC is held by the Toronto Scottish Regiment (Queen Elizabeth The Queen Mother's Own), Hodden Grey Museum, Captain Bellenden Hutcheson VC Armoury, 70 Birmingham Street, Toronto, Ontario.

24/1699 SERGEANT REGINALD STANLEY JUDSON
1st Battalion, Auckland Infantry Regiment NZEF

Reginald Judson was born on 29th September 1881 at Port Albert, Wharehine, Rodney, North Island, New Zealand. His father, Edgar Judson (1847–12th November 1922), born at Lindfield, Sussex, married Emma Frances née Holmden (18th October 1853–16th July 1930), born at Edenbridge, Kent, in 1876 at Lewisham, London. They emigrated to New Zealand, where Edgar was a sheep farmer at Port Albert in 1881. They had moved to Florida, USA by 1884 and returned to England by 1891. Edgar was living at the home of Thomas Stubbs, restaurant proprietor, at Melbourne Street, St Mary, Nottingham. He later moved to 23 New Windsor Street, Uxbridge, Middlesex before being admitted to the London County Asylum (later Bexley Hospital), The Heath, Dartford by 1901 and then to Springfield Mental Hospital, Tooting, London where he subsequently died. Emma was boarding with her children, Fanny and Thomas, at the home of her brother, Henry Holmden, at Coulden's Farm, Hazelwood, Limpsfield, Surrey in 1891. By 1901 she was boarding with her sister, Mary Alwen, and her family, at London Road, Keymer, Sussex. By 1911 she was living with two of her sons, Edgar and Thomas, at 85 Dagnall Park, South Norwood, Croydon, Surrey. She died at 29 Tonfield Road, Sutton, Surrey. Reginald had five siblings including:

- Edgar Francis Judson (1877–1955), born at Croydon, Surrey, was living at 54 Thornfield Road, Hammersmith, London in 1901, with his sisters, Fanny and Mary. He was a bank clerk by 1911. Edgar married Mary Gilson Cooper (7th April 1895–1971), born at Lewisham, London, in 1935 at Lambeth, London. Edgar died at Christchurch, Hampshire and Mary at Bournemouth, Hampshire.
- Mary 'Molly' Cordelia Judson (23rd February 1879–11th July 1958) was born at Wharehine, Rodney, Auckland, New Zealand. She was a shop assistant when

Reginald's father was born at Lindfield, Sussex. The village High Street is on the line of an ancient north-south track and has more than forty medieval and post medieval timber-framed buildings. The village is known to date back to at least 765, when King Ealdwulf granted land to build a minster church. At the time of the Domesday Book in 1086, the lands were held by the Archbishop of Canterbury. King Edward III granted the town a royal charter to hold a market every Thursday and two annual eight-day fairs in 1343. Lindfield was part of the Wealden iron industry from 1539 onwards. The Ouse Valley Railway line reached it in 1866 but was abandoned for financial reasons.

she returned to New Zealand with her sister, Fanny, aboard SS *Medic*, arriving at Sydney, New South Wales on 19th December 1901 and in New Zealand in January 1902. She married Walter Sotham (27th December 1894–18th September 1972), a bank officer born at Witney, Oxfordshire, on 31st December 1907. She died in

Reginald's mother came from Edenbridge, Kent on the River Eden, a tributary of the Medway. The town grew along the disused Roman road from London to Lewes. In the Middle Ages it was a centre of the Wealden iron industry. It expanded when the railways arrived. First the South Eastern Railway line from Redhill to Tonbridge in 1842 and the London, Brighton & South Coast Railway in 1888. Edenbridge War Memorial Hospital was established as a cottage hospital to care for soldiers returning from the Great War. In recent years it has faced closure many times but local campaigners have been successful in keeping it open. The racing driver, John Surtees (1934-2017) had a workshop in Edenbridge.

What is now Springfield University Hospital, a psychiatric hospital in Tooting, opened as the Surrey County Pauper Lunatic Asylum in 1840. It was managed by Middlesex County Council from 1888 and renamed Wandsworth Asylum. During the Great War it was Springfield War Hospital and afterwards Springfield Mental Hospital. An infirmary block opened in 1932. The hospital joined the National Health Service in 1948. At its peak there were 2,000 patients but this has reduced to under 300. Much of the original building is now disused and there are plans to convert it into residential accommodation.

Auckland and he was living at 27 Walmsley Road, St Heliers at the time of his death at Point Chevalier, Auckland. They had seven children including:
- ° Dorothy Sotham (1908–95), born at Temuka, Canterbury, married Maurice Sinclair Wells (1905–82), born at Tairei, Otago, in 1938 and they had a child. He died at Christchurch, Canterbury. She is understood to have died at Perth, Western Australia.
- ° Walter Frank Sotham (1910–41), born at Timaru, served as a private in 21st Battalion, New Zealand Infantry during the Second World War (29463) and was captured by the Germans at El Alamein, Egypt. He was being transported aboard the Italian ship, SS *Sebastiano Venier*, to Italy with about 2,000 British, South African, New Zealander and Australian POWs when she was hit by a torpedo from the submarine, HMS *Porpoise*, about five miles south of Navarino on the Greek Peloponnese on 9th December 1941. She was not flying a POW flag. The ship was beached at Point Methoni near Pilos but 320 lives were lost, including Walter (El Alamein Memorial, Egypt).
- ° Yvonne Mary Sotham (1914–91) married John McNeil Curtis-Taylor (born 1911) in 1939.
- ° Richard John Sotham (1917–42), born at Timaru, married Gwenyth Florence Battson (born 1920) on 1st September 1941 at St Heliers Presbyterian Church. They lived at Thames, Coromandel, where she was born. He served as a pilot officer in the Royal New Zealand Air Force during the Second World War (413717). He was on a ferry flight over the Atlantic when

The Alamein Memorial is the entrance to El Alamein War Cemetery. The memorial commemorates almost 12,000 servicemen of the Commonwealth who died in the Western Desert campaigns of the Second World War and have no known grave. The Land Forces panels commemorate more than 8,500 soldiers of the Commonwealth who died in Egypt and Libya and in Eighth Army operations in Tunisia up to 19th February 1943. It also commemorates those who died in Syria, Lebanon, Iraq and Persia. The Air Forces panels commemorate over 3,000 airmen who died in Egypt, Libya, Syria, Lebanon, Iraq, Greece, Crete, the Aegean, Ethiopia, Eritrea, the Somalilands, Sudan, East Africa, Aden and Madagascar. It includes those serving with the Rhodesian and South African Air Training Scheme. The memorial was dedicated on 24th October 1954 by Field Marshal Bernard Montgomery.

The Air Forces Memorial (Runnymede Memorial), near Egham, Surrey was dedicated in 1953 to commemorate 20,456 airmen and women who were lost on operations during the Second World War and have no known grave.

his aircraft was lost (Runnymede Memorial, Englefield Green, Surrey). Gwenyth married Edward Archie Cameron on 7th July 1948 (1911–96) at Thames. He was born at Whangarei, Northland and died in Auckland.
° Nelson Clifford Sotham (1918–97) married Mary and died in Auckland.
° Helen Rosalie Sotham (1922–2007) married twice and had two children.

St Augustine, on the Florida Atlantic coast, founded in 1565 by Spanish explorers, is the oldest continuously inhabited European settlement in the continental United States. The city was the capital of Spanish Florida for more than two centuries. On 28–29th May 1586 it was burned by English privateer, Sir Francis Drake. It was sacked again by English buccaneer, Robert Searle, in 1668. The Spanish strengthen the city's defences, including a permanent masonry fortress. The British failed to take the fort in 1702 and burned St Augustine to the ground as they retreated. In 1740 the British again failed to take the fort. The Treaty of Paris in 1763, after the Seven Years' War, ceded Florida to Britain, in exchange for Cuba and the Philippines. St Augustine became the capital of British East Florida. During the American Revolutionary War, St Augustine was a Loyalist haven. The second Treaty of Paris in 1783 recognised the independence of former British colonies north of Florida, which was ceded back to Spain. Spain ceded Florida to the United States in 1819 and St Augustine was the capital until it moved to Tallahassee in 1824. Three Seminole Wars against local Creek and Miccosukee peoples were fought during the 19th century. In 1845 Florida Territory was admitted into the Union as the State of Florida. During the American Civil War, Florida joined the Confederacy and the Union gained control of St Augustine in 1862 for the rest of the war. John D Rockerfeller had the idea of making St Augustine a winter resort. In 1885 he combined several railways to form the Florida East Coast Railway. Hotels followed and St Augustine became the winter retreat of American high society until Palm Beach and Miami gained favour in the early 20th century. However, St Augustine remained a major tourist resort. It was also a centre of civil rights protests in the 1960s, including appearances by Dr Martin Luther King, who was arrested there on 11th June 1964. In 2015, the 450th anniversary of the founding of the city was celebrated with a four-day festival, including a visit by King Felipe VI of Spain. The singer, songwriter, musician and composer Ray Charles (1930–2004), attended the Florida School for the Deaf and the Blind in St Augustine 1937–45.

- Fanny Louisa Judson (28th March 1884–April 1976) was born at St Augustine, Florida, USA and was boarding with her uncle, Henry Holmden, at Coulden's Farm, Hazelwood, Limpsfield, Surrey in 1891. She was a shop assistant in 1901. She married John Bertie Desborough (19th March 1874–15th December 1928), a mining engineer born at Sheerness, Kent, at St Mathew's Church, Auckland on 7th April 1908. He was the son of Major General John Desborough (1824–1918). They moved to England. He was living at Pinelands, Hurn, Christchurch, Hampshire at the time of his death there. Fanny's death was registered at Chichester, West Sussex. They had a daughter, Mary Margaret 'Molly' Desborough (1909–98), born at Calama, Chile. She married Harold Lewis in 1926 at Romford, Essex.
- Thomas Carter Judson (c.1885–20th August 1973) was an assistant in an engineering drawing office in 1911. He was living at Farleigh View Home, Selsdon Park Road, South Croydon, Surrey at the time of his death there.

Reginald's paternal grandfather, John Ebenezer Judson (14th November 1818–27th May 1892), was born at High Wycombe, Buckinghamshire. He married Emily née Edger (18th October 1821–1848), born at Chelwood Gate, Fletching, Sussex, in 1844 at East Grinstead, Sussex. John was an Independent Minister of Lindfield Chapel, Sussex in 1851 and at Clutton Chapel, Sussex in 1871. He married Gertrude Jane Wildsmith (4th September 1821–1858), born at Clerkenwell, London, in 1851 at Islington, London. She died at Cuckfield. By 1881 John was living with his daughter, Eleanor, at Hillside Villas, Pensford St Thomas, Somerset. He died at the Alderbury Union, Salisbury, Wiltshire. In addition to Edgar, John had three other children from his two marriages:

- William Frederick Judson (1845–16th September 1931), born at Cuckfield, Sussex, emigrated to New Zealand, where he married Emily Marian Edger (1850–16th April 1935), possibly his cousin, on 6th January 1879 at Auckland Registrar's Office. She was born at St Neots, Huntingdonshire. There were no children. They both died in Auckland.
- Eleanor Jane Judson (1852–1893) married her brother-in-law, Thomas Payne Nicholls (see below), on 2nd April 1877 at St Nicholas Church, Bristol, Gloucestershire. Eleanor had reverted to her maiden name by 1881. Thomas married Jessie Louisa Harris (1847–2nd March 1930) on 29th January 1880 at Bedminster, Somerset. They were living at 11 Exeter Buildings, Redland, Bristol in 1911 and later at 5 Glenhurst Road, Mannamead, Plymouth, Devon. Jessie and Thomas both died there. They had two sons – Thomas Bruce Nicholls (1881–1973) and Charles Donald Nicholls (1883–93).
- Gertrude Mary Judson (1855–1875) married Thomas Payne Nicholls (1849–3rd October 1934), a leather merchant born at Abingdon, Berkshire, at Clifton, Gloucestershire in 1873. Gertrude almost certainly died giving birth to her daughter, Caroline, who also died. Thomas married his sister-in-law, Eleanor in 1877 (see above).

Reginald's maternal grandmother was born at Westerham, Kent. The town's history dates back to at least 2000 BC. In the Domesday Book it appears in its Norman form of Oistreham. There is a town in Normandy of very similar name. By 1227 Henry III had granted Westerham a market charter. General James Wolfe was born there in 1727. Alice Liddell, the inspiration for Lewis Carroll's *Alice's Adventures in Wonderland*, lived in the Vicarage briefly. In 1922 Winston Churchill purchased Chartwell Manor on the outskirts of Westerham which, apart from periods in Downing Street, became his home for the rest of his life.

His maternal grandfather, Richard Holmden (20th April 1813–2nd February 1890), was a farmer born at Edenbridge, Kent. He married Ann Elizabeth née Wood (25th February 1824–15th July 1866), born at Holmes Hill, Westerham, Kent, in 1842 at St George, Southwark, London. He was a farmer of one hundred acres at Edenbridge in 1861. Ann died at Coulden's Farm, Hazelwood, Limpsfield, Surrey. Richard married Frances 'Fanny' Wood (11th November 1832–1919), sister of his first wife, c.1870 but no record has been found. By 1871 he was a farmer of fifty acres at Coulden's Farm, Hazelwood, Limpsfield, Surrey. He died at Coulden's Farm. Fanny was living with her daughter, Jessie, at The Rushetts, Edenbridge, Kent in 1911. She died at Sevenoaks, Kent. In addition to Emma, Richard had eighteen other children from his two marriages:

- Richard Holmden (16th August 1842–9th June 1897) was living in Ireland c.1871. He married Mary Elizabeth Ball (c.1848–79), who was possibly born in Ireland and died at Wellington, Somerset, almost certainly as a result of complications with the birth of her son, William. Richard was a huntsman in 1881 living at Duddiscombes, Holcombe Rogus, Devon. Later he was the licensee of the White Hart Hotel, Cullompton, Devon and died there. They had six children – Richard James Holmden 1869, Mary Anne Holmden 1872, Ada Sarah Holmden 1873, Ellen Elizabeth Holmden 1875, Henry Edward Holmden 1877 and William Alfred Holmden (1879–1917). William was serving as a private in 9th Devonshire

William Alfred Holmden's name on the Tyne Cot Memorial, Belgium.

(290762) when he was killed in action on 26th October 1917 (Tyne Cot Memorial, Belgium).
- Philip Holmden (2nd December 1843–9th February 1909), born at Edenbridge, was a grocer in 1871, living with his parents. He emigrated to Malta Bend, Saline Co, Missouri, USA in 1863 and married Sena Almeda Walker Schooley (5th August 1859–19th December 1917), born at Chillicothe, Ross Co, Ohio, USA, there on 5th October 1888. They both died in Alfalfa Co, Oklahoma, USA. They had five children – Mary Josephine Luella Holmden (1890–1975), Elizabeth Amanda Ellen Holmden (1892–1973), Edythe Anne Ella Holmden (1895–1983), John Richard Holmden (1898–1933) and Frances Victoria Holmden (1902).
- Thomas Holmden (1845–18th June 1877) never married and assisted on the family farm. He died at Guildables, Edenbridge, Kent.
- William Holmden (born 14th October 1846).
- Benjamin Holmden (born 25th April 1848).
- Margaret Holmden (2nd November 1849–1926) married William Noah Alwen (20th August 1854–27th August 1931), a baker and grocer born at Oxted, Surrey, on 5th October 1892 at Edenbridge Parish Church. They were living at London Road, Keymer, Sussex in 1901 and at Franklin, London Road, Burgess Hill, Sussex in 1911, where they both subsequently died. William had married Sarah Elizabeth Osborne (1848–90), born at Towcester, Northamptonshire, on 26th September 1878 at Brighton, Sussex. They were living at 5 Ivy Place, Keymer, Sussex in 1881. Sarah died at Cuckfield, Sussex. Wiliam and Sarah had five children:
    ◦ Frederick William Haines Alwen (1879–1965) served in the RFA (TF) as a gunner (901078). He married Lydia Chipper (née Westgate) (1881–1933) in 1921 at Newhaven, Sussex. She was the widow of Edward Chipper (1877–1920). He was living at 8 Church Hill, Newhaven, Sussex at the time of his death at 51 Longford Road, Bognor Regis, Sussex.
    ◦ Arthur Osborne Alwen (1882–1922).
    ◦ Edwin Hopcraft Alwen (1883–1948), a butcher, served in the RFA (TF) as a driver (1573 & 900654). He qualified for the 1914–15 Star by serving in Mesopotamia and Bushire (now part of Iran) from 7th December 1915. He also qualified for the India General Service Medal 1909–35 with clasp 'Afghanistan NWF 1919'. He married Ethel May Armstrong (1890–1968), born at Brighton, Sussex, in 1925 at Steyning, Sussex. He was living at 13 Old Shoreham Road, Southwick, Sussex at the time of his death at 193 Upper Shoreham Road, Southwick.
    ◦ Sarah Ellen Alwen (1886).
    ◦ Annie Alwen (1889).
- Elizabeth Anne Holmden (27th February 1852–1885) married David Chandler (born 1848) in 1882 at Sevenoaks.

- James George Holmden (28th October 1855–5th September 1925) emigrated to America and married Nancy 'Dollie' Rebecca Morton (8th December 1878–1st November 1944), born at Malta Bend, Saline Co, Missouri, on 26th September 1895 at Marshall, Saline Co. The marriage ended in divorce. He died at Malta Bend and she at Santa Ana, Orange Co, California. They had two children – Florence Mae Holmden 1896 and Leta Holmden 1898.
- Mary Martha Holmden (1857–1912), a dressmaker, married William Henry Vine (1867–1934), born at Cuckfield, on 26th March 1894 at St Andrew's Church, Portslade-by-Sea, Sussex. William had married Mary Jane Chandler (1870–92) in 1891 at Lewes, Sussex, where she was born. Mary Jane almost certainly died following complications with the birth of their son, William. In 1911 William senior was a baker and confectioner, living with Mary Martha at The Broadway, Balcombe, Sussex. They both died at Steyning. William had four children from his two marriages:
  - William Percy Vine (1892–1923) served in the RFA as a gunner (94194) and went to France on 31st May 1915. He married Elizabeth Mary Gander (born 1890) at Lewes, Sussex in 1918. He continued serving as a private in C Company RAMC (No.S/12112) at Aldershot, where he died in service on 27th December 1923.
  - Robert Henry Vine (1897–1918) was serving as a gunner in A Battery, 186th Brigade RFA (32666) when he was killed in action on 9th September 1918 (Vis-en-Artois Memorial).
  - Grace Edith Mary Vine (1899).
  - Alexandra Holmden Vine (1902).
- Edith Holmden (1858–10th September 1920) never married and died at Cullompton, Devon.
- Ellen Augusta Holmden 4th June (1860–30th August 1939) never married and died at Crockham Hill, Kent.
- Henry Edward Holmden (1862–22nd December 1943), a farm labourer, married Ann 'Annie' Marchant (January 1859–3rd April 1929), born at Lingfield, Surrey,

Robert Henry Vine, bottom left, is commemorated on the Royal Horse and Royal Field Artillery panels of the Vis-en-Artois Memorial.

in 1880 at Godstone. Henry was assisting his father on the family farm in 1881. He took over Coulden's Farm, Hazelwood on the death of his father in 1890 and was living there with his family in 1911. Henry and Ann both died at Crockham Hill, Kent. They had nine children:
  ° Henry George Marchant Holmden (1880–1923).
  ° Katherine Beatrice Holmden (1883–1901).
  ° Ellen Augusta Holmden (1885).
  ° Richard Holmden (1886–94).
  ° Charlotte Mary Holmden (1888–1910).
  ° Wilfred James Holmden (1891–1969) a twin of Winifred, served in the Army Service Corps (No.T/35506). He married Eva Jessie White (1894–1970), born at Fulham, London, in 1915 at Godstone. He was a bricklayer in 1939 and they were living at 2 Westways, Sevenoaks, Kent. They had three children.
  ° Winifred Jane Holmden (1891–92) a twin of Wilfred.
  ° Thomas Jack Power Holmden (1895–1957).
  ° Robert Alexander Holmden (1898–1984).
- Catherine Beatrice Holmden (1863–5th January 1877) died at Guildables, Edenbridge.
- Bertha Caroline Holmden (1871–3rd January 1948) married her cousin, George Alfred Wood (1867–24th June 1950), a carpenter and joiner, in 1889 at Godstone. They were living at 76 Gloucester Road, Croydon, Surrey in 1901. They were living at Sunnycroft, 25 Perryfield Road, Crawley, Sussex at the time of their deaths there. They had three children – Gilbert George Wood (1889–1968), Ethel Frances Wood (1891) and Jessica Maud Holmden Wood (1893–1978).
- Jessie Sarah Holmden (1872–28th January 1952) was living at Sunnylands, 25 Perryfield Road, Crawley, Sussex before being admitted to Goffs Park Nursing Home, Crawley, where she died unmarried.
- Frank Power Holmden (1874–1960), a bricklayer, married Isabella Dowie (1873–29th August 1952), born at Scoonie, Fife, Scotland, on 31st May 1902 at Croydon, Surrey. They were living at Carpenter's Cottage, Edenbridge, Kent in 1911 before moving to Braeside, Paines Hill, Limpsfield. Isabella died at Oxted and Limpsfield Hospital, Oxted, Surrey. They had a daughter, May Esson Holmden, in 1903.
- Arthur Power Holmden (1877–31st January 1949), a bricklayer, married Edith Friend (1881–19th June 1958), born at Wimbledon, Surrey, on 27th January 1906 at Edenbridge Parish Church, Kent. She was a barmaid in 1901. They were living at Hope Cottage, Marfitt Hill, Edenbridge in 1911. Arthur enlisted in the Royal Fusiliers on 3rd June 1916 at Guildford, Surrey (51562) and was mobilised on 27th July. He transferred to 61st Labour Company, Labour Corps (581254) on 24th May 1918 and was discharged on 4th March 1919. He died at 11 Redlane Cottages, Limpsfield and she was living there when she died at 16 St

John's Hill, Tonbridge, Kent. They had three children – Dennis Richard Charles Holmden (1907–47), Maurice Arthur Robert Holmden (1908–73) and Grace Nelly Holmden (1915).
- Alice Ruth Holmden (22nd December 1878–23rd March 1963) married James Bates (4th October 1874–19th July 1934), born at Worth, Sussex, on 25th December 1907 at Balcombe, Sussex. He was a garden contractor in 1911 and they were living at Diamond Cottage, Balcombe, Sussex. He died at Cuckfield, Sussex and she at Lewes, Sussex. They had a daughter, Frances Mary Bates (1908–85).

Reginald sailed on his own from London to Port Chalmers, New Zealand aboard SS *Kaikoura* on 26th June 1890. At the time he was aged just nine. With both parents still living, there appears to be no reason why he should have been shipped off to the other side of the world, when his siblings remained in Britain. It may be that his mother could not afford to bring up all the children, as her husband appears to have been suffering some form of mental illness. However, Edgar appears to have been relatively well off. When he died in 1922, he left £2,356/0/11 (£110,000 in 2018). Emma on the other hand left just £86/9/9 in 1930 (£5,195 in 2018).

Reginald was educated at Oratia District School, Shaw Road, Oratia, Auckland from 12th August 1891 as Stanley Judson. His parent was listed as 'F Judson of Waikomiti'. He left to attend Henderson School, Montel Avenue, Henderson, Auckland from 15th September 1892. Reginald completed a mechanical engineering apprenticeship. He was employed as a mechanical engineer and boilermaker at Senior Foundry Co, Auckland and lived at Dedwood Terrace, Ponsonby, Auckland.

SS *Kaikoura* (4,474 tons), built in 1884 by John Elder & Co for the New Zealand Shipping Co, was a three masted barque-rigged clipper-bowed ship able to carry 95,000 sheep and twenty-four passengers. In 1888 the English Footballers (rugby) travelled to New Zealand aboard her, starting a tradition that continues to this day. While in New Zealand and Australia, the team played thirty-five matches, winning twenty-seven, drawing two and losing just six. Those were the days! In 1900 *Kaikoura* was sold to the British India Steam Navigation Co and renamed *Zaida*. She was scrapped in 1907.

On 19th April 1905, Reginald married Ethel May/Maie Grice (21st August 1885–13th August 1976), born at Wharehine, Albertland, Auckland, at Mareretu, the house of Mrs EJ Flower, her sister, in Northland. They had four children:

The original Oratia School building became the school hall and library in 1963. It was destroyed in a fire in 1974.

- Vera Maie Judson (20 October 1905– 6th September 1996), born at Mount Roskill, Auckland, married George Harry Bird (2nd December 1899– 3rd May 1985), born at Lewisham, London, at Auckland on 26th April 1923. He died at Kaukapakapa, Auckland. They had two daughters:
  ○ Dorothy May Bird (1923–2000), born at Ponsonby, Auckland, married Noel Edward Lord (1945–1983). They both died at Rodney, Auckland.
  ○ Valerie Merle Bird (1927–1992) married C Sweeney of Palmerston North.
- Edgar Stanley Judson (21st April 1907–17 April 1970) married Eleanor Maria Kidd (1907–December 1947), born at New Plymouth, Taranaki, in 1934. Eleanor had married Francis William Loose (21st September 1899–18th September 1972), born at Nuneaton, Warwickshire, England, in 1927 in New Zealand. The marriage ended in divorce. Eleanor died at Stratford, Taranaki and Edgar at Taumarunui, Waikato.

Dedwood Terrace, where Reginald lived, begins on the left.

- Reginald Frank Judson (25th March 1911–17th January 1978) married Margaret Jones (5th February 1910–25th September 2009), born at Cwmnantgam, Llanelli, Wales, on 24th March 1938 at Trust Church, Ruawai. He served as a chaplain to the forces, 4th class (major), with 24th Battalion during the Second World War (31604). He was awarded the MC while serving in Italy, when he was instrumental in organising a medical aid post under heavy enemy fire. He assisted in dressing wounds and also acted as a stretcher-bearer. He had been involved in similar actions earlier in the war, LG 4th May 1944. They were living at 65 Rockfield Road, Ellerslie, Auckland in 1944. Reginald was appointed Mayor of Manurewa Borough Council 1948–53. Margaret died at Howick and he at Bucklands Beach, Auckland. They had three children, including Glyn Reginald Judson, who died in 2016 at Auckland.
- Raymond Thomas Judson (30th October 1913–4th December 2005) married Violet Strong (6th January 1911–22nd August 1988) on 10th December 1938 at Auckland, where she was born. They both died at Warkworth.

Ethel's father, Marshall Thomas Grice (17th December 1843–16th August 1931), born at Waltham, Lincolnshire, emigrated to New Zealand. He married Margaret née Cray (25th February 1851–29th July 1901), born at 15 East Street, Southampton, Hampshire, England, on 15th May 1868 at Wharehine, Rodney, Auckland. She died at Albertland, New Zealand. Marshall married Mary Roberts Bailey (1862–1951), born in New Zealand, in 1904. Marshall died at Maungaturoto. In addition to Ethel, Marshall and Margaret had seven other children:

- William Marshall Grice (8th March 1869–15th March 1961) married Mary Turner (c.1875–17th March 1942) in 1898. He died at Warkworth. They had six children – Margarette Louise Grice (1899–1969), Florence Alice Clara Grice (1900–91), Harold William Grice (1904–76), Edmund Marshall Grice (1908–76), Evelyn Mary Grice (1911) and Charles John Grice (1916–45).
- Harriette Marian Grice (3rd February 1872–20th May 1909) had a daughter, Phyllis Dorothy Grice (25th April 1896–6th December 1956). Harriette married Friedrich Wilhelm Wellm (c.1859–1920), a seaman born in Germany, in 1897. He was naturalised on 26th October 1899. Harriette died at Wharehine. They had two sons – Frederick Percy Wellm (1898–1986) and William Edmund Wellm (1905–2000).
- Frederick Henry 'Harry' Grice (1873–1935), a carpenter, married Sarah Edith Keane (1873–1946) in 1904. He died at Dargaville. They had seven children – Marjorie Eunice Grice 1907, Freda Maud Grice 1908, Frederick George Bertram Grice 1909, Gladys Mary Grice 1910, Doreen Mildred Grice 1912, Evelyn Una Grice 1915 and Thomas Marshall Grice 1917.
- Annie Louise Grice (23rd June 1875–1st June 1959) married Edmund John Flower (26th December 1869–28th January 1931), born at Maungaturoto, Kaipara, on

29th December 1896. They had three children – William Edmund Leslie Flower (1898–1988), Edna Lillian Flower (1900–89) and Winnifred Margaret Flower (1903–2000). William Edmund Leslie Flower enlisted voluntarily on 27th August 1918 at Hastings (91876), described as a postal clerk working for New Zealand Post & Telegraph, living at Waipawa, Hawkes Bay, 5' 8" tall, weighing 158 lbs, with dark brown hair, brown eyes, dark complexion and his religious denomination was Congregationalist. He was serving in the Territorial Post & Telegraph Engineers at the time. He was posted to A Company, 50th Reinforcements on 10th October and was in hospital with influenza 18th–23rd October. He had a discharge medical at Trentham Military Hospital on 21st November and was demobilised next day. Annie married Francis Thomas Moore (19th May 1867–17th November 1940), born at Porirua, on 21st July 1934 at Tauranga. He died at Auckland and she at Epsom, Auckland.

- George Bertrum Grice (7th April 1877–6th March 1931), a blacksmith, married Evelyn 'Eva' Jane Heaps (1883–1927) in 1901. She died in Auckland and he at Ashburton, Canterbury. They had three sons – Thomas Lionell Grice (1901–63), George Reginald Grice (born and died 1903) and George Bertram Grice (1904–95).
- Charles Percy Grice (2nd November 1878–1st August 1960), a platelayer, married Jeannie Downie (6th January 1882–1962), born at Pahi, Northland, in 1902. They both died at Pukekohe. They had nine children – John William Marshall Grice (1903–73), Leonard Percy Grice (1905–87), Margaret Doreen Grice (1906–75), twins Rex Douglas Grice (1909–85) and Maxwell Woolsey Grice (1909–76), Jean Winnifred Grice (1912–63), Thomas Ralph Grice (1917–39), Florence Mary Grice (1920–2002) and Zoe Grice (1924–2001).
- Florence Margaret Grice (6th February 1884–20th January 1964) married Ernest David Stallworthy (7th February 1883–14th May 1967), born at Aratapu, Kaipara, Northland, in 1905. He was a manager in 1947 and they were living at 6 Sarsfield Street, Ponsonby, Auckland. They had three daughters – Hannah Freda Stallworthy 1908, Amy Florence Stallworthy 1914 and Florence Jean Stallworthy 1919.

Reginald enlisted on 19th October 1915 in the New Zealand Rifle Brigade, New Zealand Expeditionary Force, described as 5' 7½" tall, weighing 147 lbs with brown hair, fair complexion and blue eyes. He was assigned to 9th Reinforcements, 3rd New Zealand Rifle Brigade (24/1699). He embarked for Egypt aboard HMNZT *37 Maunganui* on 8th January 1916 and transferred to 2nd Auckland on 15th March. Soon after arrival he transferred to 15th North Auckland Company, 1st Auckland and sailed for France in April.

Promoted temporary lance corporal on 3rd April and temporary corporal on 1st August. He was seriously wounded in the abdomen on the Somme on 15th September. It was later discovered that eight pieces of shrapnel had lodged

1st General Hospital occupied most of the large buildings in Étretat, including La Villa Orphée, the former summer home of the composer Jacques Offenbach.

near his heart. He relinquished temporary corporal on being wounded and was admitted to 1st General Hospital, Étretat on 18th September. Reginald was evacuated to Britain and was admitted to 1st New Zealand General Hospital, Brockenhurst, Hampshire on 27th September.

Reginald transferred to A Company, New Zealand Command Depot, Codford, Wiltshire on 3rd February 1917. He was appointed temporary sergeant while employed on the staff as foreman of works at the New Zealand Command Depot on 11th September. He reverted to corporal having ceased to perform the duties for which he was granted temporary rank on 8th April 1918. Next day he joined 3rd Reserve Battalion, Auckland Regiment, No.2 Reserve Brigade, Sling Camp, Bulford and returned to France on 8th May. He joined No.1 New Zealand Entrenching Battalion on 12th May and transferred to 1st Auckland on 1st June. Promoted sergeant on 21st June.

In 1914 Brockenhurst was selected for one of the large number of temporary military hospitals. Close to railway links and the port of Southampton, it was ideally situated to receive wounded from the Western Front. Initially it was The Lady Hardinge Hospital for Wounded Indian Soldiers and almost 3,000 Indian soldiers were treated before the Indian Corps was sent to Egypt in November 1915. The hospital was named after Lady Hardinge, wife of the British Viceroy of India, who died shortly before, in honour of the many hospitals she founded in India. Balmer Lawns and Forest Park Hotels were commandeered, with temporary structures in the grounds to provide additional accommodation. Within months the facilities were overcrowded and 500 extra bed spaces were provided in tents and galvanised huts, known as 'Tin Town'. Unusually for the time Indian patients were treated by British nurses. In 1916 the hospital was taken over by the New Zealanders and became 1st New Zealand General Hospital, one of three in Britain staffed and operated by the New Zealand Medical Corps. Over 21,000 casualties were treated before its closure in January 1919. In the nearby Commonwealth War Graves Commission cemetery at St Nicholas' Church, there are ninety-three New Zealanders, three Indians, a Canadian, an Australian, three unknown Belgian civilians, a South African and three British soldiers.

The building of Sling Camp commenced in 1903, but it expanded rapidly once war broke out. By 1916 it had been taken over by New Zealand forces and comprised four main sections - Auckland, Wellington, Otago, and Canterbury Lines. Its main purpose was to train reinforcements and recovering casualties. At the end of the war, there were 4,600 New Zealand troops there and it became a repatriation centre. No troopships were available due to overuse during the war and strikes. Eventually the men rioted in frustration and in the aftermath they were put to work carving an enormous Kiwi into the chalk hillside in February and March 1919. Although Sling Camp was removed in the 1920s, the Bulford Kiwi remains to this day. It covers 6,100 m2 and is 130m long. In the post-war years the Kiwi Polish Co maintained it and during the Second World War it was covered over to prevent it being used by enemy aircraft as a navigation marker. In 1948 local Boy Scouts removed the covering and added fresh chalk. Military units then took over the maintenance including the author's own unit, 249th Signal Squadron (AMF(L)), in the 1980s and 90s.

Awarded the DCM for his actions near Hébuterne, France on 24th July 1918. He led a patrol along a sap and continued bombing the enemy, forcing them to retreat for a distance of 550m. This enabled the troops who were following to garrison and hold the captured trench. His skill in organising the trench during the next twenty-four hours under heavy bomb and machine gun fire was inspiring and he personally bombed the enemy out of an angle in the sap where they were collecting, LG 30th October 1918. Awarded the MM for his actions near Puisieux-au-Mont, France on 16th August 1918 when he led a bayonet charge against a machine gun nest that was harassing the Otago Battalion, which was fighting in Ford Wood and Crayfish Trench. Two machine guns and sixteen men were captured, LG 30th October 1918.

Awarded the VC for his actions near Bapaume, France on 26th August 1918, LG 30th October 1918. Eight men have been awarded all three major gallantry awards for soldiers, but none achieved this in just thirty-four days. Reginald suffered the effects of gas in September. He transferred to No.5 Officer Cadet Battalion, Trinity College, Cambridge on 21st October and was commissioned on 14th February 1919, supernumerary to establishment in the New Zealand Staff Corps. The VC, DCM and MM were presented by the King in the ballroom of Buckingham Palace on 26th February 1919. Reginald was admitted to 2nd New Zealand Hospital, Walton-on-Thames, Surrey 20th–29th May 1919 with deafness. He embarked for New

Zealand on SS *Marama* on 9th June 1919 and arrived on 28th July. Reginald was struck off strength of the New Zealand Expeditionary Force on 14th August 1919 and was absorbed into the Unattached List, General List. His address at that time was 20 Dedwood Terrace, Ponsonby. Auckland. Reginald was promoted lieutenant on 1st October 1919 and joined the Permanent Staff Corps of the New Zealand Military Forces. He was based at Auckland 1920–29.

Reginald and Ethel divorced in 1920. She married Edward Roy Becroft (20th May 1887–16th October 1946), born at Albertland, in 1921. He died at Port Albert and Ethel at Albertland. They had two children – Clifford Roy Becroft (5th October 1922–25th March 1992) and Philip Verne Becroft (25th November 1925–17th April 1988).

Reginald married Kate Marion Lewis née Bailey (28th October 1888–April 1977), born at Maungaturoto, a draper, on 27th March 1928 in Auckland. Kate was living at 19 Pollen Street, Grey Lynn, Auckland in April 1916, later at Green Lane, Great South Road, Auckland. They had a daughter, Claire Marion Judson (22nd March 1929–2nd November 2014).

Kate had married George Forrester Lewis (21st October 1894–2nd October 1917), a farmer born in Sydney, New South Wales, Australia, at Hamilton on 20th April 1916. They lived at 19 Pollen Street, Grey Lynn, Auckland, later at 111 Green Lane Road, Remuera, Auckland. He was medically examined on 19th January 1916 at Kaipara and enlisted on 7th

From 1803 to 1916, young military officers had been trained in conjunction with University education through the Officers' Training Corps, forming the National Reserve of Officers. However, due to the unforeseen number of casualties in the first two years of the Great War, conscription was introduced in 1916 and the Officer Cadet Battalions were formed. They produced 73,000 commissioned officers at locations around the country, including 5th OCB, based at Trinity and St John's Colleges, Cambridge.

SS *Marama* was built by Caird & Co at Greenock for the Union Company of New Zealand in 1907. In the Great War she was commandeered as HMNZHS No.2. She was refitted in 1920 for trans-Pacific services to San Francisco and Vancouver. In 1925 she was converted to oil and employed on the Tasman run. She was broken up in Osaka in 1938.

February (24026). He was a senior cadet in 15th North Auckland Regiment at the time, described as 5′ 9½″ tall, weighing 140 lbs and his religious denomination was Church of England. He was a farmer working for F Lewis Bickerstaffe. His next of kin was his brother, Roderick Forrester Lewis of Pukerata, Kaipara until he married Kate. George was posted to A Company, 13th Reinforcements on 12th February and was admitted to Trentham Military Hospital with influenza 15th–16th February. He overstayed his leave from 3.15 p.m. on 30th April to 10.30 a.m. on 4th May, for which he forfeited five days' pay. He overstayed his leave again on 24th May, for which he forfeited a days' pay. In the field he lost a shirt and his pay was reduced by 6/3d to replace it. George embarked at Wellington on 30th May aboard HMNZT *54 Willochra*, sailed next day and disembarked at Devonport, England on 26th July. While aboard, he was awarded seven days detention on 7th July. He was posted to Auckland Company, 3rd Reserve Battalion, Sling Camp, Bulford on 27th July and to the Machine Gun Depot, Grantham on 14th September. He was admitted to Grantham Military Hospital with pyrexia 5th–20th September. George went to France on 1st November and joined the New Zealand Base Depot, Étaples on 3rd November. He was posted to No.2 Company, New Zealand Machine Gun Corps on 14th November. On 28th December he was evacuated sick to 3rd New Zealand Field Ambulance and was admitted to 1st Australian Casualty Clearing Station on 1st January 1917, transferring to 2nd Australian General Hospital, Boulogne with otitis media on 3rd January. He embarked at Boulogne for England aboard HMHS *Cambria* on 13th February and was admitted to No.2 New Zealand Hospital, Walton-on-Thames. On 2nd March he transferred to the New Zealand Convalescent Hospital, Hornchurch and was sent on leave 5th–20th March, then reported to the Machine Gun Depot, Grantham. He embarked for France on 6th June and joined the Machine Gun Corps Base Depot, Camiers next day. He returned to his unit on 24th June and was killed in action on 2nd October 1917 (Tyne Cot Memorial, Belgium).

Kate's father, William John Bailey (1845–15th June 1927), born in Birmingham, Warwickshire, England, married Emma Barrington (15th March 1848–10th June 1897), also born in Birmingham, in 1880 at Aston, Warwickshire. He was a beer housekeeper in 1881 and they were living at 52 St Luke's Road, Birmingham. They emigrated to New Zealand and lived at Maungaturoto.

In July 1924 a medical report concluded that Reginald was suffering total nervous exhaustion. A heart condition was detected, probably resulting from his exposure to phosgene gas in September 1918. Due to his war wounds and the effects of gas

George Forrester Lewis is commemorated in the New Zealand Apse of the Tyne Cot Memorial. His name is on the far right.

Mount Albert Grammar was founded in 1922 as a subsidiary of Auckland Grammar School. It was originally for boys but became co-educational in 2000. Boarding accommodation opened in 1927. A former pupil was Sir Robert Muldoon, New Zealand Prime Minister 1975–84.

he had two periods of extended sick leave in 1924 and 1934. On 21st April 1929 he attended the presentation of new Colours to the Auckland Regiment by the Governor-General, Sir Charles Fergusson. That October Reginald was appointed Adjutant, Taranaki Regiment and Area Officer at New Plymouth. He attended the New Zealand VC Dinner in Wellington on 9th November. He was promoted captain and applied for a four months extension of service to increase his pension benefits on reaching fifty-five years, which was approved. Reginald transferred to the Retired List on 31st January 1938.

Reginald was employed as secretary to the principal of Mount Albert Grammar School 1938–39. In 1938 he was one of six candidates who stood for selection for the National Party in Auckland East, but was not selected. In 1939 Reginald was voted onto Auckland City Council for the Citizens and Ratepayers Association until 1947.

On 21st October 1939 Reginald attested and was recalled on 23rd November from the National Military Reserve (5045). He was posted to No.4 Platoon, Oil Tanks, Auckland and was appointed captain the same day. His address at the time was 21 (or 11) Ely Avenue, Remuera. On 2nd January 1940 he commanded a group of ex-servicemen at Auckland Town Hall when Major General Bernard Freyberg VC was given a civic welcome. Reginald was granted annual leave 4th–17th January 1941. On 27th August 1942 he was posted from 5th Battalion, Auckland Regiment as a temporary captain (seniority 4th December 1941) to Army HQ, Wellington and retained the appointment of OC No.2 Post, Guard Vital Point. On 7th September 1942 he transferred to the Territorial Force, Guard Vital Point, Auckland (800942). He was admitted to Auckland Public Hospital from No.2 Guard, Guard Vital Point 3rd–12th April 1943. On 31st December he was transferred to 1st Battalion, Auckland Regiment but remained seconded to Army HQ. He transferred to the National Military Reserve Guard Company for Guard Vital Point, Auckland on 28th March 1945 and was promoted temporary major on 1st May. Reginald transferred to the Retired List on 16th September 1946.

He became a farmer at Mangonui before returning to Auckland. He address in April 1957 was 29 Speight Road, Kohimarama, Auckland. Reginald died at Jane

Cavenis Private Hospital, Mount Eden, Auckland on 26th August 1972. He is buried in Waikumete Cemetery, Auckland (Soldiers Block M, Section 13, Plot 69). Reginald is commemorated in a number of other places:

- Judson Barracks, Linton Military Camp, Linton, near Palmerston North.
- Judson Place, Taradale, Napier.
- Judson's oak tree planted by him on ANZAC Day 1926 at Stockade Hill, Howick. It was grown from an acorn from the King's estate, Windsor Great Park, Berkshire. A memorial plaque was unveiled on 25th April 2006.
- Oratia School War Memorial gates, Shaw Road, Oratia, Auckland, dedicated by Rex Mason MP on Anzac Day 1948.

Reginald's grave marker in Waikumete Cemetery.

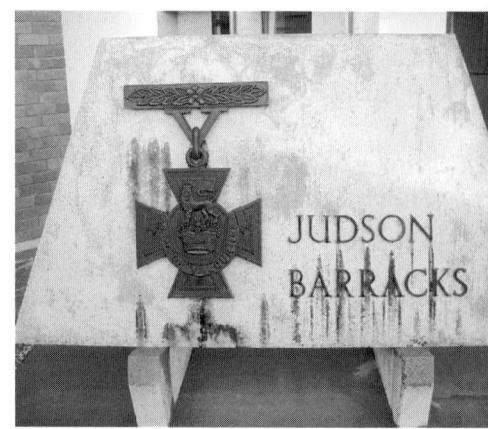
Judson Barracks at Linton Military Camp.

Oratia School War Memorial gates. Reginald's name is about one third down in the right hand column.

Judson's oak tree (Olivier Longley).

- An obelisk surmounted with a sundial in the centre of the War Memorial Wall, Caroline Bay, Timaru bears the names of eleven New Zealand VCs.
- Victoria Cross memorial dedicated by the Reverend Keith Elliott VC outside the Headquarters of the Dunedin Branch of the Returned Services Association and unveiled by Governor General Sir Charles Willoughby Moke Norrie GCMG GCVO CB DSO MC on 29th January 1956, the centenary of the institution of the VC by Queen Victoria. The memorial was later transferred to Anzac Square in front of the railway station. It was moved again to near Dunedin Cenotaph in Queen's Gardens and rededicated on 11th November 2001.
- Named on one of eleven plaques honouring 175 men from overseas awarded the VC for the Great War. The plaques were unveiled by the Senior Minister of State at the Foreign & Commonwealth Office and Minister for Faith and Communities, Baroness Warsi, at a reception at Lancaster House, London on 26th June 2014 attended by The Duke of Kent and relatives of the VC recipients. The New Zealand plaque was unveiled on 7th May 2015 at a ceremony attended by Defence Minister Gerry Brownlee and Defence Force Chief Lieutenant General Tim Keating. Corporal Willie Apiata VC read the names of the sixteen men on the plaque, which is displayed in the grounds of Parliament in Wellington.
- An issue of twenty-two 60c stamps by New Zealand Post entitled 'Victoria Cross – the New Zealand Story' honouring New Zealand's twenty-two Victoria Cross holders was issued on 14th April 2011.
- Communities and Local Government commemorative paving stones for the 145 VCs born in Australia, Belgium, Canada, China, Denmark, Egypt, France, Germany, India, Iraq, Japan, Nepal, Netherlands, Newfoundland, New Zealand, Pakistan, South Africa, Sri Lanka, Ukraine and United States of America were unveiled at the National Memorial Arboretum, Alrewas, Staffordshire by Prime Minister David Cameron MP and Sergeant Johnson Beharry VC on 5th March 2015.

The New Zealand VC plaque in Wellington.

The Judson stamp in New Zealand Post's 'Victoria Cross – the New Zealand Story' series.

The New Zealand War Service Medal was awarded to members of New Zealand armed forces, National Military Reserve, Home Guard, Merchant Navy and Naval Auxiliary Patrol Service. Qualification was twenty-eight days' full-time aggregated service or six months' part-time aggregated service between 3rd September 1939 and 2nd September 1945. Service ended by death, wounds or honourable discharge automatically qualified for the medal, About 238,000 medals were issued.

The New Zealand Long and Efficient Service Medal was the first medal awarded in New Zealand for long and efficient services. It was issued between 1st January 1887 and 22nd September 1931. Eligibility changed over time and from 1920 could be issued to all members of New Zealand Military Forces for sixteen or twenty years' service. Active service between 5th August 1914 and 28th January 1919 counted as double.

In addition to the VC, DCM and MM he was awarded the British War Medal 1914–20, Victory Medal 1914–19, War Medal 1939–45, New Zealand War Service Medal 1939–45, George VI Coronation Medal 1937, Elizabeth II Coronation Medal 1953 and New Zealand Long & Efficient Service Medal. The medals were presented to Queen Elizabeth II Army Memorial Museum by his daughter, Mrs C Sweeney, in 1982. They were received by Deputy Chief of the General Staff, Brigadier AC Hamilton. On 2nd December 2007, ninety-six medals were stolen from the Museum by James Joseph Kapa and Ronald van Wakeren, including nine VCs (Andrew, Elliott, Frickleton, Grant, Hinton, Hulme, Judson, Laurent and Upham) and two GCs. A $300,000 reward was offered by medal collector, Lord Michael Ashcroft, and Nelson businessman, Tom Sturgess. The collection was recovered on 16th February 2008 and the medals were returned to the Museum in October. Kapa was jailed for six years and van Wakeren for eleven years for this and other crimes. Upgrades to security at the Museum cost NZ$1.4 million. The VC is held by the since renamed National Army Museum, State Highway One, Waiouru.

The National Army Museum, formerly the Queen Elizabeth II Army Memorial Museum, in the military town of Waiouru, was built by 2nd Field Squadron, Royal New Zealand Engineers and opened in October 1978.

426402 SERGEANT ARTHUR GEORGE KNIGHT
10th Battalion (Canadians) CEF

Arthur Knight was born on 26th June 1886 at Franklyn Road, Haywards Heath, Sussex, England. His father, Edward 'Ted' Henry Knight (2nd October 1861–1942), also born at Haywards Heath, was a carpenter with Bagaley & Sons of Redhill, Surrey. He married Ellen née Stoner (1850–28th December 1923), born at Staplefield, West Sussex, on 3rd August 1884 at Haywards Heath. She was working as a housemaid for George Catt and family, a corn merchant, at Lunt House, Lindfield, Sussex in 1871. By 1881 she was head of household, living with some of her siblings at 7 Osborne Cottages, Cuckfield. Ted and Ellen lived at Franklyn Road, Haywards Heath and by 1891 had moved to Railway Stables, Haywards Heath. They were living at 11 Copse Road, Reigate, Surrey by 1901, at 1 Somerset Road, Mead Vale, Redhill, Surrey by 1911 and had moved to 39 Somerset Road by 1921. Arthur had three siblings:

- Lily Annie Knight (16th February 1888–1953) was a servant at The Oaks, Wray Common, Reigate, Surrey in 1911. She married Percy Wratten (17th April 1891–1953), a gardener born at Hastings, Sussex, in 1918. They were living at 39 Somerset Road, Reigate in 1921, at The Lodge, Salmons Lane, Caterham, Surrey in 1926, at Spreakley Villas, Hambledon, Surrey in 1939 and later at The Lodge, Woodhatch House, Reigate. She died at Wokingham, Berkshire and he at Reading, Berkshire. They had a daughter, Joan Lily Wratten (1919–99), who married Arthur W James in 1947 at Wokingham. They were living on City Road, Newbury, Berkshire in 1960.

Arthur was born on Franklyn Road, Haywards Heath.

- Ellen 'Nellie' Alice Knight (27th February 1890–1974) was a servant at 2 The Grange, Frenches Road, Redhill, Surrey in 1911. She married Ernest James Stoner (21st May 1893–1969), a plumber born at Cuckfield, Sussex, at Reigate

in 1923. They had a daughter, Josephine Ellen Stoner (1924–2004). She was living at 39 Somerset Road, Reigate in 1939 and married Denis Quarendon Barker (1910–84) in Surrey in 1946. Denis and Josephine were living at 63 London Road, Reigate soon after their marriage.
* Rose Knight (6th November 1892–1893).

The family was living at 1 Somerset Road, Mead Vale, Redhill in 1911.

Arthur's paternal grandfather, Stephen Knight (c.1836–1910), a journeyman carpenter born at Buxted, near Uckfield, Sussex, married Alice née Ridley (c.1841–92) in 1860 at Brighton, Sussex. She was living with her parents at Bents Cottage, Cuckfield in 1851. They were living at Middle Farm, Cuckfield, Sussex in 1861, by when she was a dressmaker. By 1871 they had moved to 2 Springfield Cottages, Cuckfield and by 1881 to 1 South Road, Cuckfield. In 1891 they were living at Wivelsfield, Sussex, where Alice died. By 1901 Arthur was living with his daughter, Alice Watts and her family, at 185 South Road, Haywards Heath. In addition to Edward they had six other children, all born at Haywards Heath:

* Thomas Jesse Knight (1863–1904), a gardener, married Ellen Elizabeth Maskell (1860–1939), born at Beeding, Sussex, on 14th May 1882. They were living at 8 The Square, Patcham, Sussex in 1891 and at Church Hill, Patcham in 1901. Both their deaths were registered at Brighton. Ellen was living at 12 Church Hill, Patcham in 1911 with her sons Albert and Arthur. They had five children:
  ○ William Frederick Knight (1885–1902).
  ○ Edith Alice Knight (1889–1967) was a servant at 38 Brunswick Place, Hove, Sussex in 1911. She married Christopher Henry Seager (1890–1965), a plumber born in Brighton, on 2nd June 1915 at Patcham Parish Church and they were living there at 12 Church Hill. He enlisted in the Royal Sussex Regiment on 11th December 1915 at Hove, Sussex (G/12005) and transferred to the Reserve next day. He was living at 35 Alpine Road, Hove at the time. He was described as 5′ 2¾″ tall, weighing 114 lbs and his religious denomination was Church of England. He was mobilised on 8th April 1916 and was posted to 10th Battalion at Chichester, Sussex on 24th May. He transferred to 23rd Training Reserve Battalion on 1st September (8889) and to 25th Garrison Battalion, Middlesex Regiment on 13th September (39135). He disembarked at Cape Town, South Africa on 7th February 1917, embarked again on 26th February and disembarked in Hong

Kong on 1st April. Awarded the Good Conduct Badge on 8th April 1918 and transferred to 40th Company RE in Hong Kong on 20th July (368879). He was discharged from the Crystal Palace, London on 18th December 1919. They were living at 350 Old Shoreham Road, Hove in 1939. He died at Brighton and she at Richmond upon Thames, Surrey. They had three children – Christopher T Seager 1916, Nora J Seager 1925 and Vera Beryl Seager 1929.
- ° Rose Ellen Knight (1892–1968) was a housemaid for Thomas Crawshay Ralston and his family at Patcham in 1911. She was a domestic servant at Stoner House, Petersfield, Hampshire in 1939. She is understood to have died at 34 Harmsworth Court, Hove.
- ° Albert Thomas Knight (born 1896) was an assistant journeyman baker in 1911.
- ° Arthur George Knight (1898–1993), a gardener, married Muriel Frances Pretty (1899–1988), a nurse born at Bishops Lydeard, Somerset, on 14th April 1928 at St John the Evangelist, Stoke-next-Guildford, Surrey. He was living at 12 Church Hill, Patcham and she at 3 Onslow Road, Guildford at the time. They had a son. By 1939 Arthur was a head gardener and an Air Raid Precautions warden and they were living at Stoner House Lodge, Petersfield.

- Alice Jane Knight (20th November 1865–1945) married Charles Frederick James Watts (1867–24th March 1946), a greengrocer born at Ditchling, Sussex, on 14th October 1893 at Cuckfield. They were living at 34 Blatchington Road, Hove in 1911 and at 47 Portland Villas, Hove in 1939. They both died at Hove, Sussex. He was living at 11 Chelston Avenue, Hove at the time of his death at 62 Pembroke Crescent, Hove. They had three sons:
  - ° James Stephen Watts (born and died 1894).
  - ° George Frederick Watts (1896–1915) served as a private in 7th Royal Sussex (G/968) and was killed in action on 28th September 1915 (Bailleul Communal Cemetery Extension, France).
  - ° Cecil Thomas Watts (1900–71) married Dorothy Ailsa Weekes Drewe (1910–80), born at Braughing, Hertfordshire, in 1939 at Hove. They were living with his parents in 1939 and at 59B The Drive, Hove in 1958. At that time they were running their business, Anne Valeting Service, Credit Drapers, at 82 Goldstone Villas, Hove.

Arthur's cousin, George Frederick Watts, is buried in Bailleul Communal Cemetery Extension.

- Minnie Knight (1867–71).
- Ann 'Annie' Knight (born 1870).
- William Knight (born 1873) was a carpenter's apprentice in 1891, living with his parents.
- Stephen Wilfrid Knight (1876–1958) was an errand boy in 1891 and later a carpenter. He married Amy Shuttleworth (1877–1953), born at West Horsley, Surrey, in 1899 at Horsham, Sussex. They were living at New Road, Wivelsfield in 1901 and at Chilgrove, near Chichester, Sussex by 1911. They had two children:
    ◦ Florence Millie Knight (1901–65) married Frederick E Hammond (1901–81), born at Thakeham, Sussex, in 1929 at Cuckfield. They had six children. She was living with her children on Grant's Lane, Bognor Regis, Sussex in 1939 but Frederick was not with her at the time of the Census.
    ◦ Stephen William Knight (1906–85) married Lilian 'Lily' Jesse Elliott (1910–80) in 1935 at Chichester, where she was born. He was a lorry driver in 1939 and they were living at 23 Caledonian Road, Chichester. They had a daughter, Dianne Knight in 1940.

His maternal grandfather, Thomas Stoner (July 1822–1879), an agricultural labourer born at Slaugham, Sussex, married Elizabeth née Falkner (c.1824–78), born at Cuckfield, Sussex, on 24th July 1847 at Slaugham. They were living at Staplefield (Upper), Cuckfield in 1851 and at 3 Forge Row, Haywards Heath in 1861. By 1871 he was a gardener (domestic servant) and they were living at 2 Harlands Cottage, Cuckfield. They both died at Cuckfield. In addition to Ellen they had seven other children, all born at Cuckfield:

- Mary Elizabeth Stoner (1848–5th June 1909) was a servant in 1861 working for George Button of Lucaster Farm, Cuckfield. She married Thomas Gates (29th July 1849–21st March 1934), born at Scaynes Hill, Lindfield, Sussex, on 30th August 1873 at St Wilfrid's Church, Haywards Heath. He was a gamekeeper in 1881 and they were living at Pease Pottage, Sussex. They were living at Tilgate, Forest Row, Sussex in 1891 and 1901 when he was a bailiff on a farm. George was still living there with his four youngest children in 1911. They both died at Slaugham. They had eight children:
    ◦ Ellen Alice Gates (1874–1915) married William Stubbs (born 1871), born at West Dean, Sussex, in 1898 at Cuckfield. He was a chauffeur in 1911 and they were living at The Cottage, Moonhill Place, Cuckfield. They had three children.
    ◦ Elizabeth Mary Gates (born 1876) was a castor oil worker in 1901 living with her parents. She married Ernest Albert Ruff (1875–1950), born at Westhampnett, Sussex, in 1903 at Cuckfield. Ernest was a gardener (domestic) in 1911 and they were living at Fair Oaks, Wineham Lane, Henfield, Sussex. They had two children. It is not clear what became of

Elizabeth but Ernest married Jessie Mignon Forty (1885–1958), born at Cheltenham, Gloucestershire, in 1922 at Paddington, London. Jessie was living with her mother at 10 Montpelier Street, Brighton, Sussex in 1939 and Ernest was living with his daughter, Sybil, at Southwood Garage, Silverdale, Lewisham, London. Ernest's death was registered at Cuckfield. Jessie was living at 5B Springfield Road, Brighton at the time of her death without issue at 14 Beaconsfield Villas, Brighton.
- Lucy Minnie Gates (1879–1960), known as Minnie, married Henry 'Harry' Ray (1874–1960), born at Forest Hill, Oxfordshire, on 24th March 1902 at Slaugham Parish Church. He was a coachman (chauffeur) in 1911 and they were living at Pease Pottage. Harry enlisted in the Army Service Corps at Brighton on 23rd April 1918 (M/401367), described as 5′ 5″ tall, weighing 110 lbs and was living with his family at Tilgate Forest Lodge, near Crawley. He joined at Grove Park next day and was posted to 776 Mechanical Transport Company ASC. He transferred to the Class Z Reserve on demobilisation from the Crystal Palace on 16th March 1919. They were living at Upper Tilgate, near Crawley in 1939. Minnie was living at 1 Hill Cottage, Pease Pottage at the time of her death at Redhill County Hospital, Surrey. Harry's death was at Horsham, Sussex. They had four children.
- Emma Gates (born 1881).
- Edith Annie Gates (1884–1942) was a housemaid in 1901 for John James Burrough, a grocer, and his family at Slaugham. She was living with her brother, Ernest, at 7 Tilbury Forest Row, Pease Pottage in 1939. She never married and her death was registered at Lewes, Sussex.
- Ernest Gates (1887–1964) was a gamekeeper in 1911, living with his father. He never married and was an agricultural labourer in 1939 living with his sister, Edith.
- Thomas 'Froggy' Alfred Gates (1890–1971), a twin of Charles, was a gamekeeper in 1911, living with his father. He married Margaret Elizabeth Hanley (1902–68), born at Newington, London, on 11th June 1932 at Slaugham. She was living with her mother and sister, Lucy, at 8 Victoria Place, Bermondsey, London in 1911. They had three daughters.
- Charles 'Chadder' Gates (1890–1962), a twin of Thomas, was a gamekeeper, living with his father in 1911. By 1939 he was a gamekeeper at The Acre, Horsham and was recorded as married.

- Thomas Stoner (born 20th March 1853) was a gardener in 1871 living with his parents.
- Andrew James Stoner (1856–1909).
- Charles Henry Stoner (1858–1913) married Emily Newnham (1852–1912), born at Wivelsfield, Sussex, in 1888 at Lewes, Sussex. She had a daughter, Daisy Emily Newnham (born 1886), who was a housekeeper for her uncle, Ernest Stoner, at Railway Stables, Haywards Heath in 1911. Charles was a whitesmith in 1891 and

they were living at 5 Pelham Place, South Road, Cuckfield. In 1901 he was a fitter to the waterworks. They were still at 5 Pelham Place in 1911. They had three children:
- ° Charles Henry Stoner (1888–1964), a gardener, enlisted in 9th Royal Sussex at Haywards Heath on 5th September 1914 (G3308). He was described as 5' 9½" tall, with fresh complexion, light blue eyes, dark brown hair and his religious denomination was Church of England. He went to France on 31st August 1915 and was promoted sergeant on 18th March 1916. He was shell shocked on 20th August and returned to England on 3rd September. On 16th August 1917 he attended a special medical board at 78 Lancaster Gate, London and was found to be suffering from shell shock. He was discharged on 6th September 1917, giving his home address as 38 Gower Road, Haywards Heath. He was unable to return to his previous employment as he had to use crutches and was granted a weekly pension of £1/12/6, to be reviewed after six months. He was issued Silver War Badge No.249159 on 26th September. He married Alice Hodges (born 1887) in 1918 and they had four children. He was living at 1 Lyoth Villas, Lyoth Lane, Lindfield in August 1919. Charles emigrated to Canada and died in British Columbia.
- ° Andrew James Stoner (1890–1962) married Edith Leeves (1892–1965), born at Buxted, Sussex, in 1916. She was a housemaid at Lindfield Place, Lindfield in 1911. He was a bookbinder in 1939 and they were living at 53 College Road, Cuckfield. They had three children.
- ° Alfred Joseph Stoner (1892–1973) was a greengrocer when he enlisted as a driver in 1st Sussex Royal Field Artillery Battery, 1st Home Counties Field Artillery Brigade TF at Brighton on 6th June 1912 (1053), described as 5' 4½" tall and his religious denomination was Church of England. He attended annual training in 1912, 1913 and 1914 at Okehampton, Bordon and on Salisbury Plain. He was embodied at Brighton on 5th August 1914 with a new number (920371) and was posted to the 2nd Line on 29th October. On 28th June 1915 he was serving in 2/1st Sussex Royal Field Artillery Battery, 2/1st Home Counties Field Artillery Brigade at Westerham, when he consented to serve abroad as a TF soldier. In June 1917 he was serving in No.1 Section, 67th Divisional Ammunition Column at Blackheath and was posted to 67th Division RA HQ on 4th October. He embarked at Southampton on 7th October, went to France on 10th October, embarked at Marseille on 20th October and disembarked at Basra, Mesopotamia on 12th November. He served under CRA 18th Division and was in hospital 29th May–2nd June 1918. He joined A/336th Brigade RFA, 18th Division on 28th August. Posted to CRA 18th Division on 2nd January and embarked for India aboard HT *Northbrook* on 19th April, arriving at Bombay on 24th April. Taken on strength of No.34 Specialist Battalion (Elephanta) at Bangalore on 26th April. On 30th May he moved to Military Base Depot,

Murree Hills. Posted to No.1 Divisional Ammunition Column on 5th August. He embarked aboard HT *Merkara* at Bombay on 22nd September and was disembodied on demobilisation on 14th December 1919, giving his home address as 53 College Road, Haywards Heath. Alfred married Ruth Sandell (1893–1969), born at Holborn, London, on 5th April 1920 at Brighton. Ruth was at Holy Cross Convent, Bolnore Road, Haywards Heath in 1911. They had four children.

- Alfred William Stoner (14th March 1861–1946) was the manager of a railway bookstall. He married Mary Ann Smith (22nd November 1864–1950), born at Norwood, London, in 1885 at Croydon, Surrey. He was living at 14 Avenue Park Villas, Lambeth, London at the time of the 1891 Census but his wife and daughter, Dorothy, were living with her parents at 31 Laud Street, Croydon. Alfred and Mary were living at 14 Maley Avenue, Norwood, London in 1901 and at 44 Links Road, Tooting, London in 1911. In 1939 they were living at 13 Davidson Road, Croydon. They both died in Croydon. They had four children, all born at Lambeth:
  ◦ Dorothy May Stoner (born 1890) was a clerk in 1911, living with her parents.
  ◦ Ernest William Stoner (1891–1979) was an ironmonger's assistant in 1911, living with his parents. He married Edith Elizabeth Friend (1890–1981), born at Lambeth, on 20th March 1920 at St John the Divine, Balham, London. He was an ironmonger's manager in 1939 and they were living at Windyridge, Dartford, Kent. He died at Canterbury, Kent. Edith was living at 26 Bridgefield Road, Tankerton, Whitstable, Kent at the time of her death there. They had two sons.
  ◦ Lewis Thomas Stoner (1894–1982) was a coal merchant's clerk in 1911, living with his parents. He married Marie Lilian Lang (1896–1952), born at Lambeth, London, in 1924 at Wandsworth. Her death was registered at Croydon. Lewis married Rose Ethel Daisy Chislett née Smith (1909–2001), born at Godstone, Surrey, in 1954. She had married James Henry Chislett (1904–51), a carpenter born at Clapham, London, on 29th April 1933 at St Mary, Caterham, Surrey. James was living at 202B Queens Road, Battersea, London and Rose at 7 William Road, Caterham at the time. James was a hospital porter at London County Council Hospital, Caterham in 1939 and they were living at 7 William Road, Caterham. Rose died at East Surrey Hospital, Redhill.
  ◦ Frederick Charles Stoner (1899–1978) married Gladys Edna Pays (1899–1982) in 1927 at St Olave, London. He was a shopkeeper living at 214 Putney Bridge Road, London and she at 15 Longley Street, London at the time. Their deaths were registered at Bromley, Kent.
- George Albert Stoner (1863–1905) was an unemployed footman in 1881, living with his sister, Ellen, and siblings at 7 Osborne Cottages, Cuckfield. Later he was a house painter. He married Emily Jenner (1870–29th June 1955) in 1892

at Cuckfield, where she was born. They lived at Lindfield Villas, Haywards Heath, Sussex. He died at Brighton, Sussex. George and Emily had three children:
- ° Albert Stuart Stoner (1893–1919) was a private in 1st Royal Sussex (L/9972) in India when he died on 24th July 1919 (Nowshera Military Cemetery, North West Frontier Province, Pakistan). As the cemetery is difficult to maintain, he is also commemorated on the Dehli Memorial (India Gate).
- ° Evelyn Gladys Stoner (1895–1977) married William George Jenner (1879–1955) in 1931 at Horsham. He was a bricklayer in 1939 and they were living at 15 Ellen Street, Hove. They had a daughter.
- ° Sylvia Dorothy Stoner (1900–02).

Arthur's cousin, Albert Stuart Stoner, is commemorated on the Dehli Memorial (India Gate). It commemorates 13,300 Commonwealth servicemen. Of these, just over 1,000 are buried in cemeteries west of the River Indus, where maintenance is not possible. The remainder died on the North West Frontier or during the Third Afghan War and have no known grave. The Delhi Memorial is also the national memorial for all 70,000 servicemen of pre-independence India who died in the years 1914-21. The majority of these are also commemorated outside India on other memorials or graves. The Dehli Memorial was designed by Sir Edwin Lutyens and was unveiled by Lord Irwin on 12th February 1931.

Emily married Harry Murrant (1882–1951), a house painter born at Guildford, Surrey, in 1908 at Horsham, Sussex. They were living at 6 Park View Terrace, Horsham in 1911 and had moved at 70 New Street, Horsham by the early 1920s, where Emily subsequently died. They had a daughter.

- Ernest Stephen Stoner (1866–1933) was a railway porter in 1881, living with his sister, Ellen, and siblings at 7 Osborne Cottages, Cuckfield. By 1891 he was lodging with his sister, Ellen and family, at Railway Stables, Cuckfield. He married Harriett French (1868–1909), born at Cuckfield, in 1892 at Brighton. She was a servant at Holly Wood, Cuckfield in 1891. They were living at Market Place, Haywards Heath in 1901. He was living with his children at Railway Stables, Haywards Heath in 1911. Living with them was his niece, Daisy Emily Newnham, recorded as Daisy Stoner, housekeeper. He was living at 5B Wharf Road, Eastbourne in 1918. Both their deaths were registered at Cuckfield. They had six children, all registered at Cuckfield:
    - ° Ernest James Stoner (1893–1969), a plumber, married his cousin, Ellen 'Nellie' Alice Knight (1890–1974), in 1923 at Reigate, Surrey. She was a servant at 2 The Grange, Frenches Road, Redhill, Surrey in 1911. They had a daughter.

- Clement Stephen Stoner (1894–1974) married Dorothy Viola Attwood (1894–1961) in 1918 at Cuckfield. He was a hairdresser in 1939 and they were living at 24 Junction Road, Burgess Hill, Cuckfield. They were living at 89 Church Road, Burgess Hill at the time of Dorothy's death there. They had three daughters.
- Archibald Maurice Stoner (1896–1922) was a journeyman butcher in 1911, lodging at 11 Gladstone Cottages, Barcombe, Sussex. He enlisted in the Royal Navy (J/4922) and reached the rank of petty officer. He married Henrietta Mabel French (1896–1984), born at Shoreditch, London, in 1919 at Steyning, Sussex. His death was registered at Alverstoke, Hampshire. They had two children. Henrietta married William George Barnden (1891–1943), born at Brighton, in 1937 at Worthing, Sussex. They were living at 7 Orchard Parade, Lancing, Sussex at the time of his death at Worthing Hospital. Her death was registered at Brighton. William had married Gladys Irene Carter (born 1894) in 1915 at Steyning and they had a son in 1918.
- Harold Victor Stoner (1898–1993) married Gladys Ruby Long (1900–93) in 1922. Her birth was registered at Brighton and she was fostered by Ezra, a brewer's foreman, and Mary Richardson, of 116 Malling Street, Lewes in 1901. Harold was a postman and Gladys was a stationery shop assistant in 1939, living at 122 South Road, Cuckfield. Her death was registered at Haywards Heath. He was living at Flat 33, Elizabeth Court, 1 The Avenue, Croydon, Surrey at the time of his death there.
- Cyril Thomas Stoner (1900–1965) was a hairdresser living at 5B Wharf Road, Eastbourne when he was called up for service in the Rifle Brigade on 20th August 1918 at Brighton (60022), having been deemed to have enlisted on 4th August. He declared previous service in the Post Office Rifles. He joined at Winchester next day, was posted to 53rd Battalion on 21st August and was appointed acting paid lance corporal on 21st March 1919. He transferred to 51st Battalion on 22nd October and was based at Benrath, Dusseldorf, Germany and was discharged on 3rd April 1920. He married Violet Maude Coleman (1904–90) in 1923 at Eastbourne, Sussex, where she was born. They were living at 46 Langley Road, Eastbourne when he died at St Marys Hospital there.
- Percival John Stoner (1904–95) was educated on TS *Arethusa* on the Thames. The ship prepared boys for maritime careers. He enlisted in the Royal Navy as a boy 2nd class aboard HMS *Ganges* on 26th February 1920 (J96567), described as 4′ 11¼″ tall, with brown hair, blue eyes and fresh complexion. He was promoted boy 1st class on 10th October and served on HMS *Orion* 26th January 1921 and HMS *Iron Duke* 9th March. He passed education for men's rating on 2nd November 1922 and on his eighteen birthday (17th November 1922) signed on as an ordinary seaman for twelve years, by when he had grown to 5′ 3¾″ tall. He passed education for petty officer on 5th December and was promoted able seaman on 7th May 1923.

He served aboard HMS *Excellent* 24th October, HMS *Victory I* 27th April 1924 and HMS *Revenge* 6th January 1926. Awarded the Good Conduct Badge on 17th November 1925. Appointed acting leading seaman on 17th February 1927 and passed proficiency for petty officer on 28th March. He returned to HMS *Victory I* on 11th January 1928 and was promoted leading seaman on 17th February. Drafted to HMS *Vernon* 26th September and HMS *Warspite* 23rd January 1929. On 9th January 1930 he qualified in seamanship for warrant rank. He was presented the Greek Medal and Diploma of Naval Valour on 5th September but the circumstances are unknown. Percival joined HMS *Excellent* on 1st January 1931, passed education for warrant rank on 30th April and was recommended for the rank on 31st May. Appointed acting petty officer on 10th November. He qualified as and was appointed gunner's mate on 27th July 1932. Appointed acting gunner RN on 1st October. Percival married Patricia Long in New Zealand in 1936. She was reportedly born in England c.1900. He was based at Portsmouth, Hampshire in 1939, living with his daughter, Jill, at 65 Wadham Road. The entry for his spouse was redacted from the Census. He reportedly died at Auckland, New Zealand and she in New Zealand c.2004. They had two children.

Arthur was educated at St John's School, Meadvale, Surrey and Redhill Technical & Trade School. He was a choirboy at St John the Evangelist Church, Redhill and was a member of the Reigate Company of the Church Lads' Brigade. He worked as an odd boy in Budder's Rag and Bone Yard, Reigate before 1901 and then became an apprentice carpenter and joiner with Bagaley & Sons Builders, Redhill. He emigrated to Canada in June 1910, where he worked as a carpenter at Regina, Saskatchewan. He lived at 1843 Rae Street and later at 1646 Albert Street (North) in Regina.

In 1840 a claim for compensation was made against the London, Brighton & South Coast Railway Co for the loss of grazing and other rights when it built the railway across common land. Four years later it was decided to spend one third of the compensation on the poor rate and two thirds on a new National School at St John's, which opened in 1845. It is still operating as a Community Primary School (Ian Capper).

Arthur is understood to have served for a year in the Territorial Force in England before he went to Canada. He enlisted in 46th Battalion at Regina on 19th December 1914 (426402), described as 5′ 9″ tall, weighing 160 lbs, with fair complexion, blue eyes, fair hair and his religious denomination was Church of England. He carried out basic training with the 1st Reinforcement Draft. In his will, completed in May 1915, he left everything to his mother. Arthur embarked

St John the Evangelist Church, Redhill was built in 1843. Aisles were added in 1867 but in 1889 it was remodelled by John Loughborough Pearson, founder of modern Gothic architecture in England. The original building was replaced with a new nave and chancel but retained the aisles. In 1895 a new southwest steeple was added and eight bells by Mears & Stainbank were installed. One of the stained glass windows is a memorial to Field Marshal Earl Kitchener. The church has suffered considerable elemental damage. It was struck by lightning in 1945, causing damage to the interior. In March and October 1987 severe storms caused extensive damage to the roof and in January 1990 storms again damaged the roof, which had to be replaced.

on SS *Elele* on 5th July 1915, arriving in Britain on 18th July. He assigned $15 per month from his Army pay to his mother. On 19th July he transferred to 32nd Reserve Battalion at Shorncliffe, Kent, where he carried out further training. He was charged with being absent without leave on 14th August and forfeited seven days' pay. On 28th August he transferred to 10th Battalion and sailed for France, arriving next day.

On 19th November, Arthur was admitted to 3rd Canadian Field Ambulance where he was diagnosed with albuminuria and nephrites in the kidneys. He was transferred to No.2 Casualty Clearing Station the same day and to 1st Canadian General Hospital, Étaples on 21st November. He was evacuated to England aboard HMHS *Stad Antwerpen* on 8th December suffering from myalgia and was admitted to Manor Court VAD Hospital, Folkestone, Kent and was the same day, on the strength of 9th Reserve Battalion, Shorncliffe. On 18th January 1916 he transferred to Granville Canadian Special Hospital, Ramsgate, Kent and was on the strength of the Canadian Casualty Assembly Centre, Folkestone from 15th February. On 4th May he was discharged to the Canadian Casualty Assembly Centre. A medical board at Shorncliffe the same day declared him fit for twelve weeks' light duties and he was attached to Granville Canadian Special Hospital for base duties 9th May–4th August, then returned to the Canadian Casualty Assembly Centre under command of 1st Canadian Command Depot, Monks Horton, Hythe, Kent. A standing medical board at Shorncliffe on 3rd August declared him fit for four weeks' physical training. On 20th September a medical board at 1st Canadian Command Depot declared him fit for General Service.

Arthur was struck off strength on transfer to 9th Battalion on 22nd September. He transferred to 10th Battalion on 27th September and sailed for France, arriving next day. He was appointed lance corporal on 16th June 1917. **Awarded the Belgian**

Croix de Guerre, LG 12th July 1918. Appointed acting corporal with pay on 22nd August and was promoted corporal on 25th September. He was granted fourteen days' leave in Britain 17th November–3rd December. On the night of 9th/10th December he was in charge of C Company's ration party at Lievin. He was carrying a bag of rations from the train in the dark at 7.30 p.m., when his coat caught in some loose barbed wire. He tripped and injured his left ankle. He told his comrades that it was

The Manor House at 38 Manor Road, Folkestone, built c.1900 for the Earl of Radnor, was converted into a VAD hospital during the Great War. The building has since been converted into apartments.

The Belgian Croix de Guerre was established by Royal Decree on 25th October 1915, primarily for bravery or other military virtue on the battlefield. It was re-established on 20th July 1940 by the Belgian government in exile to recognise bravery and military virtue but could also be awarded to units. It was re-established again on 3rd April 1954, but only for individuals. The Croix de Guerre in the Great War was also awarded for three years service on the front line and for good conduct on the battlefield. It was also awarded to volunteers aged forty or more or younger than sixteen after a minimum of eighteen months service, to escaped prisoners of war and to military personnel placed on inactive duty because of injury.

The Granville Hotel in Ramsgate, designed by Edward Welby Pugin, son of Augustus Pugin, opened in 1869. It became a spa hotel, with more than twenty-five different kinds of baths, in December 1871. In January 1915, the Granville was requisitioned and became The Granville Canadian Special Hospital. It accepted its first patients on 20th November 1915, although it was not officially opened until 30th June 1916. By April 1917 it had 809 patients. Because of air raids in the Ramsgate area, a more suitable location was sought in Buxton, Derbyshire. The move began in late October 1917 and by 8th November the new site was ready to receive patients. The Granville reopened in 1920. A corner of the hotel was destroyed by enemy action on 12th November 1940 but there were no casualties. It remained a hotel until 1946 and has since been converted into apartments and renamed Granville House, which was Grade II listed in 1973.

just a scratch and nothing to worry about but the following morning his ankle had swollen significantly. He was admitted to 1st Canadian Field Ambulance on 11th December and returned to duty on 15th December. Arthur attended the Machine Gun School 26th December–14th January 1918.

On 3rd March 1918, Arthur was appointed lance sergeant and acting sergeant on 10th August. **Awarded the VC for his actions at Villers-lès-Cagnicourt, France, on 2nd September 1918, LG 15th November 1918.** The following day at about 3 p.m. he was struck in the head by a shell fragment 450–550m 'left of Buissy'. He was rushed to a field ambulance near Hendecourt but died shortly afterwards. He is buried in Dominion Cemetery, Hendecourt-lès-Cagnicourt, near Arras (I F 15). The VC was presented to his parents by the King at Buckingham Palace on 19th December 1918. His sisters were also present. Arthur is commemorated in a number of other places:

The plaque outside 1843 Rae Street, Regina, where Arthur once lived. The house is not the original.

Arthur's grave in Dominion Cemetery. Also buried there is Lieutenant Alex Campbell-Johnston, who was involved in William Metcalf's VC action, and his brother, Ronald Alfred Campbell-Johnston.

The Saskatchewan War Memorial commemorates those who died in the two World Wars, Korean War and during military training and peacetime operations. The first part, dedicated in November 1995 by former Lieutenant Governor, Jack Wiebe, includes the names of 6,000 people from Saskatchewan who died in the Great War. The second dedication was in October 2005, the Saskatchewan centennial, by former Lieutenant Governor, Lynda Haverstock, and includes the names of 5,000 more people who died after the Great War.

- Saskatchewan
    - Knight Crescent, Regina.
    - Plaque at his former home at 1843 Rae Street, Regina.
    - Saskatchewan War Memorial, Regina.
- Ontario
    - Victoria Cross obelisk to all Canadian VCs at Military Heritage Park, Barrie, Ontario dedicated by Princess Royal on 22nd October 2013.
    - Plaque No.86 on the York Cemetery VC Memorial, West Don River Valley, Toronto, Ontario dedicated on 25th June 2017.
    - Named on one of eleven plaques honouring 175 men from overseas awarded the VC for the Great War. The plaques were unveiled by the Senior Minister of State at the Foreign & Commonwealth Office and Minister for Faith and Communities, Baroness Warsi, at a reception at Lancaster House, London on 26th June 2014 attended by The Duke of Kent and relatives of the VC recipients. The Canadian plaque was unveiled outside the British High Commission in Elgin Street, Ottawa on 10th November 2014 by The Princess Royal in the presence of British High Commissioner Howard Drake, Canadian Minister of Veterans Affairs Julian Fantino and Canadian Chief of the Defence Staff General Thomas James Lawson.
- Two 49 cents postage stamps in honour of the ninety-four Canadian VC winners were issued by Canada Post on 21st October 2004 on the 150th Anniversary of the first Canadian VC's action, Alexander Roberts Dunn VC.
- Haywards Heath, Sussex
    - War Memorial.
    - Plaque at Town Hall.
    - A Department for Communities and Local Government commemorative paving stone was dedicated at Muster Green War Memorial on 2nd September 2018.
    - Knight Close.
    - St Wilfrid's School War Memorial.

Arthur's memorial at Haywards Heath Town Hall.

The Haywards Heath War Memorial commemorates 167 servicemen who died during the Great War and was unveiled on 30th November 1924 by the Lord Lieutenant of Sussex, Lord Leconfield. Unusually it includes those who died subsequently as a result of their war service. A plaque commemorates ninety-six people who died in the Second World War.

- Reigate
  - Borough of Reigate War Memorial, Reigate and Banstead Town Hall, Castlefield Road, Reigate.
  - St Mary's Church War Memorial, Chart Lane, Reigate.
- Named on the Roll of Honour inside St John the Evangelist Church, Redhill, Surrey.
- Boys' Brigade VC & GC Memorial, National Memorial Arboretum, Alrewas, Staffordshire.
- France
  - Ring of Remembrance (L'Anneau de la Mémoire), Ablain-Saint-Nazaire, Pas-de-Calais, France.
  - Plaque, Villers-lès-Cagnicourt, France.

The Church Lads & Church Girls Brigade Memorial Plot at the National Memorial Arboretum. The twenty-two Berberis shrubs are either side of the central walkway (Memorials to Valour).

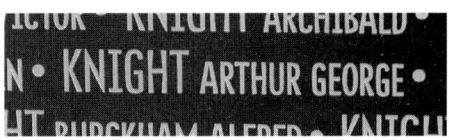

Arthur's name on the Ring of Remembrance.

In addition to the VC he was awarded the 1914–15 Star, British War Medal 1914–20, Victory Medal 1914–19 and Belgian Croix de Guerre. As he died on operational duty, his next-of-kin is eligible to receive the Canadian Memorial Cross. The VC was sold in 1966 to Glenbow Museum, 130–9th Avenue SE, Calgary, Alberta, where it is held.

LIEUTENANT DAVID LOWE MACINTYRE
Princess Louise's (Argyll & Sutherland Highlanders), attached 1/6th Battalion, The Highland Light Infantry

David Lowe Macintyre was born on 18th June 1895 at the Free Church Manse, Portnahaven, Isle of Islay, Argyll, Scotland. His father, the Reverend Archibald Stewart Macintyre (14th January 1856–20th May 1936), was born at Glenelg, Inverness-shire. Prior to Archibald the surname was also seen as MacIntyre, McIntyre or Mcintyre. He was educated at Garvan School, Locheilside and at Fort William Grammar School. In 1875–76 he studied at the Free Church Training College, Glasgow, Lanarkshire (BA). He was appointed second master at Tarbert (Loch Fyne) Public School, Argyll in 1877 and headmaster of Shiskine Public School, Isle of Arran 1879–87. Archibald studied at New College, Edinburgh (BD) and was ordained at the Free Church, Portnahaven, Islay in 1891, where he remained until 1913. Archibald married Elizabeth née Lowe (19th May 1868–3rd May 1908) on 22nd June 1893 at 25 Downie Terrace, Corstorphine, Edinburgh. She was born at 35 Grove Street, Edinburgh and died at Portnahaven, Islay. Archibald married Annie McFadyen (15th October 1884– 22nd March 1966), born at Portnahaven, on 19th December 1913 at the United Free Church, Dean Street, Edinburgh. Archibald returned to teaching and had various posts at Falkirk, Campbeltown, Kildrummy and Out Skerries in the Shetland Islands. He and Annie lived at 20 Downie Terrace, Corstorphine until his death there. Annie died at Rosslynlee Hospital, Roslin, Midlothian. In addition to David, Archibald had ten other children from his two marriages, the first six born at Portnahaven:

The Free Church at Portnahaven with the Manse, where David was born, on the right.

The Free Church Training College in Glasgow was established by the Free Church of Scotland in 1845. In 1900, it became the United Free Church Training College when the Free Church merged with the United Presbyterian Church of Scotland. In 1907 it merged with the Glasgow Church of Scotland Training College to form the Glasgow Provincial Training College, later Jordanhill College of Education. It became part of the University of Strathclyde in 1993 (Chris Upson).

- Alexander Macintyre (14th June 1894–13th February 1960) was educated at Portnahaven School, George Watson's Boys' College in Edinburgh and Edinburgh University, where he studied medicine from 1913 and joined the OTC, Royal Field Artillery in August 1915. He enlisted in General Service Cavalry at 71 Princes Street, Edinburgh on 23rd February 1916 and was posted to 2nd Cavalry Cadet Squadron (GS25015) in Kildare, Ireland on 31st March. Alexander was described as 5' 7" tall and weighed 143 lbs. He was commissioned into 2/1st Scottish Horse Yeomanry on 1st October 1916 and was promoted lieutenant on 2nd February 1917. He applied for a commission in the Indian Army on 11th October while serving at Well Camp, Alford, Lincolnshire. He had a medical as part of the acceptance process at Sutton-on-Sea, Lincolnshire on 17th October, by when he had grown 2" and added 20 lbs since enlisting. He was seconded to the Indian Army Reserve of Officers on probation on 21st December 1917 and embarked on HMT *Walmer Castle* at Devonport, Devon the same day. He

Rosslynlee Hospital opened as the Midlothian and Peebles Asylum in 1874. Two wings were added in 1898. In 1948 it joined the National Health Service as Rosslynlee Mental Hospital and became Rosslynlee Hospital in 1960. It closed in 2011 and there are plans to redevelop the site for residential use (MJ Richardson).

served in India and Egypt before returning to Britain. Alexander returned to Edinburgh University 1919–20. He was appointed senior assistant at Sendayan Estate, Kerling, Malaya in 1928. He married Margaret Alice Barnet (16th January 1892–7th December 1976), born at 38 Thistle Street, Aberdeen, Scotland, on 2nd December 1928 at St Andrew's Presbyterian Church, Penang. When they returned to Britain, they farmed at Drem, East Lothian. There were no children. Alexander died at Drem and Alice, as she was known, died at Broomhill Park, Broomhill Road, Aberdeen.
- Archibald Stewart Macintyre (1st November 1896–4th January 1899).
- George Lowe Macintyre (24th August 1898–4th November 1968) served during the Great War as a lance corporal in 5 Platoon, B Company, 4/5th Black Watch (40855). He emigrated to New Zealand aboard SS *Ruahine* in 1921 to work on his uncle's (John Macintyre) farm at Clandeboye, near Temuka, Canterbury. George married Jessie Currie (13th October 1896–12th August 1976), born at Shiskine, Isle of Arran, Scotland, there on 17th January 1924. She emigrated to New Zealand either in 1923 aboard SS *Suffolk* or SS *Ruahine* on 29th November 1921 with her future brother-in-law, Donald (see below). George and Jessie lived variously at Timaru, Canterbury, at Blenheim, Marlborough, at Dargaville, Northland, at Napier, Hawkes Bay and finally back to Dargaville, where George retired and they both subsequently died. They had six children, all born at Timaru:

- Elizabeth Lowe Macintyre (born 1924) married Malcolm Wilfred Campion (1922–c.2004), born at Christchurch, New Zealand, on 18th December 1945 at Dargaville. He served in the New Zealand Army during the Second World War. They had six children.
- Ronald Currie Macintyre (1926–91) married Mavis Edith Elaine Boakes (1928–62) on 11th May 1948 at Dargaville. They had two children. Ronald married Frances Merle Rountree on 10th March 1964 at Dargaville and they had four children. He died at Auckland, New Zealand.
- Marion Janet Macintyre (1927–34) died at Blenheim, Marlborough, New Zealand.
- Jean Freda Macintyre (1930–2011) married Mervyn Albert Wycherley (1927–89), a university technician. They were living at 135A College Street, Wanganui in 1972 and at 155 Limbrick Street, Palmerston North in 1981. They had a daughter.
- Ester Mary Macintyre (1931–2011) married Ian Gibbon Fisk on 18th February 1958. He was a director in 1978 and they were living at 407 Frederick Street, Hawke's Bay, New Zealand. They had four children.
- Heather Wilma Macintyre (1933–90).

• John Macintyre (1901–02).
• Robert 'Bertie' Dudgeon Macintyre (10th January or 30th July 1904–19th July 1972) was educated at George Watson's College, Edinburgh and Edinburgh University (BSc). He went to Malaya in 1927 as an assistant engineer in the Public Works Department, Federated Malay States in Kuala Lumpur. He was appointed Executive Engineer by 1940. He was engaged to Beatrice Mary Inglis (1904–3rd June 1979) from Cockenzie, East Lothian in October 1933. She sailed to Singapore aboard SS *Erria* from Southampton, Hampshire on 14th February 1934 and they were married on 14th March at Penang, Malaya. Bertie served as a captain in the Volunteer Force and was evacuated to Padang, Malaya then Colombo, Ceylon and finally to India, while Beatrice and their two children were evacuated from Singapore ahead of the Japanese invasion in February 1942. Their ship was reportedly torpedoed but they survived and were rescued by an Australian warship and taken to Australia. Robert joined his family there. Beatrice and her children returned to Scotland in August 1945 and were living at Parkeston, Cockenzie before moving to 4 Matilda Road, Glasgow, Lanarkshire by 1956 and were still there in 1959. They emigrated to Australia and retired to 4/60 Bower Street, Manly, New South Wales, where both Robert and Beatrice subsequently died. They had two children:
- Colin David Macintyre (c.1935–2013) became at veterinary officer in Sydney, New South Wales. He married Norma Loris Broadbent in 1964 at Muswellbrook, NSW. He later married Mairead/Maighread Forde (1936–2008), born at Ballinrobe, Ireland. They were living at 12 Cranstons Road, Dural, NSW in 1972 and were still there in 1980. They were living at

Balgowlah, NSW at the time of her death there. Colin was living at Pymble, NSW at the time of his death there. Colin had at least a daughter.
  ◦ Alison Macintyre (born c.1940).
- Donald Alexander Macintyre born (10th January 1906) was raised by Jessie Currie at Balmichael Farm, Isle of Arran following the death of his mother. He emigrated to New Zealand with Jessie, where she later married Donald's brother, George.
- Catherine Ann Macintyre (10th September 1914–13th May 1957), born at Downie Terrace, Corstophine, never married and died at the Royal Infirmary of Edinburgh.
- Jessie Jane Macintyre (13th May 1917–14th December 1947) never married and died at the Western General Hospital, Edinburgh.
- Helen Macintyre (3rd October 1918–26th January 2000) never married and died at 10 Clifton Road, Bournemouth, Dorset.
- Elizabeth Mary Macintyre (14th May 1921–29th September 1967), born at Whalsay Skerries, Shetland, married Norman Cameron Osborne (born 1925) on 19th June 1953 at the Old Church Manse, Lasswade, Midlothian. She died at the Royal Infirmary of Edinburgh. Norman married Mabel Elaine Cowdy (born December 1921), born in Armagh. Ireland, in 1968 at Morningside, Midlothian.

David's paternal grandfather, Alexander McIntyre (12th March 1806–23rd August 1877), born at Kilmallie, Argyll, was a shepherd and crofter. He married Catherine née McDonald (c.1812–20th March 1893), born at Fortingall, Perthshire, on 12th

David's paternal grandmother was born at Fortingall, Perthshire. The area is rich in prehistoric sites, including Càrn nam Marbh (Cairn of the Dead), a Bronze Age tumulus. The churchyard yew tree is believed to be the oldest living thing in Europe, over 5,000 years old. The church is on an early Christian site that is dedicated to Coeddi, Bishop of Iona, who died in 712. The current village, with its large hotel was built 1890–91 by shipowner and Unionist MP, Sir Donald Currie (1825–1909), who bought the Glenlyon Estate and village in 1885. The thatched cottages are examples of a planned village, combining Lowland Scottish and English influences, an important example of the 'arts and crafts' style.

June 1844 in the parish of Glenorchy and Inishail, Argyll. He died at Duisky, Kilmallie, Argyll and she at Ledcharrie, Killin, Perthshire. In addition to Archibald they had five other children:

 * Donald Macintyre (c.1845–5th January 1928), born at Rannoch, Fortingall, Perthshire, emigrated to New Zealand from Greenock aboard SV *City of Tanjore*, arriving at Port Chalmers, near Dunedin on 16th January 1874. He managed a sheep farm and lived at Lovell's Flat, Balclutha and at Kaitangata, Otago. He returned to Scotland and married Helen Flora Mitchell (c.1851–13th October 1940), born at Inverness, on 30th May 1901 at the United Free Church, Fort William. The couple returned to Kaitangata, where he retired.
 * John Macintyre (c.1845–24th August 1924), born at Glen Lyon, Perthshire, married Mary Bell (c.1845–1920) on 18th September 1883 at Stirling. With her baby daughter, Christina, they sailed from Glasgow aboard SV *Trevelyan* on 30th September for New Zealand, arriving at Port Chalmers on 30th December. Initially they lived with John's brother, Donald, at Lovell's Flat before moving to Clandeboye, Temuka, South Canterbury, where John had a sheep farm.
 * Alexander McIntyre (sic) (c.1850–27th February 1879) was born and died at Kilmallie, Argyll.
 * Jessie Macintyre (c.1852–9th May 1938), born at Glenelg, Inverness-shire, accompanied her brother, Archibald, to Shiskine, Isle of Arran c.1879 as his housekeeper. She married Colin Currie (1848–8th February 1919), a farmer born at Kilmory, Isle of Arran, at Torbeg, Arran on 14th February 1884. He died at Balmichael, Isle of Arran and she at Drumadoon, Blackwaterfoot, Isle of Arran. They had six children – Catherine Currie (1885–1960), John Currie (1886–1936), Jessie Ann Currie (1888–1971), Alexander Currie (1890–1969), Mary Elizabeth Currie (1892–1916) and Colina Jane Currie (1897–1960). John Currie was a mail contractor and public carrier when he enlisted in the RGA (170336) on 6th July 1917, described as 5′ 9½″ tall. He was posted to 10th Company on 4th August and to a reserve brigade on 20th December. He joined the BEF on 30th January 1918 and was posted to 41st Siege Battery on 5th February. He severely sprained his right ankle and fractured the base of his skull on 31st May and was treated at 5th General Hospital, Rouen from 7th June. On 26th June he returned to Britain and was admitted to the Military Section, London Hospital, Whitechapel next day. He was discharged on 31st December 1918 no longer physically fit for war service with right facial paralysis. John married Christian Black Jenkins (6th May 1891–1979), born at Kincardine, Perthshire, on 1st March 1922 at St Molios Church of Scotland, Shiskine.
 * Catherine McIntyre (sic) (c.1853–8th December 1940), born at Glenelg, Invernessshire, never married and moved to the Isle of Arran in her later years to be near her sister, Jessie. She died at Blackwaterfoot.

His maternal grandfather, David Lowe (1st October 1828–26th November 1901), born at Gladsmuir, Haddington, East Lothian, married Margaret née Dudgeon (1st June or 23rd May 1830 – 29th June 1906), born at West Barns, Dunbar, East Lothian, on 3rd June 1852 at Haddington, East Lothian. The ceremony may have been conducted by John Cook DD, Minister of Haddington at the time, the uncle of John Cook VC. David founded David Lowe & Sons, Horticultural Builders & Heating Engineers, in 1855, trading in Edinburgh and Manchester. In 1881 they were living at the Farm House, Blackford Avenue, Edinburgh, Midlothian and later at Gilmore Park, Edinburgh. They both died at 26 Downie Terrace, Corstorphine, Midlothian. After David's death, the firm continued under the direction of various sons until about 1947. In addition to Elizabeth they had thirteen other children:

West Barns, a small village a few miles west of Dunbar, is the birthplace of David's maternal grandmother.

- Marion Lowe (1855–12th July 1931), born at Chorlton, Manchester, Lancashire, never married and lived at 26 Downie Terrace, Corstophine, where she died.
- George Lowe (10th April 1856–1st May 1924), a horticultural builder born at Liberton, Midlothian, married Annie Moffat Fleming (c.1852–2nd August 1906) on 21st June 1876 in Edinburgh. George died at 26 Temple Park Crescent, Edinburgh. They had a son, David Lowe (1876–1932).
- Robert Dudgeon Lowe (28th December 1857–13th May 1916), a horticultural builder, married Ada Lillian Holgate (1875–2nd July 1944), born at Salford, Lancashire, in 1906 at Barton upon Irwell, Lancashire. She was a telegraph clerk in 1891, living with her parents at 1 Barrett Street, Stretford, Lancashire. They were living at 32 Darley Road, Manchester in 1911. Robert died at the Sanatorium, Ruthin, Denbighshire. Ada was still living at 32 Darley Road at the time of her death at the Memorial Hospital, Stretford, Lancashire. They had a son, Robert Cecil Holgate Lowe (1912–86), who married Mary W Kelly in 1957 at Bucklow, Cheshire.
- David Lowe (18th October 1859–20th March 1933), a heating engineer, married Annie Cossar Radcliffe (27th April 1860–4th January 1921), born at Easthouses, Newbattle, Midlothian, on 7th June 1888 at 15 Downie Terrace, Corstorphine. She died at her home at 24 West Holmes Gardens, Musselburgh, Midlothian and David at 33 Joppa Road, Portobello, Edinburgh. They had eight children:

- ○ Margaret Cossar Lowe (1889–1934) married Thomas Walker Stewart (1889–1981) on 2nd April 1920 at St Andrew, Edinburgh.
- ○ Annie Ruth Radcliffe Lowe (1891–1966) never married and died at Borthwick, Midlothian.
- ○ David Alexander Lowe (1892–1955) was commissioned in 3rd (Reserve) Battalion, King's Own Scottish Borderers on 5th August 1916. He was promoted lieutenant on 5th February 1918 and served in 4th (The Border) Battalion. He last appears in the Army List in August 1920. He married Ella Margaret Rankin (1896–1991), born at Duns, Berwickshire, on 16th February 1918 in Edinburgh. The marriage ended in divorce on February 1935. He died at St Andrew, Midlothian and she in Aberdeen.
- ○ Robert Lowe (1893–1915) was a clerk and served in 3rd (Reserve) Battalion, The Royal Scots in Edinburgh for two years before emigrating to Canada. He served for a year in 5th Royal Highlanders of Canada before enlisting in the CEF at Valcartier, Quebec on 23rd September 1914 (24370). He was described as 5′ 11″ tall, weighing 149 lbs, with grey eyes, brown hair, fair complexion and his religious denomination was Presbyterian. His brother, George, was recorded as his next-of-kin. The Battalion became 13th Battalion and sailed aboard RMS *Alaunia* from Québec on 4th October, arriving in Britain on 17th October. Promoted lance corporal on 1st December at West Down Camp South, Wiltshire but reverted to private at his own request on 15th December. He was confined to barracks for three days at Larkhill, Wiltshire on 8th January 1915 for being absent without leave. He went to France on 11th February and on 1st April assigned $15 per month from his Army pay to his mother, living at his brother George's address at 12 Braid Road, Edinburgh. Robert was killed in action on 24th April 1915 (Ypres (Menin Gate) Memorial, Belgium).
- ○ George Cossar Lowe (1894–1918) was living at 12 Braid Road, Edinburgh in September 1914. He enlisted in the Royal Scots (2503 & 350572), was promoted corporal and was awarded the MM, LG 11th October 1917). He was wounded, evacuated to England and admitted to Catterick Military Hospital, Yorkshire where he died on 7th December 1918 (Inveresk Parish Churchyard, Musselburgh, Midlothian).
- ○ William Allister Lowe (1897–1957) was educated at George Heriot's School, Edinburgh and became an insurance clerk. He enlisted in 9th Royal Scots (4113 & 351461) in Edinburgh on 30th November 1915, giving his address as 12 Braid Road, Edinburgh. He was described as 5′ 8¾″ tall, weighing 132½ lbs and transferred to the Army Reserve next day. He was mobilised on 4th January 1916, embarked at Folkestone and disembarked at Boulogne, France on 11th July and joined 5/6th Scottish Rifles from 20th Infantry Base Depot, Étaples on 23rd July. In his will dated 26th July 1916 he left everything to his mother. William was admitted to 19th

Field Ambulance with pneumonia on 31st July and transferred to No.45 Casualty Clearing Station. He transferred by 15 Ambulance Train to 10th General Hospital, Rouen on 14th August. He was invalided home on 21st August aboard HMHS *Maheno* and was treated at 4th Scottish General Hospital, Glasgow 23rd August–3rd November. He applied for a commission on 6th December 1916 while serving with 3/9th Royal Scots at Hipswell Camp, Catterick, Yorkshire. He was appointed unpaid lance corporal on 18th December and was on the strength of 4th Reserve Battalion when he joined No.16 Officer Cadet Battalion, Kinmel Park, Rhyl on 5th May 1917. William was commissioned in 3rd (Reserve) Battalion, Border Regiment on 29th September. He served in 8th Border and later transferred to 7th North Staffordshire. He embarked at Boulogne for Dover on 14th February 1918 with disorderly action of the heart and was admitted to the Royal Free Hospital. Medical boards on 13th March and 7th May found him unfit for Category A and B service for two to four months. The latter found him fit for Category C1 and he was sent to an officers' convalescent hospital. When leave ended on 28th May, he joined 3rd Reserve Battalion but was admitted to hospital again on 24th July. A medical board on 12th August found him unfit for Category A & B service for three months and C1 for two months and he was sent to an officers' convalescent hospital. A medical board on 15th October found him permanently unfit for further service and he was sent on leave after 23rd October. He relinquished his commission on account of ill-health on 19th November 1918. William married Georgina Lawler Gray (1898–1986), born at St Andrew, Edinburgh, on 9th October 1925 at Inveresk and Musselburgh, Midlothian. They were living at 1 Beulah, Musselburgh at the time of his death there. She died at Newington.
  ◦ John Lowe (1899–1994).
  ◦ James Lowe (1903–96).
- Margaret Lowe (12th February 1861–1st April 1862).
- Janet Lowe (24th October 1862–8th May 1917) was housekeeper to her father and brothers in Manchester, Lancashire. She never married and died at 33 Coates Gardens, Edinburgh.
- John Lowe (born 29th January 1864) was an ironmonger's traveller in 1891 and a wheelwright's traveller in 1901, boarding at 45 Walmer Street, Moss Side, Lancashire.
- Alexander Lowe (15th September 1865–14th December 1948), born at 18 Grove Road, Edinburgh, was educated at George Watson's College, Edinburgh, the University of Edinburgh 1884 (MA) and New College, University of Edinburgh 1890 (BD). He was ordained in Newcastleton Free Church, Roxburghshire in 1896, where he remained until his retirement. Thereafter he lived at 26 Downie Terrace, Corstorphine. He died at the City Hospital, Edinburgh.

Portnahaven School, built in 1878, where David commenced his education, is now holiday accommodation.

George Watson's College is a Merchant Company of Edinburgh school. George Watson (1654–1723) bequeathed the bulk of his fortune to found a school to provide boarding education. Land was purchased opposite George Heriot's School and the school opened as George Watson's Hospital on 17th May 1741, with a roll of just eleven boys. By 1749 there were thirty pupils and in 1842 there were eighty-six. The governors remained responsible for pupils until they were twenty-five and helped to find apprenticeships. By the 1860s the hospital school system was in disrepute and there was concern about government intervention. In 1869 the original building was sold to the Royal Infirmary of Edinburgh and the school moved to the former Merchant Maiden Hospital building in Archibald Place. Watson's was refounded as George Watson's College Schools for Boys, reopening on 26th September 1870 as a fee-paying day school with 800 boys. In 1902 the College was the first prestigious Scottish secondary school to appoint a woman head. In 1927 the site of Merchiston Castle School was secured, building commenced in August 1929 and the new building was opened on 22nd September 1932 by Prince George (later Duke of Kent). Back in February 1871, Melville House in George Square was taken over and became George Watson's College Schools for Young Ladies. In 1877 it was renamed George Watson's College for Ladies and in 1890 George Watson's Ladies College. Plans to combine the two Watson's Colleges in Colinton Road required building work and the first joint assembly was held on 1st October 1974. It became the largest co-educational school in Scotland, with over 2,400 pupils. Amongst its many famous alumni are:

- David Steel, Baron Steel of Aikwood (born 1938) KT KBE PC – Liberal Democrat politician and leader of the Liberal Party.
- Sir Malcolm Rifkind (born 1946) KCMG QC – Conservative politician.
- Gavin Hastings (born 1962) OBE – Scottish rugby captain.
- Sir Chris Hoy (born 1976) MBE – six-times Olympic gold medal winning track cyclist.

- Mary Jane Lowe (13th February 1867–4th April 1916), born at 35 Grove Street, Edinburgh, was housekeeper to her brother Alexander. She died at Newcastleton, Roxburghshire.
- Margaret Lowe (7th February 1870–5th March 1876) died at 108 Gilmore Place, Edinburgh.
- Alice Lowe (26th July 1871–14th June 1892) was born at 106 Gilmore Place, Edinburgh and died at 15 Downie Terrace, Corstorphine.
- James Lowe (4th October 1873–16th June 1947), born at 108 Gilmore Place, Edinburgh, was a horticultural builder. He died at 32 Oldfield Road, Sale, Lancashire.
- Peter Lowe (1875–27th March 1914), born at 106 Gilmore Place, Edinburgh, was a horticultural builder. He died at Newcastleton, Roxburghshire.

David was educated at Portnahaven School, Islay, at George Watson's College, Edinburgh 1907–14, where he was a cadet, and at the University of Edinburgh 1914–15 as a student of arts. He served in the OTC February – May 1915. While studying at George Watson's College and Edinburgh University he lived at his aunt Marion's home at 26 Downie Terrace, Corstophine.

David applied for a commission on 23rd March 1915, described as 5′ 8¾″ tall and weighing 140 lbs. He was commissioned in 13th (Reserve) Battalion, Argyll and Sutherland Highlanders on 8th May 1915 and was attached to 1/6th Highland Light Infantry on 16th January 1916. He sailed from Southampton, Hampshire, aboard RMS *Olympic* on 17th February. After passing Gibraltar an enemy submarine

The University of Edinburgh, originally a college of law founded in 1582, is the sixth oldest in the English speaking world. Amongst its alumni are twenty-one Nobel Prize winners. It currently admits about 6,300 students per year. Its numerous famous alumni include:

- Charles Darwin – naturalist who formulated the theory of evolution.
- Joseph Lister – pioneer of antiseptic surgery.
- Alexander Graham Bell – inventor of the telephone.
- British Prime Ministers – Gordon Brown, Lord Palmerston and Lord John Russell.
- Authors – Arthur Conan Doyle, Robert Louis Stevenson, JM Barrie and Walter Scott.
- Poet – William Wordsworth.
- MI5 Director – Stella Rimington.
- First President of Tanzania – Julius Nyerere.
- Captain Eric 'Winkle' Brown CBE DSC AFC RN (1919–2016) – world record holder for flying 487 aircraft types and undertaking 2,407 aircraft carrier take-offs and 2,271 landings.

was spotted but it was forced to break off its attack after *Olympic* fired a few shots. The ship arrived at Mudros on 24th February, where David may have joined the Battalion as it moved from there to Egypt that month. David sailed to Egypt on the *Olympic*, arriving on 17th March.

The Battalion carried out training for desert warfare. Due to the heat the soldiers trained from 2 a.m. until 7 a.m. before breakfasting and from 4 p.m. until 7 or 8 p.m. Camps were set up along the Suez Canal at Oghretina, Katia and Dueidar. The Turks made a raid in April 1916 and 157th Brigade moved eight kilometres into the desert in support. The enemy was defeated and withdrew, pursued by British mounted troops. The Battalion moved to Mahamdiya on the Mediterranean coast in early July. The Turks launched their final attempt on the Canal in August and were defeated at the Battle of Romani. The British then advanced, reaching El Arish by January 1917. The Battalion moved to El Burj and Sheikh Zowaid, only nineteen kilometres from the Turkish/Egyptian frontier by early March. It was involved in the attack on Gaza on 19th April but the British were unable to break through.

David was promoted lieutenant on 1st July and temporary captain on 31st October. The British resumed the offensive on 1st November, beginning the Third and final Battle of Gaza. There were heavy losses on both sides but the Turks began retreating again and General Allenby's force pressed on to about nineteen kilometres south of Jaffa, where they switched direction sharply eastwards and advanced to just ten kilometres from Jerusalem. The Battalion was relieved and moved to the coast at Ramleh before entering Jaffa. The Turkish guns remained in range of Jaffa, denying the use of the port facilities, so the force moved against the enemy on 21st December and pushed them back out of range of the docks. Jerusalem was surrounded and the Turks gave it up without a shot being fired. David was granted two days leave there in March 1918.

The Battalion returned to Egypt and embarked for France on 2nd April, arriving at Marseille on 10th April. David was appointed acting captain and Adjutant

Macintyre Pasha in the desert (Alasdair Macintyre).

The strategically vital Suez Canal during the Great War.

of 1/6th Highland Light Infantry in June. **Awarded the VC for his actions near Hénin Fontaine, France on 24th August 1918, and Croiselles on 27th August 1918, LG 26th October 1918.** He was wounded on the Canal du Nord at Moeuvres on 27th September by a gunshot to the left thigh. The bullet was removed at 2nd Stationary Hospital, Abbeville on 29th September and he was evacuated to Southampton from Le Havre, arriving on 2nd October. He was treated at 3rd London General Hospital, Wandsworth for about ten weeks.

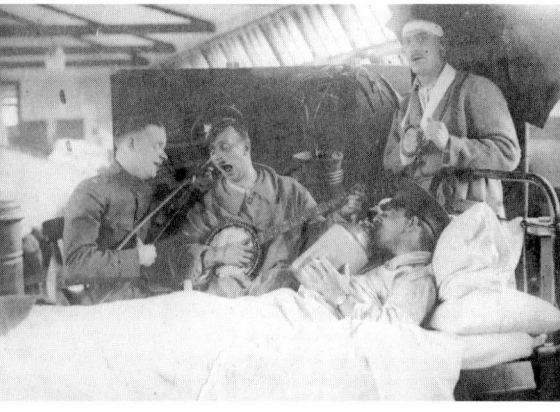

David in hospital being entertained by other patients (Alasdair Macintyre).

The VC was presented by the King in the ballroom at Buckingham Palace on 13th December 1918. A medical board at Wandsworth on 23rd November found him unfit for Category A & B Service for three months and C1 for two months. A medical board there on 16th December found him fit for Category A Service and recommended leave until 6th January 1919. While on leave he applied for a wound gratuity from 25 Downie Terrace, Murrayfield. David was discharged on 14th January 1919 and relinquished his commission on 1st September 1921, retaining the

3rd London General Hospital started life in 1859 as the Victoria Patriotic Asylum for orphan daughters of soldiers, sailors and marines. It was renamed the Royal Patriotic School and in 1914 became a Territorial Force hospital, with the staff provided by the Middlesex, St Mary's and University College Hospitals. It originally had 200 beds but eventually expanded to almost 2,000. A temporary railway enabled wounded to be brought from the south coast ports. The Hospital had its own newspaper, *The Gazette*, run by RAMC orderlies drawn from the Chelsea Arts Club. It closed in August 1920, having treated almost 63,000 patients. In recent times the Royal Victoria Patriotic Building was converted into apartments, studios, workshops, a drama school and a restaurant.

rank of lieutenant, although he does not appear in the Army List after June 1920. The people of Corstorphine presented him with an illustrated address and an inscribed gold watch and chain. The Glasgow Islay Association presented him with a smoker's cabinet, a silver inkstand and a wallet containing £131 at the 57th Annual Gathering of Natives and Friends of Islay at St Andrew's Halls, Glasgow on 19th March 1919. Over 3,000 people were in attendance.

David went back to University in 1919 to finish his studies. He and three other students decided to go to London for the Civil Service examinations in October 1919 but there was a railway strike, so they hired a taxi on Princes Street, Edinburgh. The journey took two days and the taxi broke down about fifty kilometres from London. However, they managed to board a bus and arrived just in time for the examination. David joined the Civil Service and was appointed second class clerk at the Office of Works (later Ministry of Works), London in 1920. He was promoted to assistant principal of the Secretariat Branch in 1926 and in 1936 returned to Edinburgh as Principal Assistant Secretary, Office of Works, Scotland. He was promoted Assistant Secretary, Scottish Division, Ministry of Works in January 1940 and returned to the Ministry of Works in London, where he was involved in rebuilding the House of Commons after the Blitz. He returned to Edinburgh as Principal Assistant Secretary, Scottish Division, Ministry of Works in 1943 and was Under Secretary Ministry of Works, Scotland in 1946. In this appointment he was responsible for the design, furnishing and maintenance of all Government buildings, maintenance and preservation of Ancient Monuments and the management and maintenance of Royal Park and Gardens, including The Royal Botanic Gardens, Edinburgh, the Younger Botanic Gardens, Dunoon, Argyll and elsewhere in Scotland. **Awarded the CB for this work, LG 1st January 1949**. David retired in 1959 and then undertook Civil Service Examination Boards and was for some time Chairman of Arran Piers Ltd in the 1960s, the company running and maintaining the various piers and facilities for ferries and shipping on the Isle of Arran. He was also appointed JP for Ross-shire.

David married Elspeth Moir Forsyth (9th January 1903–19th October 1996), born at 64 Hamilton Place, Edinburgh, on 20th February 1929 at Crown Court Church of Scotland, Covent Garden, London. They met as members of the London Gaelic Choir. Initially they lived at Cruachan, Wieland Road, Northwood,

St Andrew's Halls, Charing Cross, Glasgow opened in 1877. It included a grand hall holding 4,500 people, a number of smaller halls and a ballroom. In 1962 it was almost totally destroyed in a fire. The surviving Granville Street facade was incorporated into an extension of the Mitchell Library, which occupies much of the original site.

Middlesex. In Edinburgh they lived at various addresses including 20 Inverleith Row 1945–59 and 39 Buckingham Terrace from 1959. David was a fluent Gaelic speaker and they often attended the Royal National Mòd organised by An Comunn Gàidhealach (The Highland Association), Scotland's premier Gaelic festival, with the London Gaelic Choir. They had two children:

- Jean Marion Macintyre (born 28th November 1929), born at Northwood, Middlesex, was educated at Fort Augustus Village Primary School, Inverness Academy, St Georges School for Girls in Edinburgh and University College Leicester, where she qualified with a social services degree. She was appointed Personnel Manager at MacDonald's Biscuits, Hillington, Glasgow. Jean married Archibald 'Archie' Lachlan Campbell (18th March 1928–5th March 2013), born at Lochgilphead, Argyll, on 31st July 1956 at St Giles Cathedral, Edinburgh. He was a first officer in the Merchant Navy before training as a purchasing officer with Hoover at Cambuslang, Glasgow. He then joined Cummins Diesel Co, at Shotts, Lanarkshire and later at New Malden, South London. From 1975 he was with the company HQ at Columbus, Indiana, USA and retired as International Sources Planning Manager. They returned to Britain in October 2007. Archie died at Chichester, West Sussex. They had two children:
  ◦ David Lachlan Campbell (born 1959), born at Glasgow, was educated at Kelvinside Academy in Glasgow, at Reeds School in Surrey, at Columbus East High School in Indiana and at Washington University, St Louis, Missouri

David and Elspeth leaving Crown Court Church after their wedding on 20th February 1929 (Alasdair Macintyre).

The first Scottish Presbyterian congregation was established in London during the reign of King James I of England and VI of Scotland, following the Union in 1603. Crown Court Church was established near Covent Garden in 1711 and is named after a small adjacent courtyard. The church was extensively rebuilt in 1909 on the same site. The entrance in Russell Street, opposite the Theatre Royal, is difficult to find as the church exterior is shared with other buildings.

(AB & MBA). He married Jennifer Selby in 1982 at Baton Rouge, Louisiana. He married Tracey Helen Adams (born 1965), born at East Molesey, Surrey, on 19th July 1995 at Altnaharrie, Ullapool, Wester Ross, Scotland. David worked for Sir Richard Branson's Virgin Group for eleven years as head of Virgin Radio and with Chris Evans at his Ginger Media Group, masterminding the sale of Virgin Radio for £225M in 2000 to Scottish Media Group. He also worked for Pepsi, the Ministry of Sound and was head of Visit London. David was recruited by US billionaire Philip Anschutz's sports and entertainment group, AEG Europe, as President and CEO in 2005 to oversee the £350m redevelopment of the Millennium Dome in London into The O2, the most popular entertainment venue

39 Buckingham Terrace, Edinburgh, where David and Elspeth lived.

The O2 Arena on the Greenwich Peninsula opened in its present form in 2007. Only the Manchester Arena has greater seating capacity in the United Kingdom. In 2008, the O2 overtook New York's Madison Square Garden as the world's most popular concert venue in terms of ticket sales. The arena was built under the former Millennium Dome, and is often referred to simply as the Dome.

in the world in terms of ticket sales. He joined Bernie Ecclestone's Formula One Group in 2012 but left after a year and was appointed Chief Executive of restaurant group Wagamama in 2013. He stepped down in 2017 to become a special adviser to the company. David and Tracey have four children.
  - Jane Margaret Campbell (born 1961) was educated at Westbourne School for Girls in Glasgow, at Parsons Mead School, Ashstead, Surrey and at Columbus East High School, Indiana, USA. She graduated from St Mary's College, Indiana with a BSc in social work and psychology. She married Matthew Edward Haber (born 1965), born at Frankfurt am Main, West Germany, on 9th September 1989 at Columbus, Indiana. He served as an officer in the United States Air Force, completed two operational tours in Iraq and retired in 2012 as a colonel. They have two children.
- Alasdair David Macintyre (23rd June 1932–25th October 2015), born at Northwood, Middlesex, was educated at St George's School for Girls (sic – a nursery) in Edinburgh, at Fort Augustus Village Primary School 1939, at Rochester House School in Edinburgh, where he played rugby at Murrayfield Stadium, at Edinburgh Academy, where he played for the Hockey XI, and at Heriot-Watt College in Edinburgh. He completed National Service in the Royal Engineers 1950–52 and then a five-year apprenticeship with Philips, Knox & Arthur, qualifying ARICS in 1959 and was later FRICS. He worked for Iain Shaw & Partners, later becoming a partner. The firm evolved into Macintyre, McNish & Partners, with offices in Edinburgh, Glasgow, Dundee and Aberdeen. The company was sold in the late 1980s and he continued to work with the new firm of Turner Townsend as an independent consultant until he retired in 1992. Alasdair married Sheila Elizabeth Campbell (21st May 1932–7th September 2014), born at Lochgilphead, Argyll, on 7th August 1959 at St Giles Cathedral, Edinburgh. She was the sister of Archibald Lachlan Campbell, who married Alasdair's sister. Sheila qualified as a nurse at The Royal Infirmary of Edinburgh and as a midwife at Queen Charlotte's Hospital, London, later working at The London Clinic. They lived at Ivy Tree Cottage, Pencaitland, East Lothian from the early 1980s. During his later years, Alasdair assisted the Victoria Cross Database Users Group with Scottish biographical research, much of which has been used in this series. He always gave his time selflessly and his contribution to both projects was invaluable. Sheila died at The Royal Infirmary of Edinburgh. Alasdair moved to 3/24 Western Gardens, Edinburgh in August 2015 and died at Western General Hospital. Both their funerals were held at the Cloister Chapel, Warriston Crematorium, Edinburgh. They had three children, all born at the Western General Hospital, Edinburgh:
  - Caroline Julie Macintyre (born 1960) was educated at St Margaret's School, Edinburgh and Edinburgh Academy. She worked for the Bank of Scotland Portfolio Management Services as an investment manager for about thirty years before moving to Rathbones Investment Management, Edinburgh as an investment director (FCSI & CWM).

- Graeme Campbell Macintyre (born and died 1962).
- Gillian Elspeth Macintyre (born 1965) was educated at St Margaret's School, Edinburgh and was there with Lucy Muriel Campbell, granddaughter of Lorne MacLaine Campbell VC. Gillian went on to Aberdeen University (LLB) and was employed as a compliance officer with Scottish Widows, Royal Bank of Scotland, Lloyds of London and actuaries Hewitt, Bacon & Woodrow. She later founded her own company, GEM Compliance as a compliance consultant. Gillian married John Kevin Gallacher (born 1964), born in Nairobi, Kenya, on 6th August 1993 at King's College Chapel, Aberdeen.

Alasdair and Sheila Macintyre. Alasdair provided much of the Scottish biographical input to this series (Alasdair Macintyre).

Elspeth's father, William Mathieson Forsyth (4th August 1876–11th January 1964), a stereotyper born at Raes Buildings, Canongate, Edinburgh, married Jane Lind née Chisholm (8th January 1877–6th July 1964), born at Fleshmarket Close, Edinburgh, on 29th July 1898 at 3a Chalmers Crescent, Edinburgh. They were living at 50 Greenfield Crescent, Brighton, Sussex at the time of his death at the General Hospital, Elm Grove, Brighton. She was living at 3 St Andrews Close, Stanmore, Middlesex at the time of her death there. In addition to Elspeth they had three other children:

- Alexander Steele Forsyth (18th October–2nd November 1898).
- Margaret Rankine Forsyth (6th February 1901–18th April 1986), born in Edinburgh, married Albert Victor Antram (7th March 1897–28th January 1965), born at Brighton, Sussex, on 5th August 1925 at Holy Cross, St Pancras, London. Prior to the Great War he was a Post Office Telegraphist. He enlisted in the Royal Engineers (TF) at Brighton as a pioneer (3546 & 538417) in 3/1st Home Counties Division Signal Company on 7th April 1915. His next of kin was his mother, Edith Annie Antram, 9 Gladstone Terrace, Brighton, Sussex. He was described as 5′ 11″ tall. On 31st January 1916 he re-mustered as a sapper and was employed as a telegraph operator. He overstayed his leave by almost a day and was confined to barracks for four days on 12th December, while serving in 67th Divisional Signal Company. On 15th October 1917 at Bedford he had lights on in the billet at 10.30 p.m. and was confined to barracks for two days. Two days later he was absent from the defaulters parade at 6 p.m. and was confined to barracks for three more days. Albert served in

the Egyptian Expeditionary Force from 1st January 1918 and was employed with 75th Divisional Signal Company. He caught malaria in Syria on 1st November 1918 and was treated at 21st General Hospital, Alexandria, Egypt, where a medical board recommended he return to Britain, with disability assessed at 80%. He transferred to 20th Territorial Force Depot RE on returning to Britain on 7th February 1919 and was treated at 1st Western General Hospital, Fazakerley, Liverpool. Albert was discharged no longer physically fit for war service on 18th March 1919, with Military Character assessed as Very Good. He gave his address as 13 Lupus Street, London. He was assessed as 40% disabled due to malaria and was awarded a pension of 11/- per week to be reviewed after a year. Margaret and Albert were publicans of The Bear Inn and Race Hill Inn in Brighton and The Wick, Palmeira Square, Hove, Sussex. They were living at 63 Western Road, Hove, Sussex at the time of his death at Bevendean Hospital, Brighton. She was living at Bristol Lodge, 7 Bristol Road, Brighton at the time of her death there.

- John Chisholm Forsyth (6th October 1904–5th October 1991), a stereotyper born at 64 Hamilton Place, Edinburgh, married Josephine Dillon (29th June 1903–October 1990), born at Newport, Gwent, on 5th September 1936 at Westminster, London. They were living at 3 St Andrews Close, Harrow, Middlesex in 1939. He was living at 15 Tenby Avenue, Kenton at the time of his death there. They had a son, Ian William Forsyth (born 1937).

On 15th May 1930 thieves broke into David's house in Wieland Road, Northwood, Middlesex and stole gramophone records, clothing and jewellery. The maid found the house had been ransacked and sent for the police. Mrs Macintyre's first concern was for her husband's VC, but fortunately the thieves missed it. Thereafter it was kept in the bank for safekeeping.

David served in No.4 Relief Battery Home Guard in Hyde Park, London during the Second World War as a captain. When he returned to Scotland he was presented

Fleshmarket Close in Edinburgh, where David's mother-in-law was born. In Edinburgh a close means a narrow alleyway and there were many such running off the Royal Mile. The Fleshmarket was where meat was prepared and sold. Fleshmarket Close stretched from High Street North to Market Street before Cockburn Street, built c.1860, cut through many old closes. In the Close is Jinglin' Geordie Tavern, named after George Heriot (1563–1624), jeweller and goldsmith, who left his estate to build a school, which still exists. In 2004 Ian Rankin's novel *Fleshmarket Close* was released, the fifteenth in the Inspector Rebus series. It formed the basis of one of the episodes in the *Rebus* television series starring Ken Stott in 2006.

No.4 Relief Battery Home Guard in Hyde Park. David Macintyre is on the left (Alasdair Macintyre).

with an inscribed gold wristwatch. He attended a number of VC reunions – the VC Garden Party at Buckingham Palace on 26th June 1920, the VC Dinner at the Royal Gallery of the House of Lords, London on 9th November 1929, the Victory Day Celebration Dinner & Reception at The Dorchester, London on 8th June 1946 and the VC Centenary Celebrations at Hyde Park, London on 26th June 1956. He was a member of the Scottish Arts Club (Edinburgh) and was also a Fellow of the Royal Geographical Society.

David was called upon to participate in a number of ceremonies over the years, including:

- He unveiled a large, hand drawn Roll of Honour at the North United Free Church, Newcastleton, Roxburghshire on 29th March 1919, listing the names of eighty-six members of the congregation who served during the Great War.
- He was one of the VC Honour Guard at the burial of the Unknown Warrior at Westminster Abbey on 11th November 1920.
- Took part in the presentation of colours to the Liverpool Scottish on 31st July 1936.
- He attended a civic luncheon hosted by the Lord Provost, Sir William Young Darling CBE MC in Edinburgh on 21st September 1944. John Alexander Cruickshank VC was the guest of honour. Other VCs present were William Robertson, Charles George Bonner and Adam Archibald.
- He assisted the Duke of Buccleuch to open a museum at Melrose Abbey on 28th August 1946.
- He presented the key of the United Services Museum to the Governor of Edinburgh Castle on 14th April 1949, who then formally opened the Museum.
- He accepted the Eagle captured from the 45e Régiment de Ligne on 18th June 1815 at the Battle of Waterloo by Sergeant Charles Ewart, 2nd Royal North British Dragoons (Scots Greys), on behalf of The United Services Museum, Edinburgh

Castle (now National War Museum) on 7th July 1956. The Governor of the Castle, Lieutenant General Sir Horatius Murray KBE CB DSO and Colonel of The Royal Scots Greys, Brigadier George Herbert Norris Todd MC DL, both played important roles in the ceremony.

David died at the Civil Service Nursing Home in Drummond Place, Edinburgh on 31st July 1967. His funeral was held at Corstorphine Parish Church on 3rd August, followed by cremation at Warriston Crematorium, Edinburgh. His ashes were scattered in the Garden of Remembrance there. He is commemorated in a number of other places:

Corstorphine Old Parish Church (St John's Collegiate Church until 1646) was built in the 15th century in the churchyard of a 12th century or earlier chapel. When it became the parish church, the 12th century church was razed and a new aisle was added, with stone from the former church being used in the porch. It was extensively restored in 1828 and 1903-05.

- His mother's headstone in the old churchyard at Port Charlotte, Isle of Islay, Argyll.
- His Smith & Wesson .455 revolver was donated to the Museum of the Argyll & Sutherland Highlanders, Stirling Castle, where it is displayed in a mock-up Great War front-line trench.
- A Department for Communities and Local Government commemorative paving stone was dedicated at the junction of Crown Street and King Street, Portnahaven, Isle of Islay on 24th August 2018.
- Display in the National War Museum of Scotland, Edinburgh Castle.

In addition to the VC and CB he was awarded the British War Medal 1914–20, Victory Medal 1914–19, George VI Coronation Medal 1937 and Elizabeth II Coronation Medal 1953. After his death the medals were held by his widow and kept in a bank for safekeeping. It was her wish that they should be donated to the United Services Museum,

David's commemorative paving stone overlooking Portnahaven.

The Most Honourable Order of the Bath was founded by King George I on 18th May 1725. The name derives from the medieval ceremony for appointing a knight, which involved bathing as a symbol of purification. The Order consists of the Sovereign, the Great Master (currently Charles, Prince of Wales) and three classes of members:

- 120 Knights or Dames Grand Cross (GCB) – including the Great Master as Principal.
- 355 Knights Commander (KCB) or Dames Commander (DCB).
- 1,925 Companions (CB).

Members belong to either the Civil or the Military Division and recipients are usually senior military officers or civil servants. Foreign nationals may be made Honorary Members. Members appointed to the Civil Division must *by their personal services to the crown or by the performance of public duties have merited … royal favour*. Appointments to the Military Division are restricted by the rank of the individual.

Edinburgh Castle. On 23rd November 1998 her daughter and son handed over the medals at a luncheon in the Officers' Mess, Edinburgh Castle. At the time, the Museum was being refurbished and the medals were loaned to the Argyll & Sutherland Highlanders Museum, Stirling Castle. The refurbished and renamed National War Museum of Scotland was opened on 17th April 2000 by the Princess Royal and the medals are displayed there. Alasdair Macintyre represented the family at this event and was presented to the Princess. The then Scottish Naval and Military Museum (later United Services Museum), Edinburgh Castle closed in 1939 and its collection was put into safe storage for the duration of hostilities. At war's end the Museum's future was far from assured. However, David Lowe Macintyre VC CB, Under-Secretary of the Ministry of Works, ensured that the government took on the running of the Museum and thereby saved it. It is therefore fitting that his medals are held there.

The National War Museum of Scotland in Edinburgh Castle was formerly the Scottish United Services Museum and prior to this the Scottish Naval and Military Museum.

22614 LANCE CORPORAL WILLIAM HENRY METCALF
16th Battalion (Canadian Scottish) CEF

William 'Billy' Metcalf was born on 29th January 1894 at Talmadge, Washington Co, Maine, USA. His father, Henry William Metcalf (23rd May 1858–21st October 1900), a labourer born at Talmadge, was recorded as married in the 1880 Census of Talmadge, but details of his spouse were not shown. He was living with his parents at the time. Henry married Theresa Lorinza née Varnum (8th August 1869–16th June 1945), born at Princeton, Washington Co, possibly on 18th December 1882. She was aged sixteen and was single in the 1880 Census of Princeton, living with her parents. Henry died at Lubec, Washington Co. Theresa married Thomas Henry Rice (3rd December 1868–2nd September 1946), a farmer born at Digby, Nova Scotia, on 27th October 1906 at St Stephen, Charlotte Co, New Brunswick, Canada. They lived at Dennysville, Washington Co. He died at Bangor, Penobscot Co, Maine and she at Dennysville. Billy had eleven siblings from his mother's two marriages:

- Mabel Bertha Metcalf (born c.1880), born at Princeton, Washington Co, was a domestic when she married Ralph Belmore Pike (born 13th May 1876) on 11th November 1899. He was a labourer working for St Croix Paper Co, Woodland, Washington Co in September 1918 and they were living at 5 Harrison Street, Calais, Washington Co. They had five children:
  ○ Hattie M Pike (1902–03) died at Princeton of whooping cough.
  ○ Geneva Fern Pike (born 1906) married Kenneth James Barnes (1905–76), born at Eastport, Washington Co, in 1925. They had five children. He died at Dennysville.

Billy's mother was born at Princeton in Washington Co, Maine, which was named after Princeton, Massachusetts.

○ Vera Gertrude Pike (born 1909) married Leroy 'Roy' Eugene Dee (1904–80), a clerk born at Portland, Cumberland Co, on 20th May 1927 at Portsmouth, New Hampshire. She was a waitress in a tearoom in 1930, living in Boston, Massachusetts. Her husband was not with her at the time. The marriage ended in divorce. Roy married Alice Emma Rollins (1916–76) on 17th October 1938 at Portland, Massachusetts. He served as a private in the US Army infantry. The marriage ended in divorce. Roy died at Bangor, Maine. Alice served in the US Cadet Nursing Corps (236548) and trained at Maine Eye and Ear Infirmary, Portland about 1942, while living

Billy's family lived at Dennysville for some time. The town takes its name from the Dennys River and was first settled from Hingham, Massachusetts in May 1786.

Billy's mother married for the second time at St Stephen, Charlotte Co, New Brunswick. The town is on the east bank of the St Croix River, which is the border between Canada and the United States. The French explorer, Samuel de Champlain, wintered there in 1604 and the indigenous Passamaquoddy were forced off their lands thereafter. In response to the French raid on Deerfield, New Englander Major Benjamin Church raided Castine, Maine in 1704. Church learned that Michel Chartier was building a fort on the present site of St Stephen. On 7th June 1704, Church surprised Chartier and his family fled into the woods. A three-hour battle followed and the settlement was pillaged and plundered. Church moved on to raid other Acadian villages. St Stephen was incorporated as a town in 1871 and in 1877 the business district was almost destroyed by fire. The local economy was based on lumber and shipbuilding. At the end of the 18th century there were one hundred dry docks and slips along the river. However, by the end of the Second World War the town's main employer was Ganong Bros Ltd, Canada's oldest candy company established in 1873, and St Croix Cotton Mill, established in 1882 with its own hydro-electric generating station. In 1957, the textile mill closed and Ganong remains a key employer. In the 1970s St Stephen and Milltown municipalities joined together to become simply St Stephen. Every August since 1985 the town hosts the Chocolate Fest and in 2000 St Stephen was given the title of 'Canada's Chocolate Town'.

at Higgins Beach, Scarborough, Maine. She was appointed senior cadet on 14th February 1945, was admitted to the Corps on 14th August 1945 and graduated on 22nd February 1948. Alice married Paul Leon Simonin (1922–94), born at Zion, Lake Co, Illinois, on 6th June 1958 at San Diego, California. He enlisted as a seaman 3rd class in the US Navy Coast Guard (266-64-20) and was assigned to the armed guard crew at Castle Garden and Ellis Island, New York in 1943. She died in Los Angeles, California.
º Belmont Ralph Pike (born 1911) married Geraldine Patricia Hutchinson (1914–99), born at Farmingdale, Maine, on 4th April 1932 at Portsmouth, New Hampshire. The marriage ended in divorce. Geraldine married Charles Edwin Pease (1912–50), born at Augusta, Kennebec Co, Maine, on 25th November 1936 in Maine. He was an attendant at a gasoline station and she was a clerk in 1940, when they were living at Augusta. He died there and she at Lewiston, Androscoggin Co, Maine. They had two children. Belmont married Marie Georgiana Josephine Tondreau (born 1913), born at Brunswick, Cumberland Co, Maine, on 22nd September 1935 at Portsmouth, New Hampshire. The marriage ended in divorce. Belmont married Stella M Foley (née Dubowick) (1913–2011), born in Cumberland Co, on 8th February 1944 in Maine. She graduated from South Portland High School in 1931, was apprenticed to a hairdresser and later ran a salon in Portland, working until she was eighty-eight. She attended exercise classes until aged ninety-three. She died at Scarborough, Cumberland Co.
º Dorothy Pike (1919–85), born at Baileyville, Maine, married James Walter Harvey (1912–74), born at Lubec, Washington Co, on 23rd March 1935 in Maine. He died at Suffield, Hartford Co, Connecticut and she at Hartford, Hartford Co. They had two children.
• Irving Leeds Metcalf (5th May 1882–21st October 1900) was born at Lubec, Maine.
• Alice Evelyn Metcalf (born 25th December 1884–25th March 1966), born at Topsfield, Maine, was a servant when she married Alonzo Stickney Bacon (1880–13th November 1913), a labourer born at Topsfield, Washington Co, Maine, on 3rd July 1903 at Milltown, Maine. He was a registered guide living at Grand Lake Stream by 1907. He was employed by the Federal Fish Hatchery and c.1905 he conceived the idea of using the white tail feathers of a barnyard cock as a lure for landlocked salmon. The idea was developed by others into the basic feather streamer of modern times. Alonzo was shot in mistake for a deer and died at Sysladobsis Lake, Maine. He was buried with his daughter, Dorothy, at Grand Lake Stream Cemetery. Alice married William Ed Brown (1884–1959), a guide born at Grand Lake Stream, on 24th December 1914 at Princeton. In the 1920 Census she is recorded as Alice E Beacon, a widow, and as Alice Bacon, a single mother-in-law in 1940, living with her daughter, Vivian, and son-in-law Chandler Swift. William died at Waltham, Middlesex Co, Massachusetts and Alice at

Ellsworth Nursing Home, Hancock, Maine. She is buried with her first husband and daughter, Dorothy, at Grand Lake Stream Cemetery. Alice had seven children from her two marriages, all born at Grand Lake Stream:
- ° Stanley Mitchell Bacon (1903–97), a labourer, married three times:
  - ❏ Rose Emma Fecteau (born 1907), born at Coaticook, Québec, Canada, on 22nd June 1928 in Vermont. Stanley was a machinist and Rose was a worker in a bag mill in Lunenburg in 1930. The marriage ended in divorce without issue in April 1936. She was a housekeeper for Robert Montini at Lunenburg in 1940.
  - ❏ Florida Octavia Perreault (née Filion) (1910–74), born at Newmarket, New Hampshire, on 29th August 1938. Florida had married Arthur Edmond Perreault (born 1909), a salesman born at Danielson, Connecticut, on 17th September 1934 at Rockingham, Windham Co, Vermont. The marriage ended in divorce and Arthur married Beatrice Esther Spofford (1913–2005) in New Hampshire. He was serving as a fireman second class in the US Naval Reserve (8069122) aboard USS *Franklin* about fifty miles off the Japanese mainland, when she was hit by two bombs from a Japanese aircraft on 19th March 1945. Arthur and 806 other crewmen were lost (Purple Heart). He was buried at sea (Honolulu Memorial, Hawaii in the Courts of the Missing). Stanley was a shipper in a paper mill in 1940 and they were living at Lunenburg. Florida died at Canaan, Essex Co, Vermont.
  - ❏ Augusta 'Gusta' Alice Robinson (née Balch) (1913–2000), born at Cornish, Sullivan Co, New Hampshire, on 9th August 1975 at Gilman, Essex Co, Vermont. She was living at Amerherst, Merrimack, New Hampshire at the time of her marriage. Augusta had married Albert Irving Robinson (1904–69), born at Westmore, Orleans Co, on 11th June 1932 at Lunenburg. He was a grain merchant in 1940 and died at Barnet, Caledonia Co, Vermont. Gusta and Albert had three children. Stanley and Augusta died at Lunenburg, Essex Co, Vermont.
- ° Maude M Bacon (1905–92), a hotel waitress, married Edward Hugh Burrell (1902–63), a bag maker born at Skowhegan, Somerset Co, Maine, on 11th March 1925 at Baptist Parsonage, St Stephen, Charlotte Co, New Brunswick. He was a labourer on dam construction in 1930 and they were living at Waterford, Caledonia Co, Vermont. By 1940 he was an attendant at a gasoline station and they were living at Auburn Road, Boston, Massachusetts. They were living at Ellsworth, Hancock Co, Maine in 1966. He died at Bar Harbor, Mount Desert Island, Maine and she at Ellsworth.
- ° Willis Alton Bacon (1907–91), a bag-mill employee, married Marcella M La Valley (1908–97), born in New Hampshire, on 16th October 1926 at Luneburg. They had at least one daughter. They were living at Pittsfield, Somerset Co in 1966 and both died there.
- ° Lloyd Granville Bacon (1908–78) married Laura Viola Palmer (1898–1989), born at Lancaster, Coos Co, New Hampshire, on 29th May 1950 at

Guildhall, Essex Co, Vermont. Laura had married Fred Henry Richards (23rd September 1887–October 1966) on 12th December 1914 at Lancaster, Coos Co and they had a son, William Frederic (sic) Richards (c.1917–99). The marriage ended in divorce in December 1922. Fred married Thelma Scott (born c.1889) on 3rd August 1921 at Whitefield, New Hampshire and they had a son, Nolan Wilbur Richards (1922–92). They divorced on 21st June 1938. Laura married Lewis Holman Archer on 14th July 1924 at Campton, Grafton Co, New Hampshire and John Joseph Corcroan (29th May 1890–28th August 1947) on 3rd March 1930. Lloyd and Laura were living at Gilman, Vermont in 1966. He died at Hartford, Windsor Co and she at Whitefield, Coos Co.
- Vivian R Bacon (1911–90) married Chandler Swift (1909–84), a mill hand in a paper mill born at Groveton, New Hampshire, on 18th June 1933 at Essex, Vermont. They were living at 49 State Street, Northumberland, Coos Co in 1940 and later at Groveton, New Hampshire. He enlisted in the US Army on 7th April 1942 at Manchester, New Hampshire and was discharged on 13th October 1945. It is assumed that the marriage ended in divorce. Chandler died in Connecticut. Vivian married Rowden Clyde Fisk (1906–78) in 1945 at Boston, Massachusetts. He died in Coos Co and she at Ellsworth, Hancock Co, Maine.
- Dorothy Fay Bacon (1913–14) died of cholera.
- Kenneth Edward Brown (1915–86) married Glennie A MacArthur (1923–77) on 27th December 1941 in Maine. He enlisted in the US Army on 17th March 1943, was promoted private first class and was discharged on 29th October 1945. They were living at Waltham, Middlesex Co in 1966. Glennie died at Waltham and Kenneth at Calais, Washington Co. They had two sons.

• Lee A Metcalf (10th July 1885 or 10th June 1886–3rd June 1962), born at Princeton, Washington Co, Maine, married Gertrude Odley Watt (16th April 1885–28th February 1982), born in Canada, on 23rd October 1907 at St Stephen, Charlotte Co, New Brunswick, Canada. Lee was employed as a carpenter in milling and building. He died in California, USA. They had four children:
- Henry Lee Metcalf (born 1908), born at Edmunds, Washington Co, married Pauline Louise Allen (born c.1910), born in Massachusetts, on 26th March 1927 at Hanson, Massachusetts. They had a son.
- Harold Cameron Metcalf (1910–82), born at Lubec, Maine and died at Wareham, Massachusetts.
- Arlene Elizabeth Metcalf (1912–46), born at Hanson, Massachusetts, married Albert Victor Holmes (1905–75) there on 16th April 1932. He was born in New Jersey and died in Lowell, Middlesex Co, Massachusetts. She died at Malden, Middlesex Co, Massachusetts.
- Irma Winifred Metcalf (1915–2003), born at Lubec, married Francis Joseph Burke (1915–91), born in Boston, Suffolk Co, Massachusetts, on 9th December 1943 at St Patrick's Cathedral, New York. They lived at

34 Winter Street, Hanson, Massachusetts. He died at Hanson and she at Warwick, Rhode Island. They had four children.
* Earl Metcalf (4th October 1888–1st February 1969), a mill man born at Grand Lake Stream, Maine, married Eudavilla Winslow (11th August 1889–19th March 1964), a factory worker born at Grand Manan, Charlotte Co, New Brunswick, Canada, on 2nd November 1907 at Lubec. He was a labourer with Globe Canning Co, Lubec in June 1917. She died at Lubec and he at Machias, Washington Co. They had five children born at Lubec:
    ○ Delilah Gertrude Metcalf (1908–93) married John Edgar Fernald (1900–72), a boilerman born at Channel-Port aux Basques, Newfoundland, on 21st June 1925 at Campobello, Charlotte Co, New Brunswick. They were living at Lubec in 1930 and 1940. The marriage ended in divorce. They had five children. Delilah married Vance E Barker (1916–93). They both died at Lubec.
    ○ Earle Elzymore Metcalf (1914–56) married Mae Melda Brown on 30th September 1934 at Campobello. They had a daughter. He died at Lubec.
    ○ Percy M Metcalf (1916–44) married Kathleen Gretchen Eaton (1922–86), born at Campobello, on 10th July 1938 at Wilson's Beach, New Brunswick. They had a daughter. He was working in a sawmill when he enlisted in the US Army Air Force on 12th August 1942 at Bangor, Maine. He was a staff sergeant/gunner aboard a B-24D Liberator of 90th Bomb Group (H) (Jolly Rogers) on a bombing mission off the coast of New Guinea, when the plane was shot down into the Bismarck Sea. He was reported missing and subsequently declared deceased in 1946 (Purple Heart). His body was never recovered and he is commemorated with his crewmates in the Manila American Cemetery and Memorial in the Philippines and on a plaque to 90th Bomb Group at Wright-Patterson Air Force Base, Montgomery Co, Ohio. Kathleen married George F Burns (1910–93) in 1948. They both died at Lubec.
    ○ Byard Winslow 'Bill' Metcalf (1919–2009) married Rowena Marie Mulholland (1917–78), born at Campobello Island, on 17th May 1939 and they had five children. Bill served in the US Navy during the Second World War aboard USS *Pennsylvania* in the Pacific. He was awarded the Purple Heart for wounds received in a shore battle on Okinawa. He was discharged in 1945 and returned to Portland, Cumberland Co, Maine, where he joined the Portland Fire Department as a fire fighter in 1947. He spent most of his career on the Portland fireboat as senior engineer and was involved in commissioning *City of Portland III* in 1959. Bill was promoted captain in 1968 and retired in 1972. Rowena died at Portland. Bill was appointed senior engineer with the Moran Tug Co for fourteen years, until forced to retire due to injuries received in a serious engine fire aboard *Patricia Moran*. His life was saved by the crew of the Portland fireboat. Bill married Lora (died 2002) in 1986. He was President of the Portland Fire Fighters Local 740 of

the International Fire Fighters Union. He was aboard *City of Portland IV* in September 2009 when she was commissioned. Bill died at Portland and was buried with his first wife.
  ◦ Helena Ardelia Metcalf (1926–28).
- Margaret M Metcalf (21st August 1890–26th September 1971), born at Talmadge, married John Vance Brown (20th April 1889–12th November 1925) on 1st September 1906 at Grand Lake Stream Plantation, where he was born. He was a timber worker in 1920 living with his family at Grand Lake Stream. He died at St Stephen, Charlotte Co, New Brunswick. She was living at Grand Lake Stream with her son, Leslie and his family, in 1940. Margaret died at Calais, Washington Co. She and John had four children, all born at Grand Lake Stream:
  ◦ Mazie Evelyn Brown (1906–94) married Lewis F Smallbridge (1904–81), born at Eden, Hancock Co, Maine, on 26th June 1926. He was a gardener on a private estate in 1940 and they were living at Mount Desert, Hancock Co, Maine. They had five children.
  ◦ Iola Theresa Brown (1909–2001) was a student nurse in 1930 at Newark Memorial Hospital, Newton Street, New Jersey. She qualified as a state registered nurse in 1953. She married as Mahoney and died at Bridgewater, Somerset Co, New Jersey.
  ◦ Leslie Metcalf (also seen as Vance) Brown (1910–96) married Irene Maclauglin (born c.1917) on 12th April 1935 in Maine. He was a truck driver in 1940 and they were living at his mother's home in Grand Lake Stream. They had a daughter.
  ◦ Maurice Lyle Brown (1911–14).
- Leeds Coleman Metcalf (28th December 1892–June 1960), born at Princeton, was a teamster for Proctor Bros Co, Manchester Co, Hillsborough, New Hampshire in June 1917 and was living at 4 Groman Avenue, Nashua. He married Alfreda M Bishop on 8th August 1914 at Nashua, New Hampshire. By 1920 he was a hotel reporter. The marriage ended in divorce. He married Helena May Murphy (23rd July 1896–July 1985), a bookkeeper born at Kearney, New Jersey, on 1st June 1925 at Manchester, New Hampshire. He was a chauffeur at the time of the marriage and in April 1930 he was an overseer at a cotton mill. They were living at 112 West Pearl Street, Nashua in 1942. He died in Gadsen Co, Florida and she at Nashua.
- Grace M Metcalf (25th September 1896–12th April 1964), born at Talmadge, Washington Co, married Payson Urquhart (10th April 1889–18th October 1960), a labourer born in Grand Manan, Charlotte Co, New Brunswick, Canada, on 15th November 1910 at Lubec, Washington Co. He died at Ellsworth, Hancock Co, Maine and she at Portland, Cumberland Co, Maine. They had three children:
  ◦ Florence Urquhart (1911–91), born at Dennysville, Maine, married Carl D Cook (1908–83), born at East Machias, Washington Co, on 11th January 1930. He was a travelling salesman in 1940 and they were living at Dennysville. They both died at South Portland, Cumberland Co. They had three children.

- ○ Darrell William Urquhart (1917–97), born at Edmunds, Washington Co, married Beatrice Margaret Sullivan (1923–2007), born at Eastport, Washington Co. They both died at Bangor, Penobscot Co. They had two children.
- ○ Dorothy Evelyn Urquhart (1918–2002), born at Dennysville, Maine, married Earle Eugene Hanson (1904–58), born at Springvale, York Co, Maine on 17th May 1945.
• Jennie May Metcalf (24th May 1898–27th April 1992), born at Princeton, Maine, married Elmer Stickney Bacon (25th March 1894–22nd March 1963), born at Grand Lake Stream Plantation, on 3rd December 1914. He was a boatman in 1917. He died at Lincoln, Penobscot Co, Maine. Jennie married as Gardiner in 1965 and as Perkins in 1985. She also died at Lincoln. Jennie had four children from her first marriage, all born at Grand Lake Stream:
- ○ Twins Annette and Jeanette Bacon (born and died March 1915).
- ○ Eugene 'Wrig' Elmer Bacon (1916–85) married Doris Janet Strand (1923–2005), born at Boston, Suffolk Co, Massachusetts, in 1943 at Dedham, Norfolk Co, Massachusetts. He was a maintenance man at Harvard Research Center, Southborough, Worcester Co, Massachusetts. They were living at 20E Mayberry Drive, Westborough, Massachusetts at the time of his death there. She died at West Wareham, Plymouth Co, Massachusetts. They had four children.
- ○ Ethel May Bacon (1918–2015) had a son in 1934. She married Nathaniel 'Nathan' Eli Chambers (1912–69), born at Oakfield, Aroostook Co, Maine, on 2nd July 1935. Ethel was living with her parents at Grand Lake Stream at the time of the 1940 Census, while her husband, a truck driver, was lodging at 28 Western Avenue, Henniker, Merrimack Co, New Hampshire. Nathan enlisted in the US Army Air Force on 22nd July 1942 at Rockingham, New Hampshire and was discharged as a corporal from 1466 Army Air Force Base Unit, Eielson Air Force Base, Moose Creek, near Fairbanks, Alaska. They had two children. The marriage ended in divorce. Ethel married Leroy Robert Foss (1918–76) on 1st April 1962. He served as a sergeant in the US Army Air Force during the Second World War. They both died at Lee, Penobscot Co. Nathan married Wanita Fay Carter (1921–96) on 15th March 1947 at Manchester, New Hampshire, where she was born. Nathan was a mechanic at the time, living at 22 Concord Street, Manchester, Hillsborough Co, New Hampshire. He died at Houlton, Aroostook Co.
• Harry Chester Metcalf (born and died 15th April 1900).
• Henry 'Harry' E Rice (4th January 1905–1st April 1968), born at St Stephen, Charlotte Co. He married Madeline Sophia Clark (born 9th July 1905), born at Lubec, on 11th July 1925. He died at Pembroke, Washington Co. They had eight children:

- Janice Theresa Rice (1925–93), born at Pembroke, married Percy Ivan Leighton (1926–97), also born at Pembroke, on 31st December 1948. She died at Orange City, Volusia Co, Florida and he at Debary, Volusia Co.
- Edwin S Rice (1928–2017) served as a corporal in the US Army. He married Nancy on 1st July 1949 at Pembroke and they lived at Robbinston, Maine. He died at Sanford, York Co, Maine. They had six children.
- Robert A Rice (1930–2004) married three times and had five children. He died at Clinton, Kennebec Co, Maine.
- Thomas Harry Rice (1932–91), born at Ellsworth, Hancock Co, Maine, died at Sanford, York Co.
- Wayne W Rice (1934–2010), born at Pembroke, married Lorraine J Andrews (1935–2010), born at Eastport, Washington Co, on 17th October 1953. They were driving in icy conditions in Township 28 between Aurora, Hancock Co and Beddington, Washington Co on 29th January 2010 when the car skidded and collided with another vehicle. Lorraine died instantly and Wayne was flown by helicopter to Eastern Maine Medical Center, Bangor, where he died later that day. They were buried with their three children, who predeceased them, in Clarkside Cemetery, Pembroke.
- Clark W Rice (1935–2009), born at Bangor, Penobscot Co, married and had two children. He married Pat in 1961 and they had four children. He owned Clark's Auto Body for thirty-five years at Berwick, Washington Co and died at Pembroke.
- Kathleen J Rice.
- Wilma R Rice married Herbert A Pulk on 21st April 1956 in Maine. She later married Richard 'Dick' Henry Barnsley (1936–2014), born at Fitchburg, Worcester Co, Massachusetts and they lived at Palermo. Dick served as a corporal in the US Marines in the Korean War. Dick had married Katherine Marie McCann (1910–83), born at Groton, Middlesex Co, Massachusetts, in 1958. He is buried in Maine Mount Vernon Road Veterans Memorial Cemetery. Augusta, Kennebec Co, Maine.

Billy's paternal grandfather, Amos Metcalf (28th September 1820–19th July 1883), a farmer born at Amherst, Cumberland Co, Nova Scotia, married Margaret 'Maria' née Eagles (22nd May or 11th November 1823–12th February 1905), born at Five Islands, Nova Scotia, on 16th November 1841 at Folly Village, Nova Scotia. They were living at Talmadge, Washington Co, Maine in 1860. He enlisted in the Union Army on 15th November 1861 and served in 6th Battery Light Artillery, 1st Battalion, Maine Light Artillery during the American Civil War. He was detached as a hospital cook on 1st January 1863. He fought in the Battle of Antietam on 17th September 1862 and contracted rheumatism from lying in wet mud for prolonged periods. He was discharged on 17th June 1865, was granted an invalidity pension on 13th December 1875 and was completely disabled by 1881. He died at Talmadge and his invalidity pension was transferred to Margaret on 29th October 1883. She was living with her son, Amos, and his family at Talmadge in 1900, where she subsequently died of senility. In addition to Henry they had eight other children:

- James 'Jimmy' E Metcalf (1842–9th July 1905), a farmer, enlisted with his father in 6th Battery Light Artillery, 1st Battalion, Maine Light Artillery on 15th November 1861 and fought at the Battle of Gettysburg. He was discharged on 17th June 1865. Jimmy married Ann 'Annie' Roix c.1858 and they lived at Talmadge. She died before 1900, when Jimmy was living with his younger brother, Amos, at Talmadge. He died there of malarial poisoning affecting his brain, contracted during his war service in the south. They had five children – Lillian T Metcalf (1875–1967), John W Metcalf (1877–1958), Percy Allen Metcalf (1878–1949), Effie Mae Metcalf (1881–1966) and Fred Benjamin Metcalf (1883–1953).
- George William Metcalf (9th December 1845–21st August 1920), a labourer, married Elvira Lavinia Sprague (born c.1842) c.1866. He married Elizabeth 'Lizzie' Arvilla Varnum (25th May 1860–23rd May 1932), born at Princeton, Washington Co, c.1886. She was the daughter of Billy's maternal grandparents (see below). George died at Calais, Washington Co and had six children from his two marriages – Chadbourne Metcalf (born and died 1867), Wesley Edward Metcalf (1868–1938), Eva Metcalf (1872–1918), Jessie Nora Metcalf (1883–1981), Bert Metcalf (1887) and Sterling Everett Metcalf (1889–1976).
- John W Metcalf (15th June 1847–14th May 1932), a farmer born at Amherst, married Adeline 'Addie' Fogg (22nd May 1857–19th July 1943), born at Talmadge Plantation, Washington Co, on 13th June 1874 at Topsfield, Washington Co. In 1880 they were living at Talmadge next door to his brother, Oliver. In 1900 they were living at Codyville, Washington Co. They had twelve children – Edith Evelina Metcalf (1875–1959), Alfred E Metcalf (1877), Sarah Alice Metcalf (1878–83), George Burnham Metcalf (1880–1945), Willard F Metcalf (1883–87), Eleanor Alma Metcalf (1884–1938), Leon Eugene Metcalf (1885–1956), Harry Alden Metcalf (1889–1953), Glinnis Evelyn Metcalf (1893–1944), Theresa R Metcalf (1895–1969), Carl Raymond Metcalf (1898–1982) and Guy L Metcalf (1901–87).
- Oliver Metcalf (22nd October 1850–28th October 1896), a farmer born at Talmadge Plantation, married Helena 'Helen' Eulalie Leon (7th July 1855–27th June 1950), born at Boston, Suffolk Co, Massachusetts, on 15th August 1875 at Topsfield. In 1880 they were living at Talmadge next door to his brother, John. Oliver died at Middleboro, Plymouth Co, Massachusetts. Helen died in Los Angeles, California. They had two children – Frank Leon Metcalf (1879–1946) and Eulalie Frances Metcalf (1887–1960).
- Franzella/Francella 'Ella' E Metcalf (15th February 1854 (1853 in 1900 Census)–2nd July 1906) had a daughter, Helen Mae Metcalf (1874–1952). Ella married Joseph B Smith (born August 1852), born at Oak Bay, Charlotte Co, New

Brunswick, between 1st January and 22nd June 1880. She died of pulmonary tuberculosis at Talmadge. They had a son, Henry Edward Smith (1881–1969).
- Alice Sarah Metcalf (15th April 1856–26th June 1934) married Frank B Fickett (26th March 1853–26th January 1900), a timberman born at Princeton, Washington Co, on 26th October 1878 at Grand Lake Stream Plantation, Washington Co. They had three children – Thomas Crory Fickett (1883–1936), John S Fickett (1887–1903) and Roland H Fickett (1893–1911). Frank died at Mapleton, Aroostook Co, Maine. Alice married John Young (born 7th February 1882), born at Danforth, Washington Co, on 1st October 1904 at Princeton, Washington Co. He was a carpenter in a machine shop in 1910 and they were living at 337 Main Street, Milford, Worcester Co, Massachusetts. By 1911 they had moved to 351 Main Street. John was working for John McLee at Hollie, Framingham, Middlesex Co, Massachusetts in September 1918 and they were living at Waushakum Avenue, Ashland, Massachusetts. Sarah is understood to have died at Bangor, Penobscot Co, Maine.
- Amos Metcalf (3rd August 1860–14th August 1924), a farmer, married Nellie E Young (born June 1874) on 28th March 1890 at Danforth, Washington Co. They were living at Talmadge in 1900 and at Calais, Washington Co in 1920. Amos died at Milltown, Washington Co. Nellie was living at 219 North Street, Calais in 1940. They had four children – Bertha Mae Metcalf (1891–1936), James Edward Metcalf (1893–1974), Herbert Innis Metcalf (1898) and Sarah Alice Metcalf (1901–77).
- Helen 'Ellen' Metcalf (May 1874–15th April 1930) married Edward Wesley Metcalf (born November 1868), born at Forest City Township, Washington Co, on 19th April 1893.

His maternal grandfather, Leonard Eaton Varnum (also seen as Varnam) (1st May 1829–5th April 1901), born at St James, New Brunswick, Canada, married Susan Maria née Hill (13th February 1837–5th May 1899), born at Topsfield, Washington Co, Maine, in 1855 at Princeton, Maine. He was a farmer in 1880 and they were living at Princeton, Washington Co. He died there of acute lobar pneumonia. In addition to Theresa they had four other children born in Princeton, Washington Co:

- Dora Varnum (20th February 1857–May 1949) married Joseph Edwin Tucker (1846–1912), born in Robbinston, Washington Co, on 5th August 1876. They had four children – Eva Maude Tucker (1878–1956), Pearl M Tucker (1889–1967), Regina Tucker, Florence Tucker (1896) and Harold Tucker (1900–54).
- Elizabeth 'Lizzie' Arvilla Varnum (25th May 1860–23rd May 1932) married George William Metcalf (9th December 1842–21st August 1920), a labourer born in Nova Scotia, the son of the VC's paternal grandfather. George had married Elvira Lavinia Sprague (born c.1842) c.1866 and they had three children – Chadbourne Metcalf (born and died 1867), Wesley Edward Metcalf (1868–1938)

and Eva Metcalf (1872–1918). Lizzie and George had three children – Jessie Nora Metcalf (1883–1981), Bert Metcalf (1887) and Sterling Everett Metcalf (1889–1976). He died in Milltown, Washington Co.
* Cyrena L Varnum (born c.1863) does not appear in census returns after 1870.
* George W Varnum (1st December 1876–17th August 1961) married Julia Almira Smith (25th June 1889–23rd October 1965), born in Worcester Co, Massachusetts, on 4th May 1910 at St Stephen, Charlotte Co, New Brunswick. He was a machinist in 1920 and they were living at 124 Freedom Street, Hopedale, Worcester Co. By 1930 they were living at Limington, York Co, Maine. He died there and she at Camden, Maine. They had seven children including – Doris Elizabeth Varnum (1911–90), Elsie Madelene Varnum (1913–2006), Esther Marie Varnum (1916–82), Leonard Eaton Varnum (1921–2001), Thelma L Varnum (1924) and Charles R Varnum (1928).

Billy was educated at the Grammar School, Waite, Washington Co, Maine. He worked as a garage mechanic and later became a barber. He was on a fishing trip with friends on the Miramachi River, New Brunswick when he heard about the outbreak of war. He enlisted in 71st Regiment, Canadian Militia at Fredericton, New Brunswick on 13th or 15th August 1914 (22614), described as 5′ 6″ tall, with dark complexion, brown eyes, brown hair and his religious denomination was Church of England. When his mother learned that he had enlisted she appealed to Canadian and United States government officials to have him sent home but without success. Billy was found medically fit to serve on 29th August.

He transferred to 12th Battalion CEF at Valcartier, Québec on 23rd September, embarked at Québec on 1st October aboard SS *Scotian* and disembarked in England on 14th October. He assigned $23 per month from his Army pay to his mother from October, reducing to $20 per month from January 1916. From January 1919 it was assigned to his wife. Billy transferred to 16th Battalion and embarked for France on 13th May 1915. He was involved in the later stages of the Second Battle of Ypres. He was slightly wounded and returned to the Battalion on 7th July.

Billy was granted seven days' leave from 20th January 1916. He was appointed paid acting lance corporal on 12th September and was confirmed in the rank from the same date on 1st February 1918. **Awarded the MM for his actions at Courcelette on the Somme 7th–9th October 1916. On the night of 7th October word was brought to Battalion HQ that a man lying in a trench was bleeding to death some distance away. Metcalf volunteered to go and bind up the wound, although the trench was under terrific shell fire. During the next two days he repeatedly went over the heavily shelled area repairing broken telephone wires, thus maintaining communication with Brigade HQ. During twenty months service his conduct was of uniform bravery and cheerful devotion to duty, LG 6th January 1917.** He was granted ten days' leave from 24th December 1916 and returned on 6th January 1917.

Billy was posted to First Army Signal School 22nd July–2nd September. He was granted fourteen days' leave from 30th December and returned on 16th January 1918. He was reprimanded and forfeited two days' pay for overstaying his leave from 6.30 a.m. on 14th January until 6.30 a.m. on 15th January. **Awarded a Bar to the MM for his actions during the opening day of the Battle of Amiens on 8th August 1918 when he was in charge of a signal section. With great perseverance and judgement he carried a telephone line forward with the first wave and, upon arriving at the final objective, established a signal station, which he maintained for the remainder of the day under heavy shell fire. He went out into no man's land several times to carry out repairs to his lines. His conduct was responsible for keeping HQ in touch with the situation and this contributed valuable assistance to the success of the operation, LG 24th January 1919.**

Awarded the VC for his actions at Arras, France on 2nd September 1918, LG 15th November 1918. Billy received a gunshot wound to the right leg on 4th September and was treated at 22nd General Hospital, Camiers until being evacuated to England on 6th September. He was admitted to Reading War Hospital on 7th September 1918 and was taken on strength of the Manitoba Regiment Depot, Seaford the same day. He transferred to Princess Patricia's Canadian Red Cross Hospital, Bexhill on 11th October.

A tented camp was established at Cooden in 1914 and huts were constructed in the Upper Camp at the end of the year. In September 1914, Colonel Lowther recruited for the Royal Sussex Regiment, forming 11th, 12th and 13th Battalions, known as 1st, 2nd and 3rd Southdown Battalions or Lowther's Lambs or the Southdowners. They trained at Cooden until summer 1915. That September a 700 strong detachment of the South African Heavy Artillery arrived and were joined by two training units of the Royal Garrison Artillery, including a small contingent of Australian Artillery. By the summer of 1916 the Royal Garrison Artillery controlled the entire site, which was renamed No.1 Reinforcing Depot Royal Siege Artillery. In January 1918 the artillery departed and were replaced by the Canadian Engineers. The camp was reconstructed as a Canadian convalescent hospital, Princess Patricia's Canadian Red Cross Hospital, which brought together Canadian hospitals from Uxbridge and Ramsgate. The capacity was 2,000 casualties and the first 131 patients arrived in March 1918. The hospital closed in February 1919.

Billy married Dorothy Winifred Holland (2nd February 1898–3rd August 1992), born at Westham, Sussex, on 20th November 1918, registered at Eastbourne, Sussex. They were living with his mother and her second husband in Dennysville, Washington Co, Maine, USA in 1920. They later lived at 111 Margaret Street, South Portland, Maine. They were living at Eastport, Washington Co, Maine in 1930 and were still there in 1940. Dorothy died after a short illness in a nursing home at Eastport and is buried with her husband. They had four children:

Billy's wife was born at Westham, close to Pevensey, near Eastbourne. It is recorded in the Domesday Book.

- William Scott Metcalf (27th November 1919–12 January 1993), known as Scott, served in the US Navy 22nd May 1944–20th January 1946. He married Mary Katherine Campbell (19th November 1920–15th November 2010), born at Perry, Washington Co, on 31st December 1940 at Eastport. They were living at Perry in 1991. Scott died at Chelsea, Kennebec Co, Maine and Mary at Orrington, Penobscot Co, Maine. They had three children, including Lee Scott Metcalf (born and died 1941) and Sheila Rae Metcalf.
- Sheila Dorothy Metcalf (1924–16th January 1978) married George Lacono (15th August 1918–11th March 2000), a State Department employee born at Tarrytown, New York, on 23rd August 1941 in the District of Columbia, USA. He was living with his widowed mother and three older siblings at 30 Wells Street, Malden, Middlesex Co, Massachusetts in 1930. They returned from Europe aboard SS *America*, departing Le Havre, France on 31st July 1951 and arriving in New York on 6th August. They were living at 11 South Hillside Avenue, Elmsford, New York. By 1955 they had moved to 43 Beckett, Portland, Cumberland Co, Maine. She died at Portland, Maine and he at Staten Island,

Billy and Dorothy lived at 111 Margaret Street, South Portland, Maine.

In the 1930s and 1940s they lived at Eastport, a small city consisting of a number of islands in Washington Co. The area was home to the Passamaquoddy tribe for at least 10,000 years. The St Croix colony, founded by French explorer Samuel de Champlain in 1604, was the first European settlement in the area. Fishermen and traders visited in the 17th century. Moose Island was settled in 1772 by James Cochrane of Newburyport, Massachusetts, who was joined by other fishermen from Newburyport and Portsmouth, New Hampshire. On 24th February 1798 Eastport was incorporated as a town. From 1807 to 1809 the town was a centre for smuggling during the Embargo Act imposed by President Thomas Jefferson. In 1809 Fort Sullivan was built and was captured by a British fleet under Sir Thomas Hardy on 11th July 1814, during the War of 1812. The British claimed that Moose Island was on their side of the border agreed in 1783. However, the town returned to the United States in 1818. In 1833 Eastport was the second largest trading port in the country after New York City. The island's economy was primarily maritime and the harbour was ice-free year round. The first sardine factory was built c.1875 and the population grew because of it and related canning businesses. By 1886 the town had thirteen sardine factories, employing about 800 people. Eastport was incorporated as a city on 18th March 1893. As the fishing industry declined, so did the population (5,311 in 1900 falling to 1,331 in 2010). Fishing remains the principal industry but tourism has increased.

Richmond Co, New York. They had two children, both reportedly adopted in Germany:
- ° William George Lacono (born 1950), born in Germany, was studying at Carnegie Mellon University, Pittsburgh, Pennsylvania at the time of his marriage to Mary Jane Foster (born 1951), born in North Carolina, on 17th June 1970 at St Mary, Alexandria, Fairfax Co, Virginia. She was living at 6110 Edgewood Terrace, Alexandria at the time.
- ° Sheila Lacono.

- Stuart Holland Metcalf (17th October 1925–21st April 1998), born at Dennysville, Washington Co, served as a corporal in the US Army during the Second World War. He married Liberty Bell/Belle Worrey (née Barter) (22nd February 1918–25th July 2007), born at Bath, Seghadoc Co, Maine, on 1st July 1958. They lived at South Portland, Maine. Stuart and Liberty Belle are

Billy's son, Stuart, is buried in the Maine Veterans Memorial Cemetery, Augusta.

buried in the Maine Veterans Memorial Cemetery (RC Section, Row 8, Site 5), 129 Blue Star Avenue, Old Augusta, Kennebec Co, Maine. Liberty had married Herbert Lester Worrey (born 10th January 1909), born at Bath, Seghadoc Co, on 18th November 1933 at Portland. They were living with his mother, Lena, and her second husband, Eli Paul Pelkey at 69 Chestnut, Portland in 1940. Herbert and Liberty had three children – Clinton William Worrey (1934–78), Marilyn Leona Worrey (1935–2006) and Herbert Lester Worrey (1936–2014). The marriage ended in divorce.

* Stanley Harold Metcalf (19th September 1938–26th August 2018), born at Calais, Washington Co, graduated from Portland High School. He served in the US Army 1954–57 and then the US Coast Guard. He was serving as captain of a gunboat in Vietnam at the time of his father's death in August 1968 (Bronze Star and Meritorious Service Medal). On returning to the USA he was stationed at Burnt Island Light, Maine and later at Coast Guard Stations at Rockland and Southwest Harbor in Maine, at Race Point Light Search & Rescue, Cape Cod, Provincetown, Massachusetts and at Portsmouth Station Search & Rescue, New Hampshire. During his Coast Guard career he served aboard USCG *Cutters Point Mast*, *Garnet*, *Swivel* and *Eastwind*. He retired as a boatswain's mate senior chief petty officer in 1978. He was an active member of the Veterans of Foreign Wars and American Legion posts wherever he lived, including the Winslow-Holbrook-Merritt American Legion Post No.1 in Rockland. He was a life member of the Canadian Scottish Regimental Association, Victoria, New Brunswick. He married Patricia Ruth Adams (9th May 1940–6th December 2000) at Perry, Maine and they lived at Bucksport, Maine. Stan was a restaurateur there and was a board member and volunteer of the Maine Lighthouse Museum. Patricia died at Andover, New Hampshire. Stanley was engaged to Dorothy Black of Union, Maine at the time of his death at Rockport, Knox Co, Maine. Stanley and Patricia had four children:
  ◦ John Stuart Metcalf (born 1961) married Ann Deskyster and they lived at Rollinsford, New Hampshire. They had two children.
  ◦ Marianne Helen Metcalf (born 1963) married as Green (born c.1953) and they had a son. She married Michael Thompson (born c.1960). She married Edward Scully and they lived at Coxsackie, New York. Marianne and Edward had seven children.
  ◦ Stanley Herbert Metcalf (born 1965) married and had a son. He married Mary Ann Devanna (born 1965) and they had three children.
  ◦ Richard G Metcalf married Deborah and settled in York Co, Maine.

Dorothy's father, Havelock Thomas Holland (1866–24th July 1948), born at Netherfield, Sussex, married Charlotte née Elphick (1873–19th December 1857), born at Westham, Sussex, on 16th May 1896 at Eastbourne, Sussex. He was a gas stoker and they were living at Blacknest, Westham, Sussex in 1901 and at The Rookery, Friday Street, Westham, near Eastbourne, Sussex in 1911. They were both

living at 2 Friday Street, Eastbourne at the time of their deaths there. In addition to Dorothy they had two sons:
- Frederick Thomas Holland (17th February 1900–10th December 1965) was a motor mechanic when he enlisted in the Royal Naval Volunteer Reserve on 19th February 1918 (MB2353). He served on HMS *Hermione*, then HMS *Arrogant* 4th April, HMS *Hermione* again 22nd May, HMS *Victory* 29th May, *Deal Castle* 17th July, HMS *Hermione* once again 29th October and was demobilised on 22nd February 1919. He married Florence Helena Sandford (8th July 1895 -1979), born at Fulham, London, in 1924 at Eastbourne. They had a daughter, Phyllis A Holland the following year. He was a fitter in 1957. They were living at 6 Middlesex Court, Leslie Street, Eastbourne at the time of his death at St Mary's Hospital, Eastbourne.
- Gilbert Havelock Holland (20th February 1906–23rd September 1994), born at Westham, married Alice Edith Baulcomb (5th February 1905–February 1988) in 1923 at Eastbourne, where she was born. He was a generating station shift engineer in charge in 1939 and they were living at 12 South Avenue, Eastbourne. They had six children – Joan Alice Holland (1924–2009), Dora Winifred Holland (1930–2009), Yvonne Holland (1934), Rita V Holland (1938), Teresa E Holland (1940) and David J Holland (1944). The marriage ended in divorce. Gilbert married Valerie C Boden in 1955. He was living at 34 Holmbush Way, Southwick, West Sussex at the time of his death there. Alice married as Short and died at Bedford, Bedfordshire.

Billy's wife received separation allowance of $30 per month from 4th January 1919. The VC was presented by the King at York Cottage, Sandringham on 26th January. Billy was discharged from hospital on 4th April and joined 18th Reserve Battalion on 15th April. He was attached to the Canadian Discharge Depot, Buxton on 7th May for return to Canada. Billy embarked on SS *Metagama* at Liverpool on 24th May and disembarked at Québec on 2nd June, joining the Québec Depot Clearing Services Command next day. He was demobilised on 5th June 1919. His trade was given as grocer, although he was a barber when he enlisted. Billy returned to live in Maine, USA, where he became a mechanic/electrician.

York Cottage, Sandringham, Norfolk where Billy Metcalf and his CO, Cyrus Peck, received their VCs from the King.

Billy attended two VC Reunions – the VC Dinner at the Royal Gallery of the House of Lords, London on

9th November 1929 and the VC Centenary Celebrations at Hyde Park, London on 26th June 1956. He also attended the coronation of Elizabeth II in June 1953. Billy was an honorary life member of St Croix, New Brunswick Branch No.9 of the Canadian Legion (Royal Canadian Legion from 1960). He attended the 18th Annual Convention of the Maine State Command, Canadian Legion at Orchard, Maine in August 1956, at which he gave an account of the VC Centennial celebrations in London.

Billy was admitted to a nursing home in Lewiston, South Portland, Cumberland Co, Maine in the spring of 1968 and died there on 8th August 1968. His funeral, with full military honours, on 12th August was conducted by the Provincial Command Chaplain, Reverend JFN Jones, and was attended by more than forty members of

Billy Metcalf's grave in Bayside Cemetery, Eastport.

the Royal Canadian Legion. The coffin was draped in the Union Flag over the flags of Canada and the United States, as it was the Union Flag that he and his buddies fought under. Dorothy was presented with the Union Flag after the funeral. Billy is buried in Bayside Cemetery, Eastport, Maine, USA (Section D, Plot 11-NW). He had requested to be buried there close to the border between Canada and the USA across the St Croix River. Billy is commemorated in a number of other places:

- Victoria Cross obelisk to all Canadian VCs at Military Heritage Park, Barrie, Ontario dedicated by Princess Royal on 22nd October 2013.
- Named on two of eleven plaques honouring 175 men from overseas awarded the VC for the Great War. The plaques were unveiled by the Senior Minister of State at the Foreign & Commonwealth Office and Minister for Faith and Communities, Baroness Warsi, at a reception at Lancaster House, London on 26th June 2014 attended by The Duke of Kent and relatives of the VC recipients. The Canadian plaque was unveiled outside

The VC memorial plaque, presented to the United States by the people of the United Kingdom, is displayed at Arlington National Cemetery in Virginia.

the British High Commission in Elgin Street, Ottawa on 10th November 2014 by The Princess Royal in the presence of British High Commissioner Howard Drake, Canadian Minister of Veterans Affairs Julian Fantino and Canadian Chief of the Defence Staff General Thomas James Lawson. The United States plaque is at Arlington National Cemetery, Arlington Co, Virginia, USA.
* Plaque No.80 on the York Cemetery VC Memorial, West Don River Valley, Toronto, Ontario dedicated on 25th June 2017.
* Two 49 cents postage stamps in honour of the ninety-four Canadian VC winners were issued by Canada Post on 21st October 2004 on the 150th Anniversary of the first Canadian VC's action, Alexander Roberts Dunn VC.
* Communities and Local Government commemorative paving stones for the 145 VCs born in Australia, Belgium, Canada, China, Denmark, Egypt, France, Germany, India, Iraq, Japan, Nepal, Netherlands, Newfoundland, New Zealand, Pakistan, South Africa, Sri Lanka, Ukraine and United States of America were unveiled at the National Memorial Arboretum, Alrewas, Staffordshire by Prime Minister David Cameron MP and Sergeant Johnson Beharry VC on 5th March 2015.
* Plaque at Villers-lès-Cagnicourt Church, near Arras, France.

In addition to the VC and MM & Bar he was awarded the 1914–15 Star, British War Medal 1914–20, Victory Medal 1914–19, George VI Coronation Medal 1937 and Elizabeth II Coronation Medal 1953. He should have been entitled to receive the Canadian Centennial Medal 1967 but accurate records are not available. It does not appear in his medal group or miniatures. The Canadian Scottish Regimental Museum has included a replica with the other replica medals on display but it is not included with the real medals. The medals were owned by his son, Stanley, who kept them in a manila envelope at his home at Bucksport, Maine.

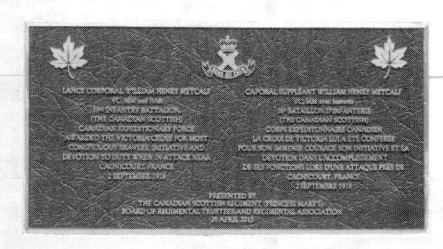

Billy Metcalf's memorial in Villers-lès-Cagnicourt.

The Canadian Scottish Regiment (Princess Mary's) Museum in Bay Street Armoury, Victoria, British Columbia. The Bay Street Drill Hall was completed in 1915 for militia units, such as 5th Regiment of Artillery, and for two new units, 50th Gordon Highlanders of Canada and HQ Military District No.11. It was designated a historic building in 1989. Currently based there are 89th Royal Canadian Air Cadet Squadron, 5th (British Columbia) Field Artillery Regiment RCA and the Canadian Scottish Regiment (Princess Mary's) (Michal Klajban).

The Canadian Scottish Regimental Museum in Victoria, British Columbia asked Stanley if they could borrow his father's VC for an 80th Anniversary display in 1998. Stanley decided instead to present the medals, together with his father's other war memorabilia, to the Museum in a ceremony on 1st October 1998. The VC is held by the Canadian Scottish Regiment (Princess Mary's) Museum, Bay Street Armoury, 715 Bay Street, Victoria, British Columbia, Canada.

410935 PRIVATE CLAUDE JOSEPH PATRICK NUNNEY
38th Battalion (Ottawa) CEF

Claude Nunney was born on 19th July 1892 at 42 Bexhill Road, St Mary, Bulverhithe, St Leonards-on-Sea, Sussex, registered as Stephen Sargent Claude Nunney. His father, William Percy Nunney Nunney (21st June 1857–1940), born at Burford, Oxfordshire, married three times:

- Mary née Sargent (c.1865–1899), born at Leeds, Yorkshire. No marriage has been traced. William was a laundry machinist in 1891 and they were living at Laundry Cottage, St Mary, Bulverhithe, St Leonards-on-Sea. By 1892 he was a grocer's assistant. She suffered from retinitis pigmentosa and was almost blind. She died of food poisoning in February 1899, registered at Pancras, London.
- Amelia Long (1874–1950), born at Buckhurst Hill, Essex, on 22nd October 1900 at West Ham Register Office, London. He was a gas engine driver in 1901 and they were living at 75 Parkside, Walthamstow, London. William appears to have deserted Amelia around August 1903. Amelia and her daughter, Emily, were living with Alphonsus Paul Aggio (1857–1939), a railway signalman, born at Colchester, Essex, as his housekeeper at 101 Whitta Road, Manor Park, East Ham in 1911. Amelia and Alphonsus married in West Ham in 1914. Alphonsus (registered as Aggis) had married Margaret Mosely (born 1858), born at Limehouse, London, in 1880 at Stepney, London. They were living at 63 Morgan Street, West Ham in 1891. He was living with his sons at 9 Florence Road, South Leyton, London in 1901. Margaret was not with them and her fate is unknown. Alphonsus and Margaret had three children:
    ◦ Lilian Catherine Aggio (registered as Aggis) (1880–84).
    ◦ Percy J Aggio (1885–1940) at Bow, London was a tea merchant's clerk in 1901. He was a bachelor living at 74 St George's Square, Westminster, London in 1939.

Biographies 231

- ◦ Alphonsus Sydney Aggio (born 1887) was a grocer's assistant in 1901. He changed his name to Sidney Allen by deed poll on 27th May 1921 (LG 28th June 1921).
- Mary Ann Smith (née Sweetman) (1863–June 1921), born at Poplar, London, on 12th June 1905 at Brentford, Middlesex. She had married George Philemon Smith (born 1860), a labourer, on 27th July 1890 at Acton Parish Church, London. George was living at 7 Richard Cottage, Acton. He was a soldier in 1891 and she was living at 14 Nelson Place, Acton in 1894. George is understood to have died in service between 1893 and 1901, by when Mary Ann was a laundress, living with her sons at 14 Nelson Place, Acton. Mary and George had two sons:
  - ◦ Charles George Smith (1891–1946) was a coal carman (unemployed) in 1911 boarding with his future wife and her parents at 1 Back Street, The Steyne, Acton. He married Ethel Louisa Keen (1891–1976) on 11th August 1914 at Acton Parish Church. He was a council lorry driver in 1939 and they were living at 3 Cheltenham Place, Acton. They had a daughter.
  - ◦ Matthew William Smith (1894–1977) married Mary Elizabeth Evers (born 1895) in 1922. He was an omnibus driver and she was a charwoman in 1939, living at 74 Brouncker Road, Acton.

About August/September 1905, Mary Ann was visited at home by William's second wife, Amelia. William was ill and was confined to his bed. Mary took Amelia into the bedroom and William immediately recognised her, calling her by her name.

St Leonards-on-Sea, west of Hastings, was laid out in the early 19th century as a new town of elegant houses for the wealthy. The area was owned by the Levett family of Norman origin. Their descendants, the Eversfields, prospered from iron foundries and property holdings in Tudor times. James Burton, a London property developer, purchased land from the Eversfield estate to establish a seaside resort and work started in 1826. A turnpike road was included and the railways arrived in 1845. A second phase commenced in 1850 under his son, Decimus Burton (1800–81). About the same time, Hastings was expanding westwards and the area between the two towns was gradually filled with new properties. In 1875 the two towns merged into the County Borough of Hastings. The pier, which opened in October 1891, was cut in half during the Second World War as an anti-invasion precaution and the remains were demolished in 1951. A number of prominent people have lived in the town:

- Queen Adelaide (1792–1849), consort of William IV, lived there as a widow.
- Author Henry Rider Haggard, who wrote *King Solomon's Mines*, lived at North Lodge, Maze Hill.
- Prince Rainier III of Monaco attended Summerfields School.
- George Monger, awarded the VC for his part in the Siege of Lucknow 1857, lived in Tower Road, where he died in 1887.
- Archibald Belaney (1888–1938), known as 'Grey Owl', a famous conservationist.

Witney is an ancient market town and important crossing point on the River Windrush in Oxfordshire. It appears as Wyttannige in a Saxon charter of 969 and the Domesday Book in 1086 records it as Witenie. The parish church of St Mary was originally Norman and the market dates back to the Middle Ages. West End, actually on the northern side of the town, is one of Britain's best-preserved streets. Witney became famous for its woollen blankets and mops, which were used aboard every Royal Navy ship. The railway arrived in 1861 and closed in 1970. In recent times the Witney MP has been former Foreign Secretary, Douglas Hurd (1983–97) and former Conservative leader and Prime Minister, David Cameron (2001–16). Patrick Steptoe, the pioneer of fertility treatment, attended Henry Box School in Witney.

Mary reported the matter to the police and William was arrested by Detective Sergeant Joseph Thompson. The case was heard at The Old Bailey, London on 12th September 1905. William stated that he wrote several letters to Amelia without reply and had assumed that she had passed away. He was recorded as a widower when he married Mary Ann. He admitted his guilt and was sentenced to six months imprisonment. The marriage was annulled. Mary Ann died at 62 The Steyne, Acton.

By 1939, William was in Tooting Bec Hospital, Wandsworth, recorded as incapacitated. Claude had six siblings from his father's first two marriages:

- William Nunney (1885–18th February 1939) was born in Natal, South Africa according to various census returns but when he enlisted he gave his birthplace as Hastings, Kent (sic). No evidence has been found that he was born in South Africa, or that his parents were ever there. William was a jobbing gardener and later a costermonger working for Mr J Aldridge of 4 Colva Mews, Colva Street (later Colva Walk), Highgate. He enlisted in 4th Battalion, East Surrey Regiment (Militia) on 8th June 1903 in London (3463). He was described as 5′ 2½″ tall, weighing 116 lbs, with fresh complexion, blue eyes, light brown hair and his religious denomination was Church of England. He attended annual training every year 1904–13 and was promoted corporal on 10th August 1908. William enlisted in 4th Battalion, East Surrey Regiment (Special Reserve) on 6th September 1908 at Shorncliffe, Kent, by when he had grown to 5′ 4½″ tall and weighed 120 lbs. Promoted sergeant 24th July 1911 and re-engaged for another four years from 6th September 1912. William was mobilised on 5th August 1914, transferred to 2nd Battalion and reverted to private on 28th December. He went to France on 14th January 1915 and was diagnosed with retinitis pigmentosa. He returned to the Depot on 20th September. A medical board at Lincoln on 3rd October

recommended discharge. He was discharged at Kingston-upon-Thames, Surrey as permanently unfit for war service on 24th November 1915. William married Sarah Tilley (7th December 1877–1970), a domestic servant born at Islington, London, on 1st December 1905 at Pancras, London. She had two daughters prior to her marriage:
- Sarah Tilley (1895–1982) married George Herbert Mewett (1896–1965) in 1924.
- Maria Elizabeth Tilley (1900–70) married Edward James Coker (1903–60) in 1929. They were living at 9 Balmore Street, Highgate in 1939 and were still there when he died at Whittington Hospital, Archway Wing, London. They had a son.

Sarah and her two daughters were living with her mother at 3 Litcham Street, Pancras in 1901. William and Sarah were living at 21 Balmore Street, Highgate, London in 1911 and at 9 Balmore Street by 1918. They were still there at the time of William's death at Archway Hospital, Highgate. William and Sarah had seven children, all born at St Pancras:

- William Percy Nunney (1906–76) had been diagnosed with retinitis pigmentosa by 1908. He was a general labourer and an Air Raid Precautions warden in 1939 living with his mother. His death was registered at Stevenage, Hertfordshire.
- Ellen Nunney (1908–85) married Frederick Barron (1907–90), born at Marylebone, London, in 1929. He was a general labourer in 1939 and they were living at 7 Balmore Street, Highgate. They had a son.
- Alfred 'Tim' Nunney (1911–46) married Eva Mary Kimber (1910–76), born at Harwich, Essex, at Holy Trinity Church, Sheerness, Kent on 12th August 1934. They had four children. Tim was a general labourer in 1939 and they were living at 149 High Street, Sheerness. He served as a bombardier in 178th Field Regiment RA (1148236). He contracted meningitis and died at County Hospital, Sheppey. Eva married Albert J Jones in 1954. She died at St Bartholomew's Hospital, Rochester, Kent.
- Dorothy 'Doll' Mary Nunney (1913–55) married John 'Jack' Stanley Farrow (1914–75), born at Barnet, Hertfordshire, in 1938. He was a navvy (heavy worker) in 1939 and they were living at 12 New Trinity Road, Finchley, London. He was living at 7 Balmore Street, London at the time of his death there. They had five children.
- Lilian 'Lily' Nunney (1916–99) married Edward George Simmonds (1916–83), born at Marylebone, London, in 1934. He was a dispatch clerk in 1939 and they were living at 9 Balmore Street, Highgate. They had four children.
- Florence M Nunney (1919–21).
- Gladys WR Nunney (1922–24).

- Percy Colin Nunney (25th July 1888–17th March 1951), born at North Hinksey, Berkshire, married Gertrude 'Gerty' Stanton (31st December 1889–1963), born at 17 Goth Street, Liverpool, at West Derby, Lancashire in 1909. He was a typefounder in 1911 and they were living at 5 Marlsford Street, West Derby. Percy served as a gunner in the Royal Garrison Artillery (92204). By 1939 he was a linotype operator and they were living at 52 Hannan Road, Liverpool. They had nine children all registered at West Derby:
    - William Claude Nunney (1910–80) was an assistant pantry man in 1939. He married Edith Grace Mackenzie (1919–90) in 1942. They had two sons.
    - Norah Gertrude Nunney (1911–74) married Eric Francis Palmer (1907–69) in 1933. They had two daughters.
    - Winifred Nunney (1913–99) was a shop assistant in a greengrocer's in 1939. She married George W Pickering in 1947 at Blackpool, Lancashire.
    - Dorothy Nunney (born 1915) married Stanley Edmund Cooksley (born 1916), born in Bristol, Gloucestershire, in 1937. They were living at 42 Jubilee Drive, Liverpool in 1950 and at 93 Thomas Lane, Liverpool in 1970. They had three children.
    - Louisa Nunney (1925–80) married Thomas J Winker (born 1925) in 1950. They had a son.
    - Twins Edith Margaret Nunney and Olive M Nunney (born and died 1927).
    - Raymond C Nunney (born 1929) married Florence Dineley (born 1929) in 1954. They had two sons.
    - George Kenneth Nunney (born 1932) was a warehouseman living with his mother at the time of his marriage to Irene Fell (born 1933) on 23rd February 1955 at All Saints, Toxteth, Lancashire. They had three children.
- George Frederick Nunney (9th February 1890–1946), born at Lambeth, London, married Edith Rosina 'Rose' Honeysett (9th February 1890–12th July 1956), born at Wandsworth in 1916. He was a builder's labourer in 1939 and they were living at 18 Meyrick Road, Battersea. His death was registered at Battersea, London. She was living at 39 Grant Road, Battersea at the time of her death at St Luke's Hospital, Paddington. They had a son, George Frederick Nunney (1919–60), who was an electrician. He was living at 69 Elsenham Street, Southfields, Wandsworth at the time of his death at St James Hospital, Balham, London.
- Alfred E Nunney (7th October 1893–10th August 1918). On attestation he stated that he was born at Hastings, Sussex, but the 1901 Census shows Woodford, Essex. The birth of an Alfred Edmund F (sic) Nunney was registered at Hastings in the 4th quarter of 1893. Alfred emigrated to Canada with his brother Claude. He enlisted in 80th Overseas Battalion CEF (219320) at Belleville, Ontario on 13th September 1915, described as a labourer, 5′ 2½″ tall, weighing 120 lbs, with dark complexion, light blue eyes, dark brown hair and his religious denomination was Roman Catholic. He gave his next of kin as his brother, Stephen (Claude), 325 Victoria Street, Kingston, Ontario. He joined 80th Battalion at Barriefield.

The Battalion sailed for England aboard SS *Baltic*, departing Halifax, Nova Scotia on 22nd May 1916 and disembarking on 31st May. He assigned $15 per month from his Army pay to a friend, Ray Murray, 325 Victoria Street, Kingston (same address as Claude) from 1st June. Alfred was included in drafts of 408 and 461 men from 80th Battalion at Bramshott to 74th Battalion at Bordon in June 1916. Alfred transferred on 13th June and transferred again to 44th Battalion at Bramshott on 15th July. In his will, dated 20th July, he signed as Alfred E Nunney and left everything to his fiancée, Miss Bessie Nicholson, City Hospital, Belleville, Ontario. Alfred embarked for France with 44th Battalion on 10th August, disembarking on 12th August. He was attached to 4th Division Train and detached to 4th Division Salvage Company CASC 23rd–31st August. He received a gunshot wound to the neck on 27th October and was admitted to 12th Canadian Field Ambulance next day. He transferred to the Corps Rest Station the same day and rejoined the Battalion on 5th November. The wound cannot have been serious. He attended a Lewis gun course 8th–14th January 1917. On 1st April he was admitted to No.23 Casualty Clearing Station with boils and was transferred by 14 Ambulance Train to 11th General Hospital, Camiers on 2nd April. He was moved to 20th General Hospital, Camiers with scabies on 6th April, transferred to No.6 Convalescent Depot, Étaples on 10th April and to Base Details Étaples on 23rd May. Alfred joined the Canadian Base Depot on 24th May. On 1st June he forfeited four days' pay for making an improper remark to a NCO on 22nd May. He transferred to 4th Entrenching Battalion on 2nd June and returned to the Battalion on 7th June. He was granted leave to England 8th–20th September and was awarded a Good Conduct Badge on 13th September. He was granted fourteen days leave to Paris from 14th March 1918 and returned to 4th Canadian Infantry Base Depot on 31st March. Alfred was admitted to 51st General Hospital, Étaples with gonorrhea on 1st April and was discharged to duty on 16th May. While in hospital his pay was stopped as gonorrhea was regarded as a self-inflicted wound. He joined the Canadian Base Depot on 17th May and the Canadian Corps Reinforcement Camp on 6th June. He was admitted to No.59 Casualty Clearing Station with an injury to his right shoulder on 25th June and transferred to the Canadian Corps Reinforcement Camp on 29th June. On 9th July his pay was stopped by 9d to make up the cost of a housewife (sewing and clothing repair kit). Alfred returned to the Battalion on 15th July.

Claude's brother, Alfred Nunney, is buried in Fouquescourt British Cemetery. Also buried there is James Edward Tait VC, who appears in the eighth volume in this series.

He was killed in action and is buried in Fouquescourt British Cemetery, France (I C 6). His medals, plaque and scroll were sent to his fiancée, who had married as Mrs Bessie Marshall, 587 University Street, Montréal, Québec.

* Mary Angelina Nunney (born 1898) was a resident at Nazareth House, Fulham, London in 1901. Nazareth House was a convent and home for the aged, infirm and destitute children.
* Emily 'Peggy' Amelia Nunney (22nd January 1904–5th January 1984), born at West Ham, London, changed her surname to Aggio following her mother's marriage to Alphonsus Paul Aggio in 1914. She married Ernest J Day in 1939 at Ilford, Essex. She married Donald Coxshall (1st December 1910–15th October 1994), born at Sewardstone, Essex, in 1952 at East Ham, London. They were living at 13 Albion Terrace, Sewardstone Road, Chingford, Essex at the time of her death there. Donald had married Eileen Heather E Wright (11th July 1915–4th January 1988) in 1938 at Edmonton, Middlesex. Donald was a motor mechanic in 1939, when he and Eileen were living with her parents at 42 Eastbrook Road, Waltham Cross, Essex. The marriage ended in divorce without issue. Eileen married Joseph JA Stapleton in 1951 at Epping, Essex. She died at 30 Buckingham Court, 12 Mount Pleasant Road, Poole, Dorset.

Claude's paternal grandfather, William Nunney (26th September 1811–2nd September 1877), born at Burford, Oxfordshire, married three times:

* Rebecca Rawlings (died 1839) on 26th June 1838 at St George, Hanover Square, London.
* Anne Clarke (c.1816–11th August 1852) in 1840 at Witney, Oxfordshire. They were living on High Street, Burford in 1851, where she died the following year.
* Angelina Davis née Baugham (4th April 1812–20th February 1890), the VC's grandmother, born at Salford, Oxfordshire, on 6th March 1855 at Chelsea, London. Angelina had married Thomas Davis (c.1815–26th January 1853), a plumber and glazier born at Upton-upon-Severn, Worcestershire, on 22nd June 1836 at Salford, Oxfordshire. There were no children. William was a building broker employing two men and three boys in 1861 and one man, two boys and a labourer in 1871. They were living on the High Street, Burford at the time of both censuses and he subsequently died there. She was still living on High Street in 1881 with her grandson, Harry Frederick William Cunningham.

William had eight children from his three marriages:

* Frederick William Nunney (born and died 1839), birth registered at Witney and death at Chipping Norton, Oxfordshire.
* Charlotte Susannah Nunney (1842–26th October 1893) married George Currell (c.1838–90), born at Winchester, Hampshire, on 4 November 1867 at St Mary's,

The High Street in Burford on the River Windrush in the Cotswold hills of Oxfordshire. In 685 one of various synods to resolve when Easter Day should be celebrated was held there. There was a battle between the West Saxons and Mercians at Burford in 752. Burford Priory, now a private house, stands on the site of a 13th century Augustinian priory hospital. The town began near the Priory and moved to its current site after the Norman Conquest. From the 14th until the 17th centuries, Burford was an important centre for the wool trade. The parish church of St John the Baptist was used as a prison during the Civil War in 1649. Burford has twice had bell foundries, one in the 17th century and another in the 19th and 20th centuries.

Portsea, Hampshire. He was a tobacconist and she was a dressmaker in 1871, living at 11 Southgate Road, Winchester. By 1881 George was a tobacconist assistant and Charlotte was employing five hands in her dressmaking business, living at 1 and 2 Parchment Street, Winchester. They both died in Winchester. They had seven children – Fanny Alice Currell 1871, Florence Annie Currell 1872, Ethel Charlotte Currell 1874, Neva Mary Currell 1875, Mabel Ida Currell 1877, Loela Ella Currell 1879 and Nora Evelyn Currell 1881.
- Alice Malinda Martha Nunney (19th February 1843–2nd July 1919) was living with her sister, Evelina and family, at 1 High Street, Rocester, Staffordshire in 1881 and 1891. She married Daniel Coleman (1847–1927) in 1895 at Uttoxeter, Staffordshire. Daniel was living with the Nunney family in 1861 as a fourteen year old assistant, born at Chadlington, Oxfordshire. By 1901 he was a grocer's manager and they were living at 10 Edith Road, Oxford. By 1911 Daniel was a grocer's assistant and later a commercial traveller. Daniel had married Constance Isabella Smith (c.1841–94), born at Brize Norton, Oxfordshire, in 1870 at Witney. He was a grocer and outfitter in 1871 and they were living at their shop in Oddington, Gloucestershire. By 1881 he was a grocer's assistant, and they were living at 1 Holybush Row, Oxford. They were still there in 1891, by which time he was a grocer's manager. Daniel and Constance had three chidren – Lily Esther Coleman 1871, Wilfred Alick Coleman 1875 and John George Coleman 1875.
- Eveline Mary Ann Nunney (1844–14th September 1920) married Edmund Langton (c.1833–30th May 1901), born at Elsham, Lincolnshire, on 7th

November 1867 at St John the Baptist Church, Penistone, Yorkshire. He was a licensed victualler in 1871 and they were living at 134 Mill Street, Toxteth Park, Lancashire. By 1881 he was a grocer and they were living at 1 High Street, Rocester. Staffordshire. He was a grocer and baker in 1901 and they were living at Churnet Row, Rocester, by which time he was suffering from paralysis and died there shortly after the census. Eveline also died there. They had twelve children – Annie Mary Langton 1871, Rosa Jane Langton 1872, Alice Malvinna Langton 1873, Angelina Florence Mabel Langton 1875, Edmund Langton 1877, Lily Langton 1879, Evelina Minna Langton 1880, Jessie Eleanor Langton 1882, Daisy Adeline Langton 1884, Elsie Violet Langton 1886, Flora Kate Langton 1888 and Thomas William Langton 1891.

- Harriett Mathilda Nunney (1846–2nd April 1911) never married and was living with her sister, Alice Coleman, and her husband at 10 Edith Road, Oxford at the time of her death there.
- Sarah Annie Nunney (1847–85) married Thomas Charles Cunningham (27th April 1846–1938), an upholsterer born at Portsea, Hampshire, on 21st October 1868 at Burford. She died at Hastings, Sussex. They had nine children – William Thomas Percy Cunningham 1870, Percy Nunney Cunningham 1871, Harry Frederick William Cunningham 1873, Walter Edward Cunningham 1875, Millicent Ida May Cunningham 1876, Thomas Charles Cunningham 1878, Hubert Frank Cunningham 1880, Alan Douglas Cunningham 1881 and Arthur Rupert Cunningham 1882. Thomas married Teresa Haseltine (c.1846–1911) on 25th December 1886 at Emmanuel, Forest Gate, London. They were living at 2 Abergavenny Villa, Frant Road, Tunbridge Wells, Kent in 1901. Teresa died at Ticehurst, Sussex. Thomas was living at 2 Abergavenny Villa with his daughter, Mary, in 1911. He died at Tonbridge, Kent. Thomas and Teresa had three daughters – twins Annie Harriet and Mary Teresa Cunningham 1888 and Dorothy Mabel Cunningham 1889.
- Florence Laura Nunney (19th January 1856–24th March 1894), born in Burford, Oxfordshire, was a schoolmistress in 1881, living with her mother. She married Frederick Cunningham (1859–16th September 1923), born at Portsea, Hampshire, on 6th March 1882 at Burford. She died in Poole, Dorset. He was living at 21 Seamoor Road, Bournemouth at the time of his death at Stagsden Nursing Home, Bournemouth. They had six children – Winifred Florence Cunningham (1883–1983), Percy Frederick William Mitchell Cunningham (1884–1947), Temple Charles Cunningham (1885–1915), Ina Alison Cunningham (1888–1974), Lillian Mary Cunningham (1889–1976) and Herbert Victor Cunningham (born and died 1892).
- Rosa Clementina Nunney (17th April 1859–1933) was an assistant in a school in 1881, living with her mother. She married Samuel Richard Langmaid (1863–1941), born at Haverfordwest, at Witney in 1886. He was an upholsterer's salesman in 1881 and they were living at 205 St George's Road, Hastings, Sussex. He was a

St Vincent's Boys' Home was on Harrow Road, Westbourne Green. It 1901 it was headed by Charlotte P Boyd, who was born at Macau, China c.1837. The Incorporated Society of the Crusade of Rescue and Homes for Destitute Catholic Children formed in 1899 to bring together various childcare initiatives in the Catholic Archdiocese of Westminster. The Society operated a number of homes, the first of which was St Patrick's Home for Working Boys founded c.1896 at 90 Charlotte Street, Fitzroy Square. At the end of 1896 the home was taken over by St Vincent's Boys' Home on Harrow Road, founded in 1859. In 1902, it relocated to larger premises at 14 Manette Street, Soho. In 1910, the Society opened a new headquarters at 48 Compton Street, Bloomsbury, which was also a receiving home for the reception, examination, classification and distribution of children coming into the Society's care.

New Orpington Lodge (later St George's Home), established in October 1895 on Wellington Street, Hintonburg, Ottawa, acted as a receiving and distributing home for Roman Catholic children from the United Kingdom.

life assurance agent in 1891 and they were living at 5 Beatrice Street, West Ham, London. By 1901 he was a furniture shop assistant and they were living at 13 Regents Park Road, Aston, Warwickshire. He was a furniture salesman in 1911 and they were living at 49 Victoria Street, Small Heath, Birmingham, Warwickshire. She died at Tenbury, Worcestershire and he in Birmingham. They had seven children – William Thomas Nunney Langmaid (1889–1946). Richard Samuel Langmaid (born and died 1889), Rosa Angelina Lowe Langmaid (1889–1971), Elsie Margaretta Langmaid (1891), Gladys Evelyn Langmaid (1893–1949), Edwin Victor Samuel Langmaid (1897–1982) and Alice Florence Stapp Langmaid (1899–1978).

No details of Claude's maternal grandparents are known. By 1901 Claude and his brother, Alfred, were living at St Vincent's Boys' Home, 337–339 Harrow Road, Westbourne Green. While there they were educated at Harrow Road School. From 1903 the government had a migration programme to offer children a better life in Canada, which continued into the 1930s. Claude and Alfred emigrated to Canada as wards of New Orpington Lodge, Wellington Street, Hintonburg, Ottawa. They departed Liverpool, Lancashire on 5th October 1905 aboard SS *Tunisian* in a group of forty-two children from the Catholic Emigration Association, Coleshill, Birmingham, Warwickshire, arriving at Québec on 13th October. Claude was renamed Claude Joseph Patrick Nunney at this time and was adopted by Dr DD MacDonald, who placed him in the care of his mother, Mrs Donald Roy McDonald, Pine Hill, North Lancaster, Glengarry Co, Ontario. Claude lived there until she died in 1912 and then lived mainly with Mr DH McGillis in North Lancaster. He continued his education in Canada at Separate School No.9, Lancaster. He was employed as a painter.

SS *Tunisian* (10,576 tons) was built for the Allan Line in 1900. In 1914 she was used as a troopship transporting the CEF to Europe. In 1915 she was an accommodation ship for prisoners of war off Ryde, Isle of Wight and later that year returned to trooping to India and Gallipoli. In 1917 the Allan Line was taken over by the Canadian Pacific Line. *Tunisian* was renamed *Marburn* in 1922 and was scrapped in 1928.

Separate School No.9, Lancaster, Glengarry Co, Ontario.

Claude served in 59th Stormont & Glengarry Regiment, (Militia) from 16th June 1913. He was found fit for service with the CEF on 8th February 1915 and enlisted for war service on 8th March at Alexandria, Ontario (410935). He was attested on 29th July, described as 5′ 5″ tall, with fair complexion, blue eyes, red hair and his religious denomination was Roman Catholic. He stated incorrectly that he was born in Dublin, Ireland on 24th December 1892. He gave his next of kin as Mrs DJ McDonald, North Lancaster, Ontario, although it is understood that she had died three years previously. The next of kin was later amended to Gordon Calder, a friend, of RR2, Green Valley, Ontario, to whom he assigned $15 per month from his Army pay from June 1916.

RMS *Caledonia* (9,223 tons), built by David & William Henderson & Co Ltd, Glasgow for the Anchor Line, was the third vessel of five so named for the Line. Launched on 22nd October 1904, she commenced her maiden voyage on 25th March 1905 and operated on the Glasgow–New York route. *Caledonia* was requisitioned on the outbreak of war in August 1914. Her passenger accommodation in peacetime of 1,468 (383 in 1st, 216 in 2nd and 869 in 3rd class) was increased to 3,074 troops and 212 horses. She operated as a troopship between Dublin and France, to Bombay and Canada and then in the Mediterranean. On 5th December 1916, she was en route from Salonica to Marseille when she was torpedoed by U-65, 200 kilometres east of Malta. Captain James Blaikie attempted to ram and sink the submarine and did strike her. Only one person was lost on *Caledonia*. Blaikie was taken prisoner and might have been shot for his attack on U-*65* had the British Government not let it be known, through the US Ambassador in Berlin, that a German officer prisoner would be shot in retaliation. Blaikie was sent to a prison camp instead.

Claude was assigned to 38th Battalion and sailed with the Battalion from Montréal aboard RMS *Caledonia* to Bermuda on 1st August to relieve the Royal Canadian Regiment, disembarking on 12th August. He forfeited five days pay in September but the reason is now known.

The Battalion moved to England, embarking aboard SS *Grampian* on 29th May 1916 and arriving on 9th June. He continued training at Bramshott, Surrey. In

SS *Grampian* (10,187 tons) docked at Glasgow. She was one of the largest vessels in the Allan Line, completed by Alexander Stephen & Sons of Linthouse in 1907. During the Great War, *Grampian* was used as a troopship for the CEF and also continued commercial work. On 10th July 1919 she was steaming between Montréal and Liverpool with 750 passengers and 350 crew aboard. Off Cape Race, Newfoundland she encountered an iceberg and, despite travelling slowly, a collision could not avoided. The captain avoided exposing the vulnerable side plates of the ship that had sealed the fate of *Titanic* seven years before, by deliberately striking the iceberg head-on. The bow was crushed and two crewmen were killed but *Grampian* was not damaged below the waterline and was able to reach St John's, Newfoundland. In 1921 *Grampian* was gutted in a fire during a refit at Antwerp and was scrapped in 1925.

his will, dated 26th July 1916, he left everything to Gordon Calder. He sailed for France with the Battalion on 13th August, arriving at Le Havre next day. **Awarded the DCM for his actions on Vimy Ridge in April 1917, when he had gunshot wounds to the left shoulder and right leg and his section was wiped out. However, he continued to advance and stopped an attack by over 200 enemy single-handed and continued for a total of three days under such conditions, 16th August 1917.**

He was admitted to 12th Canadian Field Ambulance for two days on 12th April, suggesting that the wounds were not serious. Claude was promoted corporal and lance sergeant on 28th April and sergeant on 16th June, all with seniority from 16th April. He was granted leave from 1st June and rejoined the Battalion on 16th June. **Awarded the MM for his actions after the capture of Avion Trench, near Avion, France. On the evening of 28th June 1917, Lieutenant William Cameron MacLennan took his platoon to form patrols and outposts in the village to connect with posts on either flank. Nunney was in charge of the platoon's machine gun section. MacLennan was wounded in the feet and body and was forced to retire. Nunney assumed command and remained on duty, personally superintending patrols until relieved on 30th June. That afternoon, 410548 Private William Murray was wounded. Unable to find a stretcher-bearer, Nunney proceeded to dress the injury himself. Throughout he displayed energy, strength and courage by his continuous action, LG 17th September 1917.**

Bramshott Military Camp on Bramshott Common, Hampshire, was one of three facilities set up in Aldershot Command by the Canadians in the Great War. There were five Canadian camps at Bramshott, named mainly after the Great Lakes:

- Huron and Ontario were on Bramshott Common.
- Superior was at the Grayshott end of Ludshott Common.
- Erie was at Headley Down.
- Connaught Military Hospital was also on Bramshott Common, adjacent to the A3 road.

Many men died there, some having survived the war fell victim to Spanish Influenza. In the churchyard of St Mary the Virgin are 318 Canadian burials. Another ninety-five Roman Catholics are buried in St Joseph's churchyard, Grayshott. Some battalions rested their colours in St Mary's when they left for France. In the church are stained glass windows and a priest's stall, desk and lectern presented in 1945 and 1954 to commemorate the Canadian association. At the rear of the nave hangs the Canadian Red Ensign that flew over the last Canadian Camp (Huron) in 1946. On 1st July, Canada's National Day, a service is held at the church, attended by Canadian representatives, Canadian Veterans' Association and the local Royal British Legion. The section of the A3 road at Bramshott was planted with maple trees but most have been removed since during road widening. Bramshott was one of two Canadian camps providing additional accommodation in preparation for the Normandy invasion in June 1944. The other was at Witley.

In July 1917 he suffered from gas poisoning and was admitted to No.23 Casualty Clearing Station on 29th July. He was transferred by 38 Ambulance Train on 31st July to 1st Canadian General Hospital, Étaples, arriving on 1st August. He was transferred to 3rd Stationary Hospital, Rouen, on 5th August and to No.2 Convalescent Depot, Rouen on 7th August. He was discharged on 21st September to 4th Canadian Base Depot, which he left on 29th September and rejoined the Battalion on 2nd October.

Claude was granted fourteen days leave in England from 19th January 1918 and rejoined the Battalion on 5th February. He was confined awaiting trial from 13th April, charged with striking a superior officer when he threw the CSM down the steps of a dugout, breaking his arm and causing other minor injuries. He was tried and convicted by field general court martial on 25th April, found guilty and sentenced to be reduced to the ranks and to serve one year of intensive hard labour. The sentence was confirmed by Brigadier General James Howden MacBrien CMG DSO, GOC 12th Canadian Brigade, who recommended mercy on account of his previous service. On 3rd May, whilst he was under guard in the horse lines, a British plane crashed and burst into flames. Claude broke through his guard, entered the burning plane and carried the pilot out. He was badly burned on the hands and face and was evacuated to No.57 Casualty Clearing Station. While there the Germans launched a heavy air attack, causing considerable damage, and he dashed from his bed to assist in bringing in the wounded over a period of some hours. As a result of the Brigade Commander's recommendation, the sentence was suspended on 6th May by the GOC First Army. Claude transferred to 7th Canadian General Hospital, Étaples on 4th May and was discharged on 4th June to the Canadian Infantry Base Depot. He transferred to the Canadian Corps Reinforcement Camp on 5th August and rejoined the Battalion on 18th August.

Brigadier General (later Major General) Sir James Howden MacBrien KCB CMG DSO CStJ (1878–1938) joined the Militia and transferred to the North-West Mounted Police. During the Second Boer War he served with the South African Constabulary and, on returning to Canada, was commissioned in the Royal Canadian Dragoons. In the Great War he was a general staff officer and from 1916 commanded 12th Canadian Brigade. After the war he was Chief of the General Staff 1920–27, head of the Canadian Militia, which was renamed the Canadian Army in 1940. He was Commissioner of the Royal Canadian Mounted Police 1931–38.

Awarded the VC for his actions on 1st–2nd September 1918 on the Drocourt-Quéant Line near Villers-lès-Cagnicourt, France, LG 14th December 1918. The court martial sentence was remitted on 10th September on account of his gallantry in action. Claude was wounded by a gunshot in the face and throat on 12th September and was evacuated to 3rd Canadian Field Ambulance and No.42 Casualty Clearing Station, Mingoval, near Aubigny-en-Artois, where he died of his wounds on 18th September 1918. He is buried in Aubigny Communal Cemetery Extension, Aubigny-en-Artois (IV B 39). The VC was never presented formally. He is commemorated in a number of other places:

Claude Nunney's grave in Aubigny Communal Cemetery Extension.

- Ontario
    ◦ Claude Nunney VC Memorial Branch No.544, Royal Canadian Legion (Ontario Command), 119 Military Road North, Lancaster, Ontario. There is a memorial plaque outside.
    ◦ War Memorial, Duncan Street, Lancaster, Glengarry Co.
    ◦ Victoria Cross obelisk to all Canadian VCs at Military Heritage Park, Barrie, Ontario dedicated by Princess Royal on 22nd October 2013.
    ◦ Named on one of eleven plaques honouring 175 men from overseas awarded the VC for the Great War. The plaques were unveiled by the Senior Minister of State at the Foreign & Commonwealth Office and Minister for Faith and

The War Memorial on Duncan Street in Lancaster, Glengarry.

Communities, Baroness Warsi, at a reception at Lancaster House, London on 26th June 2014 attended by The Duke of Kent and relatives of the VC recipients. The Canadian plaque was unveiled outside the British High Commission in Elgin Street, Ottawa on 10th November 2014 by The Princess Royal in the presence of British High Commissioner Howard Drake, Canadian Minister of Veterans Affairs Julian Fantino and Canadian Chief of the Defence Staff General Thomas James Lawson.

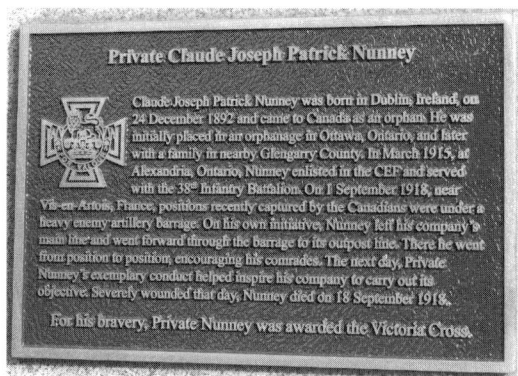

Claude Nunney's plaque on the York Cemetery VC Memorial. Unfortunately it includes a number of errors – date and place of birth (probably taken from his incorrect service record) and the wound that killed him was received on 12th September 1918 and not during the VC action.

- ○ Plaque No.94 on the York Cemetery VC Memorial, West Don River Valley, Toronto, Ontario dedicated on 25th June 2017.
- Two 49 cents postage stamps in honour of the ninety-four Canadian VC winners were issued by Canada Post on 21st October 2004 on the 150th Anniversary of the first Canadian VC's action, Alexander Roberts Dunn VC.
- Blue plaque was dedicated at his birthplace in St Leonards-on-Sea, Sussex in July 2017.
- Department for Communities and Local Government commemorative paving stones were dedicated at Hastings War Memorial, Alexandra Park, St Helens Road, Hastings, Sussex on 2nd September 2018 and at the Cross of Sacrifice, Glasnevin Cemetery, Dublin on 11th November 2018. The latter appears to be based on his statement when he enlisted that he was born in Dublin. No evidence of any Irish connection has been found.
- Vis-en-Artois named a small square 'Place du 38éme Bataillon de la Force Expéditionnaire Canadienne' and erected a plaque there to Nunney in 2018.
- Ring of Remembrance (L'Anneau de la Mémoire), Ablain-Saint-Nazaire, Pas-de-Calais, France.

The memorial to Claude Nunney in Place du 38éme Bataillon de la Force Expéditionnaire Canadienne, Vis-en-Artois.

Claude Nunney's unique medal group (Iain Stewart).

Claude was the mostly highly decorated other rank in the Canadian Army in the Great War. In addition to the VC, DCM and MM he was awarded the British War Medal 1914–20 and Victory Medal 1914–19. As he died on operational duty, his next-of-kin is eligible to receive the Canadian Memorial Cross. The VC is held at Cornwall Armoury, 505 Fourth Street East, Cornwall, Ontario.

LIEUTENANT COLONEL CYRUS WESLEY PECK
16th Battalion (Canadian Scottish) CEF

Cyrus Peck was born on 26th April 1871 at Hopewell Hill, Albert, New Brunswick, Canada. His father, Wesley Peck (18th June 1827–5th November 1920), also born at Hopewell, married Mary 'May' Susan née Rogers (25th February 1840–12th January 1928), born in New Brunswick of Irish extraction, on 27th August 1863 at Hopewell. Wesley was a ship's carpenter. The family moved to New Westminster, British Columbia on 27th June 1887, settling at 29 Wellington Street. He worked in the lumber business on the Fraser River on the lower British Columbia mainland. Cyrus had four siblings, also born at Hopewell:

- Haliburton Peck (13th June 1864–13th October 1923) moved to New Westminster, BC in 1882. He married Mabel Seraphina/Sophronia Kendall (20th October 1869–2nd January 1963), born at Gore, North Nation Hills, Québec, on 20th July 1891. Her name has also been seen as Mary Shendall and the year of marriage as 1890. She moved to New Westminster in 1887 and her father was involved in building Fraser Mills. Haliburton was the manager of the cannery at Namu and was later involved with Georgetown Sawmill, BC. He was the first vice president of the Abbotsford and District Board of Trade and the first postmaster of Georgetown Mills, Skeena until he resigned on retirement on 18th October 1919.

While hunting pheasant at Abbotsford, British Columbia, Haliburton slipped in a rut and his gun discharged both barrels into his abdomen. His wife and other family members heard his scream and rushed to his assistance but he died before medical aid arrived. An inquest found the cause of death was accidental. They had five children:
- Avery Lorne Peck (1892–1967), born at New Westminster, BC, married Kathryn Wrenn, born at Winona, Idaho, USA, on 18th January 1924. They had two children. Avery died in North Vancouver.
- Donald Wesley Peck (1894–1980) married Winifred Eva Jacklin (1896–1945), born at Prince Rupert, on 28th March 1916. They had three children. In 1916 Donald was a sawmill manager at Big Bay (Georgetown) for his father, who was the owner or part owner. The marriage ended in divorce. Winifred married Robert Thomas Cameron, born c.1890 in Ireland. Donald married Lilian Winifred Scammell (1898–1968) in Vancouver on 22nd May 1930. The marriage was dissolved in December 1938. He was a commercial fisherman before the Second World War and was a principal in Don Peck & Co Ltd, Cowichan Bay, BC. He was involved with the 'Gumboot Navie' of experienced fisherman who patrolling the British Columbia coast looking for Japanese invaders during the Second World War. Officially he was a skipper coxswain (Fishermen's Reserve) Royal Canadian Naval Reserve with seniority from 2nd April 1942. He served on HMCS *Ehkoli*, *Spray* and *Merry Chase*, then on HMCS *Burrard* as recruiting officer and HMCS *Chatham* for HMCS *Moolock* in command. He was later a master mariner and was involved in accident investigations. Donald married Doris Mary Campbell (1899–1995) at Tehama, California, USA on 22nd December 1958.
- Ruth Ida Peck (1897–1983), born at Vancouver, BC, married Rufus Seymour Wright (born 1891) on 30th August 1913 at Georgetown, BC. They had two children. She died at Burnaby, BC.

HMCS *Moolock*, built by Victoria Motor Boat & Repair Works Ltd, was commissioned into the Royal Canadian Navy Fisherman's Reserve on 2nd December 1941. Her first task was to assist in seizing Japanese-Canadian fishing vessels on 8th December. She was sold in 1947 and renamed *Western Crusader*. Thereafter she had at least seven owners and sank at Shelter Island Marina on the Fraser River on 12th May 2015.

- ○ Clarence Charles Peck (1900–13) born in Vancouver and died at Prince Rupert.
- ○ Eleanor Gloria Peck (1905–91) married Thomas W Power on 14th October 1925 at Premier Mines, BC. They moved to Ketchikan, Alaska where he was a dock superintendent for a gold mine in 1930. Eleanor married Brendan O'Farrell (1899–1982), born at Spokane, Washington, on 11th January 1936 in Los Angeles, California. When she applied for US naturalization in 1942, she was living with her husband at 13410 Saticoy Street, Van Nuys, California. They had three children.
* Irene K Peck (16th September 1866–9th January 1876).
* Seraphine Ada 'Sada' Peck (11th February 1869–22nd May 1952) married Hugh Duncan MacDiarmid (3rd January 1868–21st November 1916) on 3rd January 1905. They both died at Tappen, BC.
* Gaius La Forest Peck (25th August 1875–30th September 1954) married Maria Louise Swain (c.1879–27th June 1961) on 27th November 1899. He was a lumberman and in 1910 was manager of the Georgetown Sawmill Co, in business with his brother Cyrus. Gaius had a nervous breakdown in 1913 and was unable to work for nine months. He had an unusual military career. He enlisted in 6th Regiment (Duke of Cornwall's Own Rifles) (Militia) on 14th September 1915 and transferred to 67th Battalion on 21st September (102751 later 1039484) at Victoria, BC. He was described as a civil engineer and lumberman, 5′ 7″ tall, weighing 148 lbs, with dark complexion, blue eyes, dark hair and his religious denomination was Baptist. He gave his wife's address as 527–9th Street, New Westminster, BC and later 535–5th Avenue. He was found fit for service on 25th September and was commissioned from sergeant on 15th February 1916. He transferred to the Railway Construction Battalion on 24th February and attested for 143rd Battalion CEF as a lieutenant on 16th March, declaring previous service in 68th Regiment (Earl Grey's Own Rifles.) In May he was appointed OC 3rd Company Railway Troops and reported sick in July. Unusually Gaius resigned his commission on 9th August but attested again in Vancouver on 23rd August, declaring five months previous service with 67th Battalion (Western Scots) and six months with 143rd Battalion. He departed Halifax, Nova Scotia on RMS *Olympia* on 15th December and arrived at Liverpool on 26th December. He was promoted acting sergeant on arrival at Bramshott, with effect from 18th December. On 3rd February 1917, 239th Battalion became 3rd Battalion Canadian Railway Troops at Purfleet. Gaius went to France, landing at Boulogne on 11th March. He was confirmed in the rank of sergeant on 1st July and was commissioned as a temporary lieutenant on 4th September. On 20th September, he was struck on the right side of his head by a large piece of shrapnel and was unconscious for six hours but remained at duty, although very shaky next day. He was admitted to 63rd West Lancashire Field Ambulance and No.42 Casualty Clearing Station on 27th November with neuritis on the left side. He was discharged to duty on 8th December and was

granted leave 30th December–17th January 1918. On 12th September Gaius was granted fourteen days' leave in Britain. On 27th September, while in London he was referred by the Canadian Senior Medical Officer, 3 Southampton Street, Strand, London to the Canadian Convalescent Officers' Hospital, Matlock Bath with insomnia. He was discharged on 17th October and rejoined his unit on 21st October. He was sick with bronchitis at Valenciennes on 28th October. On 22nd November he was admitted to 10th Canadian Field Ambulance and No.4 Canadian Casualty Clearing Station with influenza and was transferred to 20th General Hospital, Camiers on 25th November. On 4th December he was discharged to the Canadian Infantry Base Depot. Medically he was classified B1 for six months from 11th December and was posted to the Canadian Railway Transportation Depot, Witley, Surrey, England on 24th December for return to Canada. In London on 20th January 1919 he injured his coccyx when he slipped on stairs in a tube station. He was carried to a hotel and was unconscious for ten hours. Gaius tried to find his brother, Cyrus, who was on leave at Marlborough House, Jermyn Street but could not find it. He was admitted to McCaul Hospital, 52 Welbeck Street on 27th January and was transferred to the Canadian Red Cross Officers' Hospital, Audley Street, London on 6th February. A medical board at 13 Berners Street, London recommended further treatment and no return to Canada. He was treated at the Canadian Convalescent Officers' Hospital, Matlock Bath from 19th March. A medical board there on 24th March found him physically fit but recommended return to Canada. He was transferred to the Canadian Railway Troops Depot, Knotty Ash Camp, Liverpool on 2nd April. While there he was found unconscious in his room having had had a drink with an American officer at the American Inn the previous day. Gaius was on the held strength of the Canadian General Depot from 29th April. He was admitted to Fazakerley Hospital, Liverpool on 1st May, transferred to 2nd Western General Hospital, Manchester on 9th May and to the Canadian Convalescent Officers' Hospital, Matlock Bath on 30th May, suffering from amnesia. He was transferred to Granville Canadian Special Hospital, Buxton next day. Gaius went for a walk and found himself back in Manchester four days later, with no idea of how he got there. A medical board at Buxton on 15th June found him unfit for any service for six months. He was transferred to the Canadian Red Cross Officers' Hospital, Audley Street, London on 16th July, was discharged on 8th August and was invalided to Canada the same day aboard HMAT *Araguaya*. He was posted to the Hospital Section, Esquamalt, Vancouver Island on 24th August and was granted fourteen days' leave from 12th September. He transferred to the Casualty Company on 3rd October and was demobilised on 7th October 1919 medically unfit for further service. He was a civil engineer in 1921 and they were living at 535 Fifth Street, New Westminster. Maria died at Courtenay, Vancouver Island. Maria and Gaius had at least six children, all born in New Westminster:

- ○ Miriam Louise Peck (1900–78) became an artist and never married. She died at Bellingham, Whatcom Co, Washington.
- ○ Evelyn May Peck (born 1903).
- ○ Frederick Gaius Peck (born c.1906).
- ○ Aubrey Charles Peck (1909–94) died at 23078 70A Avenue, Langley, BC.
- ○ Phyllis Victoria Peck (born c.1911) is believed to have married Magnus Oppel.
- ○ Lois A Peck (1913–88) married Les Morrisette. She died at White Rock, BC.

Cyrus' paternal grandfather, Joseph Peck (4th December 1798–2nd November 1879), married Melissa/Mittisa née Akerly (c.1800–14th May 1875) at Hopewell, Albert, NB, where both were born. In addition to Wesley they had six other children, all born at Hopewell:

- Thomas Peck (9th August 1825–28th January 1870), a farmer, married Catharine Kenne (born 1828). He took his horse to collect firewood. When felling a tree, it sprang back and struck him. He walked home leading his horse and told his wife what had happened. He died two hours later and an autopsy revealed that the back of his skull had been broken and his chest was badly bruised.
- Seraphine Peck (24th July 1829–27th May 1913) married Millidge West (1828–1900) on 16th September 1873. Millidge had married Emily Canon (1829–16th October 1872) on 27th November 1851 at Harvey Parish, NB.
- Amy Peck (16th March 1832–24th December 1904) married Pierce Kennie (19th January 1824–26th October 1888) on 2nd February 1860. They both died at Germantown, Albert Co. They had two children – Seraphine Kennie (1862–63) and Isaac Gladstone Kennie (1867–1927).
- Mary E Peck (6th April 1833–January 1904) married Judson Freeman Pearson (born c.1830), a farmer, on 24th September 1856. They were living at Mountain Lake, Cottonwood Co, Minnesota, USA in 1880. She died at Heron Lake, Minnesota. They had four children – Mittissa J Pierson (1858), Hattie Pierson (1874), Judson Frank Pierson (1871–1940) and Joseph A Pierson (1873).
- Asahel (also seen as Asael) William Peck (20th December 1834–16th November 1912) married Martha Ann Edgett (19th November 1841–4th November 1925), born in Albert Co, NB. He died at Hopewell. She was living at 140 Highfield Street, Moncton, Westmoreland Co, NB at the time of her death there, caused by apoplexy. They had five children – Annie Mary Peck (1871–1940), Hilyard C Peck (1874–1969), Byron Akerly Peck (1876–1949), Asael W Peck (1880) and William A Peck (1880–1931).
- Harriet Peck (16th March 1842–15th January 1932) married Hiram Edgett (22nd May 1833–24th May 1898), a ship's captain, on 14th January 1863. He died at South Portland, Cumberland Co, Maine, USA and she at Hopewell, where both are buried. They had two children – Arvilla M Edgett (1867–96) and Mary T Edgett (1868–1914).

His maternal grandfather, John Rogers (24th February 1801–2nd September 1881) was born at Hopewell, Albert, NB. His family had moved from New England to New Brunswick in 1763. John married Eleanor Plumer née Dodge (20th August 1811–2nd February 1901), born at Damariscotta Lodge, Lincoln, Maine, USA, on 8th June 1836 at Hopewell. In addition to Mary they had four other children all born at Hopewell:

* Ann Eliza Rogers (12th July 1837–16th July 1896) married John McAuley Gallacher (12th January 1819–15th January 1867), born in Glasgow, Lanarkshire, Scotland, in March 1854. He came to Hopewell via Boston, Massachusetts to help set up a chemical works. When it failed, he returned to the USA to seek work. Over the next decade they lived in Boston, Hopewell Hill and Saint John. In 1866 he found work in Philadelphia, USA but was killed there in an industrial accident. Anna and John had four children – Isabella Plumer Gallacher (1855–1941), Ella Frances Gallacher (1858–64), Francis John Howe Gallacher (1861–1948) and Achsah Georgia Gallacher (1864–96). Ann married Lemuel Robinson Moore (2nd November 1842 or 1843–16th April 1895) at Hopewell on 12th September 1869. He was a farmer, carpenter, storekeeper, school trustee, county assessor and census enumerator. Ann and Lemuel had five children:
  ◦ Ellen Kate Moore (1870–1900).
  ◦ Jennie Eliza Moore (1872–1965).
  ◦ Charles Archibald Moore (1874–1961) married Dorothy Dean Manning (1888–1977), born in Nova Scotia, on 7th November 1916 at Vancouver, BC. They had two children.
  ◦ Donald MacKenzie Moore (1877–1915) attested as a lieutenant in 30th Battalion CEF on 9th November 1914 at Victoria, BC. He was described as a canneryman, 5′ 10″ tall, weighing 150 lbs, with fair complexion, grey eyes, dark brown hair and his religious denomination was Wesleyan. He declared current service in Earl Grey's Own Rifles (Militia). His next of kin was C Archie Moore (brother), of Prince Rupert and later of Kimsquit and 925–29th Avenue, East Vancouver, all in British Columbia. He was promoted captain with effect from 11th February 1915 and sailed with the Battalion for Britain from Halifax, Nova Scotia on 23rd February aboard SS *Missanabe*, *Vaderland* and *Megantic*. He went to France on 26th April and transferred to 16th Battalion. Donald was reported wounded and missing on 21st May. On 20th October he was assumed to have died on or since 22nd May 1915 (Canadian National Vimy Memorial, France).

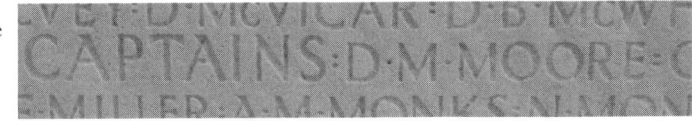

Donald MacKenzie Moore is commemorated on the Canadian National Vimy Memorial.

○ James Dodge Moore (1879–1950), a clerk, married Ethel W Batchelor (1881–1974) on 27th February 1901 in Boston, Massachusetts, where she was born. They had two children.
• Margaret Emeline Rogers (15th March 1844–6th January 1928) married Luther Archibald (21st December 1844–14th August 1919) on 1st October 1883. He was born at Truro, Nova Scotia and died at Hopewell. Margaret died at Sussex, Kings Co, NB. They had two children – Mary Elizabeth Archibald Archibald (1884–1924) and Margaret Eleanor Archibald (1887).
• Jason Horace Rogers (10th July 1849–21st October 1851).
• John Howe Rogers (11th January 1851–5th February 1858).

This is understood to be the former Hopewell Hill Superior School.

Cyrus was educated at Hopewell Hill Superior School, Albert, NB. He sailed to Britain in 1887, intending to join the British Army and volunteered for service in South Africa. However, his application was rejected. When he returned to Canada, he went to the Klondike, pioneering for gold. In 1903, with his partner and cousin, Donald MacKenzie Moore, they built Cassiar Cannery at Prince Rupert, where the Skeena River meets the Pacific, and four years later purchased the sawmill at Georgetown and started the Georgetown Sawmill Co. In 1910, Donald Mackenzie Moore was the President, Cyrus was the Secretary and his brother Gaius was the Manager. Cyrus also became an insurance broker representing salmon canning, sawmill and towing interests in British Columbia. Cyrus volunteered for service

Cassiar Cannery (Prince Rupert Archives).

Biographies 253

Georgetown Mill was set up by George Williscroft, Charles Thomas Frederick Morrison and Thomas Elwyn as Williscroft & Co. The partnership was dissolved on 19th March 1879 and ownership continued under George Williscroft alone. Various owners operated the mill thereafter, including Cyrus and his partners. The Mill burned down in 1978.

during the Second Boer War in South Africa but again was not accepted. He joined 5th British Columbia Regiment of Garrison Artillery (Militia) before 1st August 1899. The unit was redesignated 6th Regiment (The Duke of Connaught's Own Rifles (Militia) on 1st May 1900. He transferred to 43rd Regiment (Duke of Cornwall's Own Rifles) (Militia) on 1st March 1902 and later to 68th Earl Grey's Own Rifles (Militia), reaching the rank of lieutenant colonel on 20th August 1914.

Cyrus married Kate 'Katie' Elizabeth Chapman (21st November 1886–25th December 1988), born at Rat Portage (later Kenora), Rainy River, Ontario, on 11th March 1914 at Kansas City, Jackson Co, Missouri, USA. She was a stenographer in August 1913, travelling to Skagway, Alaska from Victoria, BC aboard SS *Princess Sophia*. They settled at Hopewell (named after his birthplace), Allbay Road, Sidney, BC. They had three sons:

- Horace Wesley Joangas 'Joe' R Peck (26th March 1915–22nd May 1987) was a chemist. He joined the Royal Canadian Artillery and was a captain in 1946, later rising to lieutenant colonel and was awarded the Efficiency Decoration on 25th May 1953. He married Dorothy Sheila A Payne-Jennings (née Young), known as Sheila, in 1943 at Hailsham, Sussex. Dorothy had married John William Victor

Rat Portage amalgamated with Keewatin and Norman in 1905 to form the City of Kenora, Ontario. The first European, Jacques de Noyon, arrived in 1688. A French trading post was established and Fort St Charles was built in 1732. France lost the post to the British in 1763 in the Seven Years' War. In 1836 the Hudson's Bay Company established a post on Old Fort Island and in 1861 opened a post on the mainland in Kenora's current location. Gold was discovered in 1850 and by 1893 there were twenty mines in the area. Kenora was claimed by Manitoba and there was a long lasting argument until the dispute was resolved in Ontario's favour in 1884. The first Canadian Atlantic to Pacific railway passed through in 1886. A highway was built through Kenora in 1932, which became part of Canada's first coast-to-coast highway in 1943. During Prohibition in the USA, the area became a smugglers' route for transporting alcohol. The importance of logging declined in the second half of the 20th century and was replaced by tourism.

Payne-Jennings (born 2nd May 1900) in 1936 at Brighton, Sussex. John was born at Ashtead, Surrey and enlisted in the RAF (137229) at Hampstead on 15th April 1918, described as a student, 5′ 7½″ tall, with dark hair, brown eyes, sallow complexion and his religious denomination was Non-Conformist. He was living at Greville Park, Ashtead at the time. John was posted to 5th Cadet Wing, Cadet Distribution Depot on 25th April, to No.2 School of Aeronautics on 14th June and the Armament School at Uxbridge on 3rd August. He went to Vendôme, France on 23rd September and returned to Britain on 12th December. Posted to 12th (Training) Group, 59th Wing on 16th December and to 59th Training Depot Station on 15th January 1919. He was demobilised as a flight cadet on 28th January and was granted an honorary commission in the Royal Air Force as a second lieutenant on 7th April 1919. He transferred to the RAF Reserve on 6th May 1919 but retained his rank for service with King Alfred's School Contingent, Junior Division, Officers' Training Corps. He relinquished his honorary RAF commission on appointment to the Territorial Force on 1st January 1920. John became a theatre manager and producer, involved in productions in London and New York. Sheila was living at 6 Cork Street, London in 1939. The marriage ended in divorce. John had married previously (Marguerite) and divorced in 1934. He married Mary E Cooper in 1952 at Westminster. Joe married Ruth Olive Prescott (1914–95), born at Paddington, London, on 7th February 1946 at Westminster, London. She was descended from Oliver Cromwell (1599–1658), Lord Protector of the Commonwealth of England, Scotland and Ireland. They sailed for New York aboard RMS *Queen Elizabeth* from Southampton, Hampshire on 15th March 1947 and settled at Westmount, Québec, Canada. They had a son, James Peck, born in 1951 in Vancouver. The marriage ended in divorce. Ruth married George Field and died in Vancouver. Joe married Muriel Shirley MacDonald (7th September 1920–9th June 1979), known as Shirley, born at Vernon, North Okanagan, BC. She had two children – Brian Plummer and Gillian Anglin. Joe and Shirley are buried in Holy Trinity Anglican Cemetery, North Saanich, BC.
- Edward Richard Peck, wrote and published a biography of his father, CY PECK VC: A Biography of a Legendary Canadian, Colonel Cyrus Peck.
- Douglas Cyrus Peck married Isobel Fairley Wilkinson in November 1955 and died before 1987.

Katie's father, Edward Arthur Chapman (8th May 1850–18th April 1902) was a publisher, born in Québec, Canada. He married Cordelia 'Sis' Jane née Ritchie (17th October 1859–17th April 1935) of Irish extraction, born at Thurso, Outaouais Region, Québec. In 1901 they were living at Algoma, Ontario. He died at Rat Portage, Kenora District, Ontario and she at Sidney, BC. Both are buried in Lake of the Woods Cemetery, Kenora. In addition to Kate they had a son, Charles E Chapman (born 20th April 1876), who was a printer in 1901.

Cyrus was commissioned as a captain in 30th Battalion CEF on 1st November 1914 and was attested on 8th November. He was described as 5" 8" tall, weighing 225 lbs, of fair complexion, with hazel/grey eyes, light hair and his religious denomination was Church of England. His address was Suite 11, Royal Mansions, 1183 Pacific Avenue, Vancouver. His wife was recorded as living at various other addresses in British Columbia before the above – Prince Rupert, Empress Hotel in Victoria, 1324 George Street in Victoria, 84 Moss Street in Victoria and 17 Wellington Street in New Westminster. She was in receipt of Separation Allowance of $20 per month from December 1914, increasing to $40 in January 1915, $50 in November 1915 and $60 in May 1917. Cyrus sailed for Britain from Halifax, Nova Scotia on 23rd February 1915 on SS *Missanabie*. He qualified as a musketry instructor on a course at Shorncliffe, Kent 6th–14th April. On 25th April he was promoted temporary major, transferred to 16th Battalion and sailed for France, arriving next day. He was wounded in the left thigh at La Quinque Rue during the Battle of Festubert on 20th May and was evacuated to Britain on 23rd May aboard HMHS *St Patrick*. He was treated at 3rd London General Hospital, Wandsworth. A medical board there on 24th May found him unfit for three weeks and he was taken on the strength of 30th Reserve Battalion CEF at Shorncliffe 4th–28th June while on sick leave. A medical board at Caxton Hall, London on 7th June found him unfit for service for five weeks but a medical board there on 30th June found him fit for General Service. Cyrus returned to France on 5th July and rejoined the Battalion on 7th July. He was granted seven days leave 14th–22nd October.

Cyrus was granted nine days' leave from 5th January 1916 and seven days from 4th May, extended to 14th May. He was involved in the Battle of the Somme and assumed command of 16th Battalion as a temporary lieutenant colonel on 15th

The cap badge of 16th Battalion (Canadian Scottish) CEF.

SS *Missanabie* (12,469 tons), launched by Barclay Curle & Co, Glasgow for the Canadian Pacific Railway Co on the Liverpool–Canada route, commenced her maiden voyage on 7th October 1914. During the Great War she was a defensively-armed passenger liner. On 9th September 1918 she was torpedoed by UB-87, fifty-two miles off Daunts Rock, Ireland and forty-five lives were lost.

St Patrick, one of three ships that started the Fishguard - Rosslare service in 1906, was one of the first five ships to be requisitioned at the outbreak of the Great War. She was converted into a hospital ship and remained in service until January 1919. In April 1929 she caught fire at Fishguard and was sold for scrap the following year after her engines had been transferred to *St Andrew*.

November. He was known as 'MacPeck' and was promoted lieutenant colonel on 6th January 1917. **Awarded the DSO for his actions during the attack on Vimy Ridge during the Battle of Arras on 9th April 1917, LG 4th June 1917.** Cyrus reported sick with vomiting and malaise (gastritis) on 10th April and was admitted to 14th General Hospital, Boulogne on 14th April. He was evacuated to Britain aboard HMHS *St Andrew* and was admitted to 1st London General Hospital, Camberwell next day on the strength of the Manitoba Regimental Depot, Shorncliffe, Kent. He was declared unfit for General or Home Service on 18th April following a medical board at 76 Strand, London and was sent on two weeks' leave. A medical board there on 2nd May also found him unfit for General or Home Service for two weeks and he was again granted leave. A medical board at 13 Berners Street, London on 17th May found him fit for General Service and he returned to the Canadian Base Depot, France on 1st June. He rejoined the Battalion on 3rd June.

Cyrus was granted five days special leave to Britain 9th–16th July and during this time he was probably invested with the DSO at Buckingham Palace. He was also granted leave in Britain 15th November–4th December. In the Canadian federal election (khaki election) on 17th December 1917 he was elected Unionist Member of Parliament for Skeena, BC in absentia, the first time a member had been elected

Caxton Hall, on the corner of Caxton Street and Palmer Street, Westminster has hosted many political and artistic events. It opened as Westminster Town Hall in 1883 and had two public halls for concerts and public meetings. In 1900 the First Pan-African Conference was held there. From 1907 the Women's Social and Political Union, part of the Suffragette movement, held a 'Women's Parliament' there at the beginning of each parliamentary session. During the Second World War, it was the venue for press conferences held by Churchill and government ministers. In 1940, Udham Singh assassinated Michael O'Dwyer, former Lieutenant Governor of the Punjab, there in revenge for the 1919 Amritsar massacre. On 12th May 1960 the first public meeting of the Homosexual Law Reform Society was held in Caxton Hall. By contrast, on 7th February 1967 the National Front was formed there. Caxton Hall was also a register office 1933-79 and many celebrity weddings were held there, including Donald Campbell twice, Billy Butlin, Elizabeth Taylor, Diana Dors, Peter Sellars, Roger Moore, Orson Welles, Joan Collins, Ringo Starr and, in August 1952, future Prime Minister Anthony Eden, who married Clarissa Spencer-Churchill, niece of then Prime Minister Winston Churchill. In 2006 Caxton Hall was redeveloped as apartments and offices.

In August 1914, 1st London General Hospital took over St Gabriel's College in Camberwell, built in 1900. The neighbouring Cormont Secondary School was used for convalescent cases. Extensive work to both buildings to add toilets and baths was completed within three months. The medical and nursing staff came from St Bartholomew's Hospital. Patient accommodation was extended in April 1915, when 71 Upper Tulse Hill (Margaret Hall Nursing Home) was leased as a relief hospital with twenty beds. In December 1915 huts were erected in Myatt's Fields to accommodate 520 more patients and by 1917 the Hospital had expanded to 231 beds for officers and 1,038 for enlisted men. The King and Queen visited in April 1918. Vera Brittain, author of *Testament of Youth*, worked there as a VAD Nurse. The Hospital closed in 1919. The main building is now an apartment block and Cormont Secondary School is Charles Edward Brooke Girl's School.

while overseas. He could have returned to Canada to take up his seat but chose to remain at the front. Cyrus assumed temporary command of 3rd Canadian Brigade 31st December 1917–5th January 1918, 10th–15th January and 15th February –15th March. He was admitted to 4th Canadian Field Ambulance with pyrexia of unknown origin 23rd–25th January. He was admitted to 1st Canadian Field Ambulance on 15th March with bronchitis, transferred to No.1 Canadian Casualty Clearing Station next day and rejoined his unit on 27th March. He was granted fourteen days' leave in Britain 9th–24th June.

Awarded the VC for his actions at Cagnicourt, near Bapaume, France on 2nd September 1918, LG 15th November 1918. Cyrus was gassed on 4th October and was treated at No.1 Canadian Casualty Clearing Station 5th–15th October. **Awarded a Bar to the DSO when he led his Battalion under difficult conditions in heavy mist, reaching his final objective nearly three miles distant after severe fighting. He personally led his men in an attack on nests of machine guns protecting the enemy's artillery, which he captured, LG 11th January 1919.** On 5th January 1919 Cyrus was granted one month's leave in Britain and was struck off strength of 16th Battalion on 6th January to the Manitoba Regimental Depot, Seaford, Sussex. The VC and Bar to the DSO were presented by the King at York Cottage, Sandringham, Norfolk on 26th January. Cyrus sailed for Canada and was struck off strength of the Overseas Military Forces of Canada and transferred to CEF Canada on 20th February. He was demobilised in Ottawa on 1st June 1919. **Mentioned in Sir Douglas Haig's Despatches dated 30th April 1916, 13th November 1916, 9th April 1917, 7th April 1918 and 8th November 1918, LG respectively 15th June 1916, 4th January 1917, 1st June 1917, 28th May 1918 and 31st December 1918.**

The Canadian Museum of Nature (formerly Victoria Memorial Museum) was the venue for the House of Commons of Canada from 1916 until 1922, when it moved to the current Parliament building. The House of Commons was established in 1867, when the British North America Act (Constitution Act) created the Dominion of Canada by uniting the Province of Canada (Québec and Ontario), Nova Scotia and New Brunswick. It was modelled on the British House of Commons but extensive powers were vested in the provincial legislatures. The Parliament of Canada also remained subordinate to the British Parliament until the Statute of Westminster in 1931. Before then Westminster was the supreme legislative authority for the entire British Empire but after the Act new legislation of the British Parliament did not apply to Canada, with some exceptions that were removed by the Canada Act 1982. The Canadian Commons met in the chamber previously used by the Legislative Assembly of Canada until the building was destroyed in a fire in 1916 (RealGrouchy).

Cyrus took his seat in the Canadian House of Commons as MP for Skeena on 4th March 1919. On 14th March he heard Sir Sam Hughes, the former Minister of Militia & Defense, attack Sir Arthur Currie, who had led the Canadian Corps from June 1917 to the end of the war. Peck, in his maiden speech, defended Currie, who he believed …to be one of the great Canadians, and one of the great commanders we have had in this war … I hope that the Canadian Parliament and the Canadian people will reward and pay fitting tribute to Sir Arthur Currie and all those distinguished commanders who led us in the field. Currie wrote to Cyrus and thanked him for his support. During his time in Parliament, he was active in veterans' affairs. He was defeated in the federal election on 6th December 1921. Cyrus won the seat for Saanich and the Islands in the British Columbia Legislature election on 20th June 1924. He was re-elected in 1928 and held the seat until 1933. Having left politics he sat on the Canadian Pensions Commission 1936–41.

Cyrus transferred to the Canadian Scottish Regiment (Princess Mary's) on 28th April 1920 and was appointed lieutenant colonel. He commanded the Canadian Bisley Rifle Team in 1921. On 26th November 1921 he was promoted colonel and transferred to the Reserve of Officers the same day. He was appointed Honorary ADC to King George V on 14th January 1922. He served again as a lieutenant colonel in 2nd Reserve Battalion, Canadian Scottish Regiment from 7th April 1925 until transferring to the Reserve in 1937. He was appointed ADC to two Canadian Governors General, Lord Byng and Lord Tweedsmuir. He attended two VC reunions – the VC Dinner at the Royal Gallery of the House of Lords, London on 9th November 1929 and the VC Centenary Celebrations at Hyde Park, London on 26th June 1956. Cyrus was a Freemason.

Biographies 259

Sir Samuel Hughes KCB PC (1853-1921) was the Canadian Minister of Militia & Defence 1911–16. His father was from Co Tyrone, Ireland and his mother was descended from Huguenots and Ulster Scots. In 1866 he joined 45th West Durham Battalion and fought against the Fenian Raids in the 1860s and 1870s. He was a teacher 1875–85 then bought *The Victoria Warder*, which he published 1885–97. He was elected to Parliament in 1892. He served in the Second Boer War, predicting accurately that the Boers would outride the British on the veld. He had a stormy relationship with the British, while also being a staunch imperialist. Hughes believed that part-time citizen soldiers were better than full-time professionals and this view influenced his decisions during the Great War. In South Africa he became convinced that the Ross rifle was the ideal infantry weapon. The British Army rejected it as it overheated and jammed easily. Hughes was dismissed from Boer War service in the summer of 1900 for military indiscipline and sent home. Although competent, he was boastfulness and impatient. His demand for a VC was refused but he was knighted for his Boer War service, albeit in 1915. Hughes was an agent for the Canadian Northern Railway 1902–05 and in 1906 his motion calling for the government to give preference in allocating land in the Prairies to veterans of the British Army was accepted. Hughes told the House of Commons that Catholic immigrants from Europe were 'a curse upon Canada' and repeated this two months later at the Orange Order's national convention. Despite the controversy, Hughes was able to muster Orange Order votes for the Conservatives and ensured that he was not expelled from the Party. In 1911 Hughes was appointed Minister of Militia, with the task of creating a Canadian Army, including an expeditionary force. Despite his great charm, wit, … driving energy [and] …. consummate political skills, he was also a stubborn, pompous racist, who did little to disguise his dislike of Catholics. This did much to put off French and Irish Canadians from supporting the war effort. Hughes was a colonel in the Militia and wore his uniform at all times, including during cabinet meetings. In 1912 he promoted himself to major general. Under him there was a significant increase in the Militia budget. He was openly hostile to the Permanent Force Militia, Canada's small professional army, in favour of the Non-Permanent Force Militia. Following a tour of European volunteer forces in 1913 he intended to make militia service compulsory for able-bodied males on the Swiss model. This caused much public opposition. When the Great War broke out an expeditionary force of an infantry division, a cavalry brigade and artillery and support units from the Permanent Force was assembled but, much to everyone's surprise, Hughes refused to mobilise the Militia. Instead he created a new organisation, the Canadian Expeditionary Force, and a new camp at Valcartier. This threw mobilisation into chaos as a new bureaucracy had to be created as thousands of volunteers came forward and needed to be housed, trained and equipped. Despite all the problems, on 3rd October 1914 the First Contingent boarded ships at Québec to take it to Europe. However, his speech to them sitting astride his horse, was booed and jeered. He went to London to ensure that the CEF fought together and was not dispersed within British formations. Hughes insisted that the CEF be equipped with Canadian Ross rifles, although there were many complaints raised about it during training. As the war progressed, it became clear that many policies of the Ministry of Defense & Militia were inefficient and wasteful. Various functions were taken away from the Ministry, to be handled by an independent board or commission consisting of men who were not Hughes cronies, including the creation of the Ministry of the Overseas Military Forces of Canada. Hughes was widely resented by the CEF and political opposition grew. He was forced to resign in November 1916. Only then was the hated Ross rifle abandoned in favour of the SMLE.

General Sir Arthur William Currie GCMG KCB (1875–1933) started his military career as a pre-war Militia gunner in 1897 and rose to become the first Canadian commander of the Canadian Corps. He is among the most capable commanders on the Western Front and one of the finest commanders in Canadian history. He was in the Militia while working as a teacher and later as an insurance salesman and real estate speculator. He was a corporal when he was commissioned in 1900 and by 1909 was an artillery regimental commander. In 1913 he was appointed to command the newly created 50th Regiment, Gordon Highlanders of Canada. When he found himself in debt, following a real estate crash in Victoria, he embezzled $10,000 into his personal accounts to pay off his debts. Currie was appointed by Sam Hughes to command 2nd Canadian Brigade and, after the Second Battle of Ypres, 1st Canadian Division. In June 1917 he was promoted lieutenant general to command the Canadian Corps. At the same time news of the embezzlement reached the Canadian Cabinet. Currie borrowed

money from two wealthy subordinates to pay back the money he had taken from the 50th Regiment. After the Great War Currie was promoted general and was appointed Inspector General of the Canadian Army. He resigned and became Principal and Vice-Chancellor of McGill University 1920–33. In 1927, Mons in Belgium erected a plaque commemorating its liberation by the Canadians. Canadian newspapers and Currie's enemies took the opportunity to question the necessity of the final day of fighting. An editorial published on 13th June 1927 by the Hughes supporting *Port Hope Evening Guide* argued that Currie was negligent or deliberate in wasting lives by taking Mons on the final day of the war. Currie sued the newspaper for libel, seeking $50,000 ($733,000 today) in damages. At the hearing in April 1928, Currie testified that he was under orders from the Allied Supreme Commander, Foch, to pursue German forces. Many of his senior officers testified that Currie urged them to advance with caution to avoid unnecessary casualties. The jury found the newspaper guilty of libel but awarded Currie only $500 ($7,300 today) in damages, plus costs. The trial helped to restore Currie's reputation. He was elected Dominion President of the Canadian Legion of the British Empire Service League in 1928. Currie died on 30th November 1933 and his funeral in Montréal was the largest to that time in Canadian history. Approximately 150,000 people lined the streets, eight generals acted as pallbearers and there was a seventeen-gun salute. A memorial service was held in a packed Westminster Abbey, London the same day.

Cyrus suffered a heart attack on 18th September 1956 and died at his home at Allbay Road, Sidney, Vancouver on 27th September 1956. He was cremated at New Westminster Crematorium, Vancouver and his ashes were divided into two portions. One was scattered at sea at Metlakatla Pass, off Rupert Sound, BC and the second was buried in the family plot at Fraser Cemetery, Vancouver (Range 23, Block 54, Lot B). He is commemorated in a number of other places:

Cyrus Peck's grave in Fraser Cemetery, Vancouver. His parent's grave is behind.

- Ontario
    ◦ Plaque in the Canadian House of Commons, Ottawa, Ontario.
    ◦ Named on one of eleven plaques honouring 175 men from overseas awarded the VC for the Great War. The plaques were unveiled by the Senior Minister of State at the Foreign & Commonwealth Office and Minister for Faith and Communities, Baroness Warsi, at a reception at Lancaster House, London on 26th June 2014 attended by The Duke of Kent and relatives of the VC recipients. The Canadian plaque was unveiled outside the British High Commission in Elgin Street, Ottawa on 10th November 2014 by The Princess Royal in the presence of British High Commissioner Howard Drake, Canadian Minister of Veterans Affairs Julian Fantino and Canadian Chief of the Defence Staff General Thomas James Lawson.
    ◦ A wooden plaque bearing fifty-six maple leaves each inscribed with the name of a Canadian-born VC holder was dedicated at the Canadian Forces College, Toronto on Remembrance Day 1999.
    ◦ Plaque No.99 on the York Cemetery VC Memorial, West Don River Valley, Toronto, Ontario dedicated on 25th June 2017.
    ◦ Victoria Cross obelisk to all Canadian VCs at Military Heritage Park, Barrie, Ontario dedicated by Princess Royal on 22nd October 2013.
- British Columbia
    ◦ SS *Daily* (339 tons), a ferry built in 1913 by Crawford & Reid Shipbuilding Co Ltd, Tacoma, Washington State, USA, was owned at various times by McDowell & Co, British Columbia Coast Service, Gulf Islands Ferry Co, British Columbia Toll Highways Authority, British Columbia Ferries,

The ferry, MV *Cy Peck* and her wheelhouse on the dockside in Ganges Harbour, Salt Spring Island, where it is used as a float plane waiting room.

JH Todd & Sons, JW Russell and Dale R Forsberg. She operated on various routes before being used as a supply store and floating logging camp bunkhouse. She was renamed SS *Island Princess* in 1918 and MV *Cy Peck* in 1930, because as British Columbia Legislative Assembly Member for The Islands he had pressed for a ferry service. In 1979 she was partially sank after grounding in Nanaimo Harbour. The hulk was scuttled as a reef off Salt Spring Island on 14th March 1986. The wheelhouse was salvaged and is displayed at Ganges.
  ° Plaque provided by the British Columbia Veterans Commemorative Association was dedicated on 31st August 2017 at Kwinitsa Station overlooking Metlakatla Pass, where half of his ashes were scattered at sea. The rock on which the plaque is mounted was provided by the City of Prince Rupert.
  ° Plaque dedicated in 2001 at the old Post Office, Beacon Avenue, Sidney. As a member of the British Columbia Legislative Assembly he brought the Post Office to the Saanich Peninsula, helped to establish Sidney Spit Provincial Park and co-founded the ferry service between Fulford Harbour and Swartz Bay.
* Two 49 cents postage stamps in honour of the ninety-four Canadian VC winners were issued by Canada Post on 21st October 2004 on the 150th Anniversary of the first Canadian VC's action, Alexander Roberts Dunn VC.
* Communities and Local Government commemorative paving stones for the 145 VCs born in Australia, Belgium, Canada, China, Denmark, Egypt, France, Germany, India, Iraq, Japan, Nepal, Netherlands, Newfoundland, New Zealand, Pakistan, South Africa, Sri Lanka, Ukraine and United States of America were unveiled at the National Memorial Arboretum, Alrewas, Staffordshire by Prime Minister David Cameron MP and Sergeant Johnson Beharry VC on 5th March 2015.
* Plaque at Villers-lès-Cagnicourt Church, near Arras, France.
* His VC action featured in Issue No.869 of the Victor Comic entitled 'A True Story of Men at War' dated 14th October 1978.

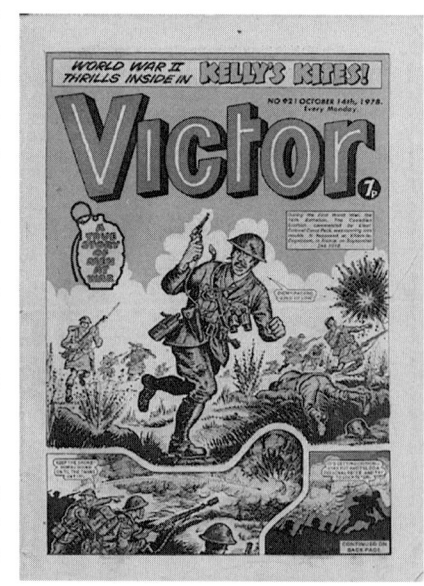

Victor Comic told the story of Cyrus Peck's VC in October 1978.

In addition to the VC and DSO & Bar he was awarded the 1914–15 Star, British War Medal 1914–20, Victory Medal 1914–19 with Mentioned-in-Despatches Oakleaf, George V Silver Jubilee Medal 1935, George

Cyrus Peck's medals are held by the Canadian War Museum in Ottawa.

VI Coronation Medal 1937 and Elizabeth II Coronation Medal 1953. His medals passed to his widow and subsequently to his sons. They were presented on loan to the Canadian Scottish Regiment (Princess Mary's) Museum, Victoria, BC at a ceremony at Bay Street Armoury in 1987. Edward, the last surviving son, and a nephew approached the Canadian War Museum in 1993 and reached a satisfactory arrangement before the medals were formally donated on 2nd September 1993, exactly seventy-five years after the VC action. The VC is held by the Canadian War Museum, 1 Vimy Place, Ottawa, Ontario, Canada.

WZ/424 CHIEF PETTY OFFICER GEORGE HENRY PROWSE
Drake Battalion, Royal Naval Division

George Prowse was born on 29th August 1886 at 8 Brynsion Terrace (later 133 High Street), Gilfach Goch, Llantrisaint, Glamorgan, Wales. He was known as Harry. His father, John Prowse (c.1856–1922), was born at Maiden Bradley, Wiltshire. He married Harriett née Grantham (1852–1912), born at Ettington, near Stratford, Warwickshire but no record has been found. She was a domestic servant in 1871 and 1881 living with her parents. John was a colliery banksman living at Meadgate Cottages, Camerton, Somerset in 1891 but Harriett was not with him. They were still there in 1911. She was admitted to Mendip Hospital (Wells Asylum), near Wells, Somerset in 1911 and subsequently died there. Harry had four siblings:

* John Grantham (1881–97) was born at Radford, Nottinghamshire. His natural father may have been John Prowse, as his surname had changed to Prowse by 1891.

Harry's mother died at Mendip Hospital. It opened in 1848 as the Somerset and Bath Pauper Lunatic Asylum at Horrington, near Wells. The first patients came from local workhouses and some of the male patients tended the hospital's farm. Land adjacent to the hospital was bought to establish a cemetery, which was used until 1963. It contains 2,900 burials. In 1897 Tone Vale Hospital took over the role of county asylum but Mendip Hospital continued to house long-stay elderly and mentally infirm patients. It closed in 1991 and the buildings were converted into houses and apartments.

The earliest reference to the village that became Maiden Bradley is in a Saxon land charter of 878, but archaeological remains date back to at least the Bronze Age. By the mid 11th century Bradley was a large manor and its lord was Tostig Godwinson, brother of King Harold. The village features in the Domesday Book. In the early 12th century, the village came into the hands of Manasser Biset, steward to Henry II, who in 1154 founded an asylum for girls with leprosy, which in 1189 became an Augustinian Priory. The Priory was dissolved in 1538 and the land was awarded by Henry VIII to local landowner Thomas Seymour, brother of the 1st Duke of Somerset. The property is still in the family. In 1646 the plague struck and for ten months no one was allowed to leave the village. In 1851 the population reached its peak of 619. The village school was built in 1847 by the Duke of Somerset and closed in 1969.

- Reuben Prowse (born c.1882), born in Lincolnshire or at Camerton, Somerset (no record found), enlisted in the Somerset Light Infantry (5647) at Bath on 17th October 1899, giving his age as eighteen years and seven months. He was described as 5′ 4¼″ tall, weighing 115 lbs, with fresh complexion, grey eyes, fair hair and his religious denomination was Church of England. He joined at Taunton next day but was discharged on 28th February 1900 not being likely to become an efficient

The Meritorious Service Medal was instituted on 19th December 1845 to recognise meritorious service by non-commissioned officers of the British Army. During the period 1916-19, NCOs could be awarded the medal immediately for meritorious service in the field. It could also be awarded for acts of non-combat gallantry. Awards for gallantry ceased after 7th September 1928 with the institution of the Empire Gallantry Medal. Variations between the medals awarded to each service and their criteria have been removed and today the same medal is issued for all three services. During the Great War, the Royal Warrant of 4th October 1916 allowed for non-commissioned officers below the rank of sergeant and men to be awarded the MSM without the annuity, for acts of gallantry not necessarily on active service, or in saving or attempting to save the life of an officer or soldier.

soldier. He was a coal miner in 1901. Reuben later served in the Royal Welch Fusiliers and was awarded the MSM for dealing with a live bomb dropped by a nervous recruit. He returned to coal mining after the Great War.
* Elizabeth Jane Prowse (born 1884) was born at Gilrock, Glamorgan.
* Dora Harriet Prowse (1896–1925), born at Camerton, Somerset, married Frederick Ruddick (16th February 1893–1976) in 1917. They had a daughter, Isabel C Ruddick (born 1919), who married Harold D Moon (1914–55) in 1938 at Norton Radstock, Somerset. They had six children. Frederick married Annie Plummer (29th March 1902–1989) in 1926. They had a son, Frederick John Ruddick (1927–94), born at Mansfield, Nottinghamshire and died at Worksop, Nottinghamshire.

Nothing is known about Harry's paternal grandparents. His maternal grandfather, William Grantham (c.1823–24th September 1910), born at Pillerton Prior, Warwickshire, enlisted in 34th Regiment of Foot (2023) at Coventry on 14th December 1841 and was discharged on 7th August 1846, being unfit for further service. He was a pensioner from 15th October 1846 and this was made permanent from 1st January 1849. He married Sarah née Alibone (c.1821–72), born at Ettington, Warwickshire, in 1848 registered at Stratford-upon-Avon, Warwickshire. William was an agricultural labourer and a Chelsea Out Pensioner in 1871, when they were living at Ettington. He was living with his children at Hockley Lane, Ettington in 1881 and was still there in 1891. By 1901 he was lodging with his granddaughter, Florence Mary East, and her family at Ettington. In addition to Harriett they had ten other children, all born at Ettington:

* Anna/Hannah Maria Grantham (1849–21st October 1915) emigrated to New Zealand, where she married James Stone in 1887. They had a daughter, Harriet Ethel Stone, in 1888.
* Sarah Ann Grantham (c.1851–1925) had a daughter, Florence Mary Grantham, in 1872. Sarah married William Hoare (1858–1948), an agricultural labourer born at Brailes, Worcestershire, in 1877. His surname has also been seen as Hoar and Hore. They were living at Village Street, Ufton, Warwickshire in 1891 and at Radford Barn, Radford Semele, Warwickshire in 1901 and 1911. They had four children – Ada Louisa E Hoare 1878, Emily Etta Hoare 1885, Ethel Lilian Hoare 1893 and William Walter John Hoare 1895.
* William Grantham (1854–1900) was a railway platelayer. He married Harriet Clarke (1858–1937) on 28th May 1877 at Ettington. They were living at the Station, Cotham, Nottinghamshire in 1891. His death was registered at Newark. She was living with her children at 62 Grove Street, Balderton, Nottinghamshire in 1901. She was living at Ettington, Stratford-upon-Avon in 1916. They had nine children including:
    ◦ William Thomas Grantham (1877–1924).
    ◦ Jane Elizabeth Grantham (1879–1960).
    ◦ George Edward Grantham (1881–1960).

- ○ Rose Grantham (1886–1957).
- ○ Eliza Grantham (1889).
- ○ Charles Henry Grantham (1891–1972), a chauffeur and gardener, was called up in the ASC (M/205623) on 12th December 1916 at Warwick and was deemed to have been enlisted on 2nd March. His address was Stone Villas, Ettington, Stratford-upon-Avon and he was described as 5′ 6″ tall and weighing 118 lbs. He joined at Grove Park, London on 13th December and was posted to the MT Training Depot, Isleworth, London on 30th December for learner driver training. He passed the course on 8th April 1917. On 19th May he embarked at Southampton and travelled via Le Havre and Marseilles, disembarking at Alexandria, Egypt on 31st May. He was posted to 955th MT Company on 16th June. He was admitted to 19th General Hospital, Alexandria with dysentery on 19th July and to the Convalescent Depot, Mustapha on 22nd July. He was at the Base MT Depot, Egyptian Expeditionary Force 8th–12th August on general duties awaiting return to his unit. At Mustapha on 10th August he failed to report for duty after the medical inspection having been warned on the 11.45 a.m. parade, for which he was confined to barracks for ten days and forfeited three days pay. On 13th August he returned to 955th MT Company on general duties in the QM stores as a storekeeper. He was upgraded to 2nd class driver and 3rd rate Corps pay on 18th September 1918 and served in 955th MT Company until 25th February 1919. He was upgraded to 1st class driver and 2nd rate Corps pay on 29th August. He embarked on HT *Caledonian* at Alexandria for four weeks leave in Britain on 3rd September. On 17th November he had a discharge medical and transferred to the Class Z Reserve on 4th December 1919 from Woolwich Dockyard. Charles married Sarah Christine Carrick (1893–1968), born at Waddesdon, Buckinghamshire, in 1929 at Aylesbury, Buckinghamshire. He was a gardener in 1939 and they were living at 1 Mobwell Terrace, Great Missenden, near Amersham, Buckinghamshire. She died at Banbury, Oxfordshire. He was living at Cedar Cottage, North Street, Aston, Oxfordshire at the time of his death there. They had a son.
- ○ May Grantham (1893–1982).
- ○ Gertrude Grantham (1896–1967).
- Charles Grantham (1856–58).
- John Thomas Grantham (birth registered as Thomas) (1858–1910) was a general labourer living with Mary Rebecca Mayfield (1865–1900) as his wife at 31 Chamber Street, Alvaston and Boulton, Derbyshire in 1891. She was born at Barnby in the Willows, Nottinghamshire. John and Mary's marriage was registered during the June quarter of 1894 (sic) at Derby. He was living with his children at 5 Simes Avenue, Chellaston, Derbyshire in 1901. Both their deaths were registered at Shardlow. They had six children – Beatrice Grantham (1887), Florence Mary Grantham (1888), William Grantham (1890), Alice Grantham (1893–93), Lily Grantham (1895) and Emma Grantham (1896–97).

- George Grantham (1859–73) was a ploughboy in 1871.
- Jane Elizabeth Grantham (1861–6th April 1931) was a general domestic servant in 1881, living with her father. She had two children (father unknown) – Charles Henry J Grantham (1880) and Rosetta Bailey Grantham (1882–1973). Jane married Henry Walsh McConnell (1840–9th February 1908), born in Ireland, on 29th November 1883 at St Mary's Roman Catholic Church, Warwick. He was a corporation labourer in 1901 and they were living at 39 Union Road, Leamington Spa, Warwickshire. He was admitted to the Warwick County Lunatic Asylum, Warwick on 23rd September 1905, where he subsequently died. Jane was living with her children near White Lion Cemetery Road, Cannock, Staffordshire in 1911. She died at Cannock, Staffordshire. They had eight children – William Henry McConnell (1884), Victoria Maud E McConnell (1887–1972), Mary Winifred McConnell (1889), Sarah Agnes McConnell (1891–1971), triplets Edith Imelda McConnell (1896), Phillip Reginald McConnell (1896–1967) and Theresa Monica McConnell (1896–1927) and Francis Robert McConnell (1901–87).
- Edwin Grantham (1863–1936), an agricultural labourer, married his first cousin, Ellen Selina Grantham (1862–1901), on 10th February 1885 at Pillerton Hersey, Warwickshire. She was born at Pillerton Priors, Warwickshire. Ellen had a daughter (father unknown), Lucy Chamberlain Grantham (1882–1951). Edwin and Ellen lived at Ettington. He was a railway platelayer in 1901. His death was registered at Bromsgrove, Worcestershire. They had four children – Edwin Ernest Grantham (1884–1955), George Grantham (1888–1964), Amy Grantham (1890–1918) and Eliza Grantham (1893–1932).
- Rosetta Grantham (1865–66).
- Ada Matilda Grantham (1866–67).

Harry was probably educated at Camerton School, Somerset. He played for the local soccer team, Camerton Football Club, and captained the reserve team. He was a coal miner general labourer in 1901 and in 1907 found employment in a coalmine at Grovesend, Swansea, Wales, and later at Mountain Colliery, Gorseinon, Wales, where he played for Gorseinon Colliery FC.

Harry married Sarah Lewis (c.1890–1968), a barmaid born at Llangyfelach, Glamorgan, on 8th November 1913 at Swansea Registry Office. He was living at 22 New Road, Grovesend, Pontarddulais and she was living at 65 Pentre-Treharne Road, Landore, Swansea. They moved to 60 Pentre-Treharne Road. Sarah worked in a war factory in Swansea during the Great War. There were no children.

Camerton Church School opened in 1846 and closed in August 2018. It is understood that Harry was educated there.

Harry moved to Gorseinon near Swansea to work at Mountain Colliery. It opened in 1846 as a drift and a shaft was added in 1900. On 31st May 1910 an explosion killed two men and injured four more. It reached its peak of employment about 1918 when 933 men worked there. At peak production over 200,000 tons of coal were mined each year. The mine was closed by the National Coal Board in 1969. Gorseinon (originally Gors Eynon) was just a tiny village until the late 19th century, when it grew considerably as a

result of the coal and tinplate industries expanding in the area. The town has produced a number of famous inhabitants including:

- Richard Moriarty (born 1957), Welsh rugby union player with twenty-three caps, who captained the team on eight occasions, losing only one match.
- Michael Howard, Baron Howard of Lympne CH PC QC (born 1941), born Michael Hecht, son of Bernat Hecht born in Romania who came to Britain in 1939. His mother was Hilda Kershion. Both parents were from Jewish families. Howard was Conservative MP for Folkestone & Hythe 10th June 1983–12th April 2010 and leader of the Conservative Party November 2003–December 2005. He held Cabinet positions under Margaret Thatcher and John Major as Secretaries of State for Employment, Environment and Home Secretary. He received a life peerage on 13th July 2010.
- Keith Howell Charles Allen (born 1953), actor, singer, comedian and television presenter, father of singer Lily Allen and actor Alfie Allen and brother of actor and director Kevin Allen.

Sarah's father, David Lewis (born c.1852), born at Carmarthen, married Hannah née Rees (born 1848), born at Dryslwyn, Llanarthney, Carmarthenshire, in 1872 in Swansea. He was a copper furnace man at a steelworks in 1881. They were living at 2 Hughes Row, Clase, Swansea at the time. They were living at 7 Pentre-Treharne Hill, Llangyfelach, Swansea in 1901. David had moved to 65 Pentre-Treharne Road, Landore by 1911. In addition to Sarah they had six other children including:

- Mary Rachael Lewis (born 1874), born at St John, Swansea, married William Jones in 1898. They had at least a son, David John Jones, c.1898.
- Elisabeth Lewis (1877–78) was born at Llangyfelach, Glamorgan.
- David John Lewis (1880–91).
- Margaret Hannah (born 1884).
- Jane Lewis (born 1886).

Harry enlisted in the Royal Naval Volunteer Reserve at Swansea Naval Recruiting Office on 25th February 1915 (WZ/424). He gave his year of birth as 1896. He was posted to 5th Battalion on 28th April and to 2nd Reserve Battalion at Blandford, Dorset on 18th June. Promoted petty officer on 20th June and was drafted to the Drake Battalion, Royal Naval Division at Gallipoli, departing Britain on 9th September and arriving on 21st September. He was admitted to 1st (Royal Naval) Field Ambulance with jaundice on 12th October and was evacuated to Malta on HMHS *Rewa* on 22nd October, where he was treated for gastro-enteritis at the

Members of the Royal Naval Division at Blandford Camp prior to embarking for Gallipoli. The camp has a long history, dating back to prehistoric times. There was a racecourse there, with meetings held from the late 16th until the end of the 19th centuries. In the 18th and 19th centuries local volunteer units used the area for training. In 1756, during the Seven Years' War, a force of 10,000 men formed near Blandford in case of a French invasion and exercised on the site of the camp. In 1806, an Admiralty Shutter Telegraph Station was built near the racecourse, in the chain between London and Plymouth. It closed in 1816. During the Great War the Royal Naval Division established a base depot and training camp, with a German prisoner of war camp alongside it. In 1918 the RFC/RAF took over the camp and a branch railway line was built. At the end of 1919 the camp closed and the wooden huts and railway line were removed. Blandford Camp was reactivated in 1939 as a mobilisation and training centre for reservists, with new wooden huts being erected, a few of which remain. After Dunkirk, the camp was used by anti-aircraft units and a reconnaissance battalion. It then became a Battle Training Camp for units prior to being sent to operational theatres. In April 1944 an American hospital complex was established. The first patients arrived two weeks after D-Day, many via the nearby airfield at Tarrant Rushton. The Roosevelt Garden and Memorial were dedicated on 30th May 1945 and a memorial service is held there annually. The camp was used by the Royal Army Service Corps 1946–62 to train National Service drivers and also by the Royal Electrical and Mechanical Engineers, the Army Catering Corps and the Army Physical Training Corps. A five kilometres motor racing circuit operated from July 1948 until December 1960 for Formula 2, road and motorcycle racing. It was the first UK post-war road racing circuit. In 1960, 30th Signal Regiment (in which the author served 1976–78 and 1996–98) moved into the camp and in 1967 the School of Signals (now Royal School of Signals) moved there. In 1995 Royal Signals soldier training moved there from Catterick and the HQ Royal Signals came from London.

SS *Rewa*, launched on 14th February 1906 for the British India Steam Navigation Co, operated for two years before becoming a troop transport (HMT) and was later converted to a hospital ship (HMHS). On 4th January 1918, she was returning to Britain from Malta carrying 279 wounded officers. Neutral inspectors from Spain had boarded the ship in Gibraltar to confirm that she had no military function. However, thirty-one kilometres off Hartland Point, Devon she was torpedoed by *U-55*. The ship took two hours to sink, allowing sufficient time for the wounded and crew to board lifeboats, except for four engine room men who died in the explosion. The sinking caused outrage in Britain and the Germans denied it, blaming a British mine for the explosion. The captain of *U-55*, Wilhelm Werner, perhaps fearing the consequences of his actions, wrote in the ship's log that he sank a cargo vessel and not a clearly lit and painted hospital ship. He was hunted after the war in an effort to bring him to trial for war crimes, but he disappeared. The wreckage lies in sixty metres of water and during the Second World War was often mistaken by sonar for a U-boat. As a result Allied ships dropped depth charges to ensure that a U-boat was not hiding on the seabed. The wreck was totally destroyed. In 2002 a memorial was erected near Hartland Point.

The Royal Naval Hospital Bighi (Bighi Hospital), in Kalkara, near Valletta, Malta, was built on the site of the gardens of Palazzo Bichi, built in 1675. The site was chosen by Nelson in 1803 but it was not until 1827 that George IV granted permission to develop the site and turn it into the current building, on the request of the Governor, Frederick Cavendish Ponsonby. The site was handed over in 1830 and the new hospital building started operating in 1832 with 200 beds. Bighi Hospital made Malta 'the nurse of the Mediterranean' and casualties from the Crimean War were treated there. In 1863, Queen Victoria's son Prince Alfred was a patient suffering from typhoid, whilst serving as a Royal Navy officer. During the Great War, Bighi accommodated a large number of casualties from Gallipoli and elsewhere in the Mediterranean theatre. During the Second World War some of its buildings were damaged or destroyed in the bombing. As part of the rundown of British forces, Bighi Hospital closed on 17th September 1970. In 1977 part of the building was occupied by the Senglea Trade School. Other sections accommodated a secondary school. Since 2010 the site has housed the head office of Heritage Malta, the national agency for museums, conservation and cultural heritage. It is scheduled as a Grade 1 national monument.

Horton Asylum opened in 1902 with 2,000 beds, the second London County Asylum, in Epsom, an exact replica of Bexley Asylum. A cemetery opened in 1899 and closed in 1955, with each grave usually containing three or four bodies. In 1915 the Asylum was taken over by the Army and the 2,143 inmates were transferred to other asylums. It became the Horton (County of London) War Hospital and was visited by King George V and Queen Mary in July 1916. In 1919, having treated over 46,000 patients, it was returned to London County Council and in 1920 was renamed Horton Mental Hospital, treating mainly female patients. In 1925 the Malaria Therapy unit moved into the Hospital's isolation block. Just before the outbreak of the Second World War, psychiatric patients were transferred to neighbouring hospitals in just eight hours and Horton became a general hospital with 2,178 beds (later 2,330). It was named Horton Emergency Hospital and treated battle and air raid casualties as well as civilian sick. After the war the first mental patients were admitted in July 1947 and it ceased to be an emergency hospital in March 1948. In 1959 it became Horton Hospital. Numbers declined as patients were rehabilitated into the community and in 1997 the Hospital closed, but a small unit, Horton Haven, opened on the edge of the site. Redevelopment began in 2002 and most buildings were demolished for new housing but some original buildings have been converted to residences.

Royal Naval Hospital from 13th November. He embarked for Egypt on HT *Nile* on 3rd December and was taken on strength of the Base Depot, Mustapha on 26th December. He embarked at Alexandria and rejoined his Battalion on 9th January 1916. On 31st May he transferred to the Base Depot, Mudros, embarked on HT *Menominee* on 1st June and landed at Marseille, France on 7th June.

Biographies

HMHS *Cambria* (1,842 tons) was launched by William Denny & Bros at Dumbarton on 4th August 1897 as a passenger ferry for the London & North Western Railway Co on the Holyhead–Dublin service. In August 1914 she was requisitioned as an armed boarding steamer but in August 1915 became a hospital ship with accommodation for 189 casualties. She was used between Dover and France until May 1917, when she was moved to Holyhead to operate between there and Dublin. She returned to the cross Channel route in December 1917 as a troop carrier and back to the Holyhead–Dublin route in February 1918. In January 1919 she returned to her civilian owners. In 1921 she was renamed *Arvonia* and in August 1922 was requisitioned by the Irish Free State for the Irish National Army to land troops, armoured cars and field guns at Cork in an attack against the Republican Army. She was also used as a prison ship at Limerick. In 1923 she transferred to the London, Midland & Scottish Railway Co and in August 1925 was scrapped.

Harry received a gunshot wound to the left thigh on 13th November and was treated at 14th General Hospital, Wimereux before being evacuated to England on 15th November on HMHS *St David*. He was treated at Horton War Hospital, Epsom, Surrey from 17th November and transferred to A Reserve Battalion at Blandford on 9th January 1917. Harry embarked at Folkestone, Kent on 3rd March for Boulogne, France

In 1866 the West Riding County Asylum at Wakefield was overcrowded, having trebled in size in the previous twenty-five years. A site at Wadsley Park, Sheffield was selected and building commenced in 1869 of the South Yorkshire Asylum. It was to have 400 beds but this was increased to 630 and then to 750. The asylum opened on 21st August 1872. The hospital church was completed in 1875 and in 1893 a nurses' home was added. In 1888 it was renamed the West Riding Asylum, Wadsley. In March 1915 it became the Wharncliffe War Hospital with 1,500 beds and all mental patients were moved to other hospitals across the north of England. The King visited in September 1915. The War Hospital closed in July 1920, having dealt with 37,000 casualties. In 1930 it was renamed the Wadsley Mental Hospital. During the Second World War one third of the accommodation became the Wharncliffe Emergency Hospital to treat military casualties. This continued as a small general medical unit after the war named Wharncliffe Hospital, also known as Wharncliffe Side, until the mid-1970s. In 1948 the psychiatric hospital was integrated into the National Health Service and renamed Middlewood Hospital, with over 2,000 beds. The author worked there briefly before joining the Army in the mid-1970s. As psychiatric treatment became more community based a run down commenced. By 1986 patients had reduced to 600 and it closed in 1996. The site had since been redeveloped into the residential Wadsley Park Village. Some of the listed hospital buildings were not demolished, including the main administrative block (clock tower), Kingswood Ward, church and porters lodge. The first two have been converted into apartments - Middlewood Lodge and Kingswood Hall.

Swansea War Memorial on the Esplanade, Mumbles Road, designed by Ernest E Morgan, closely resembles Lutyens' Whitehall cenotaph. The foundation stone was laid on 1st July 1922 by Field Marshal Earl Haig and it was unveiled on 21st July 1923 by Admiral of the Fleet Sir FC Doveton Sturdee. It commemorates 2,274 men from the Great War and 500 from the Second World War.

Camerton War Memorial in St Peter's Churchyard (Memorials to Valour).

Harry is commemorated on the Vis-en-Artois Memorial.

and was posted to the Base Depot, Calais on 5th March. He rejoined the Drake Battalion on 28th March. On 23rd April he received a gunshot wound to the left shoulder and was treated at 22nd General Hospital, Camiers from 24th April, before being evacuated to England on 27th April on HMHS *Cambria*. He was treated at Wharncliffe War Hospital, Sheffield, Yorkshire from 28th April and was granted leave 3rd–12th July. He was posted to 2nd Reserve Battalion, Command Depot at Tidworth, Wiltshire on 11th September and later at Aldershot. He attended a course at Tidworth on 24th November and received a Good Conduct Badge on 25th February 1918.

Harry rejoined the Drake Battalion on 8th April and was appointed acting chief petty officer on 28th April (later confirmed from the same date). He was granted leave to England 26th July – 9th August.

Awarded the DCM for his actions at Logeast Wood on 21st August 1918, when he led his men against a machine gun that was holding up the advance of the flank of his company. In spite of the heavy mist the post was captured and the crew was disposed of. On a subsequent occasion he held a position against repeated counterattacks and under a heavy bombardment for twenty-four hours, LG 16th January 1919.

Awarded the VC for his actions on 2nd and 4th September 1918 at Pronville, France, LG 30th October 1918. Harry was informed that he had been recommended for the VC but was killed in action at Pronville on 27th September 1918 before it was confirmed. He is commemorated on the RNVR Panels of the Vis-en-Artois Memorial, France. The posthumous VC was presented to his widow by the King at Buckingham Palace on 17th July 1919. It was the last VC issued with the blue Royal Navy ribbon. Harry is commemorated in a number of other places:

- Prowse VC Senior Rates single living accommodation block at HMS *Collingwood*, School of Maritime Warfare.
- War Memorial in St Peter's Churchyard, Camerton, Somerset.
- War Memorial, Mumbles Road, Swansea, West Glamorgan.
- Heritage Blue Plaque on his birthplace at 133 High Street, Gilfach Goch, Llantrisaint, Glamorgan, unveiled on 21st October 2006.
- A Department for Communities and Local Government commemorative paving stone was dedicated at Gilfach Goch Community Council Grounds, High Street, Gilfach Goch on 29th September 2018.
- The Ring of Remembrance (L'Anneau de la Mémoire or Ring of Memory) at Ablain-Saint-Nazaire, France, inaugurated on 11th November 2014.

Sarah married Gwyn Jones (15th May 1888–1970) in 1928 at Swansea.

In addition to the VC and DCM he was awarded the 1914–15 Star, British War Medal 1914–20 and Victory Medal 1914–19. The medals were sold for £950 at a Glendining's auction on 15th December 1966 and were purchased by Messrs Spinks. They were owned later by Captain Douglas-Morris RN, who loaned them to the Royal Naval Museum. He reclaimed them in 1990 and they were sold to Lord Ashcroft at a Sotheby's auction in 1992. The VC is held by the Michael Ashcroft Trust, the holding institution for the Lord Ashcroft Victoria Cross Collection and displayed in the Imperial War Museum's Lord Ashcroft Gallery.

2204279 PRIVATE WALTER LEIGH RAYFIELD
7th Battalion (1st British Columbia) CEF

Walter Rayfield was born on 7th October 1880 at 22 Sydney Villas, Richmond upon Thames, Surrey, England, registered as Walter Leigh Lockett. When Walter married for the first time, his father was recorded as Thomas Rayfield. When he married for the second time, his father was recorded as Thomas Guy Rayfield. However, no trace of this man has been found with any degree of certainty. A theory is that his stepfather, Thomas Henry Mills, worked at St Thomas and Guy's Hospital, and perhaps Walter picked on these two names. However, that does not explain his adopted surname. At the time of the 1881 Census he was being cared for by Charlotte Kitchen, a domestic nurse at Grove Cottage, Boston Road, Hanwell.

Walter's mother, Anna 'Annie' Maria Lockett (2nd October 1842–1909), born in Manchester, Lancashire, was a dressmaker, visiting her father and stepmother at the White Lion public house, Etnam Street, Leominster, Herefordshire in 1861. She was a domestic servant at the time of Walter's birth. Annie married Thomas Henry Mills (c.1849–c.1927), a porter born at Southwark, London, on 22nd March 1885 at St Mary Magdalen Church, Bermondsey, London. Their address at the time was 96 Snowsfields, London. In 1891 Thomas was a hospital bath man and they were living at 28 Newcomen Street, St Saviour, London. He was still there in 1911, living with his daughter Elizabeth, and was a nurse porter at St Thomas and Guy's Hospital, London. Thomas had married Elizabeth Hill (c.1849–84) on 30th July 1871 at St Paul, Bermondsey, London, where she was born. Thomas and Elizabeth had four children, all educated at Laxon Street School:

In 1861 Walter's maternal grandparents were living at the White Lion in Leominster, Herefordshire.

St Mary Magdalen, Bermondsey, where Walter's mother married Thomas Henry Mills in 1885. A church was first recorded on the site in 1290. In 1680 it was demolished, except for the medieval tower. A rebuilt church was completed about 1690, with extensions added in 1705 and 1794 and alterations in 1830, 1852 and 1883. The west end was damaged by fire in 1971. It is now the oldest building in the district.

 * Alice Elizabeth Mills (21st November 1872–1959) married David Balcombe (c.1873–1934), born at Wandsworth, London, on 15th October 1893 at Southwark. In 1901 he was a poulterer's assistant and they were living at 202 Whitehorse Lane, Croydon and at 16a Harrington Road, South Norwood, Surrey by 1911. They had four children:
   ◦ Mabel Annie Florence Balcombe (1894–1983) married Arthur Daniel Hancock (1890–1978), born in Kensington, London, in 1922. Arthur died at 31 Lincoln Road, South Norwood, London. Mabel was living at 110 Croydon Road, Penge, London at the time of her death. They had two children.
   ◦ Dorothy Eleanor Balcombe (1895–1970) married Francis Alfred Clatworthy (1892–1970), born in Greenwich, London, in 1918. She was living at 53 Kensington Avenue, Thornton Heath, Croydon at the time of her death there. They had three children.
   ◦ David Balcombe (1897–1971).

- Alice Elizabeth Balcombe (1900–85) married Charles Horace Dunster (1899–1963) in 1921 at Reigate, Surrey. They were living at 38 Carlyon Avenue, South Harrow, Middlesex at the time of his death there. She was living at 113 Kingsland, Harlow, Essex at the time of her death. They had two daughters, one of whom, June Molly Dunster (born 1926) married her step-cousin, Victor Charles Rayfield, in 1945 at Croydon. He was the son of Walter Leigh Rayfield VC. The marriage ended in divorce. June remarried as Murphy and settled in Canada.
- Albert George Mills (26th November 1876–10th March 1947) was an office boy in 1891. He enlisted in the Royal Artillery (15435) at Dover Castle, Kent on 28th May 1896, described as a telegraph messenger, 5′ 9¼″ tall, weighing 145 lbs, with fresh complexion, blue eyes, light brown hair and his religious denomination was Church of England. He declared previous service in the Kent Artillery. His father was his next of kin, living at 113 Albert Road, South Norwood, London. Albert joined No.10 Company RGA on 27th July and was posted to Woolwich on 29th October 1897. He was in hospital there with pneumonia 12th April–13th May 1898. He qualified as a 1st class gunner on 30th April and was granted Good Conduct Pay of 1d per day on 28th May. He returned to Dover Castle on 20th June and to Shoeburyness on 9th July, returning to Dover Castle again on 27th August. He qualified as a Telephonist (Specialist) on 11th October. He was in hospital with pneumonia 28th April–24th May 1900 and was granted Good Conduct Pay of 2 d per day on 28th May. On 9th April 1903 he extended to complete twelve years service and qualified in International Code Signalling on 4th August. He was granted Service Pay of 7 d per day 1st April 1904–28th May 1908 and was posted to 40 Company on 1st April 1906. Albert gained 3rd class education on 28th June 1906. At Dover on 3rd April 1908 he extended to complete twenty-one years service. He was declared fit to serve in Sierra Leone on 27th June 1910 and in Gibraltar on 8th September 1910. He served in Gibraltar from 9th September 1910 in 54 Company and was posted to 6 Company on 21st May 1913. Awarded the Long Service & Good Conduct Medal in 1915 with gratuity. On 10th December 1917 he agreed to continue serving for the duration of the war and, on 19th September 1918, elected to draw his pension while still serving. He volunteered to serve for one year from 1st February 1919 in the Army of Occupation. Albert was Mentioned in a War Office Despatch of 23rd August 1919. He embarked for Britain on 18th February 1920 and was discharged on 23rd March. Albert was living at 84 Albert Road, South Norwood, Surrey at the time of his death at Guy's Hospital, London.
- Mary Elizabeth Mills (28th February 1879–1957) was living with her father in 1911. She died unmarried.
- Thomas Henry Mills (3rd January 1883–1948) joined the Royal Navy on 17th April 1898 as a boy 2nd class (198957) and was described as 5′ 1¾″ tall, with fresh complexion. He served aboard HMS *Ganges* and was promoted boy 1st class on 2nd February 1899. He served on *Impregnable* 17th March 1899,

Minotaur 6th May 1899, *Agincourt* 23rd August 1899, *Australia* 29th September 1899, *Revenge* 23rd November 1899, *Victorious* 16th May 1900, *Caesar* 7th July 1900 and *Victorious* 9th November 1900. He engaged as an ordinary seaman on his eighteenth birthday on 3rd January 1901, by when he had grown to 5' 4" tall. He continued aboard *Victorious* and then served aboard *Cruiser* 15th July 1901, *Victorious* 9th November 1901, *Cruiser* 20th May 1902 and *Victorious* 20th July 1902. Promoted able seaman 24th August 1902 and served aboard *Duke of Wellington* 8th August 1903, *Firequeen* 1st October 1903, *Racer* 4th November 1903, *Goliath* 9th May 1905, *Victory I* 15th March 1907, *Spartiate* 21st June 1907, *Hampshire* 20th August 1907, *Victory I* 1st April 1909, *Grafton* 4th April 1909, *Prince George* 29th December 1909, *Swiftsure* 22nd November 1910 and *Victory I* 26th May 1911, when he was invalided ashore. At the Royal Naval Hospital Haslar, Gosport, Hampshire he was declared medically unfit and was discharged on 30th June 1915. Thomas married Elizabeth 'Lizzie' Rachel Pearse (28th August 1882–1948), born at St Saviour, London, on 25th December 1908 at Southwark. Lizzie was living with her mother at 48 Great Dover Street, Newington St Mary, London in 1911. They had five children – Thomas H Mills 1911, Richard A Mills 1912, Edward A Mills 1913, Elizabeth A Mills 1915 and Leonard H Mills 1919.

Little is known about Walter's paternal grandparents. His maternal grandfather, Jeremiah Bibby Lockett (1816–18th July 1877), born in Cheshire, was a labourer/platelayer. He married Charlotte Lockett (née Etches) (c.1827–13th December 1873), born in Scotland, on 14th January 1838 in Manchester, Lancashire. The marriage ended by mutual consent. In addition to Annie they had two other children:

- William Lockett (19th June 1839–9th February 1840).
- Sarah Elizabeth Lockett (1845–1921) was a cotton weaver in 1861 living with her mother and stepfather, recorded as Sarah L Hanson. She married William Oakley in 1869 at Oldham, her maiden name registered as Locket (sic). They had a son, Joshua Oakley (1869–1951), who was a brickmaker's labourer in 1891, living with his mother. Sarah married Jeremiah Horrigan (registered as Horigan) (c.1844–95), born at Warrington, Lancashire, in 1872 in Oldham. Her maiden name was registered as Holklay. In 1881 he was a jobber and she was a washerwoman. They were living at 1 Rowland's Place, Oldham. By 1891 he was a labourer in an iron works and they were living at 3 John Street, Oldham. They had three sons – John Horrigan (1875), William Horrigan (1878–1914) and George Horrigan (1882–1918). Sarah married Michael Boyle (c.1857–30th July 1930) in 1902 at Oldham. He was a textile machine labourer in 1911 and they were living at 9 John Street, Oldham. William Horrigan enlisted in 4th Manchester on 15th February 1899 in Manchester (6679), described as eighteen years old labourer working for Platt & Co, Engineers, Oldham, 5' 2½" tall, weighing 122 lbs, with fresh complexion, grey eyes and brown hair. He was confined to barracks for five days for being dirty on parade on 7th March 1899. He was embodied in 6th Battalion on 4th May 1900,

disembodied on 18th October, embodied again on 24th December and embarked for South Africa on 4th January 1901. He was admonished, having been found tampering with another man's kit on the line of march on 5th August. William embarked for Britain on 4th September 1902 and was disembodied on 30th September with the war gratuity. He was a labourer when he re-enlisted in the King's Own (Royal Lancaster Regiment) at Ashton-under-Lyne on 7th January 1903 (7639), claiming he was nineteen years and ten months old. He joined at the Depot and was awarded Good Conduct Pay of 1d per day on the same day (based on his previous service). He was described as 5′ 3¼″ tall, weighing 135 lbs, with fresh complexion, light grey eyes, brown hair and his religious denomination was Roman Catholic. He was posted to 2nd Battalion at Blackdown on 7th April 1903. He extended his service to complete eight years on 2nd February 1904. Two years and eighty-four days embodied service in 6th Manchester was allowed to count towards his current service. On 9th February 1904 he embarked on SS *Sicilia* to join 1st Battalion in India and disembarked at Calcutta on 15th March. He was treated for syphilis at Barrackpore 24th April–31st May 1904, at Calcutta 14th–29th June 1905 and at Shwebo, Burma 31st March–6th May and 13th July–7th August 1906. He was awarded Good Conduct Pay of 2d per day on 15th October 1905 and was granted Service Pay 7th January 1905–15th July 1908. William was treated for scabies 5th January 1908 and for syphilis at Rangoon 6th January–15th February. He was based at Lebong, India, then Lucknow from 21st December 1908. He returned to Britain on 27th January 1911 and transferred to the Army Reserve next day from Gosport. His address was 9 John Street, off Manchester Road, Oldham. William was recalled and went to France with 1st Battalion on 23rd August 1914. He was killed in action or died of wounds (at Harcourt according to

La Ferté-sous-Jouarre Memorial to the Missing commemorates 3,740 officers and men of the BEF who died in the Battles of Mons, Le Cateau, Marne and Aisne between the end of August and early October 1914 and have no known grave. The land was donated by Adrien Fizeau, Mayor of Jouarre, in memory of his father, Hippolyte Fizeau, the scientist who was a member of the Institut de France and the Royal Society. The memorial was unveiled by Sir William Pulteney, GOC III Corps in 1914, on 4th November 1928.

his service record) between 26th August and 8th September 1914 (La Ferté-sous-Jouarre Memorial, Seine-et-Marne, France). Joshua Oakley signed for William's Great War campaign medals on 23rd June 1921 and for his Queen's South Africa Medal on 28th February 1925.

Jeremiah Bibby Lockett married Mary Anne Bowdler (née Sheward) (c.1820–January 1870) on 25th August 1860 at Leominster, Herefordshire. She was the proprietor of the White Lion public house, Etnam Street, Leominster in 1861. Jeremiah died there. Mary Anne had married Robert Bowdler (died 1845) in 1841 at Leominster and they had two children – Charles Bowdler 1842 and Mary Ann Bowdler 1844.

Charlotte married John Hanson (c.1822–91), born in Sheffield, Yorkshire, on 24th December 1864 at St Mary, St Denys & St George Cathedral, Manchester. They were living together as husband and wife from at least the time of the 1851 Census at Hardman's Buildings, Farnworth, Lancashire. John was a fly filer in 1851, a spindle maker by 1861 and a flyer maker by 1871. By 1861 they had moved to Manchester Road, Kearsley, Lancashire and to 9 Bright Street, Oldham by 1871, where Charlotte subsequently died. Charlotte and John five children – Mary Jane Hanson 1847, Alice Hanson 1849, John Hanson 1852, William Hanson 1855 and George Hanson 1860.

Walter was educated at Laxon Street School, Southwark, London until 14th February 1891, where he was registered as Walt Lee. Walter Lee, as he was known

Walter's grandmother, Charlotte, married John Hanson at St Mary, St Denys & St George Cathedral, Manchester in 1864. The Cathedral, formally the Cathedral and Collegiate Church of St Mary, St Denys and St George, became the seat of the Bishop of Manchester in 1847. The former medieval parish church was rebuilt in the 1420s and towards the end of the 15th century and was restored extensively and extended by the Victorians. Until 1850 the Collegiate Church was the parish church for the whole of Manchester and was the only place where marriages could be legally contracted. As the population of Manchester increased more and more christenings, weddings and funerals were conducted there, often in batches. In 1838 alone there were 5,164 christenings, 1,457 funerals, and 2,615 weddings. During the 1940 Blitz a bomb exploded near the northeast corner, severely damaging the roof and demolishing two chapels. All stained-glass windows were blown out and there was extensive damage, which took almost twenty years to repair. The chapel of the Manchester Regiment was established there. In 1996 the Cathedral was damaged in an IRA bombing. It was listed Grade 1 in January 1952.

SS *Sardinian* (4,376 tons), constructed by Robert Steele & Co at Greenock for the Allan Line, was launched on 3rd June 1874. Her maiden voyage commenced on 29th July 1875 from Liverpool to Québec and Montréal. Most of her sailings were from Liverpool or Glasgow to Canadian east coast ports and some American cities such as New York and Baltimore. On 10th May 1878, a coalbunker exploded near Moville, Ireland, killing and injuring several passengers. The ship caught fire and was scuttled to extinguish it, with only the upper decks sticking out of the water. She was salvaged, repaired and returned to service on 26th June. In November 1901 the ship transported Guglielmo Marconi to set up a wireless station at St John's, Newfoundland. In 1917, *Sardinian* was bought by Canadian Pacific Line and in December 1920 by Astoreca Azqueta. She was reduced to a coal hulk at Vigo, Spain. In 1934 she was bought by Compania Carbonera and was sold for scrap in June 1938.

in 1891, was being cared for by sisters Harriet (1841–1928) and Alice (1849–1928) Wemyss at Washwell Cottages (later Washwell House), Painswick, Gloucestershire. Washwell Cottages were a residence for children awaiting migration to Canada. Walter was sent to Canada aboard SS *Sardinian* under the care of Miss Laver, departing Liverpool, Lancashire on 21st May 1891 and arriving in Québec on 30th May, via

Annie MacPherson, born in Scotland, was educated in Glasgow and at the Home and Colonial Training College in London. She opened the Home of Industry, Spitalfield, London in 1868, in a former cholera hospital. It housed up to 120 children and was soon overflowing, so she made plans to move children to Canada. The first Marchmont Home opened in 1870 on Murney Hill, Belleville, in a former residence for invalid soldiers. Two years later the property burned down and one boy died. A property at 193 Moira Street, Yeoman's Hill, Belleville, was purchased, known as Charlement Lodge, on three and a quarter acres. It was renamed Marchmont. This building burned down in 1875. A new building of brick was constructed at the same address. That year Annie handed over the running of the Home to Ellen Bilbrough, who remained until her death in 1900 and then her husband, Reverend Wallace, carried on until retiring in 1913. Manchester and Salford Homes ceased sending children to Canada after the Great War. In 1920, Lillian Birt, Annie's niece, took over the running of the Liverpool Sheltering Home in Knowlton, Québec and assumed responsibility for Marchmont. William H Merry, a nephew of Annie's, who had been superintendent at MacPherson's Stratford Receiving Home, became the new superintendent of Marchmont until it closed in August 1925. About 10,000 children had passed through the Marchmont Homes. The building has since been converted into apartments and the address is 159 Yeomans Street.

Londonderry and Montréal. He was handed over to Mr Wallace at Marchmont Home, 193 Moira Street, Belleville, Ontario, a home for children emigrating to Canada from Britain. It is assumed that his education continued in Ontario. By 1910 he was a shingle weaver at Seattle, King Co, Washington and later studied at the Agricultural, Mining and Mechanical Arts College, Oakland, California, USA. He was a dairyman at the time of his enlistment in 1917 but recorded his trade as lumberjack on his attestation papers.

Walter married Mary 'Mamie' or 'Maude' Leona Maroney (c.1885–18th October 1974), born in Wisconsin, USA, on 8th August 1907 at the Church of Our Lady of Good Help, Seattle, King Co, Washington. She was the daughter of John Maroney and Catherine Marlan. They were living in Seattle in 1910 and the marriage ended in divorce in 1915. Mary married Jan 'John' Strating (1883–1954), a butcher, born at Zuidlaren, Netherlands, in June 1916 at King County Court House, Washington. They were living at Redmond, Washington in 1917. The marriage ended in divorce in 1934. He died in Los Angeles and she in King Co, Washington. John and Mary had a daughter, Margaret Lavon Strating (1917–87).

Seattle's first Roman Catholic Church, Our Lady of Good Help, was built in 1869 by Father Francis Xavier Prefontaine (1838–1908) on the corner of Third Avenue and Washington Street. It was enlarged several times and survived the great fire in the city in 1889 before being demolished in 1904. Bishop Edward J O'Dea moved his see from Vancouver to Seattle and Our Lady of Good Help became a pro-cathedral. However, it was located in a disreputable section of Seattle and the site was not deemed suitable for development into a cathedral. A new church was constructed almost on the same site, which has also been demolished since.

Walter married Nina Hickling (born 2nd August 1896), an office nurse born in Toronto, Ontario, on 25th July 1921 at Niagara Falls, Ontario. His address was recorded as 203 Market Street, San Francisco, California and hers as 416 Brunswick Avenue, Toronto. By 1922 they were living at 931 Bathurst Street, Toronto. Nina was living with her daughter, Isobel, at 558 Gerrard Street East, Toronto in 1949. Nina attended the VC Centenary Celebrations at Hyde Park, London on 26th June 1956. She arrived on SS *Homeric* from Québec on 20th June and stayed at the Mount Royal Hotel, London. By 1963 she had moved to 32 Joicey Boulevard, Eglinton, Toronto and to 107 Jane Street, York West by 1972.

Nina's father, Charles Hickling (born 18th February 1868) married Isabelle Sanderson (born 10th October 1872), of Irish origin, in Ontario. He was a gold refiner in Toronto in 1921. In addition to Nina they had two other daughters:

- Violet Muriel Hickling (5th April 1892–9th June 1893), born at York, Ontario.
- Gladys Hickling (born 28th November 1895), born in Ontario, was a stenographer in 1921.

Walter had three children from his two marriages:

- Walter L Rayfield (1909–4th May 1953) born in Washington, USA, was recorded as his father's next-of-kin c/o his mother, Mrs John Strating, Redmond, Washington, USA, when he attested in 1917. He was a bookkeeper in 1940 and married Irene L Hall on 15th November 1941 in King Co, Washington. He died in Seattle, USA.
- Victor Charles Rayfield (born c.1923), born in Canada, moved to England and married June Molly Dunster (born 21st June 1926) in 1945 at Croydon, Surrey. She joined him in Canada in 1946 but the marriage ended in divorce. June married as Murphy and settled in Canada. Victor married Dora Matthews c.1948 in Canada. He was working in real estate in 1965 and was living on Edith Avenue, Toronto. They had a son, Walter Leigh Rayfield, born in 1949 at Hamilton, Ontario.
- Isobel Rayfield was a secretary in 1949, living with her mother.

Walter was twice rejected on medical grounds before being accepted by the Canadian Army. He enlisted at the British Recruiting Office, Los Angeles, California in May 1917 and was attested at Victoria, British Columbia on 10th July (2204279). He was described as 5′ 6¼″ tall, weighing 140 lbs, with dark complexion, grey eyes, dark hair and his religious denomination was Church of England. He was living at Gray Hotel, Los Angeles at the time. Walter joined the Forestry Depot CEF at Vancouver, British Columbia initially but transferred to the British Columbia Regiment on 1st September. He appears to have been in Vancouver until at least 21st December. He joined the 5th Draft, 1st Depot Battalion, British Columbia Regiment.

Walter sailed for Britain from Halifax, Nova Scotia aboard SS *Justica* on 8th January 1918, arriving at Liverpool on 26th January. He was taken on strength of 16th Reserve Battalion, Seaford on 27th January and transferred to 1st Reserve Battalion there on 15th February. He went to France on 10th April and was taken on strength of 7th Battalion next day. He joined the Canadian Corps Reinforcement Camp on 15th April and the Battalion on 18th April.

Awarded the VC for his actions east of Arras, France on 2nd–4th September 1918, LG 14th December 1918. He was admitted to No.2 Canadian and No.4 Canadian Casualty Clearing Stations on 15th September and was transferred by 25 Ambulance Train to 20th General Hospital, Camiers on 16th September with pyrexia of unknown origin. On 27th September he was promoted corporal. He was transferred to 6th Convalescence Depot, Étaples on 30th September and to 10th Convalescence Depot, Ècault on 2nd October. Walter was discharged to No.5 Rest Camp, St Martins, Boulogne on 12th October and was graded medically A at the

SS *Justicia* (32,234 tons), laid down as SS *Statendam* for the Holland America Line by Harland & Woolf in Belfast, was launched on 9th July 1914. Before fitting out could be completed, the Great War broke out and work stopped. In 1915 the British government requisitioned *Statendam* as a troopship. She was given to Cunard Line to manage after the sinking of RMS *Lusitania* and renamed *Justicia* (Latin for justice). Cunard had difficulty assembling a crew, so the ship passed to White Star Line, which had the crew of the sunken *Britannic* available. On 19th July 1918, *Justicia* was thirty-seven kilometres south of Skerryvore, Scotland, sailing unladen from Belfast to New York, when she was torpedoed by UB-*64*. She listed but watertight doors prevented her from sinking. UB-*64* fired three more torpedoes but she remained afloat and escort destroyers damaged UB-*64*, forcing it to leave the area. Most of the crew were evacuated, leaving only a small number on board *Justicia*. The engines were still operable and the tug *Sonia* took her in tow, in an attempt to beach the ship near Lough Swilly. However, next day UB-*124* found her and fired two more torpedoes, which struck amidships. The remaining crew were evacuated before she rolled onto her starboard side and sank about forty-five kilometres northwest of Malin Head. Sixteen crewmen were killed in the various attacks. Destroyers HMS *Marne*, *Milbrook* and *Pigeon* attacked with depth charges and sank UB-*124* with gunfire after she surfaced.

Canadian Division Base Depot on 14th October. He moved to the Canadian Corps Reinforcement Camp on 23rd October and rejoined the Battalion on 27th October.

Walter moved to Germany with the Battalion a few weeks after the war finished. While in Germany he was pulled out of bed to be informed that his VC was listed in Army Orders. Later in the day he was escorted to the parade ground for the public announcement. He was appointed acting sergeant on 7th January 1919 and was granted fourteen days leave on 18th January, extended until 8th March. The VC was presented by the King in the ballroom of Buckingham Palace on 8th March. Walter

Don Jail, built east of the Don River in Toronto in 1858–64, was reputed to be the largest in North America at the time. It had a progressive approach to welfare and living conditions but later gained a bad reputation due to overcrowding and other factors. A new wing was added in 1958 and continued as the Toronto Jail when the original building ceased to be used in 1977. It closed on 31st December 2013 when a new facility, the Toronto South Detention Centre, was completed. About a fifth of the historic Don Jail building was saved and renovated.

was struck off strength to the Canadian Record List on 15th March and was taken on strength of H Wing, Canadian Concentration Camp, Witley on 16th March. He moved to Britain on 19th March and embarked on RMS *Carmania* on 18th April. He returned to Canada and was discharged in Vancouver on 25th April 1919. His intended residence was Santa Anita Rancho, Santa Anita, California.

Walter was a milk tester in May 1919 in Seattle, USA. He took up farming at Pontypool, Ontario in an attempt to improve his health and was also responsible for the transfer of shell-shocked and other disabled soldiers to a military hospital under the Department of Soldiers' Civil Re-Establishment Scheme. About 1922 he was appointed an official of the Toronto Harbour Commission, living at 931 Bathurst Avenue, Toronto. Later he lived at Port Huron, Michigan, USA, working as a salesman. Walter ran for Parliament on one occasion but was defeated narrowly. He moved to Toronto and was appointed Sergeant-at-Arms in the Provincial Legislature in 1934. He was appointed Deputy Governor of Don Jail, Toronto in May 1935 and was later promoted to Governor.

Walter enlisted in the Queen's Rangers, which formed in Toronto on 15th January 1921 as The West Toronto Regiment, and was commissioned as a lieutenant. He was later promoted captain. He attended the VC Dinner at the Royal Gallery of the House of Lords, London on 9th November 1929. During that visit to the United Kingdom, he visited Belfast, Northern Ireland and laid a wreath in the Garden of Remembrance on behalf of the Canadian winners of the VC. He was presented to King George VI and Queen Elizabeth at Queen's Park, Toronto on 22nd May 1939. Other VCs present on that occasion were – Colin F Barron, Benjamin H Geary, Henry H Robson, Thomas W Holmes, William Merrifield and Charles S Rutherford.

Walter died at his home in Toronto, Ontario on 19th February 1949 and is buried in Prospect Cemetery, St Clair Avenue West, Toronto, Ontario (Veteran's Plot, Section 7, Grave 4196). He is commemorated in a number of other places:

- British Columbia
    ○ Corporal Walter L Rayfield VC Memorial Bursary – awarded annually by the British Columbia Regiment Association to a serving member of the Regiment for academic achievement and loyalty to the Regiment. It is one of five bursaries honouring the VCs of units perpetuated by the Regiment.
    ○ Five park benches were dedicated to VCs – Edward Donald Bellew, Robert Hill Hanna, Graham Thomson Lyall, Michael James O'Rourke and Walter Leigh Rayfield – on 11th November 2007 in a small park adjacent to the British Columbia Regiment Museum, Beatty Street, Vancouver.

Walter's grave marker in Prospect Cemetery, Toronto. Colin Fraser Barron VC (1893–1958) is also buried there.

- Ontario
  - ◦ Victoria Cross obelisk to all Canadian VCs at Military Heritage Park, Barrie dedicated by Princess Royal on 22nd October 2013.
  - ◦ Named on one of eleven plaques honouring 175 men from overseas awarded the VC for the Great War. The plaques were unveiled by the Senior Minister of State at the Foreign & Commonwealth Office and Minister for Faith and Communities, Baroness Warsi, at a reception at Lancaster House, London on 26th June 2014 attended by The Duke of Kent and relatives of the VC recipients. The Canadian plaque was unveiled outside the British High Commission in Elgin Street, Ottawa on 10th November 2014 by The Princess Royal in the presence of British High Commissioner Howard Drake, Canadian Minister of Veterans Affairs Julian Fantino and Canadian Chief of the Defence Staff General Thomas James Lawson.
  - ◦ Plaque No.26 on the York Cemetery VC Memorial, West Don River Valley, Toronto dedicated on 25th June 2017.
  - ◦ Display at the Canadian War Museum, 1 Vimy Place, Ottawa.
- Two 49 cents postage stamps in honour of the ninety-four Canadian VC winners were issued by Canada Post on 21st October 2004 on the 150th Anniversary of the first Canadian VC's action, Alexander Roberts Dunn VC.
- A Department for Communities and Local Government commemorative paving stone was dedicated at Richmond War Memorial, Whittaker Avenue, Richmond upon Thames, Surrey on 4th September 2018.
- Memorial Plaque, Villers-lès-Cagnicourt, near Arras, France.

Walter Rayfield's memorial in Villers-lès-Cagnicourt, alongside those of Billy Metcalf, Cyrus Peck and Arthur Knight.

In addition to the VC he was awarded the British War Medal 1914–20, Victory Medal 1914–19, George VI Coronation Medal 1937 and Silver Medal of the Belgian Order of the Crown. His son, Victor, presented the medals to the Canadian War Museum, Ottawa, Ontario, Canada in February 1970, where they are held.

The Belgian Order of the Crown Silver Medal. The Order was established on 15th October 1897 to recognise heroic deeds and distinguished service in the Congo Free State. In 1908 it became a national honour of Belgium, junior to the Order of Leopold. Currently, the Order is awarded for services to Belgium, meritorious service in public employment, distinguished artistic, literary or scientific achievements or commercial/industrial services in Belgium or Africa. The Order is also bestowed on foreign nationals and is frequently awarded to military and diplomatic personnel of other countries. The Order has five classes (Grand Cross, Grand Officer, Commander, Officer and Knight) plus three medals (Gold, Silver and Bronze).

LIEUTENANT CHARLES SMITH RUTHERFORD
5th Battalion, Canadian Mounted Rifles CEF

Charles Rutherford was born on 9th January 1892 at Colborne, Haldimand Township, Northumberland Co, Ontario, Canada. His father, John Thomas Rutherford (1st June 1855–1928), a farmer also born at Colborne, married Isabella 'Bell' née Kellie (6th September 1860–1960), born at Vernonville, Northumberland Co, on 11th January 1887 in Northumberland Co. They were living at Lakeport, Northumberland West in 1911. Charles had three brothers:

- Wallace Albert Rutherford (27th September 1888–1955), a farmer, married Nora Euphemia Campbell (12th March 1897–1982), born at Peterborough, Ontario, on 6th September 1922. She died at Vernonville, Northumberland Co. They are understood to have had two children.
- James Arthur Rutherford (8th November 1893–1984) reportedly had a daughter, Marguerite Rutherford, who died in 1923. He married Helen Marjorie Walker (28th August 1904–1994), born at Cramahe Township, Ontario, on 18th November 1925. They had a son, John Douglas Rutherford (1929–2016).
- Edward Alexander Rutherford (10th April 1896–1968) was a farmer when he enlisted in the CEF on 17th May 1918, described as 5' 6" tall, with fair complexion, blue eyes, fair hair and his religious denomination was Presbyterian. He married Mary Elizabeth Chatterson (22nd May 1902–1994), born at Cramahe, on 9th April 1927.

Charles' paternal grandfather, Andrew Rutherford (16th January 1827–2nd April 1900), was born in Berwickshire, Scotland. He emigrated to Canada and married Jane née Forsythe (c.1829–24th September 1899) there in 1858. They both died at Haldimand, Northumberland Co, Ontario. In addition to John they had seven other children:

- Jane 'Jennie' Rutherford (born c.1858) married John McCarl.
- Alexander Rutherford (30th April 1859–12th November 1932) married Jennie MacKenzie (4th October 1857–1949), born at Clarke Township, Durham Co, Ontario, on 1st January 1884 at Cramahe, Ontario. They had six children:
    ○ George Andrew Rutherford (1885–1952).
    ○ Jennie Leona Rutherford (1886).
    ○ MacKenzie Rutherford (1889–1970) had medicals at Vancouver, British Columbia on 8th August and Valcartier on 7th September 1914. He was

attested on 23rd September (29596), described as an insurance agent/broker, 5' 10½" tall, weighing 168 lbs, with fair complexion, hazel eyes, fair hair and his religious denomination was Presbyterian. He embarked on RMS *Andania* at Québec on 7th October and arrived in England on 14th October. MacKenzie was admitted to Tidworth Military Hospital, Wiltshire with tonsillitis 21st February–2nd March 1915 and went to France on 1st April. He allotted $20 per month to his father from his Army pay from May 1915 until December 1918. On 20th May he was wounded by a gunshot/shrapnel to the right foot in a charge at Festubert and was admitted to Merville Hospital for one day, then the Australian Hospital, Wimereux on 22nd May. He was evacuated to Britain and treated at 1st Western General Hospital, Liverpool from 10th June. He was on the strength of 30th Battalion, Shorncliffe from 14th July and 43rd Battalion from 6th October. He transferred to the Canadian Convalescent Hospital, Monks Horton on 31st July, to the Canadian Convalescent Hospital at Epsom on 10th September and to Moore Barracks Canadian Hospital, Shorncliffe on 8th November. A medical board there on 18th November recommended permanent base duties. He was discharged on 25th November and was on leave until 6th December. MacKenzie transferred to 17th Battalion at Shorncliffe on 28th January 1916. He was admitted to Moore Barracks Canadian Hospital with influenza 13th–20th February. On 15th February he was taken on strength of the Canadian Casualty Assembly Centre, Folkestone. A medical board at Shorncliffe on 28th February found he could not march and recommended base duties for six months. Appointed acting corporal 28th September. He was attached for duty at the Trench Warfare School, Crowborough 19 February–15th March 1917. Promoted acting sergeant 5th June, lance sergeant 12th August and reverted to acting corporal on 27th August. Next day he reverted to private on proceeding overseas but this was cancelled and he was promoted corporal instead. Having joined the Canadian Base Depot in France on 28th August, he rejoined 16th Battalion on 1st September. He was wounded on 16th September but returned to duty on 18th September. MacKenzie made a will on 17th January 1918 leaving $500 to his mother, $250 to his sister, Jennie, and the remainder of his estate to his father. He was granted leave to Paris for fourteen days from 19th March and joined the Canadian Corps Reinforcement Camp on 1st April. On 5th April he rejoined the Battalion and was promoted lance sergeant on 12th August, acting sergeant on 16th August and sergeant on 21st August. On 27th August he went to England to the Manitoba Regimental Depot, Seaford and joined 1st Reserve Battalion there on 31st August. He transferred to the Canadian Training School, Bexhill pending joining the Officer's Training Centre on 8th September. Commissioned as a lieutenant in the Manitoba Regiment on 23rd November and joined 11th Reserve Battalion. On 3rd December he joined the port of embarkation for Canada and arrived at St John's on RMS

Minnedosa on 14th December. He was demobilised on 29th December and transferred to the Reserve of Officers. A medical at Barriefield, Ontario on 16th February 1919 graded him B2 due to the wound on his foot.
  ○ Bruce Alexander Rutherford (1894–1948).
  ○ Wilfred James Rutherford (1895–1953) had a medical at Port Hope, Ontario on 22nd October 1917 and was graded A2. He was called up at Barriefield, Ontario on 17th May 1918 (3060064) to 1st Depot Battalion, Eastern Ontario Regiment, described as a bank clerk, 5′ 7½″ tall, weighing 140 lbs, with dark complexion, blue eyes, black hair and his religious denomination was Presbyterian. He transferred to 75th Battery CFA on 27th May and 85th Battery CFA on 16th September at Petawawa, Ontario. He assigned $20 per month from his Army pay to his father from 1st October 1918 until 31st March 1919. Wilfred was admitted to Coquitlam Hospital, Victoria with influenza 7th–14th October. He was earmarked for the Canadian Siberian Expeditionary Force but, like many members of the 4,214 strong force, he contracted influenza before he could deploy and was not entitled to a war service grant. He was admitted to Shaughnessy Hospital, Vancouver with influenza 7th–19th February 1919. On 28th March he transferred to No.3 Military District and was taken on strength of the Casualty Company for disposal on 4th April. Demobilised at Kingston, Ontario on 8th April, having grown an inch and gained ten pounds.
  ○ Gordon Forsyth Rutherford (1900).
- Robert Andrew Rutherford (2nd March 1861–1931) married Ella F Chaplin (30th November 1867–23rd October 1925). They had three children – Charlotte Winn Rutherford 1888 and twins Cecil Douglas Rutherford and Robert Fraser Rutherford 1901.
- James F Rutherford (20th August 1863–6th August 1930) committed suicide by cutting his throat while of unsound mind at Haldimand.
- Isabella Rutherford (1866–11th June 1885).
- Mary Ellen Rutherford (1868–11th June 1885).
- Lilly Margaret Rutherford (13th June 1871–29th September 1951) married Albert Alfred Lee (born 1875) on 23rd September 1913.

His maternal grandfather, James Kellie (c.1821–25th November 1897), born at Glasgow, Lanarkshire, Scotland, married Margaret née Thompson (c.1819–27th February 1898), born at Elgin, Scotland, either in Scotland or Canada. James was a farmer and they were living at Haldimand, Ontario in 1881. In addition to Isabella they had five other children:

- Elizabeth Kellie (born c.1851), born in Ontario.
- James M Kellie (6th December 1849–12th December 1927), a farmer, married Mary Ann Webster (c.1855–83) on 11th December 1879 at Grafton, Northumberland Co. He died at Victoria, BC.

Charles' maternal grandmother came from Elgin, the administrative and commercial centre of Moray. The town is first mentioned in a charter of 1151 by David I, who created a royal burgh and in whose reign a castle was built. In 1224 Alexander II granted land for a new cathedral, which was completed in the 1240s but was destroyed by fire in 1270. It was reconstructed but the stone was of inferior quality and during the Reformation the building was stripped of its roof lead and much of the internal woodwork. In 1711 the central tower collapsed and the rubble was used for various other building projects. It remains a ruin. Prince Charles Edward Stuart stayed in the town for eleven days in 1746. The Duke of Cumberland also passed through on his way to do battle with the Prince at Drummossie Muir. In the 19th century much of the old medieval town was swept away and rebuilt. The Morayshire Railway arrived in 1852 and the town prospered. Nearby RAF Lossiemouth provides employment for many people. Lieutenant (later Lieutenant Colonel) William Rennie VC (1821–96) is buried in the town.

- Margaret Kellie (born c.1852).
- Anne Kellie (born c.1857).
- John Kellie (7th March 1858–12th November 193), a farmer, married Florence Huldy Kellogg (born c.1869) on 28th November 1894 at Colborne. He died at Vernonville.

Charles was educated at Dudley Public School, near Coleborne, Haldimand Township, Northumberland Co and then worked on the family farm. He enlisted in 83rd Overseas Battalion (Queen's Own Rifles) CEF at Riverdale Barracks, Toronto on 2nd March 1916 (172458), described as 5′ 9″ tall, weighing 160 lbs, with ruddy complexion, blue eyes, black hair and his religious denomination was Presbyterian. He sailed from Halifax, Nova Scotia aboard RMS *Olympic* on 28th April, arriving at Liverpool, England on 7th May. He transferred to 5th Canadian Mounted Rifles at West Sandling on 6th June and sailed for France next day, joining the Battalion on 9th June. Appointed acting paid lance corporal 20th September.

Charles was wounded by a bullet in the right arm at Regina Trench near Courcelette on the Somme on 2nd October and was admitted to 2nd Australian Hospital, Boulogne on 4th October. He was evacuated to England through Folkestone aboard HMHS *St Andrew* and was treated at 5th Northern General Hospital, Leicester from 6th October and at the Canadian Convalescent Hospital, Bear Wood, Wokingham, Berkshire from 24th October. He was discharged to the Canadian Casualty Assembly Centre, Folkestone on 7th November. A medical board at Shoreham, Sussex on 9th November found that he had recovered but he then suffered from jaundice. A medical board at St Leonards, Sussex on 22nd December

2nd Australian General Hospital at Wimereux near Boulogne. It arrived at Marseille from Egypt in April 1916 with a nursing staff of 115 and took over the local hospital at Moussot. Soldiers with infectious diseases identified on the voyage from Egypt were treated there. The main body left at the end of June for the tented Wimereux site, which was ready for patients on 2nd July. It expanded later with the addition of seventeen huts. The first major influx of patients was in April 1917 during the Battle of Arras. The hospital closed in February 1919 and returned to Australia in March (Australian War Memorial).

found that he had recovered and he joined 1st Canadian Casualty Training Battalion, Hastings on 27th December. On 29th January 1917 he transferred to 23rd Reserve Battalion and to 5th Canadian Mounted Rifles, Shoreham on 17th February.

On 22nd February, Charles returned to France, joined 3rd Entrenching Battalion on 25th March and 5th Canadian Mounted Rifles on 18th April. He was wounded at Avion, near Lens by a gunshot to the left cheek and temple on 7th June. He was treated at 13th Canadian Field Ambulance, 20 Ambulance Train and 11th General Hospital, Camiers next day until 4th July when he transferred to 3rd Convalescent Depot. On 6th July he transferred to the Canadian Base Depot, returned to the Battalion on 27th July and was confirmed in the rank of lance corporal on 11th August.

5th Northern General Hospital was centred on the former Leicestershire & Rutland County Asylum (now the University of Leicester). It eventually had sixty sites in Leicestershire, Lincolnshire, Derbyshire and Nottinghamshire, including local and cottage hospitals such as North Evington War Hospital, Knighton House Hospital, Gilcross Hospital and the Leicester Royal Infirmary. Private houses were also used, including Admiral Beatty's Leicestershire home, Brooksby Hall. In total there were beds for 111 officers and 2,487 other ranks and more than 95,000 casualties were treated, of whom 514 died. Of those 286 are buried close to the University in Welford Road Cemetery. 5th Northern General Hospital closed in March 1919. In 1921 the University College opened as a memorial to the men of Leicestershire who never came home. The institution's motto, *ut vitam habeant*, means 'so that they may have life'.

About 1830 the Times newspaper proprietor, John Walter (1776–1847), purchased the 5,000 acre Bear Wood estate. His son, also John Walter (1818–94), had the house built in 1865-74. It is one of the largest Victorian country houses in England. Bricks and wood from the estate were used in building the mansion and also for the Times offices in Printing House Square, London. When the clay had been extracted, a dam was constructed to form Longmoor Lake. Bearwood has been a school since 1921, when the Royal Merchant Navy School moved there from Snaresbrook. A chapel, dining hall, gymnasium, classrooms and laboratories have been added since. The Royal Merchant Navy School was originally a Merchant Seamen's Orphanage, founded in 1827 to care for and educate the children of those lost at sea. By 1961 the number of orphans being cared for had reduced considerably and fee-paying pupils were accepted and the school became Bearwood College. In 1996 it became coeducational. The school continues to accept some orphans.

Awarded the MM (LG 23rd February 1918) for his actions in the Second Battle of Passchendaele, Belgium on 30th–31st October 1917. 5th Canadian Mounted Rifles assembled successfully but the artillery on both sides was active and there were several casualties. A Company was on the right and C Company on the left, supported by B and D Companies respectively. There were difficulties negotiating the swampy areas around Woodland Plantation but by 7 a.m. large numbers of the enemy were falling back in some disorder. Despite this, A Company failed to reach the objective and suffered severe casualties. However, by 6.37 a.m., on the other flank, C Company had reached the intermediate objective, albeit with both flanks in the air. There were only fifty men of C and D Companies to hold the line gained. A footing was gained at Vapour, Source and Vanity (later lost) Farms on the western tip of the Goudberg Spur. Major George Pearkes (awarded the VC for this action) noticed that his men were becoming restless and indecisive. He stood up and moved forward, calling on them to follow. Assisted by Sergeant Charles Rutherford, he led an attack on a strongpoint, which was captured. He then held Vapour and Source Farms against repeated counterattacks.

Pearkes recommended Charles for a commission. He was promoted sergeant on 9th November, returned to Bramshott, England on 10th January

Major George Pearkes VC. His story appears in the fifth book in this series, *Victoria Crosses on the Western Front – Third Ypres 1917*.

1918 and attended a commissioning course at the Officer's Training Centre, Bexhill-on-Sea, Sussex commencing on 2nd February. He was commissioned as a lieutenant on 28th April 1918 in 23rd Reserve Battalion. He returned to the Canadian Infantry Base Depot, France on 3rd June, transferred to the Canadian Corps Reinforcement Camp on 23rd June and rejoined 5th Canadian Mounted Rifles on 22nd July. He was assigned to C Company to command 9 Platoon.

Awarded the MC for his actions at Arvillers, France on 9th August 1918, when he captured a German paymaster and a significant amount of German currency. The German HQ in the town was evacuating ahead of the Canadians and they left behind a box of pigeons and 300 new machine guns. With the right flank in the air, Rutherford and his platoon, with a tank, were ordered to clear Bouchoir. This they did most successfully, killing a large number of the enemy and taking several prisoners. He demonstrated coolness, determination and marked control over his men at all times. The position was held until relieved by the French, LG 11th January 1919.

Awarded the VC for his actions at Monchy-le-Preux, France, on 26th August 1918, LG 15th November 1918. Granted leave to Paris 11th–20th September and fourteen days leave in Britain from 4th November. While he was there the Armistice was declared on 11th November. In London he met Lieutenant Colonel George Pearkes VC by chance, who informed him that he had been awarded the VC. His leave was extended to allow him to attend the investiture. The VC was presented by the King at Buckingham Palace on 23rd November. Charles returned to France next day and rejoined the Battalion on 27th November.

Charles returned to Britain with the Battalion on 13th February 1919 and had his final medical at Bramshott on 22nd February. He was struck off strength of the CEF on sailing to Canada on 8th March and was demobilised on 20th March from 4th Military District, Toronto. He established a dairy farm at Vernonville, near Colborne, which he farmed until 1939, and was also the Clerk-Treasurer of Haldimand.

On 12th March 1921, Charles married Helen Margaret née Haig (24th December 1894–18th May 1980), born at Cobourg, Ontario and known as Margaret, at Hamilton, Northumberland Co. She graduated as a dietician from the University of Toronto. They had four children:

- Andrew John Rutherford (26th March 1922–6th March 2014) graduated from Normal School and qualified as a schoolteacher. He enlisted in the Canadian Air Force at the outbreak of the Second World War, trained as a pilot and spent three years at MacDonald Airport, near Portage la Prairie. He

Vernonville, where Charlie established a dairy farm in the 1920s.

Cobourg was settled by United Empire Loyalists in 1798, originally as a group of smaller villages that were later named Hamilton. It was renamed Cobourg in 1818. By the 1830s the town was a regional centre due to its harbour on Lake Ontario. In 1835 the Upper Canada Academy was established, which became Victoria College in 1841 and a year later was empowered to confer degrees. It remained in Cobourg until 1892, when it moved to Toronto and federated with the University of Toronto. Sir Sandford Fleming (1827–1915), a Scottish Canadian engineer and inventor lived there. He promoted worldwide standard time zones, a prime meridian and the 24-hour clock as the key elements to communicating accurate time. John Weir Foote VC CD (1904–88) made Cobourg his home with his wife. He is buried in Union Cemetery there.

then worked for Eatons, farmed for seven years, operated Ideal moving business for ten years and sold insurance for twenty years. Andrew married Anne Louisa Paul on 17th January 1945 at Winnipeg, Manitoba.
* Isobel McLeod Rutherford (born 8th May 1923), a schoolteacher, married Frederick Donald Reid on 30th December 1950 at Kingston, Frontenac Co, Ontario.
* Kathleen Rosemary Rutherford (20th August 1926–23rd October 1948), a social worker, married Donald James Gormley at Grafton, Ontario.
* Dora Margaret Rutherford (born 20th November 1928), a registered nurse, married Hugh Grant (19th September 1927–18th April 1986) on 15th August 1951 at Colborne. They had three children. Dora looked after her father in his later years.

Helen's father, Andrew P Haig, a farmer, married Margaret J née McLeod. Their daughter, Margaret, was a twin with Andrew Donald Haig.

Charles was appointed Sergeant-at-Arms for the spring session of the Ontario Legislature in 1934 under Premier Mitchell Hepburn. He took over from Walter Rayfield VC. In 1939 he was appointed Postmaster of Colborne, a position he held until 1955, broken only by his service during the Second World War. Charles was presented to King George VI and Queen Elizabeth at Queen's Park, Toronto on 22nd May 1939. Other VCs present on that occasion were Colin Barron,

Charles as Sergeant-at-Arms of the Ontario Legislature in 1934.

Benjamin Geary, Walter Rayfield, Henry Robson, Thomas Holmes and William Merrifield.

Charles enlisted in the Veteran Guard of Canada at Ottawa and was posted to Centre Lake near Petawawa in 1941. He was posted to the Bahamas in 1942, where he was a member of the guard for the Duke and Duchess of Windsor. The Duke was Governor of the Bahamas 18th August 1940–16th March 1945. In 1943 Charles was promoted captain while serving at the Monteith Internment Camp near Iroquois Falls, Ontario. He transferred to the Royal Military College, Kingston, Ontario in 1944 and served there until retiring in July 1945.

In July 1940, a lumber camp at Monteith was converted into POW Camp Q, later Camp 23, with a capacity of 4,000 prisoners. These included interned German nationals, many shipped from Britain after the fall of France in 1940. Most turned out to be Jews or political refugees from the Nazis and, after vetting, many returned to Britain to join the armed forces. One of the internees was Wulff Scherchen, who was living in Cambridge when he was arrested. He was a romantic interest of the composer, conductor and pianist, Benjamin Britten. Monteith closed as a POW camp in 1946 and became the provincial Monteith Correctional Complex.

Charles and Helen moved to Keswick, on Lake Simcoe, north of Toronto in 1955, where they ran a general and dry goods store with his brother-in-law. They retired in 1960 and moved to Cobourg in 1973. When they returned to live in Colborne in August 1979, crowds lined the main street to welcome them. They rode in an open car at the head of a motorcade that also carried two VCs of the Second World War – Fred Tilston and John Weir Foote.

Charles attended a number of VC Reunions:

- VC Dinner at the Royal Gallery of the House of Lords, London on 9th November 1929.
- VC Centenary Celebrations at Hyde Park, London on 26th June 1956.

In 1874 the Military College was established on Point Frederick, site of the Kingston Royal Naval Dockyard 1788–1853. The College opened on 1st June 1876 with eighteen cadets under Lieutenant Colonel Edward O Hewett RE. It was the first military college established in a colonial dependency. In 1878 Queen Victoria granted the College the right to use the Royal prefix. In 1886 Kingston became the birthplace of ice hockey when students of Queen's University played the Royal Military College of Canada. In 1948 the College reopened after the Second World War as a tri-service institution and in 1959 it became the first military college in the British Commonwealth to achieve degree-granting status. In 1965 the College flag formed the basis for the new Canadian national flag. The first female cadets were accepted in 1980.

- 3rd–13th inclusive VC & GC Association Reunions in London on 18th July 1962, 16th July 1964, 14th July 1966, 19th July 1968, 18th June 1970, 14th July 1972, 23rd May 1974, 22nd April 1976, 11th May 1978, 18th May 1981 and 6th October 1983. They were held at the Café Royal, except for the 7th held at the Connaught Rooms, Covent Garden and the 12th at the Savoy Hotel.

Charles was related to John MacGregor VC, whose sister, Ellen, married Charles's cousin, Gordon McGregor. Charles was described by the Reverend Victor Parsons of the Colborne United Church and Padre to the Royal Canadian Legion Branch No.187: *He walked with royalty, rubbed shoulders with the political and military leaders of our nation, yet remained a very humble, God fearing and unobtrusive person, never wanting to be elevated above his peers.*

Charles attended a dinner in honour of VC recipients hosted by the Governor General of Canada, Daniel Roland Michener, at Government House, Ottawa on 16th June 1967. Also attending were – AP Brereton, DV Currie, TF Dinesen, JW Foote, FM Harvey, JK Mahony, CC Merritt, CN Mitchell, GR Pearkes, EA Smith, FA Tilston, P Triquet and RL Zengel. He also attended a dinner in honour of the thirteen living VCs at the Royal Canadian Military Institute, Toronto on 15th August 1975. Also attending were – AP Brereton, DV Currie, JW Foote, BH Geary, MF Gregg, JK Mahony, CN Mitchell, GR Pearkes, EA Smith, FA Tilston, P Triquet and RL Zengel.

Captain John MacGregor was awarded the VC for his actions during the Battle of the Canal du Nord near Cambrai, France 29th September–3rd October 1918. His story appears in a later volume in this series.

Charles moved into Rideau Veteran's Home, Ottawa in 1987 when his health began to fail. He died there on 11th June 1989. His funeral, with full military honours, was held at Colborne United Church on 14th June, attended by Fred Tilston VC. A guard of honour was provided by 1st Canadian Signal Regiment, based at Kingston, Ontario. He is buried in Union Cemetery, Sweets Corners, Haldimand-Norfolk Regional Municipality, Colborne, Ontario. He was the last surviving VC of the Great War, and held the award for the longest, a total of seventy-one years. He is commemorated in a number of other places:

Charles and Margaret's grave in Union Cemetery, Colborne.

- Ontario
  - Charles Rutherford VC Branch No.187, Royal Canadian Legion, Colborne.
  - A wooden plaque bearing fifty-six maple leaves each inscribed with the name of a Canadian-born VC holder was dedicated at the Canadian Forces College, Toronto on Remembrance Day 1999.

Charles Rutherford VC Branch in Colborne.

  - Plaque No.20 on the York Cemetery VC Memorial, West Don River Valley, Toronto dedicated on 25th June 2017.
  - Victoria Cross obelisk to all Canadian VCs at Military Heritage Park, Barrie, Ontario dedicated by Princess Royal on 22nd October 2013.
  - Named on one of eleven plaques honouring 175 men from overseas awarded the VC for the Great War. The plaques were unveiled by the Senior Minister of State at the Foreign & Commonwealth Office and Minister for Faith and Communities, Baroness Warsi, at a reception at Lancaster House, London on 26th June 2014 attended by The Duke of Kent and relatives of the VC recipients. The Canadian plaque was unveiled outside the British High Commission in Elgin Street, Ottawa on 10th November 2014 by The Princess Royal in the presence of British High Commissioner Howard Drake, Canadian Minister of Veterans Affairs Julian Fantino and Canadian Chief of the Defence Staff General Thomas James Lawson.
- Two 49 cents postage stamps in honour of the ninety-four Canadian VC winners were issued by Canada Post on 21st October 2004 on the 150th Anniversary of the first Canadian VC's action, Alexander Roberts Dunn VC.
- Communities and Local Government commemorative paving stones for the 145 VCs born in Australia, Belgium, Canada, China, Denmark, Egypt, France, Germany, India, Iraq, Japan, Nepal, Netherlands, Newfoundland, New Zealand, Pakistan, South Africa, Sri Lanka, Ukraine and United States of America were unveiled at the National Memorial Arboretum, Alrewas, Staffordshire by Prime Minister David Cameron MP and Sergeant Johnson Beharry VC on 5th March 2015.

In addition to the VC, MC and MM he was awarded the British War Medal 1914–20, Victory Medal 1914–19, Defence Medal, Canadian Volunteer Service Medal 1939–47 (no clasp), War Medal 1939–45, George VI Coronation Medal 1937, Elizabeth II Coronation Medal 1953, Elizabeth II Silver Jubilee Medal 1977 and the Canadian Centennial Medal 1967. The current location of the VC is not known.

5046 LANCE CORPORAL HENRY WEALE
14th Battalion, The Royal Welsh Fusiliers

Henry 'Harry' Weale was born on 2nd October 1895 at Nine Houses, Brook Road, Shotton, Flintshire, Wales. His father, John Weale (1870–1928), born at Much Wenlock, Shropshire, was a general labourer in 1891 lodging in Brymbo, Denbighshire. John married Sarah née Hughes (c.1871–1944), born at Northop, Flintshire, in 1893 at Chester, Cheshire. He was a general labourer in an iron works in 1901 and they were living at Nine Houses, Shotton. By 1911 he was a dock labourer and they were living at 33 Brook Road, Shotton. Harry had seven siblings:

 * John Weale (born 1894), born at Shotton, Flintshire, was a general labourer in 1911.
 * Frank Weale (1897–1930).
 * Frederick Weale (1899–1940) married Cissie Bell (3rd September 1900–1978) in 1924 at Wirral, Cheshire. They had five children:
   ° Gilbert F Weale (born 1925) married Margaret M O'Gorman (born 1929) in 1947 at Holywell, Flintshire. They had three children.
   ° Eva Weale (born 1926) married Kenneth E Latham (born 1924) in 1950 at Hawarden. They had six children.
   ° Harold Weale (1927–80) married Dorothy Megan Jones (1923–76) in 1950. They had four children.
   ° William E Weale (born 1933) married Davida H Brotherstone (born 1938) in 1960 and they had two children. It is assumed that the marriage ended in divorce as Davida married Walter B Sumner (born 1942) in 1971 and they had at least one son.
   ° Cissie M Weale (born 1934) married Thomas Baird in 1958. They had three children.
 * William Ernest Weale (1901–53).
 * Gilbert Weale (19th August 1903–29th September 1971) married Winnie Holmes in 1934. He was living at 12a Caravan Site, Gladstone Way, Queensferry, Flintshire at the time of his death. They had two children:
   ° Sarah G Weale (born 1935).
   ° Doris A Weale (born 1936) married Ralph Clarke in 1958 and they had four children.
 * Norman Weale (20th April 1907–1976) married Beatrice Anne Bellis née Aston (20th July 1907–1971) in 1939. Beatrice had married Ernest Bellis (1908–37) in 1929. Ernest and Beatrice had a son, George E Bellis, in 1930.
 * Harriet Weale (born and died 1909).

Harry's paternal grandmother was born at Broseley, Shropshire on the River Severn. The village is listed in the Domesday Book and the world's first iron bridge was Clarke-built in 1779 across the Severn at Ironbridge Gorge to link Broseley with Coalbrookdale and Madeley. It is now part of an early industrial World Heritage Site. Broseley was a major centre for iron, brick and clay pipe production. Abraham Darby (1678–1717), who developed the process of smelting iron using coking coal, is buried there. In the latter half of the 19th century the area declined as industries moved elsewhere and there was much dereliction. Despite a revival in the latter part of the 20th century, Broseley's population is still less than 200 years ago.

Harry's paternal grandfather, John Weale (c.1836–86), born at Bridgnorth, Shropshire, married Jane A née McCoy (c.1834–93), born at Broseley, Shropshire, in 1860 at Madeley, Shropshire. He was a butcher and a grocer in 1861 and they were living at 20 Listley Street, Bridgnorth. By 1871 they had moved to 96 Newtown, Bridgnorth and were back in Listley Street by 1881. Jane was a midwife at the time of the 1891 Census, living at 57 Friar Street, Bridgnorth, Shropshire, the home of Enoch and Mary E Sargeant. There was a girl aged under one month in the family and it is assumed that Jane was the live-in midwife. In addition to John they had five other children:

- George William Weale (1861–1901).
- Ann 'Annie' Louisa Weale (1866–1940) married Enos James Raby (also seen as Rabey) (1870–1943), a farmer's son born at Chetton, Shropshire, in 1893. They were living at Penn Common, Wolverhampton, Staffordshire in 1911. Both their deaths were registered at Rowley Regis, Staffordshire.
- Martha Jane Weale (1867–1945) died unmarried at Pontypridd, Glamorgan.
- Mary Weale (born 1870) was not with the family in the 1881 Census. There is mention of another girl, Agnes Weale, born c.1871 at Bridgnorth, but no birth record has been found. It is possible that Mary and Agnes are the same child.
- Ernest Weale (born 1877) was a groom and cleaner, living with his wife, Mary (born c.1875), at 41 Pulford Street, St George, Hanover Square, London in 1911. She was born at Malvern, Worcestershire and they married c.1900 but no record has been found.

Nothing is known about Harry's maternal grandparents, except that, in addition to Sarah, they had a son, William Hughes, born c.1871 at Much Wenlock, Shropshire. He was a general labourer, lodging in the same house as John Weale, his future brother-in-law, at Brymbo, Denbighshire in 1891.

Harry was educated at St Ethelwold's School, Shotton, Flintshire. He was a general labourer in 1911 and also worked as a packer at John Summer's Steelworks in Shotton. He enlisted in 5th Royal Welsh Fusiliers (TF) on 1st November 1911 (915) and was discharged to 3rd (Special Reserve) Battalion on 8th September 1913 (5046).

Harry was mobilised on 5th August 1914 and embarked for France on 1st November, disembarking next day, probably with 1/4th Battalion. He was wounded and evacuated to Britain on 10th December, returning to France on 16th March 1915. He was wounded again on 1st October and was evacuated to Britain, returning to France on 14th September 1916. He was gassed on 16th January 1917 and was evacuated to Britain, returning to France on 22nd August. On 26th October he was appointed unpaid lance corporal and was promoted lance corporal on 8th December.

Awarded the VC for his actions at Bazentin-Le-Grand, France on 26th August 1918, LG 15th November 1918. Harry was wounded by shrapnel on 28th August and was evacuated to Britain. The VC was presented by the King in the ballroom at Buckingham Palace on 1st March 1919. He was presented with an illuminated address outside St Ethelwold's School by the head teacher, Thomas Haswell, and with a gold watch by John Summers & Sons Steelworks. Harry transferred to the Reserve on 16th April and was discharged from it on 8th September 1919. Harry returned to his position as a packer at John Summer's Steelworks, Shotton. He later became a building worker with Melvill, Dunstan & Whittley of Holywell, Flintshire and subsequently a road worker with Rhyl Urban District Council.

On 16th June 1919, Harry married Susannah 'Susie' Harrison (1899–4th October 1988), born at St Asaph, Denbighshire, at St Ethelwold's Church, Shotton, Flintshire. They lived at 22 Prince Edward Avenue, Rhyl and had seven children:

John Summers & Sons Ltd, a major iron and steel producer, was founded by John Summers (1822–76). He was a clogger, who visited the Great Exhibition in 1851 and bought a nail-making machine. He used the nails to fasten iron strips onto the soles of clogs. In 1852 he moved into Sandy Bank Iron Forge, Stalybridge to produce clog irons and nails. He built a new ironworks, the Globe Works, near the forge. After he died three of his sons, James, John and Alfred, carried on the business and were joined by another brother, Henry Hall Summers in 1869. The firm opened Hawarden Bridge Steelworks at Shotton in 1896. By 1909 the company was the largest manufacturer of galvanized steel in the country. In 1919 it took over Wolverhampton Corrugated Iron Co and also bought the Castle Fire Brick Co, Buckley and Shelton Iron, Steel & Coal Co, Stoke-on-Trent. The latter was Shotton's supplier of pig iron and resulted in the company becoming largely self-contained. John Summers & Sons Ltd was nationalised in 1951, denationalised shortly afterwards and renationalised in 1967 as part of British Steel Corporation. It became Corus in 1999 and was taken over by Tata Steel in 2007. The former HQ building at Shotton seen here is a heritage building at risk.

St Ethelwold's Church, Shotton, where Harry Weale married Susie Harrison in June 1919. The church was paid for partly by William Ewart Gladstone (1809–98), who was British Prime Minister for twelve years over four terms 1868–94. Construction commenced in 1898 and the church was dedicated by the Bishop of St Asaph on 8th August 1902. It is Grade II listed.

- Phyllis M Weale (born 2nd July 1920) served in the Women's Royal Air Force during the Second World War. She married Kenneth William Perkins (26th December 1920–November 1993) in 1944 and they had two children:
  ○ Jacqueline E Perkins (born 1943) married Michael L Ward in 1971.
  ○ Stuart Michael Perkins (1949–87).
- Edward Henry 'Harry' Weale (born 17th May 1922) served in the Royal Navy during the Second World War and was injured aboard HMS *Furious* in 1940. He married Myra Noble in 1955 at Westminster, London. They had a son, Raymond Harry Weale, in 1966 at Islington, London.
- Norman V Weale (born 20th April 1924) served in the Royal Welch Fusiliers during the Second World War and transferred to the Parachute Regiment, serving in 6th Airborne Division. He married Heather I Hughes (born 1929) in 1947. He was living at Greycroft, Dundonald Avenue, Abergele, near Conwy, Flintshire in 1983. They had a son, Paul R Weale (born 1948), who married Diana L Boeg (born 1950) in 1970. Paul may have married again, to Lorraine Griffiths in 1975 at Rhuddlan, Clwyd.
- Lillian Irene Weale (born and died 1925).
- John E Weale (born and died 1927).
- John 'Jack' F Weale (born 3rd January 1929) served in the Royal Welch Fusiliers after the Second World War. He married Olwen Thomas (born 1934) in 1956. They had three children – Gillian J Weale 1957, Geoffrey J Weale 1959 and Andrew Francis Weale 1967.
- Derek Weale (19th June 1930–19th June 1991) served in the Royal Artillery after the Second World War and became a junior and Army boxing champion. He turned professional and was sparring partner to Randolph Turpin (1928–66) of Royal Leamington Spa, who became World Middleweight Champion in 1951, when he defeated Sugar Ray Robinson, who defeated Turpin in a rematch three months later. Derek married Patricia M Davies in 1977 at Rhuddlan, Clwyd. He was living at 22 Prince Edward Avenue, Rhyl, Flintshire in 1983 and subsequently died there.

Susie's father was George Harrison of 5 Hope Place, Rhyl, who died before June 1919. Harry attended a number of VC Reunions – VC Garden Party at Buckingham Palace on 26th June 1920, the VC Dinner at the Royal Gallery of the House of Lords, London on 9th November 1929, the Victory Day Celebration Dinner & Reception at The Dorchester, London on 8th June 1946 and the VC Centenary Celebrations at Hyde Park, London on 26th June 1956.

Harry re-enlisted in 5th Royal Welch Fusiliers (TA) on 7th February 1921 and served in Ireland. He was promoted sergeant on 8th July 1921 and was discharged on 6th February 1922. He was a member of the Section D Army Reserve 12th July 1922–12th July 1926. On 20th January 1927 he was bound over in the sum of £5 for shop breaking. On 25th August 1939 he enlisted in the National Defence Corps and transferred to the Royal Welch Fusiliers, serving at Dover, Kent and on Salisbury Plain, Wiltshire as an airfield guard. He was discharged as unfit for active service on 29th January 1941.

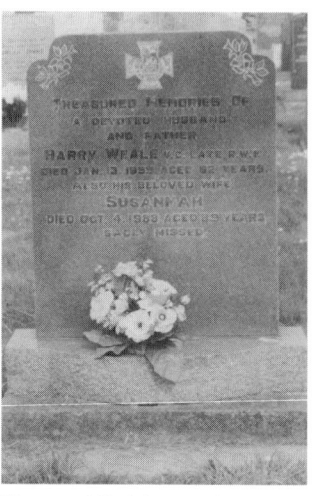

Harry and Susie's grave in Maes Hyfryd Cemetery, Rhyl.

Harry Weale died at his home at 22 Prince Edward Avenue, Rhyl, Flintshire on 13th January 1959. The cause of death was haematamosis, cirrhosis of the liver, chronic alcoholism and high blood pressure. His funeral, with full military honours, was held at St Thomas's Church, Rhyl and he is buried in Maes Hyfryd Cemetery, Dyserth Road, Rhyl (Section 10 Grave 4829). He is commemorated in a number of other places:

Harry's VC is held by the Royal Welch Fusiliers Museum in Caernarfon Castle.

- Weale Court, Hightown, Wrexham.
- Harry Weale Hall, Queensferry Army Reserve Centre, Station Road, Queensferry, Clwyd.
- Henry Weale VC Memorial Garden, Jubilee Street, Shotton, Flintshire, dedicated on 29th September 2010.
- A Department for Communities and Local Government commemorative paving stone was dedicated at Brook Road, Shotton, Flintshire on 11th November 2018.

In addition to the VC he was awarded the 1914 Star, British War Medal 1914–20, Victory Medal 1914–19 with Mentioned-in-Despatches Oakleaf, Defence Medal, War Medal 1939–45, George VI Coronation Medal 1937 and Elizabeth II Coronation Medal 1953. The VC is held by the Royal Welch Fusiliers Museum, Queen's Tower, Caernarfon Castle, Gwynedd, Wales.

177239 PRIVATE JOHN FRANCIS YOUNG
87th Battalion (Canadian Grenadier Guards) CEF

John Young was born on 14th January 1893 at 12 Crowther Street, Kidderminster, Worcestershire, England. He was baptised on 5th February at St John's Church there. His father, Robert Charles Young (1868–9th May 1949), was a grocer's assistant in 1881, living with his parents at 29 Coventry Street, Kidderminster. He married Mary Anne née Cooper (1869–29th March 1923 or 28th December 1939), born at Hoobrook, near Kidderminster, on 16th November 1890 at St George's Church, Kidderminster, where they lived until going to Canada. By 1891 he was a grocer and they were living at 12 Crowther Street. By 1901 he was a grocer's assistant and traveller and they were living at 71 Coventry Street. Later he was a newsagent at 103 Coventry Street. By 1911 he was a brewer's traveller for Hopkins, Garlick & Co, Mill Street and they were living at 16 Waterloo Street. The family emigrated to Québec, Canada in 1912, where they lived at 376 Rue St Philippe, St Henri, Montréal. By 1921 Robert was a shipper and they were living at 386 Rue St Philippe. A Mary Anne Young died on 29th March 1923 and is buried in Mount Royal Cemetery, Outremont, Québec, as is Robert Charles Young. However, some sources report that she died on 28th December 1939 at Wilkes Station, Jefferson Co, Alabama, USA. John had two brothers:

- Robert Peart Young (born 18th August 1896) was an office boy in a theatre in 1911. He served in 3rd Regiment Victoria Rifles of Canada before enlisting in 79th Depot Battery CFA (1251946) at Montréal on 21st May 1917. He was described as a draughtsman, 5′ 9″ tall, weighing 120 lbs, with fair complexion, brown eyes, brown hair and his religious denomination was Church of England. He was attached to the Divisional Artillery Column while attending the Signal School June–July 1917 to train as a wireless signaller. He embarked on SS *Megantic* at Montréal on 19th November, departed Halifax, Nova Scotia on 26th November and arrived at Liverpool, Lancashire on 7th December. He joined the Reserve Brigade CFA at Witley on 8th December. Robert allotted $20 per month from his Army pay to his mother from 1st December. He transferred to the Reserve Battery CGA, Witley on 28th April 1918, which was absorbed into the Composite Brigade, Canadian Reserve Artillery, Witley on 23rd May. He went to France on 18th June, joined the Canadian Base Depot on 20th June and left for the Canadian Corps Reinforcement Camp on 26th June, arriving next day. He was posted from the Artillery Pool to 3rd Siege Battery, 1st Brigade CGA on 14th July. On 29th August he was detached as a wireless operator for the Canadian Corps Heavy Artillery. He was admitted to 1st Canadian Casualty Clearing Station on 11th February 1919 with laryngitis and was discharged on 14th February. He returned to England on 1st April, joined at Kinmel Park on 3rd April and underwent a discharge medical there on 19th April. On 3rd May he embarked on HMT *Mauretania* at Southampton and disembarked at Halifax, Nova Scotia on 9th May. He was demobilised on 12th May 1919. Robert married Marie Shaw (born c.1895), born in Ireland. He was a mechanical engineer in 1921

John was baptised at St John's Church, Kidderminster, built in 1842–43 and rebuilt 1892–1904. It was known locally as the 'Black Church' and became a parish in 1867. The building is Grade II listed.

John's mother was born at Hoobrook.

and they were living at 362 Rue St Philippe, St Henri, Montréal. They had two children:
  ◦ Evelyn Young, born in 1920 in Québec.
  ◦ Robert John Peart Young (died 1994).
• Reginald Thomas Young (8th August 1902–17th November 1970) was a machinist in a brass works in 1921, living with his parents. He married Marion Guy (1901–58), born at West Derby, Lancashire and lived at 14 Guildhall Road, Aintree. She emigrated to Montréal aboard RMS *Minnedosa* in November 1921. They had two children including Joan, who married as Brambell.

St George's Church, where John's parents married in 1890, is a Grade II* listed building. It is a 'Waterloo' or 'Commissioners' church, built with money voted by Parliament as a result of the Church Buildings Acts of 1818 and 1824. The church was rebuilt after being gutted by fire in 1922.

John's paternal grandfather, Charles Young (1840–1917), born at Stroud, Gloucestershire, was a scholar at home living with his parents in Summer Street, Stroud in 1851. He married Mary née Peart (1837–1920), born at Winchcombe, Gloucestershire, in 1864 at Cheltenham, Gloucestershire. He was a brewer in 1871 and they were living at 29 Coventry Street, Kidderminster. By 1891 he was a newsagent and they had moved to 82 Coventry Street. In 1901 he was described as a newsagent shopkeeper. By 1911 they were living at 16 Leswell Street. In addition to Robert they had three other children but only one is known:

• John Francis 'Frank' Young (1866–90), born at West Bromwich, Staffordshire, was an apprentice carpet designer in 1881. He married Kate Keturah Cooper (January 1864–1933) in 1889 at Kidderminster, where she was born. He was a provisions dealer living with his family at Cookley, Worcestershire at the time of his death on 7th November 1890 at 82 Coventry Street, Kidderminster. They had a son:
  ◦ Charles Stephen Young (1890–1941) was a carter in 1911, living with his paternal grandparents. He married Elsie Florence Day (1891 1962) in 1912. Charles was a timekeeper in a steel rolling mill in 1939 and they were living at 1 Holmfray Road, Kidderminster. They were still there at the time of his death at The General Hospital, Kidderminster. They had four children.
• Kate married George Henry 'Harry' Butt (January 1880–12th July 1933), a carpet finisher, in 1900. George enlisted in 7th Worcestershire on 7th July 1908 and was discharged through sickness on 7th June 1916 (Silver War Badge No.56518). They were living at 50 Hincton Street, Kidderminster in 1911. George and Kate had three children:
  ◦ Leonard Arthur Butt (1900–69) married Gwladys Leah Blount (1900–72), born at Merthyr Tydfil, Glamorgan, in 1923. He was an annealer in an

John's paternal grandfather, Charles, came from Stroud, a market town in the Cotswold Hills in Gloucestershire. The town dates back to medieval times but there are Neolithic and Roman remains in the area. In the Industrial Revolution it was a cloth town, with woollen mills powered by the rivers flowing through its five valleys. They were noted for military uniforms in Stroudwater Scarlet. The area attracted a large Huguenot community fleeing persecution in France in the late 17th century. There was also a significant Jewish influx in the 19th century, linked to the tailoring and cloth industries. Transport was improved with the arrival of the Stroudwater Navigation and Thames & Severn Canals, followed by the railways. Stroud railway station was designed by Isambard Kingdom Brunel. Lord John Russell was the MP 1837–41 and later Prime Minister. The author Laurie Lee set his book, *Cider with Rosie*, in nearby Slad valley.

Winchcombe, birthplace of John's paternal grandmother, is a small Cotswold town in Gloucestershire. Nearby Belas Knap long barrow is evidence of Neolithic occupation. In Saxon times Winchcombe was a chief city of Mercia and in the 11th century was briefly the county town of Winchcombeshire. The Anglo-Saxon St Kenelm is believed to be buried in the town. Nearby Hailes Abbey was one of the main pilgrimage centres in Britain due to a phial said to contain the blood of Christ.

  iron works and she was a cop winder in 1939, living at 19 Jubilee Drive, Kidderminster. They had four children.
- ° Isabella Kate Butt (1902–82) married Albert Henry Watkins (1899–1980) in 1924. He was working in a spinning mill in 1939 and they were living at 3 Duke Street, Kidderminster. They had three children.
- ° Nellie Mabel Butt (1903–73) was a threader in a carpet works in 1939, living with her sister Isabella and family. She never married.

Shortly after Kate died, George married Maria Crossley (1879–1955) in 1933 in Birmingham, Warwickshire. Maria and George had a daughter, Marian Crossley (1917–96), whose birth was also registered as Butt. She changed her name to Butt and married Eric Victor Wearing (1915–91) in 1939. At that time he was a film despatch clerk and Marian was a grocer's shop assistant. They were living at 5/20 Ruston Street, Birmingham with Marian's mother Maria. They had a son,

John's maternal grandmother was born in Halifax. The town is not mentioned in the Domesday Book but by the 12th century it was a religious centre. It has been a centre of wool manufacturing from the 15th century and expanded hugely in the 19th century. It is also known for Mackintosh's chocolate and toffee and the headquarters of Halifax Bank. The minster's first organist in 1766 was William Herschel, who discovered the planet Uranus. Piece Hall opened in 1779 for trading woollen cloth in 315 merchant trading rooms. It is now a centre for arts, crafts and independent shops. Dean Clough Mill, built in the 1840s to 1860s for Crossley's Carpets and once the largest carpet factory in the world, became a business park in the 1980s. Halifax Town Hall was designed by Charles Barry, who also designed the Houses of Parliament. Amongst the notable inhabitants are:

- William Bramwell Booth (1856–1929), first Chief of Staff of the Salvation Army 1881–1912 and the second General 1912–29, succeeding his father, William Booth.
- John Reginald Halliday Christie (1899–1953), serial killer who carried out his murders at 10 Rillington Place, Notting Hill, London.
- Hannah Lucy Cockroft MBE DL (born 1992), wheelchair racer who has gained world and Paralympic records for 100m, 200m, 400m, 800m and 1500m. She won two Olympic gold medals in London in 2012 and three in Rio de Janeiro in 2016.
- Anne Lister (1791–1840), who lived at nearby Shibden Hall, kept diaries of her daily life, including her lesbian relationships, financial concerns, industrial activities and work on improving the Hall. A BBC HBO TV drama series, Gentleman Jack, based on her diaries, was broadcast in 2019 starring Suranne Jones.
- Eric Harold Portman (1901–69) stage and film actor.

John Wearing, in 1944. George died soon after his marriage to Maria, who was living with her daughter Marian and son-in-law at 32 Glenavon Road, Brandwood, Birmingham at the time of her death there.

His maternal grandfather, John Cooper (17th May 1839–1881), born at Stone, near Kidderminster, married Sarah Ann née Dyson (1840–1912), born at Halifax, Yorkshire, on 15th February 1863 at Stone. He was a worsted spinner labourer in 1871 and a general labourer in 1881, living with his family at Hoobrook, Stone.

Sarah was a worsted mill hand in 1891 living with her son, Charles, at 2 St Mary's, Kidderminster. She was living with her daughter, Emma, and family in 1911. In addition to Mary Ann they had three children, all born at Stone:

- Emma Cooper (1864–1923) was a worsted spinner in 1881. She married James Weavers (15th April 1863–1943), a worsted spinner born at Kidderminster, on 14th November 1885 at St Mary, Kidderminster. They were living at 7 Dudley Street there in 1891 and at 20 Plimsoll Street by 1901. By 1911 he was a fish fryer living at the same address, and Emma was assisting him in the business. He was a carpet beamer in 1939, living with his son John, at 20 Plimsoll Street. Emma and James had six children:
    ○ John Weavers (1887–1941) was a tapestry printer living with his parents in 1911. He married Mary Graham in 1920. By 1939 he was a carpet worker and an Air Raid Precautions Warden, living with his father. Mary was not with them.
    ○ Emma Weavers (born 1891) was an Axminster setter living with her parents in 1911.
    ○ Charles Weavers (1893–1971), a twin with Thomas, was an Axminster tube maker living with his parents in 1911. He enlisted in the Royal Field Artillery on 16th October 1915 at Kidderminster Recruiting Office (3634 & 314853), described as 5′ 5″ tall. He served with 2/2nd South Midland Field Artillery Brigade Ammunition Column and went to France on 20th January 1917. He was compulsorily transferred to the RGA on 25th June 1918 and was disembodied on demobilisation on 2nd March 1919. Charles married Tryphena Ada Cookson (1896–1982), born at Wolverley, Worcestershire, in 1919. They had a daughter. He was a carpet loom tuner and an Air Raid Precautions Warden in 1939, when they were living at 139 Hurcott Road, Kidderminster.
    ○ Thomas Weavers (1893–95), a twin with Charles.
    ○ Edward Weavers (1896–1964) was a cycle repairer living with his parents in 1911. He married Florence Lilian Munn (1897–1971) in 1923. She was living at 293 Turves Green, Northfield, Birmingham, Warwickshire at the time of her death there.
    ○ Harold Weavers (1903–71) married Lottie Elizabeth Webb (1897–1971) in 1936. She had a son born in 1930. Harold was a carpet weaver in 1939 and they were living at 27 Avill Grove, Kidderminster.
- Helena 'Ellen' M Cooper (1866–1937) never married.
- Charles Cooper (7th August 1877–1956) was a worsted mill hand in 1891 and a machine minder in a works in 1901, living with his mother. He married Lizzie Stanford (1879–1949) on 1st August 1904 at St George's, Kidderminster. He was an insurance agent and she was a carpet weaver in 1911, living at 17 Park Street, Kidderminster. He enlisted in the Army Reserve on 11th December

1915, described as a checker and packer, living at 78 Milner Road, Selly Oak, Birmingham and was 5′ 5″ tall. He was mobilised in the Royal Warwickshire Regiment on 16th August 1916 at Warwick (21057) and transferred to the Machine Gun Corps on 7th October (63227). He went to France on 4th March 1917 and returned to England on 29th September. He developed chronic bronchitis and was discharged no longer physically fit for war service on 7th December 1917. In 1939 he was living with his daughter, Phyllis, at 78 Milner Road, by when he was a charge hand in a chocolate factory. Charles and Lizzie had two children:
  ◦ Charles Frederick Cooper (1906–47), born at 1 Dudley Street, Kidderminster, was a correspondence clerk at Cadbury's chocolate factory and a volunteer in the Auxiliary Fire Service in 1939, boarding at 58 Willow Road, Birmingham. He died at 44 Greenland Road, Birmingham.
  ◦ Phyllis May Cooper (1909–94), born at 17 Park Street, Kidderminster, married James Baxter (c.1903–67) in 1943 in Birmingham. They had two children.

John was educated at St George's School, Kidderminster 1899–1906. He was employed at Findon's Grocers, Worcester Street and was described as an assistant in a seed warehouse, living with his parents in 1911. He emigrated to Canada with his parents in 1912 and lived with them at 376 Rue St Phillipe, St Henri, Montréal, Québec. He worked as a packer for Imperial Tobacco. John served for four months in the McGill Auxiliary Battalion in 1915.

John enlisted in 87th Battalion CEF on 20th October 1915 at Montréal (177239), was found fit for service and attested on 23rd October. He was described as 5′ 6½″ tall, weighing 121 lbs, with fair complexion, brown eyes, brown hair and his religious denomination was Church of England. The Battalion sailed for England aboard RMS *Empress of Britain* on 25th April 1916 from Halifax, Nova Scotia, arriving at Liverpool, Lancashire on 5th May. Training continued at Bramshott, Surrey. John allotted $15 per month from his Army pay to his mother from 1st May. He sailed for France with D Company on 11th August and arrived next day.

On 18th November, John was admitted to 11th Canadian Field Ambulance, not yet diagnosed, and transferred to 12th Canadian Field Ambulance and No.49 Casualty Clearing Station on 20th November. He was transferred by 10 Ambulance Train to 1st General Hospital, Étretat with pyrexia of unknown origin, later diagnosed as influenza, on 21st November. He returned to duty on 29th November and to the Battalion on 6th December.

John was wounded by a gunshot to the left side of the back of the neck on 15th August 1917 and was admitted to 2nd Stationary Hospital, Abbeville next day. He transferred to No.5 Convalescent Depot, Cayeux-sur-Mer on 4th September and was discharged to 4th Canadian Division Base Depot, Étaples on 16th October. He was awarded the Good Conduct Badge on 20th October and transferred to the Canadian Corps Reinforcement Camp on 23rd October. He rejoined the Battalion on 3rd December and was granted fourteen days' leave on 12th December, rejoining on 29th December.

Awarded the VC for his actions at Dury, near Arras, France on 2nd–4th September 1918, LG 14th December 1918. He was wounded by a gunshot to the left temple on 27th September and was admitted to 1st Canadian Casualty Clearing Station on 1st October and to 83rd General Hospital, Boulogne on 2nd October. He transferred to No.1 Convalescent Depot, Ècault, Boulogne on 9th October and to No.10 Convalescent Depot on 11th October. He was discharged on 10th November to the Canadian Infantry Base Depot and transferred to the Canadian Corps Reinforcement Camp on 13th November. John rejoined the Battalion on 9th December and was granted fourteen days' leave on 16th December, rejoining on 8th January 1919.

On 4th April 1919, John was granted fourteen days' leave. The VC was presented by the King in the ballroom at Buckingham Palace on 12th April. John married Ida May Thatcher (1893–1971) on 21st April 1919 at St Mary Church, Kidderminster, where she was born. She was a winder in the carpet trade, living with her parents at 91 Baxter Avenue, Kidderminster in 1911. They returned to Canada and her address was 989 Addington Avenue, Montréal at one time. They had two children:

2nd Stationary Hospital, Abbeville.

13th General Hospital in the casino at Boulogne, opened in October 1914 on the Boulogne docks and became the main specialist unit for the treatment of eye, face and jaw injuries. In May 1917 it was renamed 83rd (Dublin) Hospital when the staff was augmented by volunteers from Irish hospitals. It moved to Langenfeld in the Ruhr after the Armistice.

- John Francis Young (born late 1920/early 1921) lived at 10479 Laurentide Avenue, Montréal North 459, Québec.
- Marjorie Young (born and died 1929).

Ida's father, William John Thatcher (14th July 1872–20th September 1957), a postman born at Kidderminster, married Annie née Jones (1873–1921), born at Kinver, near Stourbridge, Worcestershire, on 29th May 1893 at Kinver. In 1901 they were living at 24 Baxter Avenue, Kidderminster. By 1911 they were living at 91 Baxter Avenue. He was living alone at 89 Baxter Street in 1939 and at 18

Bennett Street at the time of his death at Blakebrook Hospital, Kidderminster. In addition to Ida they had four other children, all born at Stone:

- Reginald Alfred Thatcher (1895–6th May 1918) was baptised at St Mary, Kidderminster on 18th February 1895. He was an accountant clerk living with his parents in 1911. He married Elsie Maud Briggs (14th July 1889–19th September 1974), born at Kington, Herefordshire, in 1915. They lived at 57 Blackwell Street, Kidderminster. Reginald was serving as a private in 6th Dorsetshire (204052) when he died (Doullens Communal Cemetery Extension No.2 (II A 20). Elsie married Lees Greenwood (26th April 1891–19th July 1946) in 1920. He was an insurance inspector and she was a milliner in 1939, living at 176 Chester Road North, Kidderminster. They were living at 374 Chester Road North at the time of his death at Queen Elizabeth Hospital, Edgbaston, Warwickshire. She was living at 13 Land Oak Drive, Kidderminster at the time of her death. Elsie and Lees had two children:
  - Robert Lees Greenwood (1922–2010) was studying medicine in 1939, living with his parents. He qualified MB ChB at the University of Birmingham in 1945 and was practising at Dunedin, New Zealand in 1952. He married Margarita Vablaite (born c.1930), born in Lithuania, on 22nd January 1954. He died at Aldea Blanca, Tenerife and she reportedly died in New Zealand.
  - Mabel E Greenwood (born 1928).

John and Ida were married at St Mary and All Saints' Church, Kidderminster in April 1919. The church dates back to before the Domesday Book but the current building dates from the 15th and 16th centuries. In 1847 a south aisle was added to the chancel and an organ chamber in 1874. The Whittall Chapel was added in 1921-22 and other work was carried out in 1966–67 and 1988–90. It is Grade I listed.

The grave of John's brother-in-law, Reginald Alfred Thatcher, in Doullens Communal Cemetery Extension No.2.

- William 'Willie' Thatcher (1897–2nd August 1965) was a clerk for a carpet manufacturer living with his parents in 1911. He married Kathleen Snell (c.1892–10th May 1966) in 1919. They were living at 30 Canterbury Road, Kidderminster at the time of his death at the General Hospital, Mill Street, Kidderminster. She was living at 1 Norwich Avenue at the time of her death at the General Hospital. They had five children:
    ◦ Betty Thatcher (born 1920).
    ◦ Reginald Arthur Thatcher (born 1922) married Edith M Staight (1928–96), born at Tewkesbury, Gloucestershire, in 1948. They had a son.
    ◦ Trevor Thatcher (born 1925) married Elsie Spells (born 1927), born at Auckland, Co Durham, in 1951. They had a son.
    ◦ Kathleen Sylvia Thatcher (1928–2002) married Andrew Faulkner (1922–2002), born at Birkenhead, Cheshire, in 1948.
    ◦ William A Thatcher (1931–32).
- Clifford Thatcher (1st March 1899–8th December 1971) married Amelia Olwen Harries (4th May 1895–21st November 1974), born at Llandovery, Carmarthenshire, in 1928 at Droitwich, Worcestershire. He was a coal and builder's merchant and the head Air Raid Precaution's Warden for E Sector, Kidderminster Borough in 1939, when they were living at Stone Hill, Kidderminster. They were living at The Croft, Butts Lane, Stone at the time of their deaths there.
- Doris 'Dolly' Thatcher (28th November 1901–February 1987) married Franklin George Davies (2nd August 1903–9th December 1952), born at Highly, Somerset, in 1928. He was a police constable in 1939 and they were living at Langdale, 73 Hurcott Road, Kidderminster. They were still living there at the time of his death there. They had a son, Geoffrey Franklin Davies (born 1930), who became a solicitor.

John was posted to the Québec Regiment Depot, Ripon, Yorkshire on 28th April. He was allocated to A Company on 1st May. His discharge medical at Ripon on 7th May found no disability but he had gained almost three inches in height and fourteen pounds in weight since enlisting. The allotment of $15 per month from his Army pay to his mother was switched to his wife from 1st June 1919. John was struck off strength of the Québec Regiment Depot, Ripon to H Wing, Witley on 5th June. He transferred to the Canadian Discharge Depot, Buxton for return to Canada on 28th July. He was struck off strength to Canada from London on 13th August aboard RMS *Baltic* and arrived at Halifax, Nova Scotia on 21st August. He was taken on and struck off strength of Clearing Services Command, Halifax on demobilisation on 24th August 1919.

John returned to work as a tobacco packer in Montréal. He joined the Militia and reached the rank of sergeant. He was a member of the Canadian Red Cross. John died of tuberculosis at Ste-Agathe Sanatorium, Ste-Agathe-des-Monts, Laurentian Mountain, Québec on 7th November 1929. He is buried in Mount Royal Cemetery (Cimetière Mont-Royal), 1297 Chemin de la Foret, Outremont, Montréal, Québec (Sect L2, Grave

Between 1895 and 1912, many small sanatoria and rest homes for treating tuberculosis (TB) were established in and around Ste-Agathe-des-Monts because of its cool and dry climate. Douglas Lorne McGibbon, who made a fortune in the rubber industry, was diagnosed with TB in his late thirties and was treated at Saranac Lake, New York. He and Dr Roddick Byers decided that such a facility was needed in Canada and constructed the Laurentian Sanatorium at Ste-Agathe in 1910–11. It and Mount Sinai Hospital, constructed about the same time, made Ste-Agathe the Canadian centre for TB care. The federal government requisitioned the facility in 1915 to treat soldiers gassed during the Great War. In 1924 it was handed back to the provincial government. TB spread and more buildings were added to increase the sanatorium's capacity to 350 patients. In 1941 the Laurentian Sanatorium merged with the Royal Edward Laurentian Hospital in Montréal. When TB became less prevalent in the 1950s, the 1920s buildings were demolished and in the 1970s the two hospitals demerged and Laurentian Sanatorium became Laurentian Chest Hospital. Both hospitals at Ste-Agathe went into decline. Mount Sinai has been abandoned and Laurentian Chest Hospital is used by the Centre Hospitalier Laurentien for its administrative offices and some outpatient clinics.

L2019G) and is also named on the family headstone there. He is commemorated in a number of other places:

- Worcestershire
    ◦ Young Close, Kidderminster.
    ◦ A Department for Communities and Local Government commemorative paving stone was dedicated at St Mary and All Saints Church, St Marys Ringway, Kidderminster on 3rd September 2018.
- Ontario
    ◦ Victoria Cross obelisk to all Canadian VCs at Military Heritage Park, Barrie dedicated by Princess Royal on 22nd October 2013.
    ◦ Plaque No.21 on the York Cemetery VC Memorial, West Don River Valley, Toronto dedicated on 25th June 2017.
    ◦ Named on one of eleven plaques honouring 175 men from overseas awarded the VC for

John Young's grave in Mount Royal Cemetery, Outremont, Montréal.

the Great War. The plaques were unveiled by the Senior Minister of State at the Foreign & Commonwealth Office and Minister for Faith and Communities, Baroness Warsi, at a reception at Lancaster House, London on 26th June 2014 attended by The Duke of Kent and relatives of the VC recipients. The Canadian plaque was unveiled outside the British High Commission in Elgin Street, Ottawa on 10th November 2014 by The Princess Royal in the presence of British High Commissioner Howard Drake, Canadian Minister of Veterans Affairs Julian Fantino and Canadian Chief of the Defence Staff General Thomas James Lawson.

Memorial plaque on the wall of the chapel close to Dury Crucifix Cemetery.

- Two 49 cents postage stamps in honour of the ninety-four Canadian VC winners were issued by Canada Post on 21st October 2004 on the 150th Anniversary of the first Canadian VC's action, Alexander Roberts Dunn VC.
- Plaque near Dury Crucifix Cemetery, Pas de Calais, France, on which his year of death is shown incorrectly as 1919.

In addition to the VC he was awarded the British War Medal 1914–20 and Victory Medal 1914–19. The VC was acquired by the Canadian War Museum in February 2012 and is held there at 1 Vimy Place, Ottawa, Ontario.

Sources

The following institutions, individuals and publications were consulted:

Regimental Museums

British Columbia Regiment Museum, Vancouver, Canada; Museum of Lincolnshire Life, Lincoln; Headquarters The Royal Anglian Regiment (Lincolnshire), Lincoln; Canadian War Museum, Ottawa.

Individuals

Doug and Richard Arman, Gaye Ashford, Maj (Ret'd) Marcus Beak, Norman Best, Tony Grant, DJ Huggins, Alan Jordan, Steve Lee, Alasdair Macintyre, Robert Mansell, Colin Martin, Bill Mullen, Iain Stewart, Vic Tambling, Glenys Taylor, Gemma Wade, Jackie Wood.

Schools and Universities

Oratia District School, Auckland, New Zealand; Taunton College, Southampton.

Divisional Histories

The Royal Naval Division. D Jerrold. Hutchinson 1923. (63rd Division).

Regimental/Unit Histories

Royal Navy
  Gallant Deeds. Compiler Vice Admiral W H D Boyle. Gieves, Portsmouth 1919.
The Lincolnshire Regiment
  History of the Lincolnshire Regiment 1914–18. Editor Maj Gen C R Simpson. Medici Society 1931.
The Royal Welsh Fusiliers
  That Astonishing Infantry, The History of the Royal Welsh Fusiliers 1689–1989. M Glover.
  Regimental Records of the Royal Welsh Fusiliers (23rd Foot), Volume III 1914–18 France & Flanders. Compiler Maj C H Dudley Ward. Forster Groon 1928.
The Duke of Wellington's (West Riding Regiment)
  History of the Duke of Wellington's Regiment (West Riding) 1702–1992. J M Brereton and A C S Savoury. Amadeus 1993.

Princess Louise's (Argyll and Sutherland Highlanders)
  Argyllshire Highlanders 1860–1960. Lt Col G I Malcolm. Halberd Press.
  An Reisimeid Chataich, The 93rd Sutherland, Now 2nd Battalion The Argyll and Sutherland Highlanders (Princess Louise's) 1799–1927. Brig Gen A E J Cavendish. Butler & Tanner 1928.
  Fighting Highlanders – The History of the Argyll and Sutherland Highlanders. P J R Mileham. Arms and Armour Press 1993.
The Royal Munster Fusiliers
  History of the Royal Munster Fusiliers, Volume II 1861–1922. Capt S McCance. Gale & Polden 1927.
Canadian Expeditionary Force
  Official History of the Canadian Army in the First World War – Canadian Expeditionary Force 1914–19. Col GWL Nicholson 1962.
  Gallant Canadians; The Story of The Tenth Canadian Infantry Battalion 1914–1919. Daniel G Dancocks 1950.
  The History of The 16th Battalion (The Canadian Scottish) Canadian Expeditionary Force in the Great War, 1914–1919. Lt Col HM Urquhart DSO MC ADC. Trustees & Regimental Committee of The 16th Battalion 1932.
New Zealand
  The New Zealand Division 1916–1919. A Popular History Based on Official Records. Col H Stewart CMG DSO MC. Whitcombe & Tombs Ltd, Auckland 1921.

General Works

A Bibliography of Regimental Histories of the British Army. Compiler A S White. Society for Army Historical Research 1965.
A Military Atlas of the First World War. A Banks & A Palmer. Purnell 1975.
The Soldier's War 1914–18. P Liddle. Blandford Press.
Into Battle 1914–18. E Parker. Longmans 1964.
The Times History of the Great War.
Topography of Armageddon, A British Trench Map Atlas of the Western Front 1914–18. P Chasseaud. Mapbooks 1991.
Before Endeavours Fade. R E B Coombs. Battle of Britain Prints 1976.
British Regiments 1914–18. Brig E A James. Samson 1978.

Biographical/Autobiographical

The Dictionary of National Biography 1901–85. Various volumes. Oxford University Press.
The Cross of Sacrifice, Officers Who Died in the Service of the British, Indian and East African Regiments and Corps 1914–19. S D and D B Jarvis. Roberts Medals 1993.
Whitaker's Peerage, Baronetage, Knightage & Companionage 1915.
Our Heroes – Containing Photographs with Biographical Notes of Officers of Irish Regiments and of Irish Officers of British Regiments who have fallen or who have

been mentioned for distinguished conduct from August 1914 to July 1916. Printed as supplements to Irish Life from 1914 to 1916.

The Bond of Sacrifice, A Biographical Record of all British Officers Who Fell in the Great War. Volume I Aug–Dec 1915, Volume II Jan–Jun 1915. Editor Col L A Clutterbuck. Pulman 1916 and 1919.

The Roll of Honour Parts 1–5, A Biographical Record of Members of His Majesty's Naval and Military Forces who fell in the Great War 1914–18. Marquis de Ruvigny. Standard Art Book Co 1917–19.

The Dictionary of Edwardian Biography – various volumes. Printed 1904–08, reprinted 1985–87 Peter Bell Edinburgh.

Dictionary of Canadian Biography.

Valiant Hearts. Atlantic Canada and the Victoria Cross. John Boileau. Nimbus Publishing, Halifax, Nova Scotia 2005.

Specific Works on the Victoria Cross

The Register of the Victoria Cross. This England 1981 and 1988.
The Story of the Victoria Cross 1856–1963. Brig Sir J Smyth. Frederick Muller 1963.
The Evolution of the Victoria Cross, A Study in Administrative History. M J Crook. Midas 1975.
The Victoria Cross and the George Cross. IWM 1970.
The Victoria Cross, The Empire's Roll of Valour. Lt Col R Stewart. Hutchinson 1928.
The Victoria Cross 1856–1920. Sir O'Moore Creagh and E M Humphris. Standard Art Book Company, London 1920.
Victoria Cross – Awards to Irish Servicemen. B Clark. Published in The Irish Sword summer 1986.
Heart of a Dragon, VC's of Wales and the Welsh Regiments 1914–82. W Alister Williams. Bridge Books 2006.
Devotion to Duty, Tributes to a Region's VCs. James W Bancroft. Aim High 1990.
VC Locator. D Pillinger and A Staunton. Highland Press, Queanbeyan, New South Wales, Australia 1991.
Black Country VCs. Barry Harris. Black Country Society 1985.
The VC Roll of Honour. J W Bancroft. Aim High 1989.
A Bibliography of the Victoria Cross. W James McDonald. W J Mcdonald, Nova Scotia 1994.
Canon Lummis VC Files held in the National Army Museum, Chelsea.
Recipients of the Victoria Cross in the Care of the Commonwealth War Graves Commission. CWGC 1997.
Victoria Cross Heroes. Michael Ashcroft. Headline Review 2006
Monuments to Courage. David Harvey. 1999.
Beyond the Five Points – Masonic Winners of The Victoria Cross and The George Cross. Phillip May GC, edited by Richard Cowley. Twin Pillars Books, Northamptonshire 2001.
Irish Winners of the Victoria Cross. Richard Doherty & David Truesdale. Four Courts Press, Dublin, Ireland 2000.

Our Bravest and Our Best: The Stories of Canada's Victoria Cross Winners. Arthur Bishop 1995.
A Breed Apart. Richard Leake. Great Northern Publishing 2008.

Other Honours and Awards

The Distinguished Service Order 1886–1923 (in 2 volumes). Sir O'Moore Creagh and E M Humphris. J B Hayward 1978 (originally published 1924).
Orders and Medals Society Journal (various articles).
The Old Contemptibles Honours and Awards. First published 1915. Reprinted by J B Hayward & Son 1971.

Official Publications and Sources

History of the Great War, Order of Battle of Divisions. Compiler Maj A F Becke. HMSO.
History of the Great War, Military Operations, France and Belgium. Compiler Brig Gen Sir J E Edmonds. HMSO. Published in 14 volumes of text, with 7 map volumes and 2 separate Appendices between 1923 and 1948.
Navy Lists.
Army Lists – including Graduation Lists and Record of War Service.
Air Force Lists.
Home Guard Lists 1942–44.
Indian Army Lists 1897–1940.
India List 1923–40.
Location of Hospitals and Casualty Clearing Stations, BEF 1914–19. Ministry of Pensions 1923.
London Gazettes
Census returns, particularly for 1881, 1891 and 1901.
Service records from the Library and Archives of Canada.
Service records in Archives New Zealand.
Officers and Soldiers Died in the Great War.

National Archives

Unit War Diaries under WO 95
Military maps under WO 297.
Medal Cards and Medal Rolls under WO 329 and ADM 171.
Soldier's Service Records under WO 97, 363 and 364.
Officer's Records in the Public Record Office under WO 25, 76, 339 and 374.
RAF Officer's Records under Air 76.
Births, Marriages and Deaths records.

Reference Publications

Who's Who and Who Was Who.
The Times 1914 onwards.
The Daily Telegraph 1914 onwards.
Kelly's Handbook to the Titled, Landed and Official Classes.
Burke's Peerage.

Internet Websites

History of the Victoria Cross – www2.prestel.co.uk/stewart
Commonwealth War Graves Commission – www.yard.ccta.gov.uk/cwgc
Scotland's People – http://scotlandspeople.gov.uk
Free Births, Marriages and Deaths – www.freebmd.com
Memorials to Valour – http://www.memorialstovalour.co.uk

Periodicals

This England magazine – various editions.
Coin and Medal News – various editions.
Journal of The Victoria Cross Society
Gun Fire – A Journal of First World War History. Edited by AJ Peacock, but no longer published
Stand To – Journal of the Western Front Association.

Useful Information
(Some details may be affected by Brexit)

Accommodation – there is a wide variety of accommodation available in France. Search on-line for your requirements. There are also numerous campsites, but many close for the winter from late September.

Clothing and Kit – consider taking:
Waterproofs.
Headwear and gloves.
Walking shoes/boots.
Shades and sunscreen.
Binoculars and camera.
Snacks and drinks.

Customs/Behaviour – local people are generally tolerant of battlefield visitors but please respect their property and address them respectfully. The French are less inclined to switch to English than other Europeans. If you try some basic French it will be appreciated.

Driving – rules of the road are similar to UK, apart from having to drive on the right. If in doubt about priorities, give way to the right, particularly in France. In many rural areas you have to give way to vehicles coming in from the right, even from apparently minor roads onto major routes. Obey laws and road signs – police impose harsh on-the-spot fines. Penalties for drinking and driving are heavy and the legal limit is lower than UK (50mg rather than 80mg). Most autoroutes in France are toll roads. In rural areas the speed limit is 80kph but in many places the old 90kph signs remain. The name board at the entrance to a village or town automatically imposes a 50kph speed limit.

<u>Fuel</u> – petrol stations are usually only open 24 hours on major routes and larger supermarkets. Payment by credit cards in automatic tellers is increasingly becoming the norm. The cheapest fuel is at hypermarkets.

<u>Mandatory Requirements</u> – if taking your own car you need:
Full driving licence.
Vehicle registration document.
Comprehensive motor insurance valid in Europe (Green Card).

European breakdown and recovery cover.
Letter of authorisation from the owner if the vehicle is not yours.
Spare set of bulbs, headlight beam adjusters, warning triangle, GB sticker, high visibility vest and breathalyzer. Requirements do vary, so check before departing. Emission quality sticker if driving in Paris or certain other cities.

Emergency – keep details required in an emergency separate from wallet or handbag:
Photocopy passport, insurance documents and EHIC (see Health below).
Mobile phone details.
Credit/debit card numbers and cancellation telephone contacts.
Travel insurance company contact number.
Who to contact in an emergency.

Ferries – the closest ports are Boulogne, Calais and Dunkirk. The Shuttle is quicker, but usually more expensive.

Health

European Health Insurance Card – entitles the holder to medical treatment at local rates. Issued free and valid for five years. You are only covered if you have the EHIC with you when you go for treatment. Post-Brexit, existing EHICs remain valid until expiry date. A new Global Health Insurance Card is being issued to replace EHIC. Apply through the NHS website.

Travel Insurance – you are also strongly advised to have full travel insurance. If you receive treatment get a statement by the doctor (*feuille de soins*) and a receipt to make a claim on return.

Personal Medical Kit – treating minor ailments saves time and money. Pack sufficient prescription medicine for the trip.

Chemist (*Pharmacie*) – look for the green cross. They provide some treatment and if unable to help will direct you to a doctor. Most open 0900–1900, except Sunday. Out of hours services (*pharmacie de garde*) are advertised in Pharmacie windows.

Doctor and Dentist – hotel receptions have details of local practices. Beware private doctors/hospitals, as extra charges cannot be reclaimed – the French national health service is known as *conventionné*.

Rabies – contact with infected animals is very rare but if bitten by any animal get the wound examined professionally immediately.

Money

ATMs – at most banks and post offices with instructions in English. Check your card can be used in France and what charges apply. Some banks limit how much can be withdrawn. Let your bank know you will be away, as some block cards if transactions take place unexpectedly.

Credit/Debit Cards – major cards are usually accepted, but some have different names – Visa is Carte Bleue and Mastercard is Eurocard.

Exchange – beware 0% commission, as the rate may be poor. The Post Office takes back unused currency at the same rate, which may or may not be advantageous. Since the Euro, currency exchange facilities are scarce.

Local Taxes – if you buy high value items you can reclaim tax. Get the forms completed by the shop, have them stamped by Customs, post them to the shop and they will refund about 12%. Brexit may change this.

Passport – a valid passport is required with at least six months left to run. No visa is required if staying for less than ninety days in any 180 days period.

Post – postcard stamps are available from vendors, newsagents and tabacs.

Public Holidays – just about everything closes and banks can close early the day before. Transport may be affected, but tourist attractions in high season are unlikely to be. The following dates/days are public holidays:

1 January
Easter Monday
1 May
8 May
Ascension Day
Whit Monday
14 July
15 August
1 & 11 November
25 December

In France many businesses and restaurants close for the majority of August.

Radio – if you want to pick up the news from home try BBC Radio 4 on 198 kHz long wave. BBC Five Live on 909 kHz medium wave can sometimes be received. There are numerous internet options for keeping up with the news.

Shops – in large towns and tourist areas they tend to open all day. In more remote places they may close for lunch. Some bakers open Sunday a.m. and during the week take later lunch breaks. In general shops do not open on Sundays and those that do have limited hours.

Telephone

<u>To UK</u> – 0044, delete initial 0 then dial the rest of the number.

<u>Local Calls</u> – dial the full number even if within the same zone.

<u>Mobiles</u> – check yours will work in France and the charges. Although most operators have no current plans to impose data roaming charges, this may change. Check your operator's policy before departure.

<u>Emergencies</u> – dial 112 for medical, fire and police anywhere in Europe from any landline, pay phone or mobile. Calls are free

<u>British Embassy (Paris)</u> – 01 44 51 31 00.

Time Zone – one hour ahead of UK. This may change in 2022 if the EU member states decide to abolish daylight saving time.

Tipping – a small tip is expected by cloakroom and lavatory attendants and porters. Not required in restaurants, when a service charge is included.

Toilets – the best are in museums and the main tourist attractions. Towns usually have public toilets where markets are held; some are coin operated. Otherwise on the battlefields facilities are sparse. Finding a local café may be the best option, although they are closing as rapidly as British pubs.

Index

Notes
1. Not every person or location is included. Most family members named in the Biographies are not.
2. Armed forces units, establishments, etc are grouped under the respective country, except for Britain's, which appear under the three services – British Army, Royal Air Force and Royal Navy. Royal Naval Division units appear under British Army for convenience.
3. Newfoundland appears under Canada although not part of it at the time.
4. Cemeteries/Crematoria, Cathedrals, Churches, Hospitals, Museums, Schools, Ships, Trenches, Universities and Commonwealth War Graves Commission appear under those group headings.
5. All orders, medals and decorations appear under Orders.
6. Belgium, Britain, France and Germany are not indexed in the accounts of the VC actions, as there are too many mentions. Similarly, England, Britain and United Kingdom are not indexed in the biographies.

Abbotsford, BC, 246–7
Aberdeen, 89, 91, 133, 191, 196, 205–206
Aberdeen Line, 89
Aberdour, 71, 84
Abergele, 299
Abingdon, 158
Ablain-Saint-Nazaire, 189, 245, 273
Abu Sueir, 130–1
Abyssinian expedition, 75
Acre, 118
Acton, 231–2
Addington, NZ, 126
Addison VC, William, 98
Adelaide, 116
Aden, 127, 156
Adler, Larry, 134
Adnitt MM, LCpl George, 63, 145
AEG Europe, 204
Aegean, 156
Afghanistan, 74, 160
Africa, 284
African American, 152
Aintree, 303
Air Raid Precautions, 123, 133, 177, 233, 306, 310
Aisne, Battle of, 277
Alabama, 301
Alaska, 218, 248, 253
Albany, WA, 127
Albert, 7
Albert & Co, NB, 246, 250–1
Albert MofH, Christian, 137
Alberta, 189
Albertland, 164–5, 169
Albion, Ill, 136

Albion, Neb, 141
Aldea Blanca, 309
Aldershot, 75, 110, 130, 161, 272
Alexander Co, 136, 138, 151–2
Alexander Stephen & Sons, 241
Alexandria, Egypt, 72, 126–7, 207, 266, 270
Alexandria, Ont, 240
Alexandria, VA, 225
Alexian Brothers (Cellites, Beghards), 142
Alexius of Rome, 142
Alfalfa Co, 160
Alford, 190
Algoma, Ont, 254
Alice's Adventures in Wonderland, 159
Allan Line, 240–1, 279
Allbay Road, BC, 253, 260
Allen, Keith, 268
Allen, Lily, 268
Allenby, Gen Sir Edmund, 200
Alrewas, 104, 153, 173, 189, 229, 262, 295
Alton, 81
Alvaston, 266
Alverstoke, 183
Amelia de Orleans, 89
Amerherst, 214
American Civil War, 152, 157, 219
American Legion, 226
American Medical Association, 151
American Revolutionaray War, 137, 140, 157
Amersham, 77, 266
Amherst, NS, 147, 219–20
Amiens, Battle of, 94, 145, 223
Amis, Kingsley, 134
Amistad, 137

Amritsar massacre, 256
Anchor Line, 241
Andover, NH, 226
Andrew VC, Cpl Leslie, 174
Androscoggin Co, Me, 213
Anglesey, 131
Anglo-Saxons, 304
Anschutz, Philip, 204
Antarctica, 144
Antietam, Battle of, 219
Antrim, Co, 87, 106, 132
Antwerp, 87–8, 96, 241
ANZAC Day, 172
Apiata VC, Cpl Willie, 173
Appleton, Sir Edward, 141
Aratapu, 166
Archbishop of Canterbury, 155
Archbishop of Westminster (RC), 239
Archibald VC, Adam, 208
Arctic, 139
Ardendee, 80
Argyll, 189, 193–4, 202–203, 205, 209
Arleux, 26
Arlinton Co, 153
Armagh, 81, 193
Armentières, 82, 123
Armistice, 291, 308
Armstrong, Dido, 86
Armstrong, Neil, 137
Armstrong Whitworth, 114
Aroostook Co, ME, 218, 221
Arran, 189, 191, 193–4, 202
Arran Piers Ltd, 202
Arras & Battle of, 9, 11, 14–15, 17, 22, 26–7, 43, 51, 53, 55–9, 64, 145, 223, 229, 256, 262, 281, 284, 289, 308
Artillery Hill, 22, 26
Artillery Mansions Hotel, 83
Artman Nicholls & Co, 138
Arvillers, 291
Ashburton, NZ, 166
Ashland, MA, 221
Ashstead, 205, 254
Ashton-under-Lyne, 277
Asia, 87
Askham Richard, 123
Association of Canadian Clubs, 88
Astley & Castle, 81, 83
Aston, 170, 239
Aston, Oxon, 266
Atherstone, 126
Atlantic, 96, 109, 143, 146, 156–7, 253
Attock, 74
Aubencheul-au-Bac, 112
Aubigny-en-Artois, 244
Auckland, 310
Auckland, NZ, 156–8, 163–6, 168–9, 171, 184, 192

Augusta, ME, 213, 219, 226
Augustinians, 237, 264
Aurora, ME, 219
Austen, Jane, 139
Australia/n, 87, 89, 110, 113, 115, 117, 122, 133, 153, 156, 163, 167, 173, 192, 229, 262, 289, 295
Australian armed forces,
    AIF HQ, 72
    Australian Corps, 23, 29, 31
    Australian Imperial Force, 115–16
    Medical,
        1st Australian Casualty Clearing Station, 170
        2nd Australian General Hospital, 170, 288–9
        4th Military General Hospital, 116
        Australian Hospital, Wimereux, 286
        Prince of Wales Military Hospital, Randwick, NSW, 115
    Royal Australian Artillery, 117, 223
    Tank Corps, 115, 117
    Royal Australian Air Force, 133
        76 Operational Base, 133
    Royal Australian Navy, 192
        HMAT *Araguaya*, 249
Australian Capital Territory, 117
Australian Coronation Contingent, 116–17
Australian Government,
    Government House, 116
    Governor General, 115
Auxiliary Fire Service, 307
Avion, 242, 289
Avon, 139
Avranches, 118
Axbridge, 71
Axminster, 306
Aylesbury, 266
Aylmer VC, Lt Gen Sir Fenton, 135

Baedeker Blitz, 139
Bagaley & Sons, 175, 184
Bahamas, 293
Baileyville, Me, 213
Balclutha, 194
Balcombe, 161, 163
Balderton, 265
Baldwin, Stanley, 134
Balgowlah, 193
Balham, 181, 234
Ballinrobe, 192
Ballybofey, 79–80, 83
Ballyclough Castle, 80
Ballykelly, 98
Balmer Lawns Hotel, Brockenhurst, 167
Balmichael, 194
Baltimore, 75, 279
Banbury, 266

Bangalore, 180
Bangor, ME, 211–12, 216, 218, 221
Bank/Royal Bank of Scotland, 205–206
Bankes VC, William, 86
Banstead, 189
Bapaume & Second Battle of, 1, 5–7, 16, 29, 168, 257
Baralle, 45
Barbaville, 80
Barclay Curle & Co, Glasgow, 96, 255
Barcombe, 183
Barnby in the Willows, 266
Barnet, 233
Barnet Co, VT, 214
Baron Fisher, 134
Baron Lifford, 79
Baron Montagu, 77
Baron Paton of Barnes, 139
Baron Raglan, 86
Baroness Warsi, 96, 153, 173, 188, 228, 245, 261, 284, 295, 312
Barrackpore, 277
Barrett, 2Lt A, 67
Barrie, Ont, 96 152, 228, 244, 261, 284, 295, 311
Barrie, Sir James M, 199
Barriefield, Ont, 234, 287
Barron VC, Colin, 283, 292
Barry, Charles, 305
Bart, Lionel, 134
Barton Mount Stephen, 89
Barton upon Irwell, 195
Basingstoke, 81
Basra, 180
Bath & Abbey, 79, 83, 100, 111, 138, 139, 264
Bath, ME, 225–6
Baton Rouge, 204
Battersea, 126, 181, 234
Bay of Plenty, 114
Bazentin-le-Grand, 1, 3, 298
Bazentin-le-Petit, 4
Beak, Cdr Daniel VC, 38
Bear Inn, Brighton, 207
Bearforest, 80
Beatty, Adm, 289
Beaucourt, 145
Beaulieu Abbey, 77
Beaumetz, 33
Beddington, ME, 219
Bedford, 206, 227
Bedfordshire, 133, 227
Bedminster, 158
Beechmount Castle, 85
Beeding, 176
Beharry VC, Sgt Johnson, 153, 173, 229, 262, 295
Belaney, Archibald (Grey Owl), 231
Belas Knap, 304
Belcher VC, Douglas, 98

Belfast, 127, 282–3
Belgium, 77, 111, 153, 159, 167, 173, 186, 229, 260, 262, 284, 290, 295
Bell, Alexander Graham, 199
Bell Telegraph Co of Canada, 91
Belleville, Ont, 234, 235, 279–80
Bellew VC, Edward, 283
Bellingham, WA, 250
Belton, 75
Bench Farm, 27
Benedictines, 86
Bengal, 85
Benn, Tony, 86
Benrath, 183
Berkhamsted, 79
Berkshire, 83, 113, 151, 158, 172, 175, 234, 288
Berlin, 241
Bermondsey, 179, 274
Bermuda, 108, 241
Bermuda & West Indies Steamship Co, 110
Berwick, ME, 219
Berwick-upon-Tweed, 119–20, 122–3, 128–30, 133
Berwickshire, 196, 285, 292
Beugnâtre, 7
Beugny, 33
Beverley, 75, 82, 133
Bevin, Ernest, 134
Bexhill-on-Sea, 150, 223, 291
Big Bay (Georgetown), BC, 247
Bingham Dana/McCutchen, 147
Bingham VC, R Adm Edward, 135
Birkenhead, 105, 107, 118, 310
Birmingham, 151, 170, 239–40, 304–307
Bishop Lydeard, 177
Bishop of Asaph, 299
Bishop of Iona, 193
Bishop of Llandaff, 132
Bishop of Manchester, 278
Bishop VC, William, 144
Bisley, 258
Bismarck Sea, 216
Blackdown, 277
Blackheath, 180
Blackpool, 234
Blackwaterfoot, 194
Blaikie, Capt James, 241
Blakiston, 122
Blandford & Camp, 268–9, 271
Blendon, 138
Blenheim bomber, 27
Blenheim, NZ, 115, 191–2
Blitz, 124, 202, 278
Bloody Sunday, 80
Bloomfield, 77
Bloomsbury, 239
Bloomville, 148
Blue Riband, 146

Index   325

Blyton, Enid, 134
Bocca Tigris, 73–4
Boeing 707, 122
Boer/South African Wars, 81, 89, 92, 95, 125, 243, 253, 259
Boers MofH, Edward, 137
Bognor Regis, 160, 178
Boiry-Notre-Dame, 20, 22, 26–7, 65
Bois de Bouche, 38, 45, 50
Bois de Loison, 45, 50
Bois du Sart, 22
Bois du Vert, 22
Bolan, Marc, 134
Bolton, 105–106, 110–12
Bolton Journal & Guardian, 105, 108
Bolton-le-Moors, 105
Bombay, 92, 96, 180–1, 241
Bonner VC, Charles, 208
Boone Co, 141
Booth, William Bramwell, 305
Bordon, 180, 235
Borthwick, 196
Boston, MA, 75, 147, 150–1, 212, 214–15, 218, 220, 251–2
Bouchoir, 291
Boulogne, 76–7, 90, 120–2, 170, 196–7, 248, 256, 271, 281, 288–9, 308
Boult, Sir Adrian, 86
Boulton, 266
Bourlon Wood, 26
Bournemouth, 83, 154, 193, 238
Bow, 230
Boy Scouts, 168
Boyd, Charlotte P, 239
Boys' Brigade, 189
Bradfield, 113
Bradford, 138, 141
Brailes, 265
Bramshott, Camp & Common, 94, 149–50, 235, 241–2, 248, 290–1, 307
Branson, Richard, 204
Brant Co, 87
Braughing, 177
Brentford, 231
Brereton VC, LCpl Alexander, 294
Bridge of Allan, 122
Bridgewater, 217
Bridgnorth, 297
Brighton, 112–13, 117, 143, 160, 176, 179–80, 182–3, 206–207, 254
Bristol, 158, 234
British Army (for Indian units *see* Indian Army), 99, 102, 116, 252, 264
    Army Certificate of Education, 119
    Army List, 83, 85, 132, 196, 202
    Army of Occupation, 275
    Army Reserves, 112, 119, 176, 196, 277, 298, 306

    Class Z, 125, 179, 266
    National Reserve of Officers, 169
    Regular Army Reserve of Officers, 82, 133
    Reserve of Officers, 258, 287
    Section D, 300
    Special Reserve, 78, 85, 100
    Army Reserve Centre Queensferry, 301
    British Military Missions,
        Washington DC, 90
    Chelsea Pensioners, 265
    Chief of the Imperial General Staff, 43
    Field Forces,
        British Expeditionary Force, 67, 133, 194, 277
        Egyptian Expeditionary Force, 72, 207, 266
        North Russia Relief Force, 116
    Good Conduct Badge/Pay, 119, 177, 272, 275, 277
    Inspector General, 92
    Militia, 81
    Service Pay, 275, 277
    Territorial Force, 184, 201, 206, 254
    Armies,
        First, 1, 9, 15–16, 20, 23, 26–7, 30–1, 33, 40–3, 243
        Second, 76
        Third, 1, 2, 7, 9, 15–16, 20, 23, 26–7, 30–32, 41, 43
        Fourth, 1, 4, 9, 15–16, 23, 26–7, 29, 31
        Eighth, 156
    Army Corps,
        III, 4, 23, 31, 92, 277
        IV, 1, 5, 7, 16, 30, 33–4
        V, 1, 5, 16, 31, 33
        VI, 1, 7, 16, 30, 33
        VIII, 9, 15, 43
        XVII, 1, 7, 9, 16, 23–4, 29–30, 33–4, 41, 43
        XIX, 76
        XXII, 43, 65
        Cavalry, 43
    Commands,
        Aldershot, 242
        Eastern, 133
        Ireland, 92
        Southern, 79, 133
    Corps,
        Army Catering, 269
        Army Physical Training, 269
        Army Service/Royal Army Service, 162, 179, 266, 269
        Intelligence, 76
        Labour, 132, 162
        National Defence, 300
        Queen Alexandra's Imperial Military Nursing Service, 123
        Royal Corps of Signals, 269
        Royal Electrical & Mechanical Engineers, 269

Districts,
  Aldershot, 92
  Southern, 92
Divisions,
  3rd, 33, 38
  4th, 26–7, 30, 43, 65, 67
  5th, 5, 7, 33
  6th Airborne, 299
  8th, 15
  11th, 29, 31, 65, 111
  15th, 9
  16th, 9
  17th, 5, 33
  18th, 4, 180
  21st, 5, 33
  32nd, 121
  38th, 1, 33
  39th, 9
  42nd, 33
  51st, 9, 14, 23–4, 26, 29
  52nd, 7–10, 14–16, 18, 20, 34, 36–8
  56th, 7, 8, 16, 18–19, 23
  57th, 20, 23, 30–1, 34, 37–8, 45–6, 101
  59th, 111
  62nd, 7, 33–4
  63rd (Royal Naval), 5, 31, 34, 38, 263, 268–9
  67th, 180
  74th, 31
  Guards, 7–8, 34
  HQ, 133
Brigades,
  1st Guards, 7
  2nd, 74
  3rd Tank, 9, 43
  8th, 33
  10th, 26, 28, 30
  11th, 29
  33rd, 29, 31, 65, 67, 111
  34th Foot, 81, 265
  113th, 1, 3
  115th, 1, 3
  152nd, 15
  153rd, 15
  154th, 15
  155th, 8, 18–19, 38
  156th, 16, 18–19, 37–8
  157th, 15, 16, 18–20, 200
  167th, 16, 23
  169th, 16, 19
  172nd, 20, 31, 34–5, 37, 45, 47
  177th, 111
  187th, 33
  188th, 38
  189th, 31, 38–9
  190th, 38
  Eyre's, 74
  Lowland Reserve, 121–2
Cavalry,
  1st Dragoon Guards, 74
  1st (Royal) Dragoons, 73
  2nd Cavalry Cadet Sqn, 190
  2nd Life Guards, 83
  2nd Royal North British Dragoons (Scots Greys), 208
  3rd (Prince of Wales) Dragoon Guards, 80
  6th Dragoon Guards (Carabiniers), 4, 73
  7th Dragoon Guards, 73
  Imperial Yeomanry, 92, 125
  Paget's Horse, 92
  Rhodesian Horse, 92,
  Royal Scots Greys/Dragoon Guards, 73–4, 209
  Scottish Horse,
    2/1st Scottish Horse Yeomanry, 190
  Sussex Yeomanry, 114
Infantry,
  3rd Foot, 81
  4th Foot, 80
  5th Foot, 119
  9th Foot, 119
  10th (North Lincoln) Foot, 83
  17th Foot, 81
  18th Royal Irish Foot, 73–4
  Anson Battalion (RND), 38
  Argyll & Sutherland Highlanders, 189
    13th Argyll & Sutherland Highlanders, 199
  Black Watch,
    3rd (Reserve) Black Watch, 119
    4th Volunteer Bn, Black Watch, 119–20
    4/5th Black Watch, 191
  Border,
    3rd Border, 197
    8th Border, 197
  Cameronians (Scottish Rifles),
    1st Cameronians, 84
    5th/6th Cameronians, 196
  Coldstream Guards, 70
  Devonshire, 81, 111
    9th Devonshire, 159
  Dorsetshire,
    6th Dorset, 81, 309
  Drake Battalion (RND), 31, 38–9, 263, 268, 272
  Duke of Cornwall's Light Infantry,
    6th Duke of Cornwall's Light Infantry (Pioneers), 81
  Duke of Wellington's, *see* West Riding
  East Lancashire,
    4th East Lancashire, 82
  East Surrey, 82,
    2nd East Surrey, 82, 232
    4th East Surrey (Militia) & (Special Reserve), 232
    Depot, 232
  East Yorkshire,
    1st East Yorkshire, 82
    3rd East Yorkshire, 82
  Essex,
    65th Provisional Bn TF, 78
  Galloway Rifles, 72

Hawke Battalion (RND), 39
Highland Light Infantry,
  5th (Reserve) Highland Light Infantry, 121
  1/5th Highland Light Infantry, 16
  1/6th Highland Light Infantry, 15–16, 18–20, 189, 199, 201
  1/7th Highland Light Infantry, 18
Hood Battalion (RND), 39
King's (Liverpool),
  1st King's, 110
  3rd King's, 111
  9th King's (Liverpool), 36
  10th King's (Liverpool Scottish), 208
  11th King's, 106
King's Own Royal Lancaster, 277
  1st King's Own, 277
  2nd King's Own, 277
  10th (Reserve) King's Own Royal Lancaster, 111
King's Own Scottish Borderers,
  3rd (Reserve) King's Own Scottish Borderers, 196
  4th King's Own Scottish Borderers, 196
  1/5th King's Own Scottish Borderers, 72
King's Shropshire Light Infantry,
  7th King's Shropshire Light Infantry, 33–4
Lincolnshire,
  3rd (Reserve) Lincolnshire, 111
  2/4th Lincolnshire, 111
  6th Lincolnshire, 31, 65, 67, 105, 111
London,
  Post Office Rifles, 183
Manchester, 278
  4th Manchester, 276
  6th Manchester, 276–7
Middlesex,
  25th Garrison Battalion, 176
North Staffordshire, 111
  3rd North Staffordshire, 197
  7th North Staffordshire, 197
Northumberland Fusiliers/Royal, 119
  3rd (Home Service) Garrison Battalion, 106
  1/7th Northumberland Fusiliers, 120, 123, 129
  2/7th Northumberland Fusiliers, 129
  17th Northumberland Fusiliers (Pioneers), 121
  28th (Reserve) Northumberland Fusiliers, 121
  30th (Reserve) Northumberland Fusiliers, 121
  32nd (Reserve) Northumberland Fusiliers, 121
Parachute, 299
Rifle Brigade, 78, 92, 183
  5th (Reserve) Rifle Brigade, 78
  8th Rifle Brigade, 78

  51st Battalion, 183
  53rd Battalion, 183
Royal Anglian, 117
Royal Dublin Fusiliers, 100
Royal Fusiliers, 116, 162
  45th Royal Fusiliers, 116
Royal Irish Regiment,
  1st Royal Irish Regiment, 100
  2nd Royal Irish Regiment, 38
  4th Royal Irish Regiment, 100
Royal Marine Light Infantry,
  1st Royal Marine Light Infantry, 38
Royal Munster Fusiliers, 49, 98, 102, 104
  1st Royal Munster Fusiliers, 31, 35–7, 49–50, 100
Royal Navy,
  2nd Reserve Battalion, 268, 272
  5th Battalion, 268
  A Reserve Battalion, 271
Royal Scots, 196
  1st Royal Scots, 84
  2nd Royal Scots, 33
  3rd Royal Scots, 84, 196
  4th Royal Scots, 73, 197
  7th Royal Scots, 22
  9th Royal Scots, 196
  3/9th Royal Scots, 197
Royal Scots Fusiliers,
  1st Royal Scots Fusiliers, 33
  5th Royal Scots Fusiliers, 73
Royal Sussex, 114, 176, 223
  1st Royal Sussex, 182
  7th Royal Sussex, 177
  9th Royal Sussex, 180
  10th Royal Sussex, 176
  11th Royal Sussex, 223
  12th Royal Sussex, 223
  13th Royal Sussex, 223
Royal Warwickshire, 307
  1st Royal Warwickshire, 27–8
  2nd Royal Warwickshire, 30
Royal Welsh/Welch Fusiliers, 265, 299–300
  2nd Royal Welsh Fusiliers, 3
  3rd (Special Reserve) Royal Welsh Fusiliers, 298
  1/4th Royal Welsh Fusiliers, 298
  5th Royal Welsh Fusiliers, 298, 300
  13th Royal Welsh Fusiliers, 3–4
  14th Royal Welsh Fusiliers, 1, 3–4, 296
  16th Royal Welsh Fusiliers, 3–4
  17th Royal Welsh Fusiliers, 3
Royal West African Frontier Force, 130, 133
  Sierra Leone Battalion, 130
Royal West Kent (Queen's Own),
  4th Royal West Kent, 78
  71st Provisional Bn TF, 78
Seaforth Highlanders, 30
  2nd Seaforth Highlanders, 30

Somerset Light Infantry, 264
South Lancashire,
   2/4th South Lancashire, 36
South Staffordshire,
   7th South Staffordshire, 65
South Wales Borderers,
   10th South Wales Borderers, 3
Suffolk,
   2nd Suffolk, 34
West Riding (Duke of Wellington's), 132–3
   1st West Riding, 130
   2nd West Riding, 26–30, 118, 129–30, 133
   5th West Riding, 26, 118, 120, 129
   1/6th West Riding, 120, 129
West Yorkshire,
   1st Volunteer Battalion, West Yorkshire, 132
Worcestershire,
   7th Worcestershire, 303
Machine Gun Corps, 122, 307
   3rd Battalion MGC, 33
   6th Battalion MGC, 122
   57th Machine Gun Battalion, 36
   Machine Gun Corps Base Depot, Camiers, 170
   Machine Gun Training Depot, Grantham, 170
Miscellaneous units,
   20th Infantry Base Depot, 196
   23rd Training Reserve Battalion, 176
   30th Infantry Base Depot, 120
   30th Signal Regiment, 269
   34th Infantry Base Depot, 121
   43rd Training Reserve Battalion, 111
   61st Labour Coy, 162
   67th Divisional Ammunition Column, 180
   75th Territorial Force Depot, 120
   85th Training Reserve Battalion, 121
   153 HQ Provost Company, 133
   249th Signal Squadron (AMF(L)), 168
   776 Mechanical Transport Coy ASC, 179
   955th MT Coy, 266
   Base Depot, Calais, 272
   Base Depot, Mudros, 270
   Base Depot, Mustapha, 72, 270
   Base MT Depot, EEF, 266
   Central London Recruiting Depot, 78
   First Army Signal School, 223
   L Traffic Control Group, 133
   Military Train, 75
   MT Training Depot, Isleworth, 266
   No.1 Dispersal Unit, Ripon, 122
   No.2 Dispersal Unit, Shorncliffe, 125
   No.4 Relief Battery Home Guard, 207–208
   No.34 Specialist Battalion (Elephanta), 180
Royal Army Medical Corps/Army Medical Services, 161, 201

1st British Red Cross Hospital, Le Touquet, 145
1st General Hospital, Étretat, 167, 307
1st London General Hospital, Camberwell, 91, 256–7
1st Northern General Hospital, 121
1st (Royal Naval) Field Ambulance, 268
1st Scottish General Hospital, Aberdeen, 91
1st Southern General Hospital, Edgbaston, 151
1st Western General Hospital, Liverpool, 207, 286
2 Casualty Clearing Station, 185
2/2nd (Northumbrian) Field Ambulance, 120
2nd Scottish General Hospital, Edinburgh, 149
2nd Stationary Hospital, Abbeville, 201, 307
2nd Western General Hospital, Manchester, 249
3 Casualty Clearing Station, 120
3rd General Hospital, 94
3rd London General Hospital, Wandsworth, 121, 149–50, 201, 255
3rd Stationary Hospital, Rouen, 243
4 Casualty Clearing Station, 93, 123
4th Scottish General Hospital, Glasgow, 197
5th General Hospital, Rouen, 194
5th Northern General Hospital, Leicester, 288–9
6th Convalescent Depot, Étaples, 281
7th Stationary Hospital, 76, 90
8th Red Cross Hospital, 77
10 Ambulance Train, 307
10 Casualty Clearing Station, 149
10th Convalescent Depot, Écault, 281
10th General Hospital, Rouen, 197
11th General Hospital, Camiers, 235, 289
12 Casualty Clearing Station, 149
13th General Hospital, Boulogne, 308
15 Ambulance Train, 235
14th General Hospital, Boulogne/Wimereux, 256, 271
14th Stationary Hospital, Boulogne, 91
15 Ambulance Train, 197
18 Ambulance Train, 120
19 Ambulance Train, 145
19th Field Ambulance, 196–7
19th General Hospital, 72, 266
20 Ambulance Train, 289
20th General Hospital, Camiers, 235, 249, 281
21 Casualty Clearing Station, 149
21st General Hospital, Alexandria, 207
22 Casualty Clearing Station, 145
22nd General Hospital, Camiers, 223, 272
23 Casualty Clearing Station, 235, 243
25 Ambulance Train, 281

Index

38 Ambulance Train, 243
42 Casualty Clearing Station, 244, 248
45 Casualty Clearing Station, 197
49 Casualty Clearing Station, 307
51st General Hospital, 235
57 Casualty Clearing Station, 243
58th General Hospital, Ormskirk, 123
59 Casualty Clearing Station, 235
63rd West Lancashire Field Ambulance, 248
83rd General Hospital, Boulogne, 308
Auxiliary Military Hospital, Askham Richard, 123
Bevan Military Hospital, Sandgate, 150
Catterick Military Hospital, 196
Caxton Hall, London, 72
Connaught Military Hospital, Aldershot, 242
Convalescent Depot, Mustapha, 266
Duchess of Westminster's Hospital, Le Touquet, 145
Grantham Military Hospital, 170
Highbury Auxiliary Hospital, Birmingham, 151
Horton (County of London) War Hospital, Epsom, 271
Lady Hardinge Hospital for Wounded Indian Soldiers, 167
Manor Court VAD Hospital, Folkestone, 185
Military Hospital, Shorncliffe, 91
Military Section, London Hospital, Whitechapel, 194
No.1 Convalescent Depot, Écault, 308
No.2 Convalescent Depot, Rouen, 243
No.3 Convalescent Depot, 289
No.5 Convalescent Depot, Cayeux-sur-Mer, 307
No.5 Rest Camp, Boulogne, 281
No.6 Convalescent Depot, 235
No.8 Convalescent Home for British Officers, Dieppe, 145
No.10 Convalescent Depot, 308
North Midlands Casualty Clearing Station, 150
Prince of Wales' Hospital, London, 94
Queen Alexandra's Military Hospital, Millbank, 144
Raven's Croft Military Hospital, Seaford, 143–4
Reading War Hospital, 223
Red Cross Hospital, Brighton, 78
St John's Ambulance Brigade Hospital, Etaples, 151
Springfield War Hospital, 155
Tidworth Military Hospital, 286
Voluntary Aid Detachments, 185–6, 257
Wharncliffe War Hospital, Sheffield, 271–2
Royal Artillery, 71, 81, 85, 90, 92, 275, 299
   1st & 2/1st Home Counties Field Artillery Bde TF, 180
   1st & 2/1st Sussex RFA Battery, 180
   2/2nd South Midland Field Artillery Brigade Ammunition Column, 306
   6th Company, 275
   10th Company RGA, 194, 275
   11th Field Regiment, 71
   38th (Army) Brigade RFA, 76
   40th Company, 275
   41st Siege Battery RGA, 194
   54th Coy, 275
   76th (Army) Brigade RFA, 144–5
   178th Field Regiment RA, 233
   186th Brigade RFA, 161
   298th Army Field Brigade Ammunition Column, 90
   336th Bde RFA, 180
   Artillery Base Depot, Le Havre, 76
   Donegal RFA Reserve, 81
   Kent Artillery, 275
   No.1 Reinforcing Depot Royal Siege Artillery, 223
   Royal Field Artillery, 76, 160–1, 306
   Royal Garrison Artillery, 194, 223, 234, 306
   Royal Horse Artillery, 161
Royal Engineers, 92, 105, 205–206
   3/1st Home Counties Division Signal Coy, 206
   20th TF Depot RE, 207
   40th Company, 177
   57th Traffic Company, 125
   67th Divisional Signal Coy, 206
   75th Divisional Signal Coy, 207
   Inland Waterways Transport, 125
Royal Flying Corps, 269
Tank Corps,
   6th (Light) Battalion, 33–4
   9th Battalion, 57–8
   11th Battalion, 57, 64
   12th Battalion, 33
   14th Battalion, 20–1, 44, 50, 54
   17th Armoured Car Bn, 43
Training establishments/units,
   80th Training Reserve Battalion, 121
   No.5 Officer Cadet Battalion, Trinity College, Cambridge, 168–9
   No.9 Officer Cadet Battalion, Gailes, 122
   No.10 Officer Cadet Battalion, Gailes, 120
   No.16 Officer Cadet Battalion, Kinmel Park, Rhyl, 197
   No.19 Officer Cadet Battalion, Pirbright, 78
   Officers' Training Corps, 78, 84, 190, 199
   Royal Military Academy, Woolwich, 92
   Royal Military College/Academy, Sandhurst, 78, 82, 132
   Royal School of Signals, 269
   School of Musketry, 82
   University Officers' Training Corps, 169

British Columbia, 87–9, 180, 229–30, 246–8, 250–6, 260–1, 281, 283, 285, 287, 292
   Coast Service, 261
   Legislative Assembly, 258, 262
British Columbia Ferries, 261
British Columbia Toll Highways Authority, 261
British Columbia Veterans Commemorative Association, 262
British East Florida, 157
British Embassy, Washington, 151
British Empire, 93, 258
British Empire Service League, 260
British Government Departments/Ministries, 96, 241
   Board of Trade, 111
   Cabinet, 268
   Communities & Local Government, 97, 104, 117, 135, 153, 173, 188, 209, 229, 245, 262, 273, 284, 295, 301, 311
   Employment, 268
   Environment, 268
   Faith & Communities, 96, 153, 173, 188, 228, 244–5, 261, 284, 295, 312
   Foreign & Commonwealth Office, 96, 153, 173, 188, 228, 244, 261, 284, 295, 312
   Home Office, 72, 268
   House of Commons, 73, 202, 258–9
   House of Lords, 95, 102, 151, 208, 258, 283, 293, 300
   Member of Parliament, 99, 139, 268, 304
   Parliament, 79, 103, 258, 303, 305
   Prime Minister, 139
   War Cabinet, 43
   War Office, 73, 90
   Works, 202, 210
British High Commission, Ottawa, 97, 153, 188, 229, 245, 261, 284, 295, 312
British India Steam Navigation Co, 163, 269
British Legion/Royal Britiuh Legion, 116, 242
British North America Act (Constitution Act), 258
British Overseas Airways Corporation, 122
British Steel Corporation, 298
Brittain, Vera, 257
Britten, Benjamin, 293
Brize Norton, 237
Broadway, 81
Brockenhurst, 167
Bromley, 181
Bromsgrove, 267
Bronze Age, 193, 264
Broseley, 297
Broughton, Pte John, 67
Brown, Capt Eric 'Winkle', 199
Brown, Hart & Kaplan, 147
Brown, PM Gordon, 199
Brown VC, WE, 115
Brown-Synge-Hutchinson VC, Col Edward, 135

Brownlee, Gerry, 173
Bruce, Jack, 134
Brunel, Isambard Kingdom, 304
Brunswick, Me, 213
Brunt VC, John, 98
Brymbo, 296–7
Buckhurst Hill, 230
Buckingham Palace, 94, 101–102, 130, 146, 168, 187, 201, 256, 272, 282, 291, 298, 308
Buckinghamshire, 77, 158, 266
Bucklands Beach, 165
Buckley, 298
Bucklow, 195
Bucksport, ME, 226, 229
Budder's Rag & Bone Yard, 184
Buffalo, NY, 110
Buissy, 38, 45
Bulawayo, 131
Bulford & Kiwi, 167–8, 170
Bull, William Perkins, 144
Bullecourt, 23, 30
Burford, 230, 236–8
Burgess Hill, 160, 183
Burma, 78, 277
Burmah Steamship Co, 110
Burnaby, BC, 247
Burnt Island Light, ME, 226
Bushire, 160
Butlin, Billy, 256
Butt Wood, 44–5
Buxted, 176, 180
Buxton, 186, 249

Cadbury's chocolate, 307
Caernarfon Castle, 300–301
Café Royal, London, 134, 294
Cagnicourt, 20, 23, 26, 31, 35, 38–9, 43–5, 48, 50–2, 65, 257
Caird & Co, 169
Cairo, 75, 147
Cairo, IL, 136, 138, 142, 151–2
Calais, ME, 211, 217, 220–1, 226
Calama, 158
Calcutta, 83, 85, 277
Caledonia Co, VT, 214
Calgary, Alta, 189
California, 147, 161, 213, 215, 247–8, 280–1, 283
Calling Card Wood, 35–6, 38, 44–6, 48
Camberwell, 126, 256
Cambrai, 7, 9, 11, 14, 17, 22, 26–7, 43, 51, 53, 55–9, 64, 294
Cambridge, 293
Cambridge Barracks, Portsmouth, 119
Cambuslang, 203
Camden Town, 125
Cameron, PM David, 153, 173, 229, 232, 262, 295
Camerton, 263–5, 267, 272–3

Camiers, 149, 289
Campbell, Brig Colin, 74
Campbell, Donald, 256
Campbell VC, Lorne, 206
Campbell-Johnston, Lt Alex, 46, 187
Campbeltown, 190
Campobello & Island, NB, 216
Campton, NH, 215
Canaan, VT, 214
Canada Act, 258
Canada/ians, 87–9, 91–2, 94, 96, 109, 128, 140, 143–4, 147–51, 153, 167, 173, 180, 184, 196, 211–12, 214–17, 221–2, 227–30, 234, 240–3, 246, 249, 252–60, 262–3, 275, 279–81, 283, 285–7, 291–3, 295, 301, 307–308, 310–12
Canada Post, 97, 153, 188, 229, 245, 262, 284, 295, 312
Canadian Armed Forces, 143
  Canadian Army, 9, 142, 242–3, 246, 259, 281
    Chief of the General Staff, 243
    Department of Soldiers' Civil Re-establishment Scheme, 283
    Field Forces,
      Canadian Expeditionary Force, 90–1, 95, 148, 196, 222, 240–1, 245, 248, 251, 255, 257, 259, 273, 281, 285, 292, 307
      Canadian Siberian Expeditionary Force, 287
      First Canadian Contingent, 92, 259
    Good Conduct Badge, 235, 307
    Inspector General, 260
    Military Districts,
      3rd Military District, 287
      4th Military District, 291
      11th Military District, 229
    Militia, 92, 95, 222, 240, 243, 248, 253, 259–60, 310
    Non-Permanent Force Militia, 259
    Overseas Military Forces of Canada, 257, 259
    Permanent Force Militia, 259
    Reserve, 258
    Army Corps,
      Canadian, 1, 7, 9, 16, 20, 22, 23, 26, 29, 33–4, 40–1, 43–4, 57, 64–5, 67, 145, 258, 260
      Divisions,
        1st, 25–7, 30–1, 43–4, 50, 56
        2nd, 9–11, 14–15, 20, 22–6, 93, 94, 150
        3rd, 1, 9–11, 14–15, 20, 22–3, 25–6, 90
        4th, 9, 30–1, 43, 55, 57, 64
        Canadian, 260
      Brigades,
        1st, 41, 45, 50–1
        2nd, 31, 43–4, 50, 56, 260
        3rd, 31, 43–4, 45, 50, 53, 55, 93, 257
        3rd Reserve, 143
        4th, 10, 14, 20, 22, 24–5

        5th, 10, 15, 20–1, 24–5, 93–4
        6th, 10, 14, 21, 24
        7th, 14, 25–6
        8th, 1, 10, 14, 22, 25–6
        9th, 22, 25–6
        10th, 26–7, 57–8, 60
        11th, 26, 31, 57, 59–61, 65
        12th, 30–1, 43, 57, 59–61, 64–5, 243
        Brutinel's/Independent, 26–7, 29, 43, 57, 64
        Nova Scotia Highland, 149
      Cavalry,
        14th King's Canadian Hussars, 148
        Canadian Corps Cavalry Regt, 57
        Royal Canadian Dragoons, 243
      Infantry Regiments/Battalions,
        1st, 41
        1st Reserve, 281, 286
        2nd, 41
        2nd Canadian Division Cyclists Coy, 150
        3rd, 41, 50
        3rd Entrenching, 289
        4th Entrenching, 235
        5th, 50–1
        5th Brigade Reserve Battalion, 150
        5th Regiment (Royal Highlanders of Canada), 89, 92, 196
        6th Regt (Duke of Cornwall's Own Rifles), 248, 253
        7th, 31, 50–1, 53–4, 273, 281
        7th Reserve, 143
        8th, 50, 55–6
        9th, 185
        9th Reserve, 185
        10th, 31, 50–1, 53–5, 57, 185
        11th Reserve, 286
        12th, 222
        13th, 25, 45, 50, 89, 92, 196
        13th Provisional, 143
        14th, 45, 50
        15th, 45, 50
        16th, 31, 45–50, 211, 222, 246, 251, 255, 257, 286
        16th Reserve, 281
        17th, 90, 286
        17th Reserve, 149–50
        18th, 14, 22
        18th Reserve, 227
        19th, 22
        20th, 13–14
        21st, 14
        22nd, 21–2, 24–5
        23rd Reserve, 289, 291
        24th, 15, 21–2, 24–5, 70, 93
        25th, 21, 24–5, 148–9
        26th, 21–2, 24
        27th, 10

28th, 10
29th, 21
30th, 251, 255, 286
30th Reserve, 255
32nd Reserve, 185
38th, 31, 56–60, 230, 241, 245
42nd, 26, 90
43rd, 22, 25, 286
43rd Regt (Duke of Cornwall's Own Rifles), 253
44th, 60, 235
45th West Durham Bn, 259
46th, 60, 184
47th, 60
49th, 26
50th, 60
50th Regt, Gordon Highlanders, 229, 260
52nd, 22, 26
54th, 60–2
58th, 22, 26
59th Stormont & Glengarry Regt, 240
67th, 248
68th Regt (Earl Grey's Own Rifles), 248, 251, 253
71st Regt, 222
72nd, 57–8, 60
74th, 235
75th, 31, 56, 60–2, 136
78th, 57, 59–60
80th, 234–5
83rd, 288
85th, 57–8, 60, 149
87th, 31, 60–1, 63, 301, 307
97th, 142
102nd, 60–1
116th, 22
143rd, 248
185th, 149
239th, 248
British Columbia Regiment, 281, 283
  1st Depot Battalion, 281
Canadian Corps Cyclist Battalion, 150
Canadian Mounted Rifles,
  1st Canadian Mounted Rifles, 11, 13–14
  2nd Canadian Mounted Rifles, 10–11, 14, 89
  4th Canadian Mounted Rifles, 10–11, 14, 25–6, 145
  5th Canadian Mounted Rifles, 1, 10–14, 26, 285, 288–91
  6th Canadian Mounted Rifles, 148
Canadian Scottish Regiment, 226, 229, 258
  2nd Reserve Bn, 258
Cyclists Battalion, 150,
Eastern Ontario Regiment, 287
  1st Depot Battalion, 287
Gordon Highlanders, 229
Manitoba Regiment, 223, 286

Depot, Seaford/Shorncliffe, 223, 256–7, 286
McGill Auxiliary Battalion, 307
Nova Scotia Regiment,
  Depot, Bramshott, 149–50
Princess Patricia's Canadian Light Infantry, 26, 143
Quebec Regiment,
  Depot, Bramshott, 94
  Depot, Ripon, 310
Queen's Rangers, 283
Royal Canadian Regiment, 143, 241
Toronto Scottish Regt, 152, 154
Victoria Rifles of Canada, 3rd Regt, 302
West Toronto Regiment, 283
Machine Gun Units,
  1st Canadian Machine Gun Battalion, 50, 53
  2nd Canadian Machine Gun Battalion, 10, 21
  4th Canadian Machine Gun Battalion, 57, 60, 64
  11th Canadian Machine Gun Battalion, 64
Medical/ Royal Canadian Army Medical Corps, 31, 91, 136, 143
  1 Canadian Casualty Clearing Station, 94, 257, 302, 308
  1st Canadian Field Ambulance, 187, 257
  1st Canadian General Hospital, Étaples, 120, 185, 243
  2 Canadian Casualty Clearing Station, 281
  2nd Canadian Stationary Hospital, 144
  3rd Canadian Field Ambulance, 93, 185, 244
  3rd Canadian General Hospital, Boulogne/Camiers, 91
  4 Canadian Casualty Clearing Station, 249, 281
  4th Canadian Field Ambulance, 94, 257
  6th Canadian Field Ambulance, 149
  7th Canadian General Hospital, 144, 149, 243
  10th Canadian Field Ambulance, 249
  11th Canadian Field Ambulance, 144–5, 149, 307
  12th Canadian Field Ambulance, 57, 145, 149, 235, 242, 307
  12th Canadian General Hospital, Bramshott, 149–50
  13th Canadian Field Ambulance, 145, 289
  14th Canadian General Hospital, Eastbourne, 91
  Army Medical Corps Training Depot, Toronto, 146
  CAMC Casualty Coy, Witley, 146
  CAMC Depot, Shorncliffe, 91, 144
  CAMC Training Corps, 91

Canadian Casualty Assembly Centre, Folkestone, 151, 185, 286, 288
Canadian Casualty Discharge & Exercise Depot, 91
Canadian Convalescent Depot, Hastings, 151
Canadian Convalescent Hospital, Epsom, 286
Canadian Convalescent Hospital, Monks Horton, 286
Canadian Convalescent Hospital, Wokingham, 151, 288
Canadian Convalescent Officers' Hospital, Matlock Bath, 91, 150, 249
Canadian Red Cross Hospital, London, 150, 249
Granville Canadian Special Hospital, Buxton, 249
Granville Canadian Special Hospital, Ramsgate, 185–6
Hospital Section, Esquamalt, 249
Imperial Order of the Daughters of the Empire Canadian Red Cross Hospital, London, 94–5
Moore Barracks Canadian Hospital, Shorncliffe, 286
Officers Casualty Company, Bexhill, 150
Perkins Bull Hospital for Convalescent Canadian Officers, Putney Heath, 143–4, 150
Princess Patricia's Canadian Red Cross Hospital, Bexhill, 223
Royal Canadian Artillery, 253
    2nd Brigade CFA, 50, 54
    3rd Brigade CFA, 57–8
    3rd Field Battery, 89
    3rd Siege Battery CGA, 302
    5th (BC) Field Artillery Regt RCA, 229, 253
    6th Battery CFA, 53
    39th Depot Battery CFA, 302
    75th Battery CFA, 287
    85th Battery CFA, 287
    Canadian Corps Heavy Artillery, 302
    Composite Brigade, Canadian Reserve Artillery, 302
    Divisional Artillery Column, 302
    Reserve Brigade CFA, Witley, 302
Royal Canadian Engineers, 223
    12th Battalion CE, 57
Other units,
    1st Canadian Casualty Training Battalion, 289
    1st Canadian Command Depot, 185
    1st Canadian Signal Regt, 294
    1st Reinforcement Draft, 184
    2nd Canadian Command Depot, Shorncliffe, 151

2 Repatriation Depot, South Ripon, 94
3rd Battalion Canadian Railway Troops, 248
3rd Company Railway Troops, 248
4th Canadian Base Depot, 243
4th Canadian Division Base Depot, 307
4th Canadian Infantry Base Depot, 235
4th Division Salvage Coy CASC, 235
4th Division Train, 235
11th Canadian Brigade Trench Mortar Battery, 60
ADMS HQ Ottawa, 146
Base Details, Étaples, 235
Canadian Base Depot, Étaples, 235, 256, 286, 289, 302
Canadian Concentration Camp, Kinmel Park, 150
Canadian Concentration Camp, Witley, 283
Canadian Corps Reinforcement Camp, 235, 243, 281–2, 286, 291, 302, 307–308
Canadian Corps Salvage Coy, 150
Canadian Discharge Depot, Buxton, 227, 310
Canadian Division Base Depot, 282
Canadian Forces College, Toronto, 295
Canadian General Depot, 249
Canadian Infantry Base Depot, 243, 249, 291, 308
Canadian Railway Transportation Depot, Witley, 249
Canadian Railway Troops Depot, Liverpool, 249
Canadian Training Division, Shorncliffe, 149
Canadian Training School, Bexhill, 286
Clearing Services Command, Halifax, 310
Clearing Services Command, Québec, 146
Corps Rest Station, 235
Forestry Depot CEF, 281
General Depot, Chiseldon, 151
General Depot, Hastings, 151
Machine Gun School, 187
No.2 Canadian Discharge Depot, London, 151
No.2 District Depot, Toronto, 146
No.2 Divisional Rest Station, 150
Officers' Training Centre, Bexhill, 286, 291
Québec Depot Clearing Services Command, 227
Railway Construction Battalion, 248
Royal Canadian Regt & PPCLI Depot, Seaford, 143
Royal Military College, Kingston, 293
Signal School, 302
Trench Warfare School, Crowborough, 286
Veteran Guard of Canada, 293

Canadian Forces College, Toronto, 261
Chief of Defence Staff, 97, 153, 229, 245, 261, 284, 312
Royal Canadian Air Force, 291
  89th Royal Canadian Air Cadet Sqn, 229
Royal Canadian Navy, 143
  HMCS *Ehkoli*, 247
  HMCS *Merry Chase*, 247
  HMCS *Moolock*, 247
  HMCS *Spray*, 247
  Kingston Royal Naval Dockyard, 293
  Royal Canadian Naval Reserve, 148, 247
  Royal Canadian Navy Fisherman's Reserve, 247
Canadian Government, 146
  Cabinet, 260
  Governor General, 24, 92, 144, 258, 294
  House of Commons, 258, 261
  Legislative Assembly, 258
  Member of Parliament, 258
  Militia & Defence, 258–9
  Parliament, 256, 258–9, 283
  Prime Minister, 144
  Veterans Affairs, 97, 153, 188, 229, 245, 261
Canadian Legion/Royal Canadian Legion, 228, 260, 294–5
Canadian National Day, 242
Canadian Northern Railway, 259
Canadian Pacific Line, 240, 279
Canadian Pacific Railway, 91, 96, 255
Canadian Patriotic Fund, 88
Canadian Pensions Commission, 258
Canadian Red Cross, 95, 310
Canadian Veterans' Association, 242
Canal du Nord & Battle of, 33–4, 43, 57, 60, 65, 69, 201, 294
Canary Islands, 127
Canberra, 117
Canning, NS, 148
Cannock & Chase, 122, 267
Canterbury, 181
Canturbury Frozen Meat Co, 126
Canterbury, NZ, 126, 156, 166, 168, 191
Canton & River, 73–4
Cape Cod, MA, 226,
Cape Colony, 81, 89, 92, 98
Cape Race, 241
Cape Town, 127, 176
Capitol, 143
Cardiff, 126
Carmarthen, 268
Carmarthenshire, 268, 310
Caroline Bay, 173
Carrickfergus, 132
Carroll, Lewis, 159
Carsphairn, 70–1, 97
Carter, Helena Bonham, 86
Cartwright VC, G, 115, 117
Cascais, 89

Cassiar Cannery, 252
Castine, Me, 212
Castle Douglas, 71, 97
Castle Garden, 213
Caterham, 175, 181
Cathcart, Capt, 45
Cathedrals,
  Christ Church, Montreal, 88,
  St Giles, Edinburgh, 203, 205
  St Mary, St Denys & St George, Manchester, 278
  St Patrick's, New York, 215
  St Paul's, London, 93
  St Paul's Anglican, Valletta, Malta, 131
Catholic Emigration Association, 240
Cathy Come Home, 139
Catterick, 197, 269
Cayeux-sur-Mer, 307
Cemeteries & Crematoria,
  Anfield Cemetery, Liverpool, 107
  Arlington National Cemetery, Virginia, USA, 151, 153, 228–9
  Bayside Cemetery, Eastport, ME, 228
  Clarkside Cemetery, Pembroke, ME, 219
  Dury Communal Cemetery, 153
  Fraser Cemetery, Vancouver, 260
  Fulford Cemetery, York, 122–3
  German Cemetery, Cannock Chase, 122
  Glasnevin Cemetery, Dublin, 104, 245
  Golders Green Crematorium, 116–17, 134–5
  Grand Lake Stream Cemetery, Me, 213–14
  Grangegorman (Blackhorse) Cemetery, Dublin, 103
  Holy Trinity Anglican Cemetery, North Saanich, BC, 254
  Inveresk Parish Churchyard, Musselburgh, 196
  Lake of the Woods Cemetery, Kenora, Ont, 254
  Lytham Park Cemetery, 117
  Maes Hyfryd Cemetery, Rhyl, 300
  Maine Mount Vernon Road Veterans Memorial Cemetery, Augusta, ME, 219, 225–6
  Mount Royal Cemetery, Montréal, 88, 95, 97, 301, 310–11
  New Westminster Crematorium, Vancouver, 260
  North Suburbs Crematorium, Sydney, 117
  Prospect Cemetery, Toronto, 283
  Riverside Cemetery, Oswego Co, New York, 138
  Rookwood Cemetery & Necropolis, Sydney, NSW, 117
  Rose Hill Cemetery, Mount Carmel, Ill, 151, 153
  St James Anglican Cemetery, Blakiston, SA, 122
  Union Cemetery, Colborne, Ont, 292, 294
  Waikumete Cemetery, Auckland, 172
  Warriston Crematorium, Edinburgh, 205, 209
  Welford Road Cemetery, Leicester, 289
  York Cemetery, Toronto, 97, 152, 188, 229, 245, 261, 284, 295, 311
Cenotaph, 102, 272

Index 335

Central America, 108
Centre Lake, Ont, 293
Ceylon, 78, 192
Chadlington, 237
Chamberlain, Joseph, 151
Chamberlain, Neville, 134
Channel Islands, 75
Channel-Port aux Basques, 216
Chapel-en-le-Frith, 85
Chapel Hill, 9–10
Charles, Ray, 157
Charlotte Co, NB, 211–12, 214–18, 220, 222
Chartier, Michel, 212
Chartwell Manor, 159
Chatham, 108
Chellaston, 266
Chelmsford, 98
Chelsea, 125, 236
Chelsea Arts Club, 201
Chelsea, ME, 224
Cheltenham, 83, 179, 303
Cheniote, 74
Cherisy, 15, 17, 20–22, 94, 97–8
Cherry VC, Capt Percy, 73
Cheshire, 105–107, 195, 276, 296, 310
Chester, 85, 296
Chetnole, 84
Chetton, 297
Chicago, 142
Chichester, 158, 178, 203
Chieveley, 83
Chile, 158
Chilgrove, 178
Chillicothe, 160
China, 87, 89, 148, 153, 173, 229, 239, 262, 295
China Expedition 1842, 73
Chingford, 236
Chipping Norton, 236
Chiseldon, 151
Chiswick, 112–13
Christchurch, 154, 158
Christchurch, NZ, 114, 126, 156, 192
Christie, John Reginald, 305
Church Buildings Act 1818, 303
Church Lads & Church Girls Brigade, 184, 189
Church, Maj Benjamin, 212
Churches,
    Acton Parish, London, 231
    All Saints, Toxteth, 234
    Ballykelly RC Church, 99
    Baptist Parsonage, St Stephen, NB, 214
    Carsphairn Parish Church, 97
    Christ Church, Bexley, NSW, 115
    Christ Church, Southwark, 127
    Church of Our Lady of Good Help, Seattle, WA, 280
    Church of the Advent, Montreal, 88
    Clutton Chapel, 158
    Colborne United, Ont, 294
    Corstorphine Parish, 209
    Crown Court Church of Scotland, Covent Garden, 202–203
    Edenbridge Parish, 160, 162
    Free Church, Portnahaven, 190
    Guards Chapel, London, 116
    Holy Trinity, Sheerness, 233
    King's College Chapel, Aberdeen, 206
    Lindfield Chapel, 158
    New Ross RC Church, 100
    Newcastleton Free, Roxburghshire, 197
    North United Free Church, Newcastleton, 208
    Old Church, Lasswade, 193
    Patcham Parish, 176
    St Andrew's, Edinburgh, 82
    St Andrew's, Portslade-by-Sea, 161
    St Andrew's Presbyterian, Penang, 191
    St Anne's (Richmond), Liverpool, 106
    St Ethelwold's, Shotton, 298–9
    St Gabriel's, Warwick Square, London, 79
    St George, Southwark, 159
    St George's Anglican, Montreal, 87–8, 90
    St George's, Bolton-le-Moors, 105
    St George's, Kidderminster, 301, 303, 306
    St Heliers Presbyterian, 156
    St John the Baptist, Burford, 237
    St John the Baptist, Penistone, 238
    St John the Baptist, Walton-on-the-Hill, 106
    St John the Divine, Balham, 181
    St John the Evangelist, Redhill, 184–5, 189
    St John the Evangelist, Stoke-next-Guildford, 177
    St John's, Kidderminster, 301–302
    St Joseph's RC, Grayshott, 242
    St Jude, Montreal, 88
    St Mary, Caterham, 181
    St Mary, Kidderminster, 306, 308–309, 311
    St Mary, Witney, 232
    St Mary Magdalen, Bermondsey, 274
    St Mary's, Portsea, 236–7
    St Mary's RC, Warwick, 267
    St Mary the Virgin, Bramshott, 242
    St Matthew's, Auckland, 158
    St Michael's, Liverpool, 106
    St Molios Church of Scotland, Shickine, 194
    St Nicholas, Bristol, 158
    St Nicholas, Liverpool, 106–107
    St Paul, Bermondsey, 274
    St Paul's, Montreal, 89
    St Peter's, Camerton, 272–3
    St Saviour, London, 127
    St Stephen's, Dublin, 81
    St Thomas, Seaforth, 107
    St Thomas', Rhyl, 300
    St Wilfred's, Haywards Heath, 178
    Slaugham Parish, 179
    Trust Church, Ruawai, 165

United Free, Edinburgh, 190
United Free, Fort William, 194
Villers-les-Cagnicourt, 229, 262
Churchill, PM Winston, 159, 256
Cider with Rosie, 304
Cincinnati, 136–7
Civil Rights Movement, 152
Civil Service, 202
Clapham, 181
Clarence Barracks, Portsmouth, 119
Clarendon Commission, 86
Clark-Kennedy, Lt Gen Sir Alexander, 73–4
Clark-Kennedy VC, HW, 15, 17, 21–2, 24–5, 70–98
Clarke Township, Ont, 285, 292
Clegg, Nick, 86
Clerkenwell, 158
Clews, Capt Arthur, 96
Clifton, 158
Clinton Co, ME, 219
Cloughton, 132
Cloutman VC, Lt Col Sir Brett, 135
Clwyd, 299, 301
Coalbrookdale, 297
Coates, Eric, 134
Coaticook, 214
Cobourg, Ont, 291–3
Cochrane, James, 225
Cockenzie, 192
Cockroft, Hannah, 305
Codford, 167
Codyville, ME, 220
Cojeul, 8–10, 14, 67
Colborne, Ont, 285, 288, 291–5
Colchester, 75, 230
Coleshill, 80, 84, 240
Collins, Joan, 256
Colombo, 127, 192
Colonial Mutual Life Assurance Soc, 70
Columbus, 138, 141–2, 203, 205
Colville, RAdm S, 109
Commonwealth, 76, 156, 293
Commonwealth/Imperial War Graves Commission, 82, 167
  Aubigny Communal Cemetery Extension, 244
  Bailleul Communal Cemetery Extension, 177
  Canadian National Vimy Memorial, 251
  Caterpillar Valley Cemetery, 3
  Dehli Memorial (India Gate), 182
  Dominion Cemetery, 46, 51, 187
  Doullens Communal Cemetery Extension No.2, 309
  Dury Crucifix Cemetery, 56, 153, 312
  Dury Mill Cemetery, 56, 58, 64
  El Alamein Memorial & War Cemetery, 156
  Fouquescourt British Cemetery, 235–6
  Gaza War Cemetery, 72–3
  Houplines Communal Cemetery Extension, 123
  La Ferte-sous-Jouarre Memorial, 277–8
  Lone Pine Memorial, 126–7
  Nowshera Military Cemetery, 182
  Ploegsteert Memorial, 84
  Queant Road Cemetery, Buissy, 73
  Québec Cemetery, 17, 24
  Ration Farm Military Cemetery, 82
  Runnymede Memorial, 157
  St Nicholas Church, Brockenhurst, 167
  Terlincthun British Cemetery, 63, 76–7
  Tyne Cot Memorial, 159–60, 170
  Vieille-Chapelle New Military Cemetery, 84
  Vis-en-Artois Memorial, 27, 67, 161, 272
  Ypres (Menin Gate) Memorial, 82, 196
Compania Carbonera, 279
Confederacy, 157
Congo Free State, 284
Connaught Rooms, Covent Garden, 294
Connecticut, 213–15
Conservative Party, 198, 268
Contalmaison, 3
Cooden, 223
Cook, Cordelia, 137
Cook MofH, John, 137
Cook, Peter, 134
Cook VC, John, 195
Cookley, 303
Coon Rapids, 140–1
Coos Co, NH, 215
Corfu, 93
Corio, 133
Cork, 111, 122, 271
Cork, Co, 80, 98
Cornish, NH, 214
Cornwall, Ont, 246
  Cornwall Armoury, 246
Cornwallis, NS, 148
Coromandel, 156
Corstorphine, 190, 193, 195, 197, 199, 202
Corus, 298
Cotham, 265
Cotswold Hills, 237, 304
Cottingham, 133
Cottonwood Co, MN, 250
Courcelette, 222, 288
Courcelles, 34
Courtenay, 249
Courtneidge, Cicely, 134
Covent Garden, 135, 202, 203, 294
Coventry, 80, 265
Cowichan, BC, 247
Coxsackie, NY, 226
Cramahe Township, Ont, 285, 292
Cramlington, 129
Crawford & Reid Shipbuilding Co Ltd, 261
Crawley, 162, 179
Creek people, 157

Cressing Temple, 75
Crete, 156
Crimea, 74
Crimean War, 86, 270
Croak VC, Pte John, 96
Crockham Hill, 161–2
Croisilles, 1, 7–8, 16–19, 23, 201
Cromer, 75
Cromwell, Oliver, 99, 254
Crossley's Carpets, 305
Crow's Nest, 30, 36, 43–4
Croydon, 100, 154, 162, 181, 183, 274–5, 281
Cruikshank VC, John Alexander, 208
Crusades, 118
Crystal Palace, 177, 179
Cuba, 108, 157
Cuckfield, 158, 160–1, 163, 175–83
Cullompton, 159, 161
Cumberland Co, ME, 212–13, 216–17, 224, 228, 250
Cumberland Co, NS, 219
Cumbria, 71
Cummins Diesel Co, 203
Cunard Line, Steamship Co, 87–8, 92, 146, 282
Currey VC, WM, 115, 117
Currie, Lt Gen Sir Arthur, 43, 258, 260
Currie, Sir Donald, 193
Currie VC, DV, 294
Cwmnantgam, 165

Dade Co, 101
Dad's Army, 139
D'Aguilar, Maj Gen Sir George, 73
Dakar, 108
Dale R Forsberg, 262
Danforth, ME, 221
Danielson, CT, 214
Dannes-Camiers, 91
Darby, Abraham, 297
Dardanelles, 109
Dargaville, 165, 191–2
Darjeeling, 83
Darling, Sir William, 208
Darlington, 122–3
Dartford, 154, 181
Darwin, Charles, 199
Daughters of the Empire, 95
Daunts Rock, 255
David & William Henderson & Co Ltd, 241
David Lowe & Sons, 195
Dawson, Les, 117
Day, Doris, 137
D-Day, 269
De Chair, Sir Dudley, 115
De Champlain, Samuel, 212, 225
De Gaulle, Charles, 76
De Hougham, 118

De Noyon, Jacques, 253
Dean VC, Lt Cdr Percy, 135
Debary, FL, 219
Dedham, MA, 218
Deerfield, 212
Dehra Dun, 130
Delius, Frederick, 141
Delville Wood, 4
Denbighshire, 83, 195, 296–8
Denmark, 153, 173, 229, 262, 295
Denny & Co, 110
Dennysville, ME, 211–12, 217–18, 224–5
Deputy Lieutenant, 70, 80–1, 83, 209, 305
Derbyshire, 85, 91, 150, 186, 266, 289
Detroit, 108
Devonport, 72, 108, 148, 170, 190
Devonshire, 82, 92, 144, 158–9, 161, 190, 269
Dickens, Charles, 131–2, 139, 152
Dieppe, 133, 145
Digby, NS, 211
Dinesen VC, Pte Thomas, 96, 294
Dissolution of the Monasteries, 77, 132
District of Columbia, 224
Ditchling, 177
Dixon VC, Matthew, 98
Dogger Bank, Battle of, 109
Domesday Book, 75, 155, 224, 232, 264, 297, 305, 309
Don Jail & River, Ont, 282–3
Don Peck & Co Ltd, 247
Donaghmore, 79, 83
Donegal, Co, 70, 79, 83–4
  High Sheriff, 83
Donitz, Adm Karl, 76
Donitz, Klaus, 76
Dorchester Hotel, London, 208, 300
Dors, Diana, 256
Dorsetshire, 70–1, 83–5, 111, 193, 236, 238, 268
Douai, 44
Dougall VC, Eric, 98
Douglas, 85
Douglas-Morris, Capt, 273
Dover & Castle, 118, 197, 271, 275, 300
Downham, 75
Downing Street, 159
Doyle, Arthur Conan, 199
Doyle VC, CSM Martin, 31, 35, 37, 98–104
Drake, Howard, 97, 153, 188, 229, 245, 261, 284, 295, 312
Drake, Sir Francis, 157
Drem, 191
Drocourt–Queant Line, 9, 15, 20, 23–4, 26–7, 30–1, 34–8, 40, 43–8, 50–2, 56–7, 60, 62, 65, 67, 244
Droitwich, 310
Drumboe Castle, 83
Drummossie Muir, 288

Dublin, 70, 79–80, 83, 101, 103, 240–1, 245, 271
Dubuc, Maj Arthur, 21–2
Dueidar, 200
Duke & Duchess of Connaught & Strathearn, 92
Duke & Duchess of Windsor, 293
Duke of Bussleuch, 208
Duke of Cambridge, 119
Duke of Cumberland, 288
Duke of Grafton, 86
Duke of Kent, 93, 97, 135, 153, 173, 188, 228, 245, 261, 284, 295, 312
Duke of Somerset, 264
Duke of Strathearn, 92
Duke of Wellington, 110, 124
Dumbarton, 110, 271
Dumfries, 71
Dumfries & Galloway, 97
Dumfriesshire, 70–1
Dun, Sir Patrick, 103
Dunbar, 195
Dunblane, 118, 123, 135
Dundee, 205
Dunedin, 173, 194, 309
Dunkirk, 76, 269
Dunlop, Lt, 48–9
Dunlop MC, Maj Robert, 62–3
Dunmain, 98
Dunn VC, Alexander, 97, 153, 188, 229, 245, 262, 284, 295, 312
Dunoon, 202
Duns, 196
Dunstable, 133
Dural, 192
Durham, Co, 122–3, 310
Durham Co, Ont, 285, 292
Dury, Hill & Mont, 23, 31, 43, 51, 56–60, 63–4, 145, 308
Dusseldorf, 183

Ealing, 100
Earl of Chatham, 139
Earl of Gosford, 79
Earl of Pembroke, 99
Earl of Radnor, 186
Earl of Southampton, 77
Earl of Ypres, 134
East Africa, 156
East Grinstead, 158
East Ham, 230, 236
East Indies, 81
East Lothian, 82, 191–2, 195, 205
East Machias, Me, 217
East Molesey, 204
East Vancouver, 251
Eastbourne, 144, 182–3, 224, 226–7
Easter Rising 1916, 99
Eastport, ME, 211, 218–19, 224–5, 228

Écault, 308
Ecclestone, Bernie, 205
Ecoust-St-Mein, 30, 44
Eden, ME, 217
Eden, PM Anthony, 256
Edenbridge, 154–5, 159–60, 162
Edessa, 142
Edgbaston, 151, 309
Edinburgh & Castle, 73, 82, 149, 190, 192–3, 195–7, 199, 202–10
Edmonton, 236
Edmunds, ME, 215, 218
Egham, 157
Eglinton, 280
Egypt, 72, 75, 92, 126–7, 130–1, 153, 156, 167, 173, 191, 200, 207, 229, 262, 266, 270, 289, 295
El Alamein, 156
El Arish, 200
El Burj, 200
Elandsfontein, 125
Elgin, 287–8
Eliot, TS, 134
Elizabethan Club, 72
Ellerslie, 165
Ellington, Ray, 134
Elliot VC, Rev'd Keith, 173–4
Ellis Island, 213
Ellsworth, ME, 214–15, 217, 219
Elmira, 138
Elmsford, NY, 224
Elsham, 237
Embargo Act (USA), 225
Emperor Haile Selassie, 139
Employment of Children Act, 72
England rugby team, 163
Englefield Green, 157
English Channel, 92, 271
English Civil War, 237
English Gothic, 88
Epping, 128
Epsom, 83, 270–1
Epsom, NZ, 166
Erie Canal, 140
Eritrea, 156
Erskine & Erskine, 147
Esher, 105
Esquamalt, 249
Essex, 75, 98, 100, 128, 158, 230, 233–4, 236, 275
Essex Co, IA, 141
Essex Co, VT, 214, 215
ET, 137
Etaing & Wood, 23, 31, 43, 65–9, 112
Étaples, 120–1, 170, 196
Eterpigny, 29
Ethiopia, 139, 156
Étretat, 167
Ettington, 263, 265–6

Europe, 87, 92, 139–40, 157, 224–5, 240, 259
Evans, Chris, 204
Evans VC, LSgt Arthur, 31, 67, 105–18
Everton, 107
Ewart, Sgt Charles, 208
Exhibition Camp, Toronto, 143

Fairbanks, AK, 218
Fairfax Co, VA, 225
Fairfield, NZ, 126
Fairton Ashburton, NZ, 126
Faith Chapter Order of the Eastern Star, 140
Falkirk, 190
Fantino, Julian, 97, 153, 188, 229, 245, 261, 284, 295, 312
Farmingdale, Me, 213
Farnham, 75, 77
Farnworth, 278
Federal Fish Hatchery, 213
Federated Malay States, 192
Federated Malay States Volunteer Force, 192
Fenian Raids, 92, 259
Fergusson, Sir Charles, 171
Festubert & Battle of, 93, 110, 255, 286
Fife, 84, 123, 162
Fincastle VC, Maj Alexander, 135
Finchley, 233
Findon's Grocers, 307
Finn Valley Railway Co, 79
Fisher, Adm of the Fleet John, 134
Fisher VC, LCpl Fred, 96
Fishguard, 256
Fitchburg, MA, 219
Fitzroy, Henry Duke of Grafton, 86
Five Islands, NS, 219
Flanaghan, Bud, 134
Flanders, 93
Fleming, Sir Sandford, 292
Fletching, 158
Flintshire, 296, 298–301
Florida, 141, 148, 154, 157–8, 217, 219
Florida East Coast Railway, 157
Foch, Marshal Ferdinand, 15, 260
Folkestone, 120–2, 151, 185–6, 196, 268, 271, 286, 288
Fontaine-les-Croisilles, 15–20, 22
Fontaine Wood, 22
Foochow, 89
Foote VC, John, 292–4
Forbes-Robertson VC, Brig Gen James, 8, 19
Force MofH, Manning, 137
Ford Wood, 168
Forest City Township, ME, 221
Forest Gate, 238
Forest Hill, 179
Forest Park Hotel, Brockenhurst, 167
Forest Row, 178

Formula One, 205
Formula Two, 269
Fort Defiance, 152
Fort St Charles, 253
Fort Sullivan, 225
Fort William, 194
Fortingall, 193–4
Fox MofH, John, 137
Framlington, MA, 221
France, 73, 90–9, 98, 100, 109–12, 123, 129–30, 133, 144–5, 150, 153, 161, 167–8, 170, 173, 180, 185, 189, 196, 200–201, 212, 223–4, 229, 235–6, 241–2, 245, 248, 251, 254–7, 259, 262, 269–73, 277, 281, 284, 286, 288–9, 291, 293–5, 298, 302, 304, 306–308, 312
Frankenstein, 139
Frankfurt am Main, 205
Franklin Co, 138, 141–2
Fraser Mills & River, 246–7
Fredericton, NB, 222
Freemasons, 133, 258
  Crystal Palace Preceptory, 133
  Freemason's Hall, London, 97, 135
  Maguncor Lodge, 133
  Mark Grand Lodge, 134
  Mark Masons' Hall, 133
  Rokell Lodge, 133
  Rose Croix of Heredom, 133
  St David's Lodge, Berwick-on-Tweed, 133
  St Paul's Lodge, Montreal, 95
Freetown, 133
French Army,
  Armies,
    First, 15
    Grande, 76
    Third, 15
  Regiments,
    45th, 74, 208
    105th, 73–4
French & Indian War, 140
French, FM Sir John, 134
French Red Cross, 79
Fresnes-Rouvroy Line, 20, 23–6, 41
Freud, Sigmund, 134
Freyberg, Bernard VC, 171
Frickleton VC, Samuel, 174
Frontenac Co, Ont, 292
Fulford Barracks, York, 121–2
Fulford Harbour, BC, 262
Fulham, 162, 227, 236
Funchal, 83, 108
Fylde, 106

Gadsen Co, 217
Gainsborough, Thomas, 139
Galley Wood, 67–8
Gallipoli, 72, 92, 126–7, 146, 240, 268–70

Galloway, 71
Galway, Co, 83–4
Ganges Harbour, BC, 261–2
Ganong Bros Ltd, 212
Garland's Hotel, 94
Gaza & Battles of, 72–3, 200
Geary VC, Benjamin, 283, 293–4
Geelong, 133
GEM Compliance, 206
General Post Office, 206
Genoa, 96, 110
Gentleman Jack, 305
Georgetown Mills, BC, 246–7, 248, 252
Georgetown Sawmill Co, 252
German/y, 153, 165, 173, 183, 225, 229, 262, 269, 282, 293, 295
German armed forces, 260
  Army,
    Armies,
      Second, 15
      Seventeenth, 15
      Eighteenth, 15
  Navy,
    SMS *Blucher*, 109
    SMS *Breslau*, 109
    SMS *Derfflinger*, 109
    SMS *Goeben*, 109
    SMS *Seydlitz*, 109
    U–55, 269
    U–65, 241
    UB–*64*, 282
    UB–*87*, 255
    UB–*124*, 282
    UC–*16*, 92
Germantown, NB, 250
Gettysburg, Battle of, 220
Gibraltar, 199, 269, 275
Gielgud, Sir John, 86
Gilbert, Maj Gen Sir Walter, 74
Gilbert, WS, 134
Gilbertine Order, 132
Gilfach Goch, 263, 273
Gilman, VT, 214–15
Gilrock, 265
Ginger Media Group, 204
Gladstone, PM William, 299
Glamorgan, 126, 263, 265, 267–8, 273, 297, 303
Glasgow, 87, 96, 125, 189, 190, 192, 194, 197, 202–205, 241, 251, 255, 279, 287
Glasgow Islay Association, 202
Glen Lyon, 194
Glendining's, 273
Glenelg, 189, 194
Glengarry Co, Ont, 240, 244
Glenorchy, 194
Globe Canning Co, 216
Gloucestershire, 83, 158, 179, 234, 237, 279, 303–304, 310

Gnat aircraft, 131
Godstone, 162, 181
Godwinson, Tostig, 264
Goldsmiths' Hall, 124
Good VC, Cpl Herman, 96
Goojerat, Battle of, 74
Gore, 246
Gorseinon, 267–8
Gosport, 276–7
Goudberg Spur, 290
Grafton Co, NH, 215
Grafton, Ont, 287, 292
Grand Lake Stream & Plantation, Me, 213–14, 216–18, 221
Grand Manan, NB, 216–17
Grand Pump Room Hotel, Bath, 79
Grant, Gen & Pres Ulysees, 92, 152
Grant VC, John Duncan, 98
Grant VC, John Gildroy, 174
Grantham, 75, 122, 170
Granville Hotel, Ramsgate, 186
Gravesend, 89
Gray Hotel, Los Angeles, 281
Great Exhibition, 298
Great Fire of London, 124
Great Lakes, 138, 242
Great Missenden, 266
Greece, 156
Green, Hughie, 134
Green, Lt, 50
Green Valley, Ont, 240
Greenland Hill, 14–15, 23–4
Greenock, 95, 169, 194, 279
Greenwich, 204, 274
Gregg VC, Lt Milton, 96, 294
Grenfell, Joyce, 134
Greymouth, NZ, 115
Groton, MA, 219
Grove Park, 179, 266
Grovesend, 267
Groveton, NH, 215
Guam, 148
Guardian Insurance Co of Canada, 95
Guemappe, 9–10, 14
Guernsey, 75
Guildford, 162, 177, 182
Guildhall, VT, 215
Guinness, 102–103
Gulf Islands Ferry Co, 261
Gullane, 82
Gusserane, 98
Gwent, 207
Gwynedd, 301

Habbaniya, 131
Hackney, 125
Haddington, 195
Haggard, Henry Rider, 23

Index 341

Haig, FM Sir Douglas, 15, 26, 43, 272
Hailes Abbey, 304
Hailsham, 253
Haldimand Township, Ont, 285, 287–8, 291–2
Halifax, 106, 146, 305, 310
Halifax Bank, 305
Halifax, NS, 87, 91, 95, 143, 148–50, 235, 248, 251, 255, 281, 288, 302
Hall MC, Maj Patterson, 25
Hamblain, 26
Hambledon, 175
Hamburg America Line, 96
Hamelincourt, 16
Hamilton, Brig AC, 174
Hamilton Co, 137
Hamilton, NZ, 169
Hamilton, Ont, 281, 291–2
Hamilton VC, JP, 115, 117
Hammersmith, 154
Hampshire, 71, 75, 77, 79, 81, 83–5, 90, 95, 110, 154, 158, 165, 167, 177, 183–4, 192, 199, 236–8, 242, 254, 276
Hampstead, 125, 254
Hancock Co, ME, 214–15, 217, 219
Handley, Tommy, 134
Hanna VC, Robert, 283
Hanson, Ma, 215
Hanwell, 273
Haplincourt, 33
Harbonnières, 101
Harcourt, 277
Hardin, 141
Hardy, Sir Thomas, 225
Harland & Wolff, 127, 282
Harlow, 275
Harrison GC, Barbara Jane, 122
Harrogate, 121
Harrow, 207
Hartford & Co, CT, 213
Hartford, VT, 215
Hartland Point, 269
Harvard Research Center, 218
Harvey Parish, NB, 250
Harvey VC, Lt Frederick, 294
Harwich, 233
Hastings, 81, 92, 175, 231–2, 234, 238, 245, 289
Hastings, Gavin, 198
Hastings, NZ, 166
Haucourt, 26–7, 130, 135
Haverfordwest, 238
Haverstock, Lt Gov Lynda, 187
Hawk aircraft, 131
Hawke's Bay, 166, 191–2
Hawkins, Jack, 134
Hayes MofH, Webb, 137
Hayes, Pres Rutherford, 137
Haywards Heath, 175–6, 178–83, 188
Hazelwood, 162

Headley Down, 242
Heathrow, 122
Hébuterne, 168
Hendecourt & Chateau, 18, 22–3, 30, 36, 41, 44–5, 51, 187
Henderson, 163
Hendon, 125
Henfield, 178
Henin & Hill, 9, 15–16, 18–19
Henin Fontaine, 201
Heninel, 16
Henniker, NH, 218
Hepburn, Prem Mitchell, 292
Herefordshire, 274, 278, 309
Heriot, George, 207
Herne Hill, 151
Heron Lake, MN, 250
Herschel, William, 305
Hertfordshire, 79, 131, 177, 233
Hewett, Lt Col Edward, 293
Hewitt, Bacon & Woodrow, 206
Hewitt VC, Denis, 85
High Wood, 1, 3
High Wycombe, 158
Highgate, 232–3
Highland Association, 203
Highly, 310
Hillsborough Co, NH, 217–18
Hinaidi, 130
Hindenburg Line, 7–8, 15–18, 34–5, 37–9, 41, 43, 69
Hingham, Ma, 212
Hinton VC, John, 174
Hipswell Camp, 197
Hirondelle stream, 3
Hobart, Tas, 127
Hockney, David, 141
Hoffman MofH, Heinrich, 137
Holborn, 181
Holcombe Rogus, 159
Holland America Line, 282
Holmes VC, Thomas, 283, 293
Holyhead, 271
Holywell, 296, 298
Homestead, FL, 148
Homosexual Law Reform Society, 256
Hong Kong, 139, 176–7
Honolulu Memorial, Hawaii, 214
Hoobrook, 301–302, 305
Hoover, 203
Hopedale, MA, 222
Hopewell Hill, NB, 246, 250–3
Hopkins, Garlick & Co, 301
Hornchurch, 170
Horne, Kenneth, 134
Horrington, 264
Horsham, 178–9, 182
Horsham, Vic, 133

Hospitals,
  Alexian Brothers, Chicago, 142
  Archway, Highgate, 233
  Asylum for Destitute Children, Sydney, 116
  Auckland Public, 171
  Bevendean, Brighton, 207
  Bexley, 154
  Blakebrook, Kidderminster, 309
  Blue Sisters, Malta, 72
  Broadmoor, 96
  City Hospital, Belleville, Ont, 235
  City Hospital, Edinburgh, 197
  Civil Service Nursing Home, Edinburgh, 209
  Coquitlam, Victoria, BC, 287
  County Hospital, Sheppey, 233
  Deaconess, Boston, Ma, 151
  East Surrey Hospital, Redhill, 181
  Eastern Maine Medical Center, Bangor, ME, 219
  Eastern Suburbs, Sydney, 116
  Edenbridge War Memorial Hospital, 155
  Edgware General, Stanmore, 134
  Ellsworth Nursing Home, Hancock, Me, 214
  Evangelical Protestant Deaconesses' Association & Training Hospital, 94
  Fazakerley, Liverpool, 249
  Fenwick Cottage Hospital, Lyndhurst, 81
  General Hospital, Brighton, 206
  General, Kidderminster, 303, 310
  General Hospital, Newcastle-upon-Tyne, 129
  Gilcross Hospital, 289
  Goffs Park Nursing Home, Crawley, 162
  Guy's, London, 275
  Horton Asylum/Hospital, Epsom, 270
  Jane Cavenis Private Hospital, Mount Eden, 171–2
  King Edward VII, Southampton, 78
  Knighton House Hospital, 289
  Leeds General Infirmary, 123
  Leicester & Rutland County Asylum, 289
  Leicester Royal Infirmary, 289
  London County Asylum, 154
  London County Council Hospital, Caterham, 181
  Maine Eye & Ear Infirmary, Portland, Ma, 212
  McCaul, London, 249
  Memorial Hospital, St Anne's-on-Sea, 106
  Memorial Hospital, Stretford, 195
  Mendip Hospital (Wells Asylum), 263–4
  Merville, 286
  Middlesex, 201
  Middlewood, Sheffield, 271
  Montreal Maternity Hospital, 89
  New Ross Auxiliary Hospital, 99
  Newark Memorial, NJ, 217
  North Evington War Hospital, 289
  Oxted & Limpsfield, 162
  Prince of Wales General Hospital, London, 94
  Prince of Wales Hospital, Sydney, 116
  Prince Henry Hospital, Sydney, 116
  Queen Charlotte's, London, 205
  Queen Elizabeth, Edgbaston, 309
  Redhill County Hospital, 179
  Rideau Veteran's Home, Ottawa, 294
  Rosslynlee Hospital, Roslin, 190–1
  Royal Edward Laurentian Hospital, Montréal, 311
  Royal Free, London, 197
  Royal Infirmary of Edinburgh, 193, 198, 205
  Royal South Sydney, 116
  Royal Victoria, Montreal, 90–1
  St Bartholomew's, London, 257
  St Bartholomew's, Rochester, 233
  St Faith's London County Council Hospital, Brentwood, 105
  St James, Balham, 234
  St James', Dublin, 103
  St Luke's, Paddington, 234
  St Mary's, Cairo, Ill, 151–2
  St Mary's, Eastbourne, 183, 227
  St Mary's, London, 201
  St Thomas and Guy's, London, 273–4
  Ste-Agathe Sanatorium, Ste-Agathe-des-Monts, 310–11
  Sanitorium, Ruthin, 195
  Shaughnessy Veterans, Vancouver, 287
  Sir Patrick Dun's Hospital, Dublin, 103
  South Yorkshire/West Riding Asylum, Wadsley, Sheffield, 271
  Springfield Mental/University Hospital, Tooting, 154–5
  Stagsden Nursing Home, Bournemouth, 238
  Surrey County Pauper Lunatic Asylum, 155
  The London Clinic, 205
  Tooting Bec, 232
  Tottenham Hospital, 94
  University College Hospital, London, 201
  Veterans Affairs, Hospital, Murfreesboro, TN, 138
  Wandsworth Asylum, 155
  Warwick County Lunatic Asylum, 267
  West Riding County Asylum, Wakefield, 271
  Western General, Edinburgh, 193, 205
  Wharncliffe, Sheffield, 271
  Whittington, London, 233
  Worthing, 183
Houlton, ME, 218
Hove, 114, 121, 176–7, 207
Howard, Barion Michael of Lympne, 268
Howell VC, GJ, 115, 117
Howick, 172
Hoy, Sir Chris, 198
Hudson's Bay Co, 253
Huffam VC, 2Lt James, 26–8, 30, 118–35

Index   343

Hughes, Sir Sam, 258–60
Huguenots, 259, 304
Hull, *see* Kingston
Hulme, 106
Hulme VC, Alfred, 174
Humber Redoubt, 17–20
Huntingdonshire, 158
Hurd, Douglas, 232
Hurn, 158
Hursley, 85
Hutcheson Lumber Co, 136
Hutcheson VC, Capt Bellenden, 31, 56, 60, 62–3, 136–54
Hythe, 185, 268

Iain Shaw & Partners, 205
Idaho, 247
Ilford, 98, 236
Illinois, 136, 138, 142, 147, 151–2, 213
  Governor, 152
Illinois Central Railway, 152
Illinois State Medical Society, 151
Imperial Order of the Daughters of the Empire, 95
Imperial Tobacco, 307
In Flanders Fields, 91
Inchy-en-Artois & Station, 34–5, 38–9
Incorporated Society of the Crusade of Rescue and Homes for Destitute Catholic Children, 239
India, 77–8, 82–3, 85, 92, 130, 133, 153, 167, 173, 180, 182, 191–2, 229, 240, 262, 277, 295
Indian Army, 130, 190
  Indian Army Reserve of Officers, 130, 190
  Armies,
    Bombay, 92
  Army Corps,
    Indian Corps, 167
  Cavalry,
    Bombay Light Horse, 73
  Infantry,
    1/9th Gurkha Rifles, 130
    2/9th Gurkha Rifles, 130
  Miscellaneous units,
    Military Base Depot, Muree Hills, 180–1
    No.1 Divisional Ammunition Column, 181
    No.34 Specialist Battalion (Elephanta), 180
Indian Viceroy, 167
Indiana, 140, 203, 205
Indus, River, 74, 182
Industrial Revolution, 304
Inishail, 194
Institut de France, 277
Inter City Baking Co, 88
International Code Signalling, 275
International Fire Fighters Union, 216
International Red Cross, 136
Inveresk, 197
Invergordon, 108

Inverness, 194
Inverness-shire, 189, 194
Iowa, 140–1
Iran, 160
Iraq, 130–1, 153, 156, 173, 205, 229, 262, 295
Ireland, 70, 79, 81–3, 87, 92, 98, 100, 104, 106, 111, 122, 159, 190, 192–3, 240, 245–7, 254–5, 259, 267, 279, 300, 302, 308
  British Embassy, 80
  Government, 104
  Lord Chancellor, 79
  Lord Lieutenant, 80
Irish Citizen Army, 104
Irish Civil War, 102
Irish Confederate War, 99
Irish Free State, 271
  Army, 102–103
    2nd Battalion, 102
    2nd Battalion Reserve, 103
    20th Battalion, 102
    School of Instruction, 102
Irish Home Rule Act, 99
Irish National Volunteers, 99
Irish Parliamentary Party, 99
Irish Republican Army, 102, 104, 271, 278
  Mid Clare Brigade, 102
Irish Soldiers and Sailors Trust, 103
Irish War of Independence, 102
Ironbridge Gorge, 297
Iroquois Falls, Ont, 293
Irving, Henry, 134
Islay, 189–90, 209
Isle of Sheppey, 78
Isle of Wight, 240
Isleworth, 266
Isley Brothers, 137
Islington, 124–5, 128, 158, 233, 299
Italy, 79, 96, 110, 156, 165

Jackson Co, MO, 253
Jackson, Gordon, 134
Jackson, TN, 136, 138
Jackson VC, W, 115, 117
Jaffa, 200
James, Henry, 134
James, Sid, 134
James, William, 152
Japan, 153, 173, 192, 214, 229, 247, 262, 295
Jaws, 137
Jefferson Co, AL, 301
Jefferson, Pres Thomas, 86, 225
Jerusalem, 200
Jesus Christ, 304
Jet Provost aircraft, 131
Jewish, 88, 140, 268, 304
JH Todd & Sons, 262
Jhelum, 74

Jigsaw Wood, 22, 26
Jinglin' Geordie Tavern, Edinburgh, 207
Jinsen, 148
Johannnesburg, 87
John Elder & Co, 163
John Summer's & Sons Steelworks, 298
Johnson, Ben, 86
Jones, Suranne, 305
Jouarre, 277
Judson VC, Sgt Reginald, 1, 5–7, 154–74
Jurassic Park, 137
Justice of the Peace, 70, 80–1, 83, 202
Jutland, Battle of, 109
JW Russell, 262

Kaipara, 165–6, 169–70
Kaitangata, 194
Kalkara, 270
Kansas City, MO, 253
Kantara, 72
Kanturk, 98
Katia, 200
Kaukapakapa, 164
Kearney, 217
Kearsley, 278
Keating, Lt Gen Tim, 173
Keewatin & Flour Mills, 88, 253
Kendal, 81
Kenley, 144
Kennebec Co, ME, 213, 219, 224, 226
Kennedy, John F, 99
Kennington, 113
Kenny VC, TJB, 115, 117
Kenora, 253–4
Kensington, 78, 274
Keswick, Ont, 293
Kent, 70, 78–9, 85, 91, 108, 114, 118, 125, 144, 150, 154–5, 158–63, 181, 185, 232–3, 238, 255–6, 271, 275, 300
Kenton, 207
Kentucky, 137
Kentville, 147–8
Kenya, 206
Kerling, 191
Kes, 139
Ketchikan, 248
Keymer, 154, 160
Keysor VC, Lt Leonard, 135
KGB, 86
Kidderminster, 301–11
Kildare, Co, 82, 190
Kildrummy, 190
Kilkenny, 100, 102
Killin, 194
Kilmallie, 193–4
Kilmory, 194
Kilrush, 102

Kimmage, 102
Kimsquit, BC, 251
Kincardine, 194
King Alexander II, 288
King Co, WA, 280–1
King David I, 288
King, Dr Martin Luther, 157
King Ealdwulf, 155
King Edward III, 155
King Edward VII, 94
King Edward VIII, 116
King Felipe VI, 157
King George I, 210
King George IV, 93, 270
King George V, 94, 101, 112–13, 130, 144, 146, 168, 187, 201, 227, 257–8, 270–2, 282–3, 291, 298, 308
King George VI, 116, 117, 151, 292
King Harold, 264
King Henry II, 264
King Henry III, 159
King Henry VIII, 86, 264
King James I & VI, 203
King John, 99
King Richard I, 118
King Solomon's Mines, 231
King William IV, 231
King's Co, NB, 252,
King's Co, NS, 147–8
Kingston, Ont, 234–5, 287, 292, 294
Kingston-upon-Hull, 121, 132
Kingston-upon-Thames, 112–13, 233
Kington, 309
Kinmel Park, 150, 197, 302
Kinver, 308
Kipling, Rudyard, 134
Kirkcaldy, 123
Kirkcudbright, 71
Kirkcudbrightshire, 70, 80, 85, 97
Kitchener, FM Lord Herbert, 185
Kiwi Polish Co, 168
Klondike, 252
Knight, Lt, 35
Knight VC, Sgt Arthur, 31, 51, 54–5, 175–89, 284
Knights Templar, 75
Knightsbridge, 84
Knockgray, 70–1
Knotty Ash Camp, 249
Knowlton, 90, 279
Knox Co, ME, 226
Kodak, 89
Kohimarama, 171
Korda, Alexander, 134
Korea, 148
Korean War, 187, 219
Kuala Lumpur, 192
Kwinitsa Station, BC, 262

La Quinque Rue, 255
Lady Hardinge, 167
Lagnicourt, 33–4
Lake Co, 213
Lake of the Woods Milling Co, 88
Lake Ontario, 140, 292
Lake Simcoe, Ont, 293
Lakeport, Ont, 285, 292
Lambeth, 123, 127, 154, 181, 234
Lanark Co, 89
Lanarkshire, 125, 189, 192, 251, 287
Lancashire, 105–108, 110, 117, 123, 133, 143, 195, 197, 199, 203, 234, 238, 240, 273, 276, 278–9, 302, 307
Lancashire Landing, 72
Lancaster, 273
Lancaster House, London, 96, 153, 173, 188, 228, 245, 261, 284, 295, 312
Lancaster, NH, 215
Lancaster, Ont, 244
Lancing, 183
Landore, 267–8
Langenfeld, 308
Langley, BC, 250
Larkhill, 196
Lasswade, 193
Laurent VC, Henry, 174
Laurentian Mountain, 310
Laverton, 133
Lawson, Gen Thomas, 97, 153, 188, 229, 245, 261, 284, 295, 312
Lawson, Nigel, 86
Le Cateau, Battle of, 277
Le Fanu, Sheridan, 80
Le Havre, 76, 78, 201, 224, 242, 266
Le Quesnel, 145
Le Transloy, 31, 33
Le Tréport, 94
Leamington Spa, 267
Learmonth, 133
Lebanon, 156
Lebong, 277
Lee, Laurie, 304
Lee, ME, 218
Leeds, 230
Leicester, 288
Leicestershire, 106, 289
Leigh, Vivian, 134
Leith North, 82
Lenon VC, Edmund, 86
Lens, 289
Leominster, 274, 278
Lepidoptera, 77
Lewes, 121, 155, 161, 163, 179, 183
Lewisham, 154, 164, 179
Lewiston, Me, 213
Liberal & Liberal Democratic Party, 198

Liberator bomber, 216
Liberton, 195
Libya, 156
Liddell, Alice, 159
Lievin, 186
Lillington, 81
Limehouse, 230
Limerick, 271
Limington, ME, 222
Limpsfield, 154, 158–9, 162
Lincoln, 232
Lincoln, ME, 218, 251
Lincolnshire, 75, 165, 190, 237, 264, 289
Lindfield, 154–5, 175, 178, 180
Lingfield, 161
Linnaean Society, 70
Linthouse, 241
Linton Military Camp, 172
Lister, Anne, 305
Lister, Joseph, 199
Litherland, 108
Lithuania, 309
Liverpool, 91, 96, 105–108, 110, 117–18, 143, 146, 149–50, 227, 234, 240–1, 248–49, 255, 279, 281, 288, 302–303, 307
Liverpool FC, 99
Livery Companies, 124
Llanarthney, 268
Llandovery, 310
Llanelli, 165
Llangyfelach, 267–8
Llantrisaint, 263, 273
Lloyd Webber, Lord Andrew, 86
Lloyds Bank, 112, 114
Lloyds of London Registry, 146, 206
Loach, Kenneth, 139
Lochgilphead, 203, 205
Logeast Wood, 38, 272
Loggie, Lt Warren, 12
London, 43, 70–3, 75, 77–9, 81, 83–5, 87, 89, 91–2, 94–7, 100–102, 112–13, 117, 119, 122–8, 130, 134–5, 143–4, 149–51, 153–5, 158, 159, 162–4, 173, 177, 179–81, 183, 188, 202–204, 206–208, 227–8, 230–4, 236, 238–9, 245, 249, 254–6, 258, 260–1, 266, 269, 274–6, 278–80, 283–4, 290, 293–5, 297, 299–300, 305, 310, 312
London County Council, 270
London & North Western Railway Co, 271
London, Brighton & South Coast Railway, 113, 155, 184
London, Midland & Scottish Railway Co, 271
London North Eastern Railway, 123
Londonderry, 80, 280
Londonderry, Co, 83
Longatte, 30
Longmoor Lake, 290
Longueval, 1, 3

Lord Ashcroft & Victoria Cross Collection, 104, 174, 273
Lord Byng, 258
Lord Irwin, 182
Lord John Russell, 199, 304
Lord Leconfield, 188
Lord Palmerston, 199
Lord Tweedsmuir, 258
Los Angeles, 213, 248, 280–1
Lough Swilly, 282
Loughborough, 106
Louis-Napoleon, 76
Louisiana, 204
Lovell's Flat, 194
Lowell, Ma, 215
Lowestoft, 105
Lowther, Col, 223
Lubec, ME, 211, 213, 215–18
Lucas VC, Charles, 98
Lucknow & Siege of, 231, 277
Ludshott Common, 242
Lunenburg, NS, 214
Lunenburg, VT, 214
Lutyens, Sir Edwin, 134, 182, 272
Lyall VC, Graham, 283
Lympne, 268
Lyndhurst, 81
Lys, 69
Lytham St Annes, 116

Macau, 239
MacBrien, Brig Gen James, 243
MacDonald's Biscuits, 203
MacGregor VC, John, 294
Machias, Me, 216
Macintyre, Lt David, 15, 18–19, 189–210
Macintyre, McNish & Partners, 205
Mackintosh, Charles Rennie, 134
Mackintosh's chocolate & toffee, 305
MacLennan, Lt William, 242
Madagascar, 156
Madeira, 83, 108
Madeley, 297
Madison Co, 136, 138
Madison Neb, 140
Madison Square Garden, 204
Mahamdiya, 200
Mahony VC, JK, 294
Maiden Bradley, 263–4
Maidstone, 78–9
Maine, 211–19, 221–2, 224–9, 250–1
Major, PM John, 268
Malaya, 191–2
Malden, MA, 215, 224
Malin Head, 282
Malta, 72, 108, 130–2, 241, 268–70
Malta Bend, 160–1

Malton & Priory, 131–3
Malvern, 297
Mametz Wood, 1
Manchester, 111, 195, 197, 249, 276, 278
Manchester & Salford Homes, 279
Manchester Arena, 204
Manchester, NH, 215, 217–18
Mangonui, 171
Manila American Cemetery & Memorial, 216
Manitoba, 253, 292
Manly, 192
Mansfield, 265
Manurewa, 165
Maori, 114
Mapleton, ME, 221
Marchmont Homes, 279
Marconi, Guglielmo, 279
Marigold, Pte Walter, 145
Markham, Brig Frederick, 74
Marlborough, NZ, 191–2
Marne & Battle of, 110, 277
Marquion, 38–9, 44, 50
Marseille, 180, 200, 241, 266, 270, 289
Marshall, 161
Martin Chuzzlewit, 152
Martin-Leake VC, Arthur, 86
Maryland, 75
Marylebone, 77, 81, 125, 233
Massachusetts, 75, 147, 150–1, 212–15, 218–22, 224, 226, 251–2
Matlock Bath, 91, 150, 249
Maungaturoto, 165, 169–70
Maxwell VC, J, 115
McCrae, Maj John, 91
McCullogh, Sgt Geoffrey, 63
McDowell & Co, 261
McGibbon, Douglas, 311
McKee Barracks, Dublin, 103
McMurray MC, Lt William, 25
Meadvale, 184
Mediterranean, 88, 93, 109, 200, 241, 270
Medway, 155
Meenglas, 70
Melbourne, 89
Melrose Abbey, 208
Melvill, Dunstan & Whittley, 298
Mennell DCM, Cpl Hedley, 62–3
Merchant Navy, 108, 111, 126, 203
Mercia/ns, 237, 304
Merrifield VC, William, 283, 293
Merrimack Co, NH, 214, 218
Merritt VC, CC, 294
Merthyr Tydfil, 303
Mesolithic, 139
Mesopotamia, 130, 160, 180
Metcalf VC, LCpl William, 31, 44, 47, 51, 54–5, 187, 211–30, 284

Metlakatla Pass, BC, 260, 262
Metropolis, 138
MI5, 199
Miami, 157
Miami & Erie Canal, 137
Miccosukee people, 157
Michener, Gov Gen Daniel, 294
Michigan, 108, 147, 283
Mid Somerset, 84
Middle Ages, 120, 155, 232
Middle East, 131
Middleboro, MA, 220
Middlesex, 72, 125, 131, 134, 154, 203, 205–207, 231, 236, 275
   County Council, 155
Middlesex Co, MA, 213, 215, 219, 221, 224
Middleton St George, 131
Midlothian, 190, 193, 195–7
Milford, MA, 221
Military Heritage Park, Barrie, Ontario, 96, 152, 188, 228, 244, 261, 284, 295, 311
Millenium Dome (O2), 204
Milltown, ME, 213, 221–2
Milne, AA, 86
Milwaukee, 101
Mingoval, 244
Ministry of Sound, 204
Minnesota, 250
Minster, 78
Miramachi River, NB, 222
Mississippi & River, 142, 152
Missouri, 160–1, 203, 253
Mitchell VC, CN, 294
Moeuvres, 73, 201
Molson Brewery, 90
Monaco, 231
Monchy-le-Preux, 1, 9–14, 291
Moncton, NB, 250
Monger VC, George, 231
Monks Horton, 185
Mons & Battle of, 110, 260, 277
Mont des Cats, 150
Mont St Quentin, 29, 31
Montauban, 3–4
Monteith, Internment/POW Camp, Correctional Complex, Ont, 293
Montgomery, FM Bernard, 156
Montgomery Co, OH, 216
Montréal, 87–91, 95–6, 236, 241, 260, 279–80, 301–303, 307–308, 310
Montréal Board of Trade, 88
Montréal Canadian Club, 88
Montréal Sailor' Institute, 88
Moon, 137
Moon, Keith, 134
Moon River, 137
Moore, Roger, 256

Moose Creek, AK, 218
Moose Island, ME, 225
Moran Tug Co, 216
Moray, 288
Morayshire Railway, 288
Morchies, 33
Morgan MC, Lt Frederick, 25
Moriarty, Richard, 268
Morningside, 193
Moseley, 151
Moss Side, 197
Mound City, IL, 136, 142
Mount Carmel, IL, 136, 151–2
Mount Desert Island, ME, 214, 217
Mount Pleasant, 87
Mount Roskill, 164
Mount Royal Hotel, London, 280
Mount Royal Milling & Manufacturing Co, 87
Mount Royal Rice Mills, 88
Mountain, Brig Armine, 74
Mountain Colliery, Gorseinon, 267–8
Mountain Lake, MN, 250
Moussot, 289
Moville, 279
Moylena, 87
Moylough, 84
Much Wenlock, 296–7
Mudros, 72, 200
Muldoon, PM Sir Robert, 171
Munro, Matt, 134
Muree Hills, 181
Murfreesboro, 138
Murray, Lt Gen Sir Horatius, 209
Murray, Pte William, 242
Murrayfield & Stadium, 201, 205
Museums,
   Argyll & Sutherland Highlanders, 209–10
   British, 78
   British Columbia Regiment, Vancouver BC, 283
   Canadian Museum of Nature, 258
   Canadian Scottish Regiment, Victoria, BC, 230, 263
   Canadian War Museum, Ottawa, 263, 284, 312
   Glenbow, Calgary, 189
   Hodden Grey, Toronto, 154
   Imperial War, 104, 273
   Maine Lighthouse, 226
   National Army, Chelsea, 74
   National Army, Waiouru, New Zealand, 174
   National Motor Museum, 77
   National War Museum of Scotland, 209–10
   Queen Elizabeth II Army Memorial Museum, NZ, 174
   Royal Highlanders of Canada, Montréal, 96
   Royal Navy, 273
   Royal Scots, Dragoon Guards, 74
   Royal Welch Fusiliers, 300–301

Scottish Naval & Military, Edinburgh, 210
United Services, Edinburgh, 208–10
Musselburgh, 195, 197
Mustapha, 72, 266
Muswellbrook, 192

Nairobi, 206
Namu, BC, 246
Nanaimo Harbour, BC, 262
Nankin, 73
Napier, 172, 19
Napoleon I, 74, 76
Napoleonic Wars, 93
Nash, Beau, 139
Nashua, NH, 217
Natal, 232
National Coal Board, 268
National Front, 256
National Health Service, 155, 191, 271
National Memorial Arboretum, Alrewas, 104, 153, 173, 189, 229, 262, 295
National Party NZ, 171
National Service, 205, 269
Natives & Friends of Islay, 202
Navarino, 156
Navy League of Canada, 88
Nazis, 293
Nebraska, 140–1
Neil, Lt Col Justin, 152
Nelson, Adm Lord Horatio, 142, 270
Neolithic, 75, 304
Nepal, 153, 173, 229, 262, 295
Netherfield, 226
Netherlands, 153, 173, 229, 262, 280, 295
Neuville Vitasse, 9–10
New Brunswick, 96, 211–12, 214–17, 220–2, 226, 228, 246, 250–2, 258
New Brunswick Railway, 88
New England, 251
New Guinea, 216
New Hampshire, 212–15, 217–18, 225–6
New Jersey, 77, 215, 217
New Maldon, 203
New Orpington Lodge (St George's Home), Ottawa, 239–40
New Parl, 80
New Plymouth, 126, 164, 171
New Ross, 98–101, 104
New South Wales, 115, 155, 169, 192–3
  Governor, 115
New Westminster, 246–9, 255
New York, 92, 95–6, 108, 110, 123, 141, 146, 148, 151, 204, 213, 224–5, 241, 254, 279, 282, 311
New York State, 138, 140, 148, 224–6
New Zealand, 114–15, 126–7, 153–6, 158, 163, 165, 167–70, 173–4, 184, 191–4, 229, 262, 265, 295, 309

New Zealand armed forces, 174
  Chief of Defence Staff, 174
  National Military Reserve, 171, 174
  New Zealand Army, 168, 192
    Army HQ, 171
    Commands,
      Southern, 114
    Division, 1, 5, 7, 33
    Brigades,
      1st NZ Brigade, 1, 7
      2nd NZ Brigade, 5
      2nd Reserve, 167
      3rd NZ Brigade, 5, 7
    Bns/Regts,
      1st Auckland, 1, 5, 7, 154, 166–7, 171
      1st Otago, 168
      2nd Auckland, 166
      2nd Wellington, 5, 7
      3rd Reserve Battalion, 167, 170
      5th Auckland, 171
      15th North Auckland Regt, 170
      21st Battalion, 156
      24th Battalion, 165
      Auckland Regt, 167, 171
      Canturbury Infantry Battalion, 126–7
      Nelson, Marlborough & West Coast Regt, 114
      No.1 NZ Entrenching Battalion, 167
      New Zealand Rifle Brigade, 166
        3rd New Zealand Rifle Brigade, 166
      Taranaki Regt, 171
    New Zealand Expeditionary Force, 166, 169
    Other units,
      1st New Zealand General Hospital, Brockenhurst, 167
      2nd Field Coy RNZE, 174
      2nd New Zealand Hospital, Walton-on-Thames, 168, 170
      3rd New Zealand Field Ambulance, 170
      9th Reinforcements, 166
      13th Reinforcements, 170
      50th Reinforcements, 166
      Home Guard, 174
      National Military Reserve Guard Coy, 171
      New Zealand Base Depot, Étaples, 170
      New Zealand Command Depot, Codford, 167
      New Zealand Convalescent Hospital, Hornchurch, 170
      New Zealand Machine Gun Corps, Étaples, 170
      New Zealand Medical Corps, 167
      New Zealand Staff Corps, 168
      Permanent Staff Corps, 169
      Royal New Zealand Engineers, 174
      Territorial Post & Telegraph Engineers, 166

Trentham Military Hospital, 166, 170
  Permanent Defence Staff, 114
  Territorial Force, 171
Royal New Zealand Air Force, 156
Royal New Zealand Navy,
  HMNZHS No.2 *Marama*, 169
  HMNZT 11 *Athenic*, 126–7
  HMNZT 57 *Maunganui*, 166
  HMNZT 54 *Willochra*, 170
  Naval Auxiliary Patrol Service, 174
New Zealand Government, 173
  Defence, 173
  Governor General, 171, 173
  New Zealand Parliament, 173
New Zealand Merchant Navy, 174
New Zealand Post & Telegraph, 165, 173
New Zealand Shipping Co, 163
Newark, 265
Newbattle, 195
Newbury, 175
Newburyport, MA, 225
Newcastle, NSW, 89
Newcastle-upon-Tyne, 87
Newcastleton, 199, 208
Newfoundland, 79, 153, 173, 216, 229, 241, 262, 279, 295
  Governor, 79
Newhaven, 160
Newington, 123–4, 127–8, 179, 197
Newington St Mary, 276
Newland VC, JE, 115
Newmarket, NH, 214
Newport, 207
Newtownabbey, 132
Niagara Falls, 110, 280
Nilgiri Hills, 77
Nobel Prize, 141, 199
Nore, 108
Noreuil, 33
Norfolk, 75, 257
Norfolk Co, MA 140, 218
Norman, Ont, 253
Normandy, 159, 242
Normans & Conquest, 118, 159, 231–2, 237
Norrie, Sir Charles, 173
North America, 151, 282
North Atlantic, 92
North Carolina, 225
North Dorset, 84
North Hinksey, 234
North Humberside, 133
North Island, NZ, 114, 154
North Lancaster, Ont, 240
North Nations Hills, 246
North Okanagan, BC, 254
North Saanich, BC, 254
North Vancouver, 247

North West Frontier & Province, 160, 182
North West Mounted Police, 243
Northampton, Mas, 147
Northamptonshire, 100, 160
Northern Ireland, 80, 131, 283
Northland, 157, 164, 166, 191
Northop, 296
Northumberland, 119, 128–9
Northumberland Co, Ont, 285, 287–8, 291–2
Northumberland, NH, 215
Northumberland West, Ont, 285, 292
Northwest Passage, 139
Northwood, 202–203, 205
Norton Radstock, 265
Norwood, 181, 207
Notting Hill, 305
Nottingham, 154
Nottinghamshire, 263, 265–6, 289
Nova Scotia, 91, 95, 143, 146, 148–50, 211, 219, 221, 235, 248, 251–2, 255, 258, 281, 288, 302, 307, 310
Novello Ivor, 134
Nowshera, 133, 182
Nuneaton, 164
Nunney VC, Pte Claude, 31, 56–8, 230–46
Nyerere, Pres Julius, 199

Oak Bay, NB, 220
Oakfield, ME, 218
Oakham, 100
Oakland, CA, 280
O'Connell, Daniel, 80
Oddington, 237
O'Dea, Bishop Edward, 280
O'Dwyer, Michael, 256
Oghretina, 200
Ohio & River, 136–8, 141–2, 152, 160, 216
Oistrehem (Ouistreham), 159
Okehampton, 180
Okinawa, 148, 216
Oklahoma, 160
Old Bailey, 232
Old English Poetic Metre, 147
Old Fort Island, 253
Oldham, 276–8
Olympic Games, 198, 305
Onondaga Co, 136, 138
Ontario & Fort, 87, 89, 96, 152–4, 188, 228–9, 234–5, 240, 244–6, 253–4, 258, 261, 263, 280–1, 283–5, 287, 291–5, 311–12
  Provincial Legislature, 283, 292
Orange City, FL, 219
Orange Co, 161
Orange Free State, 92, 98
Orange Hill, 9–10
Orange Order, 259
Oratia, 163, 172

Orchard, ME, 228
Orders, Decorations & Medals,
   1914 Star (Mons Star), 117, 301
   1914/15 Star, 98, 104, 135, 160, 189, 229, 262, 273
   1939–45 Star, 135
   Air Force Cross, 199
   British War Medal 1914–20, 98, 104, 111, 117, 135, 154, 174, 189, 209, 229, 246, 262, 273, 284, 295, 301, 312
   Bronze Star (USA), 137, 226
   Canadian Centennial Medal 1967, 229, 295
   Canadian Forces Decoration, 152, 293
   Canadian Memorial Cross, 189, 246
   Canadian Volunteer Service Medal, 295
   Companion of Honour, 268
   Croix de Guerre (Belgium), 185–6, 189
   Croix de Guerre (France), 93, 98
   Defence Medal 1939–45, 135, 295, 301
   Distinguished Conduct Medal, 112, 115, 117, 168, 174, 242, 246, 272–3
   Distinguished Flying Cross, 144
   Distinguished Service Cross, 199
   Distinguished Service Order, 82, 93–4, 98, 144, 173, 209, 243, 256, 257, 262
   Efficiency Decoration (Canada), 98, 144, 253
   Empire Gallantry Medal, 264
   George Cross, 122
   Greek Medal of Naval Valour, 184
   India General Service Medal 1909–35, 160
   King George V Silver Jubilee Medal 1935, 262
   King George VI Coronation Medal 1937, 98, 104, 135, 154, 174, 209, 229, 262–3, 284, 295, 301
   Legion d'Honneur (France), 76
   Long Service & Good Conduct Medal, 275
   Medal of Honor (USA), 137, 140
   Mentioned in Despatches, 73, 82, 92, 95, 98, 111, 118, 120, 133, 135, 257, 262, 275, 301
   Mercantile Marine War Medal, 111, 117–18
   Meritorious Service Medal, 264–5
   Meritorious Service Medal (USA), 226
   Military Cross, 90, 144–6, 152, 154, 165, 173, 208–209, 291, 295
   Military Medal, 101, 104, 168, 174, 196, 222–3, 229, 242, 246, 290, 295
   New Zealand Long & Efficient Service Medal, 174
   New Zealand War Service Medal 1939–45, 174
   Order of Leopold (Belgium), 284
   Order of St John of Jerusalem, 243
   Order of St Michael & St George, 81, 90, 93–4, 98, 173, 198, 243, 260
   Order of the Bath, 73, 79, 144, 173, 202, 209–10, 243, 259, 260
   Order of the British Empire, 198–9, 208–209, 305
   Order of the Crown (Belgium), 284
   Order of the Thistle, 198
   Purple Heart (USA), 137, 214, 216
   Queen Elizabeth II Coronation Medal 1953, 98, 135, 154, 209, 229, 263, 295, 301
   Queen Elizabeth II Silver Jubilee Medal 1977, 295
   Queen's South Africa Medal, 81, 89, 98, 278
   Royal Victorian Order, 173
   Service (1917–1921) Medal (Ireland), 104
   Victory Medal 1914–19, 98, 104, 111, 118, 135, 154, 174, 189, 209, 229, 246, 262, 273, 284, 295, 301, 312
   War Medal 1939–45, 135, 174, 295, 301
Orleans Co, VT, 214
Ormskirk, 123
O'Rouke VC, Michael, 283
Orrington, ME, 224
Osaka, 169
Oscar, 137
Oswego, Canal, Fort & Co, 138, 140, 142
Otago, 156, 168, 194
O'Toole, Peter, 134
Ottawa, 97, 146, 153, 188, 229, 239–40, 245, 261, 263, 284, 293–5, 312
Ouse Valley Railway, 155
Out Skerries, 190
Outaouais Region, 254
Oxford, 129, 237, 238
Oxfordshire, 71, 155, 179, 230, 232, 236–8, 266
Oxted, 160, 162

Pacaut, 26
Pacific, 109, 169, 216, 252–3
Padang, 192
Paddington, 100, 179, 234, 254
Paddington, NSW, 116
Pahi, 166
Painswick, 279
Pakistan, 153, 173, 182, 229, 262, 295
Palace of St Michael & St George, 93
Palestine, 31, 118, 130
Palluel, 44
Palm Beach, 157
Palmerston North, 164, 172, 192
Pan African Conference, 256
Panama & Canal, 108–109
Pancras, 100, 124, 230, 233
Paralympic Games, 305
Paris, 76, 88, 90–1, 150, 235, 291
Parry, R Adm Sir William, 139
Passamaquoddy, 212, 225
Passchendaele & Battles of, 145, 290
Patch, Harry, 139
Patcham, 176–7
Patten, Christopher, 139
Pavlova, Anna, 134

Pearkes VC, Maj George, 290–1, 294
Pearson, John Loughborough, 185
Pease Pottage, 178–9
Peck VC, Lt Col Cyrus, 31, 44, 47–51, 54–5, 227, 246–63, 284
Peel MC, Chap Maurice, 73
Peel, PM Sir Robert, 73, 124
Peel, Viscount, 73
Pelly, Anna, 152
Peloponnese, 156
Pelves, 22, 25–6
Pembroke, ME, 218–19
Pembrokeshire, 133
Penang, 192
Pencaitland, 205
Penge, 274
Peninsular War, 73, 110
Penistone, 238
Pennsylvania, 225
Penobscot Co, ME, 211, 218, 221, 224
Penrith, 71
Pensford St Thomas, 158
Pepsi, 204
Péronne, 31
Perry, ME, 224, 226
Persia, 156
Perth, 89, 119–20
Perth, WA, 156
Perthshire, 118–19, 121–3, 129, 193–4
Peshawar, 74, 130
Petawawa, Ont, 287, 293
Peterborough, 100
Peterborough, Ont, 285, 292
Petersfield, 177
Pevensey, 224
Philadelphia, 251
Philby, Kim, 86
Philippines, 157, 216
Philips, Knox & Arthur, 205
Pickwick Papers, 139
Pillerton Hersey, 267
Pillerton Prior, 265, 267
Pilos, 156
Pinckney, Charles, 86
Pitt, William, 139
Pittsburgh, PA, 225
Pittsfield, ME, 214
Platt & Co, 276
Plouvain, 24
Plymouth, 92, 158, 269
Plymouth Co, MA, 218, 220
Plymouth, IN, 140
Poelcapelle and Battle of, 111, 115
Point Methoni, 156
Ponsonby, Frederick Cavendish, 270
Ponsonby, NZ, 163–4, 166, 169
Pontarddulais, 267

Pontefract, 132
Pontypool, Ont, 283
Pontypridd, 297
Poole, 83, 236, 238
Poor Cow, 139
Poplar, 231
Port Albert, 154, 169
Port Chalmers, 163, 194
Port Charlotte, 209
Port Hope, Ont, 287
Port Hope Evening Guide, 260
Port Huron, MI, 147, 283
Portage la Prairie, Man, 291
Portland, 108
Portland, ME, 212, 216–17, 224, 226
    Fire Department, 216
Portman, Eric, 305
Portnahaven, 189, 190, 209
Portpatrick, 70
Portsea, 237–8
Portslade-by-Sea, 161
Portsmouth, 119, 184
Portsmouth, NH, 212, 213, 225–6
Portugal, 89
Pound, Adm of the Fleet Sir Dudley, 134
Power, Tyrone, 137
Prefontaine, Fr Francis, 280
Premier Mines, BC, 248
Preston, Sussex, 113
Priestley, John Boynton, 141
Primrose Hill, 125
Prince Alfred, 270
Prince Arthur (Duke of Kent), 198
Prince Charles Edward Stuart, 288
Prince of Wales (Edward), 94, 109, 116
Prince Rainier III, 231
Prince Rupert, BC, 247–8, 251–2, 255, 262
Princess of Wales, 94, 210
Princess Louise, Duchess of Argyle, 95, 134
Princess Louise Margaret, Duchess of Connaught & Strathearn, 134
Princess Royal, 96–8, 152, 153, 188, 210, 228–9, 244–5, 261, 284, 295, 311–12
Princeton, ME, 211, 213, 215, 217–18, 220–1
Privy Councillor, 198, 259, 268
Proctor Bros Co, 217
Prohibition, 253
Pronville, 31, 38–40, 73, 272
Prospect Farm, 65
Provincetown, MA, 226
Prowse VC, CPO George, 31, 38–40, 263–73
Pugin, Augustus, 186
Pugin, Edward, 186
Puisieux-au-Mont, 168
Pukekohe, 166
Pukerata, 170
Pulaski Co, 136, 142

Pulteney, Sir William, 277
Punjab, 256,
　Lieutenant Governor, 256
Purcell, Henry, 86
Purfleet, 248
Putney Heath, 143
Pymble, 193

Quéant, 34, 35, 38–9, 50, 101
Québec, 87–8, 90, 92, 96, 146, 151, 196, 214, 222, 227, 236, 240, 246, 254, 258–9, 279–80, 286, 301, 303, 307–308, 310
Québec Battlefields Association, 89
Queen Adelaide, 131, 231
Queen Alexandra, 94
Queen Elizabeth II, 88, 228
Queen Elizabeth, Queen Mother, 151, 283, 292
Queen Mary, 102, 144, 257, 270
Queen Victoria, 92, 173, 270, 293
Queen's Barracks, Perth, 119
Queen's Counsel, 198, 268
Queensferry, 296, 301
Queripel VC, Lionel, 98

Race Hill Inn, Brighton, 207
Rackemann, Sawyer & Brewster, 147
Radford, 263
Radford Semele, 265
Rainy River, Ont, 253
Ramleh, 200
Ramsgate, 185–6, 223
Randwick, 115
Rangoon, 89, 277
Rankin, Ian, 207
Rat Portage (Kenora), 253–4
Rathbones Investment Management, 205
Rayfield VC, Pte Walter, 31, 51–2, 54–5, 273–84, 292–3
Reading, 175
Rebus, 207
Redhill, 155, 175–6, 181–2, 189
Redmond, John, 99
Redmond, WA, 281
Reford, Robert Wilson, 87
Reformation, 288
Regina, Sask, 184, 187–8
Reigate, 175–6, 182, 184, 189, 275
Remuera, 169, 171
Remy & Wood, 26–7
Rennie VC, William, 288
Returned Services Association (NZ), 173
Revie, Don, 134
Rhodesian & South African Air Training Scheme, 156
Rhuddlan, 299
Rhyl, 150, 197, 298–300
　Urban District Council, 298

Richards, Wendy, 134
Richborough, 125
Richmond Co, NY, 225
Richmond upon Thames, 177, 273, 284
Ridley, William Arnold, 134, 139
Riencourt-*lès-Bapaume*, 18, 23, 31
Riencourt-*lès-Cagnicourt*, 34, 48, 101
Rifkind, Sir Malcolm, 198
Rimington, Stella, 199
Ring of Remembrance, 189, 245, 273
Rio de Janeiro, 305
Ripon, 94, 122, 132, 150, 310
River Barrow, 99
River Eden, 155
River Severn, 297
River Windrush, 232, 237
Riverdale Barracks, Toronto, 288
Robbinston, ME, 219, 221
Robert Reford Co, 88–9
Robert Steele & Co, 279
Robinson, Sugar Ray, 299
Robson VC, Henry, 283, 293
Rocester, 237–8
Rochester, 70, 233
Rockerfeller, John D, 157
Rockingham, NH, 218
Rockingham, VT, 214
Rockland, 226
Rockport, ME, 226
Rodney, 154, 164–5
Roeux, 15
Rollinsford, NH, 226
Romani, Battle of, 200
Romania, 268
Romans, 74–5, 139, 155, 304
Romford, 100, 158
Roosevelt, Pres Franklin D, 269
Roscommon, Co, 80
Roslin, 190
Ross Co, 160
Ross rifle, 259
Rosslare, 256
Ross-shire, 202
Rosyth, 146
Rouen, 194
Rowley Regis, 297
Roxburghshire, 199, 208
Royal Air Force, 9, 22, 72, 106, 130, 254, 269
　1st Brigade, 43–4
　5 Sqn, 44
　6 Sqn, 44
　8 Sqn, 44
　12 Sqn, 34
　12th (Training) Group, 254
　20 Sqn, 44
　40 Sqn, 44
　52 Sqn, 44

Index

54 Sqn, 44
55 Sqn, 130
59th Training Depot Station, 254
64 Sqn, 44
73 Sqn, 44
102 Sqn, 34
208 Sqn, 44
209 Sqn, 44
Advanced Flying Schools, 131
Armament School, Uxbridge, 254
Habbaniya Air Striking Force, 131
No.2 School of Aeronautics, Oxford, 254
No.4 Flying Training School, Abu Sueir, Egypt, 130–1
No.5 Cadet Wing, Cadet Distribution Depot, 254
No.7 Flying Training School, RAF Valley, 131
No.205 Advanced Flying School, Middleton St George, 131
No.211 Advanced Flying School, Middleton St George, 131
Officers' Training Corps, 254
RAF Dishforth, 133
RAF Habbaniya, 131
RAF Lossiemouth, 288
RAF Reserves, 254
RAF Valley, 131
Red Arrows, 131
Women's Royal Air Force, 299
Royal Botanic Gardens, Edinburgh, 202
Royal Canadian Legion/Canadian Legion, 244
Royal Canadian Military Institute, Toronto, 294
Royal Canadian Mounted Police, 243
Royal College of Physicians of Ireland, 103
Royal Geographical Society, 70, 208
Royal Leamington Spa, 299
Royal Mile, Edinburgh, 207
Royal Navy & Royal Marines, 108, 111, 121, 143, 183, 199, 232, 270, 272, 275, 299
  Admiralty Shutter Telegraph Station, 269
  Good Conduct Badge, 184
  Home Fleet, 109
  Invincible Class, 109
  Nore Division, 109
  Royal Naval Volunteer Reserve, 148, 151, 227, 268, 272
  Ships,
    C8, 108
    C68, 108
    HMHS *Brighton*, 151
    HMHS *Cambria*, 91, 170, 271–2
    HMHS *Grantully Castle*, 72
    HMHS *Maheno*, 197
    HMHS *Panama*, 72
    HMHS *Rewa*, 268–9
    HMHS *St Andrew*, 288
    HMHS *St David*, 271
    HMHS *St Patrick*, 255–6
    HMHS *Stad Antwerpen*, 185
    HMS *Acheron*, 108
    HMS *Agincourt*, 276
    HMS *Arrogant*, 227
    HMS *Australia*, 276
    HMS *Caesar*, 276
    HMS *Collingwood*, 273
    HMS *Columbella*, 148
    HMS *Cruiser*, 276
    HMS *Deal Castle*, 227
    HMS *Duke of Wellington*, 276
    HMS *Endymion*, 148
    HMS *Excellent*, 148, 184
    HMS *Firequeen*, 276
    HMS *Furious*, 299
    HMS *Ganges*, 183, 275
    HMS *Goliath*, 276
    HMS *Grafton*, 276
    HMS *Hampshire*, 276
    HMS *Hercules*, 108
    HMS *Hermione*, 227
    HMS *Impregnable*, 275
    HMS *Indomitable*, 108–109
    HMS *Iron Duke*, 183
    HMS *Lion*, 109
    HMS *Marne*, 282
    HMS *Milbrook*, 282
    HMS *Minotaur*, 276
    HMS *Moldavia*, 148
    HMS *Northumberland*, 108
    HMS *Orion*, 183
    HMS *Pembroke II*, 108
    HMS *Pigeon*, 282
    HMS *Porpoise*, 156
    HMS *Prince George*, 276
    HMS *Racer*, 276
    HMS *Revenge*, 184, 276
    HMS *Shannon*, 143
    HMS *Spartiate*, 276
    HMS *Swiftsure*, 276
    HMS *Teutonic*, 148
    HMS *Vernon*, 184
    HMS *Victorious*, 276
    HMS *Victory & I*, 184, 227, 276
    HMS *Warspite*, 184
    HMT *Aragon*, 72
    HMT *Mauretania*, 302
    HMT *Regina*, 91
    HMT *Walmer Castle*, 190
    HT *Caledonian*, 266
    HT *Menominee*, 270
    HT *Merkara*, 181
    HT *Nile*, 270
    HT *Northbrook*, 180
  Minotaur Class, 108
  Royal Naval Hospital,

Bighi, Malta, 270
Haslar, 148, 276
School of Maritime Warfare, 273
Squadrons,
  1st Cruiser, 109
  1st Reserve, 108
  2nd Battlecruiser, 109
  3rd Battlecruiser, 109
  Channel Squadron, 108
Royal Society, 86, 277
Roye, 145
Ruawai, 165
Rugby, 103
Rugby World Cup, 139
Ruhr, 308
Runcorn, 106
Rupert Sound, BC, 260
Russell, Lord John, 86
Rutherford Co, 138
Rutherford VC, Lt Charles, 1, 11–14, 283, 285–95
Ruthin, 195
Rutland, 100
Ryan VC, J, 115
Ryde, 240

Saanich & Peninsula, BC, 258, 262
St Abban of Magheranoidhe, 99
St Albans, 131, 133
St Andrew's Ball, 92
St Andrew's Hall, Glasgow, 202
St Anne's-on-Sea, 106
St Asaph, 298
St Augustine, 157–8
St Croix, Cotton Mill, Paper Co & River, 211–12, 225, 228
St George, Hanover Square, London, 75, 77, 81, 83, 85
St Helens, 107
St Heliers, 156
St James, NB, 221
St James's Palace, 116
St John Ambulance, 80
St John, NB, 96, 251
St John's, Newfoundland, 241, 279, 286
St Kenelm, 304
St Leger Wood, 7
St Leonards-on-Sea, 230–1, 245, 288
St Louis, 142, 203
St Marylebone, 79, 125
St Neots, 158
St Olave, 181
St Omer, 149
St Pancras, 123–4, 206
St Saviour, 274, 276
St Servin's Farm, 26–30, 130, 135
St Stephen, NB, 211, 212, 214–15, 217–18, 222
St Vincent's Boys' Home, Westbourne Green, 239–40

Ste-Agathe-des-Monts, 310–11
Saillisel, 31
Sailly-en-Ostrevent, 66–7
Sale, 199
Salford, 106, 195
Salford, Oxon, 236
Saline Co, 160–1
Salisbury, 158
Salisbury Plain, 92, 180, 300
Salonica, 241
Salt Spring Island, BC, 261–2
Salvation Army, 305
San Diego, 213
San Fernando, 151
San Francisco, 169, 280
Sandgate, 150
Sandringham, 227, 257
Sandwich, 125
Sanford, ME, 219
Santa Ana, CA, 161
Santa Anita, CA, 283
Santa Barbara, 147
Saranac Lake, 311
Saskatchewan, 184, 187–8
Saskatchewan War Memorial, 187–8
Saudemont, 44
Saving Private Ryan, 137
Savoy Hotel, London, 130, 294
Saxons, 232, 237, 264
Sayers, Dorothy L, 75
Scarborough, 82, 132
Scarborough, ME, 213
Scarpe, 1, 9–10, 15, 20, 26–7
Scherchen, Wulff, 293
Schindler's List, 137
School of Physic Act 1800, 103
Schools,
  Agricultural, Mining & Mechanical Arts College, Oakland, CA, 280
  Ashburnham, 72
  Auckland Grammar, 171
  Bearwood College, 290
  Blatchington Court, 144
  Camerton Church, Somerset, 267
  Charles Edward Brooke Girl's School, Camberwell, 257
  Charterhouse, 77
  Columbus East High, Indiana, 203, 205
  Cormont Secondary, Camberwell, 257
  Cushintown, 100
  Dexter, 147
  Dudley Public School, Haldimand, Ont, 288
  Dulwich College, 82
  Edinburgh Academy, 84, 205
  Eton College, 78
  Florida School for the Deaf and the Blind, St Augustine, 157
  Fort Augustus Village Primary, 203, 205

Fort William Grammar, 189
Free Church Training College, Glasgow, 189–90
Garvan, 189
George Heriot's, Edinburgh, 196
George Watson's Boys' College, Edinburgh, 190, 192, 197–9
George Watson's College for Ladies, Edinburgh, 198
Grammar School, Waite, ME, 222
Gusserane National School, 100
Haileybury College, 81
Harrow Road, Westbourne Green, 240
Harvard School of Public Health, 147
Henderson, Auckland, 163
Henry Box, Witney, 232
Home & Colonial Training College, London, 279
Hopewell Hill Superior, Albert, NB, 252
Illinois High, Mound City, 142
Inverness Academy, 203
Kelvinside Academy, Glasgow, 203
King Alfred's, 254
Laxon Street, Southwark, 274, 278
Lincoln College, Sorel, 88
Malton, 132
Merchiston Castle, Edinburgh, 198
Mount Albert Grammar, 171
Mount City High, 142
Naparima Girls High, San Fernanado, Trinidad & Tobago, 151
Oratia District, Auckland, 163–4, 172
Parsons Mead, Ashtead, 205
Perth Academy, 129–30
Perth Grammar, 130
Philips Exeter Academy, 147
Portland High, ME, 226
Portnahaven, 190, 198–9
Portsmouth Grammar, 119
Raven's Croft, Seaford, 144
Redhill Technical & Trade, 184
Reeds, Surrey, 203
Rimrose Hope C of E Primary, Seaforth, 117
Rochester House School, Edinburgh, 205
Royal Merchant Seaman's Orphanage/Navy School, 290
Royal Victoria Patriotic, Wandsworth, 201
Rugby, 80
St Andrew's, Southborough, 85
St Ethelwold's, Shotton, 298
St Gabriel's College, Camberwell, 257
St George's, Kidderminster, 307
St Georges School for Girls, Edinburgh, 203, 205
St John's, Meadvale, 184
St Margaret's, Edinburgh, 205–206
St Mary's College, Indiana, 205
St Thomas's, Seaforth, 108
St Wilfred's, Haywards Heath, 188

Senglea Trade School, Malta, 270
Separate School No.9, Lancaster, Ont, 240
Sharp's Institution, Perth, 130
Shiskine Public, Arran, 189
South Portland High, Me, 213
Southern District, Perth, 121
Summerfields, St Leonards-on-Sea, 231
Tarbert (Loch Fyne) Public, Argyll, 189
Upper Canada Academy, Cobourg, Ont, 292
Upper Canada College, Toronto, 88
Victoria College, Cobourg, Ont, 292
Wellington House, Westgate, 78
Westbourne School for Girls, Glasgow, 205
Westminster, 71–3, 86–7
Scioto Country Club, 142
Scone, 121–2
Scoonie, 162
Scotland/Scottish, 70, 80, 87, 97, 118–19, 133, 162, 191–2, 194, 202–204, 207, 251, 254, 259, 276, 279, 282, 285, 287, 292
Scotland Media Group, 204
Scott, Ronnie, 134
Scott, Walter, 199
Scottish Arts Club, 208
Scottish rugby team, 198
Scottish Widows, 206
Scrimger VC, Capt Francis, 91
Sculcoates, 75
Seacombe, 105, 107
Seaford, 143–4, 223, 257, 281, 286
Seaforth, 105–106, 117
Searle, Robert, 157
Seattle, 280–1, 283
Sebastopol, 74
Second World War, 72, 76–7, 106, 122–4, 127, 131, 137, 139–40, 144, 156–7, 165, 168, 187–8, 192, 207, 212, 216, 218, 225, 231, 247, 256, 269–70, 272, 291–3, 299
Seghadoc, ME, 225–6
Selby, 133
Sellars, Peter, 134, 256
Selly Oak, 307
Seminole Wars, 157
Senior Foundry Co, Auckland, 163
Sensee River & Canal, 16, 19–22, 26, 43–4, 65–69, 112
Seven Years' War, 157, 253, 269
Sevenoaks, 159–60, 162
Seventy Ridge, 26
Sewardstone, 236
Shackleton, Sir Ernest, 144
Shanghai, 89
Shardlow, 266
Sheerness, 158, 233
Sheffield, 271–2, 278
Sheikh Zowaid, 200
Shelley, Mary, 139
Sherborne & Castle, 84–5

Shetland Islands, 190, 193
Shipping Federation of Canada, 87–8
Ships,
   City of Portland III, 216
   Cutty Sark, 89
   Dunbrody, 99
   Maraval, 110
   MV *Cy Peck*, 261–2
   Pedro Nunes, 89
   RMS *Alaunia*, 90, 92, 196
   RMS *Andania*, 286
   RMS *Baltic*, 310
   RMS *Britannic*, 282
   RMS *Caledonia*, 150, 241
   RMS *Carmania*, 283
   RMS *Empress of Britain*, 307
   RMS *Lusitania*, 146, 282
   RMS *Majestic*, 146
   RMS *Mauretania*, 95, 146
   RMS *Minnedosa*, 286–7, 303
   RMS *Olympic*, 91, 143, 146, 149, 199–200, 248, 288
   RMS *Queen Elizabeth*, 254
   RMS *Queen Mary*, 95
   RMS *Titanic*, 143, 241
   Sir Lancelot, 89
   SS *America*, 224
   SS *Arvonia*, 271
   SS *Athenic*, 127
   SS *Baltic*, 235
   SS *Canadian Skirmisher*, 151
   SS *Celtic*, 150
   SS *Corinthic*, 127
   SS *Daily*, 261
   SS *Elele*, 185
   SS *Erria*, 192
   SS *Grampian*, 149, 241
   SS *Homeric*, 280
   SS *Huanchaco*, 91
   SS *Imo*, 143
   SS *Ionic*, 127
   SS *Irrawaddy*, 110
   SS *Island Princess*, 262
   SS *Justicia*, 281–2
   SS *Kaikoura*, 163
   SS *Liguria*, 96
   SS *Manchester Port*, 151
   SS *Marama*, 169
   SS *Marburn*, 240
   SS *Medic*, 155
   SS *Megantic*, 251, 302
   SS *Melita*, 94, 96
   SS *Metagama*, 91, 227
   SS *Missanabe*, 251, 255
   SS *Mont Blanc*, 143
   SS *Pelagos*, 127
   SS *Princess Sophia*, 253
   SS *Ruahine*, 191
   SS *St Andrew*, 256
   SS *St Patrick*, 256
   SS *Sardinian*, 279
   SS *Saxonia*, 148
   SS *Scotian*, 222
   SS *Sebastiano Venier*, 156
   SS *Sicilia*, 277
   SS *Statendam*, 282
   SS *Suffolk*, 191
   SS *Tunisian*, 240
   SS *Vaderland*, 251
   SS *Zaida*, 163
   Stedmound, 108
   SV *City of Tanjore*, 194
   SV *Marlborough*, 126
   SV *Thermopylae*, 87–9
   SV *Trevelyan*, 194
   TS *Arethusa*, 183
   Tug *Sonia*, 282
   Western Crusader, 247
Shiskine, 191, 194
Shoeburyness, 275
Shoreditch, 124–6, 183
Shoreham-on-Sea, 143, 288–9
Shorncliffe, 91, 144, 149–51, 185, 232, 255–6, 286
Shotton, 296, 298–9, 301
Shotts, 203
Shropshire, 296–7
Shumran, 130
Shute, Maj Gen Sir Cameron, 121
Shwebo, 277
Sidney, BC, 253–4, 260, 262
Sierra Leone, 133, 275
Sikh, Second War, 74
Sikhs, 74
Silver War Badge, 180, 303
Simpson VC, Walter, see Arthur Evans
Singapore, 192
Singh, Udham, 256
Singh VC, Maj Parkash, 135
Skagway, AK, 253
Skeena & River, BC, 246, 252, 256, 258
Skerryvore, 282
Skowhegan, Me, 214
Slad valley, 304
Slaugham, 178
Sling Camp, Bulford, 167–8, 170
Small Heath, 239
Smith & Wesson, 209
Smith, Sgt James, 19
Smith VC, EA, 294
SMLE rifle, 259
Smyth VC, Nevill, 86
Smyth VC, Sir John, 135
Snaresbrook, 290
Snowsfields, 274

Society for Destitute Children, 116
Society of Actuaries, 70
Society of Actuaries (Scotland), 70
Soho, 239
Somaliland, 156
Somerset, 71, 79, 83, 100, 111, 138–9, 158–9, 177, 263–5, 273, 310
Somerset Co, ME, 214
Somerset Co, NJ, 217
Somerset, FM Fitzroy, Baron Raglan, 86
Somme & Battle of, 15, 23, 31, 78, 105, 151, 166, 222, 255, 288
Soorjkoond, 74
Sopwith Camel aircraft, 22
Sotheby's, 104, 273
Soult, Marshal, 76
Source Farm, 290
South Africa, 70–1, 87, 89, 92, 98, 125, 132, 153, 156, 167, 173, 176, 229, 232, 252, 253, 259, 262, 277, 295
    South African Constabulary, 243
    South African Police, 70
South African armed forces,
    Heavy Artillery, 223
South America, 87, 108
South Australia, 122
South Canterbury, 194
South Croydon, 158
South Eastern Railway, 155
South Hampstead, 124
South Harrow, 275
South Island, NZ, 115
South Kensington, 71
South Leyton, 230
South Norwood, 154, 274–5
South Portland, ME, 217, 224–5, 228, 250
South Tipperary, 102
Southampton, 71, 72, 78, 95–6, 110, 146, 165, 167, 180, 192, 199, 201, 254, 266, 302
Southborough, MA, 218
Southern Rhodesia, 131
Southwark, 100, 123, 125–8, 159, 274, 276, 278
Southwick, 160, 227
Spain, 157, 269, 279
Spanish Influenza, 242
Special Operations Executive, 77
Spencer-Churchill, Clarissa, 256
Spielberg, Steven, 137
Spink & Son, 104, 118, 273
Spital, 119–20, 122, 128–9
Spitalfield, 279
Spokane, WA, 248
Springvale, ME, 218
Sri Lanka, 153, 173, 229, 262, 295
Staffordshire, 104, 153, 173, 189, 229, 237–8, 262, 267, 295, 297, 303
Staked Barrier, 74

Stalybridge, 298
Standard Life Assurance Co, 87, 95
Stanmore, 131, 134, 206
Staplefield, 175
Star Corner, 17
Starr, Ringo, 256
Staten Island, NY, 224
Statute of Westminster 1931, 258
Steel, Baron David of Aikwood, 198
Stepney, 230
Steptoe, Patrick, 232
Stevenage, 233
Stevenson, Robert Louis, 199
Steyning, 113–14, 160–1, 183
Stirling & Castle, 87, 194, 209–10
Stirlingshire, 135
Stoke-next-Guildford, 177
Stoke-on-Trent, 298
Stoker, Bram, 134
Stone, 305–306, 309–10
Storkey VC, P, 115, 117
Stott, Ken, 207
Stourbridge, 308
Strabane, 79
Stranmore Park Golf Club, 134
Stranorlar, 79, 84
Stratford, NZ, 164
Stratford-upon-Avon, 263, 265–6
Streatley, 113
Stretford, 195
Stripe Copse, 30
Stroud, 303–304
Stroudwater Navigation, 304
Stroudwater Scarlet, 304
Sturdee, Adm of the Fleet Sir FC Doveton, 272
Sturgess, Tom, 174
Sturminster Marshall, 70–1, 85
Sudan, 156
Suez Canal, 200
Suffield, Ct, 213
Suffolk, 105
Suffolk Co, MA, 215, 218, 220
Suffragette movement, 256
Sullivan Co, NH, 214
Sullivan VC, AP, 115–17, 135
Sun Quarry, 22
Surrey, 75, 77, 83, 100, 105, 119, 123, 127–8, 144, 154, 157–62, 168, 175, 177–9, 181–4, 189, 204–205, 233, 241, 249, 254, 271, 273–5, 281, 284, 307
Surtees, John, 155
Sussex, 81, 83, 92, 112–14, 117, 121, 143–4, 154–5, 158, 160–3, 175–80, 182–3, 206–207, 224, 226, 230, 234, 238, 245, 253–4, 257, 288, 291
    Lord Lieutenant, 188
Sussex, NB, 252
Sutton, 154

Sutton-on-Sea, 190
Swalcliffe, 71
Swan, Hunter & Wigham Richardson Ltd, 146
Swansea, 267–8, 272–3
   Registry Office, 267
Swartz Bay, BC, 262
Switzerland, 259
Sydney, Harbour & Sydney Opera House, 115–17, 122, 155, 169, 192
Symons VC, Lt Col William, 135
Syracuse, 136, 138
Syria, 142, 156, 207
Sysladobsis Lake, Me, 213

Tacoma, WA, 261
Taft, Pres William, 137
Tairei, 156
Tait VC, Lt James, 235
Talavera Barracks, Aldershot, 110
Tallahassee, 157
Talmadge, 211, 217, 219–21
Tanks,
   Mk IV, 33
   Mk V, 33, 43
   Whippet, 33, 34
Tanner MC, Lt Harold, 25
Tanzania, 199
Tappen, BC, 248
Taradale, 172
Taranaki, 164
Tarrant Rushton, 269
Tarrytown, NY, 224
Tasmania, 169
Tata Steel, 298
Taumarunui, 164
Taunton, 264
Tauranga, 114, 166
Taylor, AJP, 134
Taylor, Elizabeth, 256
Taylor, Pte Andrew, 19
Tehama, CA, 247
Temple VC, William, 98
Temuka, 156, 191, 194
Tenby, 133
Tenbury, 239
Tenerife, 309
Tennessee, 136, 138
Terlincthun, 76
Testament of Youth, 257
Tewkesbury, 310
Thakeham, 178
Thames & Severn Canal, 304
Thames, NZ, 156–7
Thatcher, PM Margaret, 268
The Adventures of Huckleberry Finn, 152
The Islands, BC, 262
The Sample Case, 138

The Times, 290
The Victoria Warder, 259
Theatre Royal, 203
Third Afghan War, 182
Thirsk, 113
Thompson, Det Sgt Joseph, 232
Thomson Line, 88
Thurso, Quebec, 254
Ticehurst, 238
Tidworth, 90, 272
Tigris, 130
Tilloy-les-Mofflaines, 9
Tilston VC, Fred, 293–4
Timaru, 156, 173, 191
Tintern, 98
Tobruk, 96
Todd, Brig George, 209
Tonbridge, 155, 163, 238
Tooting, 154–5, 181
Topsfield, ME, 213, 221
Torbeg, 194
Toronto, 87, 95, 97, 143, 146–7, 153–4, 188, 229, 245, 261, 280–4, 288, 291–5, 311
   Harbour Commission, 283
   Jail, 282
Torquay, 82
Tottenham, 94
Towcester, 160
Tower of London, 116
Towers, First Officer Thomas, 96
Toxteth Park, 106, 238
Trafalgar, Battle of, 142
Tranmere, 106
Transvaal, 89, 92, 98
Treaty of Paris, 157
Trenches,
   Avion, 242
   Boiry Reserve, 16
   Bottom Bridge, 22
   Buissy Switch, 39, 41, 45, 50–6, 65
   Circle, 13
   Crayfish, 168
   Cromarty, 11
   Dachsund, 36
   Dagger, 11
   East, 13
   First Avenue, 21
   Fooley, 19
   Fop Lane, 17–18
   Greyhound, 36
   Halifax, 10
   MacAulay Avenue, 33
   Mallard, 21
   Minorca, 10
   Obus, 22
   Ocean, 25
   Occident, 21–2

Olga, 22
Opera, 25
Orient Lane, 17, 21–2
Parnell, 21
Plaid, 11
Possum Lane, 35–6
Puffin, 21
Queer Street, 38, 55
Regina, 288
Sack, 29
Star Corner, 22
Summit, 19
Ulster, 17, 21, 24–5
Una Lane, 22
Unicorn, 24–5
Union, 17, 21, 24–5
Vis-en-Artois Switch, 50–1
Vraucourt Switch, 33–4
Trento, 79
Trigger Copse, 44, 46–8
Trinidad & Tobago, 151
Trinidad Shipping & Trading Co, 110
Triquet VC, P, 294
Trônes Wood, 4
Truro, NS, 252
Tsingtao, 148
Tuam, 83
Tunbridge Wells, 85, 97–8, 114, 238
Tunisia, 156
Turkey, 127, 200
Turner Townsend, 205
Turpin, Randolph, 299
Twain, Mark, 152
Tweedmouth, 120, 128–9
Twyford, 114
Tyne, 146
Tyrone, Co, 259

Uccle, 77
Uckfield, 83, 176
Ufton, 265
Ukraine, 153, 173, 229, 262, 295
Ullapool, 204
Ulster, 259
Ulverston, 133
UNESCO City of Film, 141
UNESCO World Heritage Site, 139
Union, ME, 226
Union Flag, 228
United Empire Loyalists, 292
United States of America, 75, 77, 99, 101, 108–109, 123, 126, 136, 138, 140, 142, 147–8, 150, 153–4, 157–8, 160–1, 173, 203, 205, 211–12, 215, 222, 224–9, 247–8, 250–1, 253, 261–2, 279–81, 283, 295, 301
United States armed forces, 140, 146, 269
  Union Forces, 138, 141, 152
  1st Bn, Maine Light Artillery, 219–20
  6th Battery Light Artillery, 219–20
  24th (New York Vols) Regt, 138
  48th Regt, 138
  First Army Corps Ambulances, 138
  Mississippi River Sqn, 152
  United States Army, 212, 215, 219, 225–6
    42nd Infantry Division, 146
    74th Engineers, 138
    US Army Nurse Corps, 137
    US Cadet Nursing Corps, 212–13
  United States Air/Army Air Force, 205, 216, 218
    90th Bomb Group, 216
    Eilson Air Firce Base, AK, 218
  United States Marine Corps, 219
  United States Navy, 216, 224
    US Naval Reserve, 148, 214
    US Navy Coast Guard, 213, 226
      Coast Guard Station Portsmouth, NH, 226
      Coast Guard Station Race Point, Cape Cod, MA, 226
      Coast Guard Station Rockland, ME, 226
      Coast Guard Station Southwest Harbor, ME, 226
      USCG *Cutters Point*, 226
      USCG *Eastwind*, 226
      USCG *Garnet*, 226
      USCG *Mast*, 226
      USCG *Swivel*, 226
    USS *Chesapeake*, 143
    USS *Franklin*, 214
    USS *Pennsylvania*, 216
    USS LCS(L) (3) *126*, 148
    Wright-Patterson Air Force Base, 216
United States Government,
  Public Health Service, 151
  State Department, 224
Universities,
  Aberdeen, 206
  Birmingham, 309
  Carnegie Mellon, Pittsburgh, PA, 225
  Christ Church, Oxford, 84
  Cincinnati, 137
  Columbia, 147
  Edinburgh, 190–2, 197, 199
  Exeter College, Oxford, 77
  Goldsmiths' College, London, 124
  Heriot-Watt College, Edinburgh, 205
  John Hopkins, 90
  Leicester, 289
  Marshall, 147
  McGill, Montréal, 90, 260
  Michigan, 147
  New College, Edinburgh, 189, 197
  New York, 147
  Northwestern University Medical School, Chicago, 142
  Queen's, Kingston, Ont, 293

St John's College, Cambridge, 169
Strathclyde, 190
Toronto, 291–2
Trinity College, Cambridge, 72, 168–9
University College, Leicester, 203
Washington, St Louis, 203
Unknown Warrior, 102, 208
Up the Junction, 139
Upham VC, Charles, 174
Upper Arlington, 142
Upper Dyke Village, 148
Upper Tilgate, 179
Upton-upon-Severn, 236
Upton VC, Cpl James, 135
Upton Wood, 21–2
Uranus, 305
Ustinov, Sir Peter, 86
Uttoxeter, 237
Uxbridge, 154, 223

Valcartier, 89, 92, 196, 222, 259, 285
Valenciennes, 44, 112, 249
Valletta, 131, 270
Van Nuys, CA, 248
Vancouver & Island, 89, 169, 247–9, 251, 254–5, 260, 280–1, 283, 285, 287, 292
Vanier MC, Maj Georges, 24, 144
Vanity Farm, 290
Vapour Farm, 290
Vaulx-Vraucourt, 33–4
Vaulx Wood, 33
Vauvillers, 101
Vendome, 254
Vermont, 214–15
Vernon, BC, 254
Vernonville, Ont, 285, 288, 291–2
Verona, 79
Veterans of Foreign Wars (USA), 226
Victor Comic, 117, 262
Victoria, 133
Victoria Barracks, Perth, 121
Victoria, BC, 87–9, 229–30, 248, 251, 253, 255, 260, 281, 287
Victoria Copse, 27
Victoria, NB, 226
Victoria Cross & George Cross Association & Reunions, 134, 294
Victoria Cross Centenary 1956, 95, 134, 208, 228, 258, 280, 293, 300
Victoria Cross Dinner, House of Lords 1929, 95, 102, 151, 208, 227, 258, 283, 293, 300
Victoria Cross Garden Party, 102, 208, 300
Victoria Cross Guard, 102, 208
Victoria Motor Boat & Repair Works Ltd, 247
Victorians, 278
Vietnam, 226
Vigo, 279

Vikings, 118
Villers-les-Cagnicourt & Chateau, 31, 50–1, 53–5, 58–9, 64–5, 187, 189, 229, 244, 284
Vimy Ridge & Battle of, 93, 145, 242, 256
Vincent Barracks, Valenciennes, 112
Virgin Group, Radio & Records, 204
Virginia, 153, 225
Vis-en-Artois, 17, 20, 22, 26–7, 97, 130, 245
Viscount Lifford, 79–81
Visit London, 204
Volusia Co, FL, 219

Wabash Co, 136
Waddesdon, 266
Wadsley, 271
Wagamama, 205
Waikato, 164
Waiouru, 174
Waipawa, 166
Waitara, 126
Waite, ME, 222
Wakeford VC, Richard, 86
Wales, 131, 165, 263, 267, 296, 301
Walker MofH, Mary Edwards, 140
Wallasey, 107
Walter Hood & Co, 89
Walter, John, 290
Waltham, Lincs, 165
Waltham, MA, 213, 215
Waltham Cross, 236
Walthamstow, 128, 230
Walton-on-Thames, 168, 170
Walton-on-the-Hill, 106
Walworth, 118, 126
Wancourt & Tower Ridge, 9, 14, 21
Wandsworth & Common, 77, 125, 128, 149–50, 201, 232, 234, 274
Wanganui, 192
War of 1812, 140, 143, 225
Wareham, 111
Wareham, MA, 215
Wark VC, Blair, 115
Warkworth, 165
Warlingham, 144
Warren, Samuel Russell, 88
Warrington, 276
Warwick, 266–7, 307
Warwick, RI, 215
Warwickshire, 80–1, 83–4, 103, 126, 151, 164, 170, 239–40, 263, 265, 267, 304, 306, 309
Washington Co, ME, 211, 213, 215–2, 224–6
Washington DC, 92, 138, 143, 151
Washington, George, 86
Washington State, 248, 250, 261, 280–1
Waterford, 100, 102
Waterford Co, 103
Waterford, VT, 214

Waterloo, Battle of, 73–4, 86, 208
Watson VC, Lt Col Thomas, 135
Watt, Lt G, 54
Wealdon, 155
Wealdstone Police Court, 114
Weale VC, LCpl Henry, 1, 4, 296–301
Well Camp, Alford, 190
Welles, Orson, 256
Wellington, 159
Wellington Barracks, London, 116
Wellington, NZ, 127, 168, 170–1, 173
Wells, 263–4
Wells, HG, 134
Welsh rugby team, 268
Werner, Wilhelm, 269
Wesley, Charles, 86
West Barns, 195
West Bromwich, 303
West Dean, 178
West Derby, 105, 107, 234, 303
West Down Camp, 196
West Germany, 205
West Glamorgan, 273
West Ham, 124, 230, 236, 239
West Horsley, 178
West Riding of Yorkshire, 141
West Sandling, 288
West Sussex, 158, 175, 203, 227
West VC, Lt Col Richard, 34
West Wareham, MA, 218
Westborough, MA, 218
Westbourne Green, 239–40
Wester Ross, 204
Westerham, 159, 180
Western Australia, 133, 156
Western Desert, 156
Westerville, 142
Westham, 224, 226–7
Westhampnett, 178
Westmeath, Co, 80
Westminster, Hall & Abbey, 75, 77, 79, 83–4, 86, 88, 207–208, 230, 254, 256, 258, 260, 299
Westmore, VT, 214
Westmorland Co, NB, 250
Westmount, 254
Weston Corbett, 81
Weston-super-Mare, 71
Wexford, Co, 98, 100
Whalsay Skerries, 193
Whangarei, 157
Wharehine, 154, 164–5
Whatcom Co, WA, 250
Wheeler VC, Lt Col George, 130
Whish, Lt Gen Sir William, 74
Whitby, 77
White Hart Hotel, Cullompton, 159
White House, 143

White Lion pub, Leominster, 274, 278
White Rock, BC, 250
White Star Line, 127, 146, 282
Whitefield, NH, 215
Whitehall, 272
Whitstable, 181
Whittle VC, JW, 115, 117
Wicklow, Co, 81
Wiebe, Lt Gov Jack, 187
Wigan, 105
Wigham Richardson, 146
Wigtownshire, 70
Wilde, Oscar, 80
Wilkes Station, AL, 301
William Denny & Bros, 271
Williams, Andy, 137
Williams, Ralph Vaughan, 134
Wilson, Gen Sir Henry, 43
Wilson's Beach, NB, 216
Wiltshire, 83, 92, 151, 158, 167, 196, 263, 272, 300
Wimbledon, 112, 162
Wimereux, 76, 286, 289
Wimille, 76–7
Winchcombe, 303–304
Winchcombeshire, 304
Winchester, 79, 84–5, 133, 183, 236–7
Winchester Assizes, 96
Windham Co, VT, 214–15
Windsor Great Park, 172
Winehouse, Amy, 134
Winnipeg, 292
Winona, ID, 247
Winters, Bernie, 134
Wisconsin, 101, 141, 280
Witham, 75
Witley, 149, 242, 249, 283, 302, 310
Witney, 155, 232, 236–8
Wivelsfield, 176, 178–9
Wokingham, 151, 175, 288
Wolfe, Gen James, 159
Wolverhampton, 297–8
Wolverley, 306
Women's Canadian Club, 89
Woodford, 234
Woodland, ME, 211
Woodland Plantation, 290
Woodward, Sir Clive, 139
Woolwich & Dockyard, 266, 275
Worcester Co, MA, 147, 218–19, 221–2
Worcestershire, 81, 236, 239, 265, 267, 297, 301, 306, 308, 310–11
Wordsworth, 199
Worksop, 131, 265
World Heritage Site, 297
Worshipful Company of Goldsmiths, 123–4
Worth, 163
Worthing, 183

Wren, Sir Christopher, 86
Wrexham, 301

Yeats, WB, 80
York, 100, 121
York Co, ME, 218–19, 222, 226
York Cottage, Sandringham, 227, 257
York, Ont, 280
York West, Ont, 280
Yorkshire, 75, 77, 82, 94, 100, 106, 113, 121–3, 131–3, 138, 150, 196–7, 230, 238, 272, 278, 305, 310

Young VC, Pte John, 31, 56, 64, 301–12
Younger Botanic Gardens, Dunoon, 202
Ypres & Battles of, 85, 93, 110, 145, 222, 260

Zengel VC, Sgt Raphael, 294
Zion, Il, 213
Zoological Society, 70
Zuidlaren, 280